Photoshop CC

the missing manual®

The book that should have been in the box®

Lesa Snider

O'REILLY®

Beijing | Cambridge | Farnham | Köln | Sebastopol | Tokyo

Photoshop CC: The Missing Manual

by Lesa Snider

Published by O'Reilly Media, Inc.,
1005 Gravenstein Highway North, Sebastopol, CA 95472.

O'Reilly books may be purchased for educational, business, or sales promotional use. Online editions are also available for most titles (*http://my.safaribooksonline.com*). For more information, contact our corporate/institutional sales department: (800) 998-9938 or *corporate@oreilly.com*.

June 2013:   First Edition.

Revision History for the First Edition:

    2013-05-31   First release
    2013-08-23   Second release

See *http://oreilly.com/catalog/errata.csp?isbn=0636920027591* for release details.

ISBN-13: 978-1-449-34241-8

Contents

NOTE   You can download four online-only appendixes from this book's Missing CD page at *www.missingmanuals.com/cds*. The appendixes cover installing Photoshop, troubleshooting problems, all the tools in the Tools panel, and the program's menu items.

The Missing Credits

ABOUT THE AUTHOR

 Lesa Snider is on a mission to teach the world to create—and use!—better graphics. She's an internationally acclaimed speaker, a stock photographer, and the founder of the creative tutorial site PhotoLesa.com. Lesa is the author of many video-training workshops (*www.lesa.in/clvideos*) and the coauthor of *iPhoto '11: The Missing Manual*. She writes a regular column for *Photoshop User* and *Macworld* magazines, and contributes frequently to *Design-Tools.com* and *PlanetPhotoshop.com*. Lesa is also a long-time member of the Photoshop World Dream Team of instructors and can be spotted teaching at many other conferences around the globe. You can connect with her online on Facebook (*www.facebook.com/PhotoLesa*), YouTube (*www.lesa.in/ytvideochannel*), Twitter (@PhotoLesa), and PhotoLesa.com.

During her free time, you'll find Lesa carving the twisties on her sportbike, dressed up in her Star Trek best at a sci-fi convention with her husband, or hanging with fellow Apple Mac enthusiasts. Lesa is a proud member of the BMWMOA and the First Lady of the Colorado Mac User Group (*CoMUG.com*), a.k.a. the Boulder Mac Maniacs. Email: *lesa@photolesa.com*.

ABOUT THE CREATIVE TEAM

Dawn Mann (editor) is associate editor for the Missing Manual series. When not working, she plays soccer, beads, and causes trouble. Email: *dawn@oreilly.com*.

Kara Ebrahim (production editor) lives, works, and plays in Cambridge, MA. She loves graphic design and all things outdoors. Email: *kebrahim@oreilly.com*.

Carla Spoon (proofreader) is a freelance writer and copy editor. An avid runner, she works and feeds her tech gadget addiction from her home office in the shadow of Mount Rainier. Email: *carla_spoon@comcast.net*.

Ron Strauss (indexer) specializes in the indexing of information technology publications of all kinds. Ron is also an accomplished classical violist and lives in northern California with his wife and fellow indexer, Annie, and his miniature pinscher, Kanga. Email: *rstrauss@mchsi.com*.

Shangara Singh (technical reviewer) is the author of the popular exam aids for Photoshop and Lightroom—study guides for people who want to become an Adobe Certified Expert—published by *Examaids.com*. He has also authored a keyword hierarchy for stock photographers (*Keyword-Catalog.com*) and has his own stock photo website, *SensaStockImages.com*.

David Creamer (technical reviewer) is an Adobe Certified Instructor for over 10 programs, and has been an Adobe Certified Expert in Photoshop since 1995. Creamer is owner of IDEAS Training (*IDEAStraining.com*), a training and consultation company.

ACKNOWLEDGEMENTS

This book is dedicated to my husband, Jay Nelson, for making everyday life incredibly fun and for learning to appreciate heavy metal music, namely Ozzy Osbourne. ☺

I'd like to express galactic thanks to iStockphoto.com for providing some of the imagery in this book: An image really is worth a thousand words (if you ever need high-quality, affordable graphics, visit *www.lesa.in/istockdeal*). (Full disclosure: I was their chief evangelist for over six years.) A big hug and thanks to David Pogue who so graciously wrote the foreword for this book. To Jeff and Scott Kelby for believing in me and nurturing my career in immeasurable ways. To Derrick Story for his wisdom before I got started on this project, and a great big jug of Umbrian vino rosso to Dawn Mann for editing this book and keeping me on track. Her input makes me a better writer and I'm lucky to have her on our team. To my brilliant and long-time tech editor, Shangara Singh, whose expertise has helped create the best Photoshop book yet and whose humorous comments always made me giggle.

Special thanks to Marcus Conge (*digitalmanipulation.com*) and Jay Nelson for writing the new 3D chapter, to Rod Harlan for consulting on video editing, to Richard Harrington (*photoshopforvideo.com*) for helping with actions, to Taz Tally (*taztallyphotography.com*) for helping with the print chapter, as well as Bert Monroy (*bertmonroy.com*) and Veronica Hanley for guidance on all things vector-related. To Deborah Fox (*deborahfoxart.com*) for the beautiful art in the painting chapter, to Tanya and Richard Horie for their expert advice on the painting chapter and brush customization options (as well as creating my logo), to Karen Nace Willmore (*karennace.com*) for her HDR and wide-angle photography, and to Jeff Gamet (*macobserver.com*) for keeping me sane and helping with the first edition of this book.

To my esteemed colleagues—and good friends—Jack Davis, Ben Willmore, Eddie Tapp, Judy Host, Peter Cohen, Gary-Paul Prince, Larry Becker, Kevin Ames, Terry White, Dave Moser, and Andy Ihnatko, who all expressed their pride and confidence in me. I'd also like to thank our *creativeLIVE.com* family for promoting this book and for being so fun to play with, as well as *LensProToGo.com* for supplying me with incredible Canon gear to shoot with (if you need to rent camera gear, they're the best!).

Last but not least, buckets of appreciation to my friends who gave their support—or a cocktail!—when I needed it most: Carol Morphew, Kathryn Kroll, Leslie Fishlock, Lorene Romero, and most importantly, Fran Snider, the best mama a girl could have (wish Daddy could've held this book!). To our beautiful kitties, Samantha and Baby Sherlock, who forced me to get out of my pretty purple Aeron chair and play The Laser Pointer Game with them at exactly 5:15 pm each day.

May the creative force be with you all!

—*Lesa Snider*

THE MISSING MANUAL SERIES

Missing Manuals are witty, superbly written guides to computer products that don't come with printed manuals (which is just about all of them). Each book features a handcrafted index and cross-references to specific pages (not just chapters). Recent and upcoming titles include:

Excel 2013: The Missing Manual by Matthew MacDonald

Microsoft Project 2013: The Missing Manual by Bonnie Biafore

Access 2013: The Missing Manual by Matthew MacDonald

Windows 8: The Missing Manual by David Pogue

NOOK HD: The Missing Manual, Second Edition by Preston Gralla

Kindle Fire HD: The Missing Manual, Second Edition by Peter Meyers

iPod: The Missing Manual, Eleventh Edition by J.D. Biersdorfer

CSS3: The Missing Manual, Third Edition by David Sawyer McFarland

iPad: The Missing Manual, Fifth Edition by J.D. Biersdorfer

PHP & MySQL: The Missing Manual, Second Edition by Brett McLaughlin

Adobe Edge Animate: The Missing Manual by Chris Grover

iPhone: The Missing Manual, Sixth Edition by David Pogue

QuickBooks 2013: The Missing Manual by Bonnie Biafore

WordPress: The Missing Manual by Matthew MacDonald

Photoshop Elements 11: The Missing Manual by Barbara Brundage

Go to *www.missingmanuals.com/library.html* for a full list of all Missing Manuals in print.

Foreword

In the short but crowded history of consumer technology, only two products ever became so common, influential, and powerful that their names become *verbs*.

Google is one.

Photoshop is the other.

("Did you Google that guy who asked you out?" "Yeah—he's crazy. He Photoshopped his last girlfriend out of all his pictures!")

It's safe to say that these days, not a single photograph gets published, in print or online, without having been processed in Photoshop first. It's usually perfectly innocent stuff: a little color adjustment, contrast boosting, or cropping.

But not always. Sometimes, the editing actually changes the photo so that it no longer represents the original, and all kinds of ethical questions arise. Remember when *TV Guide* Photoshopped Oprah's head onto Ann-Margaret's body? When *Time* magazine darkened O.J. Simpson's skin to make him look more menacing on the cover? Or when *National Geographic* moved two of the pyramids closer together to improve the composition?

Well, you get the point: Photoshop is magic. Thanks to Photoshop, photography is no longer a reliable record of reality.

And now, all that magic is in your hands. Use it wisely.

Trouble is, Photoshop is a *monster*. It's *huge*. Just opening it is like watching a slumbering beast heave into consciousness. Dudes: Photoshop has over *500 menu commands*.

In short, installing Photoshop is like being told that you've just won a 747 jumbo jet. You sit down in the cockpit and survey the endless panels of controls and switches. *Now what?*

You don't even get a printed manual anymore.

If there were ever a piece of software that needed the Missing Manual treatment, it was Photoshop.

In 2009, the beast was tamed at last by its new master, Lesa Snider: a natural-born Missing Manual author with Photoshop credentials as long as your arm.

She had worked on Missing Manuals, side by side with me in my office, for four years, in all kinds of editorial and production capacities. Today, when she's not writing the bestselling Photoshop book (you're reading it), she's out in the real world, teaching Photoshop seminars, writing Photoshop articles, reviewing Photoshop for magazines, and generally serving as Photoshop guru to the masses.

The Missing Manual mantra runs through her blood: Make it clear, make it entertaining, make it complete (hence the thickness of this book). And above all, don't just identify a feature: Tell us *what it's for.* Tell us when to use it. (And if the answer is, "You'll *never* use it," tell us that, too.)

Now, I'll be the first to admit that this book isn't for everybody. In fact, it's aimed primarily at two kinds of people: people who have never used Photoshop, and people who have.

But seriously, folks. If you're new to Photoshop, you'll find patient, friendly introductions to all those nutty Photoshoppy concepts like layers, color spaces, image resolution, and so on. And, mercifully, you'll find a lot of loving attention to a time-honored Missing Manual specialty—tips and shortcuts. As Photoshop pros can tell you, you pretty much *have* to learn some of Photoshop's shortcuts or it will crush you like a bug.

On the other hand, if you already have some Photoshop experience, you'll appreciate this book's coverage of Photoshop CC's new features. Some of them are pretty sweet indeed. For example, all the 3D features are built into the standard version of Photoshop; you don't need some expensive Extended Edition to get them. The Camera Raw plug-in is available as a filter, and the Image Size dialog box sports a preview and new techniques for enlargements. And Shake Reduction—unbelievable. Its ability to de-blur a picture you took with an unsteady hand is nearly miraculous.

In any case, get psyched. You now have both the most famous, powerful, magical piece of software on earth—and a 900+-page treasure map to help you find your way.

The only missing ingredients are time, some photos to work on, and a little good taste. You'll have to supply those yourself.

Good luck!

—*David Pogue*

David Pogue is the tech columnist for the New York Times *and* Scientific American, *an Emmy-winning TV correspondent (CBS News and NOVA on PBS), and the creator of the Missing Manual series.*

Introduction

Congratulations on buying one of the most complicated pieces of software ever created. Fortunately, it's also one of the most rewarding. No other program on the market lets you massage, beautify, and transform images like Photoshop. It's so popular that people use its name as a verb: "Dude, you Photoshopped the heck out of her!" You'd be hard-pressed to find a published image that *hasn't* spent some quality time in this program, and those that didn't probably should have.

The bad news is that it's a tough program to learn; you won't become a Photoshop guru overnight. Luckily, you hold in your hot little hands a book that covers the program from a *practical* standpoint, so you'll learn the kinds of techniques you can use every day. It's written in plain English for normal people, so you don't have to be any kind of expert to understand it. You'll also learn just enough theory (where appropriate) to help you understand *why* you're doing what you're doing.

> **NOTE** Adobe used to offer *two* versions of the program: Photoshop Standard and Photoshop Extended, which included extra features such as 3D tools. However, they *combined* the two versions in CC.

What's New in Photoshop CC

Adobe has added some nice new features to Photoshop CC and, as noted above, they rolled *all* of the features that used to be in Photoshop Extended into the CC version. The inclusion of 3D tools aside, Photoshop CC isn't the most feature-packed upgrade the program has seen, but it's still got some good stuff in it, especially in the realm of actions and filters. Here's an overview of the new goodies (don't worry if you don't yet understand some of the terms used here—you'll learn what they mean as you read through this book):

- **Retina ready**. Both Photoshop and Bridge now support Retina displays, Apple's super-high resolution monitors (called HiDPI on PCs) and as such, you'll spot a new 200 percent option in the View menu (which lets you see web graphics at the size they'll appear in a browser). Several plug-ins also support these mind-bogglingly crystal-clear displays including Liquify, "Save for Web," "Merge to HDR," Vanishing Point, Adaptive Wide Angle, Lens Correction, and the Filter Gallery. While the new Adobe Camera Raw 8 isn't *yet* Retina-happy, it should be soon (probably in version 8.1).

- **Conditional actions**. This super useful new feature lets you record a *conditional* action (see Chapter 18) that chooses among several *previously* recorded actions in order to meet criteria that you set. You'll learn all about it on page 768.

- **Field Blur, Iris Blur, and Tilt-Shift filters now work with Smart Filters**. Some of the most useful new features in Photoshop CS6 were the Field Blur, Iris Blur, and Tilt-Shift filters, which make creating blurry backgrounds easier than ever. Here in CC, those filters now work with Smart Filters, so you can run 'em non-destructively *without* having to duplicate your Image layer. These filters also take advantage of OpenCL, a technology found in newer graphics cards that lets Photoshop tap into the card's processing power. As a result, previewing and applying these filters to your images is noticeably faster.

- **Camera Raw filter and other Camera Raw enhancements**. One of the most useful changes in Photoshop CC is that the Camera Raw plug-in is available as a Photoshop *filter* (it works as a Smart Filter, too). Camera Raw also has a new Radial filter that lets you apply adjustments in a *circular* fashion either from the inside of your image to its edges or vice-versa (it's like a circular Gradient Filter). You can now heal areas that *aren't* round using Camera Raw's Spot Removal tool, and the new Upright feature lets you correct perspective problems. Last but not least, when merging multiple 32-bit image exposures using the "Merge to HDR Pro" dialog box, you can have Photoshop *automatically* create a Smart Object out of the result and then open it in the Camera Raw filter for fine-tuning. (Camera Raw is discussed throughout this book, but the bulk of the coverage is in Chapter 9.)

- **Shake Reduction filter**. In previous versions of Photoshop, there wasn't much hope of making a blurry image look sharp (aside from using the Emboss filter). However, Photoshop CC's new Shake Reduction filter analyzes your image and *traces* the pattern of the blurry parts in order to eradicate it. It does an *incredible* job on images that are slightly blurry due to camera shake. You'll learn all about it starting on page 462.

- **Redesigned Smart Sharpen filter**. Rounding out the improvements in the sharpening realm is the completely redesigned Smart Sharpen filter. It sports a new and improved sharpening method that keeps from introducing halos around high-contrast edges, a new noise-reduction slider, as well as a simplified, resizable dialog box.

- **Faster Liquify filter that works with Smart Filters**. The Liquify filter also takes advantage of your graphics card's processing power, so it runs up to 16 times faster than it used to (especially when you're working with big files). It now works with *Smart Filters* (page 632), too, which lets you use it nondestructively on *any* kind of layer including Shape, Type, and Video layers. Its masking controls were also simplified, it sports a new *Smooth* tool, and the new Load Last Mesh button lets you summon the last mesh you made.

- **Minimum and Maximum filter improvements**. Both of these filters were notorious for making round things appear square, though by choosing Roundness from the new Preserve drop-down menu, that won't happen. And when you choose Roundness, you can enter decimals into the filters' Radius fields, letting you be a lot more precise when you're using 'em to fine-tune a layer mask.

- **Brand-new Image Size dialog box and interpolation method**. The Image Size dialog box has been simplified and redesigned to include a resizable image preview that helps you *see* the results of your settings before applying 'em, which is incredibly helpful in choosing the right interpolation method. The new Preserve Details interpolation method sharpens areas of fine detail in your image in order to produce higher quality enlargements (this new method includes a noise-reduction slider, too). All interpolation methods now have keyboard shortcuts, and there's a handy list of size presets in the new Fit To drop-down menu.

- **Rounded Rectangle tool has editable properties**. One of the problems with using the Rounded Rectangle tool was that you had to *guess* at the Radius setting in order to produce the corner roundness that you want. That's all changed now. When you use the Rounded Rectangle tool (or the plain ol' Rectangle tool) in Photoshop CC, the Properties panel that opens includes four fields that you can use to alter the roundness of each corner individually, *after* you've drawn the shape.

- **Path improvements**. You can now activate *multiple* paths in the Paths panel by Shift- or ⌘-clicking (Ctrl-clicking on a PC) them, which lets you delete, duplicate, and change their stacking order en masse (you can also Shift-click to activate 'em in your document). And speaking of paths, Photoshop CC also lets you use the space bar to reposition an anchor point *while* you're drawing a path.

- **Selective layer filtering**. This option lets you view only the layers that are currently *active* in the Layers panel. It's really handy when your Layers panel is long and you're editing layers that don't necessarily match any of the other layer-filtering criteria, as well as when you're editing vector shapes. Page 73 has details.

- **Default character and paragraph styles**. Once you've saved frequently-used text formatting as character or paragraph styles, you can use the new Save As Defaults option to make Photoshop *automatically* add them to new documents, as well as to *existing* documents that didn't previously contain any styles. You can also activate multiple styles in the Character or Paragraphs panel and delete 'em all at once.

- **CSS support**. To the delight of web designers worldwide, the new Copy CSS command lets you copy color and formatting info into your computer's memory as fully functional CSS code, so you can then paste it into your favorite HTML editor. You'll spot the new command in the shortcut menus you get when you Control-click (right click) Type and Shape layers. Also new is the ability to point the Swatches panel to an HTML, CSS, or SVG file and have it automatically generate swatches from the color info *inside* those files (the Tip on page 494 tells you how to accomplish this).

- **3D**. The experience of painting 3D objects in Photoshop has been improved and live previews are up to a hundred times faster than in previous versions of the program. To help you get a grip on 3D, this book sports a brand-new chapter (Chapter 21) that shows you how to start creating and working with 3D text and objects.

There are also tons of little changes in Photoshop CC, too, that are the direct result of Adobe's customer feedback initiative called Just Do It (JDI). Here's a partial list: the Crop tool now includes a setting that brings back the resolution field in the Options bar, you can save more than one Photoshop document at the same time, the Color Range command is better at detecting faces, a new anti-aliasing option makes text look like it will in popular web browsers, the Type tool new supports Indic languages, the Migrate Presets feature now copies over presets that aren't currently loaded in Photoshop and doesn't require a restart, metadata and ICC profiles are now saved with PNG files, Shape layer thumbnails now accurately preview the whole document, the Color Picker's hex field is automatically highlighted when you open the dialog box, and last but not least, the Brush Preset picker now includes a brush tip preview as well as angle and roundness controls (which are also accessible from the Brush tool's shortcut menu).

About This Book

Adobe has pulled together an amazing amount of information in its online help system (see online Appendix B, available from this book's Missing CD page at *www.missingmanuals.com/cds*), but despite all these efforts, it's geared toward seasoned Photoshop jockeys and assumes a level of skill that you may not have. The explanations are very clipped and to the point, which makes it difficult to get a real feel for the tool or technique you need help with.

That's where this book comes in. It's intended to make learning Photoshop CC tolerable—and even enjoyable—by avoiding technical jargon as much as possible and explaining *why* and *when* you'll want to use (or avoid) certain features of the program. It's a conversational and friendly approach intended to speak to beginners and seasoned pixel pushers alike.

Meet the Creative Cloud

Dude, what the heck happened to Photoshop CS7? What on earth does "CC" mean?

Great question. For the first time ever, Adobe isn't shipping perpetually licensed, boxed versions of their products; instead, your only option is to subscribe to—and then download—the software.

Using a service called the Adobe Creative Cloud, you can subscribe on an annual or monthly basis to one or all of Adobe's products. For example, a Single App Creative Cloud subscription for Photoshop CC costs about $20 a month and gives you access to both Mac and PC versions of the program that you can install on up to two machines (say, a desktop and laptop). If you use two or more Adobe programs (say, Photoshop and InDesign), you might want to subscribe to all of their products which, as of this writing, includes 24 programs and services (both Mac and PC versions)—including the entire Adobe web font collection and the ability to share your projects with the collaborative Behance community (see the Note on page 2)—for about $50 a month. (Of course, these prices could change; check with Adobe for current pricing.)

Whichever option you choose, you simply download the software to your machine and install it, just like you normally would. However, once a month your Adobe software phones home via the Internet to validate your Creative Cloud account; if Adobe can't validate your account, your software stops working (along with your fonts). In other words, if you don't pay, you don't get to play with the software (though there is a 30-day grace period if, for whatever reason, your computer can't connect to the Internet).

Once you're a Creative Cloud subscriber, you get 20 GB of storage space, which you can use to hosts websites and sync documents between computers and tablets (think iPads), and to back up documents or share them with others (regardless of whether or not those folks have Creative Cloud subscriptions). You also get the ability to sync custom settings to the Cloud so they're accessible on other machines, such as actions, prefer-

ences, brushes, styles, and so on. For example, when you subscribe to the Creative Cloud (even if it's just for Photoshop) and then install the program, your Adobe ID appears in the Photoshop menu (the Edit menu on a PC) with a submenu that contains Sync Settings Now and Manage Sync Settings options. Choosing the latter opens the Sync Settings preferences (page 21) so you can decide which presets to sync. You'll also see a new sync icon near the status bar at the bottom left of an open document (it's labeled in *Figure 1-1* on page 2); give it a click to sync your goodies.

You can also sync documents between devices. For example, you can designate a folder on your hard drive for syncing, and then any items you put into it automatically sync to the Creative Cloud for access elsewhere (say, home or work). Subscribers also get their hands on new features as soon as Adobe rolls 'em out. (To learn the current version number of your copy of Photoshop CC, choose Help→System Info.)

You might ask, "Is this a good deal?" Well, if you typically upgrade your copy of Photoshop every other year, then subscribing to it costs more than twice as much as you'd pay to upgrade it over that period of time (though doing so is no longer an option). However, if you upgrade yearly, then you'll pay a mere $40 more per year for Creative Cloud but gain access to new features as soon as they're released, as well as the syncing and sharing services mentioned above. The bottom line is that now the only way to get Photoshop CC is to subscribe to it. Adobe will continue to sell and support Photoshop CS6 for a while; however, that's the last licensed copy you'll ever get (and there's nothing wrong with keeping it on your machine if you already own it). Like it or not, we're in the realm of rental software now.

If you're in North America, you can purchase a Creative Cloud subscription through Adobe.com, Amazon.com, or Staples. com. Folks in other countries should go through Adobe.com.

And that, dear friends, is why the program is now called Photoshop Creative Cloud (a.k.a. Photoshop CC).

Some of the tutorials in this book refer to files you can download from this book's Missing CD page on the Missing Manuals website (*www.missingmanuals.com/cds*) so you can practice the techniques you're reading about. And throughout the book, you'll find several kinds of sidebar articles. The ones labeled "Up to Speed" help newcomers to Photoshop do things or explain concepts that veterans are probably already familiar with. Those labeled "Power Users' Clinic" cover more advanced topics for the brave of heart.

NOTE Photoshop CC functions almost identically on Mac and Windows computers, but the screenshots in this book were all taken on a Mac for the sake of consistency. However, the keyboard shortcuts for the two operating systems are different, so you'll find both included here—Mac shortcuts first, followed by Windows shortcuts in parentheses. In a few instances, the locations of certain folders differ, and in those cases, you get the directions for both operating systems.

UP TO SPEED

What Does "64-bit" Mean?

The cool phrase in computing circles for the past few years has been "64-bit." While that term may sound pretty geeky, it's actually not that intimidating. 64-bit programs (a.k.a. "applications" or "apps") simply know how to count higher than 32-bit programs.

So what does that mean in practice? 32-bit programs can open and work with files that are up to 4 gigabytes in size—which is already huge. 64-bit programs, on the other hand, can open files that are *way* bigger than that, as long as your computer's operating system can handle 64-bit apps. (Mac OS X 10.5 [Leopard] and Microsoft Windows Vista [the 64-bit version, anyway] and later are up to the task.) 64-bit programs can also make use of more memory than their 32-bit counterparts, which is crucial when you're working with big honkin' files. For example, the 64-bit version of Photoshop lets you use more than 4 gigs of RAM, which makes it run faster. (You can change how your

machine's memory is allotted by tweaking Photoshop's preferences as described on pages 22–23.)

The bottom line is that, if you work with gigantic files, you'll want to use the 64-bit version of Photoshop. And since most third-party plug-ins (Chapter 19) and filters (Chapter 15) have now been upgraded to work in 64-bit mode, there's little reason to cast a single glance backward. In Photoshop CC, the 64-bit version is all you get on a Mac; however, when you install Photoshop on a PC, you get two full versions of the program in two separate folders: one for 64-bit mode and another for 32-bit mode (located in *Program Files\Adobe\Photoshop CC* and *Program Files (x86)\Adobe\Photoshop CC*, respectively). Simply quit one program and then launch the other.

You can still share Photoshop files with both Mac and PC folks, just like you always have.

About the Outline

This hefty book is divided into six parts, each devoted to the type of things you'll do in Photoshop CC:

- **Part One: The Basics.** Here's where you'll learn the essential skills you need to know before moving forward. Chapter 1 gives you the lay of the land and teaches you how to work with panels and make the Photoshop workspace your own. You'll also find out the many ways of undoing what you've done, which is crucial when you're still learning. Chapter 2 covers how to open and view documents efficiently, and how to set up new documents so you have a solid foundation on which to build your masterpieces.

  Chapter 3 dives into the most powerful Photoshop feature of all: layers. You'll learn about the different kinds of layers and how to manage them, the power of layer masks, and how to use layer styles for special effects. Chapter 4 explains how to select part of an image so you can edit just that area. In Chapter 5, you'll dive headfirst into the science of color as you explore channels (Photoshop's way of storing the colors that make up your image) and learn how to use channels to create selections; you'll also pick up some channel-specific editing tips along the way.

> **NOTE** In this book, the word "select" is used only to refer to the act of creating selections. In most other instances, the word "activate" is used instead, as in "activate the layer" or "activate the Crop tool."

- **Part Two: Editing Images.** Chapter 6 starts off by explaining a variety of ways you can crop images, both in Photoshop and in Camera Raw. The chapter then demystifies resolution once and for all so you'll understand how to resize images without reducing their quality. In Chapter 7, you'll learn how to combine images in a variety of ways, from simple techniques to more complex ones. Chapter 8 covers draining, changing, and adding color, arming you with several techniques for creating gorgeous black-and-white images, delicious duotones, partial-color effects, and more. You'll also learn how to change the color of almost anything.

  Chapter 9 focuses on color-correcting images, beginning with auto fixer-uppers, and then moving on to the wonderfully simple world of Camera Raw and the more complicated realm of Levels and Curves. Chapter 10 is all about retouching images and is packed with practical techniques for slimming and trimming, and explains how to use the Dodge and Burn tools in ways that won't harm your images. This chapter also covers using the various Content-Aware tools to remove objects from images or scoot an object from one spot to another, as well as how to use the Puppet Warp command to move just your subject's arms and legs. Chapter 11 covers numerous ways to sharpen your images in order to make 'em look especially crisp.

- **Part Three: The Artistic Side of Photoshop.** This part of the book is all about creativity. Chapter 12 explains the many ways of choosing colors for your documents, and teaches you how to create a painting from scratch. Chapter 13 focuses on using the mighty Pen tool to create complex illustrations and selections, along with how to use Photoshop's various shape tools. Chapter 14 teaches you the basics of typography and then moves on to creating and formatting text in Photoshop. You'll find out how to outline, texturize, and place photos inside text, among other fun yet practical techniques. Chapter 15 covers the wide world of filters including how to use Smart Filters; you'll come away with at least one practical use for one or more of the filters in every category.

- **Part Four: Printing and the Web.** In Chapter 16, you'll learn about printing images, beginning with why it's so darn hard to make what comes out of your printer match what you see onscreen. You'll learn about the different color modes and how to prepare images for printing, whether you're using an inkjet printer or sending your files to a commercial printing press. Chapter 17 focuses on preparing images for the Web, walks you through the various file formats you can use, explains how to protect your images online, and shows you how to use Bridge to create web galleries. Rounding out the chapter is info on using the Slice tool on a web page design, and step-by-step instructions for creating an animated GIF.

- **Part Five: Photoshop Power.** This part is all about working smarter and faster. It starts with an entire chapter devoted to using actions (Chapter 18), which help you automate tasks you perform regularly. Chapter 19 covers installing and using plug-ins (small programs you can add on to Photoshop) and recommends some of the best on the market. Chapter 20 teaches you how to edit videos in Photoshop, Chapter 21 gets you started creating and working with 3D objects and text, and Chapter 22 explains how to use both Adobe Bridge and Photoshop's Mini Bridge panel.

- **Part Six: Appendixes**. Appendix A covers installing and uninstalling Photoshop. Appendix B gives you some troubleshooting tips, explains Photoshop's help system, and points you to resources other than this book. Appendix C gives you a tour of the mighty Tools panel. And finally, Appendix D walks you through Photoshop CC's 200+ menu items. All the appendixes are available on this book's Missing CD page at *www.missingmanuals.com/cds*.

For Photographers

If you're relatively new to digital-image editing or you've always shot film and are taking your first brave steps into the world of digital cameras, you'll be amazed at what you can do in Photoshop, but there's a lot to learn. By breaking Photoshop down into digestible chunks that are most important to *you*, the learning process will feel less overwhelming. (There's no sense in tackling the whole program when you'll only use a quarter of it—if that much.)

The most important thing to remember is to be patient and try not to get frustrated. With time and practice, you *can* master the bits of Photoshop that you need to do your job better. And with the help of this book, you'll conquer everything faster than you might think. As you gain confidence, you can start branching out into other parts of the program to broaden your skills. Here's a suggested roadmap for quickly learning the most useful aspects of the program:

1. **Read all of Chapters 1 and 2 (or at the very least skim them).**

   These two chapters show you where to find all of Photoshop's tools and features, and explain how the program is organized. You'll learn how to open, view, and save images, which is vital stuff to know.

2. **If your photos aren't on your computer already, read Chapter 22 about Adobe Bridge.**

   Bridge is an amazingly powerful image organizer and browser that can help get your images onto your computer. It takes care of importing, renaming, and even backing up your precious photos.

3. **If you shoot in raw format (see the box on page 366) and need to color-correct your images in a hurry, skip ahead to the section on editing in Camera Raw in Chapter 9 (page 361).**

   This chapter includes an entire section on practical editing techniques you can use in Camera Raw, and a quick reference that points you to where you'll find other Camera-Raw techniques throughout this book.

4. **If you *don't* shoot in raw and you need to resize your images before editing them, read Chapter 6.**

   This chapter explains resolution and how to resize images without reducing their quality.

5. **Proceed with Chapters 8, 9, and 10 to learn about color effects, color-correcting, and retouching people, respectively.**

6. **When you're ready to sharpen your images, read Chapter 11.**

7. **Finally, when you want to print your photos, read the section on printing with an inkjet printer in Chapter 16 (page 685).**

   This chapter walks you through printing photos and includes advice on how to print borderless images.

That's all you need to get started. When you're ready to dive more fully into Photoshop, pick back up at Chapter 3, which covers layers, and then move on through the book as time permits.

The Very Basics

This book assumes that you know how to use a computer and that, to some extent, you're an expert double-clicker and menu opener. If not, here's a quick refresher:

To *click* means to move the point of your cursor over an object onscreen and then press the left mouse or trackpad button once. To *right-click* means to press the right mouse button once, which produces a menu of special features called a *shortcut menu*. (If you're on a Mac and have a mouse with only one button, hold down the Control key while you click to simulate right-clicking.) To *double-click* means to press the left button twice, quickly, without moving the cursor between clicks. To *drag* means to click an object and then use the mouse to move it while still holding down the left mouse button.

Most selection buttons onscreen are pretty obvious, but you may not be familiar with *radio buttons*: To choose an option, you click one of these little empty circles that are arranged in a list.

You'll find tons of keyboard shortcuts throughout this book, and they're huge time-savers. If you see a sentence like, "Press ⌘-S (Ctrl+S) to save your file," that means to hold down the ⌘ key (or Ctrl key, if you're using a PC), and then press the S key, too; then let go of both keys. (This book lists Mac keyboard shortcuts first, followed by Windows shortcuts in parentheses.) Other keyboard shortcuts are so complex that you'll need to use multiple fingers, both hands, and a well-placed elbow.

If you're comfortable with basic concepts like these, you're ready to get started with this book.

About→These→Arrows

In *Photoshop CC: The Missing Manual* (and in all Missing Manuals, for that matter), you'll see arrows sprinkled throughout each chapter in sentences like this: "Choose Filter→Blur→Tilt-Shift." This is a shorthand way of helping you find files, folders, and menu items without having to read through painfully long and boring instructions. For example, the sentence quoted above is a short way of saying: "At the top of the Photoshop window, locate the Filter menu. Click it and, in the list that appears, look for the Blur category. Point to the word Blur without clicking and, in the resulting submenu, click Tilt-Shift" (see *Figure I-1*).

FIGURE I-1

Choosing Filter→Blur→Tilt-Shift takes you to the menu item shown here.

About MissingManuals.com

On the Missing Manuals website (*www.missingmanuals.com*), you'll find this book's Missing CD page, which includes links to downloadable images mentioned in this book's tutorials, in case you want to practice techniques without using your own photos.

A word about the image files for the tutorials: To make life easier for people with dial-up Internet connections, the file sizes have been kept pretty small. This means you probably won't want to print the results of what you create (you'll end up with a print about the size of a matchbook). But that doesn't really matter because the files are only meant for onscreen use. You'll see notes throughout the book about which practice images are available for any given chapter.

On the website, you can also find articles, tips, and updates to this book. If you click the Errata link, you'll see any corrections we've made to the book, too; if you find something in these pages that you think is wrong, feel free to report it by clicking that link. Each time the book is printed, we'll update it with any confirmed corrections. If you want to be certain that your own copy is up to the minute, this is where to check for any changes. And thanks for reporting any errors or suggesting corrections.

We'd love to hear your suggestions for new books in the Missing Manual line. There's a place for that on *www.missingmanuals.com*, too. And while you're online, you can also register this book at *www.oreilly.com/register*. Registering means we can send you updates about this book, *and* you'll be eligible for special offers like discounts on future editions.

Safari® Books Online

Safari® Books Online is an on-demand digital library that lets you easily search over 7,500 technology and creative reference books and videos to find the answers you need quickly.

With a subscription, you can read any page and watch any video from our library online. Read books on your cellphone and mobile devices. Access new titles before they're available for print, and get exclusive access to manuscripts in development and post feedback for the authors. Copy and paste code samples, organize your favorites, download chapters, bookmark key sections, create notes, print out pages, and benefit from tons of other timesaving features.

Photoshop CC Guided Tour

Photoshop CC is bursting with fabulous features that'll help you edit and create your very own digital masterpieces. If this is your first foray into the world of Photoshop, all these features will be new to you. If you're an experienced pixel pusher, there are some surprises waiting for you, too. If you're upgrading from Photoshop CS5 or earlier, Adobe introduced *major* changes to the work environment back in CS6—like a brand-new color theme—and while these changes make Photoshop easier to use, they take some getting used to.

This chapter gives you a solid foundation on which to build your Photoshop skills. You'll learn how to work with the Application Frame and how to wrangle document windows and panels. Once you've gotten them placed just right, you'll learn how to save your setup as a custom workspace. If you're a beginner, the section on using Undo commands and history states will teach you how to fix mistakes and back out of almost anything you've done. Finally, you'll learn how to fine-tune Photoshop's behavior through preferences and built-in tools (called *presets*) that let you personalize your experience even more. Let's dive in!

Meet the Application Frame

When you launch Photoshop CC for the first time, you're greeted by the *Application Frame* shown in *Figure 1-1*. This frame confines all things Photoshop to a single resizable *and* movable window. You can grab the whole mess—documents, panels, and all—and drag it to one side of your screen (or better yet, to another monitor) so it's out of the way. And if you open more than one document, they're displayed in handy tabs that you can rearrange by dragging.

Chances are, you'll either love the Application Frame or hate it. If you're on a computer running Windows, you're used to programs looking and behaving this way. But if you're on a Mac and you're coming from an older version of Photoshop (like CS3), this arrangement may feel a little odd; in that case, you can turn off the frame by choosing Window→Application Frame to make Photoshop switch to the floating-window view used in older versions of the program. (PC folks are stuck with the frame.)

> **NOTE** In Photoshop CC, you may spot two new icons at the bottom of each document window, to the right of the zoom-level indicator. The first icon, which looks like a tiny gear with two arrows to its right (labeled in *Figure 1-1*) lets Creative Cloud subscribers sync their preferences and presets to the Creative Cloud so they can access 'em on another machine (see the box on page xxvii for more on the Creative Cloud). The second icon, which looks like a rectangle with a curved arrow inside it, lets you upload an image to the portfolio-sharing website Behance. (To learn more about Behance, visit *www.lesa.in/adobebehance*.)

Tools panel
Options bar
Document tabs   Document window   Panels

FIGURE 1-1

You can open several images at the same time; just click a document's tab to summon it front and center for editing. Photoshop stores the tools and adjustments you'll use most in the panels on the left and right sides of the Application Frame; a full introduction to panels starts on page 7. (See page 12 to learn how to make your Tools panel have two columns like the one shown here.) The upside to using the Application Frame is that all of Photoshop's bits and pieces stay together as you move things around (as long as the panels are still docked—see page 7).

Zoom level   Sync settings with Creative Cloud   Drag corner or sides to resize frame

> **NOTE** Adobe reduced clutter back in Photoshop CS6 by removing the Application bar. Introduced in CS4, it housed extras like guides, grids, and rulers, as well as several menus. As you'll learn in the next few pages, those items are now sprinkled throughout the Tools panel, the View menu, and the Window menu. Also, if you use Photoshop *alongside* other programs, the box on page 4 explains how to get Photoshop out of the way *without* quitting it.

The Almighty Options Bar

Lording over the document window is the Options bar (*Figure 1-2*, top), which lets you customize the behavior of nearly every item in the Tools panel. This bar automatically changes to include settings related to the tool you're currently using. Unfortunately, the Options bar's labels are fairly cryptic, so it can be hard to figure out what the heck all those settings do. Luckily, you can point your cursor at any setting to see a little yellow pop-up description called a *tooltip* (you don't need to click—just don't move your mouse for a couple seconds).

TIP If the tooltips drive you crazy, you can hide 'em by choosing Photoshop→Preferences→Interface [Edit→Preferences→Interface on a PC] and turning off Show Tool Tips.

When you first install Photoshop, the Options bar is perched at the top of the screen, but it doesn't have to stay there. If you'd rather put it somewhere else, grab its left end and drag it wherever you want, as shown in *Figure 1-2*, middle. If you decide to put it back later (also called *docking*), just drag it to the top of the screen and, when you see a thin blue line appear (*Figure 1-2*, bottom), release your mouse button.

TIP If a tool seems to be misbehaving, it's likely because you changed one of the Options bar's settings and forgot to change it back. These settings are *sticky*: Once you change them, they *stay* that way until you change them back.

FIGURE 1-2

Top: The Options bar is customization central for whatever tool you're currently using. However, it doesn't have to live at the top of the screen; you can undock it by dragging the tiny dotted lines circled here.

Middle: Once you've freed the Options bar, you can drag it anywhere you want by grabbing the dark gray bar on its far left.

Bottom: To redock the Options bar, drag it to the top of your screen. Once you see a thin blue line like the one shown here, release your mouse button. (If you're feeling frisky, you can dock it to the bottom of your screen instead!)

> **NOTE** The Options bar also includes the workspace menu, which lets you change the way your Photoshop environment is set up. You'll learn all about workspaces on page 10.

Swapping Screen Modes

Photoshop includes three different *screen modes* for your document-viewing pleasure. Depending on what you're doing, one will suit you better than the others. For example, you can make an image take up your whole screen (with or without the menus and Options bar), hide Photoshop's panels, and so on (see *Figure 1-3*). To give each mode a spin, you first need to open an image file: Choose File→Open, navigate to where the image lives, and then click Open.

> **TIP** You can free up precious screen real estate by pressing the Tab key to hide Photoshop's Options bar and panels (pressing Shift-Tab hides all the panels *except* the Tools panel). This trick is a great way to get rid of distractions when you're editing images, especially if you have a small monitor. To bring the panels back, press Tab again or mouse over to the edge of the Photoshop window where the panels *should* be; when you move your cursor away from the panels, they'll disappear again. (If you mouse too far away from Photoshop's edge, nothing happens.)

It's a snap to jump between modes. Just press the F key repeatedly (unless you're in the middle of cropping an image or using the Type tool—if you are, you'll type a bunch of Fs) or use the Screen Modes menu at the bottom of the Tools panel (circled in *Figure 1-3*, top). These are your choices:

UP TO SPEED

Hiding vs. Quitting

If you need to do some work on your desktop or in another program, you can temporarily *hide* Photoshop, saving you the time and toe-tapping of quitting it and then restarting it again later.

On a Mac, press ⌘-Control-H or click the yellow dot at the top left of the Application Frame to minimize the window. Your workspace disappears, but Photoshop keeps running in the background. To bring it back to the forefront, click its icon in the Dock. You can also make Photoshop temporarily disappear by pressing ⌘-H; the first time you do, a dialog box appears asking if you'd like to *assign* that keyboard shortcut to make it hide Photoshop instead of hiding text highlighting, guides,

and so on. (To change it back, edit your keyboard shortcuts as explained in the box on page 27, or delete Photoshop's preferences as described in the first Note on page 21.)

On a PC, you can hide (minimize) the program by clicking the minus button in Photoshop's upper right; Windows tucks the program down into your taskbar. To get it back, click its taskbar icon.

If your machine has at least 8 GB of memory (RAM), there's absolutely no downside to hiding the program. However, if you're low on memory and your machine's fan is cranking away, then choose File→Quit (File→Exit on a PC) instead.

FIGURE 1-3

The many faces of Photoshop: Standard Screen Mode on (top), Full Screen With Menu Bar (bottom left), and Full Screen (bottom right). You can edit images in any of these modes, though some give you more screen real estate than others. You can also hide or show the Options bar and panels by pressing the Tab key.

The Screen Modes menu used to live in the Application bar, but back in CS6 it migrated south to the bottom of the Tools panel. (Page 12 tells you how to switch to the two-column Tools panel shown here.)

- **Standard Screen Mode** is the view you see when you launch Photoshop for the first time. This mode includes menus, the Application Frame, the Options bar, panels, and document windows. Use this mode when the Application Frame is active and you need to scoot the whole of Photoshop—windows and all—around on your monitor (except for undocked panels or free-floating windows).

- **Full Screen Mode With Menu Bar** completely takes over your screen, puts your document in the center on a dark gray canvas or frame, and attaches any open panels to the left and right edges of your screen. This mode is great for day-to-day editing because you can see all of Photoshop's tools and menus without being distracted by the files and folders on your desktop. The dark gray background is also easy on the eyes and a great choice when color-correcting images (a brightly colored desktop can affect your color perception).

TIP You can change Photoshop's canvas color anytime by Control-clicking (right-clicking on a PC) the canvas itself. From the shortcut menu that appears, choose from Default (the dark, charcoal gray you see now), Black, Dark Gray, Medium Gray, or Light Gray. If none of those colors float your boat, you can pick your own by choosing Select Custom Color to open the Color Picker, which is explained on page 489.

- **Full Screen Mode** hides all of Photoshop's menus and panels, centers the document on your screen, and puts it on a black background. (If you've got rulers turned on, they'll still appear, though you can turn 'em off by pressing ⌘-R [Ctrl+R]). This mode is great for displaying and evaluating your work or for distraction-free editing. And the black background really makes images pop off the screen (though the next section shows you how to change it to another color—dark gray, say—if you wish).

Changing Photoshop's Appearance

While the dark gray interface colors introduced in CS6 are supposed to be easier on the eyes and help you see the colors in images more accurately, you may disagree. You may also want to increase the size of the text labels in the Options bar and panels. Fortunately, you can change several aspects of the program's appearance by choosing Photoshop→Preferences→Interface (Edit→Preferences→Interface on a PC), as *Figure 1-4* shows.

FIGURE 1-4

Not a fan of the dark gray color theme? Use the Appearance settings shown here to pick something lighter (click the light gray square to revert to CS5's color theme). To change Full Screen Mode's background (discussed in the previous section) to something other than black, use the Full Screen drop-down menu.

If the text labels throughout the program have you squinting, you can make 'em bigger with the UI Font Size menu near the bottom of this dialog box. Once you make a selection, you have to choose File→Quit (File→Exit on a PC) and then restart Photoshop to make it take effect.

TIP Unlike in previous versions, as of this writing, Photoshop CC *doesn't* let you cycle through its color themes by pressing Shift-F1 and Shift-F2.

The next section tells you how to customize Photoshop's look and feel even *more* by opening, closing, rearranging, and resizing panels. Read on!

Working with Panels

The right side of the Application Frame is home to a slew of small windows called *panels* (years ago, they were called palettes), which let you work with popular features like colors, adjustments, layers, and so on. You're free to organize the panels however you like and position them anywhere you want. Panels can be free floating or *docked* (attached) to the top, bottom, left, or right sides of your screen. And you can link panels together into *groups*, which you can then move around. Each panel also has its very own menu, called (appropriately enough) a *panel menu*, located in its top-right corner; its icon looks like four little lines with a downward-pointing triangle and is labeled in *Figure 1-5*.

Double-click tab to collapse panel vertically; single-click tab to expand

Panel menu

Click to expand panel horizontally

Click to collapse panel horizontally

FIGURE 1-5

Here you can see the difference between expanded panels (left) and collapsed panels (right). Double-click a panel's tab to collapse it vertically, rolling it up like a window shade; single-click the tab again to expand the panel.

You can also collapse a panel horizontally by clicking the right-pointing double arrows in its top right (circled, right), at which point it turns into a small button. To expand one of these buttons back into a panel, just click the left-pointing double arrows circled here (circled, middle).

Take a peek on the right side of your screen, and you'll see that Photoshop starts you off with three docked panel groups filled with the goodies it thinks you'll use a lot (there's more on docked panels coming up shortly). The first group contains the Color and Swatches panels; the second group contains Adjustments and Styles; and the third contains Layers, Channels, and Paths. To work with a panel, activate it by clicking its tab.

Panels are like Silly Putty—they're incredibly flexible. You can collapse, expand, move, and resize them, or even swap 'em for other panels. Here's how:

- **Collapse or expand panels**. If panels are encroaching on your editing space, you can shrink them both horizontally and vertically so they look and behave like buttons. To collapse a panel (or panel group) horizontally so that it becomes a button nestled against the side of another panel or the edge of your screen, click the tiny double arrow in its top-right corner; click this same button again to expand the panel. To collapse a panel vertically against the bottom of the panel above it, as shown in *Figure 1-5*, right, double-click the panel's *tab* or the empty area to its right; single-click the tab or double-click the empty area to roll the panel back down. To adjust a panel's width, point your cursor at its left edge and, when the cursor turns into a double-headed arrow, drag left or right to make the panel bigger or smaller (though some panels have a minimum width).

- **Add and modify panel groups**. You can open even *more* panels by opening the Window menu (which lists all of Photoshop's panels) and then clicking the name of the one you want to open. When you do, Photoshop puts the panel in a column to the left of the ones that are already open and adds a tiny button to its right that you can click to collapse it both horizontally and vertically (just click the button again to expand it). If the new panel is part of a group, like the Character and Paragraph panels, the extra panel tags along with it. If it's a panel you expect to use a lot, you can add it to an existing panel group by clicking and dragging the dotted lines above its button into a blank area in the panel group, as shown in *Figure 1-6*.

- **Undock, redock, and close panels**. From the factory, Photoshop docks three sets of panel groups to the right side of your screen (or Application Frame). But you're not stuck with the panels glued to this spot; you can set them free by turning them into *floating* panels. To liberate a panel, grab its tab, pull it out of the group it's in, and then move it anywhere you want (see *Figure 1-7*). When you let go of your mouse button, the panel appears where you put it—all by itself.

You can undock a whole panel group in nearly the same way: Click an empty spot in the group's tab area and drag it out of the dock. Once you release your mouse button, you can drag the group around by clicking the same empty spot in the tab area. Or, if the group is collapsed, click the tiny dotted lines at the top of the group, just below the dark gray bar.

To dock the panel (or panel group) again, drag it back to the right side of your screen. To *prevent* a panel from docking while you're moving it around, ⌘-drag (Ctrl-drag) it instead.

NOTE The Timeline panel (which was called the Animation panel prior to Photoshop CS6) is docked to the *bottom* of your workspace, which is a docking hotspot, too.

FIGURE 1-6

Top: When you open a new panel, Photoshop adds it to a column to the left of your other panels and gives it a handy button that you can click to collapse or expand it. The tiny dotted line above each button is its handle; click and drag one of these handles to reposition the panel in the column, add the panel to a panel group, and so on. If the panel you opened is related to another panel—like the Brush panel and the Brush Presets panel—then both panels will open as a panel group with a single handle (note the two buttons above the circle here).

Middle: When you're dragging a panel into a panel group, wait until you see a blue line around the inside of the group before you release your mouse button. Here, the Kuler panel is being added to a panel group. (You can see a faint version of the Kuler panel's button where the red arrow is pointing.)

Bottom: When you release your mouse button, the new panel becomes part of the group. To rearrange panels within a group, drag their tabs (circled) left or right.

To close a panel, click its tab and drag it out of the panel group to a different area of your screen (*Figure 1-7*); then click the tiny circle in the panel's top-left corner (on a PC, click the X in the panel's top-right corner instead). Don't worry—the panel isn't gone forever; if you want to reopen it, simply choose it from the Windows menu.

FIGURE 1-7

To undock a panel or panel group, click the panel's tab or a free area to the right of the group's tabs and then drag the panel or group somewhere else on your screen. To dock it again, drag it to the right side of your screen—on top of the other panels. When you see a thin blue line appear where you want the panel or group to land, release your mouse button.

TIP If the blue highlight lines are hard to see when you're trying to group or dock panels, try dragging the panels more *slowly*. That way, when you drag the panel into a group or dockable area, the blue highlight hangs around a little longer and the panel itself becomes momentarily transparent.

Getting the hang of undocking, redocking, and arranging panels takes a little practice because it's tough to control where the little rascals land. When the panel you're dragging is about to join a docking area (or a different panel group), a thin blue line appears showing you where the panel or group will go.

Customizing Your Workspace

Once you arrange Photoshop's panels just so, you can keep 'em that way by saving your setup as a *workspace* using the Workspace menu at the far right of the Options bar (see *Figure 1-8*). Straight from the factory, this menu is set to Essentials, which is a good general-use setup that includes panels that most people use regularly. The menu's other options are more specialized: "What's New" includes only new features, 3D is designed for working with 3D objects (new in Photoshop CC and described in Chapter 21), Motion is for video editing, Painting is for (you guessed it) painting, Photography is for working with photos, and Typography is for working with text. To swap workspaces, simply click one of these *presets* (built-in settings), and Photoshop rearranges your panels accordingly.

TIP If you don't see the Workspace menu and you've got the Application Frame turned on, position your cursor on the right side of the Photoshop window and, when the cursor turns into a double-headed arrow, click and drag rightward to increase the size of the frame.

FIGURE 1-8

Most of the built-in workspaces are designed to help you perform specialized tasks. For example, the Painting workspace puts the Brushes and Navigation panels at the top right and groups together the color-related panels you'll undoubtedly use when painting.

Take the built-in workspaces for a test drive—they may give you customization ideas you hadn't thought of. If you're familiar with Photoshop but new to this version, try the "What's New" workspace, which highlights all the menu items that include new features—a great way to see the additions at a glance.

To save your own custom workspace, first arrange things the way you want. Next, click the Workspace menu and choose New Workspace. In the resulting dialog box, give your setup a meaningful name and turn on the checkboxes for the customizations you want Photoshop to save. Aside from panel locations, you can save any keyboard shortcut and menu settings you've changed (see the box on page 27 for more on changing these items)—just be sure to turn on the options for *all* the features you changed or they won't be included in your custom workspace. After you click Save, your workspace shows up at the top of the Workspace menu.

If you've created a custom workspace that you'll never use again, you can send it packin'. First, make sure you aren't currently using the workspace you want to delete. Then, choose Delete Workspace from the Workspace menu and, in the resulting dialog box, pick the offending workspace and then click Delete. Photoshop will ask if you're *sure*; click Yes to finish it off.

The Tools Panel

The Tools panel (*Figure 1-9*, left) is home base for all of Photoshop's editing tools, and it's included in all the built-in workspaces. Until you memorize the tools' keyboard shortcuts, you can't do much without this panel! When you first launch the program, you'll see the Tools panel on the left side of the screen, but you can drag it anywhere you want by clicking the tiny row of vertical dashes near its top (*Figure 1-9*, right).

Once you expand a toolset, you'll see the tools' keyboard shortcuts listed to the right of their names. These shortcuts are great timesavers because they let you switch between tools without moving your hands off the keyboard. To access a tool that's hidden deep within a toolset, add the Shift key to the tool's shortcut key, and you'll cycle through all the tools in that toolset. For example, to activate the Elliptical Marquee tool, press Shift-M repeatedly until that tool's icon appears in the Tools panel.

Click the tool's icon to expand its toolset

Click to toggle
between 1 or
2 column view

Click and drag
to uncock the
Tools panel

Foreground/
Background
chips

FIGURE 1-9

*There's not enough room in the Tools panel
for each tool to have its own spot, so related
tools are grouped into toolsets. The microscopic
triangle at the bottom right of each toolset's
button lets you know it represents more than
one tool (the Move and Zoom tools are the
only ones that live alone). To see the other
tools, click the tool's button and hold down
your mouse button (or right-click the button
instead); Photoshop then displays a list of the
other tools it harbors in a fly-out menu, as
shown here (left).*

*Photoshop starts you off with a one-column
Tools panel (left), but you can collapse it
into two columns (right) by clicking the tiny
double triangles circled here (click them again
to switch back to one column). If you want to
undock the Tools panel, grab the dotted bar
labeled here and drag the panel wherever you
want it. You can dock the Tools panel to the left
or right edge of your screen, or leave it as a
free-floating panel.*

TIP If you need to switch tools *temporarily*—for a quick edit—you can use the spring-loaded tools feature.
Just press and hold a tool's keyboard shortcut to switch to that tool and then perform your edit. As soon as you
release the key, you'll jump back to the tool you were using before. For example, if you're painting with the Brush
and suddenly make an error, press and hold E to switch to the Eraser and fix your mistake. Once you release the
E key, you're back to using the Brush tool. Sweet!

You'll learn about the superpowers of each tool throughout this book. For a brief
overview of each tool, check out Appendix C, which you can download from this
book's Missing CD page at *www.missingmanuals.com/cds*. For a quick reminder
of what each tool does, point your cursor at its icon for a couple of seconds while
keeping your mouse perfectly still; Photoshop displays a handy tooltip that includes
the tool's name and keyboard shortcut.

■ FOREGROUND AND BACKGROUND COLOR CHIPS

Photoshop can handle millions of colors, but its tools let you work with only two
at a time: a foreground color and a background color. Each of these is visible as a
square *color chip* near the bottom of the Tools panel (labeled in *Figure 1-9*, where
they're black and white, respectively). Photoshop uses your foreground color when
you paint or fill something with color; it's where most of the action is. The program

uses your background color to do things like set the second color of a *gradient* (a smooth transition from one color to another, or to transparency) and erase parts of a locked Background layer (page 78); this color is also helpful when you're running special effects like the Clouds filter (page 662).

To change either color, click its color chip once to open the Color Picker (page 489), which lets you select another color for that particular chip. To swap your foreground and background colors, click the curved, double-headed arrow just above the two chips or press X. To set both color chips to their factory-fresh setting of black and white, click the tiny chips to their upper left or press D (in a two-column Tools panel, they're at the lower left). Remember these keyboard shortcuts; they're extremely handy when you work with layer masks, which are discussed in Chapter 3.

Common Panels

As mentioned earlier, when you first launch Photoshop, the program displays the Essentials workspace, which includes several useful panels. Here's a quick rundown of why Adobe considers these panels "essential":

- **Color**. This panel in the upper-right part of your screen includes your current foreground and background color chips. This panel lets you pick a new color for either chip *without* opening the Color Picker (which is a big dialog box that can hide part of your image, though you can always move it). This panel is discussed in detail in Chapter 12.

- **Swatches**. This panel holds miniature samples of colors, giving you easy access to them for use in painting or colorizing images. This panel also stores a variety of color libraries like the Pantone Matching System (special inks used in professional printing). You'll learn all about the Swatches panel in Chapter 12.

- **Adjustments**. This panel lets you create Adjustment layers. Instead of making color and brightness changes to your original image, you can use Adjustment layers to make these changes on a *separate* layer, giving you all kinds of editing flexibility and keeping your original image out of harm's way. They're explained in detail in Chapter 3, and you'll see 'em used throughout this book.

- **Styles**. *Styles* are special effects created with a variety of layer styles. For example, if you've created a glass-button look by using several layer styles, you can save the whole lot of 'em as a *single* style so you can apply them all with a single click (instead of adding each style individually). You can also choose from tons of built-in styles; they're all discussed starting on page 124.

- **Layers**. This is the single most important panel in Photoshop. Layers let you work with images as if they were a stack of transparencies, so you can create one image from many. By using layers, you can adjust the size and opacity of—and add layer styles to—each item independently. Understanding layers is the *key* to Photoshop success and non-destructive editing; you'll learn all about them in Chapter 3.

- **Channels**. *Channels* are where Photoshop stores the color information your images are made from. Channels are extremely powerful, and you can use them to edit the individual colors in an image, which is helpful in sharpening images, creating selections (telling Photoshop which part of an image you want to work with), and so on. Chapter 5 has the scoop on channels.

- **Paths**. *Paths* are the outlines you make with the Pen and shape tools. But these aren't your average, run-of-the-mill lines—they're made up of points and paths instead of pixels, so they'll always look perfectly crisp when printed. You can also make them bigger or smaller without losing any quality. You'll learn all about paths in Chapter 13.

- **History**. This panel is like your very own time machine: It tracks nearly everything you do to your image (the last 20 things, to be exact, though you can change this number using preferences [see page 15]). It appears docked as a button to the left of the Color panel group. The next section explains how to use it to undo what you've recently done (if only that worked in real life!).

- **Properties**. This panel, which is also docked to the left of the Color panel group, is a combination of the Adjustments and Masks panels that were in older versions of Photoshop. It gives you one-stop access to all the settings for Adjustment layers and, new in this version, Shape layers. This panel also lets you create and fine-tune *layer masks*. You'll dive headfirst into masks in Chapter 3; for now, you can think of them as digital masking tape that lets you hide the contents of a layer.

◼ The Power of Undo

Thankfully, Photoshop is extremely forgiving: It'll let you back out of almost anything you do, which is *muy importante* when you're getting the hang of things.

You've got several ways to retrace your steps, including the lifesaving Undo command. Just choose Edit→Undo or press ⌘-Z (Ctrl+Z).

The Undo command lets you undo the very last edit you made. If you need to go back more than one step, use the Step Backward command instead: Choose Edit→Step Backward or press Option-⌘-Z (Alt+Ctrl+Z). Straight from the factory, this command lets you undo the last 20 things you did, one at a time. If you want to go back even further, you can change that number by digging into Photoshop's preferences, as the next section explains. You can step *forward* through your editing history, too, by choosing Edit→Step Forward or Shift-⌘-Z (Shift+Ctrl+Z).

> **NOTE** Photoshop only lets you undo changes back to the point when you first opened the document you're working on, meaning you can't close a document and then undo changes you made *before* you closed it.

Changing How Far Back You Can Go

If you think you might someday need to go back further than your last 20 steps, you can make Photoshop remember up to *1,000* steps by changing the program's preferences. Here's how:

1. **Choose Photoshop→Preferences→Performance (Edit→Preferences→ Performance on a PC).**

2. **In the Preferences dialog box, in the History States field (it's in the History & Cache section), pick the number of undo steps you want Photoshop to remember.**

    You can enter any number between 1 and 1,000 in this field. While increasing the number of history states might help you sleep better, doing so means Photoshop has to keep track of that many more versions of your document, which requires more hard drive space and processing power. So if you increase this setting and then notice that the program is running like molasses—or you're suddenly out of hard drive space—try lowering it.

3. **Click OK when you're finished.**

Turning Back Time with the History Panel

Whereas the Undo and Step Backward commands let you move back through changes one at a time, the History panel (*Figure 1-10*) kicks it up a notch and lets you jump back *several* steps at once. (You can step back through as many history states as you set in Photoshop's preferences.) Using the History panel is much quicker than undoing a long list of changes one by one, and it gives you a nice list of *exactly* what tools or menu items you used to alter the image—in chronological order from top to bottom—letting you pinpoint the exact state you want to jump back to. And, as explained in a moment, you can also take snapshots of an image at various points in the editing process to make it easier to jump back to the state you want.

After you make a few changes to an image, pop open the History panel by clicking its button (circled in *Figure 1-10*, top) or by choosing Window→History. When you do, Photoshop opens a list of the last 20 things you've done to the image, including opening it. To jump back in time, click the step you want to go back to, and Photoshop returns the image to the way it looked at that point. If you stepped back further than you meant to, just click a more recent step in the list.

If you'd like the top of the History panel to include thumbnail previews showing what your image looks like each and every time you *save* the document—in addition to the thumbnail you automatically get by *opening* the image—choose History Options from the History panel's menu. In the resulting dialog box, turn on the Automatically Create New Snapshot When Saving checkbox. Clicking one of these saved-state thumbnails is a fast and easy way to jump back to the last saved version of the document.

FIGURE 1-10

Top: The History panel keeps track of everything you do to your images, beginning with opening them. You can even take snapshots of an image at crucial points during the editing process, like when you convert it to black and white and then add a color tint.

Bottom: If you take a snapshot, you can revert to that state later with a single click. For example, if you've given your image a sepia (brown) tint and later changed it to blue, you can easily go back to the sepia version by clicking the snapshot you took of it, as shown here, without having to step back through all the other changes you made. What a timesaver!

Create new document from current state
Take snapshot
Delete state

TIP You can also get back to the last saved version of a document by choosing File→Revert (page 19).

Taking snapshots of an image along the way lets you mark key points in the editing process. A snapshot is more than a preview of the image because it also includes all the edits you've made up to that point. Think of snapshots as milestones in your editing work: When you reach a critical point that you may want to return to, take a snapshot so you can easily get back to that particular version of the document. To take a snapshot, click the little camera icon at the bottom of the History panel. Photoshop adds the snapshot to the top of the panel, just below the saved-state thumbnail(s). The snapshots you take appear in the list in the order you take them.

NOTE History states don't hang around forever—as soon as you close the document, they're history (ha!). If you think you'll ever want to return to an earlier version of the document, click the "Create new document from current state" button at the bottom of the History panel (labeled in *Figure 1-10*). That way, you've got a totally separate document to return to so you don't have to recreate that particular state.

The History Brush

The History Brush takes the power of the History panel and lets you focus it on specific parts of an image. So instead of sending the *entire* image back in time, you can use this brush to paint edits away *selectively*, revealing the previous state of your choosing. For example, you could darken a portrait with the Burn tool (page 432) and then use the History Brush to undo some of the darkening if you went too far, as shown in *Figure 1-11*.

NOTE The Art History Brush works similarly, but it adds bizarre, stylized effects as it returns your image to a previous state, as shown in the box on page 532.

FIGURE 1-11

By using the History Brush set to the image's earlier state—see step 4 on page 18—you can undo all kinds of effects, including a little over-darkening from using the Burn tool.

You can also reduce the opacity of the History Brush in the Options bar to make the change more gradual.

Here's how to use the History Brush to undo a serious burn you've applied:

1. **Open an image—in this example, a photo of a person—and duplicate the image layer.**

   You'll learn all about opening images in Chapter 2, but, for now, choose File→Open; navigate to where the image lives on your computer, and then click Open. Next, duplicate the layer by pressing ⌘-J (Ctrl+J).

2. **Activate the Burn tool by pressing Shift-O and then darken part of your image.**

   The Burn tool lives in a toolset, so cycle through those tools by pressing Shift-O a couple of times (its icon looks like a hand making an O shape). Then mouse over to your image and drag across an area that needs darkening. Straight from the factory, this tool darkens images pretty severely, giving you a *lot* to undo with the History Brush.

3. **Grab the History Brush by pressing Y.**

   You'll learn all about brushes and their many options in Chapter 12.

4. **Open the History panel and then click a saved state or snapshot.**

   This is where you pick which version of the image you want to go back to. If you dragged more than once in step 2, you'll see several Burn states listed in the panel. To reduce some of the darkening, but not all of it, choose one of the first Burn states (or choose the Open state to get rid of *all* the darkening where you painted). Just click within the panel's left-hand column next to a state to pick it, and you'll see the History Brush's icon appear in that column.

5. **Mouse over to your image and drag to paint the areas that are too dark to reveal the lighter version of the image.**

   To make your change more gradual—if, say, you clicked the Open state but you don't want to erase *all* the darkening—just lower the Opacity setting in the Options bar. That way, if you keep painting in the same place, you'll expose more and more of the original image.

You can use the History Brush to easily undo anything you've done; just pick the state you want to revert to in the History panel and then paint away!

POWER USERS' CLINIC

Erasing to History

At some point, you'll realize that the perfect fix for your image is something you zapped 10 steps ago. For example, you may change the color of an object only to decide later that it looked better the way it was. Argh!

Happily, Photoshop's "Erase to History" feature lets you jump back in time and paint away the edits you no longer want. Erasing to history is a handy way to leave *some* changes in place while recovering your original image in other areas.

First, grab the Eraser tool by pressing E and then, in the Options bar, turn on the "Erase to History" checkbox. Next, in the Layers panel, click the layer you want to edit, and then start dragging over the areas you want to restore to their former glory.

How is erasing to history different from using the History Brush? They both do basically the same thing. The only benefit to using the History Brush instead of "Erase to History" is that the brush lets you use the Option bar's blend mode menu to create different color effects as you erase to the previous state. (You'll learn more about blend modes in Part Two of this book; they control how the colors you add to an image—by painting, darkening, filling, and so on—blend with or cancels out the color that's already there.)

The Revert Command

If you've taken your image down a path of craziness from which you *can't* rescue it by using Undo or the History panel, you can revert back to its most recent saved state by choosing File→Revert. This command opens the previously saved version of the image, giving you a quick escape route back to square one.

> **NOTE** If you haven't made any changes to your image since it was last saved, you can't choose the Revert option; it's grayed out in the File menu.

■ Tweaking Photoshop's Preferences

As you learned earlier in this chapter, Photoshop is pretty darn customizable. In addition to personalizing the way its tools behave and how your workspace looks, you can make lots of changes using the program's preferences, which control different aspects of Photoshop and let you turn features on or off, change how tools act, and fine-tune how the program performs.

> **TIP** Tooltips work on preference settings, too! So if you forget what a setting does, just point your cursor at it for a second or two and you'll get a tiny yellow explanation.

To open the Preferences dialog box, choose Photoshop→Preferences→General (Edit→Preferences→General on a PC), or press ⌘-K (Ctrl+K). When you choose a category on the left side of the dialog box, tons of settings related to that category appear on the right. The following pages give you an idea of the kinds of goodies each category contains, and you'll find guidance on tweaking preferences sprinkled throughout this book.

General

The General section of the Preferences dialog box (*Figure 1-12*) is a sort of catchall for settings that don't fit anywhere else. Most of these options are either self-explanatory (Beep When Done, for example) or covered elsewhere in this book. A few, however, are worth taking a closer look at.

Unless you tell it otherwise, Photoshop displays the Adobe Color Picker (see page 489) anytime you choose a color. If you're more comfortable using your operating system's color picker instead, you can select it from the Color Picker drop-down menu. If you download and install third-party color pickers, they show up in this menu, too. However, since the Adobe Color Picker is designed to work with Photoshop and all its built-in options, using another color picker may mean losing quick access to critical features like Color Libraries (page 492).

The HUD Color Picker setting refers to the on-image color picker you can summon when using a tool that paints, such as the Brush tool. (HUD is short for "heads-up display.") It's also available in a variety of shapes and sizes (strip or wheel in small, medium, and large), and you can choose among 'em here. (See *Figure 12-16* on page 502 for more on using the HUD Color Picker.)

FIGURE 1-12

The General preferences include the History Log settings.

If you turn on the History Log checkbox, Photoshop keeps track of everything that happens to your images. This is an invaluable tool for folks who need to prove what they've done to an image in order to bill clients or produce legal documentation of all the edits they've made (think law enforcement professionals and criminal investigators).

The Image Interpolation menu controls the mathematical voodoo Photoshop performs when you resize an image with the Image Size dialog box (page 234) or the Crop tool (page 218). In CS6, Adobe added the Automatic option, which tells Photoshop to pick the method that it thinks will work best for your image. Will it always choose wisely? Only you can tell.

Other notable options here involve a couple of cool features called animated zoom and flick-panning (both covered in Chapter 2). If your computer is running at a snail's pace, try disabling one or both features by turning off their checkboxes (both features can *really* tax slower video cards).

The other noteworthy options in the General preferences have to do with painting and drawing vectors (Chapters 12 and 13, respectively). For example, "Vary Round Brush Hardness based on HUD vertical movement" means that dragging up or down with your mouse while changing paint color with the on-image color picker (page 502) changes the brush's hardness; if you'd rather have that motion change opacity instead, turn this checkbox off. "Snap Vector Tools and Transforms to Pixel Grid" causes new vector shapes and paths to automatically snap to Photoshop's pixel grid, ensuring precise alignment when you're designing graphics for the Web. Both these settings are turned on straight from the factory.

> **NOTE** Deleting Photoshop's preferences file can be a useful troubleshooting technique. (It resets all the preferences to what they were when you first installed the program.) Just choose File→Quit (File→Exit on a PC), and then press and hold Shift-Option-⌘ (Shift+Alt+Ctrl) when you restart Photoshop. Online Appendix B (available from this book's Missing CD page at *www.missingmanuals.com/cds*) has more about this procedure.

Interface

The Interface preferences control how Photoshop looks on your screen. As you learned on page 6, you can use the Color Theme swatches at the top of these settings to change Photoshop's colors (click the light gray swatch to resurrect the color theme of CS5 and earlier versions). You can squeeze a little more performance out of slower computers by setting the Border drop-down menus near the top of the dialog box to None. That way, Photoshop won't waste any processing power generating pretty drop shadows around your images or around the Photoshop window itself.

If you're familiar with all of Photoshop's tools and don't care to see the little yellow tooltips that appear when you point your cursor at tools and field labels, turn off the Show Tool Tips checkbox. And if you'd like new documents to open in separate windows instead of in new tabs, turn off the "Open Documents as Tabs" checkbox.

> **NOTE** If you use Photoshop on a Mac laptop and you're constantly zooming and rotating your canvas with your trackpad by accident, turn off the Enable Gestures checkbox.

Sync Settings

New in Photoshop CC, these preferences let you control which of your settings and preset goodies are *synced* to the Creative Cloud so you can access 'em on another machine (as the box on page xxvii explains, you have to subscribe to the Creative Cloud for this stuff to work). To trigger a sync, click the new Sync Settings button at the bottom left of your document window, near the status bar (labeled back in *Figure 1-1*).

Photoshop displays your Adobe ID at the top of these settings, and you use a series of checkboxes to tell Photoshop exactly what you want to sync. Your options are Preferences, Actions, Brushes, Swatches, Styles, Gradients, Custom Shapes, Patterns, Contours, and Tool Presets. Use the When Conflicts Occur drop-down menu to tell Photoshop what to do if it encounters a problem (say, if the settings on your machine don't match what's on the Creative Cloud). From the factory, this menu is set to Always Ask; your other choices are Keep Remote Settings and Keep Local Settings. By leaving it set to Always Ask, you'll see a dialog box appear whenever there's a conflict so you can choose to keep the settings on your machine (local) or ones you previously stored on the Creative Cloud (remote).

File Handling

These preferences control how Photoshop opens and saves files. If you're a Mac person and you plan on working with images that'll be opened on both Macs and PCs, make sure the Append File Extension menu is set to Always and that Use Lower Case is turned on. These settings improve the chances that your files will open on *either* type of computer without a hassle. (PC users can leave their File Handling settings alone because file extensions are *required* in Windows, whereas on a Mac they're *automatically* added but can be turned off.)

Since CS6, you've had the ability to keep working while Photoshop saves your file in the *background*—meaning you don't have to wait until it's finished to do something else—plus Photoshop automatically saves your document at regular time intervals. (CC lets you save *additional* documents before the first one finishes, but there's more on that in Chapter 2.) The File Handling preferences let you turn background saving on or off (via the "Save in Background" checkbox), as well as control how the Auto Recovery feature works. To have Photoshop save your file more often than every 10 minutes, pick another duration from the Automatically Save Recovery Information Every menu (your choices are 5, 10, 15, or 30 minutes, or 1 hour).

Straight from the factory, Photoshop is set to display a dialog box each time you save a file that asks if you want to save the image for maximum compatibility with *PSD* and *PSB* files (the native Photoshop format and the format for really big files, respectively; see page 39); doing so improves the chances that your files can be understood by other programs like Adobe InDesign or QuarkXPress. If that pesky dialog box annoys you, change the "Maximize PSD and PSB File Compatibility" menu to Always and you'll never see the dialog box again (plus you'll have the peace of mind that comes with knowing your images will play nice with other programs). You also have the ability to keep Photoshop from automatically compressing these files, which makes it save 'em faster, though the end result will be bigger file size. If speed is more important to you than file size, then turn on "Disable Compression of PSD and PSB Files."

> **NOTE** The Adobe Drive option lets you connect to a *digital asset management* program (also called a DAM) in order to organize, track, and store files in a central location that other folks can access (so they can work on those files too). Visit *www.lesa.in/adobedrive* for more info.

Another handy option lies at the very bottom of the dialog box. It lets you change the number of documents Photoshop lists in the Recent files menu (found by choosing File→Open Recent). This field is automatically set to 10, but feel free to change it if you frequently need to reopen the same documents.

Performance

The Performance preferences control how efficiently Photoshop runs on your computer. For example, the amount of memory the program has to work with affects how well it performs. In the Memory Usage section, the Let Photoshop Use field's factory setting tells the program to use up to 60–70 percent of your machine's available memory (the exact number may vary). If you're tempted to increase it to 100 percent for better performance, *don't*. Other programs need to use your computer's memory, too, and leaving it set between 60 and 70 percent ensures that all of them get their fair share (after Photoshop takes the biggest chunk, that is).

The History & Cache section lets you change the number of history states that Photoshop remembers, as explained on page 15. You can also let the program set optimal cache levels and tile sizes *for* you; all you have to do is pick the kind of document you work on the most. Your options are "Tall and Thin," "Default," and "Big and Flat"; just click the one that's the closest match to what you regularly use. Here's why this matters: Cache levels controls how much image info is temporarily stored in your computer's memory for things like screen and histogram refreshing (you'll learn about histograms on page 373). The cache tile size is the amount of info Photoshop can store and process at one time (for example, larger tile sizes can speed things up if you work with documents with really large pixel dimensions). See? Now you *appreciate* Photoshop managing these settings for you!

If your computer's hard drive is running low on space, consider adding another drive that Photoshop can use as a *scratch disk*—the place where it stashes the bazillions of temporary files it makes when you're editing images (so *that's* where those history states are stored!). If you don't have a separate scratch disk, Photoshop stores those temporary files on your computer's primary hard drive, taking up space you could be using for other documents. When you add a new internal hard drive or plug in an external drive, that drive appears in the Scratch Disks list shown in *Figure 1-13*. To give Photoshop the green light to use it, put a checkmark in the disk's "Active?" column, and then drag it upward into the first position. After you do this, Photoshop will be a little zippier because it'll have *two* hard drives reading and writing info instead of one.

NOTE   When it comes to Photoshop's scratch disk, speed matters, and faster is better. Since the speed at which the disk spins plays a big role in scratch disk performance, stick with disks rated at 7200 RPM (revolutions per minute) or faster. Slower 5400 RPM disks can take a toll on Photoshop's performance, and 4200 RPM drives slow...Photoshop...to...a...crawl. Better yet, spend the extra money for a solid state drive (SSD), which has no moving parts and uses an electronic system to read and write data, making it much faster than its spinning cousins.

More than ever before, Photoshop CC takes advantage of your computer's built-in ability to draw and process graphics. This results in faster and smoother performance when you're resizing images with Free Transform, rotating your canvas temporarily with Rotate View, using the HUD Color Picker—the list goes on and on (you'll learn about all these features throughout this book). If you turn off the Use Graphics Processor checkbox at the bottom right, you lose all these superpowers, though you might squeeze a little more performance out of your machine. If you've got a newer machine, be sure to leave this setting turned on. That said, you can control *how much* your graphics processor is being tapped by clicking the Advanced Settings button (your choices are Basic, Normal, and Advanced).

FIGURE 1-13

To add one or more scratch disks, click the square in the "Active?" column next to each hard drive you want to use, and then drag the drives up or down into the order you want Photoshop to use them. For the zippiest feel, use a solid-state drive (SSD) that's at least 256 GB in size (and is separate from the one where your operating system is installed). Also, avoid using USB2-based drives, as they tend to be sluggish and can actually make Photoshop run slower (USB3-based drives work just fine).

Cursors

These preferences control how your cursor looks when you're working with images. There are no right or wrong choices here, so try out the different cursor styles and see what works best for you. Photoshop includes two types of cursors: painting cursors and everything else. When you choose different options here, Photoshop shows you a preview of what each cursor looks like. At the bottom of the dialog box is a Brush Preview color swatch that controls the color of the brush preview when you resize your brush by Control-Option-dragging (Alt+right-click+dragging on a PC) left or right. To change the preview's color, click the color swatch, choose a new color from the Color Picker dialog box, and then click OK. (See page 497 to learn how these options affect the Brush tool.)

> **TIP** If you turn on your keyboard's Caps Lock key when you're working with a tool that uses a brush cursor, Photoshop switches it to the precise cursor instead (it looks like a tiny crosshair). To switch back to the regular cursor, turn Caps Lock *off*.

Transparency and Gamut

The Transparency settings let you fine-tune what a layer looks like when part of it is transparent. Like the cursor settings, these options are purely cosmetic, so feel free to experiment. (You'll learn more about transparency in Chapter 3.) The Gamut

Warning option lets you set a highlight color that shows where colors in your image fall outside the safe range for the color mode you're working in or the printer you're using. (Chapter 16 has more about these advanced color concerns.)

Units and Rulers

The Units & Rulers preferences (*Figure 1-14*) let you pick the unit of measurement Photoshop uses. The Rulers menu, not surprisingly, controls the units displayed in your document's rulers (though you can change them on the fly, as described on page 61); your choices are pixels, inches, centimeters, millimeters, points, picas, and percent. If you work on a lot of documents destined for print, using inches, points or picas are probably your best bet (in the USA, that is). If you create images primarily for the Web, choose pixels instead. Leave the Type menu set to Points unless you need to work with type measured in pixels or millimeters, which can be handy if you need to align text in a web page layout.

The Column Size settings are handy when you're designing graphics to fit into specific-sized columns in a page-layout program like Adobe InDesign. Just ask the person who's creating the InDesign layout which measurements to use.

FIGURE 1-14

To really save some time, take a moment to adjust the settings in the New Document Preset Resolutions section (resolution, as you'll learn on page 233, controls pixel size).

From that point on, Photoshop automatically fills in the New Document dialog box with the settings you entered here (you'll learn about creating new documents on page 31).

Guides, Grid, and Slices

These preferences let you choose the colors for your document guides (page 60), grid (page 62), and slice lines (page 738). You can also set the grid's spacing and the number of subdivisions that appear between each major gridline with the "Gridline every" and Subdivisions fields, respectively.

Plug-ins

You can make Photoshop do even more cool stuff by installing third-party programs called *plug-ins*. There are so many useful plug-ins that this book has an entire chapter devoted to them (Chapter 19). The preferences in this category used to let you store plug-ins somewhere other than your computer's Photoshop folder, but in Photoshop CC that option has been removed (evidently this was causing confusion as some folks used the same plug-in folder for multiple versions of the program, which resulted in a lot of crashes).

Leave both checkboxes in the Extension Panels section turned on so Photoshop can connect to the Internet if a plug-in or panel needs to grab information from a website. For example, the Kuler panel (page 487) lets you use color themes posted on the Web by folks in the Kuler community; if you turn off these checkboxes, Photoshop can't connect to the Internet and you can't use Kuler. To make any changes in this section take effect, you need to restart Photoshop.

Type

Photoshop has an amazing text engine under its hood and you'll learn all about it in Chapter 14. The preferences here let you toggle smart quotes (the curly kind) on or off, as well as enable other languages. If you work with Asian characters, turn on the East Asian option in the Choose Text Engine Options section and make sure the Enable Missing Glyph Protection checkbox is also turned on. That way you won't end up with weird symbols or boxes if you try to use a letter or symbol that isn't installed on your machine. Photoshop can now work with Middle Eastern and South Asian languages, too. (Any changes you make in the Choose Text Engine Options section take effect only after you restart Photoshop.)

Because seeing a font in its typeface is so handy when you're choosing fonts, Adobe turned on font previews automatically in CS5, and then in CS6 they *removed* the Font Preview Size from preferences altogether. These days you can adjust the preview size not in the Preferences dialog box, but by choosing Type→Font Preview Size, where you can pick among six handy options, including none to huge.

3D

As you learned on page xxiii, Adobe merged the Extended and Standard versions of the program into Photoshop CC, meaning *everyone* now has access to its 3D tools. (Chapter 21 teaches you how to get started creating and working with 3D objects.)

You can use the preferences in this section to adjust the amount of video card memory (VRAM) Photoshop can use while you're working in the 3D environment, as well as the color and size of the various overlays you'll encounter when creating or editing 3D text and objects. The options on the right side of the dialog box let you change how Photoshop displays 3D objects, their interactive controls, and how much detail the program displays when you load a 3D object that was made in another program. (Unless you're an expert in working with 3D objects, it's probably best to leave most of these settings alone.)

Customizing Keyboard Shortcuts and Menus

Keyboard shortcuts can make the difference between working quickly and working at warp speed. They can drastically reduce the amount of time you spend taking your hands off the keyboard to move your mouse to do things like choose menu items or grab tools. Photoshop has a ton of built-in keyboard shortcuts and menus, but that doesn't mean you're stuck with 'em. You can reassign shortcuts, add new ones, and show or hide menu options. Here's how to add or change keyboard shortcuts:

1. Choose Edit→Keyboard Shortcuts to open the "Keyboard Shortcuts and Menus" dialog box.

2. Choose which type of shortcuts you want to add or change from the Shortcuts For menu. Your options are Application Menus (like the File and Edit menus), Panel Menus (the menus on the program's various panels), and Tools.

3. In the list below the Shortcuts For menu, pick the shortcut you want to change. (If a list item has a flippy triangle next to it, click the triangle to see all the options nested within that menu item.)

4. Enter a new shortcut in the Shortcut field and then click Accept.

5. To save your new shortcut to Photoshop's *factory* set of shortcuts, click the first hard-disk icon near the top of the dialog box (to the right of the Set menu). Click the Save button in the resulting dialog box, and Photoshop names your shortcuts Photoshop Defaults (Modified). To create a brand-new set of shortcuts instead, click the *second* hard-disk icon with the little dots underneath it; in the Save dialog box that appears, give your custom shortcut set a meaningful name and then click Save. Creating separate keyboard shortcut sets lets you quickly switch back to Photoshop's factory shortcuts, or switch between sets you've made for specific tasks by using the Set menu at the top of the dialog box.

You can also clear an existing keyboard shortcut for something else. First, make note of which menu the existing shortcut currently lives in. Next, find the same menu in middle of the "Keyboard Shortcuts and Menus" dialog box, click its flippy triangle to expand the menu, and then click to highlight the shortcut. Finally, click the Delete Shortcut button on the right and consider it free at last.

To help you remember the new shortcuts, Photoshop lets you print a handy chart to tack up on the wall. In the "Keyboard Shortcuts and Menus" dialog box, pick your custom set from the Set menu and then click Summarize. In the resulting Save dialog box, give the list of shortcuts a name, choose where to save it, and then click Save. Photoshop creates an HTML file that you can open in any Web browser or HTML-savvy software and then print. When you're finished, you can impress your colleagues by telling them that you *reprogrammed* Photoshop to do your bidding; unless they've been in this dialog box themselves, they'll have no idea how easy this stuff is to change.

What if you need to reinstall Photoshop or upgrade to a newer version? The Migrate Presets feature introduced in CS6 copies over your keyboard shortcuts so you don't lose 'em (see the Note on page 29).

The "Keyboard Shortcuts and Menus" dialog box also lets you modify the program's menus: If there are commands you rarely use, you can hide 'em to shorten and simplify the menu. Click the Menus tab near the top of the dialog box and then, from the Menu For drop-down menu, choose Application Menus or Panel Menus, depending on which ones you want to tweak. Next, click the little flippy triangle next to each menu's name to see the items it includes. To hide a menu item, click its visibility eye; to show a hidden item, click within its Visibility column. (If you suddenly need to access a hidden menu item, choose Show All Menu Items from the very bottom of the affected menu.) You can even *colorize* menu items so they're easier to spot. To do that, pick the item you want to highlight, click the word None in the Color column, and then choose a color from the resulting drop-down menu. Click OK and enjoy your new customizations.

Working with Presets

Once you get comfortable in Photoshop, you can customize the behavior of almost every tool in the Tools panel. If you find yourself entering the same settings in the Options bar over and over again for the same tool, then saving those settings can save you time. In fact, Photoshop includes a bunch of built-in tool recipes, called *presets*, such as frequently used crop sizes, colorful gradient sets, patterns, shapes, and brush tips. You can access 'em through the tool's Preset Picker at the far left of the Options bar. *Figure 1-15* (top) has the scoop.

The Preset Manager handles loading, saving, and sharing the built-in presets, as well as the ones you create yourself. You can open it by choosing Edit→Presets→Preset Manager. Each group of settings, like a category of brushes, is called a *preset library*. To see a certain preset library, choose it from the Preset Type drop-down menu at the top of the Preset Manager dialog box (*Figure 1-15*, bottom).

Click to reset tool or load more presets
Create new tool preset

FIGURE 1-15

Top: To access a tool's presets or create new ones, open its Preset Picker at the far left of the Options bar (circled). Click a preset in the list to activate it and then use the tool as you normally would. To save a new preset, enter your custom settings in the Options bar and then click the Create New Preset button labeled here. Give the preset a name in the resulting dialog box, click OK, and it appears in the Preset Picker list. To reset a tool to its factory fresh settings, load additional presets, or access the Preset Manager, click the little gear icon.

Bottom: The Preset Manager gives you access to all the presets for all of Photoshop's tools (except for the Convert Point tool—see page 541). Click the gear circled here to open this menu, which lets you change the size of the previews, as well as reset, replace, and otherwise manage presets. To save your eyesight, it's a good idea to set the preview size to Large List so you can actually see what your options are. Changing the preview size here also changes it in the Preset Picker.

Clicking the little gear icon that's labeled in *Figure 1-15*, top, lets you set the category of presets you're viewing to the factory-fresh settings (choose "Reset [name of category] Presets" and then click OK) or load new ones. You can make these adjustments when you're using the tools themselves, but the Preset Manager gives you a bigger preview space, which makes these organizational chores a little more tolerable.

NOTE The Migrate Presets option lets you easily transfer presets from the previous version of Photoshop (in CC it only transfers presets from the most *current* version of Photoshop; other versions are simply ignored). The first time you crack open Photoshop CC, the program kindly asks whether you want to transfer your presets from the most recent version hanging around on your machine. If you accept, your goodies are copied over to CC (if the older presets have the same name as the newer ones, Photoshop copies only the newer ones). (If you don't encounter the Migrate Presets option when you first launch CC, it means the installer didn't find any presets to copy over.) If you didn't migrate your presets when you first launched the program, you can do it anytime by choosing Edit→Presets→Migrate Presets, or by resetting your preferences (see the first Note on page 21 to learn how). Happily, migrating presets in CC doesn't require you to *restart* the program before you can use 'em.

Sharing Presets

Once you've got your own custom settings for tools, styles, or what have you, feel free to share them with the masses. You can share them with other computers (handy when the whole team needs to use the same color swatches or brushes) and upload them to the Web (for the whole world to download).

In Photoshop CC, managing and sharing presets is easy. You've got a couple of ways to import and export these little gems:

- **To share** *all* **your presets**—including actions, keyboard shortcuts, menu customizations, workspaces, brushes, swatches, gradients, styles, patterns, contours, custom shapes, and tools—choose Edit→Presets→Export/Import Presets. In the resulting dialog box, tell Photoshop which goodies you want to share (say, actions and workspaces) in the Export Presets tab, and then click Export Presets (see *Figure 1-16*). Photoshop opens the "Choose a Folder" dialog box—just pick a spot that's easy for you to find and then click Open. Photoshop creates a new folder named Exported Presets in the location you picked and dutifully lets you know that it has put your presets there.

    To *import* presets, click the Import Presets tab and then click the Select Import Folder button at the bottom of the dialog box. In the resulting dialog box, navigate to where the presets live on your hard drive and click Open. Back in the Export/Import Presets dialog box, choose the presets you want to import from the left-hand list (or click the Add All button) and then click Import Presets.

- **To share just a** *few* **presets** (excluding actions, keyboard shortcuts, menu customizations, and workspaces) create a preset library of your own by opening the Preset Manager (Edit→Presets→Preset Manager) and choosing the presets you want to share (Shift-click or ⌘-/Ctrl-click to highlight 'em). Next, click the Save Set button, and in the resulting Save dialog box, give your custom library a name. Unless you pick a different location on your hard drive, Photoshop automatically saves it in the folders where it stores *all* custom settings. When everything looks good, click Save. Once you've saved your custom library, you can email it to folks or upload it to a website for others to download. If you're uploading it to the Web, make sure the file keeps the extension Photoshop gave it (.abr for brushes, for example), and that it doesn't have any *spaces* in its name. For example, instead of naming the file "Dragon Scales Brush," use "DragonScalesBrush."

FIGURE 1-16

Using the Export/Import Presets command is a great way for big companies and design firms to share their presets across a whole army of computers. Doing this ensures consistency and accuracy in the artwork they create, and can boost production speed through the use of carefully crafted actions (see Chapter 18).

To choose an item for exporting or importing, double-click it in the column on the left, or single-click it and then use the direction buttons (circled) to add or remove presets from the list.

If you're on the receiving end of a preset library, open the Preset Manager and then click the Load button. Navigate to where the library lives and then click Open. (Alternatively, you can choose Edit→Presets→Export/Import Presets, and then click the Import Presets tab shown in *Figure 1-16*.) The next time you use a tool that has custom presets, you'll see the new library's options in the tool's Preset Picker menu.

To add to the fun, you can also rename individual presets. In the Preset Manager dialog box, choose the relevant library from the Preset Type menu and then click to activate the soon-to-be-renamed preset. Click the Rename button, type a new moniker in the Name field, and then click OK.

To delete a preset library you never use, choose it from the Preset Manager's Preset Type menu and then click Delete.

TIP If you've managed to mess up one of Photoshop's built-in preset libraries by adding items that don't work the way you want, you can easily restore it: Open the Preset Manager and choose the library you want to reset. Then, click the gear icon that's circled back in *Figure 1-15*, bottom, and choose "Reset [type of preset]" (for example, Brushes). Photoshop asks if you want to replace the current brushes or append (add to) them instead. Click OK to replace the brushes, and you'll be back to the factory-fresh settings.

Opening, Viewing, and Saving Files

C hances are good that if you're holding this book, you're spending a lot of time in Photoshop. So the ability to shave off a minute here and there from routine stuff can really add up. Heck, if you're lucky, you'll save enough time to read a book, ride your bike, or catch an episode of *The Big Bang Theory*.

One way to steal back some of that time is to work more efficiently, and that means learning tricks for the less glamorous stuff like opening, viewing, and saving files. And since you'll be doing these things so often, it's important to form good habits so your documents are set up properly from the get-go. (It would be truly heartbreaking to find the artwork you've spent weeks creating is too small to print, or that you saved the file in such a way that you can't change it later on.) Finally, since a key part of working with images is navigating vast pixel landscapes, this chapter teaches you some handy ways to move around within images onscreen.

▇ Creating a New Document

Photoshop gives you a variety of ways to accomplish most tasks, including creating a new document. Sure, you can choose File→New, but it's faster to press ⌘-N (Ctrl+N). Either way, you'll be greeted with the New dialog box shown in *Figure 2-1*.

You'd think naming a document would be simple: Just type something in the Name box and you're done, right? Not quite. Here are a few things to keep in mind:

- If you're working on a Mac, don't start file names with periods. Files whose names start with periods are invisible in Mac OS X (meaning neither you *nor* Photoshop can see them), which makes 'em darn hard to work with.

FIGURE 2-1

The New dialog box (top) is where life begins for any Photoshop file you make from scratch. The settings here let you pick, among other things, the document's size, resolution, and color mode, all of which affect the quality and size of the image. You'll learn more about these options in the following pages.

Whatever you enter in the Name box appears in the document's title bar (circled, bottom).

- If folks need to open your files on both Mac and Windows machines, don't put slashes (/), colons (:), angle brackets (<, >), pipes, (|), asterisks (*), or question marks (?) in the file names, either.

- Leave *file extensions* on the file name (the period and three letters at the end of the name, like .psd, .jpg, and so on). The file extension makes it easier for your computer to tell what *kind* of file it is so it can pick a program that can open it.

Photoshop's Ready-Made Documents

After you've named your document, you need to pick a size for it. You've got two choices here: Enter the dimensions you'd like in the New dialog box's Width and Height fields, or pick one of Photoshop's canned choices (4"×6" landscape photo, 640×480–pixel web page, and so on) from the Preset and Size menus shown in *Figure 2-2*.

FIGURE 2-2

Once you choose an option from the Preset menu (which includes different types of paper, electronic formats, and recently opened document sizes), Photoshop fills the Size menu and its related fields with the appropriate settings—including Width, Height, Resolution, and Color Mode. Presets are great timesavers, and they can help you avoid mistakes when creating new documents.

The advantage of picking a canned option is that, in addition to filling in the dimensions for you, Photoshop plugs in resolution and color mode settings. You'll learn more about these two options in a minute, but if you're new to the program, these *presets* (document recipes) are a great way to make sure you're starting off with a well-configured document. If you use a preset in the Film & Video category, for instance, you automatically get document guides that help you keep important parts of the image or text within a safe viewing area (see page 60 for more on guides). Besides, the presets can be helpful even if they're not *exactly* what you need. For example, if you find one that's the right size but the wrong resolution, just pick it, adjust the resolution, and you're on your way. (The box below explains how to create a document that has the same size and resolution settings as an existing one.)

UP TO SPEED

Stealing Document Settings

Need to create a document that's the same size and resolution as an *existing* document? No problem—just snag the original file's settings and use 'em to make another. You can swipe a document's settings in several ways:

- Open the existing document and then press ⌘-N (Ctrl+N) to open the New dialog box. Click the Preset drop-down menu, which includes the names of all open documents. Simply pick the document you want and Photoshop adjusts all the dialog box's settings to match.

- With the existing document open, press ⌘-A (Ctrl+A) to create a selection around the document's edges and then press ⌘-C (Ctrl+C) to copy the document's contents

to your computer's memory (a.k.a. the Clipboard). Next, choose File→New or press ⌘-N (Ctrl+N) and Photoshop automatically fills in the document's settings for you. (You can also use this maneuver to create a new document that matches your selection's *rectangular* dimensions, even if that selection is smaller than the document itself; see Chapter 4 for the full story on selections.)

- If you want to base your new document on the *last* new document you created since you launched the Photoshop, press ⌘-Option-N (Ctrl+Alt+N) or hold down the Option key (Alt on a PC) while you choose File→New.

TIP Photoshop CC includes a bunch of presets for common video formats as well as devices such as the iPhone and iPad. Choose Film & Video or Mobile & Devices from the New dialog box's Preset menu and you'll see a slew of useful goodies!

Setting Size and Resolution

In Photoshop, "size" refers to two different things: file size (640 kilobytes or 2.4 megabytes, for example) and dimensions (like 4"×6" or 640×480 pixels). You'll find plenty of advice throughout this book on how to control file size, but this section is about the size of your document's *canvas*.

Photoshop can measure canvas size in pixels, inches, centimeters, millimeters, points, picas, and columns. In the New dialog box, just pick the unit of measurement that's appropriate for your project—or the easiest for you to work with—from the drop-down menus to the right of the Width and Height fields. If you're designing a piece for the Web or for use in presentation software, pixels are your best bet. If you're going to print the image, inches are a common choice. Columns come in handy when you're making an image that has to fit within a specific number of columns in a page-layout program, such as InDesign or QuarkXPress.

NOTE Photoshop assumes you want to use the same unit (say, inches) to measure width and height, so it automatically changes both fields when you adjust one. If you really *do* need to work with different units, just hold the Shift key while you pick the second unit to make Photoshop leave the other field alone.

The Resolution field controls pixel size by specifying the number of pixels per inch or per centimeter in your document. High-resolution documents have smaller pixels, as they contain more pixels per inch than low-resolution documents of the same size. You'll learn all about resolution in Chapter 6. For now, here's some ready-to-use guidance if you haven't mastered the fine art of resolution just yet: If you're designing an image that will be viewed only onscreen (in a web browser or a slideshow presentation, for example) enter *72* in the New dialog box's Resolution field. If you're going to print the image at home, set the resolution to at least 240 pixels per inch (if it's headed to a professional printer, enter *300* or more instead).

TIP If you don't know the exact size your document needs to be, it's better to make it really big; you can always shrink it down later. See page 232 for more on resizing images.

Once you enter values in the Width, Height, and Resolution fields, Photoshop calculates the document's *file size*—the amount of space it takes up on your computer's hard drive—and displays it in the New dialog box's lower right corner (in *Figure 2-1*, for example, the file size is 2.25 MB).

Just because you make a document a certain size doesn't mean you can't have artwork in that file that's *bigger* than the document's dimensions. Photoshop is perfectly fine with objects that extend beyond the document's edges (also called *document boundaries*), but you can't see or print those parts. It may sound odd, but if you paste a photo or a piece of vector art (page 43) that's larger than your document, those extra bits will dangle off the edges (text that you make with the Type tool can dangle off, too). To resize your document so you can see everything—even the stuff that doesn't quite fit—choose Image→Reveal All to make Photoshop modify the document's dimensions so everything fits.

Choosing a Color Mode

The New dialog box's Color Mode menu (see *Figure 2-1*) determines which colors you can use in the document. You'll spend most of your time working in RGB mode (which stands for "red, green, blue"), but you can switch modes whenever you like. (The drop-down menu to the right of the Color Mode menu controls the document's *bit depth*, which is explained in the box on page 36.)

Unless you choose a different color mode, Photoshop automatically uses RGB. The Color Mode menu gives you the following options:

- **Bitmap** restricts you to two colors: black and white. (Shades of gray aren't welcome at the Bitmap party.) This mode is useful when you're scanning high-contrast items like black-and-white text documents or creating graphics for handheld devices that don't have color screens.

- **Grayscale** also contains no color, but expands on Bitmap mode by adding shades of gray between pure black and pure white. The higher the document's bit depth, the more shades of gray—and so the more details—it can contain. Eight-bit documents include 256 shades of gray; 16-bit documents extend that range to over 65,000; and 32-bit documents crank it up to over 4.2 *billion* (see the box on page 36 for more on bit depth). Use this mode if you're designing an ad for a newspaper printed in black and white.

- **RGB Color** is the color mode you'll use the most, and it's also the one your monitor and digital camera use to represent a wide range of colors. This mode shows colors as a mix of red, green, and blue light, with each having a numeric value between 0 and 255 that describes the brightness of each color present (for example, fire-engine red has an RGB value of 250 for red, 5 for green, and 5 for blue). As with Grayscale mode, the higher a document's bit depth, the more details it can contain. In this mode, you can choose among 8-, 16-, and 32-bit documents. (See Chapter 5 for more on RGB mode.)

- **CMYK Color** simulates the colored inks used in printing (its name stands for "Cyan, Magenta, Yellow, blacK"). This mode doesn't have as wide of a color range as RGB because it's limited to the colors a printer—whether it's an inkjet, commercial offset, or digital press—can reproduce with ink and dyes on paper. You'll learn more about CMYK in Chapter 5, and Chapter 16 explains if and when you should switch to CMYK mode.

- **Lab Color** mode, which is based on the way we see color, lets you use all the colors human eyes can detect. It represents how colors *should look* no matter which device they're displayed on, whereas RGB and CMYK modes limit a file's colors to what's visible onscreen or in a printed document, respectively. The downside to this mode is that many folks have a hard time learning to create the colors they want in it. You'll find various techniques involving Lab mode sprinkled throughout Part Two of this book.

Understanding Bit Depth

You may have heard the terms "8-bit" and "16-bit" tossed around in graphics circles (confusingly, neither has anything to do with Photoshop being a 64-bit program, as the box on page xxviii explains). When people refer to bits, they're talking about how many colors an image contains. Photoshop's color modes determine whether a document is an 8- or a 16-bit image (other, less common options are 1-bit and 32-bit). Since you'll run into these labels fairly often, it helps to understand what these numbers mean.

A *bit* is the smallest unit of measurement that computers use to store information: either a 1 or a 0 (on or off, respectively). Each pixel in an image has a *bit depth*, which controls how much color information that pixel can hold. So an image's bit depth determines how much color info the image contains. The higher the bit depth, the more colors the image can display. And the more colors in your image, the more info (details) you've got to play with in Photoshop.

To understand bit depth, you need to know a little about *channels.* Photoshop stores your image's color info separated into a single channel for each color (see Chapter 5 for details). For example, in an RGB image you have three channels: one each for red, green, and blue. By viewing all the channels at once, you see a full color image.

With all that in mind, here's a quick tour of your various bit choices in Photoshop:

- In **Bitmap** color mode, your pixels can be only black or white. Images in this mode are called 1-bit images because each pixel can be only one color—black or white (they're also known simply as *bitmap* images).

- An **8-bit image** can hold two values in each bit, which equals 256 possible color values. Why 256? Since each of the eight bits can hold two possible values, you get 256 combinations. (For math fans, that's 2^8). Images in Grayscale mode contain one channel, so that's 8 bits per channel, equaling 256 colors. Since images in RGB mode contain three channels (one each for red, blue, and green), folks refer to them as 24-bit images (8 bits per channel × 3 = 24), but they're still really just 8-bit images. With 256 combinations for each channel (that's $2^8 \times 2^8 \times 2^8$), you can have over 16 million colors in an RGB image. Since CMYK images have four channels, folks refer to them as 32-bit images (8 bits per channel × 4 = 32), but again, these are *still* 8-bit images. Over 200 combinations per channel and four channels add up to a massive number of possible color values, but since you're dealing with printed ink, your color range in CMYK is dictated by what can actually be reproduced on *paper*, which reduces it to about 55,000 colors.

- **16-bit images** contain 65,536 colors in a single channel and are produced by high-end digital cameras (*digital single-lens reflex*, or DSLR, cameras) shooting in raw format and/or by really good scanners. On your screen, these files don't look any different from other images, but they take up twice as much hard drive space. Pro photographers love 16-bit images because the extra color range gives them more editing flexibility, even though the larger file sizes can *really* slow Photoshop down. Also, not all of Photoshop's tools and filters work on 16-bit images.

- **32-bit images**, referred to as *high dynamic range* (HDR), contain more colors than you can shake a stick at. See page 396 for more info.

For the most part, you'll deal with 8-bit images, but if you've got a camera that shoots at higher bit depths, by all means, take a weekend and experiment to see if the difference in quality is worth the sacrifice of hard drive space (and editing speed). And if you're restoring a really old photo, it may be helpful to scan it at a high bit depth so you have a wider range of colors to work with. (See the box on page 48 for more scanning tips.)

Choosing a Background

The New dialog box's Background Contents menu lets you choose what's on the Background layer—the only layer you start out with in a new document or when you open a photo. Your choices are White, Background Color (which uses the color that your background color chip is set to [page 12]), and Transparent (which leaves the background completely empty).

What you choose here isn't crucial—if you change your mind, you can fill the Background layer with another color (page 83), turn off its visibility (page 74), or delete it once you start adding other layers (your document has to contain *at least* one layer). The Transparent option is handy if your document is part of a bigger project where it'll be placed on top of other artwork; when you choose this option, you see a gray-and-white checkerboard pattern, as explained in the box below.

Advanced Options

The Advanced section at the bottom of the New dialog box contains the following menus:

- **Color Profile**. A *color profile* is a set of instructions that determine how computer monitors and printers display or print your document's colors. This menu is set to the same profile listed in the Color Settings dialog box (page 676), which, unless you've changed it, is "sRGB IEC61966-2.1." Leave this setting alone unless you know you need to use a specific color profile for your project; otherwise, the image's colors may not look the way you expect them to. You'll learn all about color profiles on page 674.

- **Pixel Aspect Ratio**. This setting determines the shape of the image's pixels by changing their size. This setting gets its name from the term *aspect ratio*—the relationship between an image's width and height. (For example, a widescreen television has an aspect ratio of 16:9.) From the factory, Photoshop's pixels are square. Although square pixels are fine for photos, printed images, and onscreen use, they look funky and distorted in video, which has a tendency to make everything appear short and fat (including people). So if you're using Photoshop to make a video, try to find out which video format you need and then choose it from the Preset menu's Film & Video category. That way, Photoshop adjusts this setting for you according to the format you pick.

FREQUENTLY ASKED QUESTION

Seeing Transparency

What's up with the gray-and-white checkerboard pattern in my new document? I thought it was supposed to be blank!

When you tell Photoshop to make your Background layer transparent, it fills your new document with a checkerboard pattern. Don't worry: That checkerboard is just what the program uses to *represent* transparency on the Background layer. In other words, the checkered pattern is just a reminder that there aren't any pixels on that layer (or on that particular *part* of a layer).

You can change how the checkerboard pattern looks by choosing Photoshop→Preferences→Transparency & Gamut (Edit→Preferences→Transparency & Gamut on a PC). In the Transparency Settings area, tweak the options to make the squares bigger or smaller or change their colors. If you can't stand seeing the checkered pattern no matter *what* it looks like, turn it off by setting the Grid Size option to None. When you've got things set the way you want, click OK.

■ SAVING YOUR CUSTOM SETTINGS

If you've gone to the trouble of getting your document's settings just right and you expect to create *lots* of similar documents, save those settings as a preset *before* you click OK to create your new document. In the New dialog box, click the Save Preset button to open the dialog box shown in *Figure 2-3*, and then type a descriptive name for your time-saving preset.

FIGURE 2-3

Use these checkboxes to tell Photoshop which settings you want it to remember. When you create a new document using a preset you've made, the program grabs any settings you didn't include in the preset from the last new document you made. For example, if you turn off the Profile checkbox shown here, your preset doesn't include a color profile, so Photoshop assigns the currently active color profile (from Color Settings—see page 676) to the new document.

■ Saving Files

After you've put a ton of work into whipping up a lovely creation, don't forget to save it or you'll never see it again. As in any program, be sure to save early and often so your efforts don't go to waste if your computer crashes or the power goes out.

> **TIP** Photoshop sports a life-saving Auto Recovery feature that automatically saves your document every 10 minutes (though you can change the time interval; see the box on page 41). You can also keep working *while* Photoshop saves your file in the background, meaning you don't have to wait until it's finished to do something else. And new in Photoshop CC is the ability to trigger yet *another* document save before the first one finishes!

The simplest method is to choose File→Save or press ⌘-S (Ctrl+S). If you haven't previously saved the file, Photoshop summons the Save As dialog box so you can pick where to save the file, give it a name, and choose a file format (your options are explained in the next section). If you *have* already saved the file, Photoshop replaces the previously saved version with the *current* version without asking if that's what you want to do. In some situations, that's fine, but it can be disastrous if you wanted to keep more than one version of the image.

You can play it safe by using the Save As dialog box every time you save. It *always* prompts you for a new file name (see *Figure 2-4*), which is handy when you want to save another version of the document or save it in a different format. Choose File→Save As or press Shift-⌘-S (Shift+Ctrl+S) to open the dialog box. From the factory, the format menu is set to Photoshop, which is perfect because that format keeps all your layers and Smart Objects intact in case you need to go back and change them later. This is the format you want to use while editing images. Then, when you're finished and ready to save the image for use in another program—or for posting on the Web or sending in an email—you can save it in a different file format, as the next section explains.

FIGURE 2-4

The Save As dialog box lets you save a copy of your file with a different name in a different location and in a different format.

When you save a file as a Photoshop document (also known as a PSD), its layers remain intact and fully editable even after you close the document. In fact, you may want to store all your PSDs from a single photo shoot—right alongside the originals from your camera—in a folder named "in progress," as shown here.

NOTE When you run the Save As command, Photoshop assumes you want to save the document in the original folder from whence it came. To change this behavior, choose Photoshop→Preferences→File Handling (Edit→Preferences→File Handling on a PC) and turn off the "Save As to Original Folder" checkbox.

File Formats

You'll learn all about file formats in Chapters 16 and 17, but here's a quick overview:

If you remember nothing else, remember to save your images as *PSD files* (Photoshop documents) because that's the most flexible format (as explained in the previous section). That said, sometimes you need to save a document in other formats because of where the file is *headed*. For example, InDesign and recent versions of QuarkXPress (two popular page-layout programs) are adept at handling PSD files, but not all programs understand what the heck a PSD file is. In that case, try saving the document as a TIFF file; nearly every image-handling program on the planet can open TIFFs.

NOTE If you need to save a document that's bigger than 2 GB, save it in Large Document Format (.PSB format) instead, which gets you past Photoshop's 2-gigabyte limit on PSD files. Photoshop also supports BIGTIFF format, which lets you circumvent the 4-gigabyte size limit of TIFF format.

Graphics destined for the Web are a different animal because they're specially designed for onscreen viewing and faster downloading. Here's a quick cheat sheet to tide you over until you've got time and energy to make your way to Chapter 17:

- **JPEG** is commonly used for graphics that include a wide range of colors, like photos. It compresses images so they take up less space, but the smaller file size comes at a price: loss of quality.

NOTE Because JPEGs can't be saved as 16-bit files, Photoshop automatically converts 'em to 8-bit. If that sentence is as clear as mud to you, flip back to the box on page 36 to learn more about image bit depth.

- **GIF** is a popular choice for graphics that include a limited number of colors (think cartoon art), have a transparent background, or are animated (page 732).

- **PNG** is the up-and-comer because it offers true transparency and a wide range of colors. It produces a higher-quality image than JPEG format, but it generates larger files. In Photoshop CC, metadata (page 48) and ICC profiles (page 675) are now included with the file when you save it as a PNG.

For more on creating and preparing images for the Web, hop over to Chapter 17. If your image is headed for a professional printer, visit Chapter 16 instead.

■ Opening an Existing Document

Opening files is simple in most programs, and that holds true in Photoshop, too. But Photoshop gives you a few more options than you'll find elsewhere because it's amazingly versatile at working with a wide range of images. Photoshop knows how to open Adobe Illustrator, Camera Raw (page 48), JPEG, GIF, PNG, TIFF, EPS, and PDF files (page 46), along with Collada DAE, Google Earth 4 KMZ, Scitex CT, Targa, and several other file types most folks have never heard of.

NOTE These days, Photoshop supports more formats than ever, including JPS and PNS (a stereo image pair that's captured by cameras with two lenses or one lens that's split in half to produce 3D images), as well as BIGTIFF (for TIFFs larger than 4 GB). It also allows for more bit depth (think "colors") in TIFF files. (For more on bit depth, see the box on page 36). New in Photoshop CC is the ability to open JPEGs that are 65,535 pixels in width or height (in previous versions, the limit was 30,000 pixels).

You can open files in Photoshop in several ways, including the following:

- Double-clicking a file's icon whose format is associated with Photoshop (like JPEG or TIFF), no matter where it's stored on your computer.

TIP To change file association on a Mac, single-click the file's icon and then press ⌘-I. In the resulting Info dialog box, locate the Open With section and then pick a program from the drop-down menu. If you want to change the association for *all* files of that kind on your computer, click the Change All button.

On a Windows machine, right-click the file's icon and choose "Open with"→"Choose default program." Select the program you want and make sure the "Always use the selected program to open this kind of file" checkbox is turned on; then click OK.

Now you can double-click the file and the program you specified will pop open. Nifty, eh?

- Dragging the file's icon onto the Photoshop Dock icon (the blue square with "Ps" on it) on a Mac. (This trick *doesn't* work in the Windows taskbar.)

UP TO SPEED

Photoshop's Magical Auto Recovery

Every time you lose a Photoshop document to a computer crash, a baby frog dies.

OK, not really, but it sure can ruin an otherwise perfectly good day.

Happily, Photoshop includes an Auto Recovery feature that automatically saves all your open Photoshop documents as fully layered PSD files every 10 minutes. If you've ever used Microsoft Word, you've encountered a similar feature already. That's right: If the program crashes, the documents pop back open the next time you launch Photoshop.

These back-up, or *recovered*, documents are stored in a folder named PSAutoRecover on your *scratch disk*, the hard drive that's specified in the Performance pane of Photoshop's Preferences (see page 23 for more on scratch disks). The only caveat is that if you run out of hard-drive space on your scratch disk, the back-up documents won't be saved.

These back-up documents are temporary and don't hang around forever (which isn't a big deal if you remember to save your file every so often). They disappear if you do any of the following:

- Choose File→Save in your original document.
- Choose File→Revert in your original document.
- Close your original document without ever saving it first.
- Close a back-up document without saving it first.
- Save a back-up document to another location.

This fabulous, derrière-saving feature is turned on straight from the factory, though all of this automatic saving can take a toll on performance. If you notice that Photoshop feels sluggish—say, if you frequently work with a lot of big documents open at the same time—you can always turn it off. Choose Photoshop→Preferences→File Handling (Edit→Preferences→File Handling on a PC) and turn off the Automatically Save Recovery Information Every checkbox. You can also change the auto-save interval to every 5 minutes by using the drop-down menu to the right of the checkbox (handy if you're doing detailed retouching and your image is changing significantly every few minutes). If you want to leave Auto Recovery on but have it happen *less* frequently (to increase performance), you can set the auto-save interval to 15 minutes, 30 minutes, or an hour.

- Control-clicking (right-clicking on a PC) the document's icon and, from the resulting shortcut menu, choosing Open With→Adobe Photoshop CC. (This method works only for files formats that are associated with Photoshop.)

- Launching Photoshop and then choosing File→Open or pressing ⌘-O (Ctrl+O) to rouse the Open dialog box, discussed in the next section.

- Dragging the document's icon into the Photoshop program window.

- Choosing File→"Open as Smart Object" as discussed later in this chapter (page 45).

You can also use Adobe Bridge—or the Mini Bridge panel—to preview and open documents. Head over to Chapter 22 to learn more about installing Bridge and Mini Bridge for use with Photoshop CC.

The Open Dialog Box

When you choose File→Open or press ⌘-O (Ctrl+O), Photoshop summons the dialog box shown in *Figure 2-5*. All you need to do from there is navigate to a file on your hard drive and then click the Open button.

NOTE The Windows version of Photoshop CC sports a brand-new Open dialog box; it looks just like the standard Windows Explorer window, complete with a search box that helps you locate files faster. Nice!

FIGURE 2-5

The Open dialog box lets you navigate to the image you want to open. The format drop-down menu at the bottom automatically changes to match the format of the document you pick.

PC users see different options in the Open dialog box than Mac users do. For example, they don't see the Enable drop-down menu, and their format drop-down menu is unlabeled.

Raster Images vs. Vector Images

The images you'll work with and create in Photoshop fall into two categories: those made from *pixels* and those made from *points and paths*. It's important to understand that they have different characteristics and that you need to open them in different ways to *preserve* those characteristics:

- **Raster images** are made from pixels, tiny blocks of color that are the smallest elements of a digital image. The number of pixels in an image depends on the device that captured it (a digital camera or scanner) or the settings you entered when you created the document in Photoshop (page 31). The size of the pixels depends on the image's resolution (see page 233), which specifies the number of pixels in an inch. Usually pixels are so small that you can't see them individually; but, if you zoom in on a raster image, the pixels get bigger and the image starts to look like a bunch of blocks instead of a smooth image. JPEGs, TIFFs, GIFs, and PNGs are all raster images. (Technically raw files are rasters too; that is, once you open 'em in a program that can interpret them, such as Camera Raw).

- **Vector images** are made up of points and paths that form shapes; these shapes are then filled and *stroked* (outlined) with color. (In Photoshop CC, you can create vector images as easily as in drawing programs such as Adobe Illustrator or CorelDraw.) Paths are based on mathematical equations that tell monitors and printers exactly how to draw the image. Because there aren't any pixels involved, you can make vector images as big or small as you want, and they'll still look as smooth and crisp as the original. Photoshop can open vector images, but unless you open them as Smart Objects (discussed later in this chapter), Photoshop will turn them into pixel-based raster images through a process called *rasterizing*.

In the figure below, the upper image is a vector image (the right-hand version shows the paths it's made from) and the bottom image is a raster image. Vectors are handy when you're designing logos and other illustrations that you might need to make bigger at some point. You'll end up working with rasters more often than not because *photos* are raster images and Photoshop is a pixel-based program (as are all image-editing and painting programs). That said, Photoshop has a slew of tools you can use to draw vectors (see Chapter 13), and it lets you open vector files, as discussed in the next section. And as page 300 explains, you can create amazing artwork by combining raster and vector images.

In addition to letting you peruse the murky depths of your hard drive, the dialog box also lets you narrow your search by choosing a format from the Enable drop-down menu. If you pick just the format you want to find, Photoshop will dutifully dim everything else (you can't choose dimmed items), which is handy when you've saved the same image in several different formats—like PSD, JPEG, and TIFF.

TIP To open more than one file from the Open dialog box, ⌘-click (Ctrl-click) to choose files that aren't next to each other in the list or Shift-click to choose files that are. When you click Open, Photoshop opens each file in a separate tab if you've got the Application Frame turned on (page 1) and you've kept Photoshop's Interface preferences set to "Open Documents as Tabs" (page 21).

If you leave the Enable drop-down menu set to All Readable Documents (or leave the unlabeled format menu set to All Formats on a PC), you're telling Photoshop it's OK to open *any* file format it recognizes. If you try to open a format Photoshop *should* know how to open but for some mysterious reason thinks it doesn't (see page 40 for a list of formats Photoshop recognizes), someone may have saved the document with the wrong file extension. (Since all programs, including Photoshop, rely on the file extension to figure out which type of document they're looking at, be careful not to change these multi-letter codes that appear after a document's name.) If you run into this problem, Mac users can use the Format drop-down menu (PC users can choose File→Open As instead) to tell Photoshop which format the document *should* be, and the program will ignore the file's extension and try to open it based on the format you pick.

TIP If you're looking for a specific image but can't remember its name, try using Bridge or the Mini Bridge panel to find it (see Chapter 22). Both show you a preview of each image along with tons of other info like keywords, ratings, and more. Bridge also gives you filtering and search options to help hunt down the image you want. Unfortunately, in CC, you have to install Bridge separately from Photoshop (Mini Bridge tags along when you do). See page 848 for the dirty details.

Opening Multiple Files within a Single Document

If you're creating one image from many—say, to combine several images into a collage or several group shots into one perfect image where everyone's eyes are open—it's helpful to know how to open multiple files within the same document. As with most things in Photoshop, there are a few ways to get it done:

- **Dragging and dropping files into a Photoshop document**. Simply ⌘-click (Ctrl-click) to activate multiple files and then drag 'em into an open Photoshop document. One by one, the images appear in the document on separate *Smart Object* layers (you'll learn all about layers in Chapter 3). Photoshop surrounds each image with resizing handles; if you need to resize the image, you can go ahead and do that now (page 232 has more on resizing). Press Return (Enter) to accept the size change—even if you didn't make one—and the *next* image appears on a separate layer, also with resizing handles. Repeat this process until you're finished adding images to the document.

You can also drag and drop files from the Mini Bridge panel into an open Photoshop document to accomplish the same thing (the figure on page 867 has the scoop). Unfortunately, in CC, you have to install Bridge and the Mini Bridge panel separately from Photoshop (see page 848).

- **Using the "Load Files into Stack" command**. To use this command, choose File→Scripts→"Load Files into Stack." In the resulting Load Layers dialog box, the Use drop-down menu lets you choose what you want to open: individual images or whole folders of images. Click the Browse button to tell Photoshop where the images or folders are stored on your hard drive; you can ⌘-click (Ctrl-click) files within the Browse dialog box to select more than one at a time. Click Open and you're deposited back in the Load Layers dialog box, where you can see the list of images you're about to load. If you're combining several shots into one, turn on the "Attempt to Automatically Align Source Images" checkbox. If you want Photoshop to convert all the layers into a single Smart Object, turn on the "Create Smart Object after Loading Layers" checkbox. (For more on using Smart Objects, see page 118.)

When you click OK, Photoshop opens the files at warp speed and then copies and pastes them into a *new* document, all on separate layers. (Unfortunately, you can't use this command to add files to an *existing* document. Bummer!)

TIP   You can trigger the same behavior in Bridge by activating multiple files in Bridge's Content panel and then choosing Tools→Photoshop→"Load Files into Photoshop Layers." (For more on Bridge, see Chapter 22.)

Opening Files as Smart Objects

Smart Objects are one of those glorious features that make Photoshop truly amazing. You'll learn a lot more about them in Chapter 3, but here's a quick overview: Smart Objects are basically containers that can store raster, vector, or raw files (page 43) in their original formats. Using Smart Objects forces Photoshop to keep track of important information about the original file—including its original pixel dimensions and any superpowers inherent to that format, like the ability to resize vectors without sacrificing quality—so you can experiment with size without losing quality, and quickly open the program from whence the image came (such as Illustrator or Camera Raw). In addition to the image types just mentioned, you can also open TIFF, PDF, and JPEG files as Smart Objects, as well as convert multiple layers or an *entire* Photoshop document into a Smart Object.

To open an image as a Smart Object, choose File→"Open as Smart Object." In the resulting dialog box, choose the file you want to open. When you click Open, Photoshop loads the file as a Smart Object in a new document. (To include an image as a Smart Object in a document that's *already* open, choose File→Place instead.) See Chapter 3 for more about layers and Smart Objects.

TIP   Photoshop opens some images as Smart Objects *automatically*. Any time you choose File→Place or drag a raster image into a Photoshop window, it'll open as a Smart Object without you having to think twice about it.

Opening Recent Files

This one's a real timesaver. Like many programs, Photoshop keeps track of the documents you've recently opened (see *Figure 2-6*). Choose File→Open Recent to see a list of the last 20 documents you worked on, with the latest one at the top of the list. If you've moved or renamed the file since you last opened it in Photoshop—put it in a different folder on your hard drive, say—the program will try to find it for you when you choose it from this list. If the document isn't on your hard drive anymore, Photoshop displays a message box letting you know it can't find the file.

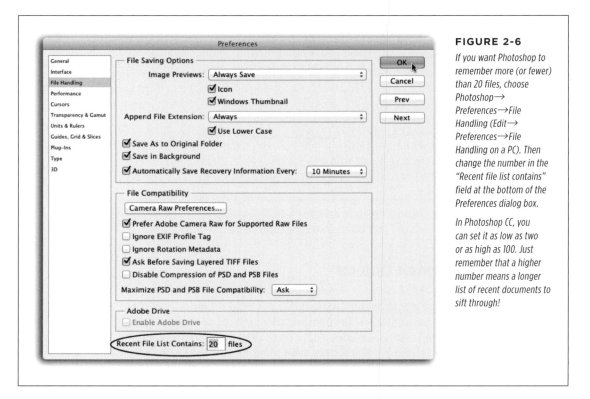

FIGURE 2-6

If you want Photoshop to remember more (or fewer) than 20 files, choose Photoshop→Preferences→File Handling (Edit→Preferences→File Handling on a PC). Then change the number in the "Recent file list contains" field at the bottom of the Preferences dialog box.

In Photoshop CC, you can set it as low as two or as high as 100. Just remember that a higher number means a longer list of recent documents to sift through!

Working with PDFs

Saving a document as a PDF file is like taking a *picture* of the document so others can open it without needing Photoshop—they just need the free Adobe Reader (or any other PDF-viewing program, like Preview on the Mac). PDFs can store text, images, and even video at a variety of quality settings. They're also *cross-platform*, which means they play nice with both Macs and PCs. It's an amazingly useful file format that will only become more common (see Chapter 16 for a peek into the future).

You open PDFs the same way you open any file: Choose File→Open, find the PDF you want, and then click the Open button. If someone created the PDF in Photoshop, it opens right up. If someone created it in another program, Photoshop displays the Import PDF dialog box (*Figure 2-7*) so you can choose which parts of the document you want to import (full pages or just the images) and set the resolution, dimensions, and so on.

FIGURE 2-7

If you decide to import multiple pages (as shown here), Photoshop creates a new document for each one. If you're lucky and the person who created the document was a PDF pro, she may have included size-specification goodies like crop size, bleed area, trim, and art size (you'll learn about most of these terms in Chapter 16). In that case, you can eliminate some resizing work on imported files by choosing one of the size options from the Crop To menu (shown here, right).

Working with Scanned Images

It *used* to be the case that, if you had a scanner that knew how to talk to Photoshop, you could use it to import images straight into the program. However, the TWAIN plug-in, which lets Photoshop communicate with scanners, is an older technology that's no longer being updated. These days, Adobe wants you to use the scanning software that came with your scanner instead. Another option is to use the third-party program VueScan (*www.hamrick.com*). If you go that route, save your image as a TIFF *and then* open it in Photoshop.

> **TIP** The Mac version of Photoshop CC includes an Import→"Images from Device" command; however, if you're using Mac OS 10.8, it won't work (to find out why, read the educational yet complex *Macworld* article available at *www.lesa.in/scanninginps*). One solution is to use Apple's Image Capture program to scan the image, and *then* open it in Photoshop.

The bottom line is that these days Adobe *really* doesn't want you scanning images straight into Photoshop because they'd have to keep up with the ever-evolving technological gymnastics that allow scanners and different operating systems to communicate with each other.

Each scanner has its own flavor of software, so there's no standard set of steps to work through to perform an actual scan—they're all different. Unfortunately, that means you have to read the documentation that came with your scanner to figure out how to get it done (the nerve!). Nevertheless, the box below has some scanning tips for your reading pleasure.

Working with Raw Files

Of all the file formats you can work with, *raw* may be the most useful and flexible. Professional-grade digital cameras (and many high-end consumer cameras) can capture images in this format. The info in a raw file is the exact, unprocessed information the camera recorded when it took the picture. (When shooting in JPEG format, in contrast, the camera processes the image by applying a little noise reduction, sharpening, and color boosting.) Raw files contain the most detailed information you can get from a digital camera, including what's known as *metadata*: info on all the settings the camera used to capture the image, like shutter speed, aperture, and so on. You can edit raw files using the pre-installed Photoshop plug-in called *Adobe Camera Raw* (shown in *Figure 2-8*), which you'll learn more about in Chapter 9.

> **TIP** Photoshop CC even lets you open Camera Raw from within Photoshop as a *filter*. Flip ahead to page 367 to learn about this super handy new feature.

■ OPENING RAW FILES

Opening a raw file in Photoshop is just like opening any other kind of image except that it opens in the Camera Raw window instead of the main Photoshop window. You can open raw files by:

- **Double-clicking the file's icon**. Your computer launches Photoshop (if it wasn't running already) and then opens the Camera Raw window.

- **Control-clicking (right-clicking on a PC) the file's icon and then choosing Open With→Adobe Photoshop CC**. Since Camera Raw is a plug-in that runs in conjunction with Photoshop and Bridge, it isn't listed separately, but your computer knows to open the file in Camera Raw.

UP TO SPEED

Scanning 101

Just because all scanning software is different doesn't mean there aren't a few guidelines you can follow to produce good scans. Keep these things in mind the next time you crank open your scanner's lid:

- **Scan at a higher bit depth than you need for the edited image**. Yes, the files will be larger, but they'll contain more color info, which is helpful when you're editing them. (See the box on page 36 for more on bit depth.)

- **Scan at a higher resolution than you need for the finished image so the files include more details**. You can always

lower the resolution later, but it's best not to increase it. However, Photoshop CC includes some new math that makes it pretty darn good at creating enlargements (see the box on page 238 for the scoop).

- **If your scanner software lets you adjust the image's color before you import the file into Photoshop, do it**. Making adjustments before you import the image lets you take advantage of all the info your scanner picked up.

FIGURE 2-8

Adobe Camera Raw (a.k.a. ACR or just Camera Raw), launches automatically when you open a raw file. If you've got a brand-new camera, you may have to update Camera Raw before you can open your photos. To do that, choose Help→Updates; online Appendix A has more on checking for updates. (This abstract image was created by keeping the camera's shutter open while pointing it at a flower, and then swirling the camera body around, which is a great way to make your own background images!)

- **Using Bridge to find the file and then choosing File→"Open in Camera Raw" or pressing ⌘-R (Ctrl+R).** You can also Control-click (right-click) the file in Bridge or the Mini Bridge panel and then choose "Open in Camera Raw" from the resulting shortcut menu. Bridge and Mini Bridge are a separate installation as discussed in Chapter 22.

TIP If you've got a bunch of raw images that need similar edits (cropping, color-correcting, and so on), you can open them all at once by Shift- or ⌘-clicking (Ctrl-clicking) them in Bridge or the Mini Bridge panel—if you've installed Bridge, that is; see page 848—or by choosing them on your desktop and then double-clicking or dragging them onto the Photoshop icon. When you click the Select All button in the top-left corner of the Camera Raw window, any edits you make from then on affect *all* your open images. See the box on page 403 for more on editing multiple files.

Duplicating Files

If your client or boss asks you to alter an image and you suspect he'll change his mind later, it's wise to edit a *copy* of the image instead of the original. That way, when he asks you to change everything back, you don't have to sweat bullets hunting for a backup of the original or try to recreate the earlier version. Duplicating files is also handy when creating duotones (page 322) and when you want to experiment with a variety of different treatments.

You can duplicate an open file by choosing File→Save As and renaming the image, but there's a faster way: Make sure the file you want to copy is in the currently active window (just click its window to activate it), and then choose Image→Duplicate. In the Duplicate Image dialog box (*Figure 2-9*), give the file a new name and then click OK. You've just set yourself up to be the office hero.

FIGURE 2-9

A duplicate PSD file is exactly the same as the original, including layers, layer styles, and so on. If you need to create a single-layer (flattened) version—for use in a program that doesn't support PSDs, say—turn on the Duplicate Merged Layers Only checkbox. (Page 108 has more about flattening files.)

Changing Your View

Photoshop gives you a variety of ways to view images, and different views are better for different editing tasks. For example, you can get rid of the Application Frame (page 2), view images full screen, zoom in and out, or rotate your canvas to view images at an angle. This section teaches you how to do all that and more.

Zooming In and Out

Being able to zoom into your image is crucial; it makes fixing imperfections, doing detailed clean-up work, and drawing accurate selections a zillion times easier. One way to zoom is to use the Zoom tool, which looks like a magnifying glass. You can click its icon at the bottom of the Tools panel or simply press Z (see *Figure 2-10*); then click your image, hold down the mouse button, and drag right to zoom in or drag left to zoom out. Alternatively, you can click repeatedly with the Zoom tool to get as up close and personal with those pixels as you want, and then Option-click (Alt-click on a PC) to zoom back out. You can also zoom using your keyboard, which is faster if your hands are already on it: Press ⌘ and the + or – key (Ctrl-+/–).

> **TIP** To turn off the pixel grid that appears when you're zoomed in to 501 percent or more, choose View→Show→Pixel Grid.

If your computer has a graphics processor that supports *OpenGL* (see the box on page 58), you can hold down your mouse button while the Zoom tool is active to *fly* into your image, zooming to a maximum of 3,200 percent; simply Option-click (Alt-click) and hold down your mouse button to zoom back out. This animated zooming makes you feel like you're flying into and out of the image—and it saves you several mouse clicks along the way.

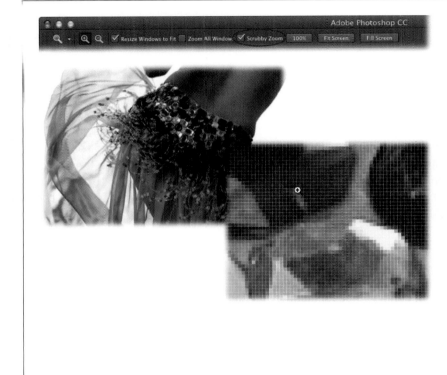

FIGURE 2-10

Top: You can also use the Zoom tool to dive into your image, though you have to turn off the Scrubby Zoom checkbox in the Options bar first. Then drag with the Zoom tool to draw a box around the pixels you want to look closely at. Release your mouse button, and Photoshop zooms in so the area you selected fills your document window. You can also zoom by typing a percentage into the lower-left corner of the document window next to the status bar (see the box on page 54).

Bottom: Zoom in to 501 percent or closer and you'll get a pixel-grid view that lets you edit precisely, pixel by pixel. If you're moving items around, this grid makes it easy to see whether pixels are perfectly aligned horizontally and vertically.

When the Zoom tool is active, the Options bar gives you the following choices:

- **Resize Windows to Fit**. To have Photoshop resize your document window to accommodate the current magnification level, leave this checkbox turned on.

- **Zoom All Windows**. Turn on this checkbox to use the Zoom tool to zoom in on *all* open windows by the same amount *simultaneously*. This setting is helpful if you've opened a duplicate of an image in order to see what your edits look like at roughly the size the image might print. You can also use the Window→Arrange submenu to do pretty much the same thing. Your options there include:

  — **Match Zoom**. Zooms all open windows to the same magnification level.

  — **Match Location**. Zooms to the same spot in each window.

  — **Match Rotation**. Rotates each window's canvas to the same angle.

  — **Match All**. Does all of the above.

- **Scrubby Zoom**. This option lets you click and *drag* to zoom. Drag right to zoom in, or left to zoom out.

TIP   If you've got a scroll wheel on your mouse, you can use that to zoom, too. Just choose Photoshop→ Preferences→General (Edit→Preferences→General on a PC), turn on the "Zoom with Scroll Wheel" checkbox, and then click OK.

- **100%**. Click this button—which was labeled Actual Pixels in previous versions—to see your image at 100 percent magnification. You can do the same thing by pressing ⌘-1 (Ctrl+1), by double-clicking the Zoom tool in the Tools panel, by entering *100* into the zoom percentage field at the bottom-left corner of the document window, or by choosing View→100%. Whew!

- **Fit Screen**. Clicking this button makes Photoshop resize the image so the whole thing fits inside your document window. (You can also press ⌘-0 [Ctrl+0] or choose View→"Fit on Screen" to do the same thing.) This is incredibly handy when you're using Free Transform (page 259) on an image that's larger than your document—it's tough to grab bounding-box handles if you can't see 'em!

- **Fill Screen**. This button enlarges your image so that it fills all available space inside the document window, both horizontally and vertically. Clicking Fill Screen makes your image a little bigger than it gets when you use Fit Screen, so you'll need to use the document window's scroll bars to see the whole thing.

The View menu also includes two additional zoom options that you won't find anywhere else:

- **200%**. New in Photoshop CC, this option lets you jump to a zoom level of 200% in order to compensate for the extra pixel density found in Apple's super high-resolution Retina displays (called HiDPI in Windows). Because those displays have twice as many pixels as regular displays, images designed for onscreen use look half their size. You can do the same thing by ⌘-double-clicking (Ctrl-double-clicking) the Zoom tool in the Tools panel. To set the zoom of *all* open documents to 200%, Shift-⌘-double-click (Shift-Ctrl-double-click) the Zoom tool in the Tool's panel. Alternatively, you can Ctrl- or right-click your canvas while the Hand or Zoom tool is active and choose 200% from the shortcut menu. And if all that isn't fast enough for you, you can give this command its own keyboard shortcut; the box on page 27 tells you how.

- **Print Size**. Previously a button in the Options bar when the Zoom tool was active, this option lives solely in the View menu in CC. When you choose it, Photoshop *previews* your image at the size it'll be when you print it. Keep in mind that your monitor's resolution settings can make the print-size preview look bigger or smaller than it will really be, so use this feature only as an approximation. (That said, you can use the Screen Resolution field in Photoshop's Units & Rulers preferences to control size in conjunction with monitor resolution.)

TIP If your image is smaller than the document window (meaning you see a gray border around the edges of the image) or if the document window itself is smaller than the available space in the Application Frame, double-click the Hand tool in the Tools panel and Photoshop enlarges your image to fill the window.

Moving Around in an Image

Once you've zoomed in on an image, you can use the Hand tool to move to another area without zooming back out. Grab this tool from the Tools panel or just press and hold the space bar on your keyboard (unless you're typing with the Type tool—then you'll type a bunch of spaces!). When your cursor turns into a hand, hold your mouse button down and then drag to move the image. When you get to the right spot, just let go of your mouse button.

TIP If you press and hold the Shift key while you're using the Hand tool, Photoshop moves *all* your open windows' contents at the same time. (You can do the same thing by turning on the Scroll All Windows checkbox in the Options bar.)

Back in Photoshop CS5, Adobe introduced a couple of other ways to move around a document: *flick-panning* and the *birds-eye view* feature. If you've got a computer that can run OpenGL (see the box on page 58), you can use these fast and efficient ways to scoot from one point to another. Here's how they work:

- **Flick-panning** lets you "toss" an image from one side of the document window to the other. Just grab the Hand tool, click the image, and hold down the mouse button. Next, quickly move your mouse in the direction you want to go and then release the button—the image slides along and slowly comes to a stop. You can do the same thing by holding the space bar and then moving your mouse quickly while pressing the mouse button, or while using gestures on a Mac (see the box below).

Zooming with Gestures

If you use a Mac with a multitouch trackpad or a Wacom tablet, you've got yet *another* way to zoom even if the Zoom tool isn't active: Use the finger pinch and spread gestures. You can also flick left or right with two fingers to move across the image or twist with your finger and thumb to rotate the canvas.

You can see examples of each of these gestures in the Mouse Preference pane. Choose ⌘→System Preferences→Mouse, and then click the Trackpad tab. Pick an item in the action list on the left side of the pane to see that gesture in action.

Zooming with gestures is all well and good...until you accidentally zoom or rotate your canvas by accident. That's why it's helpful to have the ability to turn Photoshop gestures *off*. Choose Photoshop→Preferences→Interface and, in the Options section, turn off Enable Gestures.

If you're using Windows and you've got a touch screen or a graphics tablet (see the box on page 517 for more on the latter), you can use gestures, too, though you don't get the Enable Gestures checkbox described above.

- **Birds-eye view** lets you zoom out of a *magnified* document quickly to see the whole thing (helpful when you're zoomed in so far that you don't know *where* you are in the image). To use it, just press and hold the H key and then click your image and hold the mouse button down: You'll get an instant aerial view of your image with a box marking the area you're zoomed in on. Let go of your mouse button (and the H key) to zoom back in.

GEM IN THE ROUGH

The Status Bar: Document Info Central

At the bottom of each document window is the *status bar*, shown below, which gives you a quick peek at important info about your document. When you first start using Photoshop, the status bar shows the size of the document; K stands for kilobytes and M for megabytes. (If you don't see any status information, the document's window may be too small. Just drag the lower-right corner of the window to enlarge it. The two buttons to the *left* of the status bar are discussed on page 2.)

Click the little triangle next to the status bar (circled) and you get a menu that lets you control what the bar displays. Here's what you can choose from:

- **Adobe Drive** connects to *Version Cue* servers. Version Cue was Adobe's method of attaching versions and enabling asset management throughout all of its programs, but they discontinued Version Cue back in Photoshop CS5. For more on Adobe Drive, see the Note on page 22.

- **Document Sizes** displays the image's approximate size for printing (on the left) and its approximate saved size (on the right). This option is selected from the factory.

- **Document Profile** shows the image's color profile (page 675).

- **Document Dimensions** displays the width, height, and resolution of the image.

- **Measurement Scale** lets you see the scale of pixels compared with other units of measurement. For example, an image from a microscope can measure objects in microns, and each micron can equal a certain number of pixels. Prior to CC, this option was available only in Photoshop Extended.

- **Scratch Sizes** tells you how much memory and hard disk space Photoshop is using to display your open documents.

- **Efficiency** lets you know if Photoshop is performing tasks as fast as it possibly can. A number below 100 percent means the program is running slowly because it's relying on scratch-disk space (page 23).

- **Timing** shows how long it took Photoshop to perform the most recent activity.

- **Current Tool** displays the name of the currently active tool.

- **32-bit Exposure** lets you adjust the preview image for 32-bit HDR images (see page 395).

- **Save Progress** displays the world's tiniest status bar, which indicates Photoshop's progress in saving a file. (New in Photoshop CC is the ability to save *another* file before the program finishes saving the *first* one—see page 38.)

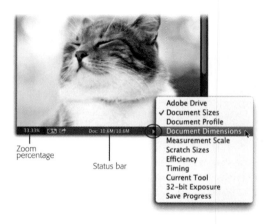

Zoom
percentage

Status bar

Adobe Drive
✓ Document Sizes
Document Profile
Document Dimensions
Measurement Scale
Scratch Sizes
Efficiency
Timing
Current Tool
32-bit Exposure
Save Progress

TIP If you're not a fan of flick-panning, you can turn it off by choosing Photoshop→Preferences→General (Edit→Preferences→General on a PC) and turning off the Enable Flick Panning checkbox.

Getting Oriented with the Navigator Panel

You can think of the Navigator panel as your GPS within Photoshop. If you want to know *exactly* what part of an image you're zoomed in on, it can show you. To open it, choose Window→Navigator. The panel displays a smaller version of your image called a *thumbnail* and marks the area you're zoomed in on with a red box called the *proxy preview*. At the bottom of the panel, the percentage field shows your current magnification level. You can zoom into or out of the image by clicking the zoom buttons at the bottom of the panel (they look like little mountains) or by using the slider nestled between them (see *Figure 2-11*). To zoom to a specific level, enter a number in the percentage field in the panel's lower left.

Your current viewing area

Drag to increase panel size

Zoom out   Zoom slider   Zoom in

FIGURE 2-11

As you zoom in on an image, the proxy preview box shrinks because you're looking at a smaller area. You can drag the box around to cruise to another spot in the image.

To make the Navigator panel bigger, drag its bottom-right corner downward. You can change the color of the proxy preview box by choosing Panel Options from the Navigator panel's menu. In the dialog box that appears, click the red color swatch, pick another color from the resulting Color Picker, and then click OK.

Rotating Your Canvas

If you're an artist, you're gonna love this feature! The Rotate View tool rotates your canvas—without harming any pixels—so you can edit, draw, and paint at a more natural angle (see *Figure 2-12*). It's like shifting a piece of paper or angling a canvas, but it doesn't rotate the actual image—just your *view* of the image. (The box on page 60 explains the difference between document size and canvas space.) Bear in mind, though, that your computer needs to be able to run OpenGL for this feature to work (see the box on page 58). To use this tool, choose it from within the Hand tool's toolset in the Tools panel.

NOTE MacBook, MacBook Air, and MacBook Pro users with multitouch trackpads can rotate the canvas by using the two-finger rotate gesture. See the box on page 53 for more on Mac gestures.

FIGURE 2-12

Grab the Rotate View tool, mouse over to your image, and then drag diagonally up or down to rotate it. When you drag, a compass appears that shows how far from "north" you're rotating the canvas, as shown here. If you're not the dragging type, you can enter a number into the Options bar's Rotation Angle field or spin the little round dial to the field's right. To straighten your canvas back out, click the Reset View button (also in the Options bar). To rotate all open images, turn on the Rotate All Windows checkbox.

This tool is especially handy if you use a graphics tablet (page 517) and you're retouching people (Chapter 10) or using Photoshop's painting tools (Chapter 12).

Arranging Open Images

The Application Frame and tabbed-document workspace help you manage several open documents; if you turn off the Application Frame, your documents can get scattered across your screen. However, you can herd those open windows together by using the commands listed under Window→Arrange (see *Figure 2-13*).

The Window→Arrange submenu offers a slew of choices:

- **Tile All Vertically** resizes your windows so you can see them all in vertical columns.

- **Tile All Horizontally** does nearly the same thing, but arranges them in horizontal rows.

FIGURE 2-13

*Use the Window→
Arrange commands to
create order out of chaos
by tiling (top) or cascading
(bottom) your windows.
(You can't cascade tabbed
documents because
they're attached—or
rather, docked—to the top
of the Photoshop window.
The fix is two choose
Window→Arrange→
"Float All in Windows"
first, and* then *choose
Cascade.)*

*When the Application
bar was removed in CS6,
the Arrange Documents
menu disappeared along
with it; however, Adobe
moved its commands to
the Window→Arrange
submenu.*

- **2-up, 3-up Horizontal** resizes two or three windows so they fit one on top of the other in horizontal rows.

- **2-up, 3-up Vertical** resizes two or three windows so they fit side by side in vertical columns.

- **3-up Stacked** resizes three windows side by side with one in a vertical column and two in horizontal rows.

- **4-up, 6-up** resizes four or six windows side by side in a tic tac toe–style grid.

NOTE You can only pick a 2-up option if you have two images open, a 3-up option if you have three images open, and so on. If you've got fewer images open, the commands listed above are grayed out.

- **Consolidate All to Tabs** groups your open images in a single, tabbed window (as shown in *Figure 2-14*, top).

- **Cascade** stacks your windows on top of one another, putting the largest one on the bottom and the smallest on the top.

- **Tile** resizes your windows to identical sizes and arranges them in rows and columns.

- **Float in Window** puts the current document in its own window if it's part of a tabbed group of documents that share the same window.

- **Float All in Windows** splits all tabbed documents out into their own windows and cascades the new windows.

UP TO SPEED

Understanding the GPU, OpenGL, and OpenCL

You might not know it, but your computer actually has *two* brains: a CPU (central processing unit) for interpreting and executing instructions, and a GPU (graphics processing unit, also called a *video card*) for displaying images and videos.

Newer GPUs take advantage of a technology called *OpenGL,* which helps computers draw and display graphics faster and more efficiently. (To learn more about it, go to *www. opengl.org.*) You can tell whether your GPU uses OpenGL by choosing Photoshop→Preferences→Performance (Edit→Preferences→Performance on a PC). In the Graphics Processor Settings at the bottom right, check whether the graphics processor listed includes "OpenGL" in its name and whether the Use Graphics Processor checkbox is turned on (it probably will be). If the checkbox is grayed out (meaning you can't turn it on), then your computer's video card isn't fast enough or doesn't have enough memory to run OpenGL—bummer.

If your computer can't run OpenGL, some Photoshop features will take a long time to run; others won't work at all, such as the Rotate View tool, birds-eye zooming, smooth pan and zoom, pixel-grid overlay (*Figure 2-10*), flick-panning, scrubby zoom, HUD Color Picker, rich cursor info, the Eyedropper tool's sampling ring, on-canvas brush resizing, and brush bristle tip preview. Other nifty features in CC that require OpenGL include all the 3D features, Auto Recovery, Free Transform's Warp option, Puppet Warp preview, the Liquify filter, the Adaptive Wide Angle filter, the Oil Paint filter, the Lighting Effects Gallery, as well as the Field Blur, Iris Blur, and Tilt-Shift filters.

In *addition*, GPUs that are brand-spanking-new also support *OpenCL*, a technology that lets Photoshop use the GPU for processing tasks that *aren't* specifically related to viewing graphics. Features that can use OpenCL include the Field Blur, Iris Blur, and Tilt-Shift filters, which all perform better now than they did before.

Bet you feel like *you* have two brains now, too!

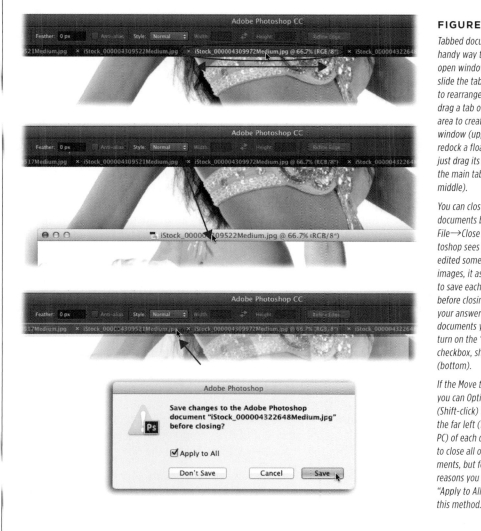

FIGURE 2-14

Tabbed documents are a handy way to organize open windows. You can slide the tabs left or right to rearrange them (top) or drag a tab out of the tab area to create a floating window (upper middle). To redock a floating window, just drag its tab back into the main tab area (lower middle).

You can close all tabbed documents by choosing File→Close All. If Photoshop sees that you've edited some or all of those images, it asks if you'd like to save each edited image before closing it. To apply your answer to all the documents you're closing, turn on the "Apply to All" checkbox, shown here (bottom).

If the Move tool is active, you can Option-click (Shift-click) the tiny X at the far left (far right on a PC) of each document tab to close all open documents, but for unknown reasons you don't get the "Apply to All" option with this method. Weird!

TIP You can Control-click (right-click) a document's tab to reveal a shortcut menu that lets you close that document's window, close all windows, create a new document, open an existing one, or reveal where that document lives on your hard drive.

TIP   You can cycle through all open documents by using the ⌘-tilde (~) keyboard shortcut (Ctrl+Tab on a PC). To cycle through documents in the reverse order, press Shift-⌘-tilde (Shift+Ctrl+Tab). This is especially handy when you're showing off images in Full Screen mode, as described on page 5.

◼ Guides, Grids, and Rulers

Placing all the components of your design in the right spots can be challenging, and if you're a real stickler for details, close isn't good enough. This section teaches you how to use Photoshop's guides, grids, and rulers to get everything positioned *perfectly*. Adobe calls these little helpers *extras*, and you access them via the View menu.

Rulers and Guiding Lines

Properly positioning objects on your canvas can be the difference between a basic design and a masterpiece. The quickest way to position and align objects is by drawing a straight line to nestle them against. You can do just that using Photoshop's nonprinting *guides*—vertical and horizontal lines you can place anywhere you want (see *Figure 2-15*).

The easiest way to add guides is to drag 'em into your document, but before you can do that, you need to turn on Photoshop's *rulers* by pressing ⌘-R (Ctrl+R); you can also turn them on by choosing View→Rulers. Whichever method you use, the rulers appear on the top and left edges of the document window.

Once you've turned rulers on, you can add a guide by clicking either the horizontal or vertical ruler, and then dragging the guide into your document as shown in *Figure 2-15* (you won't see the guide until you start dragging). After that, you can do any of the following:

- **Move the guide** by grabbing the Move tool (see Appendix C, online) from the Tools panel or by pressing V, and then dragging the guide to a new position (your cursor turns into a double-sided arrow like the one circled in *Figure 2-15*).

UP TO SPEED

Document Size vs. Canvas Space

One thing that's super confusing to Photoshop beginners is the difference between document size (also known as image size) and canvas size. In Photoshop, the *canvas* is the amount of viewable and editable area in a document (it's the same as the document's dimensions) and you can add to or subtract from it anytime. By doing so, you add or subtract pixels from the *image*, which either increases or decreases the document size.

For example, say you're designing a poster for a chili cook-off and you're experimenting with the design. Instead of limiting your work area to the final size of the poster, you can make the canvas bigger than that (page 248) so you have room to spread out and try different design ideas. Then, once you've nailed down the final design, you can crop (page 216) or trim (page 226) it back down to size.

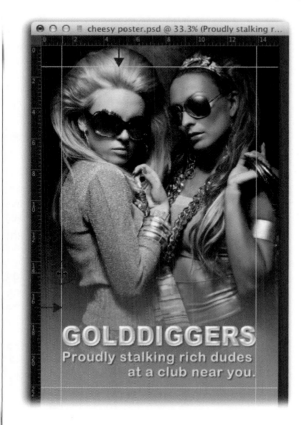

FIGURE 2-15

Guides help you position items exactly where you want 'em. Here, the light blue (cyan) guides help make sure all the text is the same width and the edges of the poster are free of clutter. The guides won't show up when you print the image, so you don't have to worry about deleting them.

To add a guide in a certain spot in a document, choose View→New Guide and then enter the position in the resulting dialog box. If you have trouble grabbing a guide to move it, try making the document window bigger than the canvas by dragging any edge of the document window, or its lower-right corner, diagonally. That way, the guides extend beyond the canvas and don't overlap other elements that you might accidentally grab.

You can change the rulers' unit of measurement on the fly by Control-clicking (right-clicking) the ruler itself and then choosing the unit you want from the resulting shortcut menu. Alternatively, you can change it in the Units & Rulers preferences.

- **Snap objects to the guide** by turning on Photoshop's *snap* feature. Snapping makes it super easy to align objects because when they get close to one of your guides, they jump to it as if they were magnetized. You can tell that an object has snapped to the nearest guide because it pops into place. After the object aligns to a guide, you can move it along that line to snap it into place with other guides, too. If you don't want an object aligned with a certain guide, just keep moving it—it'll let go of the guide as soon as you move it far enough. This feature is turned *on* initially, though you can turn it off by choosing View→Snap To→Guides (handy when you can't position an object where you want to because it keeps snapping to align with a guide).

NOTE Straight from the factory, layer content snaps to grids, layers (Chapter 3), slices (Chapter 17), *and* the edges of your document. You can choose among these items by choosing View→Snap To and then picking the elements you *actually* want objects to align with. For example, choosing both Guides and Layers makes the object you're moving snap to guides *and* the edges of objects on other layers.

- **Hide all guides** temporarily by pressing ⌘-; (Ctrl+;) or by choosing View→Show→Guides.

- **Delete a guide** by dragging it into the ruler area.

- **Delete all guides** by choosing View→Clear Guides.

- **Lock all guides** by choosing View→Lock Guides or pressing Option-⌘-; (Alt+Ctrl+;)—useful when you don't want to accidentally move a guide.

■ SMART GUIDES

Smart Guides are a little different from regular guides in that they automatically appear onscreen to show the spatial relationship between objects. For example, they pop up when objects are aligned or evenly spaced in your document. As you drag an object, Smart Guides appear whenever the current object is horizontally, vertically, or centrally aligned with other objects on other layers. To turn on Smart Guides, choose View→Show→Smart Guides. You can see 'em in action on page 95.

■ USING THE DOCUMENT GRID

If you want *lots* of guides without all the work of placing them, you can add a grid to your image instead by choosing View→Show→Grid. Straight from the factory, Photoshop's gridlines are spaced an inch apart with four subdivisions, although you can change that by choosing Photoshop→Preferences→"Guides, Grid & Slices" (Edit→Preferences→"Guides, Grid & Slices" on a PC), as *Figure 2-16* explains.

The Ruler Tool

In addition to the rulers you learned about earlier, Photoshop also gives you a virtual tape measure and protractor: the Ruler tool, which lets you measure the distance between two points in a document. Just grab the tool by pressing Shift-I repeatedly (it's hiding in the eyedropper toolset and it looks like a little ruler), and then click and hold your mouse button where you want to start measuring. Drag across the area or object, and you'll see a line appear in your document (see *Figure 2-17*).

When you're using the Ruler tool, the Options bar's measurements get a little confusing. Here's what they mean:

- **X and Y**. These *axes* mark the horizontal and vertical coordinates (respectively) at the start of your ruler line. For example, if you start the line at the 4-inch mark on the horizontal ruler and the 7-inch mark on the vertical ruler, your coordinates are X: 4 and Y: 7.

- **W and H**. Calculates the distance your line has traveled from the X and Y axes.

FIGURE 2-16

Photoshop's grid is helpful when you need to align lots of different items, like the text shown here. You can turn it on by pressing ⌘-' (Ctrl+' on a PC).

In the Preferences dialog box, adjust the gridline marks by changing the number in the Gridline Every field, and use the drop-down menu next to it to change the grid's unit of measurement: pixels, inches, centimeters, millimeters, points, picas, or percent. Use the Subdivisions field to control how many lines appear between each gridline—if any.

To turn off all of Photoshop's extras—that is, guides, grid, and slices—in one fell swoop, choose View→Extras. But even if you do that, any extra that's individually turned on in the View→Show menu will reappear the next time you open a document or create a new one, which could drive you bonkers. The fix is to specifically turn off the offending item—say, the grid—in the View→Show menu. Who knew?

FIGURE 2-17

To measure a perfectly straight horizontal or vertical line, hold the Shift key as you drag. When you release your mouse button, Photoshop displays the measurement between the line's start and end points in the Options bar.

- **A**. Displays the angle of the line relative to the X axis.

- **L1**. Indicates the length of the line.

- **L2**. You see a number here only if you use a virtual *protractor*. (Thought you left protractors behind in high school, didn't you? Quick refresher: Protractors help you measure angles.) To create a protractor, Option-drag (Alt-drag on a PC) at an angle from the end of your ruler line, or just double-click the line and then drag. This number represents the angle between the two lines.

- **Use Measurement Scale**. Photoshop includes a set of rulers, but it has nothing upon which to *base* the measurements you make with those rulers. For example, a photo of a garden gnome doesn't indicate its actual size; if you measure the width of the gnome in Photoshop, it could be .25 inch or 25 pixels—depending upon the unit of measurement you've picked in Units & Rulers preferences—rather than its real-world size of 6 inches. However, by choosing Image→Analysis→Set Measurement Scale→Custom and then entering the logical (real-world) length of an inch or pixel, you give Photoshop a scale upon which to base its measurements. Photoshop then uses this new scale when you turn on Use Measurement Scale in the Options bar. (Prior to CC, this setting was available only in the Extended version of the program.)

- **Straighten Layer**. To use the Ruler tool to straighten your image, draw a line across an area that should be straight (like the horizon). Then click this button, and Photoshop straightens and crops the image. To make Photoshop straighten the image *without* cropping it, Option-click (Alt-click) this button instead. (If you forget to press Option [Alt], you can undo the crop by pressing ⌘-Z [Ctrl+Z].)

NOTE   You can straighten images with the Crop tool, too (see page 227 for the scoop). You can also straighten images using Camera Raw, as explained on page 229.

- **Clear**. Any ruler line you draw hangs around until you tell it to go away by clicking this button or drawing another ruler line. But ruler lines don't print even if you forget to clear them, so don't lose any sleep over 'em.

TIP   To change the angle of a ruler line, just grab one of its end points and drag it to another spot. To move a ruler line, grab it anywhere *other* than its end points and drag it to another location.

Layers: The Key to Nondestructive Editing

Photoshop gives you two ways to edit files: destructively and nondestructively. *Destructive editing* means you're changing the original image—once you exceed the History panel's limit (page 15) and save your document, those changes are (gulp) permanent. *Nondestructive editing* means you're not changing the original file and you can go back to it at any time. Folks new to image editing tend to use the first method and experienced pixel-jockeys the second—and you'll likely see a tiny cloud of smugness floating above the latter.

When you're working in Photoshop, it's best to keep your documents as flexible as possible. People (even you!) change their minds hourly about what looks good, what they want, and where they want it—all of which is no big deal if you're prepared for that. But if you're not, you'll spend a ton of time *redoing* what you've already done from scratch. To avoid that kind of suffering, you can use *layers*, a set of stackable transparencies that together form a whole image (see *Figure 3-1*). Layers are your ticket to nondestructive and therefore safer, *non-committal* editing (if only we had layers in real life!).

> **NOTE** Another argument for using layers is that they let you easily apply the same effect you're creating in one image to other images (by dragging and dropping the relevant layers into another open document), as well as reverse-engineer a technique or effect that you created years ago in order to apply it to a *new* image today.

FIGURE 3-1

You can think of layers like the ingredients on this pizza (really!).

Left: In the Photoshop workspace, most folks keep their document window on the left and Layers panel on the right. So by looking straight down at this pizza, you get a bird's-eye view of it, which represents what you see in your document window. Even though the pizza is made up of many layers (the different toppings, sauces, and dough), you see a single image.

Right: However, the Layers panel shows you an exploded view. If some of the toppings don't cover the pizza's entire surface—like the bell peppers and mushrooms shown here—you can see through that layer to what's on the other layers below. In this example, that's the pepperoni, cheese, sauce, and dough.

This kind of image is called a composite: *a seemingly single image that's made from many. The act of creating an image like this is called* compositing.

With layers, you can make all kinds of changes to an image without altering the original. For example, you can use one layer to color-correct your family reunion photo (Chapter 9), another to whiten Aunt Bessie's teeth (page 420), and yet another to add a photo of the Great Pyramid to make it look like the reunion was held in Egypt instead of at the local park (page 270). Using layers also lets you:

- Resize an object independently of everything else in the document, without changing the document's size (page 91).

- Move an object or text around within the document without moving anything else (page 93).

- Combine several images into one document to make a collage (Chapter 7).

- Make most of an image black and white while leaving a small part of it in color (see page 316).

- Fix the color and lighting of a photo (or just parts of it) without harming the original (see *Figure 3-31* on page 115).

- Remove blemishes and other objects without harming the original (Chapter 10).

- Add editable text on top of an image (page 582).

The best part about using layers is that once you save a document as a PSD file (page 39), you can close it, forget about it, and open it next week to find your layers—and all your changes—intact. Learning to love layers is the key to a successful Photoshop career because they let you edit with maximum flexibility.

In this chapter, you'll learn about the different kinds of layers, when to use them, and how to create them. You'll also find out about the fun and useful features that tag along with layers, like layer styles and layer masks. By the time you're done, you'll be shouting the praises of nondestructive editing from the highest rooftop! (Whether you do it smugly or not is up to you.)

Layer Basics

Layers come in many flavors, all of which have their own special purpose:

- **Image layers**. These layers are pixel-based (see page 43)—in fact, Photoshop also calls 'em *pixel layers*—and you'll work with them *all* the time. If you open a photo or add a new, empty layer and paint on it (Chapter 12), you've got yourself an Image layer.

- **Fill layers**. When it comes to changing or adding color to an image, these layers are your best friends. They let you fill a layer with a solid color, gradient, or pattern, which comes in handy when you want to create new backgrounds or fill a selection with color. Just like Shape layers (which are explained in a sec), you can double-click a Fill layer's thumbnail to change its color anytime. The next time you're tempted to add an empty layer and fill it with color (page 83), try using one of these layers instead.

- **Adjustment layers**. These ever-so-useful layers let you apply changes to one or all the layers underneath them, though the *changes* actually happen on the Adjustment layer. For example, if you want to change a color image to black and white, you can use a Black & White Adjustment layer (page 308) and the color removal happens on its *own* layer, leaving the original unharmed. These layers don't contain any pixels, just instructions that tell Photoshop what changes you want to make (which is why you can't use any of the program's painting tools on them). Adjustment layers are also handy for creating *reusable* effects; to apply the same effect to another image, just drag the Adjustment layer from one document to the other.

  You can access these handy helpers in the Adjustments panel on the right side of the Photoshop window (if you don't see it, choose Window→Adjustments), via the Adjustment layer menu at the bottom of the Layers panel (its icon is a half-black/half-white circle), or in the Layer menu (choose Layer→New Adjustment layer). There are 16 kinds of Adjustment layers, and you'll learn how to use 'em in Part Two of this book.

- **Smart Objects**. Adobe refers to this kind of layer as a *container*, though "safe layer" is a better description. You can put anything you want into a Smart

Object—pixel-based images, raw images (page 48), vector files (page 43), other layers, or even whole Photoshop documents—and Photoshop keeps that content safe by making changes to the *container* instead of the *content*. This lets you resize the contents of a Smart Object without trashing its quality (as long as you don't exceed the file's original pixel dimensions, unless it's a vector), swap content with another image, run filters non-destructively, and much more. Flip to page 118 for more info.

- **Shape layers**. These layers are vector-based, meaning they're made from points and paths, not pixels (see page 43). Not only can you create useful shapes quickly with these babies, but you can also resize 'em without losing quality *and* change their fill color by double-clicking their layer thumbnails or using the Fill and Stroke settings in the Options bar. Photoshop creates a Shape layer automatically anytime you use a shape tool, unless you change the tool's mode as explained on page 555.

- **Type layers**. In Photoshop, text isn't made from pixels, so it gets its own special kind of layer. Any time you grab the Type tool and start pecking away, Photoshop automatically creates a Type layer. See Chapter 14 for the full story on creating text in Photoshop.

- **Video layers**. Want to edit video in Photoshop? No problem. These layers give you the ability to import, trim, and split video clips, as well as add transitions, motion, and even audio tracks to a document. (Prior to CS6, these options were available only in the now-deceased Extended version of the program.) You can use Photoshop to color-correct, apply filters, and layer styles to video as easily as other layers. You'll learn all about editing videos in Chapter 20, where you'll also pick up some practical project ideas.

- **3D layers**. Previously found only in the Extended version of Photoshop, these layers let you create three-dimensional objects from scratch, make text that looks 3D, and import existing 3D files so you can add custom paint and other details to 'em. To get started using Photoshop's 3D tools, head on over to Chapter 21.

The Layers Panel

No matter how many or what kind of layers your document contains, the one that's most important to you at any given time is the *active* layer. You can tell which layer is active by peeking at the Layers panel, where Photoshop highlights it in blue, as shown in *Figure 3-2*. (To open the Layers panel, click its tab in the panel dock on the right side of your screen, or choose Window→Layers.) The next edit you make will affect *only* that layer.

Activating Layers

About the easiest thing you'll ever do in Photoshop is activate a layer—just mouse over to the Layers panel and click the layer you want to work on. However, just because this process is easy doesn't mean it's unimportant. As you learned in the last section, most of Photoshop's tools and commands affect only the *currently active layer* (save for things like cropping or changing your document's color mode).

Double-click tab to collapse vertically

Panel menu

Layer thumbnail

Smart Object

Type layer

Adjustment layer

Shape layer

Highlight indicates active layer (image layer)

Solid Color Fill layer

Drag to resize
Delete layer
New layer

FIGURE 3-2

In the Layers panel, Photoshop highlights the currently active layer in blue, as shown here (the exact color of blue depends on the color theme you're using [page 6]).

Each layer has its own little preview of what the layer contains, called a layer thumbnail (circled). To make layer thumbnails bigger so they're easier to see, open the panel menu labeled here and then choose Panel Options. The resulting dialog box includes a list of thumbnail sizes to choose from. Alternatively, you can Control-click (right-click) the layer thumbnail and choose a size from the resulting shortcut menu.

If you're trying to use a tool and Photoshop doesn't seem to be responding, take a peek at the Layers panel and make sure you've got the right layer activated. Nine times out of ten, you'll find that you don't!

As your document gets more complex and your Layers panel starts to grow (and it will), it can be hard to figure out which layer each part of the image lives on. If you want, you can make Photoshop *guess* which layer an object is on: Press V to activate the Move tool, head up to the Options bar at the top of your screen, turn on the Auto-Select checkbox, and then choose Layer from the drop-down menu to its right. After that, when you click an object in the document, Photoshop activates the layer it *thinks* that object is on (it'll do this next time you use the Move tool, too, unless you turn off the Auto-Select checkbox). The program may or may not guess right, and it really works only if your layers don't completely cover each other up. If you've got a document full of isolated objects—ones without backgrounds—on different layers, give this feature a shot. But if you're working on a multilayered collage, forget it. For that reason, you'll probably want to leave Auto-Select turned *off*.

TIP You can have Photoshop narrow down your layer-hunting options by prodding it to give you a list of layers it *thinks* an object is on. Press V to grab the Move tool, Control-click (right-click) an object in your document, and then choose one of the layers from the resulting shortcut menu. This trick only works if the layer's visibility eye is turned on and you click an area that's more than 10 percent opaque (the requirement was 50 percent in older versions of the program).

■ ACTIVATING MULTIPLE LAYERS

You'd be surprised how often you need to do the same thing to more than one layer. If you want to rearrange a few of them in your layer stack (page 76), move 'em around in your document together (page 93), or resize them simultaneously (page 91), you need to activate 'em first. Photoshop lets you activate as few or as many as you want, though how you go about it depends on where they live in the Layers panel:

- **All layers**. To activate the whole kit and caboodle, choose Select→All Layers. Choose Deselect→All Layers to (you guessed it) deactivate everything. Keyboard shortcut: Option-⌘-A (Alt+Ctrl+A). (Note that, on PCs, this command activates all layers *except* a locked Background layer.)

- **Consecutive layers**. To activate layers that are next to each other in the Layers panel, click the first one and then Shift-click the last one; Photoshop automatically activates everything in between (see *Figure 3-3*, left).

- **Nonconsecutive layers**. To activate layers that *aren't* next to each other, click near the first one's name and then ⌘-click (Ctrl-click on a PC) the rest of them (see *Figure 3-3*, right).

- **Linked layers**. If you've linked any layers together (page 99), you can activate them all by choosing Layer→Select Linked Layers. This command also lives in the Layers panel's menu—the one in its upper right—as well as the shortcut menu you get by Control-clicking (right-clicking) to the right of the layer thumbnail.

NOTE Activating a layer is *completely* different from loading a layer's contents as a *selection*. When you load a layer as a selection, you see marching ants running around whatever is on that layer. Activating a layer simply makes that layer active so you can perform other edits. See Chapter 4 for more on creating selections.

■ FILTERING LAYERS

If your list of layers is *really* long, you'll have to scroll through the Layers panel to find the ones you want to activate. However, you can make Photoshop *hide* layers based on conditions you specify using the row of filtering controls at the top of the Layers panel (labeled in *Figure 3-4*, top). You tell Photoshop which layers you want to view, and it temporarily hides the rest in the Layers panel (though the content of those layers is still visible in your document).

Click in this area to activate a layer

FIGURE 3-3

You can activate consecutive layers (left) or nonconsecutive layers (right). To avoid loading a layer as a selection (page 136) when you're activating nonconsecutive layers, make sure you ⌘-click (Ctrl-click) the area to the right of the layer thumbnail (near the layer's name), as shown here.

To filter layers, pick an option from the drop-down menu in the upper left of the Layers panel, and then use the controls to the menu's right to refine your search. Here are your options:

- **Kind**. This is what the drop-down menu is set to unless you change it. This option lets you tell Photoshop what *type* of layers you want to see. Use the buttons to this menu's right to have Photoshop display only the Image, Adjustment, Type, or Shape layers, or Smart Objects. For example, to see only the Type layers—so you can activate 'em all and change their fonts, say—make sure the drop-down menu is set to Kind (it should be unless you've changed it) and then click the T button to its right, and Photoshop hides all the layers in the Layers panel *except* the Type layers (see *Figure 3-4*, bottom). You can also click more than one button to see more than one kind of layer—like the Type and Shape layers, say.

- **Name**. If you've given your layers meaningful names, choose this option from the drop-down menu and a search field appears to the menu's right. Enter some text (it's not case-sensitive) and Photoshop displays only the layers whose names include what you entered. You don't need to press Return/Enter—Photoshop begins filtering layers as soon as you start typing.

> **TIP** When you choose Select→Find Layers or press Shift-Option-⌘-F (Shift+Alt+Ctrl+F), Photoshop automatically sets the filtering drop-down menu to Name and plops a cursor into the text field to its right so you can start typing.

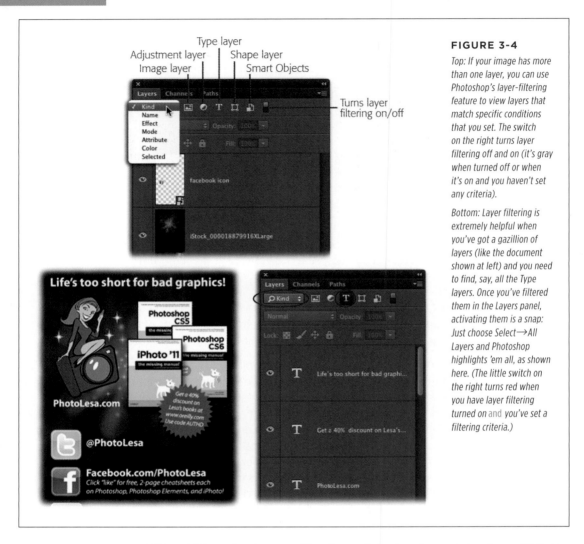

FIGURE 3-4

Top: If your image has more than one layer, you can use Photoshop's layer-filtering feature to view layers that match specific conditions that you set. The switch on the right turns layer filtering off and on (it's gray when turned off or when it's on and you haven't set any criteria).

Bottom: Layer filtering is extremely helpful when you've got a gazillion of layers (like the document shown at left) and you need to find, say, all the Type layers. Once you've filtered them in the Layers panel, activating them is a snap: Just choose Select→All Layers and Photoshop highlights 'em all, as shown here. (The little switch on the right turns red when you have layer filtering turned on and you've set a filtering criteria.)

- **Effect**. This option lets you filter layers based on layer styles (page 124). For example, to see all the layers that have a drop shadow, choose this option and then choose Drop Shadow from the drop-down menu that appears to this menu's right.

- **Mode**. To filter layers based on their blend modes (page 276), pick this option and then choose the blend mode you're after from the drop-down menu that appears on the right.

- **Attribute**. When you pick this option, a drop-down menu appears that lets you filter layers based on whether or not they're visible, empty, locked or linked to other layers (page 99), clipped to other layers (page 119), include a pixel- or vector-based layer mask (page 109), include effects (think layer styles [page 124]), or use advanced blending options (page 108).

- **Color**. If you've color-coded your layers (page 98), you can use this option to view layers labeled with a certain color. For example, if you applied a red label to all the layers you used to fix skin imperfections in a portrait, choose this option and then pick Red from the drop-down menu that appears to its right and Photoshop displays only those layers.

- **Selected**. New in Photoshop CC, this option lets you see only the layers that are currently *active* (see page 68 for more on activating layers); Adobe calls this maneuver *isolating layers*. This is handy when your Layers panel is long and you're experimenting with size, placement, or effects of certain layers that don't necessarily match any of the criteria listed above, or when you're editing certain Shape layers in a document that contains several.

Once you've isolated the active layers, you can deactivate 'em selectively—thus removing that particular layer from your current Layers panel list—by Control-clicking (right-clicking) the layer and choosing "Release from Isolation" from the resulting shortcut menu. If you add a new layer while Selected layer filtering is turned on, Photoshop adds it to the Layers panel's list (because new layers are active when you make 'em). To see all your layers again, choose Select→Isolate Layers or click the switch labeled in *Figure 3-4* (top).

TIP If you've used one of Photoshop's shape tools to create a Shape layer, you can isolate that layer by double-clicking its gray outline with the Path Selection or Direct Selection tool. When you do, you see only that layer in the Layers panel. However, if you double-click a path that *doesn't* live on a layer—you drew the path using the Pen tool or a shape tool in Path drawing mode (page 536), say—layer filtering is indeed turned on, but nothing is isolated in your Layers panel.

After you've filtered the layers so that only the ones you're interested in are visible, you can quickly activate all the visible ones—save for a locked Background layer—by choosing Select→All Layers. You can work with filtered layers just like any other layers: Delete 'em, change their stacking order, and so on. Your filter remains in effect until you turn it off or close the document (Photoshop doesn't save your layer filter settings when you save the document).

When you're ready to see *all* the layers again, *Option*-click (Alt-click on a PC) the little red switch near the top right of the Layers panel; it turns gray to let you know that filtering is turned off. Photoshop reveals all your layers and then sets the filtering controls to their factory settings so you can use 'em again. If you just *click* the switch, Photoshop still shows all your layers but it takes several more clicks to use layer filtering again: You have to click the switch *again* to turn filtering back on and *then* tweak the filtering options to reveal the layers you want. Yuck.

NOTE None of Photoshop's layer-filtering options currently work with actions (Chapter 18).

Adding New Layers

Most of the time, Photoshop creates new layers *for* you, like when you copy and paste an image (page 83), create text (page 582), draw a shape (page 547), and so on. But if you want to do something like paint with the Brush tool—to colorize a grayscale image (page 339), say—you need to create a new layer manually; otherwise, you'll paint right on your original image. Photoshop gives you five ways to create a new layer:

- Click the "Create a new layer" button at the bottom of the Layers panel (it looks like a piece of paper with a folded corner).

- Choose Layer→New→Layer.

- Choose New Layer from the Layers panel's menu.

- Press Shift-⌘-N (Shift+Ctrl+N).

- Drag a file from your desktop, Bridge, or Mini Bridge (Chapter 22) into an open Photoshop document; the item you dragged appears on its own layer in the document—as a Smart Object to boot!

When you click the "Create a new layer" button, Photoshop creates an empty layer called *Layer 1*, though you can double-click this name in the Layers panel to change it. (If you already have a layer called *Layer 1*, Photoshop names the new one *Layer 2*, and so on.) If you use the menu options or keyboard shortcut instead, the program displays the New Layer dialog box (*Figure 3-5*), where you can name the layer, color-code it (page 98), choose its blend mode (page 276), set its opacity, and use it in a clipping mask (see the box on page 119). Whichever method you use, Photoshop adds the new layer above the one that was active when you added it.

TIP If your fingers are flexible enough, you can create a new layer *and* bypass the New Layer dialog box by pressing Shift-*Option*-⌘-N (Shift+Alt+*Ctrl*+N). This shortcut is handy if you want new layers and don't care what they're called.

To create a new layer *below* the one that's currently active, ⌘-click (Ctrl-click) the "Create a new layer" button at the bottom of the Layers panel. (If the only layer in your document is the locked Background layer, you've got to double-click it or choose Layer→New→"Layer from Background" to unlock it before you can add a new layer below it.) This shortcut saves you the extra step of dragging the new layer to a lower position later; over the course of a year, this tip has been known to produce an *entire* vacation day!

Hiding and Showing Layers

The little visibility eye to the left of each layer thumbnail in the Layers panel lets you turn that layer off and on (*Figure 3-5*, bottom). Photoshop calls this incredibly useful feature *hiding*. Here are some examples of what hiding layers lets you do:

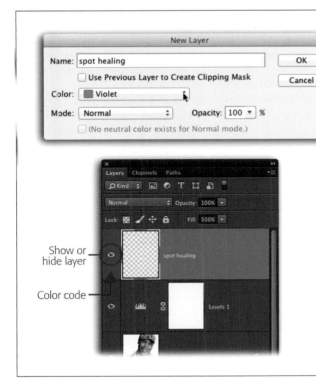

FIGURE 3-5

In the New Layer dialog box (top), you can give your new layer a name and a colored label. Color-coding layers makes them easier to spot in a long Layers panel (bottom), so it's especially helpful to use on layers that you may need to return to for additional editing.

In the Layers panel, you can double-click a layer's name to rename it, and turn its visibility on or off by clicking the little eye icon to the left of its thumbnail. The new layer's thumbnail shown here is a checkerboard pattern because the layer is empty and transparent. (See the box on page 37 for more on transparency.)

- **See an instant before-and-after preview**. If you've spent some time color-correcting (Chapter 9) or retouching people (Chapter 10) on duplicate layers, hiding the layers you used to do that is an easy way to see the effect of your handiwork.

- **Experiment with different looks**. If you're trying out different backgrounds or background colors, you can add them all to your document, hide them, and then turn them on one at a time to see which one looks best.

- **See what you're doing**. When you're working on a document that has a bunch of layers, some of them may hide an area you need to see or work on. The solution is to hide in-the-way layers while you're working on those parts of the image and then turn 'em back on when you're done. That said, in Photoshop CC, it's faster to use layer filtering instead (page 70).

- **Print certain layers**. Only layers that are visible in your document will print, so if you want to print only parts of an image, hide the other layers first.

To hide a layer, simply click the little eye to the left of its layer thumbnail; to show it again, click the empty square where the eye was. To hide *all* layers except one, Option-click (Alt-click on a PC) the visibility eye of the layer you want to see; to display the other layers again, Option-click (Alt-click) that same layer's visibility eye again. Alternatively, you can Control-click (right-click) a layer's visibility eye (or, if the layer is hidden, the spot where the eye was) and then choose "Show/Hide this layer" or "Show/Hide all other layers" from the shortcut menu. You can also find the Show/Hide Layers command in the Layer menu.

> **TIP** To hide or show several layers, drag up or down over their visibility eyes in the Layers panel while holding down your mouse button. To hide or show a *single* layer in a document that contains a slew of layers, Option-click (Alt-click) its visibility eye.

Restacking Layers

Once you start adding layers, you can change their *stacking order*—the order they're listed in the Layers panel—to control what's visible and what's not. When you think about stacking order, pretend you're peering down at the Layers panel from above: The layer at the very top can hide any layers below it. For example, if you fill a layer with color (page 83) and then place it above another layer containing a photo, the color will completely cover the photo (just like a piece of bread hides all the sandwich ingredients beneath it). But if you've merely painted a swish or two with the Brush tool, your brushstrokes will cover only the *part* of the photo where the two overlap.

POWER USERS' CLINIC

Shortcuts for Activating and Moving Layers

It's a little-known fact that you can use keyboard shortcuts to activate and move layers. This trick can be a real timesaver since you don't have to lift your hands off the keyboard. It's also mission critical to use these shortcuts when you're creating actions (the box on page 764 tells you why). Here's the rather complicated list of shortcuts:

- To activate the layer *below* the current layer (and deactivate the current layer), press Option-[(Alt+[on a PC). To activate the layer *above* the current layer, press Option-] (Alt+]). You can also use these two keyboard shortcuts to cycle through all layers.

- To grab a bunch of layers in a row, activate the first layer and then press Shift-Option-[(Shift+Alt+[) to activate the layer below it (while keeping the first layer active), or Shift-Option-] (Shift+Alt+]) to activate the layer above it. This shortcut lets you grab one layer at a time; just keep pressing the [or] key to grab more layers while continually holding down the other two keys.

- To activate the top layer in the Layers panel, press Option-. (Alt+.)—that's Option or Alt plus the period key. To activate

the bottom layer, press Option-, (Alt+,)—Option or Alt plus the comma key.

- To activate all the layers between the currently active layer and the top layer, press Shift-Option-. (Shift+Alt+.)—Option or Alt plus Shift and the period key. To activate all the layers between the currently active layer and the bottom layer, press Shift-Option-, (Shift+Alt+,)—Option or Alt plus Shift and the comma key.

- To activate every layer *except* the locked Background layer, press ⌘-Option-A (Ctrl+Alt+A). If you've unlocked the Background layer (page 78), it gets activated by this keyboard shortcut, too.

- To move the current layer up one slot in the layer stack, press ⌘-] (Ctrl+]). To move it down one slot, press ⌘-[(Ctrl+[).

- To move the current layer to the top of the layer stack, press Shift-⌘-] (Shift+Ctrl+]). To move it to the bottom of the layer stack—but still above the Background layer, if you've got one—press Shift-⌘-[(Shift+Ctrl+[).

Page 93 has more about moving layers around.

You can rearrange layers manually, or make Photoshop do it for you:

- **By dragging**. Click a layer's thumbnail and drag it up or down to change its position as shown in *Figure 3-6*. (Technically, you can click the layer *anywhere* to grab it, but targeting the thumbnail is a good habit to get into, lest Photoshop think you want to rename the layer instead.) When you get the layer in the right place, let go of the mouse button.

FIGURE 3-6

To rearrange layers, simply drag a layer's thumbnail up or down. When you drag, your cursor turns into a tiny closed fist as shown here (left). As you drag, you see a ghost image of the layer you're dragging, which is helpful visual feedback. When the dividing line between two layers changes so it looks more like a gap (left), let go of the mouse button to make the layer you dragged hop in between them (right).

- **Using the Arrange command**. If you've got one or more layers activated, you can choose Layer→Arrange to move them somewhere else in the layer stack. Depending on the location of the layer(s) in the Layers panel, you can choose from these commands:

  - **Bring to Front** moves the layer(s) all the way to the top of the layer stack. Keyboard shortcut: ⌘-Shift-] (Ctrl+Shift+] on a PC).

  - **Bring Forward** moves the layer(s) up one level. Keyboard shortcut: ⌘-] (Ctrl+]).

  - **Send Backward** sends the layer(s) down one level. Keyboard shortcut: ⌘-[(Ctrl+[).

  - **Send to Back** sends the layer(s) all the way to the bottom of the layer stack (or just above the Background layer, if you've got one). Keyboard shortcut: ⌘-Shift-[(Ctrl+Shift+[).

  - **Reverse**. If you've got two or more layers activated, this command inverts the stacking order of the active layers. You probably won't use this command very often, but give it a try just for fun; it can produce some mildly interesting results. (There's no keyboard shortcut for this command, but you can make one yourself if you use it a lot, as the box on page 27 explains).

> **NOTE** If you've got a long Layers panel, these keyboard shortcuts can save you lots of time. And, as mentioned previously, these shortcuts are mission critical when creating actions (see Chapter 18).

The only layer you *can't* move around is a locked *Background layer*. The Background layer isn't really a layer, although it looks like one. It behaves a little differently from other layers, as the box below explains, so if you want to move it around it in the Layers panel, you first have to double-click its thumbnail and then rename it—or simply click OK—in the resulting New Layer dialog box. Once you do that, it becomes a normal, everyday layer that you can position wherever you want.

To *really* understand how layer stacking works, it helps to put theory into practice. Let's say you want to make a photo look like one side of it fades to white and then add some text on top of the white part. To do that, you need to place the photo at the bottom of the layer stack, the white paint layer in the middle, and the text layer on top (see *Figure 3-7*).

UP TO SPEED

The Background Layer and You

Only a handful of image file formats understand Photoshop's layer system: PSD (Photoshop) and TIFF are the two most popular. Most other image file formats can handle only *flat* images (unlayered files). So if you save a multilayered PSD file as a JPEG, EPS, or PNG file, for example, Photoshop flattens it, smashing all the layers into one. (See page 108 for more on flattening files.)

When you open an image created by a device or program that *doesn't* understand layers, like a digital camera or desktop scanner, Photoshop opens it as a flat image with a single layer named Background. Though a Background layer looks like a regular layer, it's not nearly as flexible as the layers you create in Photoshop. For example, you can paint on it with the Brush tool (page 494), select part of it and then fill the selection with color (page 181), or use any of the retouching tools on it (Chapter 10), but you can't use the Move tool to make it hang off the edges of your document or make any part of it transparent—if you try to use the Eraser tool, nothing happens other than painting with the background color (and you can almost *hear* Photoshop snickering at your efforts). Also, if you make a selection and then press Delete (Backspace on a PC) or use the Crop tool to make your canvas bigger (page 224), Photoshop fills that area with the color of your background chip (page 12).

The same thing happens when you create a *new* document in Photoshop: The program opens a more universally compatible flat file containing only a Background layer. You can unlock this Background layer to make it a fully editable and movable layer in a couple of different ways. The easiest way is to double-click the Background layer in the Layers panel and then click OK (you can also give it a new name if you'd like). You can also activate the Background layer in the Layers panel and then choose Layer→New→"Layer from Background," or ⌘-click (right-click) the Background layer and choose "New layer from Background" from the resulting menu.

The only way to create a new document *without* a Background layer is to choose Transparent from the Background Contents menu (see page 37). Otherwise, you're doomed to double-clicking and renaming the Background layer each time you create a new document.

If you want, you can convert a normal layer into a Background layer by choosing Layer→New→"Background from Layer," but it's tough to think of a reason why you'd want to. If you do this, Photoshop politely moves it to the bottom of the layer stack for you.

FIGURE 3-7

The stacking order of layers determines what you can and can't see.

Top: With the Type layer at the top of the stack, you can see the text because it's sitting above everything else. And because the Gradient Fill layer is partially transparent (you can tell by the checkerboard pattern in its thumbnail), you can see through it to the photo at the bottom of the stack.

By the way, this technique is great for ensuring that text remains readable atop a photo when creating postcards, invitations, and the like.

Bottom: If you drag the Type layer below the Gradient Fill layer, you can't see the text anymore because it's hidden by the white paint.

Here's a quick lesson in how to softly fade a photo to white and then add some text to it:

1. **Open a soon-to-be-faded photo and set your foreground color chip to white.**

   Peek at the color chips at the bottom of the Tools panel (page 12). If they're black and white, just press X to flip-flop them until white hops on top. If the chips are other colors, press D first to reset them to black and white.

2. **Create a Gradient Fill layer and pick the "Foreground to Transparent" gradient preset.**

Click the half-black/half-white circle at the bottom of the Layers panel to open the Adjustment layer menu, and then choose Gradient. In the resulting Gradient Fill dialog box, click the down-pointing triangle next to the gradient preview to open the Preset picker. In the drop-down menu of gradient previews, click the second preset in the top row for a "Foreground to Transparent" gradient. Don't close the dialog box just yet!

3. **Set the gradient style to Linear, change the angle to 180 degrees, enter 10% for scale, and then click OK.**

In the Gradient Fill dialog box, make sure the Style menu is set to Linear (it probably is unless you've changed it). Enter *180* in the Angle field so the color appears on the right side of your document. Next, enter *10* in the Scale field, and then click OK. The Scale field controls the size of the gradient, or rather the size of the faded area between the two colors you picked (white and transparency, in this example). The lower the number, the narrower the fade; the higher the number, the wider the fade. For more on gradients, see pages 218 and 344.

4. **Press T to grab the Type tool and add some text.**

You haven't learned about the Type tool yet, but be brave and press T to activate it, and then hop up to the Options bar and pick a font and text size from the drop-down menus (see Chapter 14 for a proper introduction to the Type tool). Click once in your document where you want the text to begin and then start typing. When you're finished, click the little checkmark in the Options bar to let Photoshop know you're done (pressing Enter on your keyboard's numeric keypad—*not* Return—or grabbing another tool works, too).

You're finished! If you want to move the text around, you can temporarily activate the Move tool by holding down the V key. When your cursor turns into a little arrow, click and move your mouse to move the text.

Duplicating and Deleting Layers

Duplicating a layer comes in handy when you want to do something destructive like remove an object using the Edit→Fill command (page 408) or soften Great Grandma's skin (page 430). By duplicating the Image layer first, you can work on a *copy* of the image instead of the original. But duplicating isn't limited to whole layers; you can duplicate just *part* of a layer. That technique comes in handy when you want to do some quality head swapping (page 180) or make multiple copies of an object and move it around (like the hippie chicks in *Figure 3-8*).

You can duplicate a layer in a gazillion ways:

- **Press ⌘-J (Ctrl+J) or choose Layer→New→"Layer via Copy"** to copy the active layer onto another layer just like it.

FIGURE 3-8

By selecting each of the silhouettes (top) and then pressing ⌘-J (Ctrl+J), you can put copies of them onto their own layers (bottom). To move them around in your document, activate one of the new layers, press V to grab the Move tool, and then drag to reposition the selected figure. (Chapter 4 has more on how to make selections.)

Photoshop automatically adds the word "copy" to duplicated layers' names. To keep it from doing that, open the Layers panel's menu, choose Panel Options, and then turn off the "Add 'copy' to Copied Layers and Groups" checkbox at the bottom of the resulting dialog box.

You can follow along by visiting this book's Missing CD page at www.missingmanuals.com/cds and downloading the file Chicks.jpg.

TIP You can duplicate multiple layers at the same time. Just activate the layers by Shift- or ⌘-clicking (Ctrl-clicking) them, and then press ⌘-J (Ctrl+J). Think of this as "jumping" the content onto other layers—it makes the keyboard shortcut easier to remember. (So many shortcuts, so little time to memorize 'em!).

- **Drag the original layer atop the "Create a new layer" button at the bottom of the Layers panel**. When Photoshop highlights the button (which looks like a piece of paper with a folded corner), let go of your mouse button.

- **Option-drag (Alt-drag on a PC) the layer somewhere else in the Layers panel**. Your cursor turns into double black-and-white arrowheads as soon as you start to drag. When you let go of your mouse button, Photoshop duplicates the layer.

- **Choose Layer→Duplicate Layer or, from the Layers panel's menu, choose Duplicate Layer**. This method gives you a chance to name the new layer, as well as to send it to a new document. If you decide to send it to a new document, in the Duplicate Layer dialog box, pick an open document from the Document drop-down menu or choose New to create a brand-new document (enter a name for the new document in the Name field).

- **Control-click (right-click) the layer in the Layers panel**. From the resulting shortcut menu, choose Duplicate Layer.

- **To duplicate** *part* **of layer, create a selection using any of the tools discussed in Chapter 4 and then press ⌘-J (Ctrl+J)** to move your selection onto its own layer. If you want to *delete* the selected area from the original layer and *duplicate* it onto another layer at the same time, press Shift-⌘-J (Shift+Ctrl+J). You can think of this trick as *cutting* to another layer since you'll have a hole in the original layer where the selection used to be.

Adding layers can *really* increase your document's file size, so it's always a good idea to delete layers you don't need (*especially* if you have a slow computer or very little memory). To delete a layer (even a locked Background layer, provided your document has more than one layer), activate it in the Layers panel and then do one of the following:

- **Press Delete (Backspace on a PC)**. This is the fastest deletion method in the West.

- **Drag it onto the trash can icon at the bottom of the Layers panel**.

- **Click the trash can icon**. When Photoshop asks if you're *sure* you want to delete the layer, click Yes and then turn on the "Don't show again" checkbox if you don't want to see this confirmation box in the future.

> **TIP** If you delete a layer and then wish you had it back, just use the Undo command: Choose Edit→Undo or press ⌘-Z (Ctrl+Z).

- **Control-click (right-click) near the layer's name in the Layers panel and choose Delete Layer from the shortcut menu**. (Be sure to click near the layer's *name*—if you click its thumbnail, you won't see Delete Layer in the shortcut menu.) When Photoshop asks if you really want to delete the layer, click Yes to send it packin'.

- **Choose Layer→Delete or open the Layers panel's menu and then choose Delete Layer**. You'll get a confirmation dialog box this way, too, so just smile sweetly, click Yes, and be on your way.

TIP If you've hidden multiple layers (page 74), you can delete 'em all at once by opening the Layers panel's menu and choosing Delete→Hidden Layers (hey, if you're not using them, you might as well toss 'em!). Getting rid of extra layers shortens the Layers panel *and* reduces the document's file size.

Copying and Pasting Layers

You can use the regular ol' copy and paste commands to move whole or partial layers between Photoshop documents, too:

- **To copy and paste a whole layer into another document**, choose Select→All (or press ⌘-A [Ctrl+A]) to select everything on the layer and then press ⌘-C (Ctrl+C). Next, click the other document's window and press ⌘-V (Ctrl+V) to add the layer.

- **To copy part of a layer into another document**, create your selection first and then press ⌘-C (Ctrl+C) to copy it. Then open the other document and press ⌘-V (Ctrl+V); Photoshop pastes those pixels onto a new layer.

Photoshop's Edit menu also includes a Paste Special option, which is incredibly handy when you're combining images. It's discussed at length starting on page 265.

TIP When you copy an image from another program and paste it into a Photoshop document, it lands on its very own layer. If the pasted image is *bigger* than your document, you may need to resize the new layer using Free Transform (page 256). Alternatively you can choose Image→Reveal All, and Photoshop resizes the canvas so you can see everything it contains. However, a better option is to use File→Place instead, because that way the image *automatically* appears on a separate layer surrounded by resizing handles. See page 45 for more on using this handy command.

Filling a Layer with Color

One of the most common things you'll do with a new layer is fill it with color. If, for example, you've hidden your image's original background with a layer mask (page 108) or added an interesting edge effect (see page 510), you can spice things up by adding a solid-colored background. Photoshop gives you a couple of different ways to tackle this task:

- **Fill an existing layer with color**. After you've created a new layer using one of the methods listed on page 74, choose Edit→Fill. In the resulting Fill dialog box (*Figure 3-9*), pick a color from the Use menu and then click OK. You can also fill the active layer with your foreground color by pressing Option-Delete (Alt+Backspace on a PC), or your background color by pressing ⌘-Delete (Ctrl+Delete on a PC).

FIGURE 3-9

The Use menu lets you tell Photoshop to fill a layer with your foreground or background color, or summon the Color Picker by choosing Color.

The downside to this method is that if you increase your canvas size (page 249) after filling a layer with color, you'll need to refill the layer or it'll be smaller than your document. To avoid this extra step, use a Fill layer instead, as discussed in this section.

- **Create a Fill layer.** If you're not sure which color you want to use, choose Layer→New Fill Layer→Solid Color, or click the half-black/half-white circle at the bottom of the Layers panel and choose Solid Color. In the New Layer dialog box that appears, name the layer and then click OK. Photoshop then displays the Color Picker so you can choose a fill color. If you decide to change this color later, simply double-click the Fill layer's thumbnail and Photoshop opens the Color Picker so you can choose a new color or *steal* one from your image as shown in *Figure 3-10*. Fill layers come with their own layer masks, making it super simple to hide part of the layer if you need to.

> **TIP** If you create a selection before adding a fill layer, when you add the Fill layer, Photoshop automatically fills the selection with color *and* fills in the mask for you in the shape of your selection. Sweet!

One of the many advantages of using a Fill layer is that, unlike an Image layer, the *whole* layer gets filled with color even if you enlarge the canvas. In addition to using Fill layers to create solid backgrounds, you can use 'em to fill a layer with a gradient or a repeating pattern, as shown in *Figure 3-11*. Simply choose Layer→New Fill Layer, and then pick either Gradient or Pattern.

> **NOTE** Photoshop includes a bunch of pattern preset categories that you can access in the Pattern Fill dialog box by clicking the down-pointing triangle labeled in *Figure 3-11* (bottom), and then clicking the tiny gear icon in the upper right of the resulting menu. For example, the Artists Brushes Canvas and Erodible Textures categories are useful when creating paintings from scratch, as described on page 502.

FIGURE 3-10

Top: Dragging a Fill layer to the bottom of the layer stack creates a solid-colored (in this case, white) background for your image. To change the color, double-click the Fill layer's thumbnail (circled) to pop open the Color Picker.

Bottom: If you want to get super creative, you can snatch color from your image by mousing over to it while the Color Picker is open (your cursor turns into an eyedropper, circled). Click once to grab the color you want, and then click OK to close the Color Picker.

If you want to hide part of the Fill layer (to, say, have it show only in certain areas), just paint with black inside the included layer mask (see page 108).

■ CREATING CUSTOM PATTERNS

Photoshop includes oodles of pattern presets, though you can also create your own. It's surprisingly simple, as the following steps explain:

1. **Open the image that you want to create a pattern from, like the chili pepper photo in *Figure 3-12*.**

   If you want the image's background to be transparent as it overlaps and repeats in the pattern, create a selection of the background using the tool of your choice and then hide it with a layer mask. (If Photoshop masks the *opposite* of what you want, simply double-click the mask's thumbnail in the Layers panel.

FIGURE 3-11

Fill layers aren't just for adding solid color; you can use 'em to create a gradient- or pattern-filled background as shown here (top and bottom, respectively). To change the gradient or pattern after you've added the Fill layer, just double-click its thumbnail in the Layers panel to make Photoshop display the appropriate dialog box—Gradient Fill or Pattern Fill. By adjusting the Scale setting in these dialog boxes, you can make the gradient or pattern bigger or smaller. (Page 85 explains how to make your own custom patterns.)

You can also add a Fill layer via the Adjustment layer menu at the bottom of the Layers panel (it looks like a half-black/half-white circle). You'll find Solid Color, Gradient, and Pattern listed at the very top of the resulting menu.

Click to open preset menu

Click to load built-in presets and/or create your own

When the Properties panel opens, click the Invert button at the bottom of the panel to flip-flop the mask.) Next, choose Image→Trim and, in the Trim dialog box (*Figure 3-12*, bottom), pick Transparent Pixels to crop the document to the object's edges, and then click OK. Choose File→Save As and, in the resulting dialog box, give the document a name—say, "chili pattern"—and pick Photoshop from the Format drop-down menu. Doing so gives you the ability to tweak the pattern later on.

2. **In the Layers panel, click the Image layer's thumbnail to activate it, and then choose Edit→Define Pattern (this step won't work if the layer mask is active instead).**

   In the resulting dialog box (*Figure 3-13*, top), give your new pattern a meaningful name and then click OK. Photoshop adds it to your list of pattern presets (*Figure 3-13*, bottom).

FIGURE 3-12

If you want to create a pattern with a transparent background, you have to select the background first and then hide it with a layer mask, as described in step 1.

When you run the Image→Trim command, Photoshop trims your document to the smallest possible size, ensuring you don't include a lot of extra space around the object once you define it as a pattern.

FIGURE 3-13

Top: Be sure to click to activate the Image layer's thumbnail or the Define Pattern command will be grayed out and you won't be able to get to this dialog box.

Bottom: Once you define a new pattern, it appears in the Fill dialog box's Custom Pattern drop-down menu, shown here.

3. **Open the document you want to apply the pattern to and create a new layer by pressing Command-Shift-N (Ctrl-Shift-N).**

    In the resulting New Layer dialog box, name the layer "chili background" and then click OK. Alternatively, you can skip creating a new Image layer and use a Pattern Fill layer instead (though the scripted-pattern feature described below doesn't work on Fill layers).

4. **Choose Edit→Fill and then, from the Use drop-down menu, choose Pattern (*Figure 3-13*, bottom).**

    Click the down-pointing triangle next to the Custom Pattern preview and then click the pattern you created in step 3. Photoshop will repeat it in a grid-like pattern.

    If you'd like your pattern to be random in shape, color, and position, you can use *scripted patterns* instead (a feature introduced in CS6). To do that, turn on the Scripted Patterns checkbox at the bottom of the dialog box and, from the Script drop-down menu, choose one of the five built-in scripts (Brick Fill, Cross Weave, Random Fill, Spiral, or Symmetry Fill) and then click OK. For example, choosing Brick Fill makes Photoshop offset the pattern every second row by half the pattern's width and introduce a variety of colors based on the original pattern's color. (Spiral is the only one that doesn't introduce random color.) When you click OK, Photoshop fills the empty layer with your new pattern. *Figure 3-14* shows the result of creating a pattern from a chili pepper (top) and a leaf (bottom).

> **NOTE** Give these patterns a spin by downloading the practice files *chili.jpg* and *oakleaf.jpg* from this book's Missing CD page.

FIGURE 3-14

Photoshop can use a JavaScript file to make your patterns vary in ways it never could before CS6. Here, the Random Fill script was used to create the background for this fictitious farmer's market ad (top) as well as the falling leaves atop this schoolgirl's photo (bottom); the latter pattern was created from a single oak leaf. As you can see, there's no end to the interesting backgrounds and textures you can create with scripted patterns!

You can access Scripted Patterns when you're filling a path, too, though they aren't available for use with Pattern Fill layers (dang it!).

You can even customize the existing scripts or (gasp!) create your own. The scripts are written in the JavaScript programming language, and they live in the *Applications/Adobe Photoshop CC/Presets/Deco* folder on a Mac. On a PC running Photoshop in 32-bit mode, they're in the *\Program Files (x86)\Adobe\Adobe Photoshop CC*

Presets\Deco folder; in 64-bit mode, peek in the *\Program Files\Adobe\Adobe Photoshop CC (64 Bit)\Presets\Deco* folder instead. Once you modify a script or add a new one, you have to relaunch Photoshop before that script will show up in the Fill dialog box's Script menu.

Tweaking a Layer's Opacity and Fill

All layers begin life at 100 percent opacity, meaning you can't see through them (except where they're empty, as shown in *Figure 3-7*). To make a layer semitransparent, you can lower its Opacity setting, which is a good way to lessen the strength of a color or lighting adjustment (Chapter 9), or a strip of color you've added as a design element, as shown in *Figure 3-15*. (Lowering layer opacity is also a good way to make a photo look more realistic after you remove dark circles under tired eyes, as explained on page 413.) The Opacity setting affects everything on a given layer equally.

The Opacity and Fill settings live near the top of the Layers panel. Unlike Opacity, the Fill setting doesn't always affect the whole layer. For example, if you create a Shape layer or a Type layer and then add a layer style to it (say, a stroke), then lowering its Fill setting will lower only the opacity of the color *inside* the shape or letters, not the opacity of the layer styles you've added.

FIGURE 3-15

If you lower the opacity of this Fill layer to 60 percent, the blue paint becomes partially transparent, letting you see through to the photo layer below, as shown here.

To look like a real Photoshop pro, point your cursor at the word Opacity. When the cursor turns into a little pointing hand like the one shown here—known as a scrubby cursor—you can drag to the left or right to lower or raise the layer's opacity, respectively (you can even drag the cursor off the Layers panel if you want to).

This trick works for any Photoshop setting with similar controls, including the Fill setting, most everything in the Options bar (no matter which tool is active), the options in the Character and Paragraph panels, and more!

TIP If you've hidden a layer by turning off its visibility eye, you can *still* see its Opacity, Fill, and blend mode settings near the top of the Layers panel (even though they're grayed out). Nice!

To change Opacity or Fill, mouse over to the Layers panel, activate the layer you want to tweak, and then do one of the following:

- **Enter a new value in the Opacity or Fill field**. Double-click the current value in either field, enter a new value, and then press Return (Enter on a PC).

- **Use the field's slider**. Click the down arrow to the right of the Opacity or Fill field, and then drag the resulting slider to the left or right to decrease or increase that setting, respectively.

- **Use your keyboard**. Press V to activate the Move tool (think "moVe"), and then change the active layer's Opacity setting by typing *1* for 10 percent, *2* for 20 percent, *3+5* for 35 percent, and so on (type *0* for 100 percent or *0+0* for 0 percent). If you've got any other tool that works with transparency active *besides* the Move tool (such as the Brush or Healing tools), you'll change the *tool's* opacity setting instead. You can use the same keyboard trick to adjust the Fill setting, too; just hold down the Shift key while you type the numbers.

TIP You can change the opacity and/or fill of multiple layers at once: Just Shift- or ⌘-click (Ctrl-click on a PC) the layers in the Layers panel to activate them, and then adjust the Opacity and/or Fill settings.

Resizing and Rotating Layers

To resize the contents of a layer—or many layers—*without* changing the size of your document, you can use the Free Transform tool shown in *Figure 3-16*. (You'll learn a lot more about this tool in Chapter 6, so consider this a sneak peek.) To resize or rotate a layer, follow these steps:

1. **In the Layers panel, activate the layer(s) you want to adjust (see page 68 for the scoop on activating multiple layers).**

2. **Press ⌘-T (Ctrl+T) to summon the Free Transform tool.**

   Photoshop puts a box lined with small square handles (called a *bounding box*) around the contents of the active layer(s). If you're resizing a normal layer, the handles are white; if you're resizing a Smart Object (page 118), they're black instead, as shown in *Figure 3-16*. The difference is purely cosmetic—they work exactly the same way.

3. **Drag one of the corner handles toward the center of the layer to make the layer's content smaller.**

   Grab any of the white corner handles and drag diagonally inward to decrease the layer content's size. To resize the content proportionately so it doesn't get squished or stretched, hold down the Shift key as you drag.

4. **To rotate the layer(s), position your cursor outside the bounding box and then—when the cursor turns into a curved, double-headed arrow—drag up or down in the direction you want to turn the layer(s).**

5. **Press Return (Enter on a PC) or double-click inside the bounding box to let Photoshop know you're done; to bail *without* changing your image, press Esc instead.**

FIGURE 3-16

You can drag any of the bounding box's square handles to resize your object. To adjust all four sides of the box simultaneously, hold down Option (Alt) as you drag a corner handle.

The Free Transform tool shows you a handy heads-up display (HUD) of the object's size (the W and H numbers shown here) when you drag a corner handle. If you click within the bounding box and drag to reposition it, the display changes to show either your X and Y coordinates on the document relative to where you started dragging or an angle value if you're rotating it (the Move tool does the same thing).

Don't forget to press Return (Enter) when you're finished because Photoshop won't let you do anything else while you've got an active bounding box.

TIP To see the Free Transform command's resizing handles whenever the Move tool is active—without actually using the Free Transform command—press V to grab the Move tool and then turn on the Show Transform Controls checkbox in the Options bar. Seeing the handles is helpful if you're jumping between layers to resize or rotate objects and don't want to stop and summon Free Transform each time.

Do you risk reducing your image's quality by resizing layers this way? Sure. Anytime you alter pixel size, you change the image's quality a little bit, too, whether it's a single layer or the whole document. But as long as you *decrease* the Image layer's size, you won't lose much quality (though you don't want to decrease its size *repeatedly*—try to do it once or twice and be done with it). You definitely risk losing quality if you *increase* the size of a pixel-based Image layer, because when pixels get bigger, they also get blockier. However, if you increase the size of an object just a *little*, nobody will be the wiser; plus, Photoshop CC is *far* better at enlarging images than previous versions (page 238).

That said, if you're working with a Smart Object (page 118), Shape layer (page 68), or Type layer (Chapter 14), you've got no worries. You can resize those babies all day long—larger or smaller, as many times as you want—and you won't affect their quality, which is why you should use those kinds of layers whenever possible. (However, you don't want to enlarge a raster-based Smart Object *too* much beyond its original dimensions because it could become pixelated and blocky.)

TIP The rest of the transform tools—including Skew, Distort, and so on—work on layers, too. See page 255 for the details.

Moving and Aligning Layers

One of the many advantages of using layers is that you can scoot 'em around independently of everything else in your document. To move a layer, first activate it in the Layers panel, and then press V to grab the Move tool and drag the layer wherever you want. For example, to move the text in *Figure 3-15* a bit to the left, press V and drag it to the new spot. To move the layer in a perfectly vertical or horizontal line, hold down the Shift key while you drag. As soon as you start dragging, you'll see a slightly transparent, dark gray border around the item you're dragging—and t moves as you drag. This is extremely helpful when you're moving items that are really small, and thus easy to lose sight of.

NOTE You can also nudge the layer one pixel at a time by pressing the arrows on your keyboard (holding down the Shift key while you press the arrow keys scoots the layer by *10* pixels per keystroke).

If you want to move only *part* of a layer, select that portion first using one of the methods explained in Chapter 4. Then you can grab the Move tool and move just the selected bits.

ALIGNING LAYERS

When you need to position layers, Photoshop has several tools that can help you get 'em lined up just right. The program tries to help you align layers by *snapping* the one you're moving to the *boundaries* (content edges) of other layers. As you drag a layer with the Move tool, Photoshop tries to pop the layer into place when you get near another layer's edge. (To make the program stop popping them into place, choose View→Snap.) If you'd like to *see* the boundaries of your layer, press V to activate the Move tool, and then hop up to the Options bar and turn on the Show Transform Controls checkbox (*Figure 3-17*).

TIP If you're trying to visually align one layer perfectly with the layer below it, it's a good idea to temporarily lower the top layer's opacity (page 90) so you can actually *see* the layer underneath. Alternatively, set one layer's blend mode to Difference (page 287).

In addition to snapping layers and showing their boundaries, Photoshop offers you the following alignment helpers:

- **Alignment settings**. These settings come in handy if you need to align the edges of more than one layer. You'll see them in the Options bar when the Move tool is active, but you'll only be able to use 'em if you have more than one layer activated (see *Figure 3-17*). You can also find them in the Layer→Align submenu (you still need to have more than one layer activated, but you don't have to activate the Move tool). *Figure 3-18* shows you what each button does.

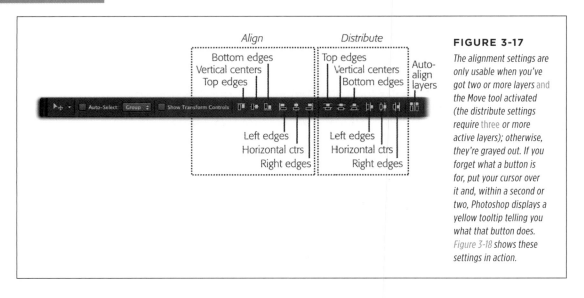

FIGURE 3-17

The alignment settings are only usable when you've got two or more layers and the Move tool activated (the distribute settings require three or more active layers); otherwise, they're grayed out. If you forget what a button is for, put your cursor over it and, within a second or two, Photoshop displays a yellow tooltip telling you what that button does. Figure 3-18 shows these settings in action.

FIGURE 3-18

Each of these guitars lives on its own layer, so you can see the effect of Photoshop's various alignment settings.

If you're a designer, these tools are huge timesavers and allow you to be very precise when aligning text and other artwork.

- **Distribute settings**. Nestled snugly to the right of the alignment settings are the distribute settings (*Figure 3-17*). Their mission is to evenly space the contents of the active layers based on each layer's horizontal or vertical center, and you need to have at least *three* layers activated to use them. For example, these options are handy when you're designing buttons for website navigation because you can use them to space the buttons equally.

- **Auto-alignment**. If you choose Edit→Auto-Align Layers or click the Auto-Align Layers button labeled in *Figure 3-17*, Photoshop does the aligning *for* you by looking at the corners and edges of the objects on the active layers. This command is really handy when you're combining multiple images of the same shot (see page 395), but it doesn't work on Adjustment layers, Smart Objects, or Shape layers.

- **Smart Guides**. Unlike the *regular* guides you learned about in Chapter 2, Smart Guides show up automatically any time you drag a layer near another layer's edge or center (see *Figure 3-19*). They're extremely helpful when you're manually aligning layers with the Move tool since they make it easier to position layers precisely in relation to each other. To turn 'em on, choose View→Show→Smart Guides.

FIGURE 3-19

With Smart Guides turned on, Photoshop alerts you with a thin red line any time you approach the edge or center of another layer so you know that you're about to move past it.

NOTE Photoshop can also do strange things when you're using the alignment commands on layers that have layer masks (page 108). Instead of aligning the layers according to what you've hidden with the mask (which is probably what you're trying to do), Photoshop ignores the mask and tries to align the layers using the *actual* pixel information. In that situation, you may need to turn on Rulers (page 60), create a few guides (also on page 60) and manually align the layers with the Move tool (page 93).

◼ MOVING LAYERS BETWEEN DOCUMENTS

In addition to copying and pasting layers from one document to another (as described back on page 83), you can also drag and drop them straight from the Layers panel to another document, as shown in *Figure 3-20*. When you do that, Photoshop leaves the layer in the original document and places a *copy* in the target document, so you don't have to worry about losing anything from either file. This technique is really helpful if you want to create a collage (Chapter 7), swap backgrounds, or share color corrections made with Adjustment layers across documents (Chapter 9). Here are the details:

1. **Open the two documents you want to combine.**

2. **Choose Window→Arrange and choose one of the 2-up options.**

   To drag a layer from one document to another document that contains *multiple* layers, you have to be able to *see* both documents, as explained in *Figure 3-20*. Choosing one of the 2-up display options makes Photoshop rearrange your document windows so you can see 'em both at the same time. (Page 56 has more on your window-arrangement options.)

FIGURE 3-20

Top: To combine two images into one document, first arrange your workspace so that you can see both windows. (The 2-up Vertical arrangement was used here.) Then drag one layer's thumbnail from the Layers panel into the other document.

Bottom: When you release your mouse button, the new layer appears in the other document's Layers panel, as shown here.

You can also drag an image file from your computer's desktop into an open Photoshop document and the object lands on its own layer as a Smart Object.

3. **Click the document that contains the layer you want to *move*, and then drag the layer's thumbnail from the Layers panel onto the other document.**

   As you drag, your cursor turns into a tiny closed fist, as you can see in *Figure 3-20*. When Photoshop highlights the inside border of the destination window in light gray, let go of your mouse button to make Photoshop add the layer to that document.

> **TIP** To center the moved layer perfectly in its new home, hold the Shift key as you drag the layer from one document to another.

■ EXPORTING LAYERS TO SEPARATE FILES

If you've got a bunch of layers that you want to separate into individual files (with each layer in its own file), choose File→Scripts→"Export Layers to Files." In the resulting dialog box (*Figure 3-21*), use the Destination field to tell Photoshop where you want it to save the files. In the File Name Prefix box, create a naming scheme (Photoshop uses whatever you enter in this field as the first part of your files' names) and, from the File Type drop-down menu, choose a format. When you're finished, click Run and sit back while Photoshop does all the work.

FIGURE 3-21

The Export Layers To Files dialog box lets you choose where to put the new files and what to name them. To exclude any hidden layers, turn on the Visible Layers Only checkbox.

In the File Type drop-down menu, you can choose from BMP, JPEG, PDF, PSD, TARGA, TIFF, PNG-8, and PNG-24. Each format gives you different options; for example, choosing JPEG lets you pick a quality setting.

Photoshop includes your document's ICC profile in each file unless you turn off the aptly named Include ICC Profile checkbox shown here.

> **TIP** If you've got a Smart Object in your document, you can export its contents to a new document by Control-clicking (right-clicking) near the layer's name in the Layers panel, and then choosing Export Contents. In the resulting dialog box, tell Photoshop where you'd like to save the document, and then click Save. (Smart Objects are covered later in this chapter, beginning on page 118.)

■ Managing Layers

If one thing's for certain in Photoshop, it's that your Layers panel will get long and unwieldy in a hurry. Now that you've seen a smidgen of the increased editing flexibility layers give you (moving, resizing, and so on), you'll want to put *everything* on its own layer—and you *should*. However, learning a wee bit about organizing layers can keep you from spending ages digging through the Layers panel to find the layer you want. This section gives you the lowdown.

> **TIP** Photoshop's layer-filtering feature is one of the best ways to manage a long Layers panel; it's covered back on page 70.

Naming and Color-Coding Layers

The simplest way to organize layers is to name the darn things something other than Layer 1, Layer 2, and so on. If you didn't name them when you made 'em, you can always double-click a layer's name in the Layers panel and rename it right there (Photoshop highlights the name when you double-click it, so you can just start typing). When you're done, press Return (Enter on a PC).

> **TIP** If you double-click in the Layers panel *near* the layer's name but not directly on it, Photoshop opens the Layer Style dialog box (shown on page 290) instead of highlighting the layer's name. No problem: Just close the dialog box and try again.

Another renaming maneuver is to choose Layer→Rename Layer. When you do, Photoshop highlights the name of the active layer; just type some text to rename it. To rename additional layers, press the Tab key to highlight the name of the next layer down in the layer stack, or Shift-Tab to highlight the name of the next layer up. (You can assign a keyboard shortcut to the Rename Layer command, too, by going to Edit→Keyboard Shortcuts; the box on page 27 has the details.)

In addition to giving layers meaningful names, another great way to keep them organized is to color-code them. For example, you could color-code various sections of a poster like the header, footer, body, and so on. As you learned back on page 74, you can assign a color to a layer when you first create it, or by activating the layer(s) and then Control-clicking (right-clicking) the layer(s) in the Layers panel and picking a color from the resulting shortcut menu. (To color-code a locked Background layer this way, you first have to *unlock* it by double-clicking it.) To remove color-coding, do the same thing but choose No Color from the shortcut menu.

Linking and Locking Layers

Editing layers can be a lot of work, and once you get them just right, you want to make darn sure they stay that way. You can protect yourself from making accidental changes by linking layers together or locking down certain aspects of them. Read on to learn how.

■ LINKING LAYERS

If you need to move something in your image that's made from several layers, it'd be a real pain to move each layer individually and then reconstruct the image. Fortunately, you can *link* layers before you grab the Move tool so that they travel as a single unit; *Figure 3-22* shows how. Linking related layers can help you avoid accidentally misaligning layers with a careless flick of the Move tool. For example, if you've zapped a blemish or removed a piercing in a portrait, linking the layers you used to make the fixes with the Image layer ensures that they stay perfectly aligned.

Link layers

FIGURE 3-22

Once you've got more than one layer activated, you can link them by clicking the tiny chain icon at the bottom of the Layers panel. When you do, the same icon appears to the right of each layer's name (circled) to show that the layers are linked. To unlink them, simply activate a layer and then click the chain icon at the bottom of the Layers panel again. Easy, huh?

The two layers that involve retouching are color-coded with red (red for retouching—get it?).

■ LOCKING 'EM DOWN

You can add a more serious level of protection with *layer locks,* which prevent layers from being edited *or* moved. At the top of the Layers panel is a row of four buttons that you can use to lock various aspects of layers (*Figure 3-23*). First activate the layer(s) you want to lock, and then click the appropriate lock button to prevent any changes. Here are your options:

- **Lock transparent pixels.** This protects the layer's transparent pixels so they don't change if you paint across them or run the Edit→Fill command. For example, if you created the faded-color effect shown on page 318, you could apply this lock to change the fade's color without affecting the layer's see-through bits. This lock's button looks like the transparency checkerboard.

- **Lock image pixels**. This won't let you do *anything* to a layer but nudge it around with the Move tool. The button for this lock looks like the Brush tool's icon.

- **Lock position**. If you've carefully positioned a layer and want to make sure it stays put, click this button, which looks like a four-headed arrow. You can still *edit* the layer, you just can't move it.

- **Lock all**. This is your deadbolt: Use it to prevent the layer from being edited *or* moved. You know this lock means business because its button is a padlock.

Lock transparent pixels
Lock image pixels
Lock position
Lock all

Layer lock

FIGURE 3-23

Use these buttons to protect your layers from accidental editing or repositioning. No matter which lock you apply, you'll see the padlock icon labeled here to the right of the locked layer's name.

When it comes to layer locks, your keyboard's forward slash key (/) acts like a switch for the last lock you applied. When a locked layer is active, tap this key once to remove that particular lock (press it again to turn that same lock back on). When an unlocked layer is active, tapping this key makes Photoshop apply the "Lock transparent pixels" lock.

You can apply locks to multiple layers at the same time. Just activate the layers first by Shift- or ⌘-clicking (Ctrl-clicking on a PC) them, and then click the appropriate lock button(s) in the Layers panel.

TIP If you've taken the time to create a layer group (as explained next), you can lock all the layers in it by activating it and then choosing Layer→"Lock All Layers in Group." (You can also find this same menu item in the Layers panel's menu.) Photoshop pops open a dialog box where you can turn on any of the locks listed above; click OK to apply them.

Grouping Layers into Folders

You can rein in a fast-growing Layers panel by tucking layers into folders called *layer groups*. You can expand and collapse layer groups just like the folders on your hard drive, and they'll save you a *heck* of a lot of time if you're designing a piece that has specific components like a front and a back, as shown in *Figure 3-24*.

Say you're creating a postcard for a concert, and you've got several layers that comprise the background, some photos of the band, some text, and so on. You can put all the layers associated with the postcard's background in a group cleverly named *Background*, the photos in a group called *Photos*, and the Type layers in a group called *Text*. Then you can add some color-coding (blue for background, red for photos, and so on) to make it easy to quickly spot the group you want to work with instead of wasting time scrolling through the Layers panel.

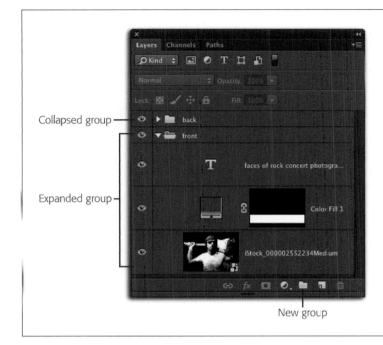

FIGURE 3-24

Just click a layer group's flippy triangle to expand or collapse that group. Here, the down-pointing flippy triangle next to the Front group's folder shows that the group is expanded, while the Back group is collapsed. You can collapse or expand all layer groups at the same time by Option-clicking (Alt-clicking on a PC) the flippy triangle to a group's left.

Layer groups not only help you shorten your Layers panel, they also let you apply masks to all the layers in the group simultaneously.

Collapsed group —

Expanded group —

New group —

Here are the different ways you can group layers:

- **Create the group first** by clicking the "Create a new group" button at the bottom of the Layers panel (it looks like a tiny folder) or by choosing New Group from the Layers panel's menu. (If you go the latter route, you'll get a dialog box where you can name the group, assign it a color, and change its blend mode and opacity if you want.) Photoshop adds the group to the Layers panel; just drag layers onto the group's folder icon in the layer stack to add them to it.

NOTE   Straight from the factory, the blend mode of a layer group is set to Pass Through, meaning any adjustment layers or blend-mode changes within the group trickle down and affect any layers underneath it. For more on this blend mode, see the box on page 289.

- **Activate the layers first** and then press ⌘-G (Ctrl+G) or choose "New Group from Layers" in the Layers panel's menu. Photoshop adds a group named *Group 1* to the Layers panel that includes all the layers you activated; double-click the group's name to rename it. Alternatively, you can Shift-click the "Create a new group" icon instead.

- **Option-drag (Alt-drag) layers** onto the "Create a new group" button at the bottom of the Layers panel.

You can do the same things to layer groups that you can to regular layers: duplicate them, hide them, lock them, color-code them, and so on. You can also create *nested* groups by dragging and dropping one group into another (see the box below for more info).

To split apart grouped layers, activate the group and then choose Layer→Ungroup Layers, press Shift-⌘-G (Shift+Ctrl+G), or Control-click (right-click) the group and then choose Ungroup Layers from the shortcut menu. Whichever method you use, Photoshop deletes the group but leaves the layers intact.

To delete a group, activate it and then choose Layer→Delete→Group, or Control-click (right-click) the group and then choose Ungroup Layers from the shortcut menu. Either way, Photoshop displays a dialog box asking whether you want to delete the group *and* all the layers inside it, or just the group itself (leaving the layers within it in the Layers panel). (If the group doesn't contain any layers, you don't see this dialog box—Photoshop simply deletes the group.) If you activate a group and then press the Delete key, Photoshop deletes the group *and* all the layers inside it.

Layer Comps: Capturing Different Document Versions

Say you're creating a poster for an upcoming concert. You'll probably want to show your client different versions of it so she can pick the one she likes best. Photoshop can help by saving multiple versions of the document as *layer comps*—snapshots of your Layers panel in various states (see *Figure 3-25*). This method is much better than having to juggle multiple files you could lose track of. Layer comps can record the position and visibility of layers, as well as the blend modes (page 276) and layer styles (page 124) you've applied.

Nested Layer Groups

Photoshop lets you nest layer groups up to 10 levels deep, meaning you can put a layer group inside of another layer group that lives inside yet *another* layer group that lives...well, you get the picture. This kind of nesting is helpful if you're a stickler for organization or are working on a complicated file and your Layers panel is a mile long. For example, a photographer might have a layer group named Retouching with another group inside it named Healing, which houses another layer group named Nose, and so on.

This kind of organization works great until you have to share the file with someone using a version of Photoshop earlier than CS5. If you open the file with Photoshop CS3 or CS4, you'll be greeted with a dialog box stating, among other things, that it encountered "unknown data" and that "groups were altered." At this point, the program gives you two choices (you can also click Cancel to close the document, but what fun is that?):

- **Flatten** makes Photoshop preserve the appearance of the original document (provided the document was saved using the Maximum Compatibility option discussed on page 22) but not its layers, which makes further editing impossible.

- **Keep Layers** makes Photoshop *try* to preserve the document's appearance and layers, though this doesn't always work. For example, if you've changed a layer group's blend mode (page 276) or used advanced blending options (page 289), they're toast.

Once you've crossed your fingers and made a choice, Photoshop opens the document (which can take a while). If you chose Keep Layers, you'll see empty layers where the nested layer groups used to be.

FIGURE 3-25

Like layer groups, layer comps work only if your document has more than one layer.

Top: Give each layer comp a name that describes that version of your design. To summon this panel, choose Window→Layer Comps. Then you can use the arrow buttons circled here to cycle through the various comps.

Bottom: Showing, hiding, and rearranging layers lets you quickly produce several versions of the same design.

You capture layer comp "snapshots" as you're working. For instance, you could start off with a baseline version and record what it looks like, then make some changes and record the new version, and so on. When you're ready to save your first layer comp, follow these steps:

1. **Choose Window→Layer Comps to summon the Layer Comps panel, and then click the Create New Layer Comp button at the bottom of the panel.**

   The button looks just like the New Layer button—a piece of paper with a folded corner.

2. **In the New Layer Comp dialog box, give the snapshot a meaningful name and then tell Photoshop what attributes to save.**

   The dialog box has three checkboxes:

   - **Visibility** captures the layers' current visibility status (whether they're on or off).

- **Position** captures the layers' positions within the document (their *location*, not their stacking order).

- **Appearance** captures any blend modes and layer styles.

It's a good idea to turn on all three settings *just in case* you decide to tweak that stuff later. Type a comment if you'd like, and then click OK.

3. **Back in the Layers panel, rearrange, show, or hide layers; add layer styles; or change blend modes to produce another version of the image.**

4. **In the Layer Comps panel, click the Create New Layer Comp button again to create another layer comp and give it a name.**

Repeat these steps as many times as you want to save lots of different versions of your document.

When you're ready to stroll through the different versions, click the little forward and back arrows at the bottom of the Layer Comps panel (*Figure 3-25*). To get back to the way the document looked when you last tweaked it (or when you saved your last layer comp), at the top of the Layer Comps panel, click the empty square to the left of the words "Last Document State."

You can duplicate and delete layer comps just like layers and layer groups. To *edit* a layer comp, activate it in the Layer Comps panel and then change whatever you want in the Layers panel. When you're finished, click the Update button at the bottom of the Layer Comps panel.

If you make certain edits, like cropping or deleting a layer, or changing a layer's color, opacity, or fill—basically, any edit that's beyond the layer-comp feature's tracking capabilities—Photoshop gets cranky and locks you out of your layer comps. You can tell which comps are affected because they'll have little warning triangles to the right of their names (see *Figure 3-26*). These triangles mean that Photoshop needs you to update the layer comp(s) because it can't keep track of every change you made. (Don't worry, it *doesn't* mean Photoshop lost your changes.) If you didn't delete any layers, then fixing the problem is easy: Just activate the affected layer comp(s) and then click the Update button shown in *Figure 3-25*. If you *did* delete a layer, then you need to create a new comp.

■ EXPORTING LAYER COMPS

When you're ready to show the client your layer comps, export them by choosing File→Scripts→"Layer Comps to Files." Photoshop creates a separate file for each layer comp in whatever format you choose (you get the same options as when you export layers to files; see *Figure 3-27*).

Older versions of Photoshop (CS3 and earlier) let you export layer comps as both a PDF file *and* Web Photo Gallery (WPG) files right from the Scripts menu. Happily, the PDF feature *reappeared* in Photoshop CS6: Choose File→Scripts→"Layer Comps to PDF," and Photoshop displays the dialog box shown in *Figure 3-27*. Creating a web gallery was offloaded to Bridge, but in Bridge CC that feature was removed; see page 750 for details.

FIGURE 3-26

If a little warning triangle appears next to your layer comp (circled), you can click it to see this dialog box, which gently chastises you for messing up the layer comp. Click Clear to get rid of the warning triangle and close the dialog box.

If you turn on the "Don't show again" checkbox, Photoshop won't display this message anymore, but you'll still have to update your layer comps when you see the warning triangle.

FIGURE 3-27

Click the Browse button to tell Photoshop where you want it to save the file (if you have multiple layer comps, Photoshop creates one PDF with multiple pages). If you want to export only the comps you've activated in the Layer Comps panel (rather than all the document's comps), turn on the Selected Layer Comps Only checkbox.

Unless you turn off the Advance Every setting, the PDF will advance from page to page like a slideshow (if you want each layer comp to remain onscreen for more than 5 seconds, enter a new number into the Advance Every field). To make the slideshow start over automatically, turn on "Loop after last page." When you're finished, click the Run button and Photoshop creates the file.

Rasterizing Layers

If you try to paint or run a filter on a Shape or Type layer (covered in Chapters 13 and 14, respectively), Photoshop puts up a fuss: It displays a dialog box letting you know that you've got to *rasterize* that layer first. Why? Because, as you learned back in Chapter 2, vectors aren't made of pixels, and to use pixel-based tools—like the

Brush, Eraser, and Clone Stamp—on a vector-based layer, you have to convert it to pixels first using a process called *rasterizing*.

> **NOTE** You see the same dialog box if you try to use one of Photoshop's healing tools on a Smart Object. While a Smart Object isn't necessarily a vector, you still can't use pixel-based tools on it.

Beware: There's no going back once you've rasterized a layer. You can't resize former Smart Objects or Shape layers without losing quality, you can't double-click a former Fill layer and change its color, *and* you can't edit a rasterized Type layer—because rasterizing converts them to pixel-based Image layers. That's why it's a good idea to do your rasterizing on a *duplicate* layer so you can always go back to the original. Just duplicate the layer by pressing ⌘-J (Ctrl+J) before you rasterize, and then turn off the original layer's visibility so you don't accidentally rasterize the *wrong* layer.

Rasterizing is easy: Activate a vector-based layer or Smart Object and then choose Layer→Rasterize→Layer. (Choose Layer→Rasterize→All Layers to rasterize *everything* in your document.) Better yet, activate the layers(s), Control-click (right-click) near the layer's name in the Layers panel, and then choose Rasterize Layer from the shortcut menu that appears.

Merging Layers

Layers are great, but sometimes you need to squash 'em together. Yes, this goes against what you've learned in this chapter so far—that you *should* keep everything on its own layer—but in some situations you have no choice but to *merge* or *stamp* layers—or worse, completely *flatten* your file. Here's what those scary-sounding commands do, along with how and why you might need to use 'em:

- **Merge**. If you've whipped pixels into perfection and know that you'll *never* want to change them, you can merge two or more layers into one (see *Figure 3-28*). Not only does that reduce the length of your Layers panel, it also knocks a few pounds off the file's size. Photoshop gives you several ways to merge layers:

  — **Merge down**. To merge two *visible* layers that live next to each other in the Layers panel—and the bottom one is a pixel-based layer—activate the top layer and then choose Layer→Merge Down, choose Merge Down from the Layers panel's menu, or press ⌘-E (Ctrl+E).

> **NOTE** You can merge any kind of layers, but you need to have a *pixel-based* layer underneath them in the Layers panel to use the merge commands, or else they're grayed out (just add a new Image layer if you need to). Photoshop then merges everything onto that pixel-based layer.

  — **Merge visible**. To merge just some of your layers, hide the ones you *don't* want to squash, activate a pixel-based layer as your target, and then go to Layer→Merge Visible, choose Merge Visible from the Layers panel's menu, or press Shift-⌘-E (Shift+Ctrl+E).

— **Merge active**. Activate the layers you want to merge (either pixel- or vector-based) and then go to Layer→Merge Layers, choose Merge Layers from the Layers panel's menu, or press ⌘-E (Ctrl+E).

— **Merge linked**. If you've linked layers together (page 99), you can merge them in one fell swoop—though you've got to activate them first by choosing Layer→Select Linked Layers or choosing Select Linked Layers from the Layers panel's menu, and then following the instructions for merging active layers (above).

FIGURE 3-28

If you need to edit a multilayer file using tools that affect one layer at a time, you can stamp layers into a merged-layer copy (like the top layer here) to avoid having to flatten the file. (Photoshop color-coded the stamped layer to match the topmost layer group.)

If you flatten your document by accident, you can get the layers back using the History panel or by pressing ⌘-Z (Ctrl+Z). Whew!

• **Stamp**. You can think of stamping as a *safer* version of merging because it combines the active layers into a *new* layer, leaving the original layers intact. This command is great when you need to edit multiple layers with tools that affect only one layer at a time (like layer styles). Here are your stamping options:

— **Stamp active layers**. Activate the layers you want to stamp and then press Option-⌘-E (Alt+Ctrl+E).

— **Stamp visible**. Turn off the layers you *don't* want to stamp by clicking their visibility eyes in the Layers panel, and then press Shift-Option-⌘-E (Shift+Alt+Ctrl+E). You can also hold Option (Alt) as you choose Merge Visible from the Layers panel's menu to make Photoshop merge everything into a new layer.

TIP An alternative to stamping layers is to use layer groups (page 100) or create a Smart Object from multiple layers, as explained on page 122.

- **Flatten**. This command makes your document flatter than a pancake, compressing all its layers into a single locked background that, as you know from the box on page 78, doesn't allow for transparency (any areas that were transparent become white instead). Alas, you have no choice but to flatten a file if you're exporting it to a format that doesn't *support* layers (like JPEG, PNG, and so on—see page 721); just be sure to save the document as a PSD file *first* so you can go back and edit that version later. You've got three flattening options:

  — **Flatten Image**. To flatten a whole file, go to Layer→Flatten Image or choose Flatten Image from the Layers panel's menu.

WARNING Danger, Will Robinson! After flattening a file, be sure to choose File→Save As instead of File→Save to avoid saving over your original, layered document.

  — **Flatten All Layer Effects**. Instead of flattening a whole file, you can flatten just its layer styles (page 124) so they become one with the layer they're attached to. But be aware that, if you've applied any layer styles to vector-based layers (like Type or Shape layers), those layers will get rasterized in the process. To flatten layer styles, choose File→Scripts→Flatten All Layer Effects.

  — **Flatten All Masks**. You can also permanently apply masks to their associated layers by choosing File→Scripts→Flatten All Masks.

Layer Blending

In Photoshop, *blending* refers to the way colors on one layer interact with colors on other layers. The program gives you some pretty powerful blending options in the form of layer blend modes, advanced blending, and "blend if" sliders. You can do some amazing stuff with these tools, as illustrated in the quick exposure fix described on page 113. However, since they're used in combining images, they're covered in depth beginning on page 276.

Layer Masks: Digital Masking Tape

Remember the last time you gave your walls a fresh coat of paint? You probably broke out a roll of masking tape and taped up the baseboards and molding so you wouldn't get paint all over them. Sure, you could've have taken the baseboards *off* and put them back on once the paint had dried, but *dadgum* that's a lot of work. Besides, masking tape covers everything just fine. Hiding and protecting is masking tape's special purpose and—what luck!—you've got its digital equivalent right in Photoshop: *layer masks*.

By adding paint to a layer mask, you can hide the content of the layer it's attached to, whether it's a pixel-based Image layer, Smart Object, Shape layer, Fill layer or—in the case of Adjustment layers—a color or lighting change. Learning to use masks will keep you from having to *erase* parts of an image to produce the effect you want. Once you erase, there's no going back, and if your hand isn't steady enough to erase around detailed areas, you may accidentally erase bits you want to keep. So, for example, instead of *deleting* a background so you can swap it with another one, you can use a layer mask to *hide* it, as shown in *Figure 3-29*. (You'll find all kinds of other uses for layer masks sprinkled throughout this book.) As long as you save the document as a PSD file, you can go back and edit the mask anytime.

FIGURE 3-29

Left: Wanna be a rock star? No problem: A layer mask can make that happen. Here you can see the original, boring, blue background, as well as the new, exciting, clamoring crowd.

Right: If you peek at the Layers panel, you can see that the original background wasn't deleted—it was hidden with a mask instead. (To make the color of the guitarist and the crowd match a bit more, a Photo Filter Adjustment layer—page 336—was added that uses the same mask.) Like layer thumbnails, a mask's thumbnail is an exact miniature of your document.

Adding Layer Masks

You can add a mask to any layer, though some layers—like Fill, Adjustment, and Shape layers—automatically come with their own masks. As you can see in *Figure 3-29*, the mask shows up in the Layers panel to the right of the layer's thumbnail.

> **NOTE** These days, the Background layer is *automatically* converted to a regular layer when you add a layer mask, alleviating the need to double-click the layer first to unlock it. Hooray for change!

Layer masks are grayscale creatures, so when you're dealing with them you work only in black, white, and shades of gray, depending on what you want to do. A black mask hides the layer completely, and a white mask reveals it completely. A gray mask falls somewhere in between—it's partially transparent. All this is easy to remember if you memorize the rhyme, "Black conceals and white reveals." Masks can be pixel- or vector-based. This section covers pixel-based masks; vector-based masks are covered on page 571.

To add a layer mask, activate the layer you want to add it to, choose Layer→Layer Mask, and then pick one of the following:

- **Reveal All**. Creates a solid white mask that shows everything on the layer, so it doesn't change anything in your image. You can also add a white (empty) mask by clicking the Add Layer Mask button at the bottom of the Layers panel (it looks like a circle within a square, as shown in *Figure 3-29*). If you want to hide just a *little* bit of a layer, Reveal All is the way to go; after you add the mask, just paint the areas you want to hide with a black brush.

- **Hide All**. Creates a solid black mask that conceals everything on the layer. (Option-clicking [Alt-clicking] the Add Layer Mask button does the same thing.) If you want to hide the majority of the layer, choose this option and then go back with a white brush to reveal specific areas.

> **TIP** You can invert a mask (flip-flop it from white to black and vice versa) by activating it and then pressing ⌘-I (Ctrl+I). This is a great keyboard shortcut to memorize, as you'll use it often.

- **Reveal Selection**. Choose this option if you've created a selection and want to hide everything *but* the selection. Photoshop adds a mask in which the selected area is white and the rest is black. (You'll learn all about selections in Chapter 4.)

- **Hide Selection**. This command adds a mask in which the selected area is black and the rest is white.

> **TIP** You can also add a pixel- or vector-based layer mask by using the Properties panel (shown on page 116).

- **From Transparency**. This command creates a layer mask from the *transparent* pixels in an Image layer (handy if you're working with an Image layer that has no background, like a brushstroke). Just activate a partially transparent layer before choosing this command, and Photoshop adds a layer mask that's black in the transparent (empty) areas, gray in the areas that are partially transparent, and white in the areas that contain info. (This command doesn't work with Shape layers or Smart Objects.)

Using Layer Masks

You can use any painting tool to add black, white, or gray paint to a layer mask, although the Brush tool is especially handy (Chapter 12 covers all your brush options), and the Gradient tool is great if you want to create a smooth transition from black to white (see the color-fade effect on page 79). Selection tools (Chapter 4) also work in masks, and once you create a selection, you can fill it with black, white, or shades of gray by choosing Edit→Fill.

One of the simplest uses for layer masks is to hide bits of text so the text looks like it's behind a person or object in a photo, as shown in *Figure 3-30*. Here's how to create that effect:

1. **Open a photo and then press T to activate the Type tool.**

   Don't worry about double-clicking the Background layer to unlock it; you don't need to touch your original image in this technique.

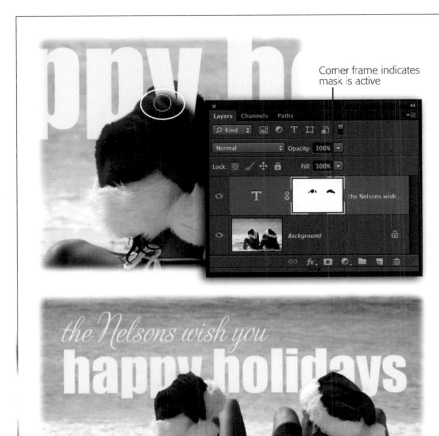

Corner frame indicates
mask is active

FIGURE 3-30

Top: Here you can see that this couple and the text live on different layers. If you add a layer mask to the text layer and then paint within the mask with a black brush (circled in white), you can hide parts of the text, revealing the couple's cute hats. Over in the Layers panel, the corner frame lets you know which part of the document is active: the Type layer or its mask.

Bottom: Magazines use this trick all the time on their covers to make text look like it's behind people.

2. **In the Options bar, pick a font, a size, and a color.**

   For this technique, select a thick font like Impact and set it to a fairly large size, like 70 points (for a high-resolution image, you'll need an even bigger size). You'll learn all about formatting text in Chapter 14.

3. **Mouse over to your document, type some text, and then commit it.**

   Click where you want the text to begin and start typing. To move the text around, mouse away from the text until your cursor turns into a little arrow; then simply drag the text wherever you'd like. To let Photoshop know you're finished, press Enter—not Return—or click the little checkmark in the Options bar.

4. **Add a layer mask to your Type layer by clicking the circle-within-a-square button at the bottom of the Layers panel.**

   Photoshop adds an all-white layer mask to the Type layer, so that everything on that layer is visible. In the Layers panel, you'll now see the mask's thumbnail next to the Type layer thumbnail. See the thin border around the corners of the mask's thumbnail (labeled in *Figure 3-30*)? That means the mask is active and you're about to paint on it (good) instead of the photo (bad).

   TIP One of the biggest mistakes folks make is not paying attention to which thumbnail they've activated in the Layers panel (it takes a single click to activate either one). The little corner frame always shows which part of the layer is active: the layer's mask or the layer itself.
   ---

5. **Press B to grab the Brush tool and pick a soft-edged brush set to black.**

   After you activate the Brush tool, head up to the left side of the Options bar and open the Brush Preset picker (page 495) by clicking the down-pointing triangle next to the little brush preview. Pick a soft-edged brush that's about 60 pixels (or larger if you're working with a high-resolution image). Since you want to *hide* bits of the text, you need to paint with black (remember, black conceals and white reveals). To do that, take a peek at the color chips at the bottom of the Tools panel and press D to set 'em to factory-fresh black and white, and then press X until black hops on top. *Now* you're ready to start painting.

6. **Mouse over to your document and paint the parts of the text you want to hide.**

   In the example in *Figure 3-30*, you'd position your cursor over one of the Santa hats and click to start painting (hiding). When you release the mouse button—you don't have to do all your painting with one brushstroke—you'll see black paint on the layer mask in the Layers panel, but *not* in your image.

7. **If you accidentally hide too much of the text, press X to swap color chips so you're painting with white, and then paint that area back in.**

   When you're working with a layer mask, you'll do tons of color-chip swapping (from black to white and vice versa). You'll also use a variety of brush sizes to paint the fine details as well as large areas. To keep from going blind when you're doing detailed work like this, zoom in or out of your document by pressing ⌘ and then the + or – key (Ctrl and then the + or – key on a PC).

TIP You can change your brush cursor's size and hardness by dragging, which is handy when it comes to painting on layer masks. To resize your brush, Control-Option-drag (Alt+right-click+drag on a PC) left to decrease brush size or right to increase it. The same keyboard shortcut also lets you change brush hardness: Drag up to soften the brush or down to harden it.

When you perform any of these keyboard shortcut+dragging maneuvers, inside your brush cursor, you'll see a red preview of what the new brush will look like—if your computer supports OpenGL, that is (see the box on page 58). To change that preview color to something other than red, flip to page 497. And if you're a creature of habit, you can *still* decrease brush size by pressing the left bracket key ([) and increase it by pressing the right bracket key (]).

That wasn't too bad, was it? You just learned *core* Photoshop skills that you'll use over and over. The more you use layer masks, the more natural this stuff will feel.

■ FIXING EXPOSURE WITH AN ADJUSTMENT LAYER AND ITS MASK

As you learned on page 109, a layer mask automatically tags along with each Adjustment layer you create, making it easy for you to hide that adjustment from certain areas in the image. For example, if you've got an over- or underexposed image (one that's too light or too dark), you can fix it with an Adjustment layer and then use the included mask to hide the lightening or darkening from the parts of the image that don't need changing. This particular exposure-fixing trick is important to have up your sleeve if you're short on time, or if other lighting fixes (see Chapter 9) aren't working. Here's what you do:

1. **Open an image and add a Brightness/Contrast Adjustment layer to it by clicking the half-black/half-white circle at the bottom of the Layers panel and then choosing Brightness/Contrast.**

   You're not actually going to adjust the Brightness/Contrast sliders (page 355); you're merely adding an empty Adjustment layer so you can swap blend modes and then use the mask that tags along with the Adjustment layer. Sure, you *could* duplicate your Image layer and then add a layer mask, but this method is faster and won't bloat the document's file size. The reason you're using a Brightness/Contrast Adjustment layer is because that kind of layer doesn't *do* anything to your image the second you add it.

2. **Using the unlabeled drop-down menu at the top of the Layers panel, change the empty Adjustment layer's blend mode from Normal to Multiply.**

   Blend modes control how colors on one layer interact with colors on other layers, which is terrific when it comes to combining images (you'll learn all about blend modes in Chapter 7). For now, you'll focus on two blend modes that you'll use often because they let you quickly darken or lighten an image, respectively: Multiply and Screen (see *Figure 3-31*). For this exercise, pick Multiply from the menu at the top of the Layers panel to darken your image dramatically. You'll hide the too-dark bits with the Adjustment layer's mask in the next steps.

FIGURE 3-31

You can quickly darken or lighten an image by adding an empty Adjustment layer and changing its blend mode to Multiply or Screen (respectively). To control where the change is visible on the image, use a brush to fine-tune the Adjustment layer's mask.

Top: This guy's shirt and arms are too light in the original image (left). If you change the Adjustment layer's blend mode to Multiply, his face and guitar are too dark (middle). But if you then hide his face and guitar using the layer mask, he looks much better (right).

Bottom: You can do the same thing to a photo that's too dark. On the left is the super-dark original. The middle image shows what happens when you change the Adjustment layer's blend mode to Screen. You can then use the accompanying layer mask to hide the over-lightened areas (mainly the background and his tattoo) as shown on the right. Now you can see the rocker dude's face (though on second thought, maybe that isn't such a good idea after all!).

3. **Press B to grab the Brush tool and set your foreground color chip to black.**

   Check to make sure the Adjustment layer's mask is active (it will be unless you clicked on another layer after adding it). To hide the over-darkened areas, you can paint them with black because—all together now!—black conceals and white reveals. Peek at your color chips, and if black isn't on top, press X (if you don't see black, press D to set your color chips to black and white first). Now you're ready to paint.

4. **With a big soft brush, paint the areas that are too dark.**

   Those keyboard shortcuts for resizing and changing brush hardness come in handy here (see the Tip on page 113). Remember, if you mess up and hide too much of the darkened part of the image, simply flip-flop your color chips by pressing X and then reveal the dark part again by painting it with white.

5. **If your image is still a little too dark, lower the empty Adjustment layer's opacity (page 90).**

Editing a Mask

Once you've gotten your hands on a layer mask, you'll undoubtedly need to fine-tune it, turn it off or on, and so on. In pre-CS4 versions of the program, you had to mouse *all* over the Photoshop workspace to do that stuff. Thankfully, these days all of your mask tasks are consolidated in the Properties panel (*Figure 3-32*).

You'll find the following controls in the Properties panel (Window→Properties) *when a mask is active* in the Layers panel:

- **Density**. If you've hidden an adjustment or effect with a mask and then want to make the mask *semi-transparent* so the adjustment or effect shows through just a *little*, drag this slider to the left (dragging it *all* the way left makes your mask completely transparent).

- **Feather**. This slider lets you soften the edges of the mask so that it blends into the background a little better. (New layer masks don't have any feathering, so their edges are sharp.) Drag it right to soften the mask's edges or left to sharpen them. You'll also use this slider when making a soft-oval vignette collage, as shown on page 142.

- **Mask Edge**. When you click this button, Photoshop opens the Refine Mask dialog box, where you can smooth the mask's edges, make the mask smaller or larger, add feathering to it, and so on. Page 165 has the details on this dialog box (which is also called Refine Edge).

- **Color Range**. This button opens the Color Range dialog box, where you can add to or subtract from the mask based on the colors in your image. You can also use this dialog box to help create a selection that you can then make a mask *from*; page 151 has more info.

- **Invert**. This button lets you flip-flop the mask so what *was* masked isn't and what *wasn't* masked is (you're gonna use this button a lot). Alternatively, you can activate a mask and then press ⌘-I (Ctrl+I) to do the same thing.

- **Load Selection from Mask**. Once you've created a layer mask, you can click this button to load it as a selection that you can then use somewhere else, like in another Fill or Adjustment layer's mask.

Add/select layer mask

Add/select vector mask

Panel menu

Mask preview

Load selection from mask

Apply mask   Show/hide mask

Delete mask

FIGURE 3-32

The Properties panel is your one-stop shop for working with layer masks and Adjustment layers (whether they're pixel- or vector-based). Heck, you can even add a layer mask right from this panel! Back in Photoshop CS5, these mask options lived in the Masks panel.

The Density slider controls mask opacity, which makes one wonder why it's not named the Opacity slider instead.

Unlinking a Layer from Its Mask

Photoshop assumes that if you reposition the contents of a layer, you want its mask to come along for the ride. But that's not always the case. For example, if you use a mask to frame a photo (see the oval vignette instructions on page 142), you may want to move what's *inside* the mask (the photo) independent of the mask itself, or vice versa. No problemo—you just need to unlink 'em first.

Over in the Layers panel, there's a tiny chain icon between the layer's thumbnail and the mask's thumbnail (you can see it in

Figure 3-31). To separate the layer from the mask, click this chain or choose Layer→Layer Mask→Unlink (you'll know they're separated because the chain disappears). Then press V to grab the Move tool, click the thumbnail of the piece you want to move (the layer or the mask), and then drag. Once you've got everything where you want it, click where the chain *used* to be (between the layer and mask thumbnails) or choose Layer→Layer Mask→Link to relink 'em. Easy, huh?

- **Apply Mask**. Once you get the mask just right, you can permanently (eek!) apply it to the layer by clicking this button. Applying a mask permanently alters the layer and limits the changes you can make later, so don't use this option unless you're *certain* you won't need to change the mask down the road. If you click this button by accident, use the History panel or the Undo command (⌘-Z or Ctrl+Z) to get the mask back or you won't be able to edit it ever again.

- **Disable/Enable Mask**. This visibility eye works just like the one in the Layers panel (page 74): Click it to turn the mask off or on.

- **Delete Mask**. If you decide you don't want the mask, you can kick it to the curb by clicking this little trash can at the bottom of the Properties panel.

- **Add or Select Layer Mask, Add or Select Vector Mask**. The two buttons at the top right of the Properties panel let you add or select (activate) a layer mask or vector mask (see page 571), depending on whether the active layer already *has* one or the other—if it does, these buttons let you activate the mask; if not, they let you add one. If you opened the Properties panel by double-clicking a mask, the appropriate mask button is darkened as if it's depressed.

TIP To copy a mask to another layer, press and hold Option (Alt on a PC), click the mask in the Layers panel, and then drag it to another layer. (You have to press Option or Alt *before* you click the mask or you'll merely move it from one layer to the other.) When you start to drag, your cursor turns into a double black-and-white arrowhead and you see a ghosted image of the mask.

When a layer mask is active, the Properties panel's menu (labeled in *Figure 3-32*) contains these goodies:

- **Mask Options**. When you're editing layer masks, you've got a few different viewing options. In the masking examples discussed earlier, the mask was edited while the image was viewed in full color. However, as *Figure 3-33* explains, you can also work on a mask while you're looking at a grayscale version of the mask itself (meaning it fills your document window), or you can turn the mask into a color overlay. Which one you should choose depends on the colors in your image and the area you're trying to select. If you go the color overlay route and Photoshop's standard red isn't doing it for you, choose this option and use the Layer Mask Display Options dialog box to pick another color that makes it easy to distinguish the mask from the unmasked parts of the image (*Figure 3-33*, bottom).

- **Add Mask To Selection**. If you create a mask and then make a selection (see Chapter 4), you can choose this option to add the area you've masked to the selection. This is an easy way to expand the currently selected area to include the mask in one quick step.

- **Subtract Mask From Selection**. This option deletes the shape of the mask from your selection.

FIGURE 3-33

Left: To get inside a layer mask and edit it in full gray-scale glory—handy for ensuring your subject is fully revealed—Option-click (Alt-click on a PC) the mask's thumbnail in the Layers panel. Once you're inside the mask, you can then copy and paste pixels—including text—right into it. (Page 622 has a cool example involving snatching texture from a photo and pasting it inside a mask to add it to text.) When you're finished editing the mask, click the layer's thumbnail.

Right: To edit the mask with a red overlay (like Quick Mask Mode; page 176), click to activate the mask and then press the backslash key (\). To change the overlay's color, open the Masks panel's menu and choose Mask Options. In the dialog box that appears (shown here), click the color square and then pick a new color from the resulting Color Picker. Press the backslash key again to send the overlay packin'.

- **Intersect Mask With Selection**. To select only areas where your selection and the mask overlap (if you need to add a color or pattern to only those places, for example), choose this option.

Using Smart Objects

A *Smart Object* is a very special, container-like layer into which you can plop all kinds of stuff, such as raw files (page 48), vectors (drawings) from programs like Adobe Illustrator (Chapter 13), other layers, and even whole PSD files. Smart Objects are smart because Photoshop protects what you put into them by applying your edits to the *container* instead of what's *inside* of the container. This lets you do the following:

- **Transform or resize it without losing quality**. Instead of resizing the *instance* (a copy) of the content that you inserted into your document, Photoshop remembers info about the *original*, resizes that, and then places that information back into your image (without altering the original file). In the blink of an eye, Photoshop updates your document with the newly resized content *without* making it look blocky (so long as you don't exceed the file's original dimensions too much—unless it's vector-based, of course). You can also use the full range of transform tools (page 255) on Smart Objects.

- **Compress a bunch of layers into a single layer nondestructively**. Unlike merging layers (page 106), converting several layers into a single Smart Object *preserves* the original layers. This ability is super helpful if you want to edit several layers as if they were one, which is great for masking several layers at once, applying filters to a composite image, applying layer styles (page 124), or using tools that work on only one layer at a time.

- **Run filters nondestructively**. When you run a filter on a Smart Object, Photoshop automatically adds a mask to the Smart Object (labeled in *Figure 3-34*), plus the filtering happens on *its* own layer (similar to layer styles) so you can tweak, hide, or undo the filter's effects. See page 632 to learn how to run filters on Smart Objects (and in Photoshop CC, more filters are Smart Object–happy than ever before).

FREQUENTLY ASKED QUESTION

Clipping Masks

What the heck is a clipping mask? Is it similar to a layer mask?

Clipping masks and layer masks are similar in that they both hide parts of an image, but that's about all they have in common. Clipping masks are like Photoshop's version of stencils: They let you take one layer's contents (a photo of bluebonnets, say) and shove it through the contents of the layer directly below (for example, text that says "Texas"). The result? The image on the top layer is "clipped" so that you only see the bluebonnets inside the text. (Hop over to page 626 for step-by-step instructions on this technique.)

You can give clipping masks a spin by opening a photo and double-clicking the Background layer to unlock it. Next, add a new Image layer *below* it by ⌘-clicking (Ctrl-clicking) the "Create a new layer" icon at the bottom of the Layers panel. Then press B to grab the Brush tool and paint a big ol' brushstroke across the new layer (don't worry about what color it is). In the Layers panel, activate the photo layer (which should be on top of your layer stack), and then choose Layer→Create Clipping Mask or press Option-⌘-G (Alt+Ctrl+G), and Photoshop makes your photo visible *only* through the brushstroke, regardless of what color the brushstroke is (layer transparency is the only thing that matters). You can also Option-click [Alt] the

dividing line *between* the two layers in the Layers panel to do the same thing.

When you use a clipping mask, you don't get another thumbnail in your Layers panel like you do with a layer mask. Instead, the photo layer's thumbnail scoots to the right and you see a tiny down arrow letting you know that it's clipped to the layer below. And in Photoshop CC, the layer that's being used as the mask—the layer on the bottom—gets an *underline* beneath its name.

You can clip as many layers together as you want. For example, you can clip three Image layers to a layer containing a brushstroke so all the photos show *through* it (provided you've adjusted their blending modes to allow that). To release a clipping mask, activate the clipped layer(s)—in this example, the three image layers—choose Layer→Release Clipping Mask, or choose Release Clipping Mask from the Layers panel's menu, or press Option-⌘-G (Alt+Ctrl+G). Alternatively, you can Option-click (Alt-click) the dividing line *above* the layer that you're shoving the images through (say, the brushstroke layer). Whew! Whichever method you use, you should see your entire photo(s) again.

- **Update multiple instances of the same content**. When you duplicate a Smart Object, the duplicate is *linked* to the original so it functions like an exact clone. So, for example, if you've placed the same content in several places in your document—like a large version of a logo, shape, or image in one spot and a smaller version of it somewhere else—and you make changes to the original Smart Object in Photoshop or you edit the contents of the original Smart Object in another program (like Camera Raw or Illustrator), Photoshop automatically updates that content wherever it appears in your document.

- **Swap content**. Once you've formatted a Smart Object just right, you can swap its contents for another image, and the new image takes on the original's attributes. This content swapping is powerful magic when it comes to making creative templates that you can use over and over with different images (photographers love this kind of thing). *Figure 3-34* has the details.

  For designers, the ability to swap content is helpful when you've got several pieces of art that need to be placed at the same size within a design (think multiple album covers in a concert ad or book covers in an author-signing event poster). You can swap the contents of one Smart Object without changing the others by creating an *unlinked* copy, as explained on page 122.

> **NOTE** Smart Objects are especially useful when you're working with raw files because you can double-click them in Photoshop to open them in Camera Raw (page 361). However, placing multiple Smart Objects in a single document—especially one that contains raw files—will bloat your file's size in a hurry and could cause Photoshop to run out of memory and run...as fast...as molasses.

The following sections teach you how to create and manage Smart Objects.

Creating Smart Objects

How you create a Smart Object depends on two things: where the original content lives and which document you want to put it in. Here are your options:

- **To create a new document containing a file that lives on your hard drive, choose File→"Open as Smart Object."** In the resulting Open dialog box, navigate to the file and then click Open to make Photoshop create a new document containing a single Smart Object (without a Background layer). The image you've opened appears at its original size, and you'll see the Smart Object badge on its layer thumbnail (circled in *Figure 3-34*).

> **TIP** You can Shift-click multiple files in the Open dialog box to open more than one file as a Smart Object. Each file opens as its own document with a single Smart Object layer.

FIGURE 3-34

You can create some pretty amazing templates using Smart Objects. Just open an image as a Smart Object (as described later in this section) and then make all the changes you want, like giving it a sepia tint, adding a dark-edge vignette, and sharpening it, as shown here. The little badge at the bottom right of the layer thumbnail (circled) indicates that the layer is a Smart Object.

Then, to swap the original photo for another one, activate the Smart Object layer and then choose Layer→Smart Objects→Replace Contents (or Control-click [right-click] near the layer's corner in the Layers panel name and choose Replace Contents from the resulting shortcut menu). Navigate to another photo on your hard drive, click Open, and it'll take on the same characteristics automatically!

Thank ya, thank ya very much.

Mask

- **To import a file into a document that's currently open, choose File→Place.**
  You get the same Open dialog box so you can navigate to the file, but this time the file opens as a Smart Object *inside* the current document, and Photoshop also puts little handles around the object so you can resize it. When you press Return (Enter on a PC) to accept the object, you'll see the Smart Object badge appear on the new layer's thumbnail. Unfortunately, you can't place multiple files using this command though you *can* do that using the Mini Bridge panel, as shown on page 867. (In CC, Mini Bridge is installed separately from Photoshop; see Chapter 22 for more.)

NOTE Photoshop includes a preference setting that makes the program automatically open dragged or placed files as Smart Objects (see page 44). This setting is turned on initially, and it's the only way to roll. If you've got a document open, the Smart Object appears on a new layer inside that document; if you don't, it opens as a Smart Object in a *new* document.

- **Copy and paste an Adobe Illustrator file**. If you copy Illustrator art into your computer's memory, you can paste it into an open Photoshop document using ⌘-V (Ctrl+V). Photoshop will then ask whether you want to paste it as a Smart Object, pixels, path, or Shape layer (the last three are covered in Chapter 13).

- **In Bridge, choose File→Place→In Photoshop**. If you're using Bridge to peruse files, this command pops 'em open as Smart Objects in Photoshop (see Chapter 22 for more on Bridge).

- **To turn existing layers into a Smart Object in the current document, activate the layer(s) and then choose "Convert to Smart Object" from the Layers panel's menu**. If you're working with an image that has a bunch of Adjustment layers associated with it (to change stuff like color and lighting), you can use this command to group the whole mess into a single Smart Object. That way, you can apply additional changes to all those layers at *once* with tools that work only on individual layers (like filters and layer styles). *Figure 3-35* has the details.

NOTE You can add a mask to Smart Objects just like you can to any other layer. Photoshop automatically *links* the mask to the layer so you can move 'em around together. To unlink them, just click the little chain icon between their thumbnails in the Layers panel. (See the box on page 116 for more on linked masks.)

Managing Smart Objects

Once you've created a Smart Object, you can duplicate it, edit it, and export its contents. You'll find the following options in the Layer→Smart Objects submenu and *most* of 'em in the shortcut menu you get by Control-clicking (right-clicking) near the layer's name in the Layers panel:

- **New Smart Object via Copy**. When you choose this command, Photoshop makes a duplicate of your Smart Object that's *not linked* to the original, so if you edit the content of the original Smart Object, the duplicate won't change. An unlinked copy is helpful if you want to place several pieces of art at the same size in your design; place the first piece of art as a Smart Object and size it just right, then make an unlinked copy of the Smart Object and swap its contents.

  You can also run this command by mousing over to the Layers panel and Control-clicking (right-clicking) near—but not *on*—the existing Smart Object's name and then choosing "New Smart Object via Copy" from the drop-down menu.

FIGURE 3-35

Top: To convert multiple layers into a Smart Object, activate them in the Layers panel and then choose "Convert to Smart Object" from the panel's menu or from the shortcut menu you get by Control-clicking (right-clicking) near a layer's name (it doesn't matter which one). Alternatively, you can choose Layer→Smart Objects→"Convert to Smart Object," or choose Filter→"Convert for Smart Filters." All these commands do the same thing.

Bottom: Photoshop converts all those layers into a single Smart Object that you can run filters on nondestructively. To edit the Smart Object's contents, choose Edit Contents from the Layers panel's menu and Photoshop opens a new temporary document containing the original layers. When you're finished editing, press ⌘-S (Ctrl+S) to save your changes and then close the document; Photoshop automatically updates your Smart Object in the original document. How cool is that?

TIP To create a duplicate Smart Object that *is* linked to the original, drag the Smart Object onto the "Create a new layer" button at the bottom of the Layers panel, or just activate the Smart Object in the Layers panel and then duplicate it by pressing ⌘-J (Ctrl+J).

This is handy when you repeat graphical element in your design—if you edit that element in the original Smart Object, Photoshop updates *all* the copies of that Smart Object in your document. For example, if you create a document that includes several sizes of the same image for printing (like the picture packages you got in grade school), using linked Smart Objects lets you swap *all* the images for a different one in two seconds flat.

- **Edit Contents**. Choose this option or double-click the Smart Object's thumbnail in the Layers panel if you want to edit the original file in the program that created it (for example, Camera Raw or Adobe Illustrator). Once you save the file in the other program (or you click Done in Camera Raw), it gets updated in your Photoshop document automatically. For this to happen, you *must* use

Photoshop to open the original file for editing; it won't work if you edit the file behind Photoshop's back.

- **Export Contents**. This command pulls the contents of the active Smart Object out of the current document and puts it into a new file that's the same format as the original. If the content began life as a raw file, for example, Photoshop will save the Smart Object's contents in raw format; if the content is a pixel-based image or Photoshop layers, you get a new Photoshop document that contains the image or layers; and so on. When you choose this command, Photoshop displays a dialog box where you can name the new file and choose where to save it.

- **Replace Contents**. As you learned back in *Figure 3-34*, you can use this command to swap the contents of a Smart Object so the new image takes on the editing treatment you gave the original one.

- **Stack Mode**. This option, which lives only in the Layer→Smart Object submenu and was previously available only in Photoshop Extended, contains a slew of processing options that you can apply to a Smart Object composed of a series of similar images (called an *image stack*) in order to produce a perfect image that's free of noise or other accidental elements that snuck into the shot (like birds flying across the sky, a car passing in front of the subject, and so on).

- **Rasterize**. As you learned on page 118, when you edit a Smart Object, you're editing the container, not its contents. That's why you can't use any of Photoshop's painting, healing, fill, or eraser tools on a Smart Object (though if the Smart Object contains other pixel-based layers, you can double-click to expand the Smart Object into a temporary document and edit that instead). However, if you're ready to give up all the goodness that comes with using a Smart Object, choose this option to rasterize it and make it behave like any other layer.

■ Layer Styles

After all that hard work learning about layers, you're probably ready for some fun. This section is all about *layer styles*: a set of 11 fully adjustable, ready-made special effects for layers that you can apply in all kinds of cool ways. Consider this section your reward for sticking with this chapter till the bitter end.

Layer styles are a lot of fun and, since they appear on their own layers, they're nondestructive *and* they remain editable as long as you save the document as a PSD file. Layer styles are great for adding finishing touches to designs, and they can really make text and graphical elements pop off the page (see *Figure 3-36*). They also update automatically as your layer *content* changes.

NOTE If you add a layer style to a path in Photoshop CC (page 536), its gray outline temporarily disappears while the Layer Style dialog box is open.

Here's how to add The Lord of All Styles, the drop shadow, to a layer:

1. **Activate the soon-to-be-shadowed layer or layer group in the Layers panel.**

   Photoshop limits you to activating a single layer when you're adding a style. That said, you *can* add layers styles to layer groups (page 100).

TIP If you apply a layer style to a *layer group*, Photoshop treats the group as if it were *flattened* so you get slightly different results than you do by adding the style to individual layers. For example, if you've got a slew of layers and you add a drop shadow to all of 'em, you end up with a shadow on top of a shadow on top of a shadow—yuck. The fix is to stuff those layers inside a layer group and then add the layer style to the *group* instead. That way you end up with one nice, subtle shadow instead of a big ol' shadowy mess.

---

2. **Click the "Add a layer style" button at the bottom of the Layers panel and choose Drop Shadow (see *Figure 3-37*, top).**

   The button looks like a tiny cursive *fx* that stands for "layer *effects*" (though this book refers to them as layer styles).

POWER USERS' CLINIC

Nested Smart Objects

Believe it or not, there will be times when you need to convert a Smart Object into *another* Smart Object, to create a *nested* Smart Object. Don't roll your eyes just yet; consider these practical scenarios:

Let's say you're retouching a portrait and you converted multiple layers into a Smart Object for sharpening that you intend to be visible across the entire image (called global sharpening). Now you decide to add *another* round of sharpening that's only visible in certain areas—say, your subject's hair, eyelashes, lips, or the iris of each eye (called selective sharpening). Sure, you can run the sharpening filter on the Smart Object a second time, but if you use the included mask you'll end up hiding *both* rounds of sharpening because you get only *one mask* per Smart Object. The fix is to create a second Smart Object out of the first in order to get another mask.

Now let's go in a completely different direction, just for fun. Say you designed a wine bottle label in a Photoshop document consisting of multiple layers and Smart Objects, and now you need to create *another* Photoshop document in order to print multiple labels on a single page. No problem! Use File→Place

to add the *first* Photoshop document—that's right, the whole enchilada—to the *second* Photoshop document as a Smart Object. Next, duplicate that Smart Object however many times you need to create multiple labels and then arrange them accordingly. Not only does this allow you to work with fewer layers in the label template, but it also gives you the ability to change *all* the labels at once. Just double-click one of the Smart Objects—it doesn't matter which one because they're all linked—to expand it into a temporary document containing the layers from the first Photoshop document, primed and ready for editing. Press ⌘-S (Ctrl+S) to save your changes, close the temporary document, and kapow! Back in the second Photoshop document, the labels change en masse.

These are but two of a *bazillion* scenarios where nesting Smart Objects is a necessity for maintaining a nondestructive workflow, wherein you can always get back to your original layers. Just activate the Smart Object(s) and use any of the methods discussed in this section to create another one. Happily, Photoshop lets you nest Smart Objects inside of Smart Objects, inside of Smart Objects...to infinity (well, maybe not *infinity*, but close!).

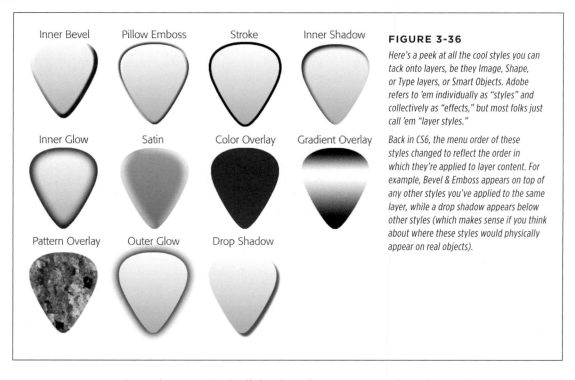

Inner Bevel   Pillow Emboss   Stroke   Inner Shadow

Inner Glow   Satin   Color Overlay   Gradient Overlay

Pattern Overlay   Outer Glow   Drop Shadow

FIGURE 3-36

Here's a peek at all the cool styles you can tack onto layers, be they Image, Shape, or Type layers, or Smart Objects. Adobe refers to 'em individually as "styles" and collectively as "effects," but most folks just call 'em "layer styles."

Back in CS6, the menu order of these styles changed to reflect the order in which they're applied to layer content. For example, Bevel & Emboss appears on top of any other styles you've applied to the same layer, while a drop shadow appears below other styles (which makes sense if you think about where these styles would physically appear on real objects).

3. **In the Layer Style dialog box that appears, adjust the settings to produce a respectable (soft)—not gaudy (black and 10 feet away from the object)— drop shadow.**

   There are a bazillion options for each style in the Layer Style dialog box, as *Figure 3-37* shows, and it's a good idea to experiment with all of 'em so you know how they work.

   > **TIP** You can also open the Layer Style dialog box by double-clicking a layer's thumbnail or double-clicking near (but not *on*) the layer's name in the Layers panel.

4. **Click OK when you're satisfied with the effect and then marvel at your very first drop shadow.**

   Photoshop closes the Layer Style dialog box and adds a couple of things to the Layers panel: a category named Effects and, beneath it, an item named Drop Shadow. (If you add *more* layer styles, they stack up beneath the word "Effects.") The program also adds a special badge to the right of the Image layer's name (it looks like a cursive *fx*).

To edit the style later on, double-click it in the Layers panel. To move it to another layer, just grab it and drag (you'll see a big *fx* as you drag). You can add as many different styles to a layer as you want, all from the Layer Style dialog box. Just turn on the checkboxes for the styles you want (they're all in the Styles column on the left) and then click a style's name to see its options. And remember the Fill setting discussed back on page 90? You can use it to make a layer's *contents* see-through while its *style* remains 100 percent solid (great for creating hollow text).

Click to change drop shadow color

Click to temporarily save settings

FIGURE 3-37

When it comes to drop shadows, the classiest ones are rarely black—instead, they pick up a darker color from the image. Just click the color swatch labeled here, and Photoshop summons the Color Picker (page 489). To snatch a color that already lives in the image, mouse over the image and, when your cursor turns into an eyedropper, click once; your shadow takes on that color.

You'll also likely need to lower the shadow's opacity so it's nice and soft, and use the Spread and Size sliders to make it wider. Don't bother messing with the Angle dial or the Distance slider because you can change those settings visually by heading over to your document and dragging the shadow around—while the Layer Style dialog box is still open—as shown here (bottom).

Once you get the drop shadow just right, click the Make Default button (labeled). The next time you need to add a drop shadow, Photoshop will use those same settings.

Managing Layer Styles

Once you've tacked on a layer style or two, you'll undoubtedly want to apply them to other layers and turn them off or on. Here's how:

- **To copy a style from one layer to another**, head over to the Layers panel and Option-drag (Alt-drag on a PC) the style to the new layer. Your cursor turns into a double black-and-white arrowhead when you drag, and you see a big, ghosted *fx*.

- **To turn a style off**, click the visibility eye to the left of the style's name in the Layers panel.

FREQUENTLY ASKED QUESTION

Hiding Styles with Masks

Help! I have a mask on my layer and Photoshop is showing the styles through the darn mask! How do I hide those pesky styles?

Ah, you seek the elusive style cloak. To summon it, you must boil the stalk of a West Texas tumbleweed, season it with eye of toad, and drink it from the shell of an armadillo three days dead...

Just kidding. To hide styles with a layer mask, you've got to change the layer's blending options. Double-click the word "Effects" in the Layers panel and Photoshop opens the Layer Style dialog box set to display the Blending Options settings.

In the Advanced Blending section in the center of the dialog box (shown here), you'll see a list of checkboxes that includes Layer Mask Hides Effects and Vector Mask Hides Effects. Turn on the appropriate option for the kind of layer you're working with (Vector Mask [page 571] for vector-based layers, and Layer Mask for all other layers), and then click OK. Back in your document, the mask should hide any styles you've applied to that layer. In the Layers panel, a tiny icon that looks like two intersecting squares appears at the far right of the layer to indicate that its blending options have been changed.

Now, back to that magic potion...

If you Control-click (right-click) a layer style in the Layers panel, you see a shortcut menu with these options:

- **Disable Layer Effects** turns off *all* the styles on that layer. To turn them back on, open the menu again and choose Enable Layer Effects. (Clicking the visibility eye to the left of the word "Effects" in the Layers panel does the same thing.)

- **Copy Layer Style** copies all the styles you've applied to the active layer so you can apply them to other layers. After you choose this command, Shift- or ⌘-click (Ctrl-click) to activate the layer(s) you want to apply the styles to, and then Control-click (right-click) to open the shortcut menu again and choose Paste Layer Style.

- **Clear Layer Style** deletes the style from the active layers. You can also drag a style to the trash can at the bottom of the Layers panel to remove it from a layer.

- **Global Light** tells Photoshop to use the same lighting angle in every style you add, which is useful when you're applying drop shadows or inner shadows. If you've got more than one drop shadow in your document, you *probably* want to turn on this option so the lighting stays consistent.

- **Create Layer** takes the style applied to the active layer and converts that *style* into an Image layer, which means you lose the ability to edit the style later. Though it sounds limiting, you can use this option to further customize a layer style into your own personal vision; once it's a regular layer, you can run filters on it, use the painting tools, and so on.

- **Hide All Effects** turns off the styles applied to *every* layer. After you've hidden them, this menu item changes to read "Show Effects" so you can choose it to turn 'em back on.

- **Scale Effects** lets you resize the style itself, independent of the layer's contents, by entering a percentage. This option is useful if you want to fine-tune drop shadows and glows by making them slightly larger or smaller.

Last but not least, there may be a time when you want to rasterize a layer style so it's part of the layer itself (though it's tough to think of a reason why). You can do that by heading to the Layers panel, Control-clicking (right-clicking) to the right of the layer's thumbnail, and then choosing Rasterize Layer Style. When you do, Photoshop *permanently* applies the layer style to the layer.

The Styles Panel

Photoshop comes with all kinds of layer-style presets made from some pretty psychedelic style combinations. You'll find a couple of them useful, but most of them are just funky. To get at them, open the Styles panel by clicking its tab in the panel dock on the right side of your screen or by choosing Window→Styles (see *Figure 3-38*).

Admittedly, the preloaded styles aren't anything to write home about, but if you open the Styles panel menu, you'll see 10 *more* sets you can load: Abstract Styles, Buttons, and so on. To load another set, just choose it from the panel's menu;

Photoshop asks if you'd like to add them to the existing styles or replace the existing ones. If you're a web designer, you may find the Glass Buttons and Web Styles sets useful for that clear, plastic look. Otherwise, you probably won't find much use for many of these styles.

To apply one of the presets, simply activate the layer you want to use it on and then click the style's thumbnail. You can tweak the style by double-clicking its layer in the Layers panel or by choosing its name from the left-hand list in the Layer Style dialog box. You can also drag and drop a style's thumbnail from the Styles panel onto a layer in the Layers panel, but doing so makes that style replace any styles you've already added to that layer. To add a saved style on *top* of existing styles, hold down the Shift key as you drag and drop or as you click the style's thumbnail.

Panel menu

Clear style | Delete style
New style

FIGURE 3-38

You'll find all manner of weird and wacky presets in the Styles panel (top). (To make the style thumbnails larger or to view them in a list, open the Styles panel's menu and choose Text Only, Small Thumbnail, Large Thumbnail, Small List, or Large List.) Some of them are more useful than others (middle).

You can add your own creations to the mix, too. Just activate the layer your style is applied to and then click the New Style button labeled here or choose New Style from the Styles panel's menu.

In the resulting dialog box (bottom), give your style a name, turn on the Include Layer Effects checkbox to make sure you don't lose any of your changes, and—if you've changed any layer blending options—turn on the Include Layer Blending Options checkbox, too. When you click OK, Photoshop saves your style for posterity and adds it to the Styles panel (though it's a good idea to safeguard your presets, as online Appendix B explains).

To bypass this dialog box next time you want to save a style, Option-click (Alt-click on a PC) the New Style button. You'll get a new Style called "Style" that you can rename later, but you don't get to change any other settings.

■ EXPORTING AND LOADING STYLES

If you're really proud of the styles you've created and want to share them with the masses (or at least load 'em onto another computer), here's what to do: From the Styles panel's menu, choose Save Styles, give your style a name, and tell Photoshop where to save it. You can then take the resulting file to another computer, launch Photoshop, and pick one of the following options from the Styles panel's menu:

- **Load Styles** adds the new style to the ones currently in your Styles panel.

- **Replace Styles** zaps the ones you've got in favor of the new one.

- **Reset Styles** returns your styles to the factory settings.

Selections: Choosing What to Edit

Life is all about making choices, and the time you spend in Photoshop is no exception. Perhaps the biggest decision you'll make is which part of an image to edit—after all, your edits don't have to affect the *whole* thing. Using a variety of tools, you can tell Photoshop exactly which portion of an image you want to tinker with, right down to the pixel, if you so desire. This process is called *making a selection*.

As you'll learn in this chapter, Photoshop has a bunch of tools that you can use to create selections based on shape, color, and other attributes. You can also draw selections by hand, although that requires a bit of mouse prowess. True selection wisdom lies in learning which tool to start with, how to use the tools together, and how to fine-tune your selections quickly and efficiently. The following pages will help you with all that and then some.

■ Selection Basics

What's so great about selections, anyway? Lots. After you make a selection, you can do all kinds of neat things with the selection itself as well as the pixels that live inside it:

- **Move it around**. To move *part* of an image, you need to select it first. You can even move selections from one document to another, as discussed on page 179. For example, a little head swapping is great fun after family reunions and breakups. If you want to stick your ex's head onto a ballerina's body, hop on over to page 180. You can scoot your selection around while you're making it, too, in case you didn't get it in the right spot at first (see the Tip on page 137).

- **Resize or transform it**. Need to change the size or shape of a selection before you manipulate the pixels inside it? No problem: Once you've made the selection, you can transform it into whatever size or shape you need (page 174). With this maneuver, Photoshop won't reshape any pixels that are in the selected area; it just changes the shape of the selection itself. This trick is handy when you're trying to select part of an image that's in perspective, as shown on page 175. Likewise, you can also transform the *pixels* you've selected, which is helpful when you're slimming your subject (page 422).

- **Fill it with color or pixels from the image's background**. Normally, the Edit→Fill command or a Fill layer floods an entire layer with color, but by creating a selection first, you can color just that area (handy when fixing animal white-eye, as described on page 440). You can also use selections in conjunction with Photoshop's Content-Aware tools to delete a person or object from a photo as if they were never there (see page 408).

- **Add an outline**. You can add a *stroke* (Photoshop's term for an outline) to any selection. For instance, you can use selections to give a photo a classy, thin black border or to circle yourself in a group photo (page 181). You can also add a stroke to shapes and paths; you'll learn all about that on page 562.

- **Use it as a mask**. When you create a selection, Photoshop protects the area outside it, so anything you do to the image affects only the selected area. For example, if you paint with the Brush tool across the edge of a selection, it paints only the area *inside* the selection (helpful when adding color to an image that doesn't have any). Likewise, if you create a selection before adding a layer mask (page 108), Photoshop loads the selected area into the mask automatically, letting you adjust only that part of the image. So selections are crucial when you need to swap backgrounds, correct color or lighting in just one area (Chapter 9), or change the color of an object (page 325).

This chapter discusses all these options and more. But first you need to understand how Photoshop indicates selections.

Meet the Marching Ants

When you create a selection, Photoshop calls up a lively army of animated "marching ants" (shown in *Figure 4-1*). These tiny soldiers dutifully march around the edge of the selected area, awaiting your command. You can select part of a layer's contents or everything on a single layer. Whenever you have an active selection (that is, whenever you see marching ants), Photoshop has eyes only for that portion of the document—any tool you use (except the Type, Pen, and shape tools) will affect only the area *inside* the selection.

> **NOTE** Selections don't hang around forever—when you click somewhere outside the selection with a selection tool, the original selection disappears, forcing you to recreate it. However, you can summon the *last* selection you made by choosing Select→Reselect. To find out how to save a selection so you can use it again later, flip to page 179.

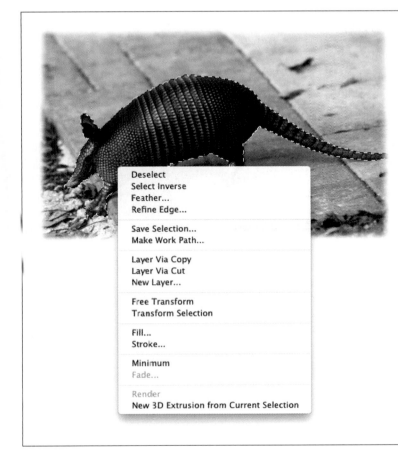

FIGURE 4-1

To let you know an area is selected, Photoshop surrounds it with tiny, moving dashes that look like marching ants. Here you can see the ants running around the armadillo.

If you Control-click (right-click) inside the selection, you see the shortcut menu shown here, which gives you super quick access to frequently-used, selection-related commands.

(FYI, the nine-banded armadillo is the state animal of Texas. Didn't think you'd learn that from this book, did ya?)

Here are the commands you'll use most often when making selections:

- **Select All**. This command selects the entirety of the currently active layer and places marching ants around the perimeter of your document, which is helpful when you want to copy and paste an image from one document into another or create a border around a photo (see page 181). To run this command, go to Select→All or press ⌘-A (Ctrl+A).

- **Deselect**. To get rid of the marching ants after you've finished working with a selection, choose Select→Deselect or press ⌘-D (Ctrl+D). Alternatively, if one of the selection tools is active, you can click once *outside* the selection to get rid of it.

- **Reselect**. To resurrect your last selection, choose Select→Reselect or press Shift-⌘-D (Shift+Ctrl+D). This command reactivates the last selection you made, even if it was five filters and 20 brushstrokes ago (unless you've used the Crop or Type tools since then, which render this command powerless). Reselecting is helpful if you accidentally deselect a selection that took you a long time to create. (The Undo command [⌘-Z/Ctrl+Z] can also help in that situation.)

- **Inverse**. This command, which you run by choosing Select→Inverse or pressing Shift-⌘-I (Shift-Ctrl+I), flip-flops a selection to select everything that *wasn't* selected before. You'll often find it easier to select what you *don't* want and then inverse the selection to get what you *do* want. The box on page 153 has more on this useful technique.

- **Load a layer as a selection**. When talking to people about Photoshop, you'll often hear the phrase "load as a selection," which is (unavoidable) Photoshop-speak for activating a layer that contains the object you want to work with and then summoning the marching ants so they run around that object; that way, whatever you do next affects *only* that object. To load everything that lives on a single layer as a selection, mouse over to the Layers panel and ⌘-click (Ctrl-click) the layer's thumbnail. Photoshop responds by putting marching ants around everything on that layer. Alternatively, you can Control-click (right-click) the layer's thumbnail and then choose Select Pixels from the resulting shortcut menu.

> **TIP**   Although you can find most of the commands in this list in the Select menu at the top of your screen (except for loading a layer as a selection), you should memorize their keyboard shortcuts if you want to be smokin' fast in Photoshop.

Now it's time to discuss the tools you can use to make selections. Photoshop has a ton of 'em, so in the next several pages, you'll find them grouped according to which *kind* of selections they're best at making: by shape, color, and so on. That way, you'll know which tool to start with the next time you need to select something.

Selecting by Shape

Selections based on shape are probably the easiest ones to make. Whether the object you want to grab is rectangular, elliptical, or rectangular with rounded corners, Photoshop has just the tool for you. You'll use the first couple of tools described in this section often, so think of them as your bread and butter when it comes to making selections.

The Rectangular and Elliptical Marquee Tools

Photoshop's most basic selection tools are the Rectangular and Elliptical Marquees. Any time you need to make a selection that's squarish or roundish, reach for these little helpers, which live at the top of the Tools panel, as shown in *Figure 4-2*.

To make a selection with either marquee tool, just grab the tool by clicking its icon in the Tools panel or by pressing M, and then mouse over to your document. When your cursor turns into a tiny + sign, drag across the area you want to select (you'll see the marching ants appear as soon as you start to drag). Photoshop starts the selection where you clicked and continues it in the direction you drag as long as you hold down the mouse button. When you've got marching ants around the area you want to select, release the mouse button.

FIGURE 4-2

You'll spend loads of time making selections with the Rectangular and Elliptical Marquee tools. To summon this menu, click and hold down your mouse button until the menu of additional tools appears.

You can use a variety of tools and techniques to modify your selection, most of which are controlled by the Options bar (*Figure 4-3*). For example, you can do the following:

- **Move the selection**. Click anywhere within the selected area and then drag to another part of your document (your cursor turns into a tiny arrow the second you release the mouse button after drawing a selection—as long as your cursor remains inside the selection, that is).

> **TIP** You can move a selection *as* you're drawing it by moving your mouse while pressing the mouse button *and* the space bar. When you've got the selection where you want it, release the space bar—but not your mouse button—and continue drawing the selection.

- **Add to the selection**. When you click the "Add to selection" button in the Options bar (labeled in *Figure 4-3*) or press and hold the Shift key, Photoshop puts a tiny + sign beneath the cursor to let you know that whatever you drag across next will get added to the current selection. This mode is handy when you need to select areas that don't touch each other, like the doors in *Figure 4-3*, or if you've selected *most* of what you want but notice that you missed a spot. Instead of starting over, simply switch to this mode and draw around that area as if you were creating a new selection.

- **Subtract from the selection**. Clicking the "Subtract from selection" button (also labeled in *Figure 4-3*) or pressing and holding the Option key (Alt on a PC) has the opposite effect. A tiny – sign appears beneath your cursor to let you know you're in this mode. Mouse over to your document and draw a box (or oval) around the area you want to *deselect*.

- **Intersect one selection with another**. If you click the "Intersect with selection" button after you make a selection, Photoshop lets you draw another selection that overlaps the first; the marching ants then surround only the area where the two selections *overlap*. It's a little confusing, but don't worry because you'll rarely use this mode. The keyboard shortcut is Shift-Option (Shift+Alt on a PC). Photoshop puts a tiny multiplication sign (×) beneath your cursor when you're in this mode.

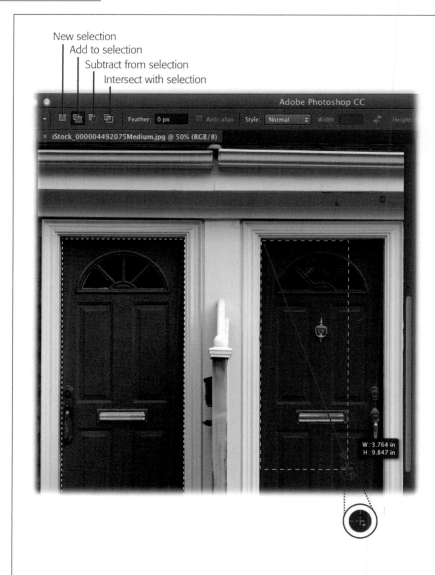

New selection
Add to selection
Subtract from selection
Intersect with selection

FIGURE 4-3

Using the buttons in the Options bar (or better yet, the keyboard shortcuts mentioned in this section), you can add to or subtract from a selection, as well as create a selection from two intersecting areas.

Since all selections begin at the point where you first click, you can easily select one of these doors by dragging diagonally from the top-left corner to the bottom right as shown here. You can tell from the tiny + sign next to the crosshair-shaped cursor that you're in "Add to selection" mode, so this figure now has two selections: the blue door and the red door.

You also get a helpful overlay that displays the width and height info as you drag to create a selection (shown here). If you move a selection, you see X and Y axis info instead that indicates how far you've moved the selection in the document.

Give this selection technique a spin by downloading the practice file Doors.jpg from this book's Missing CD page at www.missingmanuals. com/cds.

- **Feather the selection**. If you want to soften the edges of your selection so that it blends into the background or another image, use *feathering*. You can enter a value in pixels in the Options bar's Feather field *before* you create the selection, as it applies to the next selection you make. As you'll learn later in this chapter, feathering a selection lets you gently fade one image into another image or into a color. See the box on page 141 for the full scoop on feathering, including how to feather a selection *after* you create it.

- **Apply anti-aliasing**. Turn on the Option bar's Anti-alias checkbox to make Photoshop smooth the color transition between the pixels around the edges of your selection and the pixels in the background. Like feathering, anti-aliasing softens the selection's edges slightly so that they blend better, though with anti-aliasing you can't control the *amount* of softening Photoshop applies. It's a good idea to leave this checkbox turned on unless you want your selection to have super crisp—and possibly jagged and blocky—edges.

- **Constrain the selection**. If you want to constrain your selection to a fixed size or aspect ratio (so that the relationship between its width and height stays the same), you can pick Fixed Size or Fixed Ratio from the Option bar's Style menu and then enter the size you want in the resulting Width and Height fields. (Be sure to enter a unit of measurement into each field, too, such as *px* for pixels.) If you leave the Normal option selected, you can draw any size selection you want.

Here's how to select two objects in the same photo, as shown in *Figure 4-3*:

1. **Click the marquee tool icon in the Tools panel and choose the Rectangular Marquee from the menu shown in *Figure 4-2*.**

   Photoshop remembers which marquee tool you last used, so you'll see that tool's icon in the Tools panel. If that's the one you want to use, just press M to activate it. If not, in the Tools panel, click and hold whichever marquee tool icon is showing until the menu appears, and then choose the tool you want.

TIP To cycle between the Rectangular and Elliptical Marquee tools, press M to activate the marquee toolset and then press Shift-M to activate each one in turn. If that doesn't work, make sure a gremlin hasn't turned off the preference that makes this trick possible. Choose Photoshop→Preferences→General (Edit→Preferences→General on a PC) and confirm that the "Use Shift Key for Tool Switch" checkbox is turned on.

---

2. **Drag to draw a box around the first object.**

   For example, to select the blue door shown in *Figure 4-3*, click its top-left corner and drag diagonally toward its bottom-right corner. When you get the whole door in your selection, release the mouse button. Don't worry if you don't get the selection in exactly the right spot; you can move it around in the next step.

3. **If necessary, move your selection into place.**

   To move the selection, just click *inside* the selected area (your cursor turns into a tiny arrow) and drag the selection box where you want it. You can also use the arrow keys on your keyboard to nudge the selection in one direction or another (you don't need to click it first).

4. **Click the "Add to selection" button in the Options bar and then select the second object by drawing a selection around it.**

   Photoshop lets you know that you're in "Add to selection" mode by placing a tiny + sign below the cursor. Once you see it, mouse over to the second door and drag diagonally from its top-left corner to its bottom right, as shown in

Figure 4-3. (Alternatively, you can press and hold the Shift key to put the tool into "Add to selection" mode.)

If you need to move this second selection around, do that *before* you release the mouse button or you'll end up moving both selections instead of just one. To move the selection while you're drawing it, hold down your mouse button, press and hold the space bar, and then drag to move the selection. When it's in the right place, release the space bar—but keep holding the mouse button—and continue dragging to draw the selection. This maneuver feels a bit awkward at first, but you'll get used to it with practice.

Congratulations! You've just made your first selection and added to it. Way to go!

> **TIP** To draw a perfectly square or circular selection, press the Shift key as you drag with the Rectangular or Elliptical Marquee tool, respectively. If you want to draw the selection from the center outward (instead of from corner to corner), press and hold the Option key (Alt on a PC) instead. And if you want to draw a perfectly square or circular selection from the center outward, press and hold Shift-Option (Shift+Alt) as you drag with either tool. Just be sure to use these tricks only on new selections—if you've already got a selection, the Shift key pops you into "Add to selection" mode.

■ CREATING A SOFT VIGNETTE

The Elliptical Marquee tool works just like the Rectangular Marquee tool except that it draws round or oval selections. It's a great tool for selecting things that are, well, *round*, and you can use it to create the ever-popular, oh-so-romantic, soft oval vignette collage shown in *Figure 4-4*. Here's how to create such a vignette:

1. **Open two images and combine them into the same document.**

   Simply drag one image from its Layers panel into the other document's window, as shown on page 96.

2. **Reposition the layers so the soon-to-be-vignetted photo is at the top of the Layers panel.**

   Over in the Layers panel, make sure that both layers are unlocked so you can change their stacking order. If you see a tiny padlock to the right of either layer's name, double-click that layer's thumbnail to unlock it. Then drag the layer containing the photo you want to vignette (in *Figure 4-4*, that's the armadillo pic) to the top of the Layers panel.

3. **Grab the Elliptical Marquee tool and select the part of the image you want to vignette (here, the armadillo's head).**

   Peek at your Layers panel to make sure the correct Image layer is active (the armadillo) and position your cursor near the center of the image. Press and hold the Option key (Alt on a PC), and then drag to draw an oval-shaped selection from the inside out. When you've got the selection big enough, release the Option (Alt) key and your mouse button.

4. **Hide the area outside the selection with a layer mask.**

You *could* simply inverse the selection (page 153) and then press the Delete key (Backspace on a PC) to zap the area outside it, but that'd be mighty reckless. What if you changed your mind? You'd have to undo several steps or start over completely! A less destructive and more flexible approach, which you learned about back on page 108, is to *hide* the area outside the selection with a layer mask. To do that, over in the Layers panel, make sure the correct layer is active (in this case, the armadillo) and then add a layer mask by clicking the tiny circle-within-a-square icon at the bottom of the panel. Photoshop hides everything outside the selection, letting you see through to the bluebonnet layer below. Beautiful!

5. **Feather the selection's edges by using the Properties panel's Feather slider.**

With the layer mask active, open the Properties panel by choosing Window→Properties. In the panel, drag the Feather slider to the right and Photoshop softens the selection right there in the document as you watch. (Alternatively, type a number or decimal value in the text box above the Feather slider.)

FREQUENTLY ASKED QUESTION

The Softer Side of Selections

How come my selections always have hard edges? Can I make them soft instead?

While the selections you make in Photoshop start their lives with hard edges, you can apply *feathering* to soften 'em up. Feathered selections are perfect for blending one image—or a portion of an image—into another image (or another color), as in the soft oval vignette effect, an oldie but goody shown on page 142. You can also feather a selection when you retouch an image, so the re-touched area fades gently into the surrounding pixels, making it look more realistic. This technique is especially helpful when doing things like fixing animal white-eye (page 440) or swapping heads (page 180).

You can feather a selection in a variety of ways:

After you choose a selection tool from the Tools panel—but *before* you create the selection—hop up to the Options bar and enter a Feather amount in pixels (you can enter whole numbers or decimals, like *0.5*). Feathering by just a few pixels blurs and softens the selection's edges only slightly, whereas increasing the Feather setting creates a wider, more intense blur and a super-soft edge.

After you draw a selection, you can change its Feather setting either by choosing Select→Modify→Feather and then enter-

ing a number of pixels or by Control-clicking (right-clicking) the selection and then choosing Feather from the resulting shortcut menu (shown in *Figure 4-1*).

However, if the selection you made is destined to live inside a layer mask, then by far the *best* method is to use the Properties panel's Feather slider, which lets you *see* how the feathered edge will look as well as change it later on. To use this method, create a selection and then add a layer mask. Next, open the Properties panel by choosing Window→Properties and, with the mask active in the Layers panel, drag the Feather slider to the right; Photoshop shows the feathering in your document in real time. If you decide to change the amount of feathering later on, just activate the mask, pop this panel back open, and then tweak the same slider.

You can also use the Refine Edge dialog box to add and view feathering in real time, though this technique is best in cases where you need to feather the selection and tweak it in other ways (such as expanding or contracting it). That said, this method *doesn't* give you the ability to change the feathering amount later. (For more on using the Refine Edge dialog box, see page 165.)

— Mask

FIGURE 4-4

By creating a selection with the Elliptical Marquee tool, adding a layer mask (page 109), and then feathering the mask, you can create a quick two-photo collage like this one. Wedding photographers and moms—not to mention armadillo fans—love this kind of thing! By using the Properties panel to apply a feather, you gain the ability to change the feather amount later on (provided you save the document as a PSD file).

Once you get the hang of this technique, try creating it using the Ellipse tool (one of Photoshop's vector shape tools) set to draw in Path mode, as described on page 536.

6. **Choose File→Save As, and then pick Photoshop as the format.**

   Doing so lets you tweak the Feather amount later on by activating the layer mask and then reopening the Properties panel.

That armadillo looks right at home, doesn't he? You'll want to memorize these steps because this method is perhaps the easiest—and most romantic!—way to combine two images into a new and unique piece of art (although you'll learn how to use the vector shape tools to do the same thing on page 571).

The Single Row and Column Marquee Tools

The Marquee toolset also contains the Single Row Marquee and Single Column Marquee tools, which can select exactly one row or one column's worth of pixels, spanning either the width or the height of your document. You don't need to drag to create a selection with these tools; just click once in your document and the marching ants appear.

You may be wondering, "When would I want to do that?" Not often, it's true, but consider these circumstances:

- **Mocking up a web page design**. If you need to simulate a column or row of space between certain areas in a web page, you can use either tool to create a selection that you fill with the website's background color.

- **Create a repeating background on a web page**. If you're creating an image that you'll use as a repeating background on a web page, select a horizontal row and then instruct your HTML-editing program to repeat or stretch the image as far as you need it. This trick can really decrease the time it takes to download a web page.

- **Stretching an image to fill a space**. If you're designing a web page, for example, you can use these tools to extend an image by a pixel or two. Use either tool to select a row of pixels at the bottom or side of the image, grab the Move tool by pressing V, and then tap an arrow key on your keyboard while holding the Option key (Alt on a PC) to nudge the selection in the direction you need and duplicate it at the same time. However, a better option is to use Content-Aware Scale (see page 251).

- **Making an image look like it's melting or traveling through space at warp speed**. Arguably the most amusing use for these tools, you can use either one to create a selection and then stretch it with the Free Transform tool (see Figure 4-5).

The Vector Shape Tools

Technically, vector shapes aren't selection tools, but you *can* use them to create selections (turn to page 548 to learn more about vector shapes). Once you get the hang of using them as described in this section, you'll be reaching for 'em all the time.

Perhaps the most useful of this bunch is the Rounded Rectangle tool. If you ever need to select an area that's rectangular but has rounded corners, this is your best bet. For example, if you're creating an ad for a digital camera, you can use this technique on a product shot to replace the image shown on the camera's display screen with a different image. Or, more practically, you can use it to give photos rounded corners, as shown in Figure 4-6. Here's how:

1. **Open a photo and double-click the Background layer to unlock it.**

   Because you'll add a *vector* mask to the photo layer in step 5 (in lieu of a pixel-based mask), you need to make sure the Background layer is unlocked or Photoshop won't mask the image.

FIGURE 4-5

Good luck catching this hen! To achieve this look, start by using the Single Column Marquee to select a column of pixels. Then "jump" the selection onto its own layer by pressing ⌘-J (Ctrl+J). Next, summon the Free Transform tool by pressing ⌘-T (Ctrl+T), and drag one of the square, white center handles leftward. Last but not least, add a gradient mask (page 274) and then experiment with blend modes until you find one that makes the stretched pixels blend into the image (for more on blend modes, see page 276).

Unfortunately you can't activate the Single Row and Single Column Marquee tools with a keyboard shortcut; you've got to click their icons in the Tools panel instead.

Create your own speeding hen by downloading the practice file Hen.jpg from this book's Missing CD page at www.missingmanuals.com/cds.

2. **Activate the Rounded Rectangle tool in the Tools panel.**

   Near the bottom of the Tools panel lay the vector shape tools. Unless you've previously activated a different tool, you'll see the Rectangle tool's icon. Click it and hold down your mouse button until the drop-down menu appears, and then choose the Rounded Rectangle tool.

   > **TIP** To cycle through all of Photoshop's shape tools, press Shift-U repeatedly.

3. **In the Options bar, set the tool's mode to Path and change the Radius field to 40 pixels (or whatever looks good to you).**

   As you'll learn on page 535, the vector shape tools can operate in various modes. For this technique, you want to use Path mode. Click the drop-down menu near the left end of the Options bar (it s probably set to Shape) and choose Path. Next, change the number in the Radius field, which controls how rounded the image's corners will be: A lower number causes less rounding than a higher number. This field was set to 40 pixels to create the corners shown in *Figure 4-6*. However, you'll need to use a larger number if you're working with a high-resolution document.

FIGURE 4-6

If you're tired of boring, straight corners on your images, use the Rounded Rectangle tool to produce smooth corners like the ones shown here. Be sure to put the tool in Path mode first using the drop-down menu near the far left of the Options bar, or else you'll create a Shape layer that you don't really need.

You can use the same technique with the Ellipse tool to create the vignette effect shown in the previous section. To feather the mask after you've added it, double-click the mask and then drag the resulting Properties panel's Feather slider to the right.

In Photoshop CC, you can alter the roundness of these corners after you've drawn the shape. Page 554 has the scoop.

TIP   New in Photoshop CC is the ability to change the radius of individual corners *after* you've created the shape using the Properties panel. This fabulous feature is covered on page 554.

---

4. **Draw a box around the image.**

   Mouse over the image and, starting in one corner, drag diagonally to draw a box around the whole image. When you let go of the mouse button, Photoshop displays a thin gray outline atop your image called a *path*, which you'll learn all about in Chapter 13. If you need to move the path while you're drawing it, press and hold the space bar. If you want to move the path *after* you've drawn it, press A to grab the Path Selection tool (its Tools panel icon is a black arrow), click the path to activate it, and then drag to move it wherever you want.

5. **Hide the area outside the path by adding a layer mask.**

   In the Options bar, click the Mask button and Photoshop adds a *vector* layer mask to the image. You can also ⌘-click (Ctrl-click) the tiny circle-within-a-square icon at the bottom of the Layers panel to do the same thing. (Why a vector mask? Because the path you drew with the shape tool is *vector*-based, not pixel-based. As you learned on page 43, you can resize a vector any time without losing quality by activating it and then using Free Transform [page 259]. For more on vector masks, skip ahead to page 571.) Once you add the mask, Photoshop hides the photo's boring, square edges.

Who knew that giving your photo rounded corners was so simple? If you want to place your newly round-edged photo on top of another background in presentation software or on a website, choose File→Save As and pick PNG as the format. As you know from Chapter 2, the PNG format supports transparency. You'll learn more about using the PNG format on page 723.

Selecting by Color

In addition to tools for selecting areas by shape, Photoshop has tools that let you select areas by *color*. This option is helpful when you want to select a chunk of an image that's fairly uniform in color, like someone's skin, the sky, or the paint job on a car. Photoshop has lots of tools to choose from, and in this section, you'll learn how to pick the one that best suits your needs.

The Quick Selection Tool

The Quick Selection tool is shockingly easy to use and lets you create complex selections with just a few brushstrokes. As you paint with this tool, your selection expands to encompass pixels similar in color to the ones you're brushing *across*. It works insanely well if there's a fair amount of contrast between what you want to select and everything else. This tool lives in the same toolset as the Magic Wand, as you can see in *Figure 4-7*.

To use this friendly tool, click anywhere in the area you want to select or *drag* the brush cursor across it, as shown in *Figure 4-8*. When you do that, Photoshop thinks for a second and then creates a selection based on the color of the pixels you clicked or brushed across. The size of the area it selects is proportional to the size of the *brush* you're using: A larger brush creates a larger selection. You adjust the Quick Selection tool's brush size just like any other brush: by choosing a new size from the Brush picker in the Options bar, or by using the left and right bracket keys ([and]) to decrease and increase brush size (respectively). (Chapter 12 covers brushes in detail.) For the best results, use a hard-edged brush to produce well-defined edges (instead of the slightly transparent edges produced by a soft-edged brush) and turn on the Auto-Enhance setting shown in *Figure 4-7* and discussed in the box on page 149.

Add to selection
New selection | Subtract from selection

FIGURE 4-7

You can press the W key to activate the Quick Selection tool. (To switch between it and the Magic Wand, press Shift-W.)

When you activate the Quick Selection tool, the Options bar sports buttons that let you create a new selection as well as add to or subtract from the current selection.

When the Quick Selection tool is active, the Options bar includes these settings (see *Figure 4-7*):

- **New selection**. When you first grab the Quick Selection tool, it's set to this mode, which creates a brand-new selection when you click or drag (indicated by the tiny + sign that appears inside the cursor, as shown in *Figure 4-8*).

FIGURE 4-8

If the color of the objects you want to select differs greatly from their background color, like these chili peppers, use the Quick Selection tool. With this tool, you can either click the area you want to select or drag your cursor (circled) across the area as if you were painting. When you start painting with this tool, you see a tiny + sign inside the cursor (as shown here) and Photoshop puts the tool in "Add to selection" mode, which lets you add to an existing selection or make multiple selections.

- **Add to selection**. Once you've clicked or made an initial brushstroke, the Quick Selection tool automatically switches to this mode. Now Photoshop adds any areas you brush over or click to the current selection. If you don't like the selection Photoshop has created and want to start over, press ⌘-Z (Ctrl+Z) to undo it, or click the Options bar's "New selection" button and then brush across the area again. (The old selection disappears as soon as you start a new one.) To get rid of the marching ants altogether, choose Select→Deselect.

- **Subtract from selection**. If Photoshop selected more than you wanted it to, click the "Subtract from selection" button (a tiny – sign appears in your cursor) and then simply paint across the area you *don't* want selected to make Photoshop exclude it. You can also press and hold the Option key (Alt on a PC) to enter "Subtract from selection" mode.

> **NOTE** To get the most out of the Quick Selection tool, you'll probably need to do a fair amount of adding to and subtracting from your selections (unless there's a ton of contrast between the item you want to select and its background, that is). That said, you can change how picky this tool is by adjusting the Magic Wand's *Tolerance* setting (sounds strange, but it's true). Flip to page 149 to learn how.

- **Brush Size/Hardness**. Use a larger brush to select big areas and a smaller brush to select small or hard-to-reach areas. As explained earlier, you'll get better results with this tool by using a hard-edged brush instead of a soft-edged one.

> **TIP** You can change a brush cursor's size by Control-Option-dragging left or right (Alt+right-click+dragging on a PC); to adjust hardness, drag up or down instead. Alternatively, you can press the left bracket key ([) to decrease brush size or the right bracket key (]) to increase it.

- **Sample All Layers**. This setting is initially turned off, which means Photoshop selects only the pixels on the active layer (the one that's highlighted in the Layers panel). If you turn this setting on, Photoshop examines the whole enchilada—all the layers in your document—and grabs every pixel you paint across no matter which layer it's on.

- **Auto-Enhance**. Because the Quick Selection tool makes selections extremely quickly, their edges can end up looking blocky and imperfect. Turn on this checkbox to tell Photoshop to take its time and think more carefully about the selections it makes. This feature gives your selections smoother edges, but if you're working with a really big file, you could do your taxes while it's processing. The box on page 149 has tips for using this feature.

The Magic Wand Tool

The Magic Wand lets you select areas of color by clicking rather than dragging. It's in the same toolset as the Quick Selection tool, and you can grab it by pressing Shift-W (it looks like a wizard's wand, as shown back in *Figure 4-7*). The Magic Wand is great for selecting solid-colored backgrounds or large bodies of similar color, like a cloudless sky, with just a couple of clicks. (The Quick Selection tool is better at selecting objects.)

When you click once with the Magic Wand in the area you want to select, Photoshop magically (hence the name) selects all the pixels on the currently active layer that are both similar in color *and* touching one another (see page 150 to learn how to tweak this behavior). If the color in the area you want to select varies a bit, Photoshop may not select all of it. In that case, you can add to the selection either by pressing the Shift key as you click nearby areas or by modifying the Magic Wand's *tolerance* in the Options bar as described in a sec and shown in *Figure 4-9*. To subtract from the selection, just press and hold the Option key (Alt on a PC) while you click the area you don't want included.

When you activate the Magic Wand, the Options bar includes these settings:

- **Sample Size**. This menu lets you change the way the Magic Wand calculates which pixels to select (prior to CS6, you had to switch to the Eyedropper tool to see this menu). From the factory, it's set to Point Sample, which makes the tool look only at the color of the specific pixel you clicked when determining its selection. However, the menu's other options cause it to look at the original pixel *and* average it with the colors of surrounding pixels. For example, you can make the Magic Wand average the pixel you clicked plus the eight surrounding pixels by choosing "3 by 3 Average," or as much as the surrounding 10,200 pixels by choosing "101 by 101 Average." The "3 by 3 Average" setting works well for most images. If you need to select a really big area, you can experiment with one of the higher settings, like "31 by 31 Average."

- **Tolerance**. This setting controls both the Magic Wand's and the Quick Selection tool's sensitivity—how picky each tool is about which pixels it considers similar in color. If you increase this setting, the tool gets less picky (in other words, more tolerant) and selects every pixel that could possibly be described as similar to the one you clicked. If you decrease this setting, the tool gets pickier and selects only pixels that *closely* match the one you clicked.

WORKAROUND WORKSHOP

Smart Auto-Enhancing

The Quick Selection tool's Auto-Enhance feature is pretty cool, but it's a bit of a processing hog. If you have an older computer, you may have better luck using the Refine Edge dialog box to create selections with smooth edges. (See page 165 for more on the Refine Edge command.)

That said, you don't have to avoid Auto-Enhance altogether. When you're working with a large file (anything over 100 MB),

leave the Auto-Enhance checkbox turned off until you're *almost* finished making the selection. Then, when you've got just one or two brushstrokes left to complete the selection, turn on the checkbox to make Photoshop re-examine the edges of the selection it's already created to see if it needs to extend them. That way, you get the benefit of using Auto-Enhance *and* keep your computer running quickly until the last possible moment.

FIGURE 4-9

*With its tolerance set to
32, the Magic Wand did a
good job of selecting the
sky behind downtown
Dallas.*

*You've got several ways to
select the spots it missed,
like the area circled at the
bottom left: You can add
to the selection by pressing the Shift key as you
click in that area; increase
the Tolerance setting in the
Options bar and then click
the sky again to create a
brand-new selection; or
flip to page 151 to learn
how to expand the selec-
tion with the Grow and
Similar commands.*

TIP Give this selection technique a shot by downloading the practice file *Dallas.jpg* from this book's Missing CD page at *www.missingmanuals.com/cds*.

The tolerance is initially set to 32, but it can go all the way up to 255. (If you set it to 0, Photoshop selects only pixels that *exactly* match the one you clicked; if you set it to 255, the program selects every color in the image.) It's usually a good idea to keep the tolerance fairly low (somewhere between 12 and 32); you can always click an area to see what kind of selection you get, increase the tolerance if you need to, and then click that area again (or add to the selection using the Shift key, as described above).

NOTE When you adjust the Magic Wand's tolerance, Photoshop doesn't adjust your *current* selection. You have to click the area *again* to make Photoshop rethink its selection.

- **Anti-alias**. Leave this setting turned on to make Photoshop soften the edges of the selection ever so slightly. If you want a super-crisp edge, turn it off.

- **Contiguous**. You'll probably want to leave this checkbox turned on; it makes the Magic Wand select pixels that are adjacent to one another. If you turn it off, Photoshop goes hog wild and selects all similar-colored pixels no matter where they are.

- **Sample All Layers**. If your document has multiple layers and you leave this checkbox turned off, Photoshop examines only pixels on the active layer and ignores the other layers. If you turn this setting on, Photoshop examines the whole image and selects all pixels that are similar in color, no matter which layer they're on.

NOTE The Magic Wand is rather notorious for making the edges of selections jagged (that's why some folks refer to this tool as the *Tragic* Wand!). That's because it concentrates on selecting *whole* pixels rather than partially transparent ones (this doesn't happen as much with the Quick Selection tool). The fix is to click the Refine Edge button in the Options bar after you make a selection, and then adjust the Smooth slider in the resulting dialog box. Skip ahead to page 165 to learn how.

■ EXPANDING YOUR SELECTION

Sometimes the Magic Wand makes a *nearly* perfect selection, leaving you with precious few pixels to add to it. If this happens, it simply means that the elusive pixels are just a little bit lighter or darker in color than what the Magic Wand's tolerance setting allows for. You *could* Shift-click the elusive areas to add them to your selection, but the Select menu has a couple of options that can quickly expand the selection for you:

- **Choose Select→Grow** to make Photoshop expand the selection to all similar-colored pixels adjacent to it (see *Figure 4-10*, top).

- **Choose Select→Similar** to make Photoshop select similar-colored pixels throughout the *whole* image even if they're not touching the original selection (see *Figure 4-10*, bottom).

NOTE Because both of these commands base their calculations on the Magic Wand's Tolerance setting (page 149), you can adjust their sensitivity by adjusting that setting in the Options bar. You also can run these commands more than once to get the selection you want.

The Color Range Command

The Color Range command is similar to the tools in this section in that it makes selections based on colors, but it's much better at selecting areas that contain lots of details (for example, the flower bunches in *Figure 4-11*). The Magic Wand tends to select *solid* pixels, whereas Color Range tends to select more *transparent* pixels than solid ones, resulting in softer edges. This fine-tuning lets Color Range produce selections with smoother edges (less blocky and jagged than the ones you get with the Magic Wand) and get in more tightly around areas with lots of details. As a bonus, you also get a handy preview in the Color Range dialog box, showing you which pixels it'll select *before* you commit to the selection (unlike the Grow and Similar commands discussed in the previous section).

FIGURE 4-10

Top: Say you're trying to select the red part of this Texas flag. After clicking once with the Magic Wand (with a Tolerance setting of 32), you still need to select a bit more of the red (left). Since the red pixels are all touching one another, you can run the Grow command a couple of times to make Photoshop expand your selection to include all the red (right).

Bottom: If you want to select the red in these playing cards (what a poker hand!), the Grow command won't help because the red pixels aren't touching one another. In that case, click once with the Magic Wand to select one of the red areas (left) and then use the Similar command to grab the rest of them (right). Read 'em and weep, boys!

TIP   You can also use the Color Range command's Skin Tones option to select people. The box on page 155 has the details.

Open the Color Range dialog box by choosing Select→Color Range, either before or after you make a selection. If you haven't yet made a selection, Photoshop examines the entire image. If you already have a selection, Photoshop looks only at the pixels within the selected area, which is helpful if you want to isolate a certain area. For example, you could throw a quick selection around the red flower in the center of *Figure 4-11* and then use Color Range's subtract-from-selection capabilities (explained in a moment) to carve out just the red petals. By contrast, if you want to use Color Range to help *expand* your current selection, press and hold the Shift key while you choose Select→Color Range.

FIGURE 4-11

The Color Range command is handy when you need to select an area with lots of details, like the red and blue petals of these flowers. The dialog box's preview area shows which parts of the image Photoshop will select when you click OK (they're displayed in white). If you want to save your settings to use again later, click the Save button and give the preset a meaningful name. (In CC, Color Range presets are stored in the same location as the rest of your presets.)

As mentioned in the box on page 153, it's some-times easier to select what you don't *want in order to get the selection you need. To use the Color Range dialog box to select what you don't want, turn on its Invert checkbox.*

Selecting the Opposite

You'll often find it easier to select what you *don't* want in order to get the selection you *do* want. For example, look back at the photo of the Dallas skyline in *Figure 4-9*. If you want to select the buildings, it's easier to select the sky instead because its color is practically uniform. (It'd take you a lot longer to select the buildings because they're irregularly shaped and vary so much in color.)

After selecting the sky, you then can inverse (flip-flop) your se-lection to select the buildings. Simply choose Select→Inverse or press Shift-⌘-I (Shift+Ctrl+I). The lesson here is that it pays to spend a few moments studying the area you want to select and the area *around* it. If the color of the surrounding area is uniform, reach for one of the tools described in this section, select that area, and then inverse the selection to save yourself tons of time!

Use the Select drop-down menu at the top of the Color Range dialog box to tell Photoshop which colors to include in the selection. The menu is automatically set to Sampled Colors, which lets you mouse over to the image (your cursor turns into a tiny eyedropper as shown in *Figure 4-11*) and click the color you want to select. If you change the Select menu's setting to Reds, Blues, Greens, or whatever, Color Range will examine your image and grab that range of colors all by itself once you click OK.

If you're trying to select adjacent pixels, turn on the Localized Color Clusters checkbox. When you do, the Range slider becomes active so you can tweak the range of colors Photoshop includes in the selection. Increase this setting and Photoshop includes more colors and makes larger selections; lower it and Photoshop creates smaller selections because it gets pickier about matching colors.

You can tweak the point at which Photoshop *partially* selects pixels by adjusting the Fuzziness setting. Its factory setting is 40, but you can set it to anything between 0 and 200. As you move the Fuzziness slider (or type a number in the text box), keep an eye on the dialog box's preview area—the parts of the image that Photoshop will fully include in the selection appear white, and any pixels that are partially selected appear gray (see *Figure 4-11*).

TIP In Photoshop CC, the Color Range dialog box remembers the settings and sample colors you used the *last* time you opened it. In previous versions of the program, it remembered nothing, plus it automatically used your foreground color chip as the sample color. If you *want* to use your foreground color chip as the sample color, press and hold the space bar when you choose the command from the Select menu. When the Color Range dialog box opens, the Select menu reads "Selected Colors" and any areas in your image that are the same color as your foreground color chip are automatically selected and shown in white.

Use the eyedroppers on the dialog box's right side to add or subtract colors from your selection; the eyedropper with the tiny + sign adds to the selection, and the one with the – sign subtracts from it. (Use the plain eyedropper to make your initial selection.) When you click one of these eyedroppers, mouse over to your image, and then click the color you want to add or subtract, Photoshop updates the dialog box's preview to show what the new selection looks like. It sometimes helps to keep the Fuzziness setting fairly low (around 50 or so) while you click repeatedly with the eyedropper.

TIP You can use the radio buttons beneath the Color Range dialog box's preview area to see either the selected area (displayed in white) or the image itself. But there's a better, faster way to switch between the two views: With the Selection radio button turned on, press the ⌘ key (Ctrl on a PC) to temporarily switch to image preview. When you let go of the key, you're back to selection preview.

The Selection Preview menu at the bottom of the dialog box lets you display a selection preview on the image itself so that, instead of using the dinky preview in the dialog box, you can see the proposed selection right on your image. But you'll probably want to leave this menu set to None because the preview options that Photoshop offers (Grayscale, Black Matte, and so on) get really distracting!

Selecting Skin Tones and Faces

The Color Range dialog box can also help you to select skin tones. This feature is helpful for making a quick selection of skin tones in order to correct just that part of an image, or to create a layer mask that *protects* skin tones when you're sharpening, blurring, and so on.

To use it, head to the dialog box's Select menu and choose Skin Tones. Photoshop immediately hunts down all the colors in the image that are similar to those found in a wide variety of human skin (though don't expect it to work well on all ethnicities). You can then use the Fuzziness slider to fine-tune the selection; drag it left to include less skin or right to include more.

If you're after faces in particular, turn on the Detect Faces checkbox, and Photoshop locks for faces and includes 'em in your selection. (The Detect Faces checkbox becomes active when you choose Skin Tones from the Select menu; if you choose Sampled Colors instead, you have to turn on the Localized Color Clusters checkbox before you can turn on Detect Faces.) Selections made with Detect Faces turned on include partially transparent pixels around the faces' edges so the changes you make will blend better with surrounding pixels (partially transparent pixels look gray in the preview area).

When this feature was introduced in CS6, it worked on only a handful of images, though Adobe beefed up its abilities in CC. That said, if your image includes a face that's turned in profile or if skin-like colors are found elsewhere in the image—think light-colored hair, a nude-colored shirt, and so on—you're better off using the Quick Selection tool *first* and then having a go with Color Range.

The Background and Magic Erasers

These two tools let you erase parts of an image based on the color under your cursor *without* having to create a selection first. You're probably thinking, "Hey, I want to create a selection, not go around erasing stuff!" And you have a valid point except that, after you've done a little erasing, you can always *load* the erased area (or what's left) as a selection. All you have to do is think ahead and create a duplicate layer before you start erasing, as this section explains.

Say you have an image with a strong contrast between the item you want to select and its background, like a dead tree against the sky (*Figure 4-13*). In that case, Photoshop has a couple of tools that can help you erase the sky super fast (see *Figure 4-12*). Sure, you *could* use the Magic Wand or Quick Selection tool to select the sky and then delete or mask it (page 109), but the Background Eraser lets you erase more carefully around the edges of the tree.

> **TIP** The Eraser tool's keyboard shortcut is the E key. To switch among the various eraser tools in its toolset, press Shift-E repeatedly.

FIGURE 4-12

You may never see these tools because they're hidden inside the same toolset as the regular Eraser tool. Just click and hold the Eraser tool's icon until this little menu appears. Pick an eraser based on how you want to use it: You drag with the Background Eraser (as if you were painting, which is great for getting around the edges of an object), whereas you simply click with the Magic Eraser.

■ THE BACKGROUND ERASER

This tool lets you delete an image's background by painting (dragging) across the pixels you want to delete. When you activate the Background Eraser, your cursor turns into a circle with tiny crosshairs in its center. The crosshairs control which pixels Photoshop deletes, so be extra careful that they touch *only* pixels you want to erase. The size of the brush cursor controls how far into the image Photoshop hunts for pixels to erase. Up in the Options bar, you can tweak the following settings (see *Figure 4-13*):

- **Brush Preset picker**. This is where you choose the shape and size of your brush cursor. For best results, stick with a soft-edged brush. Just click the down-pointing triangle next to this menu, and then lower the Hardness setting slightly.

- **Sampling**. This setting is made up of three buttons whose icons all include eyedroppers (they're labeled in *Figure 4-13*). Sampling controls how often Photoshop looks at the color the crosshairs are touching to decide what to erase. If your image's background has a lot of color variation, leave this set to Continuous so Photoshop keeps a constant watch on what color pixels the crosshairs are touching. But if the background's color is fairly uniform, change this setting to Once; Photoshop then checks the color the crosshairs touch just once and resolves to erase only pixels that closely match it. If you're dealing with an image where there's only a small area for you to paint (like a tiny portion of sky showing through a lush tree), change this setting to Background Swatch, which tells Photoshop to erase only colors that are similar to your current background color chip (*how* similar they have to be is controlled by the tool's Tolerance setting, which is described in a sec). To choose the color, click the background color chip at the bottom of the Tools panel, mouse over to your image, and then click an area that's the color you want to erase.

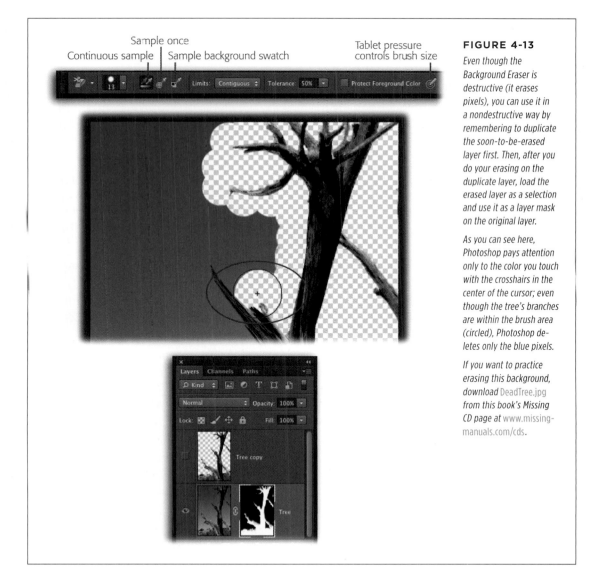

FIGURE 4-13

Even though the Background Eraser is destructive (it erases pixels), you can use it in a nondestructive way by remembering to duplicate the soon-to-be-erased layer first. Then, after you do your erasing on the duplicate layer, load the erased layer as a selection and use it as a layer mask on the original layer.

As you can see here, Photoshop pays attention only to the color you touch with the crosshairs in the center of the cursor; even though the tree's branches are within the brush area (circled), Photoshop deletes only the blue pixels.

If you want to practice erasing this background, download DeadTree.jpg *from this book's Missing CD page at* www.missing-manuals.com/cds.

- **Limits**. From the factory, this field is set to Contiguous, which means the tool erases only pixels adjacent to those you touch with the crosshairs. If you want to erase similar-colored pixels elsewhere in the image (for example, the background behind a really thick tree or a bunch of flowers), change this setting to Discontiguous. Find Edges erases only adjacent pixels, but it does so while preserving the sharpness of the object's edge.

- **Tolerance**. This setting works just like the Magic Wand's Tolerance setting (page 149): A lower number makes the tool pickier about the pixels it erases, and a higher number makes it less picky.

- **Protect Foreground Color**. If you've cranked up the Tolerance setting and you're *still* erasing some of the area you want to keep, turning on this checkbox can help. When it's on, you can tell Photoshop which area you want to keep (the foreground) by Option-clicking (Alt-clicking on a PC) that area. When the area you're erasing around changes to a different color, be sure to Option-click (Alt-click) to update the protected color (you'll do this often when erasing around hair or fur). Option-click (Alt-click) to resample the foreground area.

TIP   To use the Background Eraser on a uniformly colored background around fine details like hair or fur, try setting the Sampling method to Once, the Limits menu to Discontiguous, and turning on the Protect Foreground Color checkbox. Next, mouse over to the image and Option-click (Alt-click on a PC) one of the strands of hair. Then, when you paint across the image, Photoshop *should* protect the color of the hair, keeping it from being erased. Increase your brush size to erase bits of the background that are peeking through strands of hair. For the best results, perfect your erasing on the duplicate layer and skip adding a layer mask, as the following steps describe, because the fine edges around hair or fur won't look as good after you load 'em as a selection and add a mask.

Here's how to use the Background Eraser to remove the sky behind a dead tree *without* harming the original pixels, as shown in *Figure 4-13*:

1. **Open a photo, duplicate the image (or Background layer) by pressing ⌘-J (Ctrl+J), and then hide the original layer.**

   Because you'll do your erasing on the duplicate layer, you don't need to see the original layer. Over in the Layers panel, click the visibility eye to the left of the original layer's thumbnail to turn it off.

2. **Grab the Background Eraser tool and paint away the background.**

   This tool is in the same toolset as the Eraser tool (see *Figure 4-12*). Once you've activated it, mouse over to your document; your cursor morphs into a circle with tiny crosshairs in the center. Remember that the trick is to let the crosshairs touch *only* the pixels you want to erase; adjust the size of the brush cursor to control how far into your image Photoshop looks for pixels to delete. If you need to, increase and decrease the brush cursor's size by pressing the left and right bracket keys on your keyboard, respectively.

3. **If the tool is erasing too much or too little of the image, tweak the Tolerance setting in the Options bar.**

   If an area in the image is *almost* the same color as the background, lower the tolerance to make the tool pickier about what it's erasing so that it erases only pixels that closely match the ones you touch with the crosshairs. Likewise, if it's not erasing enough of the background, raise the tolerance to make it zap more pixels.

> **TIP** It's better to erase *small* sections at a time instead of painting around the entire object in one continuous stroke. Drag to erase some of the area around the object, let go of the button, drag again to erase a little more, and so on. That way, if you need to undo your erasing with the History panel or the Undo command (⌘-Z or Ctrl+Z), you won't have to watch *all* that erasing unravel before your eyes. This maneuver also lets you be very precise with your erasing, as you can undo small sections and adjust the tool's settings to do a better job around tough areas such as hair or fur.

4. **Once you get a clean outline around the object, switch to the regular Eraser tool or the Lasso tool (page 161) to get rid of the remaining big chunks of background.**

   After you erase the hard part—the area around the edges—with the Background Eraser, use the regular Eraser tool, set to a large brush, to get rid of the remaining background quickly. Or use the Lasso tool to select the remaining areas and then press the Delete key (Backspace on a PC) to get rid of 'em.

5. **Load the erased layer as a selection and turn off its visibility.**

   Over in the Layers panel, ⌘-click (Ctrl-click) the thumbnail of the layer you did the erasing work on to create a selection around the tree. When you see the marching ants, click the layer's visibility eye to hide it. (As the Tip at the beginning of this list explains, if you're erasing around hair or fur, skip loading the layer as a selection and adding a mask.)

6. **Activate the original layer, turn on its visibility, and then add a layer mask to it.**

   In the Layers panel, click once to activate the original layer (or Background layer) and then click the area to the left of its thumbnail to make it visible again. While you have marching ants running around the newly erased area, add a layer mask to the original layer by clicking the circle-within-a-square icon at the bottom of the Layers panel.

You're basically done at this point, but if you need to do any cleanup work (if the Background Eraser didn't do a perfect job getting around the edges, say), now's the time to edit the layer mask. To do so, click the mask's thumbnail over in the Layers panel. Then press B to grab the Brush tool and set your foreground color chip to black. Now, when you brush across the image, you'll hide more of the sky. If you need to reveal more of the tree, set your foreground color chip to white, and then paint the area you want to reveal. (See page 108 for a detailed discussion of creating and editing layer masks.) Alternatively, you can use the Refine Edge dialog box to fine-tune your selection *before* adding the mask; page 165 tells you how.

Sure, duplicating the layer you're erasing adds an extra step, but that way you're not deleting any pixels—you're just hiding them with a layer mask, so you can get 'em back if you want to. How cool is that?

■ THE MAGIC ERASER

This tool works just like the Background Eraser except that, instead of a brush cursor that you paint with, it has a cursor that looks like a cross between the Eraser tool and the Magic Wand. Just as the Magic Wand can select color with a single click, the Magic Eraser can *zap* color with a single click, so it's great for instantly erasing areas of solid color. Since this tool is an eraser, it really will *delete* pixels, so you'll want to duplicate your Background layer before using it.

You can alter the Magic Eraser's behavior by adjusting these Options bar settings:

- **Tolerance**. You guessed it: this setting works just like the Magic Wand's Tolerance setting (page 149). A lower number makes the tool pickier about the pixels it erases, and a higher number makes it less picky.

- **Anti-alias**. Turning this checkbox on makes Photoshop slightly soften the edges of what it erases.

- **Contiguous**. To erase pixels that touch one another, leave this checkbox turned on. To erase similar-colored pixels no matter *where* they are in the image, turn it off.

- **Sample All Layers**. If you have a multilayer document, turn on this checkbox to make Photoshop look at the pixels on *all* the layers instead of just the active one.

- **Opacity**. To control how strong the Magic Eraser is, enter a value here. Initially, this option is set to 100, which removes 100 percent of the image, but you can enter *50* to make it wipe away 50 percent of the image's color, for example.

◼ Selecting Irregular Areas

As you might imagine, areas selecting by colorthat aren't uniform in shape *or* color can be a real bear to select. Luckily, Photoshop has a few tools in its arsenal to help you get the job done as easily as possible. In this section, you'll learn about the three lassos and the Pen tool, as well as a few ways to use these tools together to select hard-to-grab spots.

WORKAROUND WORKSHOP

Erasing Every Bit of Background

Now that you know how to use the Background and Magic Erasers, keep in mind that you can't always believe what you see onscreen. Most of the time, you'll use these tools to erase to a transparent (checkerboard) background like the one shown in *Figure 4-13*. And while it may *appear* that you've erased all the background, you may not have. The checkerboard pattern is notorious for making it hard to see whether you've missed a pixel or two here and there, especially if the background you're trying to delete is white or gray (like clouds).

Fortunately, it's easy to overcome this checkered obstacle. The next time you're ready to use one of these eraser tools, first create a new Solid Color Fill layer, then pick a bright color

that contrasts with what you're trying to delete and place the layer at the bottom of the layer stack. That way, you can see whether you've erased everything you wanted to. (Alternatively, if you're erasing the background of one image only to replace it with another, go ahead and add the new background to your document.)

Here's how: Click the half-black/half-white circle at the bottom of the Layers panel and choose Solid Color from the drop-down menu. Select a bright color from the resulting Color Picker, and then click OK. Drag the new layer beneath the layer you're erasing, and you're good to go. (See Chapter 3 for more on Fill layers.)

The Lasso Tools

The lasso toolset contains three freeform tools that let you draw an outline around the area you want to select. If you've got an amazingly steady mouse hand or if you use a graphics tablet (see the box on page 517), you may fall in love with the plain ol' Lasso tool. If you're trying to select an object with a lot of straight edges, the Polygonal Lasso tool will do you proud. And the Magnetic Lasso tries to create a selection *for* you by examining the color of the pixels your cursor is over. The following sections explain all three tools, which share a slot near the top of the Tools panel (see *Figure 4-14*).

FIGURE 4-14

So many lassos, so little time! The regular Lasso tool is great for drawing a selection freehand, the Polygonal Lasso is good for drawing selections around shapes that have a lot of straight lines, and the Magnetic Lasso is like an automatic version of the regular Lasso—it tries to make the selection for you.

◼ LASSO TOOL

The regular Lasso tool lets you draw a selection completely freeform as if you were drawing with a pencil. To activate this tool, simply click it in the Tools panel (its icon looks like a tiny lasso—no surprise there) or press the L key. Then click in your document and drag to create a selection. Once you stop drawing and release the mouse button, Photoshop automatically completes the selection with a straight line (that is, if you don't complete it yourself by mousing back over your starting point) and you see marching ants.

The Options bar sports the same settings whether you have the Lasso tool or the Polygonal Lasso tool active. Here's what you get:

- **Mode**. These four buttons (whose icons look like pieces of paper and are labeled in *Figure 4-14*) let you choose among the same modes you get for most of the selection tools: New, "Add to selection," "Subtract from selection," and "Intersect with selection." They're discussed in detail back on page 137.

- **Feather**. If you want Photoshop to soften the edges of your selection, enter a pixel value in this field. Otherwise, the selection will have a hard edge. (See the box on page 141 for more on feathering.)

- **Anti-alias**. If you leave this setting turned on, Photoshop slightly blurs the edges of your selection, making them less jagged—page 139 has the details.

- **Refine Edge**. This button summons the mighty Refine Edge dialog box, which you can use to fine-tune your selections (and it's *especially* helpful when you're selecting hair and fur). You'll learn all about it later in this chapter, starting on page 165.

■ POLYGONAL LASSO TOOL

If your image has a lot of straight lines in it (like the star in *Figure 4-15*), the Polygonal Lasso tool is your ticket. Instead of letting you draw a selection that's any shape at all, the Polygonal Lasso draws only *straight* lines. To use it, click once to set the starting point, and move your cursor along the shape of the item you want to select; click again where the angle changes; and then repeat this process until you've outlined the whole shape. It's super simple to use, as *Figure 4-15* illustrates. To complete the selection, point your cursor at the first point you created. When a tiny circle appears below the cursor (it looks like a degree symbol), click once to close the selection and summon the marching ants.

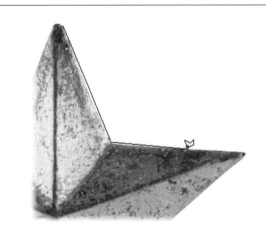

FIGURE 4-15

The Polygonal Lasso tool is perfect for selecting geometric shapes and areas that have a lot of angles. However, if you want to temporarily switch to the regular Lasso tool, press and hold Option (Alt on a PC) to draw freehand.

If you're using the regular Lasso tool, it's nearly impossible to draw a straight line unless you've got the steady hand of a surgeon. But if you press and hold the Option key (Alt on a PC) and then release your mouse button, you'll temporarily switch to the Polygonal Lasso tool so you can draw a straight line. When you release the Option (Alt) key, Photoshop completes your selection with a straight line.

TIP To bail out of a selection you've started to draw with any Lasso tool, just press the Esc key.

■ MAGNETIC LASSO TOOL

This tool has all the power of the other lasso tools, except that it's smart—or at least it tries to be! Click once to set a starting point, and from there the Magnetic Lasso tries to *guess* what you want to select by examining the colors of the pixels your cursor is over (you don't even need to hold your mouse button down). As you move your cursor over the edges you want to select, it sets additional *anchor points* for you (anchor points are fastening points that latch onto the path you're tracing; they look like tiny, see-through squares). To close the selection, put the cursor above your starting point. When a tiny circle appears below the cursor, click once to close the selection and summon the marching ants (or close the selection with a straight line by triple-clicking).

As you might imagine, the Magnetic Lasso tool works best when there's strong contrast between the item you want to select and the area around it (see *Figure 4-16*). However, if you reach an area that doesn't have much contrast—or a sharp corner—you can give the tool a little nudge by clicking to set a few anchor points of your own. If it goes astray and sets an erroneous anchor point, tap the Delete key (Backspace on a PC) to get rid of the point and then click to set more anchor points until you reach an area of greater contrast where the tool can be trusted to set its own points.

Starting point   Anchor points   Cursor   Use tablet pressure to change pen width

FIGURE 4-16

If you're trying to select an object on a plain, high-contrast background, the Magnetic Lasso works great because it can easily find the edge of the object. For best results, glide your cursor slowly around the edge of the item you want to select (you don't need to hold your mouse button down). To draw a straight line, temporarily switch to the Polygonal Lasso tool by Option-clicking (Alt-clicking on a PC) where you want the line to start and then clicking where you want it to end. Photoshop then switches back to the Magnetic Lasso, and you're free to continue gliding around the rest of the object's edges.

TIP If you're not crazy about the Magnetic Lasso's cursor (which looks like a triangle and a horseshoe magnet), press the Caps Lock key and it changes to a brush cursor with crosshairs at its center. Press Caps Lock again to switch back to the standard cursor. Alternatively, you can use Photoshop's preferences to change it to a precise cursor; page 24 explains how.

You can get better results with this tool by adjusting its Options bar settings (shown in *Figure 4-16*). Besides the usual suspects like selection mode, feather, and anti-alias settings (all discussed on pages 137–139), the Magnetic Lasso also lets you adjust the following:

- **Width** determines how close your cursor needs to be to an edge for the Magnetic Lasso to select it. From the factory, this field is set to 10 pixels, but you can enter a value between 1 and 256. Use a lower number when you're trying to select an area whose edge has a lot of twists and turns and a higher number for an area with fairly smooth edges. For example, to select the yellow rose in *Figure 4-16*, you'd use a higher setting around the petals and a lower setting around the leaves because they're so jagged.

TIP You can change the Width setting in 1-pixel increments *before* you start drawing with the Magnetic Lasso by pressing the [and] keys. You can also press Shift-[to set the width to 1 and Shift-] to set it to 256.

- **Contrast** controls how much color difference there needs to be between neighboring pixels before the Magnetic Lasso recognizes it as an edge. You can try increasing this percentage when you want to select an edge that isn't well defined, but you might have better luck with a different selection tool. If you're a fan of keyboard shortcuts—and you haven't started drawing a selection—press the comma (,) or period (.) key to decrease or increase this setting in 1 percent increments, respectively; add the Shift key to these keyboard shortcuts to set it to 1 percent or 100 percent, respectively.

- **Frequency** determines how many anchor points the tool lays down. If you're selecting an area with lots of details, you'll need more anchor points than for a smooth area. Setting this field to 0 makes Photoshop add very few points, and 100 makes it have a point party. The factory setting—57—usually works just fine. Before you draw a selection, you can press the semicolon (;) or apostrophe (') key to decrease or increase this setting by 3, respectively; add the Shift key to these keyboard shortcuts to jump between 1 and 100.

- **Use tablet pressure to change pen width**. If you have a pressure-sensitive graphics tablet, turning on this setting—whose button looks like a pen tip with circles around it—lets you override the Width setting by pressing harder or softer on your tablet with the stylus. (The box on page 517 has more about graphics tablets.)

- **Refine Edge**. If you need to fine-tune your selection, click this button to open the Refine Edge dialog box (you'll get the scoop on this powerful dialog box beginning on the next page).

Selecting with the Pen Tool

Another great way to select an irregular object or area is to trace its outline with the Pen tool. Technically, you don't draw a selection with this method; you draw a *path* (page 536), which you can then *load* as a selection or use to create a *vector mask* (page 571). This technique requires quite a bit of practice because the Pen tool isn't your average, everyday, well...*pen*, but it'll produce the smoothest-edged selections this side of the Rio Grande. Head on over to Chapter 13 to read all about it.

Creating Selections with Channels

As you'll learn in Chapter 5, the images you see onscreen are made up of various colors. In Photoshop, each color is stored in its own *channel* (which is kind of like a layer) that you can view and manipulate. If the object or area you're trying to select is one that you can isolate in a channel, you can load that channel as a selection with a click of your mouse. Chapter 5 discusses this incredibly useful technique in detail, starting on page 202.

Using the Selection Tools Together

As wonderful as the aforementioned selection tools are *individually*, they're much more powerful if you use 'em *together*.

Remember how every tool discussed so far has an "Add to selection" and "Subtract from selection" mode? This means that, no matter which tool you start with, you can add to—or subtract from—the active selection with a completely different tool. Check out *Figure 4-17*, which gives you a couple of ideas for using the selection tools together. And thanks to Photoshop's spring-loaded tools feature—press and hold a tool's keyboard shortcut to temporarily switch to it, then let go of the key to switch back to the current tool (see the Tip on page 12)—*switching* between tools is a snap.

As you can see, there are a gazillion ways to create selections, though any selection you make will likely need tweaking no matter *which* method you use. The next section is all about perfecting selections.

> **NOTE** You can also *paint* selections onto your image by using Quick Mask mode, which is discussed in the next section on page 176.

Modifying Selections

The difference between a pretty-good-around-the-edges selection and a perfect one is what separates Photoshop pros from mere dabblers. As you'll learn in the following pages, there are a bunch of ways to modify, reshape, and even *save* selections.

Refining Edges

The best selection modifier in town is the Refine Edge dialog box (*Figure 4-18*), which is great for selecting the tough stuff like hair and fur. It combines several edge-adjustment tools that used to be scattered throughout Photoshop's menus and includes an extremely useful preview option.

FIGURE 4-17

Top: It's worth taking a moment to try to see the shapes that make up the area you want to select. For example, you can select the circular top of this famous Texas building (shown in red) using the Elliptical Marquee, and then switch to the Rectangular Marquee set to "Add to selection" mode to select the area shown in green.

Bottom: Another way to use the selection tools together is to draw a rectangular selection around the object you want to select, and then switch to the Magic Wand to subtract the areas you don't want. Hold down the Option key (Alt on a PC) so you're in "Subtract from selection" mode and then click the areas you don't want included in your selection, like this grayish background.

With just a couple of clicks, you can select the prickly pear shown here (which makes superb homemade jelly, by the way!).

Any time you have a selection tool active and some marching ants on your screen, you'll see the Refine Edge button sitting pretty up in the Options bar; simply click it to open the dialog box. You can also open it by choosing Select→Refine Edge, pressing Option-⌘-R (Alt+Ctrl+R), or by clicking the Properties panel's Mask Edge button (see the figure on page 116).

Zoom tool

Click to open preview options

Hand tool

Refine tools

Refine Radius Tool   E
Erase Refinements Tool   E

Turn on
to save
settings

FIGURE 4-18

*The Refine Edge dialog
box not only lets you
see a live, continuously
updated preview of what
your selection will look
like after fine-tuning,
but you also get seven
different views to choose
from, along with two tools
you can use to refine your
selection before you click
OK (Overlay is particularly
handy if you're dealing
with hair or fur).*

*If you forget what the
dialog box's various
settings do, never fear:
Just point your cursor at
a setting, and a tooltip
appears explaining what
that item does.*

The Refine Edge dialog box gives you *seven* different ways to preview your selection. Because the preview appears in the main document window, you'll want to move the Refine Edge dialog box aside so it's not covering your image. Depending on the colors in the image, one of these View modes will let you see the selection better than the rest:

- **Marching Ants**. This view just shows the selection on the image itself. Keyboard shortcut: M.

- **Overlay**. As the name indicates, this view displays your selection overlaid with the Quick Mask (page 176), which, unless you've changed its color, is light red. (The box on page 179 explains how to change that color.) Because the red overlay is see-through, it's the best choice when your selection will include hair or fur that isn't included in the selection just yet. Keyboard shortcut: V.

TIP   You can cycle through the preview modes by pressing the F key repeatedly when you have the Refine Edge dialog box open. To temporarily see your original image, press the X key; press X again to go back to the preview mode you were using.

- **On Black**. This view displays the selection on a black background, which is helpful if your image is light colored and doesn't have a lot of black in it. Keyboard shortcut: B.

- **On White**. Choose this view if your image is mostly dark. The stark white background makes it easy to see your selection and the *object* you're selecting while you're fine-tuning it using the dialog box's settings. Keyboard shortcut: W.

- **Black & White**. This view displays your selection as an *alpha channel* (page 188). Photoshop makes your selection white and the mask black; transitions between the two areas are subtle shades of gray. The gray areas let you see how detailed your mask is, so you'll spend a fair amount of time in this mode. Keyboard shortcut: K.

- **On Layers**. To see your selection atop the gray-and-white transparency checkerboard, choose this mode. Keyboard shortcut: L.

- **Reveal Layer**. This mode displays your image *without* a selection. Keyboard shortcut: R.

Once you've chosen a View mode, you can tweak the following settings (and for the best results, Adobe suggests you adjust them in this order):

- **Smart Radius**. Turn this checkbox on to make Photoshop look closely at the edges of your selection to determine whether they're hard (like the outline of your subject's body) or soft (like your subject's hair or fur). It's a good idea to turn this setting on each time you open the Refine Edge dialog box. (If you turn on the Remember Settings option at the bottom of the dialog box, Smart Radius will *stay* on until you turn it off.)

> **TIP** If the edges of the object you're trying to select vary greatly in softness (like a girl in a hat with long hair blowing in the wind), it can be helpful to copy parts of the image onto another layer so you can use a different Smart Radius setting. To do that, create a selection and then press ⌘-J (Ctrl+J) to jump that bit onto its own layer, and then open the Refine Edge dialog box.

- **Radius**. This setting controls the size of the area affected by the settings in this dialog box—in other words, how far beyond the edge of your selection Photoshop looks when it's refining that edge. You can think of this setting as the selection's degree of difficulty. For example, if your selection is really complex, like the horse's mane in *Figure 4-19*, increase this setting to make Photoshop look beyond the original selection boundary for all the wispy stuff (which also makes the program slightly soften the selection's edge). If your selection is fairly simple, lower this setting so Photoshop analyzes just the selection's boundary, which creates a harder edge. There are no magic numbers for this setting—it varies from image to image—so you'll need to experiment in order to get your selection just right.

- **Refine Radius tool**. Once you've turned on Smart Radius, you can use this tool (shown in *Figure 4-18*) to paint over the edges of your selection to make

Photoshop fine-tune them even more in particular spots (see *Figure 4-19*, top). This is where the Refine Edge dialog box *really* works its magic: As you drag with this tool's brush cursor, you can extend your selection beyond its original boundaries, creating a more precise selection of extremely fine details. This tool is also intuitive: As you brush across the edges of your selection, it pays attention and tries to *learn* how you want it to behave.

FIGURE 4-19

Top: After creating a rough selection with the Quick Selection tool, you can use the Refine Edge dialog box's Refine Radius tool to brush across areas you want to add to the selection.

Bottom: Within minutes, you can settle this mare onto a new background, as shown here. What horse wouldn't be happier hanging out on a field of bluebonnets?

To try this yourself, trot on over to this book's Missing CD page at www. missingmanuals.com/ cds and download the file Horse.zip.

- **Erase Refinements tool**. If Photoshop gets a little overzealous and includes too much of the background in your selection as you drag with the Refine Radius tool, use this tool to drag across the areas you *don't* want to include in the selection.

TIP To temporarily switch between the Refine Radius and Erase Refinements tools while the Refine Edge dialog box is open, press and hold the Option key (Alt on a PC). Alternatively, you can flip-flop between the tools by pressing Shift-E.

- **Smooth**. Increasing this setting makes Photoshop smooth the selection's edges so they're less jagged, but increasing it *too* much can make you lose details (especially on selections of things like hair). To bring back some details without decreasing this setting, try increasing the Radius and Contrast settings.

- **Feather**. This setting controls how much Photoshop softens the edges of the selection, which is useful when you're combining images, as discussed in the box on page 141.

- **Contrast**. This setting sharpens the selection's edge, even if you softened it by increasing the Radius setting mentioned above. A higher number here creates a sharper edge and can actually reduce the noisy or grainy look that's sometimes caused by a high Radius setting. (If you spend some quality time with Smart Radius and its refinement tools, you probably won't use this slider much, if at all.)

- **Shift Edge**. You can tighten the selection (make it smaller) by dragging this slider to the left, which is a good idea if you're dealing with hair or fur. To expand the selection and grab pixels you missed when making the initial selection, drag this slider to the right.

- **Decontaminate Colors**. This option helps reduce *edge halos*: leftover colored pixels around the edges of a selection that you see only *after* putting the object on a new background (as shown on page 173). Once you turn this checkbox on, Photoshop tries to replace the color of selected pixels with the color of pixels *nearby* (whether they're selected or not). Drag the Amount slider to the right to change the color of more edge pixels, or to the left to change fewer. To see the color changes for yourself, choose Reveal Layer from the View menu near the top of the dialog box (or just press R).

- **Output To**. This setting lets you tell Photoshop what you'd like it to *do* with your new and improved selection. Here are your options:

  — **Selection** adjusts the original selection, leaving you with marching ants on the original layer just like you started with. (If you've turned on Decontaminate Colors, this option is grayed out.)

  — **Layer Mask** adds a layer mask to the current layer according to the selection you just made. You'll choose this option most of the time. (This option is also unavailable if you've turned on Decontaminate Colors.)

  — **New Layer** deletes the background and creates a new layer containing only the selected item, with no marching ants.

— **New Layer with Layer Mask** adds a new layer complete with layer mask.

— **New Document** deletes the background and sends only the selected item to a brand-new document.

— **New Document with Layer Mask** sends the selected item to a new document complete with editable layer mask.

Whew! Those settings probably won't make a whole lot of sense until you start using 'em. To get you off and running, here's how to select a subject with wispy hair, like the horse in *Figure 4-19*:

1. **Open an image and select the item using the Quick Selection tool.**

   Press W to grab the Quick Selection tool and paint across the object you want to select (*Figure 4-19*, top). Don't worry too much about the quality of the selection, because you'll tweak it in a moment.

2. **Hop up to the Options bar and click the Refine Edge button.**

   The mighty Refine Edge dialog box opens.

3. **Choose Overlay as your View mode.**

   To see the horse's mane better—in all its wispy goodness—press V to view it with a red overlay.

4. **Turn on the Smart Radius checkbox and drag the Radius slider to the right.**

   How far you should drag this slider depends on your image. Your goal is to drag it as far to the right as you can while still maintaining some hardness in the selection's edges. There's no magic Radius setting that will work on every selection (a setting of 3.2 was used in *Figure 4-19*); it varies with every image. You won't see much of anything change in your image when you tweak this setting, though a tiny rotating circle at the bottom left of the dialog box indicates that Photoshop is rethinking the selection.

5. **Use the Refine Radius tool to brush across the soft edges of your selection (*Figure 4-19*, top).**

   Press E to grab the Refine Radius tool, or click its icon near the top left of the Refine Edge dialog box (it looks like a tiny brush atop a curved, dotted line). Then mouse over to your image and brush across the soft areas you want to add to the selection, like the wispy bits of the horse's mane. Try to avoid any areas that are correctly selected (such as the horse's nose), as Photoshop tends to overanalyze them and exclude parts it shouldn't. If you end up adding too much to the selection, press Option (Alt) to switch to the Eraser Refinement tool and then brush across the areas you *don't* want selected.

6. **Turn on the Decontaminate Colors checkbox and adjust the Amount slider.**

   Turn on the checkbox and then drag the slider slightly to the right to shift the color of *partially* selected edge pixels so they more closely match pixels that are *fully* selected. Once again, this value varies from image to image (15 percent was used for *Figure 4-19*).

7. **From the Output To menu, chose "New Layer with Mask."**

   Photoshop adds a layer mask to the active layer reflecting your selection, as shown in the Layers panel in *Figure 4-19* (bottom).

Exhausted yet? This kind of thing isn't easy, but once you master using Refine Edge, you'll be able to create precise selections of darn near anything!

■ ADDING A CREATIVE EDGE

You can also use the Refine Edge dialog box to add creative edges to photos. For example, grab the Rectangular Marquee tool and draw a box around an image about half an inch inside the document's edges (*Figure 4-20*, top). Then click the Options bar's Refine Edge button and, in the resulting dialog box, drag the Radius slider to the right for a cool, painterly effect (how *far* you drag it is up to you). Be sure to choose Layer Mask from the dialog box's Output To menu before you click OK to keep from harming your original image.

FIGURE 4-20

Top: The first step to creative edges is to draw a rectangular selection around the focal point of the image. The wider the space between the edges of your selection and the edges of the document, the wider the soon-to-be-creative edge will be.

Bottom: Once you turn on Smart Radius and drag the Radius slider to the right, the edges of the image begin to change. Use the remaining sliders to tweak the look to your liking. As you can see, the Refine Edge dialog box makes short work of giving images an interesting painted edge (here, the image is shown atop a deep red Solid Color Fill layer).

Fixing Edge Halos

When you're making selections, you may encounter *edge halos* (also called *fringing* or *matting*). An edge halo is a tiny portion of the background that stubbornly remains even after you try to delete it (or hide it with a layer mask as explained on page 109). They usually show up after you replace the original background with something new (see *Figure 4-21*).

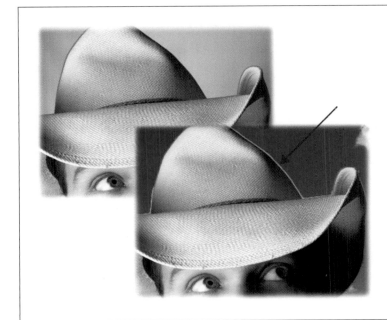

FIGURE 4-21

Here you can see the intrepid cowboy on his original green background (top) and on the new background (bottom).

The green pixels stubbornly clinging to his hat are an edge halo.

This aggravatingly tiny rim of color can be your undoing when it comes to creating realistic images because they're a sure sign that the image has done time in Photoshop. Edge halos make a new sky look fake and won't help convince anyone that Elvis actually came to your cookout.

Here are a few ways to fix edge halos:

- **Contract your selection**. Use the Refine Edge dialog box (page 165) or choose Select→Modify→Contract to contract the selection (though the latter method won't give you a preview). Use this technique while you still have marching ants—in other words, before you delete the old background (or, better yet, hide the background with a layer mask [page 109]).

- **Run the Minimum filter on a layer mask**. Once you've hidden an image's background with a layer mask, you can run the Minimum filter on the *mask* to tighten it around the object. Page 671 explains this super-useful technique. This is an *excellent* quick fix to have in your bag of Photoshop tricks.

- **Use the Defringe command**. Run this command after you delete the background (alas, it doesn't work on layer masks or while a selection is active). Choose

Layer→Matting→Defringe and then enter a value in pixels. Photoshop analyzes the active layer and changes the color of the pixels around the object's edge to the color of nearby pixels. For example, if you enter *2 px*, it'll replace a 2-pixel rim of color all the way around the object.

- **Remove Black/White Matting**. If Photoshop has blessed you with a halo that's either black or white, you can make the program try to remove it automatically. After you've deleted the background, activate the offending layer and then choose Layer→Matting→Remove Black Matte or Remove White Matte. (Like Defringe, this command doesn't work on layer masks or while you have an active selection.)

Creating a Border Selection

If you peek at the Select→Modify submenu, you'll find the same options as in the Refine Edge dialog box (but without a preview). There is, however, one addition: Border, which lets you turn a solid selection into a hollow one. Let's say you drew a circular selection with the Elliptical Marquee tool (page 136). You can turn that selection into a ring (handy if you want to make a neon sign or select the outer rim of an object) by choosing Select→Modify→Border. Just enter a pixel width, click OK, and poof! Your formerly solid selection is now as hollow as can be.

Transforming a Selection

Have you ever tried to make a slanted rectangular selection like the one shown in *Figure 4-22*? If so, you may have found the experience frustrating. Sure, you can try using one of the lasso tools, but it's quicker to *transform* (meaning "reshape") a rectangular selection instead. (Page 255 has more on the transform tools.)

> **NOTE** When you transform a selection (as opposed to part of your image), Photoshop won't mess with any of your image's pixels. Instead, the program simply changes the shape of the *selection*—in other words, the shape of the marching ants.

Once you've made a selection, choose Select→Transform Selection or Control-click (right-click) inside the selection and, from the shortcut menu that appears, choose Transform Selection. Photoshop puts a rectangular box with little, square resizing handles on its four sides around the selection (this is called a *bounding box*). You can move the selection around by clicking inside the bounding box and dragging in any direction. (If you want to get rid of the bounding box without making any changes, press the Esc key.)

The resizing handles let you do the following:

- **Scale (resize)**. Drag any handle to change the size and shape of the selection. Drag diagonally toward the center of the selection to make it smaller or diagonally away to make it bigger.

FIGURE 4-22

Top: You can easily select the center part of this playing card with the Rectangular Marquee tool. Once you see the marching ants, choose Select→Transform Selection and rotate the resulting bounding box to get the correct angle.

Bottom Left: Next, Control-click (right-click) inside the bounding box and choose Distort from the shortcut menu, as shown here. Then drag each corner handle so it's over a corner of the yellow box on the card.

Bottom Right: When you're all finished, press Return (Enter on a PC) to accept the transformation. Or, if you change your mind, press the Esc key to reject it.

- **Rotate**. When you position your cursor outside one of the bounding box's corners, the cursor turns into a curved, double-headed arrow. That's your cue that you can drag to rotate the selection (just drag up or down in the direction you want to rotate).

If you need to change the shape of the selection, just Control-click (right-click) inside the bounding box and you'll see a shortcut menu with the following options (see *Figure 4-22*, bottom left):

- **Free Transform** lets you apply any of the transformations listed below freely and in one action (instead of having to choose and apply them one at a time). See page 257 for more info.

- **Scale** and **Rotate** work as described in the previous list.

- **Skew** lets you slant the selection by dragging one of the bounding box's side handles.

- **Distort** lets you drag any handle to reshape the selection.

- **Perspective** lets you drag any corner handle to give the selection a one-point perspective—that is, a vanishing point where it seems to disappear into the distance.

- **Warp** makes Photoshop place a grid over the selection that lets you reshape it in any way you want. Drag any *control point* (the two evenly spaced points on all four sides of the selection) or line on the grid to twist the selection however you like, or choose a ready-made preset from the Options bar's Warp menu.

> **TIP** Using Warp is your ticket to creating a page-curl effect. Trot on over to this book's Missing CD page at *www.missingmanuals.com/cds* to learn how.

- **Content-Aware Scale** can intelligently resize the unimportant background areas of your image while the subject remains unchanged. You'll learn all about it on page 251.

- **Puppet Warp** lets you twist and turn the selection any which way you want, like Silly Putty. It's covered in detail beginning on page 445.

- **Rotate 180°, Rotate 90° CW**, and **Rotate 90° CCW** turn your selection 180 degrees, 90 degrees clockwise, or 90 degrees counterclockwise, respectively.

- **Flip Horizontal** and **Flip Vertical** flip your selection either horizontally (like it's reflected in a mirror) or vertically (like it's reflected in a puddle).

When you're finished transforming the selection, press Return (Enter on a PC) to accept the changes. If you change your mind and want to reject the changes, press Esc instead.

Using Quick Mask Mode

If you'd rather fine-tune selections by painting with a brush, no problem; in fact, you can even *create* a selection from scratch using this method. Just enter Quick Mask mode and you'll find all of Photoshop's painting tools (even filters!) waiting to help tweak your selection. This mode gives you the freedom to work on selections with almost any tool.

You can enter Quick Mask mode by pressing the Q key or clicking the circle-within-a-square button at the bottom of the *Tools* panel (*not* the Layers panel). When you do, Photoshop looks to see whether you have an active selection. If you do, it puts a red overlay over everything *but* the selection. (If you don't have an active selection, you won't see any change, but you can still use the directions in this section to *create* a selection.) This color-coding makes it easy to edit your selection *visually* by painting.

While you're in Quick Mask mode, you can use the Brush tool to do any of the following:

- **Deselect a portion of the selection**—in other words, add an area to the mask—by setting your foreground color chip to black and then painting across the unwanted area.

- **Extend the selection** by painting the spot you want to add with white (you may need to press X to flip-flop your color chips).

- **Create a soft-edged selection or semi-transparent area** by painting with gray. For example, by painting with 50 percent gray (to do that, lower a black brush's opacity in the Options bar to 50 percent), you'll create a selection that's partially see-through. You can create a similar effect by painting with a soft-edged brush.

All the usual tools and document tricks work while you're in Quick Mask mode: You can zoom in or out by pressing ⌘ and the + or – key (Ctrl and + or – on a PC) or by using scrubby Zoom (page 51), press and hold the space bar to move around within the document once you're zoomed in, and use any of the selection tools covered in this chapter. You can also fill the entire mask, or the selection, with black or white (see page 181), which is helpful when you have a large area to paint or when you want to paint the entire selection by hand. You can also run filters in this mode to create interesting edges (page 659).

Once you finish fine-tuning the selection, press the Q key to exit Quick Mask mode and the marching ants come rushing back, as shown in *Figure 4-23*, so you can see the newly edited selection.

Moving Selections

If you create a selection that's not in exactly the right spot or you've got several objects of the same shape that you want to alter, you may need to move the selection itself. Or maybe you need to move the pixels *underneath* the selection, or move them onto their own layer. In any of those cases, you've got plenty of options:

- **Moving the selection (the marching ants) within the same layer**. Make sure you have a selection tool active (it doesn't matter which one), and then click inside the selection and drag it to another part of the document. You can also nudge the selection into place with the arrow keys on your keyboard.

TIP To move a selection as you're drawing it, press and hold the space bar while pressing the mouse button. Drag to move the selection, release the space bar, and then continue dragging to draw the selection.

FIGURE 4-23

Top left: To select the area around this badge, start by selecting the white background with the Magic Wand tool.

Top right: When you pop into Quick Mask mode, Photoshop leaves the area you've selected in full color (in this case, white) and puts a red overlay over everything else. Now you can quickly clean up problem areas—like the drop shadow peeking out from beneath the badge—because they're so easy to spot with the red overlay. Use the Brush tool set to paint with black or white, or the Polygonal Lasso tool (and then fill the selection area with black or white).

Bottom: Once you're finished, exit Quick Mask mode by pressing Q, and you see the fine-tuned selection marked by marching ants.

- **Moving the selected object (the actual pixels) within the same document**. Press V to activate the Move tool and then drag with your mouse to reposition the object. Just be aware that a big, gaping hole will appear where the object used to be! (If you're on a Background layer, the hole will be filled with your current foreground color.) To duplicate the selection so you can move it to another part of the image *without* leaving a hole, Option-drag (Alt-drag on a PC) it instead.

NOTE You can also use the Content-Aware Move tool to scoot a selected object from one place to another. Jump ahead to page 443 for the scoop!

- **Moving the selected object onto its own new layer within the same document**. Press ⌘-J (Ctrl+J) to "jump" the selected pixels onto their very own layer, just above the current layer. That way, whatever you do to the selected area won't harm the original image. If you don't like your changes, you can throw the extra layer away or reduce its opacity if the change is a little too strong. (Flip back to Chapter 3 for more on layers.)

- **Moving the selected object to another document**. Press ⌘-C (Ctrl+C) to copy the selected pixels and then open the other document and press ⌘-V (Ctrl+V) to paste the pixels. The pasted object appears on its very own layer that you can reposition with the Move tool. This technique is *essential* for performing the classic head swap, shown in *Figure 4-24*.

- **Moving the selected object to a new document**. Copy the object as described above and then choose File→New. Photoshop opens a new document, sized to match the object you copied; press ⌘-V (Ctrl+V) to paste the object.

Saving a Selection

If you'd like Photoshop to remember a selection so you can use it again later, it's happy to oblige. After you create the selection, choose Select→Save Selection. In the resulting dialog box (*Figure 4-25*), give your selection a meaningful name (like *handsome devil*) and then click OK. When you're finished working with that document, be sure to save it as a PSD file (see page 39).

Changing Quick Mask's Color

Why is Quick Mask red? Am I stuck with red? And while we're at it, why does the mask mark unselected areas? Can I make it mark the selected areas instead?

Whoa, now! Just hold your horses; one question at a time.

First, a bit of history: The Quick Mask's default setting is red because of its real-world counterpart, rubylith plastic, which came in sheets like paper. Back in the days before desktop publishing, this red plastic was cut with X-Acto knives and placed over the parts of images that needed to be hidden.

Printing technology has come a long way since then—there's no need for X-Acto knives when you've got Photoshop. And since you're working with modern printers and not old-fashioned printing presses, you're not stuck with using a red mask; you

can change Quick Mask's color to anything you want (which is quite helpful when the area you're trying to select has red in it). So if the red overlay isn't working for you, with Quick Mask mode active (press Q), double-click the circle-within-a-square button at the bottom of the Tools panel. In the Quick Mask Options dialog box that opens, click the color swatch and choose any color you like from the resulting Color Picker. You can also make the overlay more or less intense by changing the dialog box's Opacity setting.

And, yes, you can make Quick Mask mark the areas you've selected instead of the unselected areas. Simply open the Quick Mask Options dialog box and, in the Color Indicates section, turn on the Selected Areas option and then click OK.

FIGURE 4-24

Here's a fun little prank to pull on your family, friends, and exes. Open a photo of someone and select their head using any of the selection tools discussed in this chapter (the Quick Selection tool was used here). Be sure to feather the selection so it doesn't have a hard edge (page 141) and then copy it by pressing ⌘-C (Ctrl+C). Next, open the document that contains the new body and paste your selection into it by pressing ⌘-V (Ctrl+V).

You can then use the Move tool to reposition the head onto its new body and, if you need to, add a layer mask that you can fine-tune to make the head blend a little better with the body. You can also use the Clone Stamp tool (page 418) to hide parts of the original head. Good times!

FIGURE 4-25

If you think you'll ever want to use a selection again, go ahead and save it—just in case. It's a good idea to save detailed selections that took you a long time to create, too.

When you're ready to use the selection again, pop open the document in which it was saved and choose Select→Load Selection. In the resulting dialog box, pick your selection from the Channel menu (if you've saved only one selection in this particular document, Photoshop chooses it automatically). Leave the Operation section of the dialog box set to New Selection to bring back the saved selection as a whole (instead of adding to or subtracting from another selection). Press OK and the marching ants reappear, just like you saved them.

Although the radio buttons in the Operation section of the Load Selection dialog box let you add to, subtract from, or intersect other selections with the saved selection, it's easier just to load the selection, close the dialog box, and *then* edit it using the selection tools discussed in this chapter.

Filling a Selection with Color

Filling selections with color is a great way to create shapes and add colorful photo borders to images. After you've created the selection of your dreams, you can fill it with color in a couple of ways. One option is to choose Edit→Fill and, from the Use drop-down menu, choose Color. Pick something nice from the resulting Color Picker, and then click OK twice to dismiss the dialog boxes. Photoshop fills your selection with the color you picked.

Alternatively, a more *flexible* way to fill a selection with color is to add a Solid Color Adjustment layer. Once you've made a selection, click the half-black/half-white circle at the bottom of the Layers panel and choose Solid Color (or choose Layer→New Fill Layer→Solid Color instead). Then grab a color from the resulting Color Picker and click OK. Photoshop dutifully fills the selected area with color, and you see a new Solid Color Fill layer appear in the Layers panel. To change the color of this layer, simply double-click its thumbnail to reopen the Color Picker. (Chapter 3 has more on using Solid Color, Gradient, and Pattern Fill layers.)

> **TIP**   You have yet *another* option for filling selections: Content-Aware Fill, which works with the Fill command and the Spot Healing brush. You'll learn all about it beginning on page 407.

Stroking (Outlining) a Selection

Sometimes you'll want to give your selection a *stroke* (as in an outline, not the medical condition). While you can stroke selections of any shape, this technique comes in really handy when you use it in conjunction with the Photoshop's vector tools. That's right: You can stroke *any* vector shape you create—whether it's with the Pen tool or one of the shape tools—with a variety of line widths and colors, including dashes or dots. This feature is covered on page 552.

That said, if you want to add a stroke to a pixel-based layer, you can do it with layer styles (page 124). For example, when it comes to adding a bit of class to a photo, few effects beat a thin black outline (see *Figure 4-26*). If the image lives on its own layer, click the tiny *fx* button at the bottom of the Layers panel and choose Stroke. In the resulting Layer Style dialog box, enter a size for the stroke and then choose a

FIGURE 4-26

Whether you're floating the image within text in a newspaper, newsletter, or magazine, or even if you're posting it in your blog, a thin outline gives your image's edge a little definition, making the design look nicely finished.

Location from the drop-down menu (if the image is the same size as your Photoshop document, be sure to choose *Inside* so the stroke appears inside the document's margins). Last but not least, click the colored square to pop open the Color Picker and choose a color for the stroke. Click OK to close the Layer Style dialog box and call it done. To edit the stroke's size or color later on, just double-click the Stroke layer style in the Layers panel and the Layer Style dialog box pops open.

If the object you want to stroke *isn't* isolated on its own layer—your image is comprised of several layers, say, as shown in *Figure 4-26*—then you can add the stroke to an empty Fill layer. To do this, create a selection of your whole document by pressing ⌘-A (Ctrl+A). Next, click the half-black/half-white circle at the bottom of the Layers panel, choose Solid Color, and when the Color Picker opens, immediately click OK to close it. Make sure the new Fill layer lives at the top of your layer stack and then drop its Fill setting to 0 (see page 90 for more on this setting). Now you can use the *fx* button to add a stroke as described above.

Understanding Channels

At the heart of any Photoshop file lie *channels*—storage containers for all the color information in your image, selections you've saved, masks you've created, and instructions for printing with special inks. Channels sound intimidating at first, and folks have been known to shudder at their mention and avoid them completely. But to really understand Photoshop, it's good to get a grip on channels. Luckily, you don't need a PhD to do that—just a little patience.

This chapter gets a little technical at times, but if you soldier through, you'll be rewarded with wisdom that'll help you perform some amazing pixel wizardry. You'll get a warm, fuzzy, enlightened feeling as you learn to:

- Use channels to make complex selections and masks (page 202).

- Map one image to the contours of another (page 303).

- Create a beautiful black-and-white image from a color version (pages 196 and 313).

- Perform highly targeted color adjustments (see *Figure 9-23* on page 394).

- Sharpen your images without introducing noise (page 211).

And that's just the tip of the iceberg. *Everything* you do in Photoshop involves channels (well, save for working with paths and text, which you'll learn about in Chapters 13 and 14), so it's important to get familiar with them. If you understand *how* Photoshop does what it does, you can make it do even *more* in less time and with less effort. That's called working smarter, not harder—which is why, Grasshopper, you're reading this book.

To understand how channels work, you first need to learn a bit about the two color systems you'll encounter during your Photoshop career: *additive* and *subtractive*.

Once you've got that under your belt—and fear not, there's plenty more ahead about how both systems work—you'll dive into the color channels themselves to see what kind of info lives there and how you can use it to manipulate your images. Last but not least, you'll explore *alpha channels*, an entirely different kind of channel that lets you save selections that you can use again later or access through various commands, such as Content-Aware Scale (page 251). Read on!

How Color Works

The images you see on computer monitors and TVs are made of light; without light, these screens would be completely dark. While your eyes are sensitive to hundreds of wavelengths of light (each associated with a different color), it takes just three—red, green, and blue—to produce all the colors you see onscreen. So to create color, monitors *add* individual pixels of colored light. That's why the onscreen color system is called "additive." Each tiny *pixel* (short for *picture element*) can be red, green, blue, or some combination of the three. All image-capture and input devices—digital cameras, video cameras, and scanners—use the additive color system, as do all digital-image display devices.

> **NOTE** Onscreen images are also called *composite* images because they're made up of a combination of red, green, and blue light (also known as *RGB*).

In the additive color system, areas where red, green, and blue light overlap appear white (see *Figure 5-1*). Does that sound crazy, or does it ring a bell from high school physics? Think about it this way: If you aim red, green, and blue spotlights at a stage, you see white where all three lights overlap. Interestingly, you also see cyan, magenta, or yellow where just *two* of the three lights overlap (also shown in *Figure 5-1*). Areas where no light is shining appear jet black.

That's how computer monitors and TVs create onscreen color. Now it's time to talk about printed color, which—brace yourself—works in a totally different way.

Printing presses use what's called a *subtractive* color system, where the colors result from a combination of light that's reflected (which you see) and light that's absorbed (which you don't see). In a printed photo, magazine, or book, the subtractive system operates as kind of a joint venture between the inks used (generally cyan, magenta, yellow, and black, all of which absorb color) and the paper the ink is printed on (a reflective surface). The ink serves as a filter by absorbing some of the light that hits the paper (you can think of this as the paper "subtracting" that light from what you see). The paper bounces the rest of the light back at you, so the whiter the paper, the truer the colors will look when they're printed.

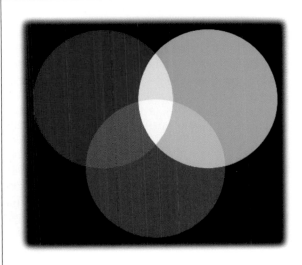

FIGURE 5-1

If you overlap red, green, and blue spotlights, you see white light. This is a prime example of the additive color system, which starts with darkness and adds light to produce different colors. Notice how cyan, magenta, and yellow appear where just two lights overlap.

You can try this spotlight experiment in Photoshop yourself by creating red, green, and blue circles on separate layers on a black background. Make the circles overlap, switch each layer's blend mode to Lighten and voilà—the other colors appear where the circles overlap.

In the subtractive system, different-colored inks absorb different-colored light. For example, cyan ink absorbs red light and reflects green and blue light back at you, so you see a mix of green and blue—in other words, cyan. Similarly, magenta ink absorbs green light and reflects red and blue light; in other words, magenta. One last example: A mix of cyan, magenta, and yellow ink absorbs *most* of the primary colors—red, green, and blue—so you see what's left over: dark brown.

NOTE In order to produce true black, grays, and shades of color (colors mixed with black to produce darker colors), the folks who ran printing presses added black as a fourth printing ink. They couldn't abbreviate it with B because they were afraid it'd be confused with blue (as in RGB), so they used K instead—as in "blacK." That's where the abbreviation CMYK comes from.

To summarize: Subtractive color is generated by light hitting an object and bouncing back to your eyes, whereas additive color is generated by different-colored light mixing together *before* you see any of it.

RGB Mode vs. CMYK Mode

Photoshop stores all the color information that gets relayed to your monitor, your printer, and so on, in separate *channels*. The channels' names change depending on which *color mode* (a.k.a. *image mode*) you're using for that particular Photoshop document. As a rule of thumb, you should use RGB mode for images destined for onscreen viewing or inkjet printing, and CMYK mode for images you plan on sending to a commercial printing press.

NOTE These days it's best to ask your printing company which color mode they prefer before you start editing. Some printing companies prefer RGB because they get better results by using their *own* software to convert images from RGB to CMYK.

To find out what color mode your image is in, choose Image→Mode; the current mode has a little checkmark to the left of its name. In *RGB mode*, your Photoshop document has a red channel, a green channel, and a blue channel. When you look at each channel individually—you'll learn how in a moment—you actually see a grayscale representation of where and at what strength that particular color appears in your image. ("Why doesn't Photoshop display them in color" you ask? The box on page 189 has the answer.) One of the best things about RGB mode is that it can display an enormous range of colors.

If you're preparing an image for a commercial printing press, they'll probably print it using a mix of cyan, magenta, yellow, and black ink. Enter *CMYK mode*, where your document includes—you guessed it—cyan, magenta, yellow, and black channels. The drawback to working in this mode is that ink reproduces *far fewer* colors than light, so this mode limits the hues at your disposal. But never fear: Even if you need to *end up* in CMYK mode, there's no harm in starting off in RGB. (Chapter 16 explains more than you ever wanted to know about when and how to change color modes.)

As you discovered in Chapter 2, Photoshop includes other color modes, such as Grayscale and Lab, which are handy for specific tasks that you'll learn about throughout this book. Nevertheless, you'll spend most of your time editing in RGB mode.

Whew! Now that the really confusing stuff is out of the way, it's time to focus on where in Photoshop you can *see* channels and the different flavors of channels you'll find there.

The Channels Panel and You

To peek inside a channel, open the Channels panel (*Figure 5-2*)—its tab is lurking in the Layers panel group on the right side of your screen. (If you don't see it, choose Window→Channels.) This panel looks and works like the Layers panel, which you learned about in Chapter 3.

When you single-click a channel in the panel, Photoshop highlights it to let you know it's active and temporarily turns off the other channels (see *Figure 5-2*); anything you do from that point on affects only that channel. This is extremely useful when you want to, say, blur only the red channel in order to soften skin (since this channel usually has the least amount of texture in it). To activate more than one channel at a time, Shift-click each one (handy for sharpening two channels at once, as shown in *Figure 5-15* on page 212).

Double-click tab to collapse vertically

Collapse panel horizontally

Close panel

Composite channel

Toggles channel visibility on/off

Color channels

Spot channel

Alpha channel

Panel menu

Currently active channel

Keyboard shortcut to activate channel (PC: Ctrl-4)

Load channel as selection

Save selection as channel

New channel

Delete channel

FIGURE 5-2

The Channels panel is your gateway to the color info that makes up your image. The composite channel at the top of the panel (here it's the one labeled RGB) shows what your image looks like with all the channels turned on; click it to turn all the channels back on if you've temporarily turned some off. You can't turn off every channel, though, since at least one has to be visible in order for you to see your image!

The little number to the right of each channel's name is its keyboard shortcut. These shortcuts changed back in CS4, but if you'd like to revert to the old ones, choose Edit→Keyboard Shortcuts and turn on Use Legacy Channel Shortcuts.

Photoshop uses several kinds of channels, all of which this chapter covers in detail:

- **Composite channels**. Technically, these aren't really channels; they're *combinations* of channels and are for your viewing pleasure only. When you're using a mode that contains more than one color channel (like RGB, CMYK, and Lab—all discussed later in this chapter), the composite channel shows all the channels *simultaneously*, revealing your image in its full-color glory. The name of the composite channel depends on which mode you're in. In RGB mode, for example, the composite channel is named RGB (creative, huh?). No matter what Photoshop calls it, the composite channel is always at the top of the Channels panel.

> **NOTE** Photoshop lets you store up to 56 channels in a single document.

- **Color channels**. As explained earlier, if you're working in RGB mode, your color channels are Red, Green, and Blue. In CMYK mode, they're Cyan, Magenta, Yellow, and Black. In Lab mode (page 195), they're Lightness, a, and b. In most other modes, you'll find only a single channel that's named after the mode you're in.

- **Alpha channels**. These ever-so-useful channels are grayscale representations of a temporary selection you're in the process of making using Quick Mask mode (page 176), or a selection that you've saved in your Photoshop document (page 179). The latter version comes in handy when you're making tough selections that you may need to tweak later, when using Content-Aware Scale (page 251), or when you can't complete the selection before your coffee break. Page 198 explains alpha channels in detail.

- **Spot channels**. Used only in commercial printing, these channels let you define areas in your image that should be printed with special premixed inks (like Pantone colors), or with a fancy coat of varnish, foil, or metallic ink. For example, if you're designing a holiday card and you want the snow to be sparkly, you can create a spot channel for the glitter so the printer knows where it goes. Page 195 has details on when to use spot channels and how to create them.

At the bottom of the Channels panel, you'll find the following buttons:

- **Load channel as selection**. This button, which looks like a tiny circle made of dots, creates a selection of whatever's in the active channel based on its lightness values (not everything gets selected). This is handy when you're using channels to swap backgrounds (page 202) or create silhouettes (page 206). You can also load a channel as a selection by ⌘-clicking (Ctrl-clicking on a PC) the channel's thumbnail.

- **Save selection as channel**. When you have an active selection in your document, click this button to save it as an alpha channel so you can continue to edit it or use it again later. Photoshop cleverly names your selections Alpha 1, Alpha 2, Alpha 3, and so on. If you want a more memorable name, simply double-click the channel's name and change it to something like "Tony's toupee" or "Nancy's nose." If you'd rather name your selection before you save it, Option-click (Alt-click on a PC) this button or choose Select→Save Selection instead.

- **Create new channel**. If you drag an existing channel onto this button (which looks like a tiny piece of paper with an upturned corner), Photoshop duplicates that channel. This is helpful if you need to lighten or darken a channel in order to create a good selection (page 209), as altering the original channel can destroy your image. If you click this button instead, Photoshop creates a new, empty alpha channel that you can use to create a selection from scratch using the red overlay of Quick Mask mode (see *Figure 5-8* on page 201).

- **Delete current channels**. Clicking this tiny trash can deletes the currently active channel(s); you can also drag and drop a channel onto this button to do the same thing. After you've tweaked a duplicate channel or an alpha channel to create the perfect selection, you can toss it by clicking this button.

Just like every other panel in Photoshop, the Channels panel has a menu tucked into its top-right corner (it looks like a down arrow next to four little lines). This handy menu includes some of the same commands mentioned earlier and a few all its own:

- **New Channel**. This command creates a brand-new alpha channel, just like click-ing the "Create new channel" button at the bottom of the panel. The difference is that, by going this route, you get a nifty dialog box where you can name the new channel and tell Photoshop how to display the channel's information (see *Figure 5-7* on page 200). However, it's quicker to Option-click (Alt-click) the "Create new channel" button.

- **Duplicate Channel**. To create a copy of a channel so you can edit it, choose this command. When you do, Photoshop displays a dialog box so you can name the new channel and choose its destination (the same document or a new one). The destination option is helpful when you're creating a displacement map (page 303) or using channels to make a high-contrast, black-and-white image (page 193).

- **Delete Channels**. This command deletes the current channel or, if you've Shift-clicked to activate more than one channel, *all* active channels. You have to keep one channel, though, so if you've activated all of 'em, Photoshop grays out this command.

- **New Spot Channel**. This option lets you create a new channel to mark an area that should be printed with a premixed, specialty ink—including varnish, foil, metallic ink, and so on—called a *spot color*. Chapter 16 has more about spot channels beginning on page 698.

FREQUENTLY ASKED QUESTION

Why Are Channels Gray?

With all this talk about color, how come Photoshop displays channels in black and white?

Although you *can* make Photoshop display channel info in color, you really don't want to; the colors would be so bright and distracting that it'd be hard to see anything useful. It's much easier to see a particular color's strength (called *luminosity*) when it's represented in shades of gray.

In RGB mode, white areas indicate a color at its full strength, and black areas indicate the color at its weakest. (In CMYK mode, the reverse is true—black indicates full strength and white indicates the weakest concentration.) For example, take a peek at the Red channel in *Figure 5-2*. The lighter-colored pixels represent high concentrations of red, whereas the darker pixels represent almost no red at all (and the tiny preview in the RGB channel shows that the image really *does* contain a lot of red).

As you can see, just glancing at grayscale channel informa-tion shows you quite clearly where a color is at full strength, where it's lacking, and what lies somewhere in between. That said, if you're determined to see channel info in color, choose Photoshop→Preferences→Interface (Edit→Preferences→Interface on a PC). In the Options section of the dialog box, turn on the "Show Channels in Color" checkbox and then see if you can make heads or tails out of anything.

Actually, there is one situation where you *do* see channels displayed in color—in your document, at least—whether you like it or not: if you activate more than one channel, Photoshop previews your image in just those colors (see *Figure 5-15* on page 212). Why? Because if the program displayed multiple channels in grayscale, you wouldn't be able to tell *which* shades of gray represented which color.

- **Merge Spot Channel**. Only commercial printing presses use spot channels, so if you need to print a proof on a regular desktop printer, you first have to run this command to merge your spot channels. See the box on page 711 for details.

- **Channel Options**. This menu item is available only if you've activated an alpha channel. When you're creating or editing an alpha channel, choose Channel Options to change the way Photoshop displays masked and selected areas. Page 200 has the scoop.

- **Split Channels**. If you need to put each channel into its own document, choose this command. Photoshop grabs each channel and copies it into a new, grayscale document (page 35 has info on Grayscale mode). This technique is useful when, for example, you're creating a black-and-white image based on one of its color channels and you need the resulting document to end up in Grayscale mode so it can be printed in a newspaper. (The box on page 314 has more on preparing grayscale images for a printing press.)

- **Merge Channels**. You might think this command merges more than one channel into a single channel. Negative, good buddy. Instead, it merges the channels of up to four Grayscale documents into a single document, whose resulting color mode depends on how many documents you had open when you began: RGB if you started with three open documents, CMYK if you started with four. You can also have Photoshop merge all the open documents' channels into a Multichannel document (see page 196). This command comes in handy if you've used Split Channels to work on each channel separately and now you want to reunite them into one document.

- **Panel Options**. In the Channels panel, Photoshop automatically displays a thumbnail preview of each channel (see *Figure 5-2*). If you want to turn off this preview or choose a different thumbnail size, pick this menu item. If you've got a decent-sized monitor (17" or larger), do your eyes a favor and go for the biggest preview possible.

- **Close** and **Close Tab Group**. Choose Close to make the Channels panel disappear, or Close Tab Group to get rid of a whole group of related panels (such as Channels, Layers, and Paths). See Chapter 1 for more on panel wrangling.

■ Meet the Color Channels

Understanding what you're seeing in each channel gives you the know-how to create complicated selections and fine-tune your images. In this section, you'll look inside the different color channels, beginning with the most common color mode: RGB.

NOTE This section doesn't cover alpha channels; they're so important, they get their very own section that begins on page 198.

RGB Channels

Unless you're preparing an image that's headed for a commercial printing press (as opposed to the inkjet printer you've probably got at home) and they *require* you to use CMYK, RGB mode is the place to be. After all, your monitor is RGB, as are your digital camera and scanner. But as the box on page 189 explains, Photoshop doesn't display individual channels in red, green, and blue—they're in grayscale so you can easily see where the color is most saturated. Because colors in RGB mode are made from light (page 184), white indicates areas where the color is at full strength, black indicates areas where it's weakest, and shades of gray represent everything in between (see *Figure 5-3*).

TIP No matter which color mode you're in, you can cycle through its various channels by pressing ⌘-3, 4, 5, and 6 (Ctrl+3, 4, 5, and 6 on a PC), though you'll only use that last one if you're in CMYK mode—which has four channels instead of three—or if you're trying to activate an alpha channel in RGB mode. To go back to the composite channel so you can see the image in full color, press ⌘-2 (Ctrl+2). When you use these shortcuts, be sure to hold down the ⌘ or Ctrl key; otherwise, typing numbers will change layer or Brush tool opacity instead (see pages 90 and 496, respectively).

Each color channel contains different information:

- **Red**. This channel is typically the lightest of the bunch and shows the greatest difference in color range. In *Figure 5-3*, this channel is very light because there's a lot of red in the woman's skin, hair, and hat. This channel can be *muy importante* when you're correcting skin tones (page 386). You can also run a blur filter on this channel to instantly soften skin (page 430).

- **Green**. You can think of this channel as "contrast central" because it's usually the highest in, well, contrast. (This makes sense because digital cameras have twice as many green sensors as red or blue ones in order to mimic the human eye, which is most sensitive to green light.) Remember this channel when you're creating an edge mask for sharpening (page 472) or working with displacement maps (page 303).

- **Blue**. Typically the darkest of the group, this channel is super useful when you want to create complex selections in order to isolate an object (page 202). It's also where you'll find problems like *noise* and *grain*. See the box on page 455 to learn how to run the Reduce Noise filter on this channel.

CMYK Channels

Though you'll probably spend most of your time working with RGB images, you may also need to work with images in CMYK mode. Its name, as you learned earlier, stands for the cyan, magenta, yellow, and black inks commercial printing presses use in newspapers, magazines, product packaging, and so on. It has a composite channel at the top of the Channels panel named CMYK. You can pop into this mode by choosing Image→Mode→CMYK Color.

Composite

Red

Green

Blue

FIGURE 5-3

Most likely, your image is already in RGB mode, especially if it came from a digital camera or a stock-image company.

See how the red, green, and blue channels differ in this cute cowgirl portrait? White areas indicate where the color in that channel is most concentrated, and black areas indicate where the color is weakest.

Back in early versions of Photoshop, if you wanted to generate a black-and-white version of a color photo, you typically picked the channel with the highest contrast and used that. Now, Photoshop gives you much better ways to convert from color to shades of gray such as Black & White and Gradient Map Adjustment layers (described on pages 308 and 311, respectively).

NOTE If you plan to print your image on a regular laser or inkjet printer, you don't need to be in CMYK mode (unless you want to create a quick, high-key effect as described in a moment). Also, this mode limits you to precious few filters (Chapter 15) and color or lighting adjustments (Chapter 9).

A professional printing press separates the four CMYK channels of your image into individual *color separations* (see page 706). Each separation is a perfect copy of the color channel you see in Photoshop, printed in its respective color (cyan, magenta, yellow, or black). When the printing press places these four colors atop each other, they form the full-color image. This technique is known as *four-color process* printing.

Because CMYK channels represent ink rather than light (as explained back on page 184), the grayscale information you see in your Channels panel represents the *opposite* of what it does in RGB mode. In CMYK mode, black indicates color at full strength and white indicates color at its weakest (see *Figure 5-4*). Does your brain hurt yet?

■ CREATING A HIGH-KEY PORTRAIT EFFECT

Even if you're not sending your image to a printing press, you can still have some fun in CMYK mode. For example, you may have noticed that the Black channel in *Figure 5-4* looks pretty darned neat. It resembles a popular portrait effect called *high-key* lighting, in which multiple light sources are aimed at the victim, er, subject to create a dazzling image with interesting shadows. Some folks labor long and hard to achieve this look in Photoshop when they could simply resort to a bit of channel theft instead. To create this effect, just extract the Black channel from a CMYK version of the image. Here's how:

1. **If your image is in RGB mode, make a copy of it by choosing Image→Duplicate.**

   Because you're going to change color modes in the next step, it's a good idea to do that on a copy of your image since you lose a bit of color info when you switch from one mode to another. If your image is already in CMYK mode, skip ahead to step 3.

2. **In the duplicate image, choose Image→Mode→CMYK Color.**

   If your document includes more than one layer, Photoshop asks if you want to combine them into one by flattening the image (compressing all layers into one). If those additional layers affect the way your image looks (for example, Adjustment layers), click Flatten. (Flattening a document is typically a scary move, but here you're working with a duplicate of your original document.)

   If you see another dialog box asking about color profiles, just click OK. You'll learn about profiles in Chapter 16. For now, all you need to know is that, since you'll end up back in your original RGB document in step 5, the CMYK profile won't affect anything.

3. **In the duplicate image's Channels panel, activate the Black channel.**

   When you click the Black channel to activate it, Photoshop automatically turns off the other channels' visibility.

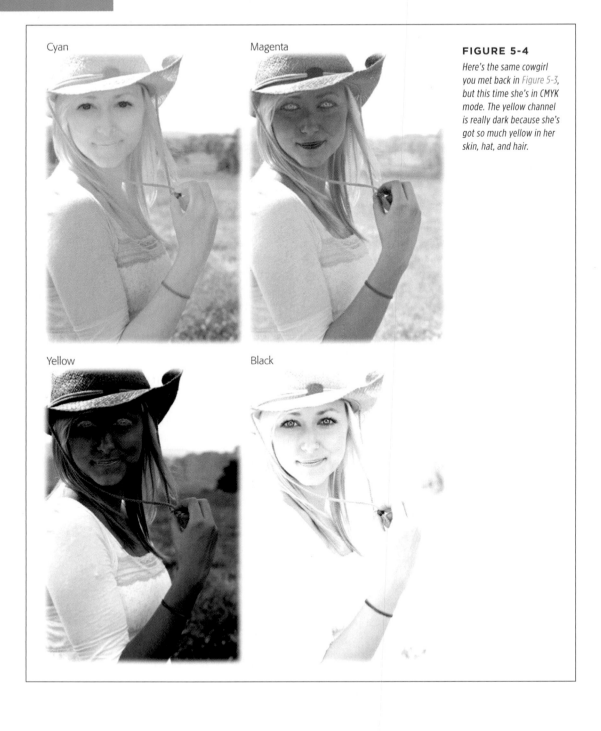

Cyan

Magenta

Yellow

Black

FIGURE 5-4

Here's the same cowgirl you met back in Figure 5-3, but this time she's in CMYK mode. The yellow channel is really dark because she's got so much yellow in her skin, hat, and hair.

TIP If you're preparing the high-key image for printing in true grayscale, meaning the image itself will be printed with black ink only (think newspapers), then you can skip the following steps and instead choose Split Channels from the Channels panel's menu. Photoshop instantly creates separate documents from each color channel. Simply find the one with "Black" in its name and call it a day. (For more on preparing grayscale images for a printing press, see the box on page 314.)

4. **Copy the Black channel.**

   Press ⌘-A (Ctrl+A) to select everything in the Black channel, and then copy it by pressing ⌘-C (Ctrl+C).

5. **Switch back to your original RGB document and paste the Black channel into the Layers panel.**

   Click the original RGB image's tab or inside its window. Next, open the Layers panel by clicking its icon in the panel dock or choosing Window→Layers. Then paste the Black channel by pressing ⌘-V (Ctrl+V). (You don't have to create a new layer; Photoshop does that for you.) The beauty of producing this effect inside your original RGB document is editing flexibility. For example, you can lower the opacity of the new Black layer for a completely different, yet interesting, partial high-key/partial color effect.

6. **Close the duplicate document (you don't need it anymore).**

That's it! You've now got yourself a beautiful, high-contrast look that took only minutes to achieve. And if the image doesn't have quite enough contrast for you, try adding a Brightness/Contrast Adjustment layer and changing its blend mode to Multiply (this maneuver is shown back on page 113).

Spot Channels

In the realm of CMYK printing, there's a special kind of premixed ink called a *spot color*, which requires a special kind of channel that tells the printer where to put that ink. If you're a graphic designer working in prepress (see the Note below), in packaging design, or at an ad agency, you need to know this stuff, and page 697 has the details. If you're a photographer or a Web designer, save your brainpower and forget you ever heard about spot channels.

NOTE *Prepress* refers to the process of preparing images and documents—usually in a page-layout program like Adobe InDesign or QuarkXPress—for printing on a commercial press.

Lab Channels

Lab mode separates an image's lightness values (how bright or dark it is) from its color information. This mode gets its name from the channels it includes: Lightness, a and b. Lab mode isn't used for output like RGB and CMYK modes; instead, it's useful when you want to alter an image's lightness values—when you're sharpening or brightening, for instance—but not its colors. (Likewise, you can adjust the color information without affecting the lightness values to, say, get rid of a color cast.) You can pop into Lab mode by choosing Image→Mode→Lab Color, and if you peek at the Channels panel, you'll see x-rayish images like the ones in *Figure 5-5*.

Here's what's in each channel:

- **Lightness**. This is where you'll find the details of your image, minus color; it looks like a really good black-and-white version.

- **a**. This channel contains half of the color information: a mixture of magenta (think "red") and green.

- **b**. Here's the other half: a mixture of yellow and blue.

Techniques that involve Lab mode are sprinkled throughout Part Two of this book.

Multichannel Mode

Unless you're preparing an image for a commercial printing press, you'll never use this mode—although you may switch to it accidentally. If you delete one of the color channels in an RGB, CMYK, or Lab mode document, Photoshop plops you into Multichannel mode without even asking. If that happens, just use the History panel to go back a step or press ⌘-Z (Ctrl+Z) to undo and bring back the channel you accidentally deleted.

Multichannel mode doesn't have a composite channel; it's strictly for two- or three-color print jobs. So whether you enter this mode on purpose by choosing Image→Mode→Multichannel or accidentally as described above, Photoshop converts any existing color channels to spot channels (page 698).

When you convert an image to Multichannel mode, Photoshop promptly does one of the following (depending on which color mode you were in before):

- **Converts the RGB channels** to cyan, magenta, and yellow spot channels.

- **Converts the CMYK channels** to cyan, magenta, yellow, and black spot channels.

- **Converts the Lab channels** to alpha channels named Alpha 1, Alpha 2, and Alpha 3.

- **Converts the Grayscale channel** to a black spot channel.

These radical channel changes cause drastic color shifts, but you can edit each channel individually—both its contents and its spot color—to create the image you want. When you're finished editing, save the image as a Photoshop (PSD) file by choosing File→Save As and picking Photoshop from the format menu.

Single-Channel Modes

The rest of Photoshop's image modes aren't very exciting when it comes to channels: They each have just one. They include Bitmap, Grayscale, Duotone, and Indexed Color mode (the latter is used in GIF files), and they're discussed back on page 35.

Lightness

a (red and green)

b (yellow and blue)

FIGURE 5-5

Here's that cowgirl again, now in Lab mode. In the a channel, lighter areas represent greens and darker areas represent magentas (reds). In the b channel, lighter areas represent blues and darker areas represent yellows.

Some folks swear that by splitting the Lightness channel into its own document and then making a few adjustments, you can create a black-and-white image worthy of Ansel Adams. See page 313 for the scoop on how to do that and then judge for yourself!

The Mighty Alpha Channel

Photoshop has one other type of channel: alpha channels. Their job is to store selections so you can use or edit them later.

These channels get their name from a process called *alpha compositing*, which combines a partially transparent image with another image. (Filmmakers use this process to create special effects and fake backdrops.) Information about the shape of the transparent area and the pixels' level of transparency has to be stored somewhere, and that somewhere is an alpha channel.

This is powerful stuff because the same technology lets you save selections. And, as you've learned, making selections can take a *ton* of time. (Heck, you may not have the stamina to finish creating a particularly challenging selection in one sitting!) And since clients change their minds occasionally—"Put the model in front of *this* bush, and change her hair color while you're at it"—the ability to save selections so you can mess with them later is a lifesaver. Likewise, a saved selection is crucial for making the Content-Aware Scale feature behave because the selection lets you tell Photoshop not to mess with certain areas in your image (see page 251 for the full scoop). As long as you save your document as a Photoshop file (page 39), that alpha channel will always be there for you to use. That ought to make you sleep better at night!

> **TIP** You can drag alpha channels between documents as long as both documents have the exact same pixel dimensions.

Folks sometimes refer to alpha channels as *channel masks* because, once you've created an alpha channel (as explained in the next section), you can use it to help you adjust certain portions of your image—kind of like when you use a layer mask (page 109). In fact, creating a layer mask by loading an alpha channel as a selection is a common use for alpha channels. That's because, as you'll learn on page 202, you can use channels to make incredibly detailed selections that are tough to get any other way.

> **NOTE** When you're in Quick Mask mode (page 176), you're actually working on a temporary alpha channel. Who knew?

Creating an Alpha Channel

It can be helpful to think of an alpha channel as a grayscale representation of your selection. Unless you change Photoshop's settings, the black parts of the channel are the unselected portion of your image—also referred to as the *protected* or *masked* part—and the white parts are the selection (see page 201 to learn how to reverse these colors). And, just like in a layer mask, shades of gray represent areas that are only partially selected, which means they're partially transparent.

Photoshop gives you several different ways to create an alpha channel:

- **Create a selection and then choose Select→Save Selection** (see page 179).

- **Create a selection and then click the "Save selection as channel" button at the bottom of the Channels panel**. It looks like a circle within a square (see *Figure 5-6*).

FIGURE 5-6

In most cases, you'll find it easier to create a selection first (even if it's rough) and then add your alpha channel, as shown here. (That way, you see the full-color image instead of a screen full of black or red.)

To do that, select something in your image and then, once you've got marching ants, click the "Save selection as channel" button (circled). Photoshop adds an alpha channel—which includes your selection—to the bottom of the Channels panel.

Alpha channel

- **Click the "Create new channel" button at the bottom of the Channels panel** (see *Figure 5-2* on page 187). When you do that, Photoshop creates an alpha channel named Alpha 1 and sticks it at the bottom of the Channels panel. The new channel is solid black because it's empty. To create a selection, turn on the composite channel's visibility to summon the red overlay of Quick Mask mode so you can see your image. Then grab the Brush tool (page 494) and paint the area you want to select white (think of this process as painting a hole through the mask so you can see—and therefore select—what's below it).

NOTE Though you can certainly start with an empty alpha channel, it's usually easier to create your selection (or at least a rough version of it) on the full-color image *before* adding the alpha channel (say, with the Quick Selection tool, discussed on page 146). Then you can fine-tune the alpha channel using the methods explained in the box on page 207.

- **Choose New Channel from the Channels panel's menu** (see *Figure 5-2*). When you choose this command, a dialog box opens that lets you name the new channel and tell Photoshop how to display the channel's info.

Straight from the factory, Photoshop shows selected areas (the parts of your image inside the marching ants) in white and unselected areas in black. Partially selected areas, which have soft edges, appear in shades of gray. If you'd rather see your selections in black and everything else in white, turn on the dialog box's Selected Areas radio button. If you want to edit your alpha channel using Quick Mask mode (as described later in this section), you can change the Quick Mask's color and opacity here. When you've got everything the way you want it, click OK to make Photoshop create your alpha channel.

TIP If you Option-click (Alt-click on a PC) the "Save selection as channel" button instead of just clicking it, you get the same dialog box as if you had chosen New Channel from the Channels panel's menu, which lets you name your sparkling new alpha channel. (You can rename a channel anytime by double-clicking its name.)

Editing Alpha Channels

Once you've got yourself an alpha channel, you can fine-tune it just like a layer mask (page 114) by painting with the Brush tool or using any selection tool. If you use a selection tool, you can choose Edit→Fill and then pick black or white from the Use menu, depending on whether you want to add to or subtract from your selection (selected areas are white, and everything else is black). If you want to reverse the way Photoshop displays the channel's info—so that your selection appears in black instead of white—just double-click the alpha channel's thumbnail in the Channels panel and, in the resulting Channel Options dialog box, turn on the Selected Areas option. When you do, Photoshop flip-flops your mask's colors, as shown in *Figure 5-7*.

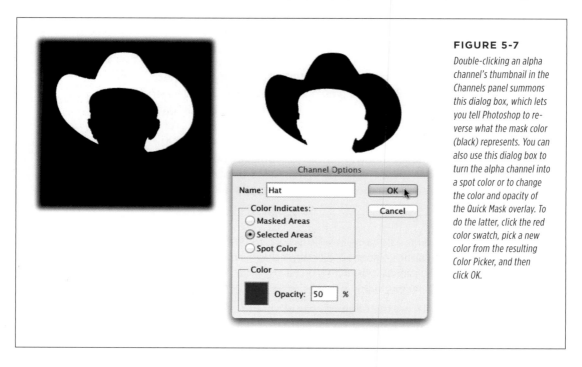

FIGURE 5-7

Double-clicking an alpha channel's thumbnail in the Channels panel summons this dialog box, which lets you tell Photoshop to reverse what the mask color (black) represents. You can also use this dialog box to turn the alpha channel into a spot color or to change the color and opacity of the Quick Mask overlay. To do the latter, click the red color swatch, pick a new color from the resulting Color Picker, and then click OK.

NOTE It doesn't matter whether you use black to mark the masked (protected) or selected (unprotected) areas of your image—it's a personal preference. Just pay careful attention to what the ants are marching 'round when you load an alpha channel as a selection, as *that's* the part of the image you'll modify when you start making changes. And keep in mind that, as you learned in the box on page 153, sometimes it's easier to select what you *don't* want and then use Select→Inverse to flip-flop your selection than to select what you *do* want.

You can also edit your alpha channel using Quick Mask mode. To do that, in the Channels panel, activate the alpha channel and then click the composite channel's visibility eye, as shown in *Figure 5-8*. When you do, Photoshop puts Quick Mask mode's signature red overlay atop your image. (If you're editing an alpha channel in an image with a lot of red in it, you won't be able to see diddly through the mask, so change the overlay's color as described in *Figure 5-7*.)

FIGURE 5-8

If you activate an alpha channel and then turn on the composite channel's visibility eye (circled), you can edit or create a selection from scratch in Quick Mask mode. Here, the Brush tool (the white circle beneath the hat brim) set to paint with black is being used to fine-tune the masked area around the little cowboy's forehead. If you mess up and mask too much—by painting with black across part of the hat, say, thereby subtracting it from your selection—press X to flip-flop your color chips and paint across that area with white to add it back to your selection (just like you would with a layer mask).

You can also run filters on an alpha channel, just like you can with a layer mask. Among the most practical are Gaussian Blur for softening the selection's edge (helpful in making the pixels you're changing blend in better with surrounding pixels) and the Minimum filter for tightening your selection (page 671). Chapter 15 shows these filters in action.

Loading an Alpha Channel as a Selection

Once you're finished editing an alpha channel, you can transform it into a selection so you can actually *do* something with it. You can summon the marching ants in several ways:

- You can ⌘-click (Ctrl-click) the alpha channel's thumbnail in the Channels panel.

- Click the "Load channel as selection" button at the bottom of the Channels panel (it looks like a tiny dotted circle) while you've got an alpha channel active.

- Drag the alpha channel onto the "Load channel as selection" button (let go of your mouse as soon as Photoshop highlights the button).

Now you can perform all the amazing color and lighting adjustments explained throughout this book, and they'll affect only the area you've selected.

Deleting Alpha Channels

When you're finished using an alpha channel (or if you want to start over with a new one), you can get rid of it by dragging it onto the Delete button (the little trash can) at the bottom of the Channels panel. Or just click the trash can while the alpha channel is active and then click Yes when Photoshop asks if you're *sure* you want to throw it away.

> **NOTE** Unless you're a panel neat freak, you don't have to throw out old alpha channels. They don't add all that much to your document's file size because they're black and white (if they contain a lot of gray, they'll add slightly more to the file size, but not enough that it's worth tossing 'em). If you've created a slew of incredibly complex alpha channels, then you might see a bump in file size. Nevertheless, if there's even the slightest chance you'll ever use them again, save your document as a PSD file (or TIFF, for that matter) to keep those hard-earned alpha channels intact.

■ Basic Channel Stunts

Now that you know what channels are all about, it's time to learn some of the cool things you can do with them. This section covers a few of the most practical channel tricks, and you'll find other techniques involving channels throughout this book.

Selecting Objects with Channels

As you learned in Chapter 4, true selection wisdom lies in knowing which tool to start with so you'll have the least fine-tuning to do later. If you have an image with a decent amount of contrast between the item you want to select and its background, you can give channels a spin. All you need to do is create an alpha channel that contains only black-and-white objects, load it as a selection, and then use it to make a layer mask. Here's how to use channels to select all the balloons in *Figure 5-9* so you can, for example, swap in a new sky:

1. **Open an image that's in RGB mode and that has a background you want to swap.**

   If your image came from a scanner or digital camera, it's already in RGB mode. To check, choose Image→Mode. If necessary, choose RGB Color to switch modes.

FIGURE 5-9

Once you find the channel where the objects you want to select appear darkest (typically the blue channel), make a copy of that channel so you don't mess up your original photo with the lightening or darkening you're about to perform.

To copy a channel, simply drag it onto the "Create new channel" button, and Photoshop adds the copy to the bottom of your Channels panel, as shown here.

Want to follow along? Visit this book's Missing CD page at www.missingmanuals.com/cds and download the practice file Balloons.jpg.

2. **Find the channel where the objects you want to select look the darkest.**

   In the Channels panel, click each channel to find the one where the balloons are the darkest. (You can also cycle through channels by pressing ⌘-3, 4, and 5 [Ctrl+3, 4, 5 on a PC].) Objects will usually be darkest on the blue channel, as is the case here.

   > **TIP** In the past, using channels was the only way to create really tough selections around hair and fur. However, in Photoshop CS5, the Refine Edge dialog box improved so much that it's becoming the preferred method. That said, it can be extremely helpful to use Channels to create a selection that you then *fine-tune* with the Refine Edge dialog box. Page 165 has more on using Refine Edge.

3. **Duplicate the blue channel so you don't destroy your original image.**

   Either Control-click (right-click) the blue channel in the Channels panel and then pick Duplicate Channel from the shortcut menu, or drag the channel onto the "Create new channel" button. (You can also choose Duplicate Channel from the Channels panel's menu, but dragging is quicker.) Whichever method you use, Photoshop puts the duplicate at the bottom of the Channels panel and cleverly names it "Blue copy."

4. **Adjust the duplicate blue channel's Levels to make the balloons black and the background white.**

   Chapter 9 covers Levels in detail, but this exercise gives you a sneak peek at how useful this kind of adjustment can be. With the duplicate blue channel active in the Channels panel, choose Image→Adjustments→Levels or press ⌘-L (Ctrl+L) to summon the Levels dialog box. To make the balloons darker, drag the shadows slider (*Figure 5-10*, top) to the right until the balloons turn *almost* black. (As you drag the slider, the background gets darker, too. That's OK—you'll fix the background in the next step.) Don't close the Levels dialog box just yet!

FIGURE 5-10

Top: Depending on the amount of contrast in your image, you may have to drag the shadows slider (circled) quite a ways to the right to make the balloons black. But be careful: If you drag it too far to the right, you'll start to lose some of the detail around their edges.

Bottom: Next, click the white eyedropper (circled) and then, over in your image, click the background area until it's as white as it'll get. When your image is pure black and white, as shown here, you're ready to load the channel as a selection. (If you can't seem to make it pure black and white, don't panic; just proceed to step 6.)

5. **Using the white eyedropper, click the gray background to make it white.**

   The little white eyedropper on the right side of the dialog box lets you tell Photoshop what should be white (pros call this technique "resetting the white point"). Click the eyedropper to activate it, mouse over to your document, and then click a gray part of the background (see *Figure 5-10*, bottom). Keep clicking on different gray areas until the background is completely white (or as close to white as you can get it). When you're finished, click OK to close the Levels dialog box.

6. **If necessary, touch up the inside of the balloons with black paint and the background with white paint.**

   If adjusting the shadows slider in step 4 didn't make the balloons *completely* black (as in *Figure 5-10*, top), use the Brush tool to touch them up (otherwise the balloons will be only partially selected). Press B to grab the Brush tool, set your foreground color chip to black (press D to set the color chips to black and white, and then press X until black hops on top), and then mouse over to the balloons and paint them solid black. And, if resetting the white point in step 5 didn't get rid of all the gray in the background—like in the upper-right corner of the balloon image in *Figure 5-10*, bottom—use the Brush tool to paint those areas white. (Alternatively, you can use the Lasso tool to hand draw a selection around an area; choose Edit→Fill, pick Black from the Use menu, and then click OK.) When you're finished, you should have a pure black-and-white image.

TIP   When you're touching up an alpha channel using the Brush tool, be sure to zoom into your image to make sure you're being precise with your brushstrokes (on a 4 MB image, for example, you need to zoom in to at least 500 percent). You may also need to switch to a hard-edged brush using the Brush Preset picker in the Options bar to ensure you don't create too soft an edge around the object you're painting. See page 50 for more on zooming and page 495 for more on changing Brush tool options.

---

7. **In the Channels panel, load the duplicate blue channel as a selection by ⌘-clicking (Ctrl-clicking) the channel's thumbnail or clicking the "Load channel as selection" button (the dotted circle) at the bottom of the panel.**

   Now that you've got a perfectly black-and-white image (it looks just like a layer mask or alpha channel, doesn't it?), you can load it as a selection. When you do, Photoshop puts marching ants around the *background* of your image, which is the opposite of what you want. No worries! You'll solve that problem in the next step.

8. **Invert the selection to select the balloons instead of the background.**

   Choose Select→Inverse or press Shift-⌘-I (Shift+Ctr +I) to flip-flop your selection so the marching ants run around the balloons instead of around the edges of the document.

9. **In the Channels panel, turn on the composite channel and hide the duplicate blue channel.**

   Scroll to the top of the Channels panel and click near the composite channel's name (RGB) to turn it back on so you can see the full-color version of your image again. (This also turns off the visibility of the duplicate blue channel.) You can delete the duplicate blue channel by dragging it to the tiny trash can at the bottom of the Channels panel or leave it hanging around in case you need to edit it later.

10. **Open your Layers panel, unlock the Background layer, and then add a mask.**

    Click the Layers tab to open the Layers panel or choose Window→Layers. If the Background layer still has a little padlock icon next to it, double-click the icon to unlock the layer. If you like, type a name for the Background layer in the resulting dialog box and then click OK. (If you're working with an image you've edited before, you may have already named your Background layer something other than "Background.") To add a layer mask, click the circle-within-a-square button at the bottom of the Layers panel. Photoshop adds a layer mask that hides the photo's original background (the sky), as shown in *Figure 5-11*, left. Sweet!

You're all finished! You can now copy and paste a new background into the Layers panel and then drag it to the bottom of the layer stack to put the balloons on a brand-new sky (see *Figure 5-11*). If you need to edit the layer mask (page 114), activate it in the Layers panel and then paint with either black or white according to what you want to do (conceal or reveal, respectively).

FIGURE 5-11

Look, Ma, no selection tools! Whenever you have an image like this one that's got a decent amount of contrast between its subject and its background, using channels is an easy way to create an accurate selection fast.

Creating a Silhouette Effect

Apple made silhouettes famous by using them in its iPod and iTunes advertising campaigns. You can use the channel-selection technique described in the previous section to create the same effect. The only difference is that, instead of adding a layer mask, you'll add a Solid Color Fill layer set to black. That way, the silhouette lives on its own layer, making it easy for you to edit it later, as the Apple-esque images in *Figure 5-12* show.

Touching Up Alpha Channels

When you're editing an alpha channel to make a selection, it's important that you end up with a pure black-and-white channel with very few shades of gray. (The alpha channel shown in *Figure 5-10*, bottom, is almost there but needs a tiny bit of touch-up on the balloons). If there are any gray areas around the edge of the object, those edges will look soft—as if you've feathered them (page 141). If there's any gray in the center of the object, those pixels will be only partially selected (and if there's any white, they won't be selected at all). Adjusting the alpha channel's Levels usually gets your image *close* to pure black and white, but that method can only do so much: You're often left with stray gray pixels here and there, a selection that isn't quite solid black or white, or some stuff in the background that you don't need. Your only choice at that point is to touch up the image by hand.

Sure, this kind of work is tedious, but it goes much faster if you use one of the following methods. Remember that when you're in Channels Land, you've got most (but not all) of Photoshop's tools at your command. With that in mind, here are a few tricks for touching up alpha channels:

- **Fill the background with black or white**. If you've managed to make your object pure black, you can use a selection tool to grab everything else in the channel and make it white. For example, use the Lasso tool to draw a rough selection around your black object and then choose Select→Inverse to select the background instead. Next, choose Edit→Fill, pick white from the Use menu, and then click OK. Now your background is solid white and your touch-up work is limited to the area right around your object. (If the object you want to select is solid white, use this method to fill the background with black instead.)

- **Fill in the object with black or white**. When the object you want to select isn't *quite* solid black or white, your best bet is to set the Brush tool to either black or white and then paint the object by hand. Or use the Lasso tool to draw a rough selection around that area and then choose Edit→Fill and pick black or white from the Use

menu. (If the area is square or oval, use the Rectangular or Elliptical Marquee tool to select it instead.) When you click OK, Photoshop fills that area with color. (For more on the selection tools, see Chapter 4.)

- **Get rid of stray gray pixels inside a black object**. If you've cleaned up the rest of your alpha channel but still see a few gray pixels in your black object, use Levels to turn them black. Remember how you used Levels to turn gray pixels white by resetting the white point (step 5 on page 204)? You can use the same technique to turn gray pixels black. Just open the Levels dialog box by pressing ⌘-L (Ctrl+L), select the *black* eyedropper, mouse over to your image, and then click one of those pesky gray pixels. Photoshop turns all the gray pixels in your document black.

- **Get rid of stray gray pixels next to a black object**. If you end up with a few gray pixels near the object you want to select, use a white brush set to Overlay mode (see page 284) to paint them white. Press B to select the Brush tool and set your foreground color chip to white. Then hop up to the Options bar and set the Mode menu to Overlay and Opacity to 100%. In this mode, the Brush tool *completely* ignores the color black and turns gray pixels white, letting you brush away gray pixels near black areas without fear of messing up the black. Even if you paint right over the black area, nothing happens to it!

- **Turn gray pixels in delicate edges black**. If you're dealing with hair or fur, some of the wispier edges may end up more gray than black. If that happens, grab the Brush tool and set your foreground color chip to black. Then trot up to the Options bar and change the Mode menu to Soft Light (page 285). Now, when you paint over the hair or fur, Photoshop turns the gray pixels black. However, you may not want to turn those delicate parts *completely* black or they'll have hard edges and won't blend into the background very well. You'll have to experiment to see what looks best.

FIGURE 5-12

Using channels to make a selection lets you create a slick silhouette in no time flat. You can even get a clean selection of curly hair (top) and dangling feathers (bottom).

When you're dealing with delicate edges like those around hair, be careful not to drag the Levels dialog box's shadows slider too far to the right or the edges will become really jagged. You'll have a little more touch-up work to do before you're finished, but it's worth it. Here, the Lasso tool was used to select areas that didn't become black by dragging the shadows slider, and then they were filled with black using the Edit→Fill command.

Heck, these two images require less fine-tuning than the balloons back in Figure 5-11!

NOTE Try this silhouette technique by visiting this book's Missing CD page at *www.missingmanuals.com/ cds* and downloading the practice file *Indian.jpg*.

To create a quick silhouette, follow steps 1–9 in the previous section so you've got a nice selection and you're looking at the full-color image. Then:

1. **Add a new Solid Color Fill layer at the top of your layer stack.**

   When you see marching ants running around your subject, you're ready to create a Solid Color Fill layer. Take a peek at the bottom of the Layers panel and click the Adjustment layer icon (the half-black/half-white circle). Choose Solid Color from the menu to make Photoshop open the Color Picker; pick black, and then click OK. (Sure, you could create a regular ol' Image layer and fill it with black, but this way is faster; see page 67 for the full story on Fill layers.) Photoshop adds the new layer to the top of your layer stack, creating a silhouette.

2. **Add a new background by creating another Solid Color Fill layer and filling it with a bright color.**

   Create another Solid Color Fill layer as you did in step 1, but this time choose a really bright color, such as lime green, and then click OK.

3. **Drag the bright-colored Fill layer below the silhouette layer.**

   This keeps the new background from covering your silhouette. You can also press ⌘-[(Ctrl+[) to move a layer down one position, or Shift-⌘-[(Shift+Ctrl+[) to move it to the bottom of the layer stack.

Now you're starting to see the power of using channels to help make selections! If you need to edit the silhouette—maybe you want to erase something or do a little touch-up with a black brush—activate the black Solid Color Fill layer's mask and have at it. Likewise, if you want to change the silhouette or background color, simply double-click the appropriate Solid Color Fill layer's *thumbnail* and then pick a new color from the resulting Color Picker (double-clicking the layer itself opens the Layer Style dialog box instead).

Lightening and Darkening Channels

There will be times when you wish a channel were lighter or darker so you'd have an easier time making a selection. Remember back in Chapter 3 when you learned how to quickly lighten and darken photos using blend modes? While there's no blend mode menu in the Channels panel, you can make a channel lighter or darker with the Apply Image command. Folks mainly use this command to blend two images together (as shown in the "The Apply Image Command" PDF available from this book's Missing CD page at *www.missingmanuals.com/cds*)—which is why the Apply Image dialog box has a blend mode drop-down menu—but you can also use it to apply a channel to *itself* (as if the channel were duplicated) and change its blend mode at the same time.

To lighten or darken a channel, activate it in the Channels panel and then create a copy of it (see page 203) so you don't destroy your original image. Then choose Image→Apply Image and, in the resulting dialog box (shown in *Figure 5-13*), choose either Screen (to lighten) or Multiply (to darken) from the Blending menu. When you click OK, Photoshop applies the channel to itself using the blend mode you picked. Depending on the image you're working with, your channel will lighten or darken by about 15 to 30 percent. If it needs to be even lighter or darker, simply run the Apply Image command as many times as necessary.

FIGURE 5-13

With the Apply Image command, you can apply a channel to itself but with a different blend mode.

As you can see here, applying the Screen blend mode to a duplicate of the red channel made this horse quite a bit whiter, making it easier to turn the horse solid white in an alpha channel.

TIP If the Apply Image command isn't lightening or darkening your duplicate channel enough to make a good alpha channel, you can always pump up the contrast by adding a temporary Brightness/Contrast Adjustment layer (see page 354) and then dragging the Contrast slider in the resulting Properties panel to the right. By using an Adjustment layer, the temporary contrast boost happens on its own layer, so you can throw it away after you've created the alpha channel.

Combining Channels

Not all images have enough contrast to let you make a good alpha channel by using just one channel—sometimes you'll have to use *two*. This process takes a bit more time, but the steps are essentially the same.

For example, if you want to select the hat and guitar in *Figure 5-14,* a quick glance at the Channels panel tells you that the hat is darkest in the red channel, but the guitar has the most contrast in the green channel. So your best bet is to build your selection one channel at a time, using the optimal channel for each part. Duplicate the red channel and adjust it using Levels, the Brush tool, and so on until the hat is solid black. Next, duplicate the green channel and work on the guitar while you erase (or paint over) the parts of that channel you don't need (the hat). When you're finished, you may want to merge them, but, alas, Photoshop won't let you. But you *can* combine them into a brand-new channel using the *Calculations* command.

Choose Image→Calculations to summon the Calculations dialog box (if this command is grayed out, check to make sure you've got only *one* channel active in the Channels panel). From the drop-down menus in the Source 1 and Source 2 sections, pick the channels you want to combine as shown in *Figure 5-14.* This dialog box also lets you set the blend mode, so if you're working with a black object and a white background as shown in the figure, set the blend mode to Multiply so Photoshop keeps the darkest parts of both channels and gets rid of everything else. (If you're working with a white object and a black background, use the Screen blend mode instead so Photoshop keep the *lightest* parts of both channels.) When everything's set, click OK, and Photoshop creates a new channel based on the two you picked.

> **NOTE** You can also use the *Channel Mixer* to simulate combining channels to create grayscale images. It doesn't actually combine channels, but it makes your image *look* like it did. The box on page 478 has the details.

Sharpening Individual Channels

As you'll learn in Chapter 11, if you sharpen an image that has a lot of noise in it, you'll sharpen the noise and grain right along with the rest of the image, making it look ten times worse than it did before (see the box on page 455). That's why it's important to get rid of—or, at the very least, reduce—those nasties *before* you sharpen an image.

> **NOTE** What's the difference between noise and grain? They both describe tiny flecks in an image, but, technically speaking, noise occurs in digital images, whereas grain occurs in analog prints, film, and transparencies. In other words, grain becomes noise once you scan the image.

However, let's say you're in RGB mode and you dutifully followed the instructions on page 455 and ran the Reduce Noise filter on your blue channel (which typically has the most noise, though sometimes noise can hide in the red channel, too), and it didn't do squat. What do you do? You can try bringing out some of the details in your image by sharpening *only* the red and green channels, as shown in *Figure 5-15.*

FIGURE 5-14

Photoshop doesn't let you merge two channels into one, but you can combine them into a new channel using the Calculations command: Choose Image→Calculations and, in the dialog box shown here, set the Channel menu in the Source 1 section to "Red copy" and the menu in the Source 2 section to "Green copy." Then choose Multiply from the Blending menu if you want to create a black object or Screen if you want to create a white one.

FIGURE 5-15

If you activate the red and green channels before running a sharpening filter, you restrict the sharpening to just those two channels. This helps you avoid sharpening—and therefore accentuating—noise or other unwanted, ahem, skin textures.

TIP The next time you need to sharpen a portrait of someone who's sensitive about his or her appearance, try sharpening only the red channel to avoid bringing out unwanted details in the person's skin. (As you learned earlier in this chapter, your camera has twice as many green sensors as red or blue, meaning that a lot of the fine details lurk in the green channel.)

Here's how to sharpen an image without making the noise in it any worse than it already is:

1. **Open your image and make a copy of the layer(s) you're going to sharpen.**

   If you're working with a document that has just one layer, activate it in your Layers panel and then duplicate it by pressing ⌘-J (Ctrl+J). If you like, double-click the layer's name and rename it *Sharpen*.

   If you're working on a multilayer document, Shift-click to activate all the layers and then choose Layer→Smart Objects→Convert to Smart Object. Photoshop combines all the layers into a single Smart Object. (To access the individual layers again, double-click the Smart Object and a new temporary document opens with the original layers fully intact; just perform your edits, choose File→Save, close the temporary document and your changes appear back in the *original* document that houses the Smart Object.)

2. **Open the Channels panel and activate both the red and green channels.**

   Click to activate one channel and then Shift-click to activate the other one, so they're both highlighted in the Channels panel. Don't panic if your image turns a weird color like the horse in *Figure 5-15*; Photoshop is just showing you the image using only those two color channels.

FREQUENTLY ASKED QUESTION

Selecting with the Lightest Channel

How come I always have to make objects black and the background white when I'm using channels to create a selection? Can I do it the other way around instead?

Trying to buck the system, are ya? Lucky for you, the answer is yes—you can make the object white and the background black instead, if you prefer. It doesn't matter whether the area you want to select is black or white; all that matters is what the marching ants surround once you load that channel as a selection.

For example, if you're trying to select a light object that lives on a dark background, it's *much* easier to make the object white and the background black. In that case, search for the *lightest* channel (which, in RGB mode, is usually red). Once you find it, duplicate that channel and then use Levels to make it pure black and white (see step 4 on page 204). You won't even need to inverse your selection: You'll see marching ants around your object as soon as you load the channel as a selection (page 205, step 7).

3. **Choose Filter→Sharpen→Unsharp Mask (page 456).**

When you run a filter while you've got only certain channels active, Photoshop applies the sharpening to just those channels. In this case, it won't apply any sharpening to the blue channel. Click OK to close the Unsharp Mask dialog box.

4. **In the Channels panel, turn on the composite channel (here, that's RGB) to see your new and improved full-color image.**

You're done! If you want to see before and after versions of the image, open the Layers panel and toggle the Sharpen layer's visibility eye—or the Unsharp Mask filter layer, if you used a Smart Object—off and on.

TIP Another, more advanced way to sharpen an image is to use the channel with the highest contrast to create an intricate edge mask, or for foolproof sharpening, try using the High Pass filter. You can read all about those techniques—including how to sharpen only certain areas of an image—in Chapter 11.

Cropping, Resizing, and Rotating

Cropping and resizing affect your entire document (not just the active layer), and are among the most basic edits you'll ever make—but they're also among the most important. A bad crop (or no crop) can ruin an image, while a good crop can improve it tenfold by snipping away useless or distracting material. And knowing how to resize an image—by changing either its file size or its overall dimensions—can be crucial when it's time to email the image, print it, or post it on a website. Cropping is pretty straightforward (though the process has changed from how it worked in previous versions of Photoshop); resizing, not so much. To resize an image correctly, you first need to understand the relationship between pixels and resolution—and how they affect image quality. (That can of worms gets opened on page 233.) And if you want to make Photoshop resize your image's background without touching its subject, the Content-Aware Scale command can get that done, though there's a trick to using it successfully. Rotating images, on the other hand, is just plain fun.

In this chapter, you'll learn more than you ever wanted to know about cropping, from general guidelines to the many ways of cropping (and straightening) in both Photoshop and Camera Raw (a powerful photo-correcting application that comes with Photoshop—see Chapter 9). Perhaps most important, you'll understand once and for all what resolution really is and when it matters. You'll also discover how to resize images *without*—and this is crucial—losing image quality for print, email and the Web, presentation software, and more. Need to resize a slew of images? No problem, this chapter will teach you how to use the Image Processor command to get it done fast. Finally, you'll glean the secrets for using the Content-Aware Scale command and spend some quality playtime with the various Transform commands.

◼ Cropping Images

There's a reason professional photos look so darn good. Besides being shot with fancy cameras and receiving some post-processing fluffing, they're also composed or cropped extremely well (or both). *Cropping* means eliminating distracting elements in an image by cutting away unwanted bits around the edges. Good crops accentuate the subject, drawing the viewer's eye to it; and bad crops are, well, just bad, as you can see in *Figure 6-1*.

FIGURE 6-1

Left: A poorly cropped image can leave the viewer distracted by extraneous stuff around the edges, like the wall and shadows here.

Right: A well-cropped image forces the viewer to focus on the subject by eliminating distractions (in this case, the empty space in the back-ground). This crop also gives the subject a little breathing room in the direction she's facing, which is always *a good idea (see Figure 6-2 for more examples).*

Technically, you can crop *before* you take a photo by moving closer to the subject (called "cropping with your feet") and repositioning the subject within the frame. However, if you don't get the shot right when you're out in the field, Photoshop can fix it after the fact. But before you go grabbing the Crop tool, you need to learn a few guidelines.

The Rule of Thirds

Once you understand the rule of thirds, a compositional guideline cherished by both photography and video pros, you'll spot it in almost every image you see. The idea is to divide every picture into nine equal parts using an imaginary tic-tac-toe grid. If you position the image's horizon on either the top or the bottom line—never the center—and the focal point (the most important part of the image) on one of the spots where the lines intersect, you create a more interesting shot. It's simpler than it sounds—just take a look at *Figure 6-2*.

NOTE The Crop tool actually *comes with* a rule-of-thirds grid, making this rule easier than ever to grasp and follow!

FIGURE 6-2

Top: Imagine a tic-tac-toe grid atop every image. Notice that the interesting bits of the photos are positioned where the lines intersect. Most digital cameras let you add such a grid to the camera's screen to help you compose shots, though to figure out how to turn it on, you may have to root through the camera's menus or (shudder) dig out the owner's manual.

Bottom: Before you crop, notice the direction the subject is facing. A good crop gives the subject room to move—or, in this case, fly— through the photo. If the image were cropped tightly to the boy's face on the right side, it'd look weird because he'd (theoretically) smack into the edge of the image if he flew away.

Creative Cropping

Along with applying the rule of thirds, pros also crop in unexpected ways, as *Figure 6-3* shows. Unconventional cropping is yet another way to add visual interest in order to catch the viewer's eye.

Creative cropping is especially important when you're dealing with super-small images, such as those in a thumbnail gallery or on a website where several images vie for attention. In such tiny images, people can see few, if any, details, and, if the photo contains people, *forget* being able to identify them. Here are some tips for creating truly enticing teensy-weensy images:

- **Recrop the image**. Instead of scaling down the original, focus on a single element in the image. You often don't need to include the *whole* subject for people to figure out what it is (*Figure 6-3*, middle, is a good example).

- **Sharpen again after resizing**. Even if you sharpened the original, go ahead and resharpen it post-resizing using one of the techniques covered in Chapter 11.

- **Add a border**. To add a touch of class to that tiny ad or thumbnail, give it an elegant hairline border (page 181) or a rounded edge (page 143).

Now that you've absorbed a few cropping guidelines, you're ready to learn the many ways you can crop in Photoshop, starting with the most common.

FIGURE 6-3

Top: Challenge yourself to think outside the box and crop in unexpected ways. You may not think cropping someone's face in half is a good idea, but here's an example where it works.

Middle: When you're close-cropping, you often don't need to reveal the whole subject. For example, this piece of zebra is more visually interesting than the whole animal, and it's still obvious what it's a photo of.

Bottom: Here's proof that you can't always trust what you see. Cropping can easily alter the perceived meaning of an image. For example, the left-hand photo has been creatively cropped to suit the headline "Sea Muffin Wins by a Mile!" But the original photo on the right reveals another story.

The Crop Tool

Photoshop tools don't get much easier to use than the good ol' Crop tool, which got a major overhaul back in CS6. Press C to grab it from the Tools panel and a crop box with transparent handles automatically surrounds your image. Grab any handle to resize the box (the handles darken when you do this), and then click *inside* the box and drag to reposition *your image* underneath it (your cursor turns into a tiny arrow). If you'd rather draw your *own* crop box instead of resizing the one Photoshop put around the image, just click and drag in your image to draw another one *inside* the automatic one (it feels weird but it works); however, if you've already adjusted the automatic crop box, press Esc to start over. To move the crop box *as* you're drawing it, press and hold the space bar while dragging; when you've got the crop box where you want it, let go of the space bar and continue drawing the box.

> **TIP** Happily, in CC, you no longer see a crop box around your image *whenever* the Crop tool is active. Once you press Return (Enter) to accept a crop, the automatic crop box is gone for good. That said, if you switch to another tool and then switch *back* to the Crop tool, the automatic crop box reappears.

Either way, as soon as you let go of your mouse, Photoshop helpfully darkens the outer portion of the image to give you an idea of what's destined for the trash can (this darkened portion is called a *shield*) and places a rule-of-thirds grid over the unshielded portion (*Figure 6-4*). When you like what you see, press Return (Enter on a PC) or double-click inside the crop box to accept it, and Photoshop deletes the unwanted pixels.

> **TIP** Photoshop includes a bushel of crop overlay options that you can access in the Options bar's Overlay drop-down menu (labeled in *Figure 6-5*). Once you click the crop box to activate it, you can cycle through the various overlays by pressing the O key repeatedly. To change an overlay's orientation (to, say, make the Golden Spiral appear at the upper left of your image instead of the lower right), press Shift-O repeatedly.

FIGURE 6-4

Top: The Crop tool lives near the top of the Tools panel; just click its icon and hold down your mouse button to expand its toolset, as shown here. It shares its toolset with the Perspective Crop tool (page 223).

Right: After you tweak the automatic crop box or draw your own, Photoshop places a rule-of-thirds grid atop the image and gives you an idea of what the end result will look like by darkening the parts that'll be cropped out. You can easily resize and rotate the crop box using the handles circled here (they look like little bars, and their color changes depending on the image colors underneath 'em). A handy info overlay appears near your cursor. If you're dragging a handle to resize the crop box, the overlay includes info about the size of the box (as shown here). If you're repositioning the crop box, the overlay indicates how much the crop box has moved, and if you're rotating the box, it indicates the angle of rotation. Handy!

> **TIP** You can toggle the crop shield off and on by pressing the forward slash key (/); Photoshop shows you a preview of what your cropped image looks like. You can also change the shield's color and transparency using the Crop Options drop-down menu (the gear icon labeled in *Figure 6-5*, too). To temporarily hide the soon-to-be-cropped edges so you can better judge what the cropped image will look like, press the H key; press it again to make the edges reappear.

Keep in mind, though, that when you accept a crop, Photoshop *deletes everything in the shielded area permanently*—that is, unless you *uncheck* the Delete Cropped Pixels checkbox in the Options bar (circled in *Figure 6-5*, top; as of this writing, it's automatically turned *on* when you install the program). So if you change your mind immediately after wielding the crop ax, press ⌘-Z (Ctrl+Z) to undo it or step backward in the History panel (page 15).

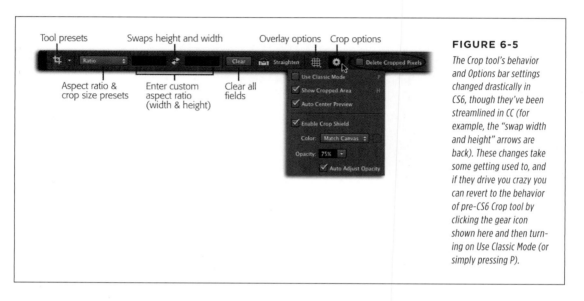

Tool presets　　　Swaps height and width　　　Overlay options　Crop options

Aspect ratio &　　Enter custom　　　Clear all
crop size presets　aspect ratio　　　fields
　　　　　　　(width & height)

FIGURE 6-5

The Crop tool's behavior and Options bar settings changed drastically in CS6, though they've been streamlined in CC (for example, the "swap width and height" arrows are back). These changes take some getting used to, and if they drive you crazy you can revert to the behavior of pre-CS6 Crop tool by clicking the gear icon shown here and then turning on Use Classic Mode (or simply pressing P).

> **TIP** You can use the Crop tool to straighten images, too. Skip to page 227 to see this technique in action.

If you turn *off* the Delete Cropped Pixels checkbox, Photoshop doesn't vaporize the cropped material; it politely dangles it outside the document's margins instead (in other words, hides it). That way, even though you don't see it onscreen, it's still part of your document. To resurrect the cropped portion—*even after you've saved and closed the document*—press C to activate the Crop tool again and then immediately press Return (Enter on a PC). Photoshop displays the previously hidden edges of the image and places an active crop box around the previously cropped area. At this point, you can resize the crop box to encompass the whole image to get those edges back, reposition the crop box, and so on.

■ CROPPING TO A SPECIFIC SHAPE, SIZE, AND RESOLUTION

The Crop tool lets you constrain your crop box to the image's original *aspect ratio*—the relationship between its width and height (a good idea if you want the cropped image to be the same shape as the original). To do so, choose Original Ratio from the aspect-ratio-and-crop-size preset drop-down menu labeled in *Figure 6-5*, top, and the crop box restricts itself accordingly (why this menu isn't labeled in the Options bar is anyone's guess). This menu also includes common aspect ratios such as 1:1, 4:5, 5:7, and so on; give one a click and that aspect ratio appears in the fields to the menu's right. If you don't see the aspect ratio you want, just enter the values into the fields yourself.

Choosing an aspect ratio from this menu or entering numbers manually changes the *shape* of the image but *doesn't* change its resolution (resolution controls pixel size, as explained on page 233). For example, if you're preparing an image for a 5"×7" frame, changing the aspect ratio lets you adjust the photo's *shape* to fit the frame; Photoshop then alters the pixel dimensions accordingly by trimming pixels off the edges of the image to make it match the aspect ratio you picked, but it doesn't mess with the image's resolution. Once the image is the right shape, you can always use the Image Size dialog box to alter its resolution manually (see page 234).

If you frequently enter the same dimensions into the Options bar's aspect ratio fields, you can save them as a preset. After you enter them in the Options bar, choose New Crop Preset from the aspect-ratio-and-crop-size drop-down menu; in the resulting dialog box, give the preset a meaningful name, and then click OK. Your new preset shows up in that same menu for easy access later on.

NOTE   In CS6, Adobe removed the resolution field from the Crop tool's Options bar in favor of a separate dialog box (so you didn't *accidentally* change an image's resolution when cropping it). In CC, that dialog box is gone and you can make the resolution field appear by choosing W × H × Resolution from the Options bar's aspect-ratio-and-crop-size preset menu. Yay!

If you *want* to change the image's pixel dimensions and resolution, choose W × H × Resolution from the aspect-ratio-and-crop-size preset menu. When you do, a new field appears in the Options bar so you can enter resolution (see *Figure 6-6*). Just enter the size you want into the width and height fields, and be sure to include a unit of measurement (use *px* for pixels or *in* for inches), or else Photoshop uses the unit of measurement you've specified in the Units and Rulers preferences (page 25). For example, if you want to print a 5"×7" image, enter *5 in* in the width field, *7 in* into the height field, and *300 in* the resolution field. If you want an 800×600 pixel image to email or post on the Web, enter *800 px* in the width field, *600 px* in the height field, and then leave the resolution field empty (it doesn't matter *what's* in the resolution field in this situation because the image is being displayed onscreen). That way, Photoshop changes the *dimensions* and *resolution* of the image rather than just its shape. Alternatively, you can choose one of the generic size-and-resolution combos listed in the presets menu. Once you accept the crop by pressing Return (Enter on a PC), Photoshop uses a mathematical formula to resize the image for maximum quality (the formula is called *Automatic* and you'll learn all about it on page 236). As a result, the image area inside the box perfectly matches the dimensions you entered or picked from the preset menu (you can pop open the Image Size dialog box [page 234] to verify the change).

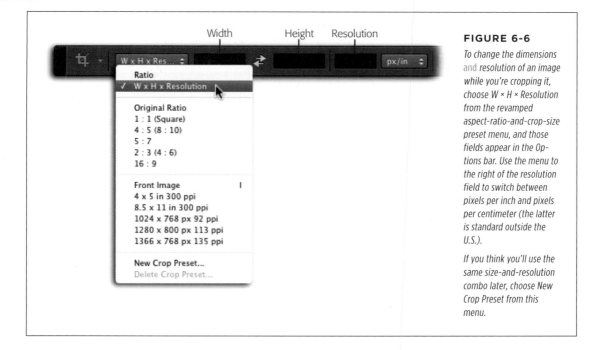

Width   Height   Resolution

FIGURE 6-6

To change the dimensions and resolution of an image while you're cropping it, choose W × H × Resolution from the revamped aspect-ratio-and-crop-size preset menu, and those fields appear in the Options bar. Use the menu to the right of the resolution field to switch between pixels per inch and pixels per centimeter (the latter is standard outside the U.S.).

If you think you'll use the same size-and-resolution combo later, choose New Crop Preset from this menu.

TIP To copy another image's dimensions so you can base a crop on those measurements, open that image, open the preset menu shown here, and then choose Front Image or press I (this keyboard shortcut is new in Photoshop CC; in previous versions it was F).

NOTE In Photoshop CC, the crop box no longer tries to rotate itself automatically to fit the aspect ratio of your image (short and wide vs. tall and thin), which is good because it rarely worked. However, once you've clicked to activate the crop box, you can rotate it by pressing the X key.

If the image gets *bigger* inside the document window after you crop to a specific size and resolution, it means you've enlarged the image by entering too high a resolution for the crop box. Depending on what you intend to use the image for (personal vs. professional projects), this may not be a big deal. If image quality is important, press ⌘-Z (Ctrl+Z) to undo the crop and then reduce the size of the crop box, or enter smaller dimensions or a lower resolution in the Options bar. (If you need to make the image bigger, skip ahead to page 236 to learn about the Photoshop CC's new enlargement voodoo.)

■ CROPPING WITH PERSPECTIVE

If you shoot an image at an angle and then need to straighten it (like the painting shown in *Figure 6-7*, top), you can crop the image *and* change its perspective at the same time using the Perspective Crop tool, which shares a toolset with the Crop tool. Just click the Crop tool's icon in the Tools panel and hold down your mouse button to pop open the toolset, and then choose Perspective Crop (or press Shift-C repeatedly to cycle through the Crop tools). To use it, click the four corners of the object you want to straighten, and Photoshop creates a crop box containing a grid overlay atop the object *for* you. (The box doesn't have to be *exactly* aligned with the object, but be sure that it surrounds the whole object.) Next, drag the box's square corner handles so the lines of the crop box are parallel to (or on top of) the angled lines of the object. When everything's lined up, press Return (Enter on a PC) or double-click inside the box to accept the crop. If the planets are properly aligned, the cropped image looks nice and straight, as shown in *Figure 6-7* (bottom).

FIGURE 6-7

As you can see here, cropping to perspective can instantly and painlessly straighten objects shot at an angle, such as this painting. This kind of thing works well on inanimate objects, but not so great on living things (unless you like that distorted, fun-house-mirror look).

(Painting by iStockphoto/ Renee Keith.)

■ ADDING POLAROID-STYLE PHOTO FRAMES

The Crop tool isn't all work and no play; you can use it for fun stuff like creating a Polaroid-style photo frame like the one in *Figure 6-8*. Besides being a fast way to add a touch of creativity to an image, this kind of frame lets you add a caption to commemorate extra-special moments. Here's how to add a frame to a photo:

1. **Open an image and double-click its Background layer to unlock it.**

   Remember, the Background layer is initially locked for the reasons explained on page 78. To unlock it, give it a quick double-click, and—if you want—type a new name in the resulting dialog box. Alternatively, you can Option-double-click (Alt-double-click on a PC) to bypass the dialog box.

> **NOTE** To practice the Polaroid maneuver yourself, visit this book's Missing CD page at *www.missingmanuals. com/cds* and download the practice file *Trekkers.jpg*.

FIGURE 6-8

Top: To create the look of a Polaroid, use the Crop tool to add canvas space around the photo as shown here. Be sure to add a little extra room at the bottom for a caption.

Bottom: When you add a solid white layer and then add even more canvas space, the Polaroid really starts to take shape. Next, add a caption, activate the layers, and then rotate 'em. Finish off the effect by adding a drop shadow large enough to show around all four edges.

Engage!

2. **Add canvas space with the Crop tool.**

   Activate the Crop tool by pressing C and then, while holding down the Option key (Alt on a PC), drag one of the crop box's corner handles outward about a quarter inch and then release the key. Holding down Option (Alt) while you drag the corner handle forces *all four sides* of the box to expand or shrink simultaneously by the same amount. (Otherwise, you'd have to move each handle one after another.) Press and hold the Shift key to resize the box as a perfect square instead.

Next, drag the bottom-middle crop handle down another quarter inch (that's where the caption goes). Finally, press Return (Enter on a PC) to tell Photoshop you want to keep the new canvas space. You should see a checkerboard background around the photo as shown in *Figure 6-8*, right.

NOTE If you don't unlock the Background layer before you increase the canvas space, the area around the photo ends up the color of your background color chip instead of transparent, so you don't see the checkerboard pattern. If you have this problem, press ⌘-Z (Ctrl+Z) and start over with step 1.

3. **Create a new layer and drag it *below* the original photo layer.**

    At the bottom of the Layers panel, click the new layer icon (it looks like a piece of paper with a folded corner). To keep from covering up the whole photo in the next step, drag the new layer's thumbnail *below* the original layer. (Alternatively, you can ⌘-click [Ctrl-click] the new layer icon to make Photoshop add the layer below the currently active layer.)

4. **Fill the new layer with white to form the Polaroid edges.**

    Choose Edit→Fill, pick "white" from the Use drop-down menu, and then click OK. Now you've got a Polaroid-style frame around the photo. (You *have* to use an Image layer for this technique rather than a Solid Color Fill layer—described on page 208—because the latter automatically resizes to fill your canvas, making the Polaroid effect impossible.)

5. **Increase your canvas space again so you have room to rotate the image and add a drop shadow.**

    Press C to grab the Crop tool again and then add equal space on all four sides by dragging any corner handle of the crop box while holding down the Option key (Alt on a PC). Press Return (Enter) to accept the crop.

6. **Add a caption with the Type tool.**

    Press T to activate the Type tool (page 582) and add a caption in the white space at the bottom of the frame. Here's your big chance to use a handwriting typeface! (Bradley Hand was used in *Figure 6-8*.) When you're done, accept your prose by clicking the checkmark in the Options bar, or just click the Type layer in the Layers panel.

7. **Activate all three layers.**

    When you have everything just right, hop over to the Layers panel and ⌘-click (Ctrl-click) to activate the Image layer, Type layer, and white Polaroid-frame layer so you can rotate the whole mess in the next step.

8. **Rotate the image just a bit to give it more character.**

   Summon the Free Transform command by pressing ⌘-T (Ctrl+T) and then rotate the photo by positioning your cursor just below the bottom-right handle of the bounding box that appears. When the cursor turns into a curved, two-headed arrow, drag slightly up or down. Press Return (Enter) to accept the rotation or Esc to reject it and try again.

9. **Activate the white background layer and add a drop shadow (page 125).**

   In the Layers panel, click the white background layer to activate it. Next, click the tiny cursive *fx* at the bottom of the panel and choose Drop Shadow, and then increase the shadow's Size setting quite a bit so it's visible on all four sides of the Polaroid frame. Move the shadow around by adjusting the Angle setting, or by clicking and dragging within your document. Soften the shadow by lowering its opacity in the Layer Style dialog box, and then click OK.

10. **Add a solid white Fill layer to the bottom of your layer stack.**

    To make your image look like *Figure 6-8* (left), you need to add another white background. Choose Layer→New Fill Layer→Solid Color or click the half-black/half-white circle at the bottom of the Layers panel and choose Solid Color. Either way, pick white in the resulting Color Picker and then click OK.

When you're all done, save the document as a PSD file in case you need to go back and edit it later. Fun stuff!

Cropping with Selection Tools

You can also crop an image within the boundaries of a *selection*. This technique is helpful if you've made a selection and then need to trim the image down to roughly that same size. The Rectangular Marquee tool (page 136) works best for this kind of cropping—though *all* the selection tools work—because Photoshop, bless its electronic heart, can crop only in rectangles (though you can remove a background from an object and then save it in a format that understands transparency, but that's a discussion for page 721).

After you draw a selection, press C to activate the Crop tool and Photoshop places a crop box atop the image that matches the shape of your selection. Easy peasy!

Trimming Photos Down to Size

If your image has a solid-colored or transparent (checkerboard) background, you may find yourself chipping away at its edges to save space in the image's final destination (a website, a book—whatever). The Trim command is *incredibly* handy in such situations, especially when you're trying to tightly crop an image that has a drop shadow or reflection. Such embellishments make the image's *true* edges hard to see—and therefore tough to crop—because they fade into the background. So it's easy to, say, accidentally chop a drop shadow in half when you're cropping. Fortunately, you can enlist Photoshop's help in finding the edges of the image and have it do the cropping for you.

To whittle a photo down to its smallest possible size, choose Image→Trim and, in the resulting dialog box (shown in *Figure 6-9*), use the radic buttons to tell Photoshop whether you want to zap transparent pixels or pixels that match the color at the document's top left or bottom right (the program needs *some* instructions to know what part of the image to trim). Next, choose which sides of the image you want to trim by turning their checkboxes on or off and then clicking OK. Photoshop trims the document down to size with zero squinting—or error—on your part.

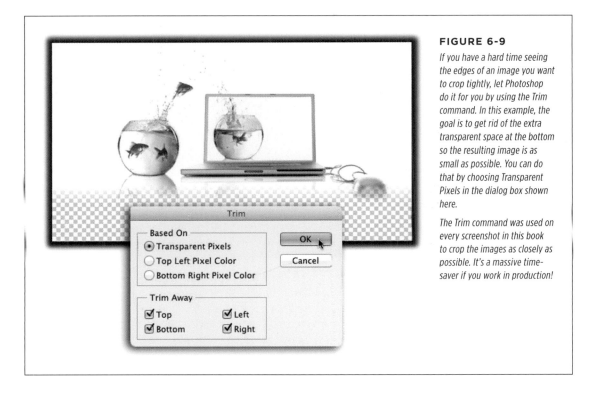

FIGURE 6-9

If you have a hard time seeing the edges of an image you want to crop tightly, let Photoshop do it for you by using the Trim command. In this example, the goal is to get rid of the extra transparent space at the bottom so the resulting image is as small as possible. You can do that by choosing Transparent Pixels in the dialog box shown here.

The Trim command was used on every screenshot in this book to crop the images as closely as possible. It's a massive time-saver if you work in production!

Cropping and Straightening Photos

You can use the Crop tool to straighten individual images in a snap. To do so, open an image and then press C to activate the Crop tool. Next, click the Straighten Image icon in the Options bar (it looks like a tiny level), mouse over to your image, and then drag to draw a line across something that *should* be straight, such as the fridge door in *Figure 6-10*. When you release your mouse button, Photoshop rotates the image. If you like the results, press Return (Enter on a PC) to accept the crop; if not, press Esc to undo it. As *Figure 6-10* shows, Photoshop gives you two ways to straighten images with the Crop tool.

Straightening one image at a time is all well and good, but if you've painstakingly scanned a *slew* of photos into a single document, you can save yourself a lot of work by having Photoshop crop, straighten, and split them into separate files *for* you—all with a single menu command. With the page of photos open, choose

File→Automate→"Crop and Straighten Photos." Photoshop instantly calculates the angle of the overall image's edge (that is, the edge of the photo bits) against the white background, rotates the images, and then duplicates all the photos into their own perfectly cropped and straightened documents, as shown in *Figure 6-11*. It's like magic!

FIGURE 6-10

Left: You can click the Straighten icon in the Options bar and then draw a line across an area that should be straight (it doesn't matter whether the line is horizontal or vertical).

Right: Or you can position your cursor just outside the crop box near one of its corner handles, and then click and drag to rotate the image (your cursor turns into a curved double arrow). Photoshop shrinks the crop box to fit the rotated photo so you don't end up with any extra space around its edges.

NOTE The "Crop and Straighten Photos" command also works on documents that contain just *one* image, provided the picture has white space on all four sides of it. It works on layered files, too. Just activate the layer that contains the image you want to extract, run the command, and Photoshop strips that layer out into its own document and deletes it from the original document. (If the layer contains several images, they'll get stripped out into their own individual documents.)

TIP If you want Photoshop to crop and straighten a *few* photos that all reside on a single layer (but not all of them), draw a selection around each of the photos before you run the command (use any selection tool and hold the Shift key to add to the selection). Photoshop then processes only those photos, provided they (and their individual selection boxes) are next to each other. If they're not, Photoshop crops and straightens everything in between, forcing you to close the unwanted new documents.

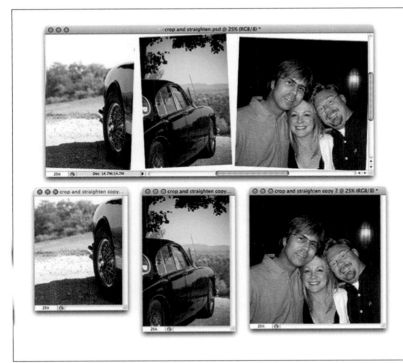

FIGURE 6-11

It's tough to get a bunch of photos perfectly straight when you're scanning (heck, just putting the lid down moves 'em!).

This is a prime opportunity to use the "Crop and Straighten Photos" command. In one fell swoop, the scanned photos (top) get straightened, cropped, and copied into their own individual documents (bottom) right before your eyes.

Cropping and Straightening in Camera Raw

Camera Raw is an amazing piece of software that photographers use to edit the color and lighting of images; you'll learn loads more about it in Chapter 9. It gets installed with Photoshop, so you don't have to download it or pay for it separately. Using Camera Raw to crop and straighten photos has two big advantages:

- **You can undo the crop or straighten (or both) any time**—whether the file you're working on is raw, JPEG, or TIFF. In Chapter 9, you'll learn how to use Camera Raw with all three file formats.

- **If you have several photos that need to be cropped in a similar manner, you can crop them all at once**. Talk about a timesaver!

While you *can* open Camera Raw as a filter from within Photoshop CC (yay!), the filter version is missing the Crop tool (darn!). So, to open an image in Camera Raw, either double-click the image's icon on your hard drive or choose File→"Browse in Bridge" (see the Note below). Once Bridge opens, Control-click (right-click on a PC) the image and choose "Open in Camera Raw" from the resulting shortcut menu. (You can also click the image in Bridge to activate it and then press ⌘-R [Ctrl+R] or use the Mini Bridge panel; see Chapter 22 for more info.) Once the image is open in Camera Raw, follow the instructions in the next section to crop one or more images.

NOTE   The bad news is that, unlike in previous versions of Photoshop, you now have to install Bridge *separately* from Photoshop CC, as page 848 explains. The good news is that when you do install Bridge, the Mini Bridge panel tags along with it.

■ CROPPING IMAGES

With one or more images open, click the Crop tool button at the top of the Camera Raw window and hold down your mouse button to reveal a handy menu that includes common aspect ratios, as well as the "Constrain to Image" option, which maintains the shape of your original, and the Show Overlay option, which places a rule-of-thirds grid atop the image (both are turned on in *Figure 6-12*). Next, click and drag diagonally downward around the part of the image that you want to keep.

If the aspect ratio you need isn't in the Crop tool's menu, choose Custom and a dialog box appears where you can enter a specific ratio or dimensions in pixels, inches, or centimeters. Click OK and Camera Raw places a crop box atop the image, which you can resize by dragging any of its handles or reposition by dragging within the box itself. Press Return (Enter on a PC) to see what the newly cropped image looks like. If you need to edit the crop, just activate the Crop tool again to make the crop box reappear.

TIP   Camera Raw lets you *undo* a crop by choosing "Set to Original Crop" from the Crop tool's menu. In the blink of an eye, Camera Raw returns your image to its original, uncropped state (though any *other* edits you've made in Camera Raw stick around).

FIGURE 6-12

Open one or more images in Camera Raw and then use the Crop tool to whittle 'em down to size. Simply drag across the image to draw a box and then press Return (Enter) to accept the crop. If you've opened multiple images (as shown here), you see their thumbnails in the filmstrip on the left side of the Camera Raw window. To crop them all at once, click the Select All button in the upper left (circled, top) and then draw the crop box. You'll see the crop, along with a tiny Crop tool icon (circled, left), applied to all active thumbnails. The blue, underlined text below the preview window (circled, bottom) changes to reflect the size of the crop box as you draw it.

> **TIP** You can exit the crop box by pressing the Esc or Delete key (Backspace on a PC) while the Crop tool is active or by choosing Clear Crop from the menu shown in *Figure 6-12*.

When you're finished, click one of the buttons at the bottom right of the Camera Raw window:

- **Save Image(s)** lets you convert, rename, or relocate the file(s)—or any combination of those tasks—so you don't overwrite the original(s). If you save them in Photoshop format, you can tell Camera Raw to preserve the cropped pixels in case you want to resurrect 'em later (see *Figure 6-13* for details).

- **Open Image(s)** applies your changes and opens the photo(s) in Photoshop.

- **Cancel** exits Camera Raw without applying the changes.

- **Done** applies your changes (which you can edit the next time you open the image[s] in Camera Raw) and exits the Camera Raw window.

> **TIP** You can use keyboard shortcuts to change how the Save, Open, Cancel, and Done buttons at the bottom of the Camera Raw window behave: To open a copy of the image in Photoshop without updating the original raw file, Option-click (Alt-click on a PC) the Open button (it changes to an Open Copy button). To open the image as a Smart Object, Shift-click the Open button (it changes to Open Object). To skip the Save As dialog box and make Camera Raw use the same location, name, and format you used last time you saved the file, Option-click (Alt-click) the Save Image button. And to change the Camera Raw settings back to what they were originally, press and hold Option (Alt) and the Cancel button's label changes to "Reset").

FIGURE 6-13

To see and work with the original, uncropped image in Photoshop, click Camera Raw's Save Images button. Next, in the Save Options dialog box shown here, choose Photoshop from the Format drop-down menu near the bottom of the dialog box, turn on the Preserve Cropped Pixels checkbox, and then click Save.

Next time you open that file in Photoshop, the photo appears on its own layer. If you want to see the hidden, cropped bits, use the Move tool to drag them back into view or choose Image→Reveal All!.

■ STRAIGHTENING IMAGES

If you need to straighten a bunch of images at a similar angle, Camera Raw can handle 'em all at once. Open the images and then click the Select All button at the top left of the Camera Raw window. Then grab the Straighten tool (circled in *Figure 6-14*) and draw a line across the horizon—or anything in the image that's supposed to be straight—as shown in *Figure 6-14*.

The image won't straighten immediately—instead, you see what looks like a rotated crop box so you can check the angle. If it's OK, press Return (Enter on a PC) and Camera Raw straightens the photo. If you didn't get it *perfectly* straight, you can have another go by choosing the Straighten tool again or, if you closed the image, by *opening* it in Camera Raw again.

FIGURE 6-14

Camera Raw's Straighten tool lets you easily straighten multiple images simultaneously; just make sure you click the Select All button at the top left of the Camera Raw window first. Next, activate the Straighten tool and draw a line across a part of the image that's supposed to be straight (circled). Just press Return (Enter on a PC) to accept the line, and Camera Raw straightens all the images instantly.

■ Resizing Images

No matter what you've whipped up in Photoshop, there will come a time when you need to change the size of your image. For example, if you want to print it, email it, or post it on a website, you need different-sized versions for each task. Changing an image's size isn't hard—Photoshop gives you oodles of options. The challenge lies in doing it *without* sending the image's quality down the tubes.

Sure, you can let the "Save for Web" dialog box (page 242) or the Print dialog box (page 686) do the resizing for you, but if you're aiming to be a serious pixel-pusher, you'll want *far* more control. That, dear friend, brings you up against the granddaddy of Photoshop principles: image resolution—the measurement that determines the *size* of the pixels in the image, which in turn controls the quality of your prints.

Resolution is arguably one of the toughest digital-image editing concepts to wrap your brain around. Many people grapple with questions like "What the heck is resolution?" "How do I change an image's resolution?" and "What's the minimum resolution I need to print good-looking photos?" In the following pages, you'll learn all the nitty-gritty you need to answer these—and other—questions.

NOTE Resolution doesn't mean a hill of beans unless you're sending the image to a printer. So if you're not going to print it, don't worry about resolution—focus on the pixel dimensions instead.

Pixels and Resolution

As you learned in Chapter 2, the smallest element of a raster image is a pixel. When they're small enough and viewed together, these tiny blocks of color form an image (see *Figure 6-15*).

FIGURE 6-15

Raster images are comprised of individual blocks of color called pixels. To see them, zoom into the image by pressing ⌘-+ (Ctrl-+) repeatedly or use the Zoom tool. (Press ⌘ or Ctrl and the - key to zoom out.)

At 3,200 percent magnification, you can see the individual pixels that make up a tiny section of this sunflower.

(Some digital images aren't comprised of pixels—they're made up of vectors, a series of points and paths. One of the best things about working with vectors is that none of the size-versus-quality challenges you run into with pixel-based images apply: You can make vectors as big or as small as you like and they'll always look great. To learn more about 'em, trot over to Chapter 13.)

Pixels have no predetermined size, which is where *resolution* enters the, uh, picture. Resolution is the measurement that determines how many pixels get packed into a given space, which in turn controls how big or small they are. It's helpful to think of resolution as *pixel size,* and it's measured in terms of pixels per inch in the USA (*ppi,* as folks typically call it) or pixels per centimeter (ppc) in most other countries.

NOTE You'll also hear resolution referred to as *dpi*, which stands for "dots per inch." This usage isn't strictly accurate because dpi is technically a measurement used by printers (since they actually print dots). Nevertheless, many folks mistakenly say "dpi" when they mean "ppi."

One helpful way to understand resolution is to relate it to something in the real world. Imagine you're baking cookies (hang in there; it'll make sense in a minute). When you pour brown sugar into a measuring cup, the sugar reaches the one-cup line. But after you pack the granules firmly into the cup, the sugar only reaches the half-cup line. You still have the same number of granules (which are like pixels); they're just smaller because they're packed more tightly together (the increased density is like a higher resolution) in the confines of the measuring cup (the Photoshop document). The loosely packed granules you started with are like low resolution, and the firmly packed granules are like high resolution. (Hungry yet?)

Since increasing image resolution—from, say, 72 ppi to 300 ppi—makes the pixels smaller because they're packed together more tightly, it results in a printed image that's physically smaller but also smoother and better-looking. Lowering image resolution, on the other hand, enlarges and loosens the pixels, which results in a physically larger image that, as you might suspect, looks like it was made from Legos because the pixels are so big you can see each one.

Printers are capable of producing much higher-resolution images than your computer monitor (*thousands* of dots per inch rather than hundreds), plus they're one of the few devices that can modify their output (that is, the print) based on image resolution. In other words, send your inkjet printer a low-res version and a high-res version of the same picture and it'll spit out images that differ vastly in size and quality. The resolution on a computer monitor, on the other hand, is handled by the computer's video driver (the software that controls what appears on the monitor) *not* the resolution specified in the image. That's why an 85 ppi image looks identical to an 850 ppi image onscreen when using View→"Fit on Screen." The bottom line: Printers can take advantage of higher resolutions (scanners can, too, but that's a story for page 48), but monitors can't.

The Mighty Image Size Dialog Box

If you can't trust your monitor to show an image's true resolution, what can you trust? Why, the Image Size dialog box, shown in *Figure 6-16*, which not only displays the current resolution of any open document, but also lets you *change* it. Adobe redesigned this dialog box in CC, and it now includes an image preview that lets you *see* the results of the options you enter in this dialog box *before* you commit to 'em, as well as the new Fit To drop-down menu, which includes a handy list of commonly-used sizes (you can also add your own presets to the list).

NOTE The chain-link icon between the dialog box's Width and Height fields locks the aspect ratio of the image (the relationship between its width and height) so it doesn't get squashed or stretched when you resize it. (In previous versions, this setting was a checkbox labeled Constrain Proportions.) It's turned on straight from the factory and you'll want to leave it that way.

Document file size   Scale styles

Turn off to lock pixel dimensions   Interpolation method

FIGURE 6-16

Behold the new Image Size dialog box! Mouse over the image preview and zoom controls appear (not shown); click the − sign to zoom out and the + sign to zoom in. Click and drag within the preview to see another part of your image. And when you resize the dialog box, the preview resizes, too. Nice!

This dialog box tells you all kinds of useful info about your image. For example, this image is 1698 pixels wide by 1131 pixels high and has a file size of 5.49 MB. If you were to fire it off to your trusty inkjet printer, the resulting print would be 23.583×15.708 inches with a resolution of 72 ppi. As you'll learn in the table on page 239, anything printed at that resolution looks blocky—like a bad Xerox that someone keeps enlarging.

To summon this dialog box, choose Image→Image Size or press Option-⌘-I (Alt+Ctrl+I). It reveals all kinds of info about the image: its file size (how much space it takes up on your hard drive), its dimensions (use the new drop-down menu to its right to see 'em in a variety of units), how big it would be if you printed it (that is, if the Width and Height fields' drop-down menus are set to Inches), and its resolution. By changing the Width, Height, and Resolution fields, you can change the size and resolution of your image.

The dialog box's Resample checkbox is your key to changing resolution *without* changing image quality. *Resampling* is the process by which Photoshop responds to your size-change request by either adding or subtracting pixels. The problem, as you'll learn in a moment, is that resampling involves guesswork on Photoshop's part, which can obliterate image quality. When the Resample checkbox is turned *on*, Photoshop increases or decreases the number of pixels in the image by either inventing pixels that weren't there to begin with or by picking which ones to eliminate, respectively. By turning this checkbox *off*, you protect the image's quality by *locking* its pixel dimensions. If you plan to print the image, turning this setting off lets you fiddle with the resolution for *hours* without altering the image's quality because you're just changing pixel *size*, not pixel *quantity*. (Take a peek at page 241 to see this concept in action.)

NOTE There are two kinds of resampling: If you delete pixels, you're *downsampling* (see page 242); if you add them, you're *upsampling* (the box on page 238 has tips for that). When you upsample, Photoshop adds pixels that weren't originally there through a mathematical process called *interpolation*, in which it uses the pixels that *are* there to guess what the new ones should look like.

When the Resample checkbox is *on*, you get to choose a resample method from the drop-down menu to its right. Why would you want to go this route? Well, if you've got a 300-ppi image that's 4"×6" but you *need* a 5"×7" *and* you have to maintain that 300-ppi resolution (say, for print), you can turn on this checkbox to make it so. On the flip side, if you've got an image that's too big to email, you can use resampling to make Photoshop reduce its pixel dimensions (and thus file size).

The menu next to the Resample checkbox determines which kind of mathematical voodoo (interpolation) Photoshop uses to either add or delete pixels. Here are your choices:

TIP In Photoshop CC, the Resample menu's options have keyboard shortcuts, making it easy for you to switch between different interpolation methods in order to find the one that works best for a particular image (and with the new preview in the Image Size dialog box, you can actually *see* the difference before you commit to it). You'll find these new shortcuts next to each entry in the bulleted list below.

- **Automatic,** which was new in CS6, tells Photoshop to pick the best method depending upon the content of your image *and* whether you're making the image bigger or smaller. Believe it or not, the Crop tool and Free Transform command use this method, too, though the resizing option in the "Save for Web" dialog box doesn't (weird!). Keyboard shortcut: Option-1 (Alt+1 on a PC).

- **Preserve Details** is new in CC; it sharpens areas of fine detail in your image in order to preserve 'em when you make the image bigger (resulting in a higher quality enlargement). The downside is that the extra sharpening can introduce noise (page 211) where there wasn't any. That's why, when you choose this option, a Noise slider appears beneath the menu; drag the slider to the right to reduce noise (effectively applying a slight blur to the areas this option just sharpened). This is where the new preview in the Image Size dialog box comes in really handy, as you can *see* the effects of the Noise slider in real-time. Keyboard shortcut: Option-2 (Alt+2).

- **Bicubic Smoother (enlargement)** is similar to Bicubic (explained in a sec) in the way it creates new pixels, but this method blurs pixels slightly to blend the new ones into the old ones, making the image smoother and more natural looking. As this method's name implies, Adobe recommends it for enlarging images. Keyboard shortcut: Option-3 (Alt+3).

- **Bicubic Sharper (reduction)** is also similar to Bicubic (see below) in the way it creates new pixels, but instead of blurring whole pixels to improve blending between the new and old like Bicubic Smoother, it softens only the pixels' *edges*. Use this method for downsizing images, though some Photoshop gurus claim that it also produces better *enlargements* than Bicubic Smoother. Keyboard shortcut: Option-4 (Alt+4).

- **Bicubic** makes Photoshop figure out the colors of new pixels by averaging the colors of pixels *surrounding* the new one. This method takes a little longer than the others but produces smoother transitions in areas where one color fades into another. Keyboard shortcut: Option-5 (Alt+5).

- **Nearest Neighbor** gives you the lowest image quality. With this method, Photoshop looks at the colors of pixels surrounding the new one and copies them. Nearest Neighbor is known for creating jagged edges, so you'll want to use it only on images with hard edges like illustrations that aren't anti-aliased (see Chapter 13). Keyboard shortcut: Option-6 (Alt+6).

- **Bilinear** tells Photoshop to guess at the color of new pixels by averaging the colors of the pixels directly surrounding the ones it's adding. Bilinear produces slightly better results than Nearest Neighbor, but you're usually better off using one of the other methods instead. Keyboard shortcut: Option-7 (Alt+7).

The Scale Styles menu at the dialog box's top right (it looks like a tiny gear icon) determines whether Photoshop resizes any layer styles you've applied to the image along with the image itself. This menu is tied to the Resample Image checkbox, so as soon as you turn *that* option on, you can click the gear icon and choose Scale Styles (otherwise the menu item is grayed out). If your document harbors layer styles, you'll want to turn this option on; otherwise, that pretty drop shadow you added might end up bigger or smaller than the image itself.

If you know your printer's *lpi* or *lpc* (lines per inch or lines per centimeter—see the box on page 238) setting, choose Auto Resolution from the Image Size dialog box's new Fit To menu to open the dialog box shown in *Figure 6-17*. Just enter the lpi, pick a quality setting, and let Photoshop calculate the proper resolution for a good print.

TIP The settings in the Image Size dialog box in CC are *sticky*, meaning they stay changed until you change them back (that is, except for the resample *method*). Nevertheless, if you find yourself entering the same settings over and over, you can use the dialog box's new Fit To menu to save 'em as a preset. The same menu also lets you *load* presets that you've gotten from somewhere else (say, a coworker who's toiling away on the same project).

FIGURE 6-17

If you know the lpi of your printer, enter it in the Screen field here, and Photoshop calculates the resolution (ppi) for you. You've got a choice of three different quality settings: Draft gives you a resolution of 72 ppi, Good multiplies the lpi by 1.5, and Best multiplies it by 2.

Upsampling Without Losing Quality

If you leave the Image Size dialog box's Resample checkbox turned on and increase an image's resolution, Photoshop adds pixels to your image that weren't originally there. Greatly increasing resolution this way is *usually* a bad idea because faked pixels never look as good as real ones (though this is much less of a problem in Photoshop CC thanks to the new Preserve Details algorithm). However, there may come a time when you've got no choice.

For example, say the image needs to be printed in an *extremely* large format (like a billboard). If you find yourself in such a pickle, you've got a couple of options. Happily, the first one is free:

- **Method 1**. Open the Image Size dialog box, make sure the Resample checkbox is turned on, and then choose Preserve Details or Bicubic Smoother from the drop-down menu to its right (use the preview to see which one works best). Next, change either the Width or Height drop-down menu to Percent (the other field changes automatically).

Then enter a number into the Width field—such as *200* to double the pixel dimensions—and click OK (the Height field changes to the same number automatically). Photoshop enlarges your image by the percentage you entered. (In pre-CS6 versions of the program, adding pixels 5 to 10 percent at a time *repeatedly* didn't damage image quality quite as much as doing it all at once, though these days you end up with an image that looks slightly mushy because the details get softened over and over again.)

- **Method 2**. Buy a third-party plug-in specifically designed to help you upsample, like Perfect Resize (formerly named Genuine Fractals) available at *www.ononesoftware.com*, PhotoZoom Pro at *www.benvista.com*, or Blow Up at *www.alienskin.com*. All of these plug-ins manage to pull off some serious pixel-adding witchery with truly amazing results. (See Chapter 19 for info on installing plug-ins and for more third-party plug-in recommendations.)

Understanding LPI

What the heck is lpi? I thought all I had to worry about was ppi!

Laser printers and professional printing presses print a little differently than inkjet and dye-sublimation printers. Inkjets spray dots of color onto paper and simulate shades of gray by using wide or narrow dot dispersal patterns. Dye-subs fuse color dyes—including shades of gray—onto paper through a heating process (they tend to produce water- and smudge-proof prints that are higher-quality than what you get from inkjets, but also more expensive).

Professional printing presses use yet another printing method: If you hold a magnifying glass to a professionally printed newspaper or magazine, you can see that the images are comprised of a gazillion tiny shapes (typically circles, though they can be diamonds or squares, depending on the printer). If

the shapes are small enough, you'll never see them with your naked eye (although some folks have been quite successful recreating them at *galactic* proportions and calling it pop art—think Lichtenstein and Warhol).

The setting that determines how many lines of little shapes get printed in an inch of space is called *lines per inch*, or lpi. (It's also referred to as screen frequency, line screen, or halftone screen.) It's important to understand lpi because there may come a day when you're forced to figure the appropriate ppi from lpi (also helpful in scanning; see page 48). When this happens, breathe deeply, smile smugly, and proceed to Table 6-1 on page 239. Or, in the Image Size dialog box, choose Auto Resolution from the new Fit To menu and let Photoshop figure out the ppi from lpi *for* you as explained in *Figure 6-17*.

■ RESOLUTION GUIDELINES FOR PRINT

Now that you understand what resolution is and how it works, you're probably wondering, "How much resolution do I need when I print?" Because different printers work in different ways—inkjets spray, dye-subs fuse, laser printers and professional presses print shapes, and so on—the resolution you need for a beautiful print depends on the *printer*.

It's tempting to practice resolution overkill just to be on the safe side, but doing that makes for larger files that take up more hard drive space and take longer to process, save, *and* print (and in some cases, the print can look every-so-slightly blurred). Instead, rein yourself in and consider the resolution guidelines in Table 6-1.

TABLE 6-1 *Resolution guidelines for print*

DEVICE	PAPER	RESOLUTION	BEST USES
Desktop laser printer	Any kind	Resolution should match the printer's dpi (which is listed in the owner's manual) up to 200 ppi. Some folks call this resolution 1:1, which just means ppi matches dpi exactly. For color or grayscale images, shoot for 200 ppi.	Business documents and line art
Inkjet printer	Regular or textured	150–240 ppi	Color and grayscale images, black-and-white documents
Inkjet printer	Glossy or matte photo	240–480 ppi. Use the upper end of this range only for large images (13×19 inches and up).	Color and grayscale images
Dye-sublimation printer	Any kind	Resolution should match the printer's dpi.	Color and grayscale images
Web offset press	Newsprint or uncoated stock	1.5–2 times the lpi, depending on how detailed you want the print to be (use 2 if what you're printing has a slew of sharp edges in it).	Newspaper ads and community papers (like *Auto Trader* and *The Village Voice*)
Commercial printing press	Uncoated or coated stock	2–2.5 times the lpi	Magazines, coffee table books, fancy brochures, business cards, and line art

NOTE   When you send files off to a professional print shop, it's *always* a good idea to ask how much resolution they want. If they don't know, find another printer—fast!

Resizing Images for Print

Throughout your Photoshop career, you'll need to resize and change the resolution of images so they'll print well. Perhaps the most common situation where you'll have to do this is when you download stock photography or import a snapshot from a digital camera.

Keep in mind that today's digital cameras can capture *tons* of info: Consumer-level, 10-megapixel cameras produce images packed with around 3648×2048 pixels (width by height), and pro-level, 21-megapixel models capture images in excess of 4080×2720 pixels. That's a veritable *smorgasbord* of pixels, letting you crop the image and alter resolution however you like.

Resizing images is a snap, but the risk of reducing image quality in the process is high. As you learned in the previous section, the key to preserving quality lies in turning on the Image Size dialog box's Resample checkbox, as *Figure 6-18* illustrates.

NOTE   If you're printing a generic-size image (like 8×10 or 5×7) straight from Photoshop, you can turn on the Print dialog box's "Scale to Fit Media" checkbox to make the program calculate the resolution for you, according to the paper size you pick (though you'll probably end up with resolution overkill). Flip to page 691 for the details.

Here's how to use the Resample checkbox to resize an image for printing without sacrificing quality:

1. **Open a photo, and then choose Image→Image Size or press Option-⌘-I (Alt+Ctrl+I) to open the Image Size dialog box.**

   The image shown in *Figure 6-18* (top) weighs in at 2592×3888 pixels at a resolution of 72 ppi. If you want to print it, you need a ridiculously big piece of photo paper (36×54 inches). Luckily, those dimensions will come way down once you increase the resolution in step 3. Remember, increasing resolution makes the pixels smaller, creating a physically smaller image whose quality (that is, resolution) is higher.

2. **Lock the image's quality by turning off the Resample checkbox.**

   In *Figure 6-18* (bottom), see how the gray line on the left side of the dialog box's fields now connects width, height, *and* resolution? That line is there to remind you that changing *one* of these fields now affects the other two.

FIGURE 6-18

A peek at the Image Size dialog box reveals that if you tried to print this image at its current resolution, you'd need a huge piece of paper—one that's 36×54 inches! Even worse, at the current resolution of 72 ppi, that massive print would look like it was made from blocks.

Turning off the Resample checkbox locks the image's pixel dimensions and protects its quality. Once you do that, you can increase the resolution without worrying about print quality—it'll get physically smaller, sure, but it won't be pixelated. Think about it this way: As the resolution goes up, the document's print size goes down because Photoshop makes the pixels smaller.

3. **Increase the resolution.**

   The value you should enter in the Resolution field depends mostly on which kind of printer you're using; see Table 6-1 for some recommended settings, and then do some tests to see which ones work best for you. For example, if you know your printer does a respectable job printing at 300 ppi, enter that value in the Resolution field, and the document's dimensions decrease to 8.64×12.96 inches (*Figure 6-18*, bottom). The pixel dimensions and file size, however, remain the same—the image is still 2592×3888 pixels and 28.8 MB; only the print size and resolution changes.

NOTE Popping open the Image Size dialog box is a handy way to learn what size print you can make with the pixel dimensions you've got. If your printer does a decent job at 240 ppi, for example, type that value into the Resolution field and see how big a print it'll create. If it's a funky size, you can always crop the image to a specific, more common shape using the Crop tool (see page 220). Alternatively, you can enter the desired print size in the Width or Height field and let Photoshop set the resolution *for* you. If that doesn't give you the exact print size you need, grab the Crop tool.

4. **Click OK when you're done.**

Now you can print the image and it'll look great.

Did you notice how much the onscreen image changed when you tweaked the resolution? That's right: Not at all. That's part of the reason resolution is so confusing. The 72 ppi image looks *just* like the 300 ppi version onscreen because your monitor's resolution can't go that high. The lesson here is that, as long as you turn off the Resample checkbox, you can tweak an image's resolution 'til the cows come home without altering its quality. Sure, you'll change the image's print size, but you won't add or delete any pixels.

Resizing for Email and the Web

Not everyone has a high-speed Internet connection...at least, not yet. Some poor souls are doomed to live with dial-up for the foreseeable future, and even wireless hotspots don't exactly provide warp-speed connections (especially when a lot of people are using 'em). That's why it's important to decrease the file size of that photo you snapped when your bird landed on your cat's head *before* emailing it to your pals—if you don't, it might take 'em forever to download it (though it'd be worth it!). The same goes for images you plan to post online: The smaller their file size, the faster they'll load in a web browser. (You'll learn a lot more about posting images online in Chapter 17, but the info in this section will get you started.)

To make an image smaller, you have to decrease its pixel dimensions. This process is called *downsampling*, and you can go about it in a couple of ways. Read on to learn both methods.

NOTE See page 719 if you'd rather resize images destined for the Web *visually* by entering a percentage instead of pixel dimensions.

■ USING THE SAVE FOR WEB DIALOG BOX

If you want to see a preview of the new, smaller image and maybe experiment with different file formats (if you're torn between a JPEG and a PNG, say), use the "Save for Web" dialog box. This method is a great way to reduce file size while monitoring image quality. Here's how to resize a photo for email or online use:

1. **Open a photo and then choose File→"Save for Web."**

The dialog box shown in *Figure 6-19* takes over your screen. It lets you choose from a variety of file formats and quality levels that Photoshop can use to make the image Web- or email-friendly. You can see up to four previews of what the image will look like in various formats before you choose one, which is why the dialog box is so darn big.

2. **In the upper-left part of the dialog box, make sure the 4-Up tab (circled in *Figure 6-19*) is active and then pick JPEG High from the preset drop-down menu in the top-right corner (also circled).**

The 4-Up tab is great for monitoring the size and quality difference between the original image and, say, a JPEG at various quality settings (as you learned on page 40, JPEG is a good choice for photos). To keep the photo's quality relatively intact while you reduce its file size, choose JPEG High from the preset drop-down menu (circled in *Figure 6-19*, top right). To make the file smaller, Photoshop tosses out some details, but the overall quality doesn't suffer much. But if you choose a quality level of Low (numeric equivalent: 10), Photoshop throws away *significantly* more details and the result is a low-quality image. (See page 366 for more about the JPEG format.)

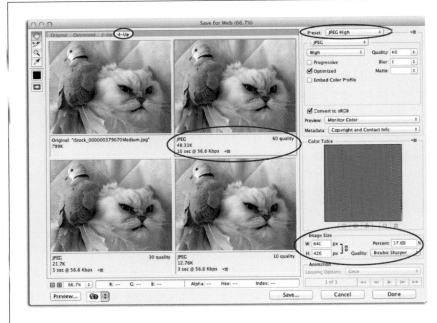

FIGURE 6-19

The quickest way to resize an image for emailing or posting online is to head straight for the "Save for Web" dialog box. It lets you reduce the image's size and save it in a different format in one fell swoop, complete with up to four previews.

That said, if you're working with a honkin' big image from a high-end digital camera (say, over 5000 pixels in width or height) this dialog box may take ages to open or you may get an error message saying the file is just too big to deal with. If that happens, reduce the image's size using the Image Size dialog box first.

3. **Reduce the image's size.**

At the bottom right of the dialog box lies a section labeled Image Size (it's circled in *Figure 6-19*). If you know the dimensions you want, enter the width or height (it's best to make the width 640 pixels or less). If you don't know what size you want and are only concerned with making the *file size* smaller, you can enter a percentage reduction, like 25 percent. (That's a good percentage if you're emailing an image captured on a 10-megapixel camera at a high quality setting.)

4. **Choose a resample method.**

   In the dialog box's Image Size section, choose Bicubic Sharper from the Quality drop-down menu (unfortunately, Automatic isn't available here). This method (explained on page 236) works particularly well when you're downsampling. As you can see in the middle of *Figure 6-19*, the resulting file is 48.31 KB at a quality setting of 60. That's a 94 percent reduction in size!

5. **Click the Save button at the bottom of the dialog box, and then give the file a new name so you don't overwrite the original.**

> **TIP** It's a good idea to sharpen images after you downsample them because they tend to get blurry from both losing details and getting compressed. (See Chapter 11 for more sharpening methods than you can shake a stick at.) However, if the image you've downsampled is for email only, you don't need to worry about it.

Resizing Web Images for Print

Unfortunately, there will come a time when you need to print an image snatched from the Web (though make sure you have the proper permissions, as the box below 245 explains). Such images are usually fairly small so they'll load quickly in web browsers, but that also means they contain precious few pixels for you to work with. As you learned on page 34, you don't have to specify resolution when creating web graphics, though when you pop one open in Photoshop, it's *automatically* given a resolution of 72 ppi—a resolution so low that, when printed, the individual pixels are big enough to see from outer space. So unless you like that blocky look, you *have* to increase the resolution first. And, as you learned earlier in this chapter, when you bump up resolution, you wind up with a print the size of a postage stamp. It's a lose-lose situation.

> **TIP** A good rule of thumb is that Web images print decently at about *half* the size they appear onscreen. So if you start with an image that's about 2×2 inches onscreen, it prints decently at 1×1.

For all those reasons, printing a Web image isn't ideal, but if you have no choice, you've got to make do. In that case, follow these steps to beef up its print quality:

1. **Save the image to your hard drive.**

   Find the image on the Web and Control-click (right-click on a PC) it to summon your web browser's shortcut menu, and then choose Save Image As. Or you can choose Copy Image from the shortcut menu and then paste the image into a new Photoshop document.

2. **Open the image in Photoshop and then choose Image→Image Size.**

   Photoshop displays the now-familiar Image Size dialog box (*Figure 6-16*).

3. **At the bottom of the dialog box, turn off the Resample checkbox, enter** *150* **in the Resolution field, and then click OK to close the dialog box.**

   A resolution of 150 ppi works OK if you're printing to an inkjet printer. The resulting print may not be frame-worthy, but it'll be identifiable.

4. **Back in the main Photoshop window, save the resulting file as a PSD or TIFF.**

   Choose File→Save As, and then pick PSD or TIFF from the format drop-down menu (see page 679 for more on TIFFs). The photo is now primed and ready for popping into Word, InDesign, or any other word-processing or page-layout program.

If the image is still too small after you follow these steps, visit the box on page 238 for tips on upsampling.

Resizing Images for Presentations

You're probably thinking, "I thought this book was about Photoshop and here you are talking about *presentations*. What gives?" Someday, you may be asked to prepare presentation graphics, and if that happens, the info in this section can save your skin. Luckily, in that situation, you don't have to worry about resolution; since your audience will view the images onscreen, it's the pixel dimensions that matter most.

Some folks claim to be more afraid of public speaking than they are of death. Standing before an expectant audience *can* be unnerving (after all, humans *are* predators); obviously, you want everything to run smoothly and the graphics to look perfect. Oversize images bloat the presentation's file size and can cause it to run slowly, or worse, crash. On the flip side, small images may look fine on a computer monitor but terribly blocky when projected onto a large screen.

The solution to both problems is to decide how big the images need to be and resize them *before* you import them into PowerPoint or Keynote. It's OK to resize images a little bit in those programs, but you don't want to put a dozen ginormous, 10 MB photos in your presentation—that's just asking for trouble.

NOTE FROM THE LAWYERS

Thou Shalt Not Steal

This whole "snatching images from the Web" business opens a copyright can of worms. You're committing image theft if you download an image created by someone else and then use it in another format—except in these situations:

- You've obtained express permission *in writing* from the photographer or artist (or other copyright holder) who created it.

- The image is clearly designated as being in the public domain.

- The image was published under a Creative Commons license (*www.creativecommons.org*).

- You're grabbing the image purely for personal use.

That said, if you're promoting a book raffle at your Mac User Group meeting and snatch cover art from the publisher's website or if you need a headshot to promote your camera club's speaker and you snag one from her blog, the chances of finding the image police at your front door are slim to none.

If you want an image to fill a whole slide, find out the pixel dimensions of the projector you'll be using (the slides should be that size, too). If you don't know, find out how big the slides are. Here's how to sniff out (and change) slide dimensions in the two most popular presentation programs:

- **Microsoft PowerPoint 2013**. Head to the Design tab and click Slide Size→Custom Slide Size. In the dialog box that appears, look for the Width and Height fields. Now, here's where things get tricky: For some unknown reason, PowerPoint lists slide dimensions in inches instead of pixels. This poses a challenge because, to ensure that the image fills the slide perfectly, you have to convert the inches to pixels. Luckily, Table 6-2 lists the most common conversions. Once you know the slide dimensions, hop on over to page 220 for instructions on how to crop the image so that it fits the slide perfectly.

- **Apple Keynote**. Open the Inspector palette by clicking View→Show Inspector. Then open the Document Inspector by clicking the icon on the far left of the palette (it looks like a piece of paper with a folded corner) and peek at the Slide Size drop-down menu at the bottom of the palette, which lists the slide dimensions in pixels; those are the magic numbers. Back in Photoshop, grab the Crop tool, set the Options bar's aspect-ratio-and-crop size drop-down menu to W × H × Resolution (page 221), and then enter those numbers in the Options bar. Technically the resolution doesn't matter because the image won't be printed, so you can leave the resolution field blank. Once you've cropped the image, save it as a PNG for maximum quality (as discussed on page 40).

> **TIP** Older projectors have a resolution of 1024×768 or 1280×720 pixels, though newer high-definition models are 1920×1080 pixels. If you've got no clue which kind of projector you'll be using, 1280×720 is *probably* a safe bet.

TABLE 6-2 *Slide size conversions*

PIXEL DIMENSIONS	PC SLIDE SIZE	MAC SLIDE SIZE
1024×768	10.66×8 inches	14.22×10.66 inches
1280×720	13.33×7.5 inches	17.77×10 inches
1920×1080	20×11.25 inches	26.66×15 inches

Resizing Smart Objects

When designing a document—a poster, a magazine cover, whatever—you'll probably do a fair amount of resizing before you get the layout just right. What if you shrink a photo down only to realize it worked better at its original size? Can you enlarge the image without lessening its quality? Negative, good buddy—unless you opened or placed it as a Smart Object.

As you learned in Chapter 3, Smart Objects are the best thing since sliced bread. They let you apply *all kinds* of transformations to files, including decreasing and then increasing their size over and over again—all without affecting the quality of that image as it appears in your document. Here's how to resize a Smart Object that contains an image:

- **To decrease the size of a Smart Object**, activate the relevant layer in the Layers panel and then choose Edit→Free Transform. Grab any of the resulting square handles and drag diagonally inward to reduce its size (hold the Shift key as you drag if you want to resize it proportionately). Let Photoshop know you're finished resizing by pressing Return (Enter on a PC).

NOTE If you've used the Place command to import the Smart Object, or if you drag and drop a raster image into an open Photoshop document, then resizing handles appear *automatically* when the image opens in your document—on its very own layer, of course. (This behavior is controlled by Photoshop's General preferences, which are described on page 19.)

- **To increase the size of a Smart Object**, make sure you've got that layer activated in the Layers panel and then choose Edit→Free Transform. Drag any of the resulting corner handles diagonally outward (hold down the Shift key if you want to preserve the image's proportions). If you don't enlarge the image beyond its original pixel dimensions, its quality remains pristine (and if you do make it a little bigger than its original size, you probably won't notice the difference, as each version of Photoshop gets better at faking pixels). Unfortunately, there's no quick and easy way to *return* the Smart Object to its original size if you forget what it was.

Automated Resizing with the Image Processor

As you'll learn in Chapter 18, you can record a series of steps as a replayable *action* that resizes and saves a batch of images en masse. But Photoshop has a niftier automatic resizing feature built right in: the Image Processor. This little *script* (similar to a program within a program) was developed specifically to convert images' file formats and change their sizes—fast (see *Figure 6-20*). It can save you tons of time whenever you need to convert files to JPEG, PDF, or TIFF format (it doesn't convert PNGs or GIFs). Here's how to run the Image Processor script:

1. **Choose File→Scripts→Image Processor.**

   Photoshop opens the aptly named Image Processor dialog box.

2. **In the top section of the dialog box, tell Photoshop which images you want to run the Image Processor on.**

   Your options are to run it on the images you currently have open (Use Open Images) or on a folder of images (Select Folder). You can also include all subfolders (if you choose Select Folder) and open the first image Photoshop changes—just to make sure everything looks OK—by turning on the appropriate checkbox(es).

3. **Pick where you want to save the images.**

   You can save the images in the same folder they're currently in or pick a new one (click the radio button next to Select Folder). If you're sending the files somewhere new, turn on the "Keep folder structure" checkbox to make Photoshop preserve your organization scheme.

4. **Pick the format(s) you want Photoshop to save the files as and, if you want to resize them, enter a new maximum size in pixels.**

> **TIP** If you're resizing images that are both portrait and landscape in orientation, then enter the *same* size in both the W and H fields.

Here's where the real magic lies. You have three options:

- **Save the files as JPEGs** and choose a quality setting (see page 725); you can also convert the color profile to sRGB (as page 729 explains, this is a good idea).

- **Save them as PSD** files and maximize their compatibility with other versions of Photoshop so you can open them with an earlier version of the program.

- **Save them as TIFFs**, with or without compression (see page 679).

You can choose one option, two, or all three. No matter what the original format, Photoshop converts the files to match the options you choose. You can also have the program resize the files while it's at it; just turn on the "Resize to Fit" checkbox next to the format(s) you picked and then enter a maximum pixel value for either width or height.

5. **In the Preferences section, enter custom settings, if you want.**

Here's your opportunity to run an additional action. Just pick an action category from the first drop-down menu and then choose an action from the second menu. You can also include copyright info in the files by entering it in the text box. Unless you turn off the ICC profile checkbox, Photoshop automatically includes an ICC profile (page 675) in the files.

> **TIP** You can save all the settings you enter in the Image Processor dialog box as an XML file so you can use them again later or share them; just click the dialog box's Save button. Likewise, you can load an existing XML file by clicking the Load button.

6. **When you've got all the settings just right, click Run to make the Image Processor work its magic.**

It may take Photoshop a while to run this script, depending on how many files you chose and how big they are. However, it certainly won't take as long as it would for you to do all this stuff yourself!

FIGURE 6-20

Russell Brown, Adobe's chief evangelist, developed the Image Processor a few years back. If you run this clever script on a folder of images, Photoshop automatically saves them in the format you choose or resizes them instantly— or both. It's amazingly cool.

You can also access this dialog box within Adobe Bridge or Mini Bridge (though in that case it doesn't work on folders, only multiple documents). See Chapter 22 for more on using Bridge and Mini Bridge.

Resizing the Canvas

In addition to resizing images, you can also resize your Photoshop canvas to make room for more artistic goodness. You can add this extra canvas space either visually by using the Crop tool (see page 224, step 2) or manually by choosing Image→Canvas Size. The manual method lets you enter specific dimensions, as *Figure 6-21* shows.

The Canvas Size dialog box includes the following options:

- **Current Size** and **New Size**. Ever informative, Photoshop lets you know how big the document is now and how big it'll be once you click OK. These sections include info on both file size and physical dimensions (width and height).

FIGURE 6-21

Using the Canvas Size dialog box, you can increase canvas space by entering dimensions or a percentage change. Use the Anchor option to determine where the existing image lands within the new space. If you don't pick an Anchor setting, the image lands in the middle.

- **Width** and **Height**. Photoshop assumes you want to measure the canvas's dimensions in inches, but you can use the drop-down menus here to change them to percent, centimeters, millimeters, points, picas, or columns. Change either the Width or Height setting and the other changes automatically.

- **Relative**. Turning on this checkbox makes Photoshop expand or contract the canvas by the amount you enter in the Width and Height fields. If you know the exact size you want the canvas to be, leave this option turned off. If you're just trying to create some extra elbow room in which to work and you've already got an image in your document, turn it on. (For example, to add an inch all the way around your document, enter 2 inches in both fields.)

- **Anchor**. Tell Photoshop where to put the existing image when you click OK. (If you don't choose anything here, it ends up in the middle of the canvas.)

- **Canvas extension color**. If you want the new space to be a certain color, choose that color here. If you don't pick a color—and the Background layer is locked (page 78)—Photoshop uses your current background color. If the Background layer is *unlocked*, the new space will be the gray-and-white transparency checkerboard (which is typically what you want).

> **TIP** If the image is in landscape orientation and needs to be portrait instead (or vice versa), you can rotate the canvas by choosing Image→Image Rotation→90° CW (clockwise) or 90° CCW (counterclockwise).

Content-Aware Scaling

Once in a blue moon, a software company adds a feature that works almost like magic. Adobe did exactly that back in CS4 with *Content-Aware Scale* (affectionately known in nerdy circles as CAS). CAS examines what's in an image and intelligently adds or removes pixels from unimportant areas as you change the overall size of the image. The magic part? It knows enough to leave the important bits—such as people—unchanged. Think of web pages you've used that resize themselves smoothly and fluidly as you make the browser window bigger or smaller; now imagine doing the same thing with an image.

With this technology, Photoshop doesn't squash or stretch the *whole* image; instead, the program adds or deletes chunks of, say, that big ol' sky in the background or the grass in the foreground, leaving the important parts unscathed. A picture really is worth a thousand words when it comes to CAS, so take a peek at *Figure 6-22* to see what this feature can do.

You can use CAS in all kinds of situations. For example, say you want to put your all-time favorite family picture in an 8×10 frame but the aspect ratio (page 37) isn't quite right, the background isn't big enough, or the photo's subjects need to be a little bit closer together. In any of these circumstances, CAS can help. You can use it on layers and selections in RGB, CMYK, Lab, and Grayscale image modes (page 35) and at all bit depths (see the box on page 36). However, you *can't* use it on Adjustment layers, layer masks, channels, Smart Objects, 3D layers, or Video layers.

When you're ready to take CAS for a spin, here's what to do:

1. **Open an image and duplicate its Background layer, and then press Q to pop into Quick Mask mode.**

   Content-Aware Scale won't work on a locked Background layer or a Smart Object, so it's best to duplicate the Image layer first by pressing ⌘-J (Ctrl+J); then turn off the original layer's visibility so it's not in your way.

   CAS isn't perfect—you'll get better results if you help it out by *masking* the areas you want to protect. Quick Mask mode is the fastest way to do that.

2. **Press B to grab the Brush tool and then set your foreground color chip to black.**

   Press D to set your color chips to factory-fresh black and white, and then press X until black hops on top.

3. **Mouse over to the image and paint the areas you want to protect.**

   When you start painting, you'll see the red overlay of Quick Mask mode (see *Figure 6-23*, top). When everything you want to protect is covered with red (like the shrubs, golfers, and flag), press Q to exit Quick Mask mode. You'll see marching ants appear around everything *except* those areas, which you'll fix in the next step.

FIGURE 6-22

As you can see, CAS does an amazing job of resizing only the unimportant background in this image.

To test-drive CAS using the images in this section, head to this book's Missing CD page at www.missingmanuals.com/cds *and download the file* CAS.zip.

4. **Flip-flop your selection by choosing Select→Inverse or pressing Shift-⌘-I (Shift+ Ctrl+I).**

   Since Photoshop selected everything *except* the area you painted in the previous step, you need to invert it.

FIGURE 6-23

*Top: The areas you paint
in Quick Mask mode turn
red, as shown here. This
mode is one of the fastest
ways to make a selection,
and you don't have to
be that careful about the
area you paint; anything
you touch with the brush
is protected. Once you
exit Quick Mask mode and
flip-flop the selection,
click the "Save selection
as channel" button at the
bottom of the Channels
panel (circled).*

*Middle: Once you've acti-
vated the Content-Aware
Scale tool, you can choose
the protective alpha
channel from the Protect
drop-down menu in the
Options bar (circled).*

*Bottom: Because you pro-
tected the shrubs, golfers,
and flag, Photoshop leaves
them alone and resizes
everything else.*

5. **Save the selection as an alpha channel and then deselect.**

   As you learned in Chapter 5, alpha channels let you save selections. Open the
   Channels panel by choosing Window→Channels. Then save the selection as
   an alpha channel by clicking the circle-within-a-square icon at the bottom of
   the panel (circled in *Figure 6-23*, top); Photoshop adds a channel called Alpha
   1 to the panel. Get rid of the marching ants by choosing Select→Deselect or by
   pressing ⌘-D (Ctrl+D).

6. **Tell Photoshop you want to resize the image by choosing Edit→Content-Aware Scale or pressing Shift-Option-⌘-C (Shift+Alt+Ctrl+C).**

   Photoshop puts see-through, square resizing handles all around the image; but don't grab them just yet!

7. **From the Options bar's Protect menu, choose Alpha 1 (*Figure 6-23*, middle).**

   Choosing the alpha channel you just created tells Photoshop which areas to protect. If the image contains people, you can preserve their skin tones by clicking the silhouette icon to the right of the Protect menu.

NOTE To make the image smaller or larger by a certain percentage, enter numbers in the W (width) and H (height) fields or the Amount field. (Most of the time, you won't mess with these fields because it's easier to resize the image visually, as you'll do in step 8.)

---

8. **Mouse over to the image, grab one of the resizing handles, and drag it toward the center of the image.**

   As you can see in *Figure 6-23*, bottom, the image has been narrowed, but the bushes, golfers, and flag remain unchanged. CAS did a great job of resizing only the unimportant parts of the image.

Is this amazing technology? Yes. Is Adobe still working to improve it? Heck, yes! Even so, it has lots of practical uses. For example, if you have to fit an image into a small space (like wedging a photo into a tiny spot in a magazine article), you can use CAS to scoot the subjects closer together instead of cropping the image. Or if you've created a panorama, you can stretch out the sky a little to fill it back in. Just don't expect CAS to work on images that don't have plain backgrounds like a portrait or other close-up image. Nevertheless, this exciting tool keeps getting better in each new version of Photoshop. And just wait till you see what this feature's cousin, Content-Aware Fill, can do! Page 408 has the lowdown.

NOTE Photoshop includes several tools based on this same technology: Content-Aware Move and Content-Aware Patch. They're both covered in detail in Chapter 10.

■ Rotating and Distorting

Photoshop gives you lots of ways to rotate, distort, and otherwise skew images, all mighty useful techniques to have in your bag of tricks. By rotating an image, you can add visual interest (as in the Polaroid technique on page 224), convert vertical elements to horizontal ones (or vice versa), and straighten crooked items. Distorting comes in handy when you want to slant an object or line of text or turn it slightly on its side, or if you want the object or text to fade into the distance with perspective. And the Puppet Warp tool lets you distort specific objects in an image while leaving the rest of it unchanged.

This chapter has touched on rotation here and there: You've learned how to rotate a crop box, rotate an image with the Free Transform command, and rotate the whole canvas. In this section, you'll learn about simple rotations as well as the tougher stuff.

NOTE To learn how to reshape pixels using the Liquify filter and Puppet Warp tool, trot on over to Chapter 10.

Simple Rotations

The Image Rotation command, not surprisingly, rotates images. You can spin the whole document—layers and all—90 degrees (clockwise or counterclockwise), 180 degrees, or by an arbitrary amount (see *Figure 6-24*). You can also flip the canvas (or layer) horizontally or vertically.

FIGURE 6-24

Choose Image→Image Rotation to view this handy menu of image- and document-rotation options. (Photoshop doesn't get any simpler than this!)

You can also rotate and flip images with the Free Transform command as explained in the next section.

The Transformers

Another way to resize and rotate (not to mention flip, skew, and distort) images is to use the Transform commands, which can help you make a selected object—or an entire layer—bigger or smaller without altering the size of the document. If you hop up to the Edit menu, you'll see the Free Transform and Transform options about halfway down the list. The Free Transform command, discussed later in this section, lets you perform *all* the tasks listed on the Transform submenu (see *Figure 6-25*).

NOTE These days the Free Transform command uses your computer's graphics card so it works in real time, meaning you don't have to wait until you've accepted the change to see the results.

FIGURE 6-25

When you choose one of the Transform commands from the Edit menu (or activate all of 'em by choosing Free Transform), you'll get a bounding box surrounded by tiny, drag-gable handles.

Left: After you pick a Transform command, you can access all the options found in the Edit→Transform submenu by Control-clicking (right-clicking) inside the bounding box to bring up this shortcut menu.

Right: By choosing Flip Horizontal, you can make this girl and her dog travel in the opposite direction.

NOTE If you're trying to transform a shape or a whole path (see Chapter 13), the Edit menu's command changes to Free Transform Path (instead of Free Transform). If you're trying to transform just *part* of a path, the menu item reads Free Transform Points instead.

Choosing one of the Transform commands summons a bounding box that has tiny square handles on all four sides. You can use these commands on objects you've selected (Chapter 4), on individual layers, or across many layers (page 70 covers activating multiple layers). The Transform commands resize the layer or selection but not the whole document; the only way to resize the whole document is by changing its image size (page 232) or canvas size (page 249).

NOTE You may find yourself wondering, "Why does Photoshop have both a Free Transform command *and* a Transform menu if I can use them to do the exact same things?" Good question! The only real difference between these two options is that choosing an item from the Transform menu locks you into performing that particular task (using the Scale tool, for example), whereas the Free Transform command lets you perform several transformations at the same time (without having to press Return [Enter] between transformations).

You can transform any objects you wish. Vectors, paths, Shape and Type layers, and Smart Objects are especially good candidates for transformation because they can all be resized *without* harming (pixelating) the image. Don't try to enlarge raster images very much because you have no control over resolution, resampling, or any of the other important stuff mentioned back on page 43. To play it *really* safe, resize images using the Transform commands for only the following reasons:

- **To decrease the size of a selection on a single layer**. Page 174 has more info about transforming a selection without altering any pixels on that layer.

- **To decrease the size of everything on a single layer or multiple layers**. You can activate multiple layers by Shift- or ⌘-clicking (Ctrl-clicking on a PC) them, and then Free Transform can change 'em all simultaneously.

- **To increase the size of a vector, path, portion of a path, Shape layer, Type layer, or Smart Object on one layer or across several layers**.

No matter what you're resizing, simply activate the layer(s) or path(s), or create a selection and then press ⌘-T (Ctrl+T) or choose Edit→Free Transform. Photoshop puts a bounding box around the item, complete with handles that let you apply any or all of the following transformations to the object (they're all illustrated in *Figure 6-26*):

- **To scale (resize) an object**, grab a corner handle and drag diagonally inward to decrease or outward to increase the size of the object. Press and hold the Shift key while you drag to resize proportionately so the object doesn't get distorted. You can drag one handle at a time or press and hold the Option key (Alt on a PC) to scale from the center outward (meaning that all four sides of the bounding box move simultaneously).

TIP   If you summon the Free Transform command to resize something big, the transform handles may end up outside the document's edges (or margins), making them impossible to see, much less grab. To bring them back into view, choose View→"Fit to Screen" or press ⌘-0 (that's the number zero, not the letter O) or Ctrl+0 on a PC.

- **To rotate an image**, put your cursor outside any corner handle. When the cursor turns into a curved, double-headed arrow, drag up or down in the direction you want to turn the image. To rotate in 15-degree increments, press and hold the Shift key while dragging.

- **To skew (slant) an object**, press ⌘-Shift (Ctrl+Shift) and drag one of the side handles; your cursor turns into a double-headed arrow.

- **To distort an image freely**, press ⌘ (Ctrl) while dragging any corner handle.

- **To alter an object's perspective**, press Shift-Option-⌘ (Shift+Alt+Ctrl) and drag any corner handle (your cursor turns gray). This maneuver gives the object a one-point perspective (in other words, a single vanishing point).

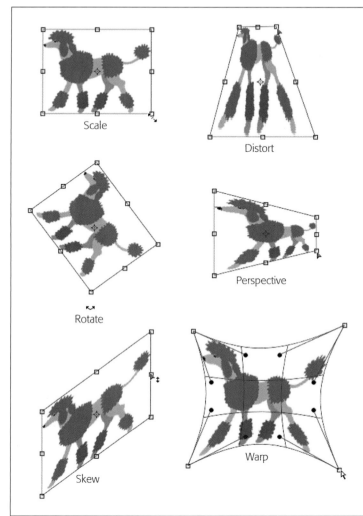

Scale

Distort

Rotate

Perspective

Skew

Warp

FIGURE 6-26

The Transform commands let you scale, rotate, skew, distort, apply perspective, and warp objects in all kinds of interesting ways.

You can apply several transformations in a row if you like; just keep choosing different options from the Transform submenu or use the keyboard shortcuts listed in this section. To undo the last change you made without exiting the bounding box, press ⌘-Z (Ctrl+Z).

- **To warp an image,** click the "Switch between free transform and warp modes" button in the Options bar (see *Figure 6-27*). Photoshop puts a warp mesh over the image so you can reshape it in any way you want. Drag a control point or line on the mesh to warp the image, or choose a ready-made preset from the Options bar's Warp drop-down menu. See page 596 for the scoop on warping text. To learn how to warp part of an image, skip ahead to page 445 to read about the Puppet Warp tool.

NOTE The warp mesh grid can help you create the slickest page-curl effect you've ever seen. Head over to this book's Missing CD page at *www.missingmanuals.com/cds* for the scoop!

- **To rotate or flip an image**, Control-click (right-click on a PC) inside the bounding box and choose one of these preset options. (Flip is shown on page 256.) If you choose one of these little jewels, you won't get a bounding box; Photoshop just rotates or flips the image.

When you're finished with the transformations, press Return (Enter on a PC), double-click inside the bounding box, or click the checkmark in the Options bar to accept them.

If you apply a transformation only to realize that it's not quite enough, you can repeat that transformation by choosing Edit→Transform→Again. You don't get a bounding box—Photoshop just reapplies the same transformation. For example, if you rotated the image 90 degrees, Photoshop rotates it *another* 90 degrees. If you're resizing a raster image, try to transform it only once: The more you transform a pixel-based image, the blurrier and more jagged it can become.

If you want more precise transformations than the ones you get by dragging handles around, you can use the Options bar to enter specific dimensions for scaling, rotating, and skewing, as *Figure 6-27* illustrates.

> **TIP** All transformations are based on a tiny *reference point* that appears in the center of a transform box—it looks like a circle with crosshairs (you can see 'em in each example in *Figure 6-26*). You can drag it around or set your own point by heading up to the Options bar and either clicking one of the reference point locator squares (shown in *Figure 6-27*) or entering X and Y coordinates.

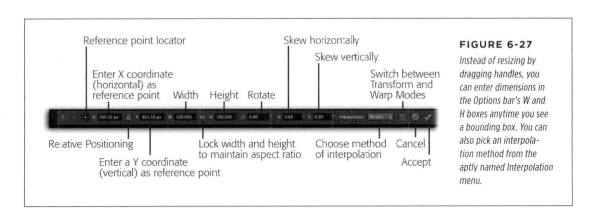

FIGURE 6-27

Instead of resizing by dragging handles, you can enter dimensions in the Options bar's W and H boxes anytime you see a bounding box. You can also pick an interpolation method from the aptly named Interpolation menu.

■ CREATING A REFLECTION

A great trick you can perform with the Transform command is adding a simple image reflection (see *Figure 6-28*). Though this technique takes a few steps, it's well worth the effort. Besides adding depth to an otherwise flat photo, a reflection can make an object look like it was shot on another surface, like a table (handy for making product shots without a proper studio setup).

FIGURE 6-28

Here's what the image looks like after you place the reflection on a black background and lower the reflection's opacity slightly to soften the effect. Adds a bit of visual interest, don't you think?

To follow along, visit this book's Missing CD page at www.missingmanuals.com/cds *and download the file* Leaves.jpg.

Here's what you do:

1. **Open a photo and duplicate the layer where the photo lives.**

   Activate the photo layer and then duplicate it by pressing ⌘-J (Ctrl+J). If your image is comprised of several layers, create a stamped copy instead (page 107). While you're at it, double-click the original Background layer to unlock it, if you haven't done so already. Name the duplicate or stamped copy *Reflection*, just to keep the layers straight.

   > **TIP** You can duplicate an item *while* you transform it by pressing Option (Alt) while choosing Edit→Free Transform or Edit→Transform. That way, the transformation gets applied to a duplicate item on a duplicate layer.

2. **Add some canvas space so you've got room to add the reflection.**

   You need room at the bottom of the document for the reflection. Press C to activate the Crop tool, and then drag the bottom handle down about 2 inches. Press Return (Enter on a PC) to accept the Crop.

3. **Flip the reflection layer.**

   Activate the reflection layer and then press ⌘-T (Ctrl+T) to summon the Free Transform command. Then Control-click (right-click) inside the bounding box and, from the resulting shortcut menu, choose Flip Vertical. When the layer is upside-down, press Return (Enter) or double-click inside the bounding box to accept the transformation.

4. **Move the reflection below the photo.**

With the reflection layer activated, press V to grab the Move tool and then hold down the Shift key while you drag the reflection toward the bottom of the document. Then press the down arrow key to nudge the two layers slightly apart (they should *almost* touch, as *Figure 6-28* shows).

TIP Holding down the Shift key while you move a layer constrains the layer so that it can only move in a straight line horizontally or vertically, depending on the direction you're dragging it. In this example, holding the Shift key ensures that the reflection lines up perfectly with the original photo.

5. **Add a gradient mask to fade the reflection.**

At the bottom of the Layers panel, click the circle-within-a-square icon to add a layer mask to the reflection layer, and then press G to activate the Gradient tool. In the Options bar, click the tiny downward-pointing triangle next to the gradient preview to open the Gradient Preset picker. Choose "Black, White" from the drop-down menu, and then choose Linear as the gradient type.

6. **Draw the gradient.**

In the document, press and hold the Shift key as you drag from the bottom of the image upward to roughly the height you'd like the reflection to be. Holding down the Shift key locks the gradient vertically so it doesn't move from side to side. If you're not pleased with your dragging attempt, just give it another go; Photoshop keeps updating the mask as you drag.

7. **Add a Solid Color Fill Adjustment layer for your new background.**

At the bottom of the Layers panel, click the half-black/half-white circle and choose Solid Color. In the resulting Color Picker, choose black and then click OK. Finally, drag the new layer to the bottom of the layer stack.

TIP By using a Solid Color Fill Adjustment layer (rather than an Image layer *filled* with color), you can experiment with the background color to see what looks best by double-clicking the Adjustment layer's thumbnail in the Layers panel to reopen the Color Picker. While this example uses black, fuchsia may be more your speed!

8. **Finally, soften the reflection by lowering its layer opacity to about 50 percent.**

This final step is really about personal preference: If you want the reflection to be faint, use the Opacity setting near the top of the Layers panel to lower the reflection layer's opacity to about 50 percent. If you want the original image to look like it's hovering above a mirror, go with an opacity of 75 percent or higher.

Now you've got yourself a professional-looking reflected image without all the hassle of setting up a reflective table. That's called working smarter, not harder!

Combining Images

One of the most rewarding projects you can tackle in Photoshop is combining images. Whether you're swapping skies, creating a complex collage, or building a panorama, this is where things start getting mighty fun. This chapter teaches you *all kinds* of techniques for mixing images together, from simply chopping a hole through one layer so you can see what's on the layer below it to a trick used by Photoshop heavyweights: mapping one image to the curves and contours of another.

Along the way, you'll learn how *layer blend modes* and *blending sliders* can help turn the images you have into the images you want. You'll also find out how to make Photoshop align and blend layers, as well as stitch multiple images into a big honkin' one.

This chapter also explains how to use the Clone Source panel to combine parts of *separate* Photoshop documents, which is helpful when you only want to use bits and pieces of an image instead of the whole thing (especially useful if you've got an older computer or limited space on your hard drive). Finally, you'll get tips on combining illustrations and photos into unique pieces of art that marry the real and the imaginary. The techniques discussed in the following pages draw on *everything* you've learned so far—layers, selections, resizing, and so on—so get ready to put your new skills to work!

■ Cut It Out

The easiest way to combine two images is to start with the images on different layers in the same document, and then simply chop a hole *through* one layer so you can see what's on the layer below. It's not elegant, but it works. For example, if you long to replace a dull window scene with something more exciting, like the sunbathing dude shown in *Figure 7-1*, you can just cut a hole through the window so the new object fills the void.

FIGURE 7-1

The simplest way to combine images: Cut a hole in one so you can see through to the other.

Once you've selected the hole (as shown in the top-left image here), you can delete it and try out new vistas.

To practice this maneuver yourself, visit this book's Missing CD page at www. missingmanuals.com/ cds and download the file View.zip.

Here's how to get yourself a brand-new view:

1. **Open an image, double-click the Background layer to unlock it, and then select the area you want to delete.**

   Since you'll delete pixels in a couple of steps, you need to convert the Background layer (if your image file has one) into a regular layer first. Then, to cut a hole in the image shown in *Figure 7-1*, use the Rectangular Marquee tool since the window is square. Press M to grab the tool and then draw a box just inside the window frame. (Chapter 4 has the full scoop on selection tools.)

2. **Use the Refine Edge dialog box to soften the selection's edges slightly.**

   Softening the edges makes the images blend together better. Click the Refine Edge button in the Options bar and, in the dialog box that appears, use the sliders to smooth the selection by 1 to 2 pixels, and then feather it by 0.5 to 1 pixel. (See page 165 for more on using Refine Edge.)

TIP If your selection is larger or smaller than the area you want to cut, adjust the Shift Edge slider near the bottom of the Refine Edge dialog box.

3. **Press Delete (Backspace on a PC) to cut a hole through the image, and then choose Select→Deselect to get rid of the marching ants.**

   Now that your selection is all set, you're ready to send it packin'. Peek in your Layers panel to make sure you're on the right layer before you perform this part of the surgery. Once you press Delete (Backspace), the transparent checkerboard pattern appears in the hole, letting you know that area doesn't contain any pixels. At this point, you're finished with the selection, so you can get rid of it by choosing Select→Deselect or pressing ⌘-D (Ctrl+D).

4. **Add other images to your document and position them below the layer with the hole.**

   Here's where you add the image that you want to appear *inside* the original one. As you learned on page 83, you can copy and paste from other Photoshop documents or from other programs. So copy an image and then paste it into your Photoshop document, where it'll land on its own layer. Or, open an image in Photoshop and then drag it from its Layers panel into the document window of the image with the hole in it. Alternatively, drag an image from your desktop into the open Photoshop document, or choose File→Place. You can add as many new layers as you want.

   When you've got all the images added, position them *below* the original layer so you can see them *through* the hole you made in step 4. (Remember, whatever's at the top of the layer stack can hide what lies below it.)

5. **Use the Move tool to position the glorious new vista(s) within the window frame.**

   Press V to grab the Move tool, activate the layer you want to move, and drag it into place. If you need to resize it so you can see *all* of it through the window frame, use Free Transform (page 257): Just press ⌘-T (Ctrl+T) and then Shift-drag one of the corner handles inward to make the image smaller or outward to make it bigger.

6. **Preview the new vistas by turning the layers' visibility on or off.**

   For example, in *Figure 7-1* you could compare dude vs. chick vs. plain beach. Click each layer's visibility eye to turn it on or off to see which view you prefer.

■ Pasting into a Selection

Instead of cutting a gaping hole through an image, you can combine two images by using the *Paste Special* submenu (Edit→Paste Special). The handy items in this submenu let you tell Photoshop exactly where to put the copied image:

- **Paste in Place**. Use this command to paste an image in the exact same position it lived within the document you copied it *from*. For example, if the image you copied was flush left in the original document, it'll be flush left when you paste it into the *new* document. The keyboard shortcut for this command is Shift-⌘-V (Shift+Ctrl+V).

- **Paste Into**. Use this command to paste an image *inside* a selection you've made (in other words, inside the marching ants). Photoshop puts the pasted image on its own layer and creates a layer mask for you, as *Figure 7-2* illustrates. You see the pasted image only in the selected area; the layer mask hides the rest. Keyboard shortcut: Shift-Option-⌘-V (Shift+Alt+Ctrl+V).

- **Paste Outside**. This option makes Photoshop paste the image *outside* your selection. You get an automatic layer mask, although this time the area *inside* the selection is hidden; the pasted image shows only on the outside. This command is useful for swapping an image frame or border. (Apparently Adobe is running short on keyboard shortcuts because this command doesn't have one.)

FIGURE 7-2

The Paste Into command tells Photoshop to create a layer mask that hides the outer bits of the pasted image so you can see it only through the selection.

This image combination was created using Paste Into to tuck the couple inside a gold frame. Add a well-placed layer style or two (for example, drop and inner shadows) and the photo of the couple looks right at home in its new digs.

Here's how to use Paste Into to combine two images without deleting any pixels:

1. **Open one image and select the area where you want the other image to appear.**

   As you learned in Chapter 4, it's wise to spend a few minutes looking at the area you want to select so you can pick the best tool for the job. For example, in *Figure 7-2*, the picture frame has a solid white interior that you can easily select based on color. So press W to grab the Magic Wand, and then click once in the white area to summon the marching ants.

NOTE Download *Framed.zip* from this book's Missing CD page at *www.missingmanuals.com/cds* if you'd like to follow along.

2. **Use Refine Edge to smooth and soften the selection slightly.**

   Once you see the selection box's marching ants, click the Refine Edge button in the Options bar. The edges of Magic Wand selections tend to be a little rough, so you can use the Refine Edge dialog box to smooth them, as well as contract or expand them, if needed. (A Smooth setting of 3 and a Feather setting of 0.25 was used in this low-resolution example.)

3. **Open the image you want to put into the frame and then copy it.**

   Press ⌘-A (Ctrl+A) to select the whole image and then copy it by pressing ⌘-C (Ctrl+C).

4. **Jump back to the frame document and then choose Edit→Paste Special→ Paste Into or press Shift-Option-⌘-V (Shift+Alt+Ctrl+V).**

   Over in the Layers panel, Photoshop plops the pasted image onto its own layer, complete with a layer mask. In the document window, you see part of the pasted image peeking out through the frame.

5. **If necessary, resize the pasted photo and adjust its position inside the frame.**

   If the photo is bigger than the frame (as in this example), you can make it smaller by using Free Transform: Press ⌘-T (Ctrl+T) and then Shift-drag one of the corner handles diagonally inward, as shown in *Figure 7-3* (top), to shrink the image proportionally. Next, position your cursor inside the bounding box; the cursor turns into an arrow that lets you drag the photo around inside the frame (*Figure 7-3*, bottom). When you're done adjusting the image, press Return (Enter).

TIP If the Free Transform bounding box hangs off the edges of your document, press ⌘-0 (Ctrl+0) to make Photoshop resize the document window *just* enough so you can see all four corners of the box. This keyboard shortcut is worth memorizing 'cause you'll use it *all* the time.

6. **Lock the pasted photo and the mask together.**

   Once you get the photo sized and positioned just right, lock it to the layer mask that Photoshop created in step 4 so everything stays in place. Over in the Layers panel, click the blank space *between* the layer thumbnail and the mask thumbnail. When you do, a little chain icon appears (you can see it in each layer in *Figure 7-2*). You're basically finished with this image-combining technique now, but you can add even *more* creativity by rotating the frame, adding a shadow, and giving it a new background. The next few steps explain how.

FIGURE 7-3

Top: If the photo is too big for the frame, you can resize it using Free Transform. Just make sure to press and hold Shift as you drag one of the corner handles (circled) so you don't squash or distort the image.

Bottom: Once you get the image sized just right, click and drag within the bounding box to move it around inside the frame. (The cursor is circled here.)

7. **Hide the white area around the frame with a layer mask.**

The frame shown in *Figure 7-2* was originally on a white background. To get rid of the white edges, activate the frame layer in the Layers panel, press W to grab the Magic Wand, and then click the white area outside the frame to select it. (If you've chosen a frame with all kinds of nooks and crannies around its edges, you can choose Select→Similar to make sure you've got *all* the white areas selected.) Once you've got a good selection, use the Refine Edge dialog box to smooth the selection's edges. Then flip-flop the selection by choosing Select→Inverse to make Photoshop place the marching ants around the frame instead of the white edges. Finally, add a layer mask to the frame layer by clicking the circle-within-a-square button at the bottom of the Layers panel.

8. **Use the Crop tool to make your canvas bigger.**

   In order to rotate the frame and add a nice, fluffy drop shadow, you need some extra canvas space. The menu command for increasing canvas size is discussed on page 249, but it's quicker to use the Crop tool: Press C to grab the tool, Option-drag (Alt-drag on a PC) one of the crop box's corner handles outward to make it bigger on all four sides, and then press Return (Enter). Now you've got all kinds of room to work!

9. **Activate the frame and photo layers and rotate them with Free Transform.**

   In the Layer's panel, Shift-click both layers to activate them, and then press ⌘-T (Ctrl+T) to summon Free Transform. Position your cursor outside the bounding box that appears and, when it turns into a curved double arrow, drag upward slightly to rotate the frame and photo. Press Return (Enter) when you've got them at an angle you like.

10. **Add an inner shadow to the photo layer.**

    To make the photo look like it's really *inside* the frame, it needs a shadow. First, click the photo layer so it's the only one activated in the Layers panel. Next, click the *fx* button at the bottom of the Layers panel and, from the menu that appears, choose Inner Shadow. Tweak the settings in the resulting Layer Style dialog box to your liking, and then click OK.

11. **Add a drop shadow to the frame layer.**

    To add a little depth and make the frame look as if it's really hanging on a wall, activate the frame layer in the Layers panel, click the panel's *fx* button, and choose Drop Shadow. (See page 125 for more on drop shadows.)

12. **Add a Solid Color Fill layer and pick a color.**

    To complete the design, put a new, colored background behind the frame. Choose Layer→New Fill Layer→Solid Color, or click the half-black/half-white circle at the bottom of the Layers panel and choose Solid Color from the menu that appears. In the resulting Color Picker, choose the color you want for the frame's background and then click OK. (To change this color later on, simply double-click the Fill layer's thumbnail to summon the Color Picker again.)

TIP   If you mouse over your image while the Color Picker is open, your cursor turns into a little eyedropper, which lets you click anywhere in the image to choose a color. Snatching a color that's already in the image is a *great* way to pick a background color that matches the image.

---

13. **Drag the Color Fill layer to the bottom of the layer stack.**

    In your document window, the background appears behind the newly framed image.

Whew! That was a lot of steps, but you're done. Be sure to save the document as a Photoshop (PSD) file in case you want to change the color of the new background. Now go find a place to digitally hang your creation.

Sky Swapping

You can also use the Paste Into technique described in the previous section to replace a bland sky with a more pleasing vista, as shown in *Figure 7-4*. Using the Paste Into command makes Photoshop add a layer mask *for* you, but it's just as easy to add a mask yourself (either method gets you the same result). Here's how:

1. **Open an image with an area that you want to replace (like the sky), and then select that area.**

    You can use any of the bazillion selection techniques you learned in Chapter 4. The channels method—discussed on page 165 and used to create the image shown in *Figure 7-4*—is a good one, as is using the Quick Selection tool with the Refine Edge dialog box.

2. **Add a layer mask to hide the old sky.**

    To do so, click the circle-within-a-square button at the bottom of the Layers panel.

TIP　If the mask hides the *opposite* of what you want it to hide, double-click the mask in the Layers panel, and the Properties panel pops open. Click the Invert button near the bottom of the panel and Photoshop flip-flops the mask. Onward ho!

---

3. **Open the image with the replacement sky and copy it.**

    Press ⌘-A (Ctrl+A) to select the whole image, and then press ⌘-C (Ctrl+C) to copy it.

4. **In the other document (the one with the mask), paste the new sky onto its own layer by pressing ⌘-V (Ctrl+V).**

    If copying and pasting isn't your thing, arrange your workspace so you can see both open documents (page 56) and then drag the sky layer from the Layers panel into the other document's window (see page 95). You can also drag the document from your desktop into the Photoshop document or choose File→Place.

5. **Position the sky at the bottom of the layer stack.**

    In the Layers panel, drag the new sky to the bottom of the layer stack and you're done.

You just swapped your first sky! If you want to try out other skies, just paste or drag them into the document and position them below the layer with the layer mask. Then hide the first new sky by clicking its visibility eye in the Layers panel.

FIGURE 7-4

*Instead of deleting the sky
in the original image, you
can hide it with a layer
mask. Doing so gives you
the ability to fine-tune
the mask later using the
methods discussed in
Chapter 4 (page 114).*

*Swapping skies makes this
rider's accomplishment a
bit more impressive, don't
you think?*

◼ Fading Images Together

So far, you've learned how to combine images with relatively high contrast such as
wedging a portrait into the white part of a digital frame or adding a brand-new sky
to an extremely light-colored background. But if your soon-to-be-combined images
don't have such stark boundaries, then you're better off using big, soft brushes to
do your erasing or, better yet, *hiding* parts of your image with a layer mask. You can
also use the Gradient tool to create a gradual transition from one image to another
as if they're faded together. Read on to learn all these methods.

Soft Erasers

Because you can set the Eraser tool to use a brush cursor, you can use a soft brush to erase part of an image so you can see the image on the layer below. Once you've wrangled the two images you want to combine into the same document (each on its own layer), grab the Eraser tool by pressing E and then, in the Options bar, set the Mode menu to Brush. Next, from the Brush Preset picker, choose a big, soft brush (see Chapter 12 for more on brushes). Then, in the Layers panel, drag the layer you want to partially erase to the top of the layer stack, and then mouse over to your image and simply brush away the parts you want to get rid of. If you mess up or change your mind, undo a step by pressing ⌘-Z (Ctrl+Z) or use the History panel to go back a few brushstrokes.

Sure, this technique gets the job done, but keep in mind that it's just as *destructive* as cutting a hole—if you change your mind about how to combine the images, you have to start over. A *better* idea is to do the erasing nondestructively by using a soft-edged brush inside a layer mask, as explained in the next section.

Soft Brushes and Layer Masks

A wonderfully practical and flexible way to fade two images together is to paint on a layer mask with a big, fluffy brush. That way you're merely *hiding* part of the image instead of deleting it. For example, say you want to create a striking image for a photography client by blending an image of a baseball player into an image of a baseball, as shown in *Figure 7-5*. Here's how:

> **NOTE** To create this collage, visit this book's Missing CD page at *www.missingmanuals.com/cds* and download the file *Player.zip*.

1. **Combine the images into one Photoshop document with each image on a separate layer.**

   If you're following along, name the layer with the boy *player* and the other layer *baseball*.

2. **In the Layers panel, position the player layer at the top of the stack and add a layer mask to it.**

   Drag the player layer to the top of the layer stack. (If you're working with your own imagery, just decide which layer you want to be on top of the collage.) Then, at the bottom of the panel, click the circle-within-a-square button to add a layer mask to it.

3. **Press B to grab the Brush tool and pick a big, soft brush.**

   In the Options bar, use the Brush Preset picker to choose a big (500-pixel, say), soft-edged brush.

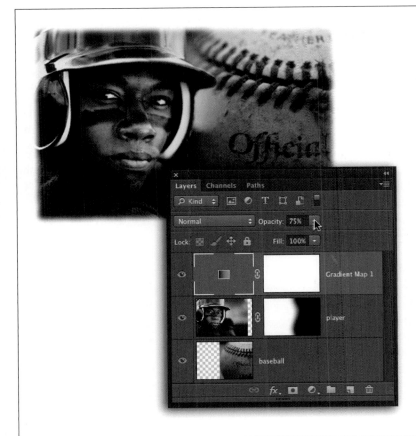

FIGURE 7-5

Combining images is a wonderful way to create eye-catching imagery. As you can see in this Layers panel, nary a pixel in the original images was harmed during the making of this collage.

The extra step of using a Gradient Map Adjustment layer to hide most of the color in the collage creates a moody and grungy feel.

4. **Set the foreground color chip to black.**

   As you learned in Chapter 3, in the realm of layer masks, painting with black *conceals*, which is exactly what you want to do here. So peek at your color chips at the bottom of the Tools panel and, if they're black and white, press X until black hops on top. If they're not, press D to reset them to black and white and *then* press X until black is on top.

5. **Mouse over to your image and paint to hide part of the player layer.**

   If you mess up and hide too much of the boy, press X to flip-flop your color chips (so white is on top) and then paint that area with white to reveal it again. You're basically done at this point, though the next step explains how to create the color effect shown in *Figure 7-5*.

6. **Add a black-to-white Gradient Map Adjustment layer to the top of your layer stack and lower its opacity to 75 percent.**

With your color chips set to black and white, press X to flip-flop them so that black is on top. Then click the half-black/half-white circle at the bottom of the Layers panel and choose Gradient Map. Photoshop drains the color from both Image layers, though you can lower the Adjustment layer's opacity a bit (to 75 percent or so) to bring back a *smidgeon* of color. (As you'll learn in Chapter 8, a Gradient Map Adjustment layer creates beautiful high-contrast black-and-white images.)

7. **Save the document as a PSD file so you can go back and tweak it later on.**

After seeing the final version, you may decide to tweak the Adjustment layer's opacity to achieve the color effect you want. In that case, you can pop open the document, activate the Adjustment layer, and then change its settings without having to start over. Whee!

If you're a pro photographer, this kind of collage is a *fantastic* additional product to offer your clients...for an extra fee, of course!

Gradient Masks

All that soft-brush business aside, the way to create the smoothest fades of all between two images is to use a *gradient*—a gradual transition from one color to another. The steps for combining two images using a gradient are basically the same as the soft-brush method in that you're adding both images to one Photoshop document and then adding a layer mask to the top layer. But instead of painting on the layer mask with a brush, you use a black-to-white gradient for a smooth and seamless fade from one image to the other, as shown in *Figure 7-6*.

NOTE   To follow along, visit this book's Missing CD page at *www.missingmanuals.com/cds* and download the file *Baby.zip*.

Once you've put two images into one document (each on its own layer), take a spin through these steps:

1. **In the Layers panel, drag the image you want on the top of the collage to the top of the layer stack and then add a layer mask to it.**

In this example, you want the baby on top, so drag it to the top of the Layers panel. Then add a layer mask to it by clicking the circle-within-a-square button at the bottom of the panel. The layer mask thumbnail appears in the Layers panel, but your document doesn't change yet because the mask is empty. (Technically the mask is white, but because "black conceals, white reveals," a white mask fully reveals the layer.)

FIGURE 7-6

Adding a black-to-white linear gradient to a layer mask is an easy and nondestructive way to softly blend two or more images together. Be sure to experiment with dragging with the Gradient tool different distances and at different angles.

To create the sepia-tint effect shown here, add a Black & White Adjustment layer and then turn on the Tint option in the Properties panel that appears.

(Trot over to page 308 for more on using Black & White Adjustment layers).

2. **Press G to grab the Gradient tool, and then choose a black-to-white, linear gradient.**

   In the Options bar, click the down-pointing triangle labeled in *Figure 7-6* (top) to open the Gradient picker. Choose the black-to-white gradient from the preset menu that appears (third from left in the top row) and, in the Options bar's row of gradient types, click the linear gradient button (circled in *Figure 7-6*, top).

3. **Mouse over to your image, click once where you want the fade to begin, drag slightly downward and to the right, and then let go of your mouse.**

   As you drag, Photoshop draws a line that represents the width of the fade: The shorter the line (the distance you drag), the narrower the fade and the harsher the transition (it won't be a hard edge, but it'll be close); the longer the line, the wider the gradient and the softer the fade. As soon as you release your mouse button, Photoshop plops the gradient into the layer mask, which effectively fades your images together. If you're not happy with the gradient, just keep clicking and dragging until you get it right; Photoshop updates the mask automatically. To empty the mask and start over, click the mask's thumbnail in the Layers panel, select the whole thing by pressing ⌘-A (Ctrl+A), and then press Delete (Backspace on a PC).

4. **Save the document as a PSD file.**

This format preserves the document's layers so you can go back and edit the gradient mask later.

Not bad, eh? Incidentally, this technique is a *great* example of how to use your own imagery along with stock photos. Just think of the possibilities: a wedding photo faded into a bouquet of flowers, piano keys faded into a sheet of music, Captain Kirk faded into a shot of the Starship Enterprise, and so on.

> **TIP** You can also *rotate* a layer to get the image in the right spot for your collage. Just activate the layer you want to twirl and then summon Free Transform by pressing ⌘-T (Ctrl+T). Next, position your cursor just outside a corner of the bounding box that appears, and when your cursor turns into a double-sided arrow, click and drag in the direction you want to rotate the image. Press Return (Enter on a PC) when you're finished.

■ Layer Blend Modes

Perched near the upper-left corner of the Layers panel is an unlabeled menu of *blend modes*, which control how pixels on different layers interact with one another. (Unless you change it, this menu is set to Normal.) For example, when layers overlap, the top one can either block the bottom one completely, or the layers can blend together in some way (these effects, and many more, are shown in *Figure 7-7*). You control exactly *how* they blend together by using blend modes.

> **TIP** To truly understand these modes, try duplicating an Image layer and then using your keyboard to cycle through 'em all. Press Shift-plus to go forward through the blend mode menu or Shift-minus to go backward.

This section covers how to use *layer* blend modes, but you can find other blend-mode menus all over the place in Photoshop:

- In the Layer Style dialog box, where you can add effects like drop shadows, glows, and so on (page 127).

- In some filters' dialog boxes and in *most* filters' Blending Options dialog box, which you get by using Smart Filters (see Chapter 15).

- In the Fade dialog box, which you can access via Edit→Fade *right* after you run a filter (see the box on page 461) or apply any of the adjustments in the Image→Adjustments menu.

FIGURE 7-7

Here's what Photoshop's blend modes do when you use them to affect how the colors on these two layers blend together. (The water image is on top in the layer stack, though the blending would look the same if the happy-face image were on top instead.)

It's hard to fully appreciate the power of blend modes from looking at this figure, but this gives you a rough idea of how they differ. As you might imagine, they're worth their weight in gold when you're combining images, whether you're using them to produce a darker or lighter version (page 113) or creating a complex collage (page 281).

- In the Options bar when you're using a tool you can paint with, like the Brush, Paint Bucket, Healing Brush, Pencil, Clone Stamp, History Brush, Gradient, Blur, Sharpen, and Smudge tools.

- In the Calculations (page 211) and Apply Image dialog boxes. (To learn how to combine two images using the Apply Image command, which lets you pick the channel Photoshop uses to do the blending, head to this book's Missing CD page at *www.missingmanuals.com/cds*.)

When you're dealing with blend modes, it's helpful to think of the colors on your layers as being made up of three parts, as shown in *Figure 7-8*:

- **Base**. This is the color you start out with, the one that's already in your image. While layer stacking order doesn't matter with *most* blend modes, you can think of the base color as the color on the bottommost layer.

- **Blend**. This is the color you're *adding* to the base color, whether it's color in an image on another layer or a color you've added to another layer using one of Photoshop's painting tools.

- **Result**. This is the color you get after mixing the base and blend colors using a blend mode.

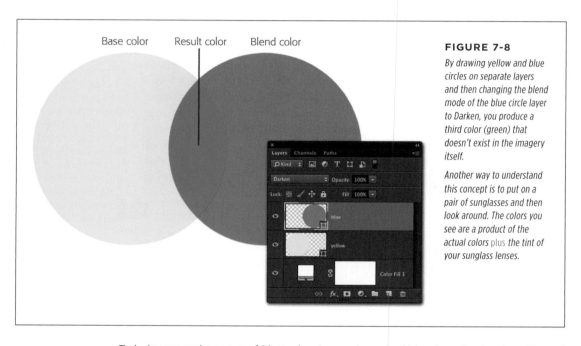

Base color   Result color   Blend color

FIGURE 7-8

By drawing yellow and blue circles on separate layers and then changing the blend mode of the blue circle layer to Darken, you produce a third color (green) that doesn't exist in the imagery itself.

Another way to understand this concept is to put on a pair of sunglasses and then look around. The colors you see are a product of the actual colors plus *the tint of your sunglass lenses.*

To help you make sense of Photoshop's growing set of blend modes (and you'll need all the help you can get), the blend mode menu is divided into categories based on each mode's *neutral color*—the color that causes *no* change in that particular mode. For example, some modes ignore white, some ignore black, and so on. This info doesn't mean a hill of beans to you just yet, but it'll start to make sense as you learn more about the various modes in the next few pages. Here's a quick tour of the Layers panel's blend mode menu.

Normal and Dissolve Blend Modes

These two modes are at the very top of the blend mode menu. Here's what they do:

- **Normal**. When you first use Photoshop, it's set to use this mode, which doesn't actually cause any blending at all; as *Figure 7-7* shows, the pixels on the top layer (the water image) totally block what lies below (the happy face). Its keyboard shortcut is Shift-Option-N (Shift+Alt+N on a PC).

NOTE Photoshop includes lots of keyboard shortcuts you can use to change the current layer's blend mode. However, if you're using one of the painting tools listed at the beginning of this section, these shortcuts change the blend mode of that particular *tool* instead of changing the *layer's* blend mode.

- **Dissolve**. This mode turns semi-transparent pixels into a spray of dots (if you don't have any semi-transparent pixels, your image won't change). You can use Dissolve to make a drop shadow look coarse instead of soft (see *Figure 7-9*), or to add shading to an object you've drawn in Photoshop (see the box on page 510). Keyboard shortcut: Shift-Option-I (Shift+Alt+I).

FIGURE 7-9

To quickly get an idea of what Dissolve mode does, apply it to a drop shadow. To create the spatter effect shown here, add a drop shadow with layer styles (page 125) and then, in the Layer Style dialog box, change the shadow's blend mode to Dissolve (because the drop shadow was made with the Layer Style dialog box, that's where you need to change the blend mode, too). Photoshop changes the formerly see-through drop shadow into a spray of pixels.

Darken Blend Modes

The modes in this category have the power to darken, or *burn*, images (see page 433 for info on the Burn tool). Simply put, when you apply these modes, the base and blend colors go to war and the darkest color wins so you end up with a darker image than you started with. These modes are incredibly useful when you want to swap a light-colored background for something darker. The neutral color in this category is white, which means that white has no effect on the blend at all, and any white parts of your images disappear.

- **Darken**. In this mode, Photoshop analyzes each channel in the image, compares the base and blend colors, and keeps the *darkest* ones, which become the result color (layer order doesn't matter). Colors darker than the blend color don't change, but colors lighter than the blend color are replaced with the result color. Darken mode is helpful when swapping a light background for something darker, and for fixing areas in an image that are too light or overexposed. Keyboard shortcut: Shift-Option-K (Shift+Alt+K on a PC).

- **Multiply**. In Multiply mode, Photoshop analyzes each channel and *multiplies* (increases) the base color by the blend color (layer order doesn't matter). You can think of this mode like a double coat of ink since the result color will always be darker than the base. Multiply does a lot of cool things, including fixing images that are too light or overexposed (see page 113), or creating an *overprint* effect in which the graphic on the top layer looks like it's been printed on the layer below (like the fake tattoo in *Figure 7-10*). Keyboard shortcut: Shift-Option-M (Shift+Alt+M).

FIGURE 7-10

By changing the blend mode of the tattoo layer to Multiply, its white background disappears so you can see through the rooster to the skin below.

All you need to do now is lower the opacity of the tattoo layer to make it look a little faded and not quite so fresh.

- **Color Burn**. In this mode, Photoshop looks at each channel and then darkens the image by *increasing the contrast* between the base and blend colors (layer order matters when using this mode). The darker the blend color, the darker and more high-contrast the base color becomes. When you use this mode on a layer filled with 50 percent gray (explained in the Tip below), it intensifies color on the layers below, which can beautify an ugly sky in a hurry. You can also use this mode on a dark-colored texture to add depth and interest to a light background on the layer below. To make the effect of this blend mode more subtle, try reducing the layer's *Fill* setting instead of its Opacity setting (page 90). Keyboard shortcut: Shift-Option-B (Shift+Alt+B).

TIP Fifty percent gray is, as you might suspect, the color exactly halfway between pure black and pure white. An easy way to fill a layer with 50 percent gray is to make a new layer, go to Edit→Fill, and then choose 50% Gray from the Use drop-down menu. Those Photoshop engineers think of everything!

- **Linear Burn**. In this mode (which is actually a combination of Multiply and Color Burn), Photoshop analyzes each channel and then darkens your image by *decreasing the brightness* between the base and blend colors (layer order doesn't matter); the darker the blend color, the darker the result. Linear Burn produces the darkest colors of any Darken blend mode, though with a bit more contrast than the others. It has a tendency to turn dark pixels solid black, which makes it ideal for grungy, textured collages like the one in *Figure 7-11*. Keyboard shortcut: Shift-Option-A (Shift+Alt+A).

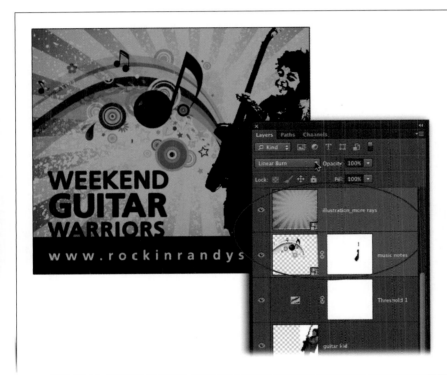

FIGURE 7-11

In this Layers panel, you can see the original image near the bottom and a Threshold Adjustment layer above it (see page 320 for more info). Popping in two pieces of art (circled) and changing their blend modes to Linear Burn created this trendy ad.

Happily, Photoshop lets you change the blend mode of multiple layers at once by activating them and then choosing a new option from the blend mode menu (this fabulous feature was added in CS6).

- **Darker Color**. This mode compares the total numeric value of all channels for the base and blend colors and then keeps the lower values, resulting in the darkest pixels. There's no blending going on here—the lighter colors just vanish, making this mode ideal for removing white backgrounds (a technique sometimes called "knocking out"), as *Figure 7-12* illustrates. (Darker Color doesn't have a keyboard shortcut, because this mode didn't come around until Photoshop CS3 when Adobe started running out of keyboard shortcut combos. Same goes for Lighter Color mode [page 284]).

FIGURE 7-12

By placing two images on separate layers, you can use Darker Color mode to zap a white background. Here, the top layer has a fairly light sunburst and the bottom layer has a dark-colored kid on a white background. If you change the blend mode of the sunburst layer to Darker Color, the white background on the layer below disappears.

Since parts of the kid's boot are lighter than the sunburst—meaning the sunburst wins the color war explained on page 279 and covers him up in those spots—you can hide that part of the sunburst with a layer mask to keep him in one piece.

Lighten Blend Modes

These modes, not surprisingly, do the *opposite* of the Darken modes: They lighten, or *dodge*, your image (see page 433 for info on the Dodge tool). Black is the neutral color for this group; it disappears in all but one of the following modes:

- **Lighten**. In this mode, the lightest pixels win the color war (layer order doesn't matter). Photoshop analyzes each channel and keeps the *lightest* ones from the base and the blend. Pixels lighter than the blend color don't change, and pixels darker than the blend are replaced with the result. Everything else is nixed (including black), which makes this mode useful for blending a dark background with something lighter (see *Figure 7-13*). Keyboard shortcut: Shift-Option-G (Shift+Alt+G on a PC).

- **Screen**. In this mode, Photoshop analyzes each channel and then multiplies the *opposite* of the blend and base colors, making everything a lot lighter as though a bottle of bleach was spilled on it (layer order doesn't matter). It's *great* for fixing images that are too dark or underexposed (like when your camera's flash doesn't fire; see page 113), and it's just the ticket for brightening eyes (page 436). Keyboard shortcut: Shift-Option-S (Shift+Alt+S).

FIGURE 7-13

To zap most of the black background of this fireball, change its blend mode to Lighten. Now the flames are visible only where they're lighter than the colors in the steel ball.

A layer mask was added to hide a few rogue flames underneath the ball.

- **Color Dodge**. The opposite of Color Burn, this mode makes Photoshop look at each channel and then lighten your image by *decreasing the contrast* between the base and blend colors (layer order matters when using this mode). The lighter the blend color, the lighter and less contrast-y the base color becomes. This mode has a tendency to turn light pixels solid white, and—unlike the other Lighten modes—it keeps black pixels, so the dark parts of the image don't change. You can use this mode on a light-colored texture to add depth and brightness to a dark background on the layer below. And by using Color Dodge on a layer filled with 50 percent gray, you can give dark hair instant highlights, as shown in *Figure 7-14*). Keyboard shortcut: Shift-Option-D (Shift+Alt+D).

- **Linear Dodge (Add)**. This mode causes Photoshop to peek at each channel and then lighten your image by *increasing the brightness* between the base and blend colors (layer order doesn't matter); the lighter the blend color, the brighter the result. This mode is a combo of Screen and Color Dodge modes, so it lightens images more than any other blend mode. But since it tends to turn *all* light colors white, it can make images look unnatural (though it can be useful in adding lighter texture to a dark background). Keyboard shortcut: Shift-Option-W (Shift+Alt+W).

FIGURE 7-14

Wish your model (or even you) had highlights? No problemo. Press ⌘-Shift-N (Ctrl+Shift+N) and, in the resulting New Layer dialog box, change the blend mode to Color Dodge. Use the Edit→Fill command to fill the new layer with 50% gray and then Option-click (Alt-click) the "Add layer mask" button at the bottom of the Layers panel to add a solid black mask to hide the lightening from the whole image. Next, reveal the lightening—in other words, paint highlights onto the hair—using a soft white brush (be sure to get close to the roots!).

Like Color Burn, Color Dodge responds differently to the Layers panel's Fill and Opacity settings, so try reducing Fill *to make this particular effect more subtle.*

- **Lighter Color**. With this mode, Photoshop compares the total numeric value of all channels for the base and blend colors and then keeps the higher values, resulting in the lightest pixels. There's no color blending in this mode; the darker colors simply disappear. If you're trying to replace a dark background with something lighter, give this mode a spin. (There's no keyboard shortcut for this mode.)

Lighting (Contrast) Blend Modes

In contrast to the Lighten and Darken modes, Lighting blend modes do a little darkening *and* a little lightening to increase the contrast of images. They have a neutral color of 50 percent gray, which doesn't affect the result color; it just disappears.

- **Overlay**. In this mode, if the base color is darker than 50 percent gray, Photoshop multiplies its color value with the base color. If the base color is lighter than 50 percent gray, Photoshop multiplies its color value with the *inverse* of the base color (like it does in Screen mode). You can use this mode to increase contrast or colorize a grayscale image, though it's commonly used in conjunction with the High Pass filter in order to sharpen an image (page 462). Keyboard shortcut: Shift-Option-O (Shift+Alt+O on a PC).

- **Soft Light**. As its name suggests, this mode is equivalent to shining a soft light on your image. It makes areas lighter than 50% gray even lighter (as if they were dodged) and areas darker than 50% gray even darker (as if they were burned). If you paint with black in this mode, you'll darken the underlying image; if you paint with white, you'll lighten it. You can use this mode to add texture to an image or to make an image look like it's reflected in metal (see *Figure 7-15*). Seasoned Photoshop jockeys use Soft Light on a layer filled with 50% gray to make the Brush tool *behave* like non-destructive versions of the Dodge and Burn tools (page 432 has the scoop). Keyboard shortcut: Shift-Option-F (Shift+Alt+F).

FIGURE 7-15

To create a quick reflection in a metal object, change the top layer's blend mode to Soft Light.

- **Hard Light**. This mode, which is equivalent to shining a harsh light on your image, combines Multiply and Screen modes: If the blend color is lighter than 50 percent gray, the image gets lighter (like Screen mode); if it's darker than 50 percent gray, the image gets darker (like Multiply). If you paint with black or white in this mode, you simply get black or white. If you *really* want to increase the level of detail in an image—say, if you're trying to fix a slightly blurry image—use this mode in conjunction with the Emboss filter (page 668). Hard Light is also used in conjunction with the High Pass filter in order to sharpen an image (page 462), and produces a slightly stronger sharpening effect than using Overlay mode. Keyboard shortcut: Shift-Option-H (Shift+Alt+H).

- **Vivid Light**. In this mode, Photoshop applies Color Burn to increase the contrast of colors *darker* than 50 percent gray and Color Dodge to decrease the contrast of colors *lighter* than 50 percent gray (layer order matters in this mode). Use Vivid Light to make an image pop or to add texture. Keyboard shortcut: Shift-Option-V (Shift+Alt+V).

- **Linear Light**. This mode combines the Linear Burn and Linear Dodge modes: It uses Linear Burn to decrease the brightness of colors *darker* than 50 percent gray and Linear Dodge to increase the brightness of colors *lighter* than 50 percent gray. Linear Light is great for adding texture to images, as shown in *Figure 7-16*. Keyboard shortcut: Shift-Option-J (Shift+Alt+J).

FIGURE 7-16

Want to turn a loved one to stone? Simply use the Quick Selection tool to select the person's skin and then add a layer mask to a layer containing marble or stone (like the top layer here). Change the marble layer's blend mode to Linear Light, and you've got an instant statue.

In this example, the opacity of the marble layer was also lowered to 60 percent to reveal some of the skin tone.

- **Pin Light**. This mode combines Lighten and Darken: If the blend color is *lighter* than 50 percent gray, it replaces areas of the base color darker than 50 percent gray with the blend color; pixels lighter than 50 percent gray don't change at all. But if the blend color is *darker* than 50 percent gray, Pin Light replaces lighter areas of the base color with the blend color, and darker areas don't change. You'll rarely use this mode because it can produce odd results (or none at all), but feel free to experiment with it—especially with filters (see Chapter 15). Keyboard shortcut: Shift-Option-Z (Shift+Alt+Z).

- **Hard Mix**. This mode greatly reduces the range of colors in your image to six (plus black and white)—an effect known as *posterizing*—so you end up with large blocks of super-bright colors like red, green, and blue. In this mode, Photoshop takes the sum of the RGB values in the blend color and adds them to the base color. For example, if the value of the red, green, or blue channel is 255, Photoshop adds that value to the base; if the value is less than 255, Photoshop doesn't add anything to the base. (See page 383 for more on color values.) You can reduce the effect of this mode to a visually pleasing level by lowering the Fill setting (of the layer you set to Hard Mix) to about 25 percent, resulting in a nice contrast boost (see *Figure 7-17*). Keyboard shortcut: Shift-Option-L (Shift+Alt+L).

FIGURE 7-17

In Hard Mix mode, Photoshop changes all the pixels to primary colors (see the figure on page 338), leaving you with solid blocks of bright, high-contrast color. By lowering that layer's Fill setting to 25 percent, you get a nice color boost.

As you can see here, combining images isn't just about using different *images; there's opportunity aplenty to combine different versions of the* same *image.*

TIP To quickly change the Layers panel's Fill setting to 25 percent, press Shift-2-5. To change its Opacity setting instead, just press the number you want to apply, such as 2-5. You can also set Fill to zero by pressing Shift-0-0, and Opacity to zero by pressing 0-0 respectively. (All of these shortcuts work only if you're *not* currently using the Brush, Spot Healing, or Healing Brush tools.)

Comparative Blend Modes

This category could be called "psychedelic" as its modes can produce freaky results that are useful only on Halloween or in grungy collages (discussed earlier in this chapter). However, as you'll soon find out, they can be *temporarily* useful. Black is the neutral color in these modes.

- **Difference**. This mode compares the brightness of both the base and the blend colors and subtracts the brightest pixels. If you use white as your blend color, Photoshop inverts (flip-flops) the base color, making the image look like a film negative. If you use black as your blend color, Photoshop doesn't change anything. You can use this mode temporarily to locate the midtones in an image (see the box on page 382 for details) or, more practically, to align two layers that contain different versions of the same image (if, say, they were shot at different exposures or if you're trying to create one perfect shot from many): Just change the top layer to Difference mode and then use the arrow keys on your keyboard to move the image until both versions line up. Keyboard shortcut: Shift-Option-E (Shift+Alt+E on a PC).

- **Exclusion**. This mode is similar to Difference but results in a little less contrast. Blending with white inverts the base color, and blending with black doesn't do anything. It produces some fairly freaky effects so you won't use it much. That said, you can also use Exclusion to align images by following the steps in the previous bullet point. Keyboard shortcut: Shift-Option-X (Shift+Alt+X).

- **Subtract**. Introduced in CS5, this mode subtracts the blend color from the base color, which significantly darkens your image (layer order matters with this mode). The results of using this mode are practically the same as inverting the colors on a given layer (see page 338).

- **Divide**. Also introduced in CS5, this mode divides the blend color by the base color, which significantly brightens your image. It's used a lot in astrophotography and microscopy.

Composite Blend Modes

All the modes in this category relate to color and luminance (brightness) values. Depending on the colors in the layers you're working with, Photoshop applies one or two of these values to produce the result color (these modes don't have a neutral color like the other ones). Hue blend modes are extremely practical because you can use 'em to change, add, or intensify colors.

- **Hue**. This mode keeps the lightness and saturation (color intensity) values of the base color and adds the *hue*—a pure color that hasn't yet been lightened with white or darkened with black—of the blend color. Use this mode to change an object's color without changing how light or dark it is (see page 332). However, Hue mode can't introduce a color that isn't already *there* to colorize grayscale images, so you have to use another mode for that (like Color, explained in a sec). Keyboard shortcut: Shift-Option-U (Shift+Alt+U on a PC).

- **Saturation**. This mode keeps the luminance and hue of the base color and picks up the saturation of the blend color. If you want to increase an image's color intensity, this mode can help (though try using a Vibrance Adjustment layer first [page 339], as it usually produces better results). You can also use Saturation to drain color from part of an image by painting that area black; because black has no saturation value, black *desaturates* any colors that intersect with it. Keyboard shortcut: Shift-Option-T (Shift+Alt+T).

- **Color**. In this mode, Photoshop keeps the luminance of the base color and picks up the hue and saturation of the blend color, which makes it handy for colorizing grayscale images (see page 339). Keyboard shortcut: Shift-Option-C (Shift+Alt+C).

- **Luminosity**. This mode keeps the base color's hue and saturation and picks up the blend color's luminance. Use Luminosity to keep your image's colors from shifting when you're sharpening it (see page 453) or using a Curves or Levels Adjustment layer (see Chapter 9). Keyboard shortcut: Shift-Option-Y (Shift+Alt+Y).

Zapping Backgrounds with Blending Sliders

If the subject of your image is radically brighter or darker than its background, you'll want to sit up and pay attention to this section. While blend modes are pretty powerful in their own right (and several of 'em can instantly pulverize a white or black background), *another* set of blending options in the Layer Style dialog box (page 127) can eat backgrounds for lunch—nondestructively!

Photoshop gives you a few different ways to open the Layer Style dialog box (*Figure 7-18*). Once you've activated the Image layer you want to work with, open the dialog box using one of the following methods:

- **Double-click the layer's thumbnail in the Layers panel**.

- **Click the *fx* button at the bottom of the Layers panel and then choose Blending Options**.

- **Choose Layer→Layer Style→Blending Options**.

> **NOTE** The Blending sliders won't work on a locked Background layer; you have to double-click the layer first to unlock it.

At the bottom of the Layer Style dialog box lie two pairs of sliders (they look like triangles): one set for the This Layer bar and another for the Underlying Layer bar, shown in *Figure 7-18*. Each slider lets you make parts of your image transparent based on the brightness value of the pixels. The left-hand sliders represent the shadows (blacks) in the image, and the right-hand ones represent the highlights (whites). To affect the currently active layer, tweak the This Layer slider (you'll learn about the Underlying Layer slider in a moment).

UP TO SPEED

Pass Through Mode

When you create a layer group (page 100), Pass Through appears at the top of the Layers panel's blend mode drop-down menu. In this mode, Photoshop makes sure that any blend modes, blending slider settings, opacity settings, and fill settings you've applied to layers in the group trickle down to layers *below* the group.

For example, let's say you've created a layer group consisting of several Image layers set to Linear Burn mode to make a grunge collage. Pass Through mode makes the Linear Burn effect trickle down to any background or text on layers below the group. If you *don't* want the blending to affect the layers below the group, change the group's blend mode to Normal instead.

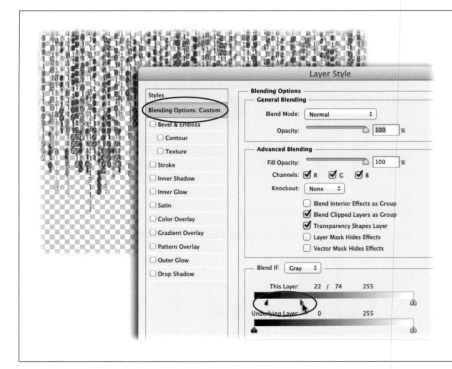

FIGURE 7-18

You can use the Blend If sliders in this dialog box to make short work of removing solid-colored backgrounds. In this image, the black background has been hidden by dragging the shadow slider to the right.

To soften the edges of the bits that remain, you can split the slider in half (as described in a sec) and then drag its left half back to the left of the This Layer slider, as shown here (circled).

For example, if the background of the active layer is black and the subject (or object in the foreground) is much brighter, you can hide the black part by dragging the shadow slider (the one on the left) right toward the middle of the This Layer bar until the black part is transparent. To hide a white background instead, drag the highlight slider (the one on the right) left toward the middle of the bar until the white part is transparent.

> **NOTE** If you save your document as a PSD file, you can adjust these sliders any time you want by activating the layer and summoning the Layer Style dialog box.

To soften the edges of what you've just hidden in the background, you can make the edge pixels partially transparent by splitting the shadow or highlights slider in half. To soften the edge pixels after you've hidden a black background, for example, Option-click (Alt-click on a PC) the left half of the shadows slider and drag it slightly back to the left (circled in *Figure 7-18*). Likewise, if you've hidden a white background, you can Option-click (Alt-click) the right half of the highlights slider and drag it slightly to the right to tell Photoshop to make pixels with that particular brightness value partially transparent.

The Underlying Layer sliders let you control the range of visible colors on layers *below* the active layer. As you drag the sliders, parts of the image on underlying layers appear *through* the pixels on the active layer as though you'd cut a hole through it. If you drag the shadows slider right toward the middle of the Underlying Layer bar, you'll begin to see the darkest parts of the underlying image show through the active layer. If you drag the highlight slider left toward the middle of the bar, you'll start to see the lightest parts of the underlying image.

As *Figure 7-19* shows, the blending sliders can do an amazing job of hiding backgrounds based on color. But if your *subject* contains some of the colors in the background, the blending sliders will zap those areas, too. In that case, you'll have to use a different method to hide the background, like another blend mode or a layer mask (as discussed earlier in this chapter).

FIGURE 7-19

Once you've hidden the black in this Matrix-like background, you can see through to the image on the layer below, which makes for a quickie collage.

In the Layers panel, Photoshop adds a special badge to the right of the layer's name to let you know its blending options have changed; the badge looks like two intersecting squares and is shown on the matrix layer here.

Auto-Aligning Layers and Photomerge

If you've ever needed to combine a few group shots to get an image where everybody is smiling and their eyes are open, you'll appreciate the Auto-Align Layers command. Sure, you can *manually* align layers, but when you run this command, Photoshop does all the hard work *for* you by examining the active layers and aligning them so identical areas overlap (see *Figure 7-20*).

Once you've got your images on different layers in the same document—they need to be exactly the same size—activate at *least* two layers by Shift- or ⌘-clicking them (Ctrl-clicking on a PC) in the Layers panel, and then choose Edit→Auto-Align Layers (this menu item is grayed out unless you have two or more layers activated). In the resulting dialog box, you can choose from these alignment methods:

- **Auto**. If you're not sure which method will work best to align your images, let Photoshop decide. When you choose this option, the program picks either Perspective or Cylindrical, depending on which one it thinks will create the best composition. It usually does a good job aligning images, though you may notice some distortion (as explained in the following bullet points).

FIGURE 7-20

The Auto-Align Layers command is great for merging a few imperfect shots into one perfect image (or at least one where each subject is smiling). To do that, combine the images into one document and place the non-smiling layer (left) atop the smiling layer (right). Then run the Auto-Align layers command. Finally, add a layer mask to the top layer and then paint the non-smile away with a black brush so your smiling pal shows through!

- **Perspective**. When you choose this method, Photoshop adjusts the four corners of your layers and repositions, stretches, and skews each one so any overlapping areas match in perspective. The final image looks slightly warped—both ends are a little larger than the center of the image, as if they were closer to you. This method can also make one of your layers look like it's coming out of the screen toward you, which can be visually interesting.

> **TIP** Photoshop picks its own *reference layer* (the layer it tries to align all the other layers with) unless you designate one *yourself* using the Lock All layer lock discussed on page 100.

- **Collage**. This method tells Photoshop to scale, rotate, and reposition the layers to align their overlapping content without changing their shape. Choose Collage if you don't want your images to get distorted in any way.

- **Cylindrical**. If you're combining several images into a panorama, choose this option. In addition to repositioning, stretching, and skewing your layers, Cylindrical helps get rid of any bow-tie lens distortion (where the subject looks like it's being pinched inward) by curving the images slightly (see *Figure 7-21*, middle).

FIGURE 7-21

Top: If you want to stitch these forest images together, you can use the Auto-Align Layers command or Photomerge (page 294) to get it done.

Middle: To compensate for bow-tie lens distortion, the Cylindrical alignment method curves the final image slightly (notice that the top and bottom edges of the image aren't straight).

Bottom: The Spherical method gives you a perfectly rectangular panorama.

Honestly, the Auto-Align feature isn't magic; the angle and the distance from the subject in all the shots need to be the same for it to work. However, since CS5, this command has taken a peek at the lens-correction profiles specified in the Lens Correction dialog box (page 639), which helps this feature do a better job of aligning layers and creating panoramas.

- **Spherical**. Like Cylindrical, this method repositions, stretches, and skews layers to match up overlapping areas. It also tries to correct barrel distortion (where the subject looks rounded) by making the panorama perfectly rectangular (see *Figure 7-21*, bottom).

- **Reposition**. If you're aligning a group shot to hide a frown or closed eyes, choose this option. It won't stretch or skew the layers; it'll just reposition them so they line up.

The Auto-Align Layers dialog box also gives you two ways to correct camera lens distortion. Turn on the Vignette Removal checkbox to get rid of darkened or soft edges caused by wide-angle lenses, or the Geometric Distortion checkbox to make Photoshop warp your image slightly to reduce the spherical look caused either by wide-angle lenses or being too close to your subject with a regular lens.

Once you've aligned the images, hop to "Auto-Blending Layers" at the end of this page to see how to make Photoshop blend 'em together seamlessly using the Auto-Blend command.

Building Panoramas with Photomerge

Photoshop has an automatic photo-stitcher called Photomerge that gives you all the same options as the Auto-Align Layers dialog box, but you don't have to combine the images into a single document first—Photoshop does that for you. This is really helpful when you're merging images into a wide shot, though you can't manually arrange your images into a panorama (that feature disappeared back in CS4).

To use Photomerge, choose File→Automate→Photomerge. In the resulting dialog box's Use menu, tell Photoshop whether you want to use individual files or a whole folder. Then click the Browse button to find the images on your hard drive, or, if you've already opened the documents, click the Add Open Files button. On the left side of the dialog box, you can pick an alignment method or leave it set to Auto and let Photoshop choose for you. If you want Photoshop to use layer masks to help cover up any seams, leave the Blend Images Together checkbox at the bottom of the dialog box turned on (this setting has the same effect as running the Auto-Blend command discussed below). The Vignette Removal and Geometric Distortion checkboxes work the same way here as they do in the Auto-Align Layers dialog box.

When you've got all the settings the way you want them, click OK. Photoshop combines your images into a new document with each image on its own layer, rotated and positioned to fit with all the others. All you need to do is crop the image to get rid of any transparent bits around the edges, or you can recreate that portion of the image by hand using the Clone Stamp tool or, even simpler, the Content-Aware Scale command.

TIP You'll find cropping and cloning easier if you stamp (page 107) or flatten (page 108) the layers first, though, if you pick the latter, be sure to choose File→Save As and give the image another name so you can flatten it without worrying about saving over the original. Also, you can choose Edit→Content-Aware Scale (page 362) to slightly stretch the image to fill in empty pixels so you don't have to crop it quite so much.

■ Auto-Blending Layers

The Auto-Blend Layers command, which was designed to be used after the Auto-Align Layers command, helps you blend images for a panorama or collage, or combine multiple exposures of the same image to create an extended *depth of field* so more of an object looks like it's in focus. When you use this command, Photoshop creates complex layer masks to blend your images, saving you a lot of hard work.

To get the best results, run the Auto-Align Layers command as explained on page 292, and then choose Edit→Auto-Blend Layers. In the resulting dialog box (*Figure 7-22*, left), choose one of the following blending options:

- **Panorama**. Select this option to have Photoshop search for overlapping areas in your images so it can piece them together into a single image.

- **Stack Images**. If you've fired off several shots of an object with different parts in focus (known as different depths of field) and you want to combine them into a single shot where the *whole* object is in focus, choose this option. Let's say you shot a tiger—with a big zoom lens, of course—that was stretched out lengthwise and facing you. If one image has his head in focus, another has the middle of his body in focus, and a third has his tail in focus, you can choose Stack Images to make Photoshop combine the three images into a single shot with the *whole* cat in focus.

> **TIP** In Photoshop CC, you can use the Field Blur, Iris Blur, and Tilt-Shift filters to produce even better and more complex depth of field effects than you can get with Stack Images.

- **Seamless Tones and Colors**. Leave this checkbox turned on to make Photoshop smooth out any noticeable seams and color differences between the images during the blending process.

As mentioned earlier, this command has a ton of potential uses. One visually interesting possibility is to make a collage of two or more action shots to create a stop-motion effect. *Figure 7-22* has the details.

UP TO SPEED

Shooting Panoramas

If you're taking photos specifically to make a big honkin' panorama, here are a few things to keep in mind while you're snapping away in order to produce the best results:

- **Use a tripod**. A tripod or some other stabilizing surface (like your mate's shoulder) helps you take steadier shots. You don't want your panorama to be blurry, right?

- **Include an overlapping element in each shot**. If you're taking three shots, make sure you include some of what's in the first shot in the second, and some of the second shot in the third (about 40 percent in each instance, if you can). That way you have overlapping bits that Photoshop can use to align the images.

- **Keep the lighting (exposure) consistent**. Though Photomerge is pretty darn good at blending images, you're going to notice if you took one shot in the shade and the other in direct sunlight. For the best results, keep the lighting constant by exposing for the brightest portion of the image manually (you may have to consult your camera's manual to figure out how).

- **Make sure the angles are the same**. Photoshop has one heck of a time matching up images shot at different angles, but mismatched shots can make for some interesting creative possibilities.

FIGURE 7-22

You can use the Auto-Blend Layers command to create interesting collages like this in mere seconds. The best part is that Photoshop does all the masking for you, as shown in this Layers panel. Woo-hoo!

Just remember that you can use the Auto-Blend Layers command only when you're working in RGB or Grayscale mode.

TIP You can also use the Auto-Blend Layers command to help scan really big images. For example, if the image is too big to fit onto your scanner in one piece, scan different sections of it—being careful to create overlapping areas—and then let Photoshop piece it together for you by first running the Auto-Align Layers command and then running Auto-Blend Layers. (Interestingly, the Photomerge command actually uses the Auto-Align and Auto-Blend commands to build panoramas.)

■ Cloning Between Documents

The Clone Stamp tool is great for tricks like banishing shiny spots (page 418) or giving someone a third eye, but it has other uses, too. You can also use it to copy bits and pieces of an image from one open document to another. Using the Clone Source panel—the *clone source* is the object you're copying—you can clone from up to five different sources whether or not they're in the same Photoshop document. Here's how to clone from one open image into another:

1. **Open the source document(s) (the image[s] you're cloning from) and the target document (the image you're cloning to) and arrange your workspace.**

    To choose clone sources in documents other than the current image, open the source documents. Then choose Window→Arrange and pick a setup that lets you see all the open documents, or just click each document's tab to activate it (see page 56 in Chapter 2 for more on working with tabbed documents).

> **NOTE** For info on using the Clone Stamp tool within the *same* document, skip ahead to page 418.

2. **Press S to grab the Clone Stamp tool, and then open the Clone Source panel.**

   Choose Window→Clone Source or click the panel's icon in the panel dock. (Full coverage of the Clone Source panel's many options starts on page 298.)

3. **Set the clone source.**

   Click the window (or tab) of the image you want to clone from (like the cats in *Figure 7-23*, top left). Then Option-click (Alt-click on a PC) the area you want to copy to set it as the clone source.

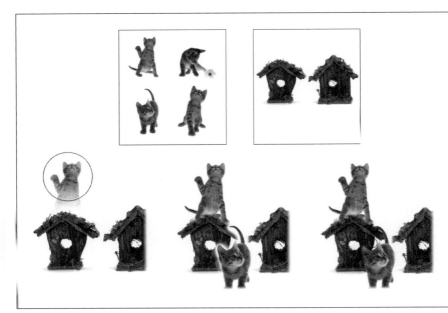

FIGURE 7-23

Top: By cloning the kitties from one image onto the birdhouses in another, you can create a mischievously cute collage.

Bottom: The brush preview is extremely helpful in positioning the cloned art (left). If you mess up and clone in a little too much (middle), grab the History Brush and paint to reveal that part of the original image (right). If you're cloning onto a new layer, you can also use the Eraser tool.

4. **Create a new layer.**

   Unless you want to clone the new image on top of your original image (and you don't!), head back to your target document and add a new layer to it by clicking the "Create a new layer" button at the bottom of the Layers panel. That way, if you don't like the result, you can simply toss the new layer instead of having to start over.

5. **Paint to clone the item.**

   As shown in *Figure 7-23* (bottom left), Photoshop displays a preview of the image you're about to paint *inside* the brush cursor. If you don't want the clone source point to move as your brush cursor moves—because you want to create multiple instances of an object, for example—turn off the Options bar's Aligned checkbox.

> **TIP** To change your brush settings, you can use the Options bar or keyboard shortcuts. You can alter brush size and hardness by Control-Option-dragging (Alt+right-click+dragging on a PC) in horizontal or vertical strokes, respectively.

You need a pretty steady hand when working with the Clone Stamp tool because it's easy to clone too much and cover up parts of your image (though a well-placed layer mask can fix that). You can solve that problem by first selecting an area to restrict your brushstrokes to that part of the image. This technique is handy when you want to fill an area with another image, as shown in *Figure 7-24*.

FIGURE 7-24

If you select the destination area first (like these silhouettes), you don't have to be as careful with your brushstrokes. As you can see here, the brush cursor (circled) extends well past the edges of these digital business dudes, but Photoshop applies the Matrix-like background only within the selected area.

If you want to get a little fancy and start doing things like pulling source points from *multiple* images and changing the *angle* of your cloned objects, then you need to enlist the help of the Clone Source panel (*Figure 7-25*).

> **NOTE** You can use the Frame Offset and Lock Frame options shown in *Figure 7-25* to clone content in video or animation frames.

The Clone Source panel includes the following settings:

- **Offset**. Use this section of the panel to move, resize, or rotate the object you're copying (a.k.a. the clone source). If you want to move the clone source, you can change its X and Y coordinates (measured in pixels) here. If you've got the Show Overlay checkbox (explained next) turned on, you see a preview of the source point on your image that moves as you tweak these settings. To clone the object at a different size, enter new percentages in the W and H (width and height) fields. To rotate your clone source—so the cloned item is turned—enter a number of degrees in the field next to the triangle icon. To reset all these options, click the curved arrow button labeled in *Figure 7-25*.

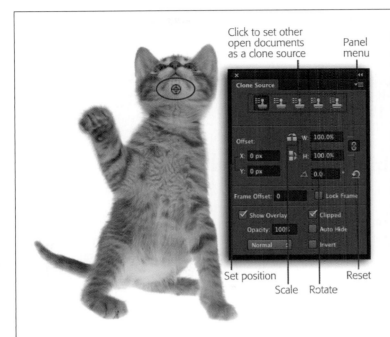

Click to set other
open documents
as a clone source

Panel
menu

Set position

Scale   Rotate

Reset

FIGURE 7-25

Assigning multiple clone sources is handy when you want to clone items between open documents or create a complex scene from different elements. For example, if you're trying to remove a cat that's standing in front of a birdhouse, one clone source can be the cat and another can be the birdhouse.

Once you've activated the Clone Stamp tool, you can use the five source buttons shown here to quickly switch between different source points without having to reset them manually each time. To set a source point, just Option-click (Alt-click on a PC) the area you want to clone, and your cursor turns into a crosshairs icon like the one circled here.

TIP You can position your cursor above any of the field labels in the Offset section—X, Y, W, and so on—to get the handy scrubby cursor (page 90). Then drag left to decrease the setting and right to increase it. You can Shift-drag to change it in larger increments or Option-drag (Alt-drag on a PC) for smaller increments. If you're a fan of keyboard shortcuts, press Option-Shift-[(Alt+Shift+[on a PC) to decrease your clone source's width and height proportionally and Option-Shift-] (Alt+Shift+]) to increase them. To rotate the source, press Option-Shift-< (Alt+Shift+<) to turn it counterclockwise or Option-Shift-> (Alt+Shift+>) to turn it clockwise.

- **Show Overlay**. With this checkbox turned on (it's on automatically), you see a preview of what you're about to paint *inside your brush cursor*. This handy feature shows you exactly what the cloning will look like before you commit to it.

- **Opacity**. Use this field to adjust the opacity of the overlay preview. (To change the opacity of what you're *cloning*—in other words, your actual brushstrokes—change the Opacity setting in the Options bar instead.)

- **Clipped**. This checkbox restricts the preview overlay to the area inside your brush cursor. For Thor's sake, leave this setting turned on. If you don't, Photoshop previews the *entire* clone source image right underneath your cursor, which keeps you from seeing anything *except* the preview.

- **Auto Hide**. If you turn on this checkbox, the overlay preview disappears as soon as you click to start painting. It's a good idea to turn it on so you can see how much you've painted so far.

- **Invert**. Turning on this checkbox makes Photoshop invert the overlay preview so it looks like a film negative, which can be helpful if you're trying to align the cloned area with something that's already in your image.

- **Blend Mode**. Use this menu to change the blend mode of the overlay preview. Your choices—Normal, Darken, Lighten, and Difference—are explained earlier in this chapter, starting on page 278. (To change the blend mode of the *cloned pixels*, use the Options bar's Mode menu instead.)

Combining Vectors and Rasters

A fun trend in the design world is to combine vectors with rasters (page 43 explains the difference); in other words, to combine illustrations with photographs, a technique that provides an interesting look and lets you get creative. Because you can place vectors as Smart Objects (page 118), they remain infinitely resizable, letting you experiment with them as backgrounds, artful embellishments, and even ornamental photo frames. As you can see in *Figure 7-26*, adding vectors to photos is a ton of fun.

FIGURE 7-26

A dash of vector art can spice up any photo. It's as if you're blending real images with imaginary ones.

Even if you can't draw these little goodies yourself, stock-image companies like iStockphoto. com and Fotolia.com sell affordable vector images so you can still join in the fun. In fact, if you visit www.lesa.in/istockdeal, you can download 10 images for free! Another great resource for vectors is GraphicAuthority.com.

You can add vector art to images in a couple of ways:

- **Place it**. With a document open, choose File→Place and navigate to the vector file on your hard drive (these files are usually in EPS [Encapsulated PostScript] or AI [Adobe Illustrator] format). This inserts the file as a Smart Object (page 118). Since you'll most likely need to resize the artwork, Photoshop considerately surrounds it with the Free Transform bounding box and resizing handles. Just Shift-drag any corner to make the art bigger or smaller. If you need to rotate it, place your cursor outside the bounding box and then drag in the direction you want to rotate. Press Return (Enter on a PC) when you're finished.

- **Paste it**. If you're working in a vector-based program like Adobe Illustrator, you can copy artwork and then paste it into a Photoshop document by choosing Edit→Paste or pressing ⌘-V (Ctrl+V). When you do, Photoshop displays the dialog box shown in *Figure 7-27* (left), asking *how* you want to paste it. If you choose Smart Object, you can resize the illustration as much as you want without losing quality.

FIGURE 7-27

When you paste a piece of vector art, Photoshop lets you decide how to paste it (left). If you choose Smart Object, the object appears in your document with helpful resizing handles, as shown here (right). It also carries the special Smart Object badge (circled) over in the Layers panel. And if the illustration includes other bits and pieces that you don't want to use, you can simply hide 'em with a layer mask, as shown here.

Framing a photo with an illustration is not only fun, it's also incredibly flexible because you can continually resize the frame without starting over. Here's how:

1. **Open the photo you want to frame and then choose File→Place to import the illustration you want to use as the frame.**

   Navigate to where the illustration file lives on your hard drive and then click the Place button.

NOTE If your image consists of *multiple* layers, either convert those layers into a Smart Object (page 122) or create a stamped layer (page 107) first. *Then* perform step 1 of this technique.

2. **Resize the illustration.**

   Conveniently, the illustration appears in your document with resizing handles around it, which you'll probably need to use to make it bigger or smaller. Grab a corner handle and drag until the frame is big enough to hold the photo. (To resize all four sides of the illustration at once, press and hold Shift-Option [Shift+Alt on a PC] as you drag a corner handle.) Drag inside the bounding box to move it around. When it's just right, press Return (Enter).

3. **Over in the Layers panel, drag the illustration layer below the Image layer.**

   The maneuver you're performing won't work if the illustration layer is *above* the photo layer.

4. **Clip the photo layer to the illustration layer.**

   With the photo layer active (or Smart Object or stamped layer, as described in step 1), choose Layer→Create Clipping Mask, or press and hold Option (Alt on a PC) while pointing your cursor at the dividing line between the two layers in the Layers panel (when the cursor turns into a square with a down-pointing arrow, click once). Either way, the thumbnail of the photo layer scoots to the right, and a tiny downward-pointing arrow appears to let you know that it's clipped (masked) to the illustration layer directly below it, as shown in *Figure 7-28*. You should now see the photo peeking through the illustration.

5. **Use the Move tool to position the photo and frame.**

   Press V to grab the Move tool and reposition the photo and/or frame layer as necessary.

6. **Activate the illustration layer and then add a Fill layer to create a colorful background for your new frame.**

   Activating the illustration layer first ensures that the new Fill layer appears *below* the photo layer, allowing you to snatch a new color from it (as described in a sec). Choose Layer→New Fill Layer→Solid Color, or click the half-black/half-white circle at the bottom of the Layers panel and choose Solid Color from the resulting drop-down menu. Once the Color Picker opens, mouse over to your image and click to steal a color from it (such as the copper color of the mermaid's hair in *Figure 7-28*). Then click OK to close the Color Picker.

7. **Save your document as a PSD file.**

You're done! To resize the frame, activate the illustration layer and summon Free Transform by pressing ⌘-T (Ctrl+T), and then use one of the corner handles to resize the illustration; press Return (Enter) when you're finished. And to give the frame a little depth, you can tack on a drop shadow using layer styles (page 125).

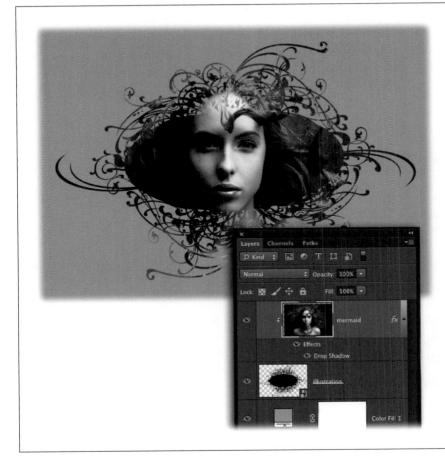

FIGURE 7-28

This detailed illustration makes a gorgeous photo frame. After you place it as a Smart Object and resize it, just clip it to a photo layer (bottom), add a new background color, and you're done!

For more ideas about how to incorporate vectors into your photos—as well as how to colorize a vector in Photoshop—see the technique on page 347.

Mapping One Image onto Another

You can combine two images in an impressive way by wrapping one around the contours of another so the first image follows every nook and cranny of the second. To perform this feat, you need to create a *displacement map*—a grayscale image that Photoshop uses to warp and bend one image to the curvature of another. Applying this technique to photos of friends and family is great fun. For example, you can take a circuit board and wrap it around a body or a face, as shown in *Figure 7-29*. Here's what you do:

1. **Open the image you want to map another image onto (like a face), and then hunt down the channel with the greatest contrast.**

   To make the best possible displacement map, you need the channel with the highest contrast. If you're in RGB mode (and you probably are), you can cycle through the channels by pressing ⌘-3, 4, and 5 (Ctrl+3, 4, and 5 on a PC). Because digital cameras tend to have so many more green sensors than red or blue ones, you'll most likely pick the green channel.

FIGURE 7-29

With a displacement map, you can apply all kinds of wild textures to skin. Know anyone who needs to be turned into a reptile?

To follow along with this tutorial, visit this book's Missing CD page at www.missingmanuals.com/cds and download the practice file Map.zip.

2. **Duplicate the high-contrast channel and send it to a new document.**

Open the Channels panel by clicking its icon in the panel dock or choosing Window→Channels. Then, from the Channels panel's menu, choose Duplicate Channel. In the resulting dialog box, choose New from the Destination drop-down menu and name the channel something memorable like *Map*. When you click OK, Photoshop opens a displacement map document that contains the grayscale channel you picked in step 1.

NOTE If the highest-contrast channel in your image isn't very contrasty, the results of this technique will be too subtle to notice. The fix is to *exaggerate* the contrast of the channel in your Map document with a Levels or Curves *adjustment* (not an Adjustment layer). To apply a Levels adjustment to the Image layer, press ⌘-L (Ctrl+L); for a Curves adjustment, press ⌘-M (Ctrl+M). For more on those adjustments, skip to Chapter 9.

---

3. **Blur the displacement map slightly.**

With the map document active, choose Filter→Blur→Gaussian Blur. Enter a value of 1–4 pixels (1 for low-resolution images, 4 for high-resolution images) and then click OK. The goal here is to blur the image just a bit so the map is slightly smooth (page 431 has more on the Gaussian Blur filter).

4. **Save the map and close the file.**

Choose File→Save As and choose Photoshop from the format menu at the bottom of the dialog box. Make sure the Alpha Channel option is turned on and then click Save. Close the file by pressing ⌘-W (Ctrl+W).

5. **Go back to the original document and turn the composite channel back on.**

When you cycled through the different channels in step 1, Photoshop temporarily turned off the composite channel (the one that shows your image in full color). Go back to the original document (the one you opened in step 1) and turn all the channels back on by pressing ⌘-2 (Ctrl+2 on a PC).

6. **Select the face.**

In the bottom image in *Figure 7-29*, it's easy to select the face because it's on a solid background. Grab the Magic Wand by pressing W, click once in the white area, and then Shift-click to select the other white parts until you have everything *except* the face selected. Then, invert your selection by pressing Shift-⌘-I (Shift+Ctrl+I on a PC) or choosing Select→Inverse; Photoshop flip-flops your selection so the face is surrounded by marching ants.

7. **Feather the edges of your selection slightly.**

Click the Options bar's Refine Edge button and feather the selection by 1 pixel. (See page 141 for more on feathering.)

8. **Save the selection by choosing Select→Save Selection.**

   Name it *Face* and then click OK. Get rid of the marching ants by pressing ⌘-D (Ctrl+D) to deselect.

9. **Add the soon-to-be-a-map image to the face document.**

   Pop open the image you want to map onto the face (like a circuit board in *Figure 7-29*), and then either copy and paste the image into the face document or drag it from the Layers panel into the face document.

10. **Choose Filter→Distort→Displace.**

    In the resulting Displace dialog box, leave the factory settings as is and click OK. If you're not sure whether the settings have ever been tampered with, press and hold the Option key (Alt on a PC) to change the Cancel button into a Reset button; click it and you're back to the original settings.

11. **In the resulting Open dialog box, navigate to the map document you saved in step 4 and then click OK.**

    If you watch your document as you click OK, you'll see the circuit board shift to the contours of the face. It's extremely cool.

12. **Load the face selection.**

    Choose Select→Load Selection→Face. You should see marching ants around the shape of the face (you can't see the actual face because it's behind the circuit board).

13. **Add a layer mask and then paint the person's eyes and teeth with black.**

    Click the circle-within-a-square button at the bottom of the Layers panel to add a layer mask. Then activate the Brush tool by pressing B and, with black as your foreground color, paint over the guy's eyes and teeth to hide them, as shown in *Figure 7-29* (bottom).

14. **Change the circuit board layer's blend mode to Multiply (page 280).**

    You should now see the face through the circuit board. If the circuit board is too dark, lower the Opacity setting at the top of the Layers panel. For even *more* creative fun, experiment with Darken, Color Burn, and Linear Burn modes.

Congratulations! You've just mapped one image to the contours of another, one of the slickest Photoshop tricks ever.

Draining, Changing, and Adding Color

When you want to make a big difference with one simple change to a photo, you can't beat converting it from color to black and white. The Ansel Adams approach doesn't just evoke nostalgia, it also puts the focus back on the *subject* in a powerful way. Going grayscale lets you salvage an image that you can't color-correct, as well as beautify a subject whose teeth need heavy-duty whitening or whose skin needs retouching. Those problems all but *disappear* when you enter the realm of black and white.

Does that mean you should set your digital camera to shoot in black and white? Heck, no! It's *much* better to photograph in color and then drain the color in Photoshop. That way, you have a truckload of artistic options like bringing back just a touch of the original color for a partial-color effect. And, speaking of color, Photoshop has several tools that let you change the color of anything, whether it's a car or the hair on your head. You can also breathe new life into *vintage* photographs by adding a dash of color.

This chapter teaches you how simple it is to drain, change, and add color to photos in a variety of ways. You'll find the following pages packed with creative color techniques you'll use again and again!

■ Draining Color

You've probably heard the saying, "You get what you pay for." In Photoshop, that saying translates to, "The quickest method ain't always the best!" In other words, some techniques just take a little extra time, and converting a color image to black and white is one of 'em—but it's well worth the effort.

To drive that point home, open a colorful image—you can download *Dragon.jpg* from this book's Missing CD page at *www.missingmanuals.com/cds* if you want to follow along—and then choose Image→Adjustments→Desaturate. (*Desaturating* means draining all color from an image.) Photoshop converts your image to black and white all right, but the results are less than inspiring (see *Figure 8-1*, top). You can also glance through your channels (Chapter 5), pick the one with the highest contrast, and then choose Image→Mode→Grayscale. Photoshop keeps the currently active channel, tosses the rest, and you're left with a black-and-white image...that *nobody* is going to write home about. As you're about to find out, Photoshop has several ways to produce beautiful black-and-white conversions, *not* including the two methods mentioned above.

FIGURE 8-1

Top: Sure, the Desaturate command lets you convert photos to black and white in one step, but as you can see, this method produces a very lame dragon.

Bottom: A Black & White Adjustment layer lets you introduce all kinds of contrast, making it a much better option for black-and-white conversions (and for producing a respectably menacing creature).

Another (older) way to create a black-and-white image is to use a Channel Mixer Adjustment layer. Cruise on over to this book's Missing CD page at www.missingmanuals.com/cds *to learn how.*

Black & White Adjustment Layers

Adding a Black & White Adjustment layer is hands down the easiest way to convert a color image to a beautiful black and white in no time flat. The process couldn't be simpler, and, best of all, it's nondestructive. As Chapter 3 explains, when you use Adjustment layers, Photoshop makes the changes on *another* layer—not on your original image—letting you tweak the opacity, toggle the visibility on or off, and so on. (You'll learn about other kinds of Adjustment layers throughout this book.)

> **NOTE** To follow along with this technique, head to this book's Missing CD page at *www.missingmanuals. com/cds* and download the practice file *Dragon.jpg*.

To create a black-and-white image, follow these steps:

1. **Pop open your soon-to-be-colorless image and add a Black & White Adjustment layer.**

   Choose Layer→New Adjustment Layer→Black & White; in the resulting New Layer dialog box, give the layer a name, if you'd like, and then click OK. Photoshop turns your image black and white, and opens the Properties panel, which contains several sliders you can use to fine-tune the image's contrast (*Figure 8-2*).

FIGURE 8-2

The Properties panel gives you access to the settings for the particular Adjustment layer you picked—in this case, Black & White—and its presets (some fairly awesome one-click, canned settings). If you click the Auto button, Photoshop shows you how it thinks the black-and-white image should look, though you can use the panel's sliders to show Photoshop what you think it should look like!

If your document contains several layers and you want the adjustment to affect only the layer directly below it—rather than all the layers underneath it—click the "Clip to layer below" button at the bottom of the panel, labeled here.

(The On-Image Adjustment button and Tint checkbox shown in this figure are explained in the next section.)

> **TIP** You can also create a Black & White Adjustment layer by clicking the Black & White icon in the Adjustments panel (choose Window→Adjustments if the panel isn't visible)—it's the same half-black/half-white square that's circled in *Figure 8-2*. Or you can click the half-black/half-white circle at the bottom of the Layers panel and then choose Black & White from the menu that appears. Whew!

2. **Move the Properties panel's various sliders to adjust the contrast of your newly black-and-white image.**

   Even though Photoshop has sapped the color from your image, there's always room for improvement. Drag a particular color's slider to the left (toward black) to make those areas darker, or to the right (toward white) to make them lighter. The colored bars under each slider give you a clue as to what dragging in each direction does to your image (*Figure 8-2*). Or, instead of adjusting a bunch of sliders, you can tweak a certain range of colors by dragging on the image itself, as *Figure 8-3* shows. Also, the Preset menu at the top of the panel has a slew of useful canned settings—just click each one to see what it looks like applied to your image (on a PC, you can use your keyboard's up and down arrow keys to cycle through the presets).

FIGURE 8-3

To adjust your image visually, click the On-Image Adjustment button circled here (right) and then mouse over to the image; your cursor temporarily turns into an eyedropper (not shown) to let you know you're about to sample a color. Position the cursor atop the area you want to adjust, then click and hold your mouse button. The cursor turns into a pointing hand with an arrow on each side (circled, left) to indicate that you can drag from side to side to adjust that range of color; drag left to make that area darker or drag right to make it lighter. With this method, you skip the "Which slider do I drag?" guessing game.

TIP For better results with the On-Image Adjustment tool, try activating the Eyedropper tool first by pressing I and, in the Options bar, change the Sample Size drop-down menu to "3 by 3 Average." That way, the On-Image Adjustment tool's eyedropper samples *several* pixels around the area you initially click instead of just one.

---

3. **Save your document as a PSD file so your layers remain intact.**

To change the Black & White Adjustment layer's settings later, just double-click its thumbnail in the Layers panel (it's that familiar half-black/half-white square icon) to reopen the Properties panel. Or, if the Properties panel *is* open, just click once to activate the layer and you'll see the sliders reappear. If you print the image and then decide it needs more contrast, being able to edit its Adjustment layer is a real timesaver.

TIP If your newly black-and-white image is headed for a professional printing press, you're not quite finished; flip ahead to the box on page 314 to learn your next step.

■ WARP-SPEED COLOR TINTING

You can give a black-and-white image a uniform color tint by using the Tint checkbox lurking near the top of the Properties panel (available only with a Black & White Adjustment layer). When you turn on this checkbox, Photoshop adds a brown tint (called a *sepia tone*) to your whole image, as shown in *Figure 8-4* (top). This technique produces what's known as a *fake duotone* (the real ones are explained on page 323).

FIGURE 8-4

Top: After you add a Black & White Adjustment layer to an image, you can give it a color overlay by turning on the Tint checkbox (circled). As you can see, adding a tint dramatically changes the image's mood. But are you stuck with brown, you ask? Heck no. To choose a different color, click the colored square to the right of the Tint checkbox to summon the Color Picker.

Bottom: Once the Color Picker opens, you can choose a range of color by clicking within the vertical, rainbow-colored bar (circled, right). Let Photoshop know how light or how dark you want the new color to be by clicking inside the large colored area (circled, left). Click OK to close the Color Picker and the new overlay color appears in the Properties panel and atop your image. Pretty slick, huh?

Gradient Map Adjustment Layers

Gradient Map Adjustment layers can also make *spectacular* black-and-white images, as *Figure 8-5* shows. In fact, many pros use this method because they believe it produces the most beautiful black-and-white images possible inside of Photoshop (that is, without using the Silver Efex Pro plug-in; see page 785). This technique is also super fast, as you can see from these steps:

1. **Open an image and set your color chips to black and white by pressing D, and then pressing X until black hops on top.**

   The Gradient Map Adjustment layer you'll add in the next step uses your foreground and background colors, so if you don't set them to black and white (respectively) *first*, the layer's effect can be rather startling—if your color chips are red and green, for example, then you get a red-and-green image (handy during the holidays, but that's about it). And make sure black is your *foreground* color, not your background color, or the image will end up looking like an x-ray.

Gradient preview
(click to open Gradient Editor)

Gradient
presets

Click to load
more presets

FIGURE 8-5

You can use a Gradient Map Adjustment layer to produce a quick yet beautiful black-and-white image. If you forgot to set your color chips to black and white before adding the Adjustment layer, just head to the Properties panel, open the Gradient presets menu (labeled), and in the resulting menu, look for the black-to-white gradient in the first row (third from the left). Give it a click, and Photoshop instantly transforms your image to black and white. And if you accidentally had white as your foreground color instead of black, just turn on the Reverse check-box beneath the gradient preview (not shown here).

2. **Add a Gradient Map Adjustment layer.**

   Choose Layer→New Adjustment Layer→Gradient Map, or open the Adjustments panel and click the Gradient Map icon (it looks like a horizontal black-to-white fade). You can also click the half-black/half-white circle at the bottom of the Layers panel and then choose Gradient Map. No matter which method you use, Photoshop maps the shadows in the image to your foreground color (black) and the highlights to your background color (white), creating a gorgeous black-and-white image.

   Told ya this method was quick! Even though you can't adjust the image's contrast like you can with a Black & White Adjustment layer, it still produces consistently good black-and-whites of most images.

> **TIP** To get more creative with this technique, you can use the Gradient Editor (page 620) to create a black-to-gray-to-white gradient, which adds extra depth and richness to a black-and-white image.

■ PHOTOGRAPHIC TONING

Photoshop also includes a bunch of gradient presets that you can use with a Gradient Map Adjustment layer to add a beautiful color overlay to an image. Just head to the Properties panel, open the Gradient presets menu, and then click the little sprocket at the top right of the resulting menu (circled in *Figure 8-6*). Choose Photographic Toning and click Append in the resulting dialog box so Photoshop adds the new gradients to the bottom of the current list...and there's a slew of 'em!

FIGURE 8-6

The 38 Photographic Toning presets you see here were introduced in Photoshop CS6, but few folks found 'em. To apply one of these beauties non-destructively to an image, just single-click its icon (if you point your cursor to a preset, Photoshop tells you its name in a little yellow tooltip). You can even tweak the Opacity setting of the resulting Gradient Map Adjustment layer to let a little of the image's original color show through.

It's well worth taking two seconds to load these goodies because you can use them to produce some amazing and, if you're a photographer, sellable results.

(Hope the bride doesn't slip off the back of this scooter!)

The Lightness Channel

As you learned back on page 195, Lab mode gets its name from its three channels. The "L" stands for the Lightness channel where Photoshop stores all the light or brightness values—and therefore the visible contours and details—of the image. The "a" and "b" are for the a and b channels, which store color info. This means the Lightness channel makes for a lovely black-and-white version of your image (see *Figure 8-7*).

To see what your image's Lightness channel looks like, first make a copy of the image by choosing Image→Duplicate (because switching color modes flattens a multi-layered document, it's a good idea to do that on a *copy* of the image). Then, choose Image→Mode→Lab Color. If your document includes any Adjustment layers, Photoshop displays a dialog box asking if you'd like to Flatten or Discard them; since you're working with a duplicate file, go ahead and click Flatten. Then, over in the Channels panel, activate the Lightness channel, tilt your head contemplatively, and see what you think. If you like the result, choose Image→Mode→Grayscale, and then click OK when Photoshop asks if it's OK to toss the image's color information. You can then return to the color mode from whence you came by choosing Image→Mode→RGB (or CMYK).

Preparing Grayscale Images for a Printing Press

Say your color image is part of a document headed for a professional printing press, and you've been assigned the task of transforming it into a grayscale image. In addition to using one of the techniques covered in this chapter to drain color from the image, you need to perform one more step: To make it a real, live grayscale image, you have to change the document's color mode to Grayscale. (If the image is headed for an inkjet printer or destined for posting on the Web, you can stop reading this box now and skip to something more interesting.)

That's right: Even though your image *looks* grayscale onscreen, it's still made from colors that have had their saturation values lowered to zero (saturation is the degree of color strength). If you're shaking your head in disbelief, open the Channels panel by choosing Window→Channels, and you'll find color channels peering back at you (exactly which channels you see depends on which color mode you're working in).

If you don't change the image's mode to Grayscale before you send it off to a printing press, the image will print with the colors listed in the Channels panel instead of with black ink alone. While the result would still *look* like a grayscale image, it would actually be made from colored inks, which costs more to print (the more colors you use on press, the higher the cost).

To prepare a grayscale image for a printing press, start by using one of the methods in this chapter to get rid of the color. Otherwise, Photoshop will do it for you when you switch to Grayscale mode—with mediocre results like those you'd get using the Desaturate command discussed on page 308. Next, save your document as a PSD file by choosing File→Save As to preserve any Adjustment layers (like a Black & White Adjustment layer) you may have added. Then, change the document's mode to Grayscale by choosing Image→Mode→Grayscale. Photoshop pops open a dialog box asking if you'd like to flatten your layers. Click OK and yet *another* dialog box appears asking if you'd like to discard color info (in other words, throw away all the color channels in the document.) Click OK and you're left with a *real* grayscale image that contains only a single channel named Gray.

If your image is headed for a local publication that's printed on *newsprint* (in other words, it's not *USA Today* or *The Guardian*) and you *haven't* attached a color profile (page 675) to it, you'll also want to adjust its *output levels* to keep the shadows from printing too dark and the highlights from printing too light. Press ⌘-L (Ctrl+L on a PC) and, at the bottom of the resulting Levels dialog box, enter 30 into the first field and 225 into the second field, and then press OK to close the dialog box. (For more about output levels, see page 676.)

To save the image for use in a page-layout program like InDesign or QuarkXPress, choose File→Save As and then, from the format drop-down menu near the bottom of the Save As dialog box, choose TIFF or PSD (see page 679 for when to use which format). Voilà—you've got yourself a *true* grayscale image!

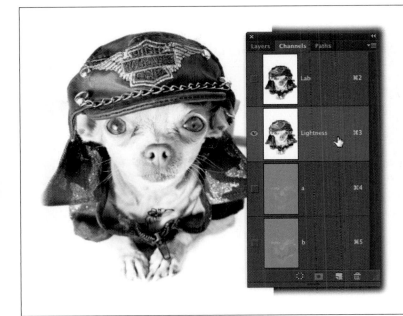

FIGURE 8-7

Because the Lightness channel holds all your image's details but none of its color, it often makes a nice black-and-white version all by itself.

To darken or lighten your newly colorless image, you can use any of the adjustments explained in Chapter 9, or the Screen and Multiply blend mode tricks mentioned back on page 113.

Going Grayscale in Camera Raw

If you're shooting photos in raw format, you may as well use the Camera Raw plug-in (page 361) to convert images to grayscale. It's easy to use and does a nice job with the conversion. Plus any edits you make in Camera Raw are nondestructive, so you can always get back to your original image. To open a raw image, just double-click its file icon, and it opens in Camera Raw automatically. If you're using Adobe Bridge (Chapter 22) to peruse your images, double-click the image's thumbnail or Control-click (right-click) it and then choose "Open in Camera Raw" from the resulting shortcut menu.

> **TIP**   New in Photoshop CC is the ability to open the Camera Raw plug-in as a *filter*. The box on page 367 has the full story on this handy feature.

Once the image is open in Camera Raw, open the HSL/Grayscale panel by clicking the button circled in *Figure 8-8*, and then turn on the panel's "Convert to Grayscale" checkbox. A set of color sliders appears that you can use to adjust contrast: Lighten a specific color by dragging its slider to the right, or darken it by dragging its slider to the left. When you're finished, click Done to close the Camera Raw window and apply your adjustments, or click Open Image to open the image in Photoshop (clicking Cancel closes the image *without* applying your adjustments).

You've now got yourself a lovely grayscale version of the image with loads of detail (though you may want to do a bit of sharpening; Chapter 11 explains how to do that *both* in Photoshop and in Camera Raw).

> **NOTE** To learn how to apply creative color effects in Camera Raw, check out your author's video workshop, *Photoshop Deep Dive: Adobe Camera Raw*, at *www.lesa.in/clvideos*.

Partial-Color Effect

One of most creative ways to accentuate part of an image is to leave that area colored and make everything else black and white. You can do that easily by using a Black & White, Channel Mixer, or Gradient Map Adjustment layer to convert the image to black and white (as discussed in the previous pages) and then use a layer mask to hide the conversion from the parts you want to keep in color. This technique is a *wonderful* way to add creativity to an image.

As luck would have it, *all* Adjustment layers come with a layer mask. It starts out empty (white) and automatically appears in the Layers panel to the right of the Adjustment layer's thumbnail (see *Figure 8-9*). So just pick whichever conversion method you like best to make the image black and white, and then follow these steps:

1. **In the Layers panel, click the Adjustment layer's mask thumbnail.**

   Photoshop puts a tiny white outline around the mask thumbnail (circled in *Figure 8-9*) as soon as you click it to let you know it's active.

> **TIP** If the thumbnails in your Layers panel are *really* small, you may not see the white outline around the mask thumbnail. Thankfully, you can make the thumbnails bigger by heading to the Layers panel's menu and choosing Panel Options. Pick the biggest thumbnail size and then click OK. *Now* you should be able to see the outline without squinting.

> **NOTE** Want to follow along? Visit this book's Missing CD page at *www.missingmanuals.com/cds* and download the file *Dragon.jpg*.

2. **Set your foreground color chip to black, press B to grab the Brush tool, and then hide part of the Adjustment layer by painting on your image.**

   Remember the layer mask rhyme, "Black conceals and white reveals?" When you're about to work with a mask, take a moment to think about what you want to do: To *hide* parts of the Adjustment layer, you need to paint with black, so press D to set your color chips to black and white, and then press X until black hops on top. Press B to grab the Brush tool, and then mouse over to your image and paint to let the image's original color show through the layer mask, as shown in *Figure 8-9*. If you reveal too much of the color, don't panic; just press X to swap color chips and then repaint that area to reveal the adjustment. (When you're working with masks, it's helpful to keep a finger poised over the X key.)

Panel menu

FIGURE 8-8

In the Camera Raw window, click the HSL/Grayscale button (circled) to see the "Convert to Grayscale" option.

Since the Camera Raw plug-in doesn't actually make changes to your original image—it saves a list of your requested edits instead, as page 361 explains—you can always change your mind. So if you decide an hour (or a year) from now that you don't want a black-and-white image, just double-click the file's icon to reopen it in Camera Raw, and then choose Camera Raw Defaults from the panel menu labeled here and presto! You'll be looking at your image exactly as it was shot. Nifty, eh?

FIGURE 8-9

All Adjustment layers come with a layer mask that lets you hide the adjustment from certain parts of the image. By painting with black to mask certain areas from a Black & White Adjustment layer, for example, you can hide the adjustment and bring back the original color (the brush cursor is circled here on the left). Just make sure you've got the mask activated before you start painting or you'll add a coat of black paint to your image.

TIP   To make sure you're painting only what you want to colorize, zoom into your image by pressing ⌘-+ (Ctrl-+). When you're zoomed in, you can toss the image from side to side with the Hand tool—very helpful if you need to view a different portion of the image. To grab the Hand tool, just press the space bar and drag, or click the hand icon near the bottom of the Tools panel. (For more tips on viewing images at close range, see page 50.) To zoom out again, press ⌘ (Ctrl) and the minus key [–].

3. **When you're finished painting the mask, save your document as a PSD file.**

    This makes Photoshop keep all the image's layers, so you can go back and edit the mask later if the mood strikes.

To see a quick before-and-after preview of your image, mouse over to the Layers panel and turn off the Adjustment layer's visibility eye. This technique is incredibly useful in *both* graphic design and photography (imagine a wedding photo where only the bridal *flowers* are in color—adorable!).

Fading Color to Black and White

You can use a technique similar to the one covered in the previous section to create a soft fade from full color to black and white (*Figure 8-10*). After you've made your image black and white using one of the *Adjustment layer* methods described earlier, follow these steps:

1. **In the Layers panel, activate the Adjustment layer's mask thumbnail (circled back in *Figure 8-9*, right).**

2. **Press G to fire up the Gradient tool and then, in the Options bar, choose a black-to-white linear gradient.**

    In the Options bar, open the Gradient Preset picker by clicking the down arrow next to the large gradient preview, and then click the gradient thumbnail circled in *Figure 8-10*, top left. (If you've got Photoshop's Show Tool Tips preference turned on [page 21], you can put your cursor over each gradient preview to see its name; the one you want is labeled "Black, White.") If your foreground and background color chips are set to black and white, respectively, you can also choose the "Foreground to Background" gradient, which is the first item in the preset menu. To the right of the Gradient Preset picker, make sure Linear Gradient is active (it should be unless you've changed gradient styles recently); you can point your cursor at each gradient-style button to see its name.

3. **Mouse over to your document and click where you want the color to start fading out, and then drag in any direction for an inch or two.**

    The beauty of using a mask for this technique is that if you're unhappy with your first gradient-dragging attempt, you can have another go at it...and another, and another until you get it right—Photoshop graciously keeps updating the mask. Try dragging from corner to corner or top to bottom and see what you get—depending on your image, one gradient angle may look better than another. For this particular image, a horizontal gradient works well.

4. **When you're finished, save your document as a PSD file and marvel at your handiwork.**

Gradient presets   Linear gradient

FIGURE 8-10

By adding a black-to-white linear gradient to a layer mask, you can create a beautiful faded-color effect. The farther you drag with the gradient cursor (it looks like crosshairs), the softer and wider the transition from color to black and white (Photoshop marks the transition width with a line like the one circled here).

As you can see, this technique can produce amazing results!

To follow along, download Facepaint.jpg from this book's Missing CD page at www.missingmanuals. com.

TIP   If you start editing a mask and then decide you want to clear it out and start over, just press ⌘-A (Ctrl+A) to select everything you've done so far and then press Delete (Backspace); Photoshop empties the mask so you can try again. Alternatively, you can activate the mask, choose Edit→Fill, and then pick White from the Use drop-down menu.

High-Contrast Black and White

The highest contrast black-and-white images are *just* black and white, with no shades of gray, like the one in *Figure 8-11* (right). It's a striking yet versatile effect that gives images an edgy look. In Photoshop, you can create this effect with a Threshold Adjustment layer, which lets you specify a brightness threshold where all the lighter-colored pixels become pure white while the darker pixels become pure black. Put more simply, Photoshop turns your shadows black and your highlights white.

> **NOTE** To practice the following technique, download the file *Girl.jpg* from this book's Missing CD page at *www.missingmanuals.com/cds*.

FIGURE 8-11

Left: Threshold Adjustment layers make shadows pure black and highlights pure white. If you use one on an image of a face that doesn't have many shadows around the cheeks, nose, or lips, you'll end up with a solid white face that's pretty creepy. The fix is to grab the Burn tool and do some darkening on a duplicate Image layer after you add the Threshold Adjustment layer (so you can see what you're doing).

Right: You can't get any contrastier than this, baby! As you can see, the effect is eye-catching and unique.

> **TIP** If you've ever wanted to create Andy Warhol–style pop art portraits (also called *serigraphs*), applying a Threshold Adjustment layer to your image is the first half of the technique. You'll learn the second half later in this chapter on page 343.

Before you get started, it's worth noting that this technique works better if your subject is on a solid white or other light-colored background; if it is, the background will disappear when you make the adjustment. If the background is dark, you may have to clean it up later with the Brush tool set to paint with white.

Here's how to use a Threshold Adjustment layer to make a pure black-and-white image:

1. **Pop open a photo and duplicate the Image or Background layer by pressing ⌘-J (Ctrl+J).**

   If your image consists of multiple layers, create a stamped copy (page 107). That way, if the image lacks shadows in areas of fine detail, you can do a little darkening with the Burn tool on that duplicate layer (or stamped copy); if not, you can skip this step. And if you like, you can turn off the original layer's visibility.

2. **Create a Threshold Adjustment layer.**

   Choose Layer→New Adjustment Layer→Threshold. You can also click either the Adjustments panel's Threshold icon (it looks like a rectangle with a couple of jagged black stripes across it), or the half-black/half-white circle at the bottom of the Layers panel and then choose Threshold. Either way, Photoshop displays a histogram (page 373) with a single slider in the Properties panel. Drag the slider to the right to increase the amount of shadows in your image (making it more black), or to the left to increase highlights (making it more white). Your goal is to achieve a nice level of detail in the image and make sure folks can still tell what it's a photo *of*.

TIP If you have trouble remembering what all the icons in the Adjustments panel are for, just put your cursor over each one to make Photoshop display its name at the top of the panel.

---

3. **If necessary, press O to grab the Burn tool, activate the duplicate Image layer (or stamped copy), and then touch up your image.**

   The lady in *Figure 8-11* has pale skin, so you need to darken her lips, nose, and cheeks with the Burn tool to make sure her features don't completely disappear. And since you've already added a Threshold Adjustment layer, your edits appear in pure black and white. If parts of the image become too dark, switch to the Dodge tool (shown in *Figure 8-11*) and lighten them. You're basically finished at this point, but with a couple more steps you can put your high-contrast face on a bright red background for a Che Guevara look shown in *Figure 8-12*.

4. **Create a Smart Object out of the face layer and the Adjustment layer.**

   Shift-click to activate both layers in the Layers panel. Next, open the Layers panel's menu, and then choose "Convert to Smart Object." Photoshop sandwiches both layers into a single Smart Object.

5. **Activate the new Smart Object and soften it slightly with a Gaussian Blur filter.**

   The high-contrast version of the image is really sharp (too many hard edges), but you can easily soften it up with a blur filter. In the Layers panel, activate the Smart Object and then choose Filter→Blur→Gaussian Blur (page 431 explains this filter). Enter a pixel value of 0.5 to 1.5 depending on the pixel dimensions of your image (use a lower number for smaller images and a higher number for bigger ones), and then click OK.

FIGURE 8-12

By adding a layer of solid color, you can create this popular look. Feel free to experiment with other background colors, too!

To change the color of the Fill layer later on, just double-click its thumbnail to summon the Color Picker.

6. **Create a new layer for the red background.**

   Click the half-black/half-white circle at the bottom of the Layers panel and then choose Solid Color. Photoshop opens the Color Picker, where you can pick a nice, bright red. Click OK to close the Color Picker, and Photoshop adds the new layer to the top of your layer stack. (If the new layer appears somewhere else in your Layers panel, just drag it to the top.)

7. **Change the red layer's blend mode to Darken.**

   With the red layer active, use the drop-down menu near the top of the Layers panel to change its blend mode to Darken. As you learned on page 279, blend modes in the darken category tell Photoshop to look at the colors on the active layer and the colors on the layers below and keep the darkest ones. In this case, those colors are black and red, so you end up with the black face on a red background. Pretty neat, huh?

8. **Save the document as a PSD file and rejoice at your creativity.**

The High-Key Effect

Another nifty black-and-white effect is known as *high key*. In the real world, you can create this effect by aiming *tons* of lights at your subject (or, in this case, victim) and shooting a picture. This gives you a high-contrast image—though not quite as high-contrast as the technique explained in the previous section—where the shadows are shades of gray and everything else is almost pure white. Fortunately, you can create this same look in Photoshop without spending a ton on light bulbs. Mosey back to page 193 for the scoop.

Delicious Duotones

There are a couple of reasons you may be interested in learning to create duotones: to save on professional printing costs and to create some *seriously* high-end looking black-and-white prints, like the ones in *Figure 8-13*. (Most black-and-white images displayed in galleries actually contain a bit of color!) To understand what's going on, you first need a quick primer on duotones—they're covered in more detail in Chapter 16—and a *brief* excursion back into some of the color mode nitty-gritty you learned in Chapter 5.

Click to save a preset

FIGURE 8-13

Top: At first glance, you might mistake this image for a black-and-white-only photo, but it's actually made from black, gray, and yellow.

Bottom: This technique is also great for making an image look like you've tinted it with color.

Duotone refers to an image that's made from two colors (black is usually one of them). Photoshop's Duotone mode lets you add special colors to genuine grayscale images. (See the box on page 314 to learn what qualifies as *true* grayscale.) If you add one color to a grayscale image, you get a duotone. If you add another color, you get a *tritone* (grayscale plus two colors), and if you add one more you get a *quadtone* (grayscale plus three colors). For the purposes of this discussion and as far as Photoshop is concerned, the term "duotone" includes tritones and quadtones, too (as confusing as that is).

As you learned in Chapter 5, printing presses generally use CMYK ink that prints on four separate plates, which correspond to the four channels in CMYK mode. A duotone or tritone has fewer channels than that, so it prints on fewer plates—grayscale plus one or two special inks (for duotone and tritone, respectively)—and *that* reduces your printing costs. So if your document is headed for a printing press, making a duotone is an affordable way to produce a striking, one-of-a-kind image. (See page 703 for the scoop on preparing duotones for print.)

Another reason to love duotones is that, because they're used so much in professional printing, Adobe has spent beaucoup bucks concocting color combinations that produce some of the most amazing images you've ever seen—and you can access them only in Duotone mode. In fact, most (if not all) award-winning black-and-white photos hanging in galleries aren't black and white at all—they're duo-, tri-, and quadtones with subtle color tints that give them extra depth and richness (see *Figure 8-13*).

Even if your image *isn't* headed for a professional printer, you'll want to get your paws on Photoshop's built-in color combos. You can get at them by popping into—and then back out of—Duotone mode. Here's how:

1. **Make a copy of your image by choosing Image→Duplicate; convert the duplicate to black and white using one of the methods described earlier in this chapter; and then save it as a PSD file.**

   Since you'll flatten your document in the next step, it's safer to work on a duplicate (so you don't *accidentally* save over your original document later). It doesn't matter which method you use; just don't let Photoshop do the conversion for you or you'll end up with a drab grayscale image like the one you saw back on page 308.

   NOTE To practice this technique at home, download the file *Car.jpg* from this book's Missing CD page at *www.missingmanuals.com/cds*.

   ---

2. **Change the image's mode to Grayscale and let Photoshop flatten the file.**

   Choose Image→Mode→Grayscale and, when Photoshop asks if you want to flatten or preserve your layers (if you've got more than one), take a deep breath and click Flatten. Then, when it asks if you want to discard the image's color information, steel yourself and click Discard.

3. **Trot back up to the menu bar and choose Image→Mode→Duotone.**

   You have to be in Duotone mode to pick one of those built-in color combos.

4. **At the top of the resulting Duotone Options dialog box, choose the color combination you want.**

Photoshop has *hundreds* of duo-, tri-, and quadtones in the Preset menu. You could spend a whole evening looking through all the options. When you choose one of these settings, Photoshop flips the dialog box's Type menu to the appropriate option.

If you'd rather have a go at mixing colors yourself, choose Duotone, Tritone, or Quadtone from the Type menu and then click the little color squares below the menu to pick your inks (remember, Duotone mode thinks you're going to send this file to a professional printing press that uses ink). If you want to save the combination you create, click the button to the right of the Preset menu (labeled in *Figure 8-13*, top) and give your combo a name to make Photoshop add it to the Preset menu. Click OK when you're finished to close the Duotone Options dialog box. (Page 703 has more on creating custom duotone combos and the printing concerns that go along with them.)

5. **Go back to the color mode from whence you came by choosing Image→Mode →RGB.**

Because Duotone mode is a special mode meant for printing (not editing), you don't want to hang around there. When you go back to RGB mode, you won't notice anything different—except the awesome new color of your image.

That's it! You've just snatched your first color combo from Duotone mode. It's like bank-robbing for Photoshop jockeys.

■ Changing Color

Photoshop is the ultimate recolorizing tool because it gives you the power to put a fresh coat of paint on *anything*. You can repaint your car, change the color of your cabinets, and even recolor your hair. You can also create cartoonish pop art or reverse the color in an image (see page 338). The next few pages describe how to do all that and more.

Hue/Saturation Adjustment Layers

If you're experimenting with color, start by creating a Hue/Saturation Adjustment layer, which offers a friendly set of sliders that let you change either the overall color of an image or a specific range of colors (see page 329). Because you're working with an Adjustment layer, any color changes take place on a separate layer, leaving the original unharmed. And since a layer mask automatically tags along with the Adjustment layer, you can use it to hide the color change from certain parts of the image.

If you select an object or specific area of the image *before* adding a Hue/Saturation Adjustment layer, you can change the color in just that one spot. Here's how:

1. **Open an image and create a selection using one of the techniques discussed in Chapter 4.**

   For example, if you want to change the color of a car, you could use the Quick Selection tool to select the car. Once it's surrounded by marching ants, you're ready for the next step.

   NOTE To practice the following technique, download the file *Corvette.jpg* from this book's Missing CD page at *www.missingmanuals.com/cds*.

2. **Create a Hue/Saturation Adjustment layer.**

   To do so, choose Layer→New Adjustment Layer→Hue/Saturation. You can also open the Adjustments panel and click the Hue/Saturation icon (which looks like three vertical stripes above a gradient), or click the half-black/half-white circle at the bottom of the Layers panel and then choose Hue/Saturation. No matter which method you use, Photoshop opens the Properties panel containing the three sliders shown in *Figure 8-14*, bottom. (In the Layers panel, notice how Photoshop filled in the Adjustment layer's mask based on the area you selected. If you don't make a selection before creating the Adjustment layer, the mask stays empty—meaning the color change affects the whole image.)

3. **To change the color of the selected area, drag the Hue slider left or right.**

   Hue is really a graphic geek's way of saying "color" (though technically it refers to pure color, before it has been tinted with white or shaded with black). As you drag the slider, the selected area's color changes. If you watch closely, you'll see one of the rainbow-colored bars near the bottom of the Adjustments panel change, too. The top rainbow bar shows the color in your original image, and the bottom one shows what you're changing that color *to*. (In *Figure 8-14*, you can see the turquoise of the original Corvette at the far left of the top bar and the purple it's been changed to at the far right of the bar below it.) It's helpful to think of these rainbow-colored bars as flattened-out color wheels; flip ahead to page 483 to see a real live color wheel.

   NOTE This color-changing trick works only on colored areas; anything that's black, white, or gray remains completely unchanged.

4. **To adjust the color's intensity, drag the Saturation slider.**

   To decrease the intensity, drag this slider to the left (if you drag it *all* the way to the left, you'll completely desaturate the image, making it grayscale). To increase the intensity, drag it to the right (if you drag it too far, the image's colors will become so vivid you'll need sunglasses, and skin tones will become an otherworldly hot pink). To get an idea of what this adjustment does, look closely at the color slider beneath the word "Saturation" in *Figure 8-14*, bottom, which ranges from gray on the left to a vivid red on the right.

FIGURE 8-14

Top: If you select an object (like the car body shown here) before you add a Hue/Saturation Adjustment layer, Photoshop automatically fills the mask (circled) with your selection, limiting the color change to that area.

Bottom: To change the colors of the selected area, grab the triangle-shaped Hue slider and drag it in either direction. If you point your cursor at the word "Hue" (without clicking), it turns into a scrubby cursor (circled) that you can drag left or right. The scrubby cursor does the same thing as the triangular sliders, but it's a bit easier to control.

Layer mask

Original color

New color

5. **To adjust the color's brightness, drag the Lightness slider.**

Lightness is what civilians call "brightness"; think of it as the amount of light shining on the selected object. Drag this slider left to darken the color or right to lighten it.

6. **Save the image as a PSD file.**

Doing so lets you go back and edit your color changes any time by double-clicking the Hue/Saturation Adjustment layer's thumbnail in the Layers panel. This is extremely handy if you're recoloring an object for a nitpicky client (even if that client is you!).

There are a few other settings lurking in the Properties panel for Hue/Saturation Adjustment layers that are worth mentioning:

- **Targeted Adjustment tool**. This tool lets you pick a range of colors to adjust and then change the saturation of those colors by clicking directly on the image instead of using the sliders. In the upper left of the Properties panel, give the tool a click—it looks like a pointing hand with a double-headed arrow—and then mouse over to your image (your cursor turns into an eyedropper). Click the color that you want to change, and Photoshop activates the appropriate color channel in the Properties panel's Edit menu (described later in this list). Then drag left to decrease the saturation (make the color less intense) or right to increase the saturation (make the color more vivid).

- **Preset menu**. This menu lets you choose from a few canned settings. Once you start tweaking the sliders, this menu changes to the Custom setting, as shown in *Figure 8-14*, bottom.

- **Edit menu**. This menu, which doesn't have a label, lets you pick the color channels you want to adjust. When you first use Photoshop, this menu is set to Master, which means you're changing the composite channel and affecting all the colors in your image. If you want to target a specific channel, pick it from this menu, and then any changes you make affect *only* the colors in that channel. For example, say you've got an image with too much red in it (a common problem in photos of people). You can choose the red channel from this menu and then drag the Saturation slider to the left to desaturate the reds without affecting the image's other colors (a great way to zap color casts that you can't get rid of any other way!). If you don't know which channel to pick, use the Targeted Adjustment tool described earlier in this list to click a color in your image and make Photoshop pick the channel *for* you. Once you've selected the color, you can drag the sliders like you normally would.

- **Eyedroppers**. The eyedroppers near the bottom of the panel also let you pick the colors in your image that you want to change. You'll see these guys in action in the next section.

- **Colorize checkbox**. This setting lets you use the Hue slider to add color to an image that doesn't have any, like a black-and-white photo. If you're working with an image that *does* have color, turning on this checkbox will add a color tint to the image's shadows and highlights, much like the kind you can make with a Gradient Map Adjustment layer or with Duotone mode.

■ TARGETING A SPECIFIC RANGE OF COLORS

When you add a Hue/Saturation Adjustment layer, Photoshop assumes you want to change *all* the colors in your image, which is why the Properties panel's Edit menu is set to Master. But if you want Photoshop to change just the reds, yellows, greens, or whatever, then choose the appropriate option from that menu first. To narrow your focus even *more*, you can use the Targeted Adjustment tool along with the eyedroppers near the bottom of the Properties panel to adjust very specific *ranges* of color.

Let's say you're thinking about repainting your scooter. If the scooter's current paint job isn't super dark, you can take a photo of it and then do your experimenting in Photoshop rather than at the body shop (if it's really dark, you can *try* lightening it first). Just follow these steps:

1. **Open the image and leave the Background layer locked.**

   If you're experimenting on an image that you've worked with before, this layer may be named something besides Background. If the image is comprised of many layers, activate 'em all and then, in the Layers panel's menu, choose "Convert to Smart Object," or create a stamped copy (page 107).

   NOTE   Download the file *Scooter.jpg* from this book's Missing CD page at *www.missingmanuals.com/cds* if you'd like to follow along.

2. **Add a Hue/Saturation Adjustment layer as described in step 2 of the previous section.**

3. **Use the Targeted Adjustment tool to choose the range of colors you want to change.**

   In the upper left of the Properties panel, click the Targeted Adjustment tool (the hand with the two arrows poking out of it), mouse over to your image, and then click the color you want to change (the red scooter, for example). Photoshop then picks the predominant color channel in the panel's Edit menu (in *Figure 8-15*, top, this menu is set to Reds).

   TIP   If you duplicate the Adjustment layer by pressing ⌘-J (Ctrl+J), you can experiment with all kinds of scooter colors before you head to the body shop!

4. **Edit the range of colors you want to adjust using the eyedroppers near the bottom of the Properties panel.**

   Once you click a color in the previous step, Photoshop marks that color range with a small gray bar that appears between the two rainbow-colored bars at the bottom of the Properties panel (circled in *Figure 8-15*, top). To edit that range, use the + and – eyedroppers near the bottom of the panel to add or subtract colors from the targeted range. For example, to expand the range to catch all the scooter's colors, grab the eyedropper with a + sign, mouse over to your image, and then click another part of the scooter (you'll see the gray bar get a little wider). To narrow the range of colors, use the eyedropper with a – sign to subtract the colors you don't want to change.

As usual, Photoshop gives you several ways to do the same thing. You can also edit the color range by dragging the tiny sliders on the gray bar, which, you may have noticed—if your eyesight is really good!—is two different shades of gray. The light gray part in the middle of the bar represents the hues that will change completely when you make a change (to see those hues, just look at the rainbow-colored bars directly above and below the gray one), and the darker gray parts on either end of the gray bar represent hues that will *partially* change. To narrow the range of colors, drag the little half triangles on the ends inward toward the middle of the gray bar; to widen the range, drag them outward.

> **TIP** If the gray bar representing your targeted color range (technically called the *range indicator*) gets split across the left and right ends of the rainbow bars, press ⌘ (Ctrl on a PC) and drag the pieces to the left or right until it becomes solid again.

5. **Recolor the scooter by tweaking the Hue, Saturation, and Lightness sliders as discussed in the previous section.**

   Photoshop reflects your changes in real time, so you can watch as the scooter changes from green to blue to magenta. Good times!

6. **If necessary, use the Adjustment layer's mask to hide the color change from other parts of your image.**

   When you start moving the Properties panel's sliders, you may notice that the scooter isn't the *only* thing that changes color. If any part of the image is similar in color to the area you're changing, it may change, too; you can try using the + and – eyedroppers to exclude these areas (as described in step 4), but they may not work if the colors are too similar. In that case, use the Adjustment layer's mask to keep the rest of the image from getting a makeover. Just activate the mask thumbnail in the Layers panel, press B to grab the Brush tool, and set your foreground color chip to black (press X if you need to flip-flop color chips). Then mouse over to your image and paint the parts that you *don't* want to change. If you hide too much, flip-flop your color chips by pressing X and paint that area white.

> **NOTE** To go back and edit the Hue/Saturation Adjustment layer later—assuming you've saved the image as a PSD file—you have to remember to change the Properties panel's Edit menu first. While Photoshop remembers all the changes you made with the sliders, it can't remember which color channel you used, so it resets this menu to Master each time you double-click the Hue/Saturation Adjustment layer's thumbnail in the Layers panel. Bummer!

FIGURE 8-15

Top: Instead of changing all the colors in an image, you can use the Targeted Adjustment and eyedropper tools to target a certain color range instead. When you click the Targeted Adjustment tool (circled, top), the Edit menu near the top of the Properties panel changes to reflect the predominant color channel for the part of the image you clicked (in this case, Red), and the color range is indicated by the small gray bar near the bottom of the panel (circled, bottom).

Bottom: If other parts of the image start changing color as you adjust the panel's sliders—such as this girl's face and skin—just grab the eyedropper with a minus sign (circled) and click those areas to make Photoshop leave 'em alone, as shown here. (You can also start over any time by clicking the Reset button labeled here.)

Or, instead of moving the panel's sliders, you can use the Targeted Adjustment tool. Once you've activated the tool, click the color in your image that you want to change, keep holding down your mouse button, and then drag left to make that color less intense (desaturate), or drag right to make it more intense (saturate). To change the hue, ⌘-drag (Ctrl-drag on a PC) left or right to move the Hue slider left or right, respectively.

Reset adjustment

You can also use this technique to experiment with hair color before heading to the salon. However, if your subject's skin color is similar to her hair color, you're better off selecting her hair *before* adding the Hue/Saturation Adjustment layer. Happily, the Refine Edge dialog box makes it easy to select those wily wisps of hair. Page 165 has the scoop.

Hue Blend Mode

Another easy way to repaint an object is to put the paint on a separate layer and then change the paint layer's blend mode to Hue. (As you learned in Chapter 7, blend modes control how color on one layer interacts with color on another; page 288 explains how the Hue blend mode works.)

To give this method a spin, open an image and then create a new layer by pressing Shift-⌘-N (Shift+Ctrl+N). In the resulting New Layer dialog box, type *paint* into the Name field, change the Mode drop-down menu to Hue (it's near the bottom of the list), and then click OK. Next, press B to grab the Brush tool, click your foreground color chip, and then pick a color from the resulting Color Picker and click OK. Then, with the new layer active, start painting over the object as shown in *Figure 8-16*.

NOTE To try this technique yourself, download the file *Superbike.jpg* from this book's Missing CD page at *www.missingmanuals.com/cds*.

FIGURE 8-16

The goal here is to repaint this red motorcycle blue. If the area you want to repaint has a lot of black, white, and gray around it (like this bike), you can paint right over those areas and they won't change a bit (note the brush cursor circled here). That's because, in Hue blend mode, the new paint affects only areas that previously contained color.

If you end up changing too much color, temporarily switch to the Eraser tool by pressing and holding the E key (the tool's keyboard shortcut). Or you can prevent the problem by adding a layer mask to the paint layer and then hiding the areas you want to leave unchanged by painting them black.

Replacing Color

Remember the Color Range command you learned about in Chapter 4 (page 151)? You can use a similar command—Replace Color—to select one color and swap in another. This command works *really* well if the color you want to replace is fairly consistent and concentrated in one area, like the car in *Figure 8-17*. It's also a little

easier to choose a paint color from the friendly Color Picker than to mix the color
yourself using a bunch of sliders.

NOTE Download *Vintage.jpg* from this book's Missing CD page to follow along with this technique.

Start by duplicating your Image layer or, if the image is comprised of multiple layers, creating a stamped copy (page 107) by activating 'em and then pressing Shift-
Option-⌘-E (Shift+Alt+Ctrl+E). Next, choose Image→Adjustments→Replace Color
to summon the Replace Color dialog box shown in *Figure 8-17*. The Eyedropper tool
is already active, so just click in your image to tell Photoshop what color you want to
change (you may need to move the dialog box to get a good view of your image),
and that color appears in the Color square in the upper right of the dialog box. In
the lower half of the dialog box, click the color square above the word "Result" to
choose a new color from the Color Picker. When you click OK, the new color appears
in the square. To make further adjustments to the color, you can use the dialog box's
Hue, Saturation, and Lightness sliders.

FIGURE 8-17

*You can use the eyedrop-
per tools to add to or
subtract from the range of
colors you want to change
(and it's helpful to zoom
into your image while
doing so by pressing ⌘-+
[Ctrl-+] repeatedly).*

*Since the Replace Color
command isn't available as
an Adjustment layer, it affects your original image,
so it's a darn good idea
to duplicate the Image
layer (or create a stamped
copy) before you use this
command. (Alas, Replace
Color doesn't won't work
on Smart Objects—darn!)*

Selective Color Adjustment Layers

Selective Color Adjustment layers are gloriously useful because they let you make a
single color in an image brighter or darker—helpful when you need to make whites
whiter or blacks blacker. You can also use them to shift one color to another, but that
technique can be a bit challenging if you don't know anything about color theory
(that is, mixing certain colors together to create *other* colors).

To add a Selective Color Adjustment layer to your document, choose Layer→New Adjustment Layer→Selective Color. You can also click the Selective Color icon in the Adjustments panel (it looks like a square divided into four triangles), or click the half-black/half-white circle at the bottom of the Layers panel, and then choose Selective Color.

Then, from the Colors menu at the top of the Properties panel, choose the color *closest* to the one you want to change. For example, to change the color of the bike and the matching leathers shown in *Figure 8-18*, choose Reds. Next, use the Cyan, Magenta, Yellow, and Black color sliders to change that color to something else. (Don't let it throw you that these sliders represent the CMYK color mode—they work just fine on RGB images.)

FIGURE 8-18

With a well-placed Selective Color Adjustment layer, you can change the red bike and matching leathers to hot pink in seconds. Just point to one of the sliders in the Properties panel until your pointer turns into a handy scrubby cursor like the one shown here (top), and then drag left or right.

To try this technique yourself, download Superbike.jpg from this book's Missing CD page at www.missingmanuals.com/cds.

The direction you drag each slider determines exactly how the color you've chosen in the Colors menu changes. By dragging a slider to the left, you decrease the percentage of that color. For example, if you choose Reds from the menu and then drag the yellow slider all the way to the left, you drain all the yellow out of the reds, making them look hot pink (as shown in *Figure 8-18*). If you drag a slider to the right, you increase the percentage of that color. (How can you know what color you'll end up with after some quality slider-dragging? Through experimentation or by learning to read a color wheel. Flip to page 482 for a short lesson that'll get you started.)

Matching Colors

The Match Color command makes the colors in one image resemble those in another. It's a *huge* timesaver when you're working with several images in a magazine spread or a book and need to make their colors somewhat consistent (see *Figure 8-19*). Since this command isn't available as an Adjustment layer, be sure to *duplicate* your Image layer first by pressing ⌘-J (Ctrl+J on a PC). (If your image consists of multiple layers, create a stamped copy instead [page 107]; this command won't work with Smart Objects.)

To get started, open two images in RGB mode: the one whose color you're trying to match (the *source*) and the one whose color you want to change (the *target*). Click within the target document to activate it and then choose Image→Adjustments→Match Color. In the resulting dialog box (*Figure 8-19*), Photoshop automatically picks the current document as the target (which is why you activated it first). Next, tell Photoshop the name of the source document by choosing it from the Source menu in the lower half of the dialog box (you'll see a thumbnail preview of the image at the bottom right).

FIGURE 8-19

The Match Color dialog box lets you copy the colors from one image (like the golds in the tiny image on the bottom left here) onto another. The result? The golden-hued bike shown at bottom right. You can use the Luminance (lightness) and Color Intensity (saturation) sliders to make the colors match a little better, and adjust the Fade slider to use more or less of the source document's original color. If your target image has a bit of a color cast, turn on the Neutralize checkbox to make Photoshop try to get rid of it for you.

If the source document has several layers, you can choose the one you want from the dialog box's Layer menu or choose Merged to have Photoshop combine those layers into one (handy if you've used several Adjustment layers to create the color you want). If the source document has only one layer, Photoshop chooses it automatically.

To confine your color-matching to specific spots in the source and target images, create selections in each document before you open the Match Color dialog box. If the dialog box detects an active selection, it lets you turn on the "Use Selection in Source to Calculate Colors" and "Use Selection in Target to Calculate Adjustment" checkboxes, both of which can be helpful when you're trying to match colors in two different images—skin tones, for example.

TIP If you've got a source color that you might want to use on other images, save your Match Color settings as a preset: When you get everything just right, click the Save Statistics button at the bottom of the dialog box and then give your preset a name. The next time you want to use those settings, you won't have to open the source image—just open the Match Color dialog box, click the Load Statistics button, and then choose your preset.

Photo Filter Adjustment Layers

Photo Filter Adjustment layers let you *gently* adjust the colors in an image, as if you'd attached a subtly colored filter to your camera's lens. For example, you can quickly warm an image with golden tones like those in the "after" photo in *Figure 8-20* (right). The effect is fairly subtle, making the image look like it's been *lightly* tinted with a color rather than having its color changed completely.

To get started, click the Photo Filter icon in the Adjustments panel (it looks like a camera with a circle on it). Then, in the Filter menu that appears in the Properties panel, choose from a list of 20 presets that range from warming and cooling filters to shades of red, violet, and so on. To choose your own color instead, turn on the Color option and click the color swatch to its right; choose a color from the resulting Color Picker and then click OK. You can use the Properties panel's Density slider to soften or strengthen the effect (just pretend the slider is called "intensity" if "Density" confuses you), and keep the Preserve Luminosity checkbox turned on to prevent Photoshop from lightening or darkening the image.

You can also use a Photo Filter Adjustment layer to reduce a color cast. For example, if your image has a strong blue cast, you can introduce a little orange with a Photo Filter adjustment to neutralize it (orange is opposite blue on the color wheel). If your image has a yellow cast, use purple to even it out. Skip to Chapter 12 to learn more about color wheels.

FIGURE 8-20

A Photo Filter Adjustment layer is really handy when you've combined images whose color doesn't quite match or when you want to add a very subtle (barely there) color tint to an image.

Though it's a little tough to see in this figure, a warming tone was added to this scooter-ridin' canine.

POWER USERS' CLINIC

Using Color Lookup Adjustment Layers

Yet *another* way to alter the color in an image is to use a Color Lookup Adjustment layer, which was introduced in CS6 but went relatively unnoticed. These layers take their name from color Lookup Tables—LUTs, in geek circles—which are used in the film industry to either apply the overall color and lighting of one film clip to another, or to apply a predetermined creative look to footage. These tables specify how the colors in an image are *remapped* to completely new ones.

To use a Color Lookup Adjustment layer, click the half-black/half-white circle at the bottom of the Layers panel and choose Color Lookup. Photoshop then opens the Properties panel, containing various presets in two categories: Abstract and Device Link menu. (If you're on a Mac, you've got six more LUTs in the Abstract category than Windows folks, simply because of how the Mac operating system handles graphics.) Simply pick a preset to see how it affects your image.

Alas, there's no way to create LUTs yourself in Photoshop; however, you *can* create 'em in video programs like Adobe SpeedGrade. If you do, you can then add 'em to Photoshop by saving them in the following locations:

- On a Mac, Abstract and Device Link profiles are stored in *Library/Application Support/Adobe/Color Profiles*. On a PC, they're in *C:Program Files\Common Files\Adobe\Color Profiles*.

- On a Mac, LUTs are stored in *Applications/Photoshop CC/Presets/3DLUTs*. On a PC, they're in *C:Program Files\Adobe\Adobe Photoshop\Presets\3LUTs*.

These presets are incredibly handy for producing creative color effects (and Photoshop CC includes a few new ones). When you've got some free time, grab your favorite beverage, pop open an image, and take 'em for a spin!

Posterizing: Your Ticket to Cartoon Art

You'll use this adjustment once in a blue moon, but if you need to make an image look like a cartoon, a Posterize Adjustment layer is just the thing. Choose Layer→New Adjustment Layer→Posterize or, in the Adjustments panel, click the Posterize icon (the one with diagonal stripes). (You can also click the half-black/half-white circle at the bottom of the Layers panel and choose Posterize.) When you do, Photoshop analyzes the image's colors and throws out the majority of 'em, leaving you with big ol' blocks of solid color. On some images, posterizing has interesting results, as the examples in *Figure 8-21* show. On other images...well, not so much.

FIGURE 8-21

Posterizing doesn't work well on portraits (unless you use a Blur filter to smooth the edges), but on images with relatively solid colors, like this one, the results are pretty neat, as you can see on the right.

Inverting Colors

Graphic designers, this one's for you! If you need to reverse the colors in an image—turning orange to blue, yellow to purple, and so on—you can add an Invert Adjustment layer.

> **TIP** To find out the reverse (or opposite) of a color, use a color wheel like the one on page 483.

If you're a photographer, you'll use this adjustment even *less* often than Posterize because it turns most images into a negative (which might be useful on Halloween). That said, if you've got an image of a black silhouette that you want to make white, this Adjustment layer can do that in one click (see *Figure 8-22*). To add an Invert Adjustment layer, choose Layer→New Adjustment Layer→Invert, or open the Adjustments panel and click the half-black/half-white icon with the half-black/half white circle in it. You can also click the half-black/half-white circle at the bottom of the Layers panel and then choose Invert.

FIGURE 8-22

An Invert Adjustment layer turns black into white, blue into orange, and so on. For graphic designers, this is an incredibly useful trick. The images on the left here are the originals.

Just for fun, try running various Smart Filters on your image— pick any one of 'em—and then add an Invert Adjustment layer to see what it does. You can use the included layer mask to hide the adjustment from certain areas of the image to create some pretty wacky—and sometimes wonderfully weird—results!

Adding Color

There will be times when you want to add color that wasn't originally part of an image, and Photoshop gives you lots of ways to do that. The techniques in this section will serve you well whether you're colorizing a black-and-white image or adding color to an empty canvas by hand. Read on!

> **NOTE** In pre-CS6 versions of Photoshop, you could use a Variations adjustment to add color that wasn't originally in an image. These days, that adjustment works only in 32-bit mode in Windows. To find out how to use it, visit this book's Missing CD page at *www.missingmanuals.com/cds*.

Colorizing Images

Due to the expense of color film, full-color images didn't become commonplace until the late '60s. So chances are good that you've got some vintage black-and-white photos lying around, just dying to be scanned. Happily, you can use Photoshop to give them a little color (which, by the way, can be a nice side business if you get really good at it). Colorizing a black-and-white (or true grayscale) photo *seems* straightforward—just grab a brush and paint the image. Unfortunately, while that method adds color, it also covers up all the photo's *details*, as shown in *Figure 8-23*, left.

FIGURE 8-23

Unless you change the paint layer's blend mode, the paint covers up all the details of this girl's cute dress (left). But once you set the blend mode to Color (right), the details come shining through.

> **TIP** Before you colorize a black-and-white image, choose Image→Mode and make sure the document is set to RGB Color mode. If it's in Grayscale mode, Photoshop won't let you add any color no matter *how* hard you try.

Fortunately, you can use blend modes to add color while keeping an image's details intact. Here's how:

1. **Add a new layer for the paint and change its blend mode to Color.**

   Since you don't want to mess up your original image by painting directly on it, you need to add a new layer. Press Shift-⌘-N (Shift+Ctrl+N) and in the resulting New Layer dialog box, name the layer *pink paint* and then set the Mode menu to Color. As explained in the box on page 342, this mode not only keeps the brightness of the gray tones in your photo, it also adds the hue and saturation values from the pink paint you're about to add, letting the details of the image show through. Make sure the paint layer is positioned above the photo layer in your layer stack.

> **NOTE** To follow along, visit this book's Missing CD page at *www.missingmanuals.com/cds* and download the file *Dress.jpg*.

2. **Grab the Brush tool and set it to whatever color you want to paint the dress (like pink!).**

   Press B to activate the Brush tool. Then, in the Tools panel, click the foreground color chip, choose a nice pastel color from the Color Picker, and then click OK.

3. **Paint the part of the image that you want to colorize.**

It's a good idea to zoom into the image when you're doing this kind of detailed work. You can use the Zoom tool, press ⌘-+ (Ctrl-+ on a PC) repeatedly, or use any of the other zooming techniques described on page 50.

4. **Use the Eraser tool set to Brush mode to fix any mistakes.**

Press E to switch to the Eraser tool and, in the Options bar, set the Mode menu to Brush and then pick a soft-edge brush from Brush preset picker. Then, to fix your mistake, mouse over to your document and paint across the areas that don't need painting. (Alternatively, you can add a layer mask to the paint layer and then use a brush set to paint with black to hide your mistakes.)

5. **When everything looks good, save the document as a PSD file.**

Saving the document in PSD format lets you go back and change the paint later. For example, after you print the colorized photo, you might decide to change the little girl's dress to yellow instead of pink. If you've saved the document with all its layers intact (as a PSD file lets you do), you can load the paint layer as a selection by ⌘-clicking (Ctrl-clicking on a PC) the layer's thumbnail and then use a Hue/Saturation Adjustment layer to change the color (page 325). That's a *heck* of a lot quicker than repainting the dress! But don't tell anyone—let 'em think it took you hours and hours.

Just think how much fun you can have using this technique with a graphics tablet and the Rotate View tool (page 55)! Another option is to select the area you want to paint and then add a Solid Color Fill layer. Which method should you use? It's one of those "six of one, half a dozen in the other" kind of things—just pick the technique you like best.

▪ ADDING DIGITAL MAKEUP TO PORTRAITS

Happily, you can use the colorization technique you just learned to add *digital* makeup to portraits. Follow the steps in the previous section but instead of picking the Color blend mode in step 1, choose Overlay instead. Then, in steps 2 and 3, paint makeup onto your subject. To help the new makeup blend in with surrounding pixels, you can blur the layer by choosing Filter→Blur→Gaussian Blur. You'll need to experiment with the filter's Radius setting; 10 pixels was used on the 1698×1131 pixel image shown in *Figure 8-24*. Photographers love this kind of thing!

TIP In some cases, you might want to run the blur filter *twice* so the new makeup blends in better with the rest of the image. To rerun the last filter you ran, press ⌘-F (Ctrl+F). And after blurring the digital lipstick, you'll likely need to add a layer mask to hide areas of paint that now extend beyond your subject's lips.

FIGURE 8-24

It's easy to add digital makeup in Photoshop, though it's important that your subject has some makeup on before *you take the picture—even if it's a subtle neutral color, as shown on the left—so you've got realistic texture to work with.*

Be sure to add each piece of makeup on a separate layer so you can soften it using a blur filter (page 648), lower its opacity if it's too strong (35% was used here), and fine-tune its color using a Hue/Saturation Adjustment layer that's attached to the layer below it (shown here—see step 5 in the previous section for details).

Adjustment Layer Blend Modes

When you're adding or shifting colors with Adjustment layers, you can experiment with changing their blend modes, too. For example:

- The **Hue** blend mode alters the image's color but doesn't change its brightness (how dark or light it is) or saturation (how intense the colors are). This mode is useful when you want to change an object's color, as described on page 332.

- The **Color** blend mode changes the image's color and saturation but leaves its brightness alone—handy when you're adding color.

- The **Luminosity** blend mode changes the image's brightness but not its color—helpful when you need to lighten or darken an image.

If you want to change the blend mode *before* you add the Adjustment layer—so you can actually see what the adjustment looks like as you're making it—Option-click (Alt-click on a PC) the half-black/half-white circle at the bottom of the Layers panel. Photoshop then opens the New Layer dialog box so you can name *and* change the blend mode of the Adjustment layer you're about to add. To learn more about blend modes, check out page 276.

Adding Solid Blocks of Color

Remember the high-contrast face from earlier in this chapter (page 320)? With just a little modification and a few well-placed blocks of color, you can turn that face into an Andy Warhol–style portrait like the one in *Figure 8-25*.

FIGURE 8-25

You can create all kinds of interesting art by adding your own color to images (this technique produces a serigraph).

If you downloaded Girl.jpg *(the practice image file for the high-contrast face tutorial back on page 320), you can use that edited image for the maneuver described in this section.*

Flip back to page 320 and follow steps 1–4 to add a Threshold Adjustment layer to create a high-contrast face. Then, once you've got yourself a Smart Object, follow these steps:

1. **Select all the black areas in the Smart Object you created.**

   Grab the Quick Selection tool (or the Magic Wand), click a black area, and then choose Select→Similar to make Photoshop grab *all* the black bits in the Smart Object (you could select 'em yourself, but it'd take days).

2. **Add a Solid Color Fill layer (page 208) and choose black from the Color Picker.**

   By creating a selection first and *then* adding the Fill layer, Photoshop hides the color from the unselected bits of the image automatically. Next, double-click the layer's name in the Layers panel and rename it *face*. (Since you're about to add a bazillion layers, it's helpful to give each one a descriptive name.) Then turn the original photo layer's visibility off because you don't need it anymore. Now you're ready to start adding more color!

3. **Grab the Polygonal Lasso tool and draw a selection around the woman's face and shoulders (see *Figure 8-26*, top left).**

   Since the Polygonal Lasso tool uses straight lines, it's perfect for creating blocks of color. Just click once where you want the selection to start and then click again each time you need to change angles. Don't worry about being precise; the point is to make it blocky. When you're finished, close your selection by putting your cursor over the starting point. When you see a tiny circle next to the cursor (it looks like a degree symbol), click once to complete your selection.

4. **Add another Solid Color Fill layer named *skin*, pick a nice peachy color for the woman's skin, and then position this layer *below* the face layer.**

   Sure, you could add a new layer and then manually fill it with color, but using Fill layers makes changing colors later on a breeze.

5. **Create a selection around the woman's lips, add a Solid Color Fill layer named *lips*, choose hot pink from the Color Picker, and then change the layer's blend mode to Darken.**

   Use the Polygonal Lasso to create your selection, as in step 3, but this time select the area around her lips. Remember, you want to make the colored areas blocky, so don't be afraid to make your selection go *outside* of her lips. Next, Option-click (Alt-click on a PC) the half-black/half-white icon at the bottom of the Layers panel and choose Solid Color. In the resulting New Layer dialog box, enter *lips* in the Name field and change the Mode menu to Darken (this lets the black face layer show through the new colors you're adding).

6. **Keep repeating step 5 to give her some eye shadow and to add color to the iris of each eye.**

   When you're all done, your Layers panel should look something like the one in *Figure 8-26*, bottom.

7. **Add a Solid Color Fill layer, pick a bright color from the resulting Color Picker, and then make this layer your new background.**

   Drag this layer *below* the skin layer so it becomes the background of the whole piece of art you're building. There's no need to change the blend mode of this layer.

Congratulations—you've just finished your first Warhol-style portrait! The really fun thing about this technique is how creative it lets you be (not to mention that you're using almost every skill you've learned in the preceding chapters). Sure, you *could* seek out Warhol's pop-style art online and use the same colors he did, but what fun is that? By using your own vision, you're creating something unique. Also, try experimenting with images of people who have light-colored hair. If the model for this portrait were blonde, you could color her hair, too. The possibilities are endless!

Building a Better Sunrise (or Sunset)

Believe it or not, you can use a Gradient Map Adjustment layer to turn a mediocre sunrise photo into something spectacular. Rather than adding one color to your image like the Tint option in a Black & White Adjustment layer or Photo Filter Adjustment layer, a Gradient Map Adjustment layer lets you add as many colors as you want. Here's how to use one to add a punch of color to a big ol' boring sky:

FIGURE 8-26

To make five more versions of this portrait, activate the layers that make up this version and stuff them into a group by choosing "New Group from Layers" from the Layers panel's menu. This helps you keep track of each version and it makes creating additional versions easier: Simply duplicate the layer group instead of each individual layer. And because you wisely used Solid Color Fill layers, changing those colors is as simple as double-clicking a layer thumbnail to reopen the Color Picker. Because your duplicated layers are all sitting on top of one another, you can toggle the visibility of each group off or on while you're changing colors. Once you've created several versions of the portrait, you can enlarge your canvas and then use the Move tool to position the layer groups next to one another to create the artwork shown back in Figure 8-25.

1. **Add a Gradient Map Adjustment layer and change its blend mode to Color.**

   Option-click (Alt-click on a PC) the half-black/half-white circle at the bottom of the Layers panel and choose Gradient Map. In the resulting dialog box, name the layer *sun* and set the Mode menu to Color. (That way, the gradient you're about to add will affect only the image's color values and not its lightness values; page 288 has more on this blend mode.) Click OK and Photoshop adds the new layer and opens the Properties panel. Don't worry about what color the gradient is—you'll pick colors in the next step.

2. **In the Properties panel, click to open the gradient preset menu.**

Click the downward-pointing triangle next to the gradient preview to open the preset menu (labeled in *Figure 8-27*). In the menu that appears, you can choose a preset gradient (best for newcomers) or make one of your own by performing the next couple of steps (which requires a bit of patience and practice).

You can load even *more* ready-made gradients by clicking the tiny gear icon at the top right of the preset menu (also labeled in *Figure 8-27*). In fact, there's a nice orange-to-yellow gradient lurking in the Color Harmonies 2 set that works quite well for this technique. If you go that route, when Photoshop asks if you'd like to replace your current gradients with the new set, click Append. That way, Photoshop adds the new gradients below the factory set. Locate the aforementioned yellow-to-red gradient and click it.

You're basically done at this point, but if you want to build your own gradient, keep on truckin' through the next two steps.

Preset menu   Click to load more presets

FIGURE 8-27

As you can see, a Gradient Map Adjustment layer set to Color mode took this sky from boring to beautiful by adding a gradual blend of colors. To reverse the gradient's colors—say, to turn a sunset into a sunrise—turn on the Reverse checkbox in the Properties panel (not shown).

If you want to keep any part of your image from being affected, click to activate the Adjustment layer's mask thumbnail, grab the Brush tool, and then paint those areas with black.

3. **In the Adjustments panel, click the gradient preview to open the Gradient Editor and then tweak the gradient's color stops to create a yellow-to-orange-to-red gradient.**

In the middle of the Gradient Editor dialog box are little colored squares called *color stops* (*Figure 8-28*) that you can drag around to control the width of the color fade. When you click a stop, its color appears in the Color field (also called a *color well*) at the bottom of the dialog box. To change the stop's color, click the color well to make Photoshop open the Color Picker so you can choose another color. If you click *between* existing color stops, you'll add a new stop. Once you click a color stop, tiny diamonds appear beneath the gradient that you can drag left and right to determine where one color stops and another one starts.

Color stops   Click to change stop color

FIGURE 8-28

The Gradient Editor lets you choose from tons of existing gradients (click the tiny gear icon circled here to load another gradient set), or create your own by editing any of the presets and adding color stops.

If you create the perfect sunset gradient, save it by clicking the Gradient Editor's Save button and then giving it a name. Photoshop adds it to the preset previews, giving you easy access to it in the future.

4. **Save the document as a PSD file in case you want to edit it again later.**

You're all finished! Nothing like a beautiful sunset, is there?

Adding Color to a Semi-Transparent Layer

If the item you want to colorize lives on its own layer *and* it has some transparent (empty) areas, you can skip creating a selection or painting the darn thing, and simply use a Fill layer that's *clipped* to that layer instead. This causes Photoshop to shove the contents of the Fill layer *through* whatever's on the layer below it.

This handy maneuver makes colorizing a vector embellishment, brushstroke, or even *text* an absolute piece of cake (see page 626 for a similar technique involving shoving a photo through text). *Figure 8-29* explains how to get it done, and gives you practical examples for photographers *and* designers.

FIGURE 8-29

The trick lies in placing the Fill layer above *the layer containing the art you want to colorize. Then all you have to do is press the Option key (Alt on a PC) while you point your cursor at the dividing line* between *those two layers in the Layers panel; when your cursor turns into a square with a down-pointing arrow (shown here), click to clip the Fill layer to the layer underneath it.*

For photographers, adding a colored vector embellishment to a photo (like the swirly stars in the top image here) can produce another sellable product. For designers, things like the colored shamrocks in the bottom image here add visual interest and depth to ads.

Correcting Color and Lighting

When you think about all the variables that come into play when you're capturing images, it's a wonder *any* photos turn out halfway decent. You're dependent on Mother Nature or the quality of artificial lighting, and, even then, it's easy to over- or underexpose an image. You need a good camera that can snap the shot before you miss it, a high-quality lens, and so on. Even if the stars are aligned and you get all that right, the camera itself may introduce a *color cast*, making your image look like it has overdosed on one particular color.

All these variables mean you need to spend some time correcting both the color and the lighting of your images. Not to worry: You've got an arsenal of tools at your disposal in Photoshop and its trusty sidekick, Camera Raw. In this chapter, you'll learn how to use all the automatic fixer-uppers (and there's a slew of 'em) like Auto Tone, Auto Color, the Shadows/Highlights adjustment, and so on. After that, you'll explore the glorious realm of Camera Raw for the easiest adjustments in the West. Then, you'll dive headfirst into professional-strength adjustments such as Levels, Curves, and merging High Dynamic Range images. And, finally, you'll learn some tricks for saving images you can't fix any other way.

> **NOTE** Photoshop lets you apply most adjustments in two different ways. One way is to run the adjustment on the currently active layer, in which case Photoshop permanently applies the change to your image (eek!). Another way is to use Adjustment layers, wherein the change happens on a *separate* layer, thereby preserving your original image and giving you the ability to tweak the adjustment later by popping open its Properties panel. The benefit of the latter method is huge, so that's the one this book uses most of the time.

This chapter also uses real-world imagery—specifically, travel photos taken by your humble author—that really needs fixing, rather than near-perfect studio shots (though the same editing techniques apply to both).

Before getting started, it's worth knowing about the three categories of brightness values that make up your images:

- **Shadows** are created when light is blocked (you knew that). Rarely jet black, shadows can be different colors depending on how much light is blocked.

- **Highlights** represent the lightest or brightest parts of an image, where the light is at full strength. When an image is overexposed, the highlights are described as "blown out."

- **Midtones** are tonal values that fall between the darkest shadows and lightest highlights. By enhancing midtones, you can increase the contrast and the details in an image.

All the color and lighting fixer-uppers covered in this chapter use this terminology.

> **TIP** A handy way to get rid of distractions so you can focus on fixing an image is to go to the bottom of the Tools panel, click the Screen Mode icon, and then choose Full Screen Mode With Menu Bar. You can also press the F key repeatedly to cycle through the screen modes.

■ Quick Fixer-Uppers

Before you dive into the murky waters of manual adjustments using Levels and Curves, it's worth trying to make Photoshop do some of this stuff automatically. As luck would have it, the program has lots of auto fixer-uppers, which were improved quite a bit back in CS6.

For example, Adobe changed the mathematical voodoo that Photoshop uses when you apply the Auto Color adjustment, *and* when you click the Auto button in a Levels, Curves, or Brightness & Contrast adjustment (all discussed in this chapter). Instead of the old Enhance Per Channel Contrast method (wherein the red, green, and blue channels were adjusted individually so that the highlights got a little lighter and the shadows got a little darker—whether they needed it or not), Photoshop now uses the new "Enhance Brightness and Contrast" method instead, which makes the program analyze your image and then adjust the brightness and contrast accordingly. Bottom line: You no longer have to change the way these automatic tools work in order to get good results. Hip hip hooray!

> **NOTE** While you may get satisfactory results using combinations of the following adjustments, they're nothing compared to what you can do if you master Levels and Curves (both covered later in this chapter). In other words, use the methods in this section only while you're learning or as quick-and-dirty fixes.

Fixing Color

If your image looks flat (like it has no contrast) or has a noticeable color cast, give the following methods a spin:

- **Auto Color**. If your image has a color cast (everything looks a little yellow, say), this command can help (see *Figure 9-1*). When you run it, Photoshop hunts down the image's shadows, highlights, and midtones and changes their color values. To use t, duplicate your Image layer by pressing ⌘-J (Ctrl+J) and then choose Image→Auto Color or press Shift-⌘-B (Shift+Ctrl+B). This command works only on images that are in RGB mode, so if the menu item is grayed out, choose Image→Mode→RGB Color first.

FIGURE 9-1

The Auto Color adjustment can help tone down oversaturated images— where all the colors look a little too intense—and fix nasty color casts (notice the extra yellow in the original snapshot on the left here).

This fix isn't available as an Adjustment layer, so be sure to duplicate your Image layer before using it.

(Morning after Krampus Day, Vienna.)

TIP Prior to CS6, you could use the Variations adjustment (Image→Adjustments→Variations) to add color to black-and-white images, as well as to fix color. These days, the Variations adjustment works only on 32-bit mode in Windows. You can see it in action by hopping online and visiting *www.missingmanuals.com/cds*.

- **Color Balance**. This adjustment changes the overall mixture of colors in an image or selection by shifting the highlights, midtones, and shadows to opposite sides of the color wheel (see page 482 for a quick lesson on color theory). It's also handy for adding color to a black-and-white image or fcr fixing a problem area, like a dull sky (see *Figure 9-2*).

The only drawback to Color Balance is that you have to know *which* color you want to shift the image *toward* (which is why color theory comes in handy). That said, when you apply this adjustment, Photoshop displays the Properties panel, which contains sliders you can drag, making Color Balance easy to play with. Because it's available as an Adjustment layer, it's nondestructive, and you can use the layer mask that tags along with it tc limit its effect to certain parts of an image.

Photoshop gives you lots of ways to summon the Color Balance adjustment:

— Choose Layer→New Adjustment Layer→Color Balance.

— In the Adjustments panel, click the Color Balance icon (it looks like a scale).

— Click the half-black/half-white circle at the bottom of the Layers panel and then choose Color Balance.

> **NOTE** To preserve an image's brightness values when you apply a Color Balance adjustment, be sure to leave its Properties panel's Preserve Luminosity checkbox turned on.

FIGURE 9-2

Left: A Color Balance Adjustment layer can zap a color cast and fix a dull sky fast. Choosing each of the three color categories in the Properties panel's Tone drop-down menu—Shadows, Midtones, and Highlights—in turn and dragging the bottom slider toward Blue for all three categories brings back some of the color and detail in this overcast sky.

Right: By using a layer mask, the adjustment is restricted to the sky and doesn't affect the rest of the image (see page 108 for more on layer masks).

(Holiday market in Nuremberg, Germany.)

- **Photo Filter**. To change an image's mood, you can add a Photo Filter Adjustment layer to warm it up with a golden tint or cool it off with a bluish tint, for example. Or, if the image has a color cast, you can neutralize it by adding the opposite color (again, a little color theory comes in handy). To use this adjustment, choose Layer→New Adjustment Layer→Photo Filter, or click its icon in the Adjustments panel (it looks like a tiny camera with a circle in front of it). See page 336 for more about this adjustment.

Fixing Lighting

Unless you're carting around a light kit with your camera, you're totally dependent on ambient light, which is less than perfect on a good day. Nevertheless, Photoshop has several tools that can help fix almost any lighting problem:

- **Auto Tone**. If your image needs a *little* lighting boost, this adjustment can get it done. It brightens your image, adding a bit of contrast. To apply it, duplicate your Image layer by pressing ⌘-J (Ctrl+J), and then press Shift-⌘-L (Shift+Ctrl+L).

  Better yet, run Auto Tone as an Adjustment layer. Click the Levels or Curves icon in the Adjustments panel—or click the half-black/half-white circle at the bottom of the Layers panel and choose Levels or Curves—and then, in the Properties panel, Option-click (Alt-click) the Auto button. In the resulting dialog box, choose the Enhance Per Channel Contrast algorithm and then click OK.

A Word on Workflow

Every adjustment you make can reduce the quality of your image a little, so the order in which you work is important. Because some techniques are more destructive than others (like sharpening), it's wise to save them for last. Here's a quick cheat sheet to follow:

1. Import pictures using Adobe Bridge (see Chapter 22) or another program.

2. Have Bridge save copies of the images to an external hard drive and then burn the originals to a high-quality DVD for off-site safekeeping.

3. View your photos, rate the best ones, and mark the bad ones as rejected (see—you guessed it—Chapter 22).

4. Crop, resize, and (if necessary) straighten your images. (There's no point in fixing pixels you're not going to keep!) See Chapter 6 for the scoop.

5. Fix whatever you can in Camera Raw (white balance, exposure, contrast, and so on). As you'll discover later in this chapter, corrections are a *breeze* in Camera Raw (you can use it to fix TIFFs and JPEGs, too).

6. Fix the remaining problems in Photoshop (like reducing wrinkles, enhancing eyes, correcting colors, and so on) using Adjustment layers, duplicate layers, and layer masks as described in this chapter.

7. Apply special effects like fancy edges, head swapping, filters, and so on.

8. Sharpen the image using the techniques you'll learn in Chapter 11.

9. Print the image (Chapter 16) or save it for the Web (Chapter 17).

If you make your edits in this order, you'll end up with the sharpest, highest-quality images possible.

NOTE   Here's a quick Auto Tone history lesson for you: In CS5 and earlier versions, the Auto button in a Levels or Curves Adjustment layer automatically used the Enhance Per Channel Contrast algorithm. But starting in CS6, the Auto button began using Enhance Brightness & Contrast by default instead. Riveting, huh?

- **Auto Contrast**. This adjustment is an automatic version of the Brightness/Contrast adjustment discussed below. It increases the contrast in an image by lightening and darkening pixels. It doesn't adjust channels individually, so if the image has a color cast, it'll still have one after you make this adjustment. And if the image is flat to begin with, it'll still be flat afterward. But if the image has a decent amount of contrast, this adjustment can boost it a little. To run Auto Contrast, duplicate the Image layer as described above and then press Shift-Option-⌘-L (Shift+Alt+Ctrl+L).

  To run Auto Contrast as an Adjustment layer, click the Adjustments panel's Levels button or click the half-black/half-white circle at the bottom of the Layers panel and choose Levels. In the Properties panel that opens, Option-click (Alt-click) the Auto button, choose the Enhance Monochromatic Contrast algorithm in the resulting dialog box, and then click OK.

- **Shadows/Highlights**. If your image's color looks good but you need to lighten its shadows or darken its highlights, this tool can do an *amazing* job in no time flat. It's discussed in detail on page 357.

- **Equalize**. This adjustment evens out the image's brightness by turning its lightest pixels white and the darkest pixels black. It's handy when some areas of a photo are decently lit but it lacks overall contrast (see *Figure 9-3*). Equalize isn't available as an Adjustment layer, so you'll definitely want to duplicate your original layer by pressing ⌘-J (Ctrl+J on a PC) before you run it by choosing Image→Adjustments→Equalize.

- **Dodge and Burn tools**. These tools are useful when you need to lighten or darken detailed areas of an image by hand, and they're no longer as harmful to images (and especially skin tones) as they were in early version of Photoshop. For example, you can use the Burn tool to selectively darken your subject's eyes and the Dodge tool to lighten deep wrinkles. But unless you duplicate the original layer first, there's no way to use these tools nondestructively. Luckily, there's a trick that makes the Brush tool *behave* like the Dodge and Burn tools. Flip over to page 432 for step-by-step instructions.

■ BRIGHTNESS/CONTRAST ADJUSTMENT LAYERS

These Adjustment layers do exactly what you'd think: They brighten an image or increase its contrast—or both. In days of old, these adjustments didn't work worth a darn because they changed your whole image the same amount, which usually resulted in nice-looking shadows but blown-out highlights. Thankfully, Brightness/Contrast got a much-needed overhaul in CS3, so now it's a useful tool, especially on lighter images and black-and-whites. (Just be sure to leave the Properties panel's Use Legacy checkbox turned off, or it'll behave like it used to!)

FIGURE 9-3

*Be careful with the
Equalize adjustment, as it
can make an image look
washed out by lightening
it too much (top). If that
happens, lessen the
adjustment's effect by
changing the duplicate
layer's blend mode to
Luminosity (so it affects
only the image's lightness
values, not its color values)
and then lowering its
opacity, as shown here
(bottom).*

(Prague from Castle Hill.)

To add one of these layers, either click the Brightness/Contrast icon in the Adjustments panel (it looks like a sun) or click the half-black/half-white circle at the bottom of the Layers panel and then choose Brightness/Contrast. In the resulting Properties panel, click the Auto button (circled in *Figure 9-4*, left) to make Photoshop analyze the image and adjust the sliders for you. If you'd rather do things manually, drag the Brightness slider left to darken the image or right to brighten it. To increase the image's contrast, drag the Contrast slider to the right; to decrease it, drag the slider to the left and watch as the image becomes flatter than a pancake (tonally speaking!).

TIP   Adjustment layers affect each and every layer beneath 'em. To restrict the adjustment to only the layer directly below the Adjustment layer, click the leftmost button at the bottom of the Properties panel (it looks like a tiny square with a downward-pointing arrow next to it).

FIGURE 9-4

Brightness/Contrast Adjustment layers do a much better job of fixing the lighting in your image than they used to. But since the brightening affects mainly the highlights (mostly leaving the shadows alone), you need to be careful that they don't get too light. You can also hide the adjustment from the lighter parts of an image by using the included mask (shown here at right). But for a quick lighting fix, this adjustment does a fantastic job. You can also use it in conjunction with other Adjustment layers to fine-tune images.

(Strahov Monastery library in Prague.)

Fixing Colored Edge Fringe

If you see a slight blue or purple fringe loitering around the edges of near-black objects in your images, you've got a dreaded *color fringe problem*. This kind of thing is especially noticeable when the object is on a white background. For example, if you take a picture of a white clock face, you may see a purplish or bluish tinge around the edges of the clock's numbers and hands. Fortunately, you can use the Gaussian Blur filter to get rid of the tinge, though there's a trick to it. Flip to page 649 for the step-by-step scoop, and see the Tip on page 650 to learn how to fix edge fringe in Camera Raw.

■ SHADOWS/HIGHLIGHTS ADJUSTMENTS

The most useful of all the quick-fix adjustments is Shadows/Highlights. If your camera's flash didn't fire and your subject is way too dark, for example, this command can bring the photo back to life by analyzing each pixel and then adjusting it according to the lightness values of neighboring pixels. This is a big deal because even the much-lauded Levels and Curves features adjust lightness values *equally* among all pixels, whether they need it or not.

You can apply this adjustment by choosing Image→Adjustments→Shadows/Highlights, but because it's destructive, be sure to duplicate your Image layer first (or better yet, convert it into a Smart Object as described in the steps below). At first you see just two sliders in the dialog box that appears: Shadows and Highlights. Because Photoshop assumes you want to lighten the shadows—and you usually do—it automatically sets the Shadows slider to 35 percent, and leaves the Highlights slider set to 0 percent. To get the most out of this adjustment, turn on the Show More Options checkbox at the bottom of the dialog box; the following steps explain all the settings that appear.

Here's how to lighten overly dark shadows in an image using a Shadows/Highlights adjustment:

1. **Activate your Image layer and then choose Filter→"Convert for Smart Filters."**

   Since the Shadows/Highlights adjustment is destructive (meaning it's not available as an Adjustment layer), it'll affect your original image. To use it non-destructively, you can either duplicate the layer first by pressing ⌘-J (Ctrl+J) or convert it into a Smart Object. The latter method forces Photoshop to list the adjustment separately in the Layers panel as if you had run a Smart Filter (see page 632). Both methods let you hide parts of the image with a mask, though by using a Smart Object, Photoshop adds the mask *for* you. (Click OK when Photoshop lets you know that to enable smart filters, it will convert your layer into a Smart Object.)

2. **Choose Image→Adjustments→Shadows/Highlights.**

   In the Shadows/Highlights dialog box that appears, turn on the Show More Options checkbox (circled in *Figure 9-5*) to see *all* the settings.

3. **In the Shadows/Highlights dialog box's Shadows section, adjust the three sliders.**

   These settings work well for most images:

   - **Set the Amount slider to between 20 and 35 percent.** If you go any higher, you'll start to see noise (graininess) in the image.

   - **Leave the Tonal Width slider set to 50 percent.** This slider controls exactly which shadows get adjusted. If you lower this number, Photoshop changes only the darkest shadows; if you raise it, Photoshop changes a wider range of shadows. The factory setting of 50 percent usually works fine, but you may want to lower it if your image looks grainy.

- **Increase the Shadows section's Radius slider to between 250 and 300 pixels.** The Shadows/Highlights adjustment works by looking at the brightness values of neighboring pixels, and this setting determines how big that neighborhood is. Pump this baby up to make Photoshop analyze more pixels.

FIGURE 9-5

Turning on Show More Options (circled) gives you a slew of sliders. If your image's shadows are OK but its highlights need darkening, apply the settings shown here in the Shadows section of the dialog box (Amount: 25, Tonal Width: 50, Radius: 275) in the Highlights section instead. Just be sure to set the Shadows section's Amount slider to 0 percent to turn that section off if you don't need to use it.

When you're finished, click the Save As Defaults button so you don't have to remember these magic numbers the next time you use this adjustment (though you'll still have to tweak them slightly for each image).

Another way to use this adjustment is to set all the sliders to 0 and then begin dragging them rightward, one at a time and in small increments, until the image looks good.

If the image needs more contrast, you can add a Brightness/Contrast Adjustment layer, as discussed in the previous section.

4. **In the Adjustments section at the southern end of the dialog box, adjust the various settings.**

   Here are some guidelines:

   - **Set the Color Correction field to 0.** Doing so keeps Photoshop from shifting the image's colors and introducing funky pinks into skin tones.

- **Leave the Midtone Contrast setting at 0.** When you use this setting, Photoshop increases the contrast in the image by making dark pixels a little darker and light pixels a little lighter. Since the point of a Shadows/ Highlights adjustment is usually to lighten shadows, increasing this setting would pretty much cancel out what you're trying to accomplish.

- **Leave the Black Clip and White Clip fields set to 0.01 percent.** Leaving these fields alone keeps your light and dark pixels from getting clipped. (*Clipping* is when Photoshop turns a light pixel pure white or a dark pixel pure black, stripping the pixel of all its details. As you might imagine, clipping is more worrisome in highlights than shadows, since highlights usually contain more important details.)

5. **Click the Save As Defaults button.**

   Photoshop saves the current settings so you don't have to reset everything the next time you use this adjustment. You'll still have to tweak the settings some because each image is different, but at least you won't have to *memorize* the magic numbers mentioned above.

6. **Click OK to close the Shadows/Highlights dialog box.**

   In the Layers panel, you'll see a new layer called Smart Filters with the Shadows/ Highlights adjustment beneath it (*Figure 9-6*), indicating that Photoshop ran the adjustment as a Smart Filter instead of applying it directly to the image.

7. **If necessary, hide the adjustment from a portion of the image by painting within the mask that came with the Smart Filter.**

   Click the Smart Filter mask's thumbnail to activate it (Photoshop puts a tiny white border around it so you can tell it's active). Next, press B to grab the Brush tool, press D to set your color chips to black and white, and then press X until black hops on top. Then mouse over to your image and paint the areas you don't want adjusted. Pretty cool, huh? You can think of this technique as Smart Shadows.

8. **For a quick before-and-after comparison, turn the Shadows/Highlights adjustment's visibility eye off and on.**

As *Figure 9-6* shows, this adjustment-run-as-a-Smart-Filter does a bang-up job of lightening shadows without introducing a funky color cast. If, for whatever reason, you don't like the adjustment, you can send it packin' by dragging the Shadows/ Highlights adjustment down to the trash can icon at the bottom of the Layers panel.

To get even *better* results, run the Shadows/Highlights adjustment on the Lightness channel in Lab mode. It sounds hard, but it's not—just follow these steps:

1. **Duplicate your original layer by pressing ⌘-J (Ctrl+J).**

   For reasons known only to the Lords of Adobe, you can't run the Shadows/ Highlights adjustment on just one channel if you've converted your Image layer to a Smart Object, which means you can't run the adjustment as a Smart Filter as described in the previous list. So to keep this adjustment from running in Super Destructo mode, you've got to duplicate the layer first. Bummer!

FIGURE 9-6

Here's an image before (left) and after (right) applying the Shadows/Highlights adjustment.

By painting with black within the mask that comes from running Shadows/Highlights as a Smart Filter, you can protect certain parts of your image from the effect (like the turret in the background here). And remember, you can also use the mask's Density setting to make the mask somewhat see-through (say, if you want to hide a little of the adjustment but not all of it). To do that, double-click the mask; its settings open in the Properties panel. Drag the Density slider leftward to make the mask partially transparent.

(Fisherman's Bastion, Budapest.)

Click to activate mask

Double-click name to reopen
Shadow/Highlight dialog box

2. **Switch to Lab mode temporarily by choosing Image→Mode→Lab Color.**

    It doesn't matter whether you were originally in RGB or CMYK mode (as you know from Chapter 2, you'll *usually* be in RGB mode). When Photoshop asks if you want to flatten layers, click Don't Flatten. If there are any Smart Objects in your document, it'll also ask if you want to rasterize them; in that case, click Don't Rasterize.

3. **Activate the Lightness channel.**

    Open the Channels panel by clicking its tab in the Layers panel group or by choosing Window→Channels, and then click once to activate the Lightness channel. As you learned back in Chapter 5, one of the great things about Lab mode is that it separates an image's light info from its color info. Since you want to lighten the image's shadows without shifting its color, you'll run the

Shadows/Highlights adjustment only on the Lightness channel, which makes the adjustment work *noticeably* better.

4. **Choose Image→Adjustments→Shadows/Highlights.**

   In the Shadows/Highlights dialog box, turn on the Show More Options checkbox and enter the following settings: Shadows Amount 20 percent, Shadows Tonal Width 50 percent, and Shadows Radius 275 pixels. Click OK when you're finished.

5. **Switch back to your original color mode.**

   Choose Image→Mode→RGB (or CMYK) to go back to the mode you started in.

6. **To see before and after versions of the image, turn the duplicate layer's visibility off and on.**

Sure, this method takes a little longer than the previous technique, but the results are well worth it. And if you need to adjust an image's highlights instead of its shadows, you can use the same magic numbers in the Highlights section of the Shadows/Highlights dialog box—just be sure to set the Shadows section's Amount slider to 0.

■ Correcting Images in Camera Raw

As you learned in Chapter 2, Camera Raw 8 is a powerful plug-in that converts images shot in raw format into editable pixels. It also gives you tools that you can use to crop, straighten, and correct the color and lighting of your images (it works on JPEGs and TIFFs, too). Since most of Camera Raw's settings are slider-based, it's hands down the easiest place to fix your images (and that's why this section comes before the ones about Levels and Curves, which are—truth be told—100 times more confusing).

Fixing Lighting with Blend Modes

If your image is *still* too dark or too light after you run a Shadows/Highlights adjustment on it, you can fix it with blend modes. The technique is described in step-by-step glory back on page 113, but it's so important that it deserves a mention here, too.

To *darken* an image, create an empty Adjustment layer by clicking the half-black/half-white circle at the bottom of the Layers panel and choosing Brightness/Contrast (it's the first one in the list that doesn't actually *do* anything to your image). Then use the drop-down menu near the top of the Layers panel to change the new layer's blend mode to Multiply (or press Shift-Option-M [Shift+Alt+M on a PC]). Finally, in the layer mask

that automatically tags along with the Adjustment layer, paint with a black brush to hide the darkened bits from areas that don't need darkening.

To *lighten* an image, add an empty Adjustment layer and change its blend mode to Screen instead (or press Shift-Option-S [Shift+Alt+S]). Then use the provided layer mask to hide the *light* bits, if necessary.

If the image needs to be darker or lighter still, duplicate the empty Adjustment layer. To reduce the effect of the darkening or lightening layer, lower its opacity using the setting at the top of the Layers panel.

NOTE In Photoshop CC, you can open the Camera Raw plug-in as a *filter* from within Photoshop. The box on page 367 has the scoop.

The adjustments you make in the Camera Raw plug-in are also nondestructive: Instead of applying them to your image, Camera Raw keeps track of them in a list it stores within the image or in a file called *Sidecar XMP* (could that name be more cryptic?). Simply put, you can undo anything you've done in Camera Raw whenever you want. Really.

The Camera Raw plug-in is covered in several places throughout this book; here's a handy cheat sheet:

- Information about the raw file format (page 48)
- Opening files in Camera Raw (page 48)
- Cropping and straightening in Camera Raw (page 229)
- Going grayscale in Camera Raw (page 315)
- Editing multiple files in Camera Raw (see the box on page 403)
- Removing dust spots in Camera Raw (see the box on page 412)
- Fixing red eye with Camera Raw (page 440)
- Sharpening in Camera Raw (page 475)

In this section, you'll learn how to use Camera Raw's various sliders to fix both color and lighting, plus you'll pick up some tricks that can make images' color leap off the page. When you're finished adjusting your image, you can use the buttons at the bottom of the Camera Raw window to do the following:

- Click **Save Images** to convert, rename, or relocate the file(s)—or any combination of those options—so you don't overwrite the original(s).

- Click **Open Images** to apply the changes you've made and then open the image in Photoshop, or Shift-click this button to open the image as a Smart Object in Photoshop.

- Click **Cancel** to bail out of Camera Raw without saving or applying changes.

- Click **Done** to apply the changes (which you can edit the next time you open the image in Camera Raw) and exit Camera Raw.

If you use Camera Raw's adjustments in the order they're presented in this section (which is also the order they appear in the Camera Raw window—how handy!), you'll be *amazed* at the results.

TIP You can zoom in/out of the Camera Raw preview window just like you can in Photoshop; just press ⌘-+/– (Ctrl-+/– on a PC). To move around within your image, press the space bar while dragging with your mouse. And to see a before/after preview of your image, press the P key to toggle the Preview option at the top right of the window off and on.

Changing White Balance

When you set an image's white balance, you're telling Camera Raw what color the light in the image *should be*. As you might suspect, changing the light's color changes *all* the colors in the image, as shown in *Figure 9-7*. Because each light source gives off its own unique color cast—whether it's a light bulb (tungsten), fluorescent light, cloudy sky, or whatever—digital cameras let you adjust the white balance accordingly (though you may have to dig out your owner's manual to find where that setting lives; if you're shooting on auto, your camera is setting the white balance for you).

> **TIP** Camera Raw lets you adjust the white balance *selectively* in certain parts of an image by using the Adjustment Brush. Skip ahead to page 368 to learn how.

One of the big advantages of shooting in raw format is that if you get the white balance wrong in your camera, you can always reset it using Camera Raw. For example, if you're shooting in an office using a white balance of Fluorescent and then walk outside and shoot in the courtyard, the color will be off in the outdoor images. But if you shot the photos in raw format, fixing their color later is a snap.

As shot   Auto   Daylight

Cloudy   Shade   Tungsten

Fluorescent   Flash   Custom

FIGURE 9-7

Here's an image with each of Camera Raw's White Balance presets applied to it. As you can see, changing the white balance makes a big difference! Cycling through the list of presets is a great way to experiment with color because it's so darned easy and it opens your eyes to more color possibilities. After all, this color-correction mumbo jumbo is purely subjective; the color that's closest to the original may not always look great or suit your taste. It's all about what looks best to you!

In Camera Raw, you change white balance by choosing one of the presets in the Basic tab's White Balance drop-down menu. Or you can set it manually (and maybe more accurately) using Camera Raw's White Balance tool (see *Figure 9-8*). Press I to grab the tool (which looks like an eyedropper) and then mouse over to your image and click an area that *should be* white or light gray. Just keep clickin' till the image looks right, and then adjust the Temperature and Tint sliders until you get the color you want (doing so changes the White Balance menu to Custom).

NOTE Compared with raw images, you don't have as much flexibility when resetting the white balance of JPEGs or TIFFs because those file formats have already been processed a bit by the camera or scanner that captured them—the only presets Camera Raw gives you are As Shot and Auto. Nevertheless, you can still tweak the color of light by adjusting the Temperature and Tint sliders.

FIGURE 9-8

When you're using the White Balance tool, be careful not to click a white reflection. For more accurate color, click an area that's really supposed to be white (or light gray), like this orchid's center.

TIP If you can't seem to get the color quite right, tweak the Temperature slider shown in *Figure 9-8*; dragging it right warms the image, and dragging it left cools it off. The Tint slider adjusts the balance of green and magenta.

Fixing Exposure

The next group of sliders in Camera Raw's Basic tab lets you adjust an image's exposure and *contrast* (the difference between light and dark pixels). Adobe upgraded these controls back in Camera Raw 7 and simplified the Basic panel to give you a more powerful—yet simpler—way to produce images with nice contrast. These six sliders (Exposure, Contrast, Highlights, Shadows, Whites, and Blacks) are all set to a consistent starting point of 0 and have a range of –100 to +100 (save for Exposure). By adjusting these sliders in the order they're listed in the Basic panel, you should be able to produce better-looking images faster than ever before.

NOTE Want to follow along? Visit this book's Missing CD page at *www.missingmanuals.com/cds* and download the practice file *Orchid.zip*.

As you learned on page 350, images consist of three categories of color: highlights, midtones, and shadows. Problems can arise in one of those categories or all three; luckily, you can fix 'em all in Camera Raw using the following sliders:

- **Exposure**. Exposure is determined by how much light your camera's sensor captures; it's measured in *f-stops* (the number indicating how much light your camera's lens lets in), and has a range of –5 to +5. You can think of this slider as controlling overall image brightness; drag it right to lighten your image or left to darken it. Be careful not to drag this slider *too* far either way or you'll start to lose details. For that reason, it's a good idea to turn on Camera Raw's clipping warnings (shown in *Figure 9-9*) so you can see if you're destroying details: Press U (as in Underexposed) to turn on the shadow clipping warning and O (for Overexposed) to turn on the highlight clipping warning. That said, it's OK to lose a *few* details because you can bring 'em back with the very next slider.

FIGURE 9-9

When you turn on the highlight clipping warning by clicking its triangular icon (top right), areas that are losing details—like the yellow part of this orchid—turn bright red. (You can tell a clipping warning is turned on because Camera Raw puts a light gray box around its icon; here, both warnings are on.) The farther you drag the Exposure slider to the right, the more red areas you see. Don't let this worry you too much because the Whites slider can bring back most (if not all) of the lost details.

Both clipping warning icons are black if no pixels are being clipped. But if either triangle turns a color, some clipping has occurred (the exact color of the triangles depends upon which channel the clipping is occurring in).

TIP If you're not up to fiddling with these six sliders, you can make Camera Raw adjust the image *for* you by clicking the word "Auto" above the Exposure slider. That said, you'll get far better results if you tweak these settings by hand.

- **Contrast**. Drag this slider right to increase the image's contrast (the difference between its light and dark pixels) or left to decrease it. Increasing contrast makes the light pixels lighter and the dark pixels darker.

- **Highlights/Shadows**. These two sliders control *tone mapping*, which is the way Camera Raw shifts (remaps) the image's colors from what was captured by your camera to what can be displayed onscreen or printed. Drag the Highlights slider left to darken an image's highlights, or right to lighten them. The Shadows slider works the same way: Drag it left to darken shadows, or right to lighten them. To produce natural-looking images, don't drag either slider past 50 in either direction. To even out the lighting in your image, try setting the Highlights to −25 and the Shadows to +25.

- **Whites/Blacks**. These two sliders let you recover lost details in overexposed highlights and underexposed shadows, and get rid of clipping warnings. If you drag the White slider *slightly* to the left, you can make the red clipping warnings in your image disappear and get some details back in those areas (dragging it to the right overexposes highlights). The Black slider works just the opposite: To lighten your image's shadows and clear any blue clipping warnings, drag this slider *slightly* to the right (dragging it to the left darkens shadows, making details in shadowy areas disappear into a big ol' black hole). Both sliders are meant for fine-tuning images, so keep your adjustments to the bare minimum.

FREQUENTLY ASKED QUESTION

Raw vs. JPEG

What's the big deal about shooting in raw format? My raw files look worse than my JPEGs! What gives?

It's true that if you compare the same image captured in both raw and JPEG format, the JPEG will look vastly better. That's because of the processing that your camera automatically performs when you shoot JPEGs. That's right: Your camera applies a little noise reduction and sharpening, and boosts color intensity before your image ever becomes a twinkle in Photoshop's eye. (To learn how to turn this stuff off, you'll have to dig through your camera's owner's manual.) But when you shoot in raw format, you get the *raw*, completely unprocessed and uncompressed info instead, which is why raw files are so much bigger and more flexible.

Think of it this way: Raw files are like raw cookie ingredients. Before you mix and roll cookie dough into balls and bake it, you've got all kinds of flexibility; you can change the ingredients, add nuts or chocolate chips, and form the cookies into fun shapes. A JPEG, on the other hand, is like a *baked* cookie; there's very little you can do to it because it's already cooked. Sure you can add a topping or two, but it's much less flexible than the raw (pun intended!) ingredients.

The point is that if you *can* shoot in raw (and you can afford the extra processing time), you *should*.

TIP To *temporarily* see clipped areas (without turning on the clipping warnings), Option-drag (Alt-drag on a PC) the Whites or Blacks sliders. The image preview turns *black* when you Option-drag the Whites slider, and *white* when you Option-drag the Blacks slider. Either way, clipped areas appear in bright colors as you drag.

Making Colors Pop

To intensify your image's colors, give the next three sliders in Camera Raw's Basic tab a tug (see *Figure 9-10*):

- **Clarity.** This slider boosts contrast in the midtones, increasing their depth so your image looks clearer. You'd be hard-pressed to find an image that wouldn't benefit from dragging this slider to about +50.

TIP If you're not a fan of the results you get using Camera Raw's toning controls—the Highlights/Shadows and Whites/Blacks sliders—you can switch back to the way they *used* to work in older versions (prior to Camera Raw 7.0) by changing the *process version* (the set of instructions Camera Raw uses to adjust images). Just click the Camera Calibration tab (its icon is a tiny camera) and, from the Process drop-down menu at the top, choose 2010. (Adobe put a lot of brainpower into improving Camera Raw, so be sure you give the newer controls a fair shake before bailing on 'em.)

On the flip side, if you open an image that you adjusted in an older version of Camera Raw, take a peek at the bottom right of your image and you'll see a small light-gray box with a blue exclamation point inside it. To switch to the new process version, give it a swift click.

UP TO SPEED

Using the Camera Raw Filter

Yes, you read that correctly: One of the exciting new features in Photoshop CC is the ability to access the Camera Raw plug-in through Photoshop's *filter menu*. This makes it easier than ever to use Camera Raw's powerful yet easy-to-use sliders on any layer content, including (but not limited to) JPEGs, TIFFs, and 8- or 16-bit images (as long as they're in RGB or Grayscale mode, though it does work on *single* channels in CMYK and Lab modes).

To give it a whirl, activate the Image layer and choose Filter→"Convert for Smart Filters" (click OK in the dialog box that appears). Then, trot *back* up to the Filter menu and choose Camera Raw Filter. Photoshop opens a version of Camera Raw that lacks a few features (such as the Crop, Straighten, the two Rotation tools; the ability to open Camera Raw's preferences;

and a few of the panel menu items), but who cares? The point is that you're accessing Camera Raw inside of Photoshop! (You don't *have* to use the new Camera Raw filter as a Smart Filter, but it's a darn good idea to do so.)

Once you make your adjustments, click OK and the filter appears in the Layers panel complete with a mask, just like any other Smart Filter (you'll learn more about 'em in Chapter 15). You can even double-click the tiny icon that appears in the Layers panel to the right of the Camera Raw filter to open a Blending Options dialog box that lets you adjust the opacity and blend mode of the changes you made using the Camera Raw filter. You can also summon it by pressing Shift-⌘-A (Shift+Ctrl+A).

- **Vibrance**. Use this slider to intensify colors without altering skin tones; it has less effect on highly saturated (intense) colors and won't destroy skin tones. If there are people in your image, this is the adjustment to use.

- **Saturation**. Intensifies *all* the colors in an image, including skin tones. So don't use it on people pictures unless you like fluorescent skin.

FIGURE 9-10

As you can see here, Camera Raw can greatly improve the look of an image. The original, underexposed image is on the left and the end result is on the right. That's an impressive result from just dragging a few sliders back and forth!

To reset any slider in Camera Raw back to its original position, simply double-click the slider itself. To reset the image to its original state, open the Camera Raw panel menu (circled) and choose Camera Raw Defaults.

Camera Raw's Adjustment Brush

The Adjustment Brush lets you selectively tweak certain areas of an image by painting them (see *Figure 9-11*). When you activate the Adjustment Brush by pressing K, a host of adjustments appears on the right side of the Camera Raw window. They're the same adjustments you've learned about so far, along with these extras:

- **Sharpness** lets you accentuate areas of high contrast in an image to make them look sharper (you'll learn all about sharpening in Chapter 11). Use this slider to add extra sharpening to important areas like the image's focal point.

> **NOTE** Camera Raw applies a round of sharpening to your *whole* image as soon as you open it. To find out how much or to turn it off (if, say, you plan on sharpening in Photoshop instead), skip ahead to page 476.

- **Noise Reduction** lets you selectively paint away the colored speckles that appear in images shot in extremely low-light conditions, or at a high *ISO* (your camera's light-sensitivity setting).

- **Moiré Reduction** helps remove the repeating pattern that sometimes appears in scans of printed images (think dots upon dots but not precisely lined up).

- **Defringe** lets you selectively remove any weird color fringe that's loitering along an object's high-contrast edges (called *chromatic aberration*). You can have Camera Raw try to get rid of the color fringe automatically by opening the Lens Correction panel (the sixth button in the row of panels on Camera Raw's right side) and then clicking the Color tab. There, turn on the Remove Chromatic Aberration checkbox and then, if necessary, adjust the Defringe sliders until the fringe is gone. (To learn how to get rid of chromatic aberration in Photoshop, see the Tip on page 650.)

- **Color** lets you paint a colored tint onto an image.

The sliders below the Color setting (you may have to scroll down to see them all) control the Adjustment Brush's cursor, and are explained in *Figure 9-11*.

To use the Adjustment Brush, choose the type of adjustment(s) you want to make using the sliders on the right, mouse over to your image, and then paint to apply the adjustment(s). Or, paint the area you want to adjust first and *then* tweak the sliders. Either way, a little greenish pin appears to mark the area you adjusted (in *Figure 9-11*, the pin is on the same flower as the cursor); press V to show or hide the pin. Behind the scenes, Camera Raw creates a mask that hides the rest of your image so you can continue to tweak the adjustment sliders even after you've finished painting. Camera Raw updates the area you painted to reflect those changes.

TIP Click the little + and – signs on either end of an adjustment's slider to strengthen or lessen that adjustment (respectively) by a preset amount (0.5 for Exposure—whose scale ranges in f-stops from –4 to +4—and 25 for most other sliders, which range from –100 to +100).

To apply an existing adjustment to more areas in your image, turn on the Add radio button in the upper-right part of the Camera Raw window and then paint across the parts that need adjusting. To add a new adjustment, turn on the New radio button, set the sliders to your liking (set any sliders you don't want applied in the new adjustment to 0), and then paint across that area. If you've added more than one adjustment and you want to add to just one of 'em, click the Add button and Camera Raw displays pins representing the different adjustments you've made; simply click the pin representing the one you want to add to, *and then* paint across that part of your image.

To *undo* part of an adjustment in your image, turn on the Erase radio button and, if necessary, click the pin that represents the adjustment you want to erase (if, say, you've used the Add button mentioned above to create multiple adjustments), and then paint the area in question or, better yet, simply Option-drag (Alt-drag on a PC) across that area. To delete a *single* adjustment, click its pin and then press Delete (Backspace on a PC). To erase *all* the adjustments you've made with the Adjustments Brush, click the Clear All button near the bottom right of the Camera Raw window.

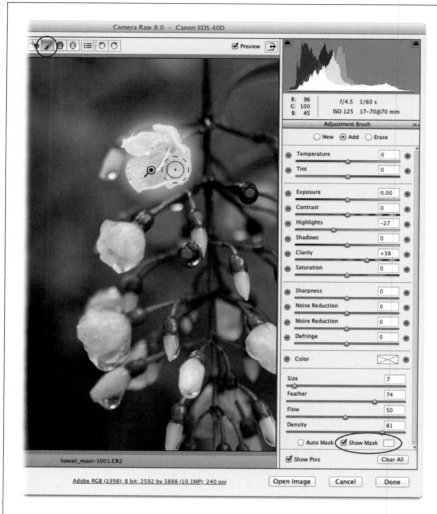

FIGURE 9-11

Here the Adjustments Brush was used to darken the highlights and add Clarity to a single flower. See the dotted line around the brush cursor? It indicates the brush's feather amount, which softens the edge of your adjustment so it blends in with the surrounding pixels. The solid line indicates brush size, and the crosshairs let you know where you're applying the adjustment. To adjust the feather amount or cursor size, drag the Feather or Size slider, respectively. The Flow slider controls the strength of the adjustment, and the Density slider controls the transparency of your brushstroke (think of it as the brush's opacity).

To see the Adjustment Brush's mask—the white overlay shown atop the flower here, which indicates your brushstrokes and, therefore, where the adjustment is visible—turn on Show Mask (circled) or press Y. You can change the color of the mask's overlay by clicking the white square to the right of the Show Mask checkbox and choosing a new color from the resulting Color Picker.

TIP Turn on the Auto Mask checkbox shown in *Figure 9-11* to limit your adjustment to pixels that are similar in color to the ones you're painting across.

Camera Raw's Graduated Filters

The Graduated Filter tool lets you apply adjustments much like a real graduated filter that screws onto the end of a camera lens. (The filter is a thin piece of glass that fades from gray to white so it darkens overly bright parts of the scene you're shooting.) When you activate this tool by clicking its button at the top of the Camera Raw window (it's circled in *Figure 9-12*) or pressing G, you get the same set of adjustments as with the Adjustment Brush (except for Erase mode). The difference is that, with the Graduated Filter tool, you apply the adjustment by dragging a line to apply a gradient (like Photoshop's Gradient tool) rather than *painting* across the area that needs adjusting with a brush cursor. This adjustment is great for fixing overexposed skies because Photoshop gradually applies it across the full width or height of your image in the direction you drag (and you can drag in any direction you want!).

Behind the scenes, this tool creates a gradient mask, which restricts the adjustment to specific parts of your image. As you click and drag, you can create a gradient at *any* angle. Even after you've used this tool, you can continue to make adjustments using the sliders on the right side of the window.

> **NOTE** Camera Raw sports several Graduated Filter adjustments: Temperature, Tint, Highlights, Shadows, Noise, and Moiré Reduction. The previous section explains what these adjustments do.

FIGURE 9-12

You can use the Graduated Filter tool to gradually darken the sky and cliffs in this image. The green-and-white dotted line across the top edge of this image that runs through the green dot represents the start of the mask, and the similar red-and-white dotted line running through the red dot represents the end.

(Santorini, Greece from the Aegean Sea.)

TIP To constrain the Graduated Filter tool's adjustment to be perfectly horizontal or vertical, press and hold the Shift key as you drag. To move the mask's midpoint (where the adjustment begins to fade), drag the green and red dots. To delete the mask, click the red dot and then press Delete (Backspace on a PC) or Option-click (Alt-click) inside the filter's overlay.

■ USING THE RADIAL FILTER

The Radial Filter is new in Camera Raw 8 (it's labeled in *Figure 9-12*). It lets you apply *circular* adjustments that gradually radiate from the outside or inside of where you place the adjustment (just scroll all the way to the bottom of the panel on the right side of the Camera Raw window and click the Outside or Inside radio button, or press X). It's like a circular Graduated Filter, but with more controls.

To create a new radial adjustment that covers the whole image (say, with the tool set to Outside in order to adjust only the *outer* edges of your image), activate the Radial Filter tool by clicking its icon or pressing J, and then double-click your image. You can also double-click an *existing* radial adjustment to make it *expand* to fit your whole image.

More Fun with Camera Raw

As you can see, the Camera Raw plug-in is crazy powerful and each version sports useful new features such as the Lens Correction panel's Automatic Upright buttons that let you fix perspective problems, and the ability to click-and-drag with the Spot Removal brush to fix problem areas that aren't round.

You can use it to adjust Curves (page 387), remove spots (page 412), softly darken the edges of an image (called *vignetting*; see page 140 to learn how to do it in Photoshop), and much more. Camera Raw deserves a whole book all to itself, and there are plenty of 'em out there. If you'd rather learn by watching a video, check out your author's online video workshops at *www.lesa.in/clvideos*.

■ Using Levels

The adjustments you've seen so far are OK when you're just starting out with Photoshop, and they're darn handy when you're pressed for time. But to become a serious pixel wrangler, you've got to kick it up a notch and learn to use Levels and Curves.

With a single Levels adjustment, you can fix lighting problems, increase contrast, and—in some cases—balance the color in your image. (If you've got *major* color problems, you need to use Curves; skip ahead to page 387 to learn how.) Levels adjustments change the intensity levels of shadows, midtones, and highlights (hence the tool's name). They're a very visual and intuitive way to improve images. And because they're available as Adjustment layers (yay!), they're nondestructive and won't harm your original image; plus they come with an automatic layer mask.

In this section, you'll learn how to use Levels adjustments in a few different ways so you can pick the one you like best. But first, you need to get up close and personal with the mighty *histogram*, your secret decoder ring for interpreting the info in your photos.

Histograms: Mountains of Information

A histogram (*Figure 9-13*) is a visual representation—a collection of tiny bar graphs, to be precise—of the info contained in an image. Once you learn how to read it, you'll gain an immensely valuable understanding of why images look the way they do. More importantly, you'll learn how to tweak the histogram itself or (more commonly) make changes with other tools while using the histogram's changing readout to monitor the image's vibrancy. It sounds complicated, but once you watch the histogram in action, you'll see that it's actually pretty straightforward—and tremendously powerful.

Double-click tab to collapse vertically

Cached data warning

Panel menu

Uncached refresh

FIGURE 9-13

Photoshop gives you three different ways to view the Histogram panel: Compact View (displays histogram only), Expanded View (displays the histogram with stats underneath it), and honkin' big All Channels View (shown here). To switch views, choose a different one from the panel's menu.

In All Channels View, you see the image's composite histogram at the top in color and the individual channel histograms below that in light gray. If the full-color composite histogram is too funky for you, from the Channel drop-down menu at the top of the Histogram panel, choose RGB and the composite histogram turns light gray, too.

The cached data warning triangle (labeled) means that the info displayed in the histogram isn't based on the current version of your image (the cache is part of your computer's memory). You'll see this icon periodically when you're editing large files. Just click the triangle or the Uncached Refresh button to make Photoshop update the histogram.

Photoshop automatically displays a histogram in the Properties panel when you create either a Levels or a Curves Adjustment layer. You can also choose Window→Histogram to open the Histogram panel shown in *Figure 9-13*.

The histogram looks like a mountain range, which is a perfectly fine way to think about it (more on that analogy in a moment). Its width represents your image's *tonal range*—the range of colors between the darkest and lightest pixels—on a scale of 0 to 255. Pure black (0) is on the far left and pure white (255) is on the far right. All told, the histogram measures 256 values. If that number sounds familiar, it should—it's the same 256-value range you learned about back in Chapter 2, which represents the minute gradations between a total absence of light (black) and full-on illumination (white).

NOTE The histogram's width is also referred to as the image's *dynamic range*, which you'll learn more about in the High Dynamic Range (HDR) section later in this chapter (page 395).

The histogram's height at any particular spot represents how many pixels are at that specific level of brightness. Using the mountain analogy, a noticeable cluster of tall, wide mountains means that particular brightness range makes up a good chunk of your image. Short or super-skinny mountains mean that particular brightness range doesn't appear much. And a big ol' flat prairie means there are few or no pixels in that range. In other words, the histogram can tell you at a glance whether you've got a good balance of light and dark pixels, whether the shadows or highlights are getting clipped, whether the image is over- or underexposed (see *Figure 9-14*), and whether it's been adjusted before.

Here are a few tips for understanding the histogram:

- An extremely jagged mountain range means the image's color info is unbalanced. The image may contain a decent amount of some colors but very little of others.

- A narrow mountain range means you've got a narrow tonal range and little difference between the darkest and lightest pixels. The whole image probably looks rather flat and lacks both details and contrast.

- If you see a sharp spike on the left side of the histogram, the image's shadows have probably been clipped (by the camera or scanner). If the spike is at the right side of the histogram, the *highlights* may have been clipped instead. (See page 359 for more on clipping.)

- If the mountain range is bunched up against the left side (near 0, a.k.a. black) with a vast prairie on the right, the image is underexposed (too dark); see *Figure 9-14*, left.

- If the mountain range is snug against the right side (near 255, a.k.a. white) with a vast prairie on the left, the image is overexposed (too light); see *Figure 9-14*, right.

- An image that has a good balance of light and dark colors has a wide mountain range—one that spans the entire width of the histogram—that's fairly tall and somewhat uniform in height. Basically, you want the histogram to look like the older, eroded Appalachians (*Figure 9-14*, center) rather than the newer, super-jagged peaks of the Himalayas (*Figure 9-14*, right).

FIGURE 9-14

These histograms—shown here in Compact View—can tell you whether an image is underexposed (left), has a good balance of color (center), or is overexposed (right).

(Great Synagogue and Szechenyi Baths, Budapest.)

- If the histogram looks like a comb—with a bunch of gaps between its spikes (see *Figure 9-16*, right)—the image is either a really lousy scan or was adjusted at some point in the past. (Anytime you shift the brightness values of pixels, you introduce gaps between the histogram's tiny bar graphs.)

All this histogram and correction business is subjective; if your histogram looks terrible but the image looks great to you, that's fine—in the end, your opinion is all that matters.

Thankfully, you can fix a lot of the problems listed above using the correction methods discussed in this chapter. For example, you can balance an image's color to smooth out the height of the histogram's mountains, and expand the image's tonal range and increase its contrast to widen the mountain range. And by keeping the Histogram panel open, you can watch how it changes in real time as you edit images.

If the whole histogram concept is clear as mud, don't fret—it'll make more sense once you start using Levels. And if you've got a little free time, you can use the Dodge and Burn tools to help gain an understanding of the relationship between what you see in an image and how the histogram looks. With the Histogram panel open, use the Dodge tool to lighten dark areas and see how the histogram changes, and then use the Burn tool to darken light areas and see how that affects it. With a little experimentation, you can get a clearer idea of what the histogram is telling you.

> **TIP**   Many digital cameras can also display a histogram, though you may have to root through your owner's manual to learn how to turn it on. Once you get comfy with histograms, you can use them to see whether the shot you're about to take will have good exposure.

The Levels Sliders

Now that you know how to read histograms, you're ready to make a Levels adjustment, which involves using a set of three sliders to reshape and expand the information in your histogram. You can add a Levels Adjustment layer by choosing Layer→New Adjustment Layer→Levels, by clicking the Levels button in the Adjustments panel (it looks like a tiny histogram), or by clicking the half-black/half-white circle at the bottom of the Layers panel and choosing Levels. (You can also summon a Levels adjustment by pressing ⌘-L [Ctrl+L on a PC] or by choosing Image→Adjustments→Levels, though in both cases the adjustment happens on your *original* image instead of on an Adjustment layer. Scary!) Whichever method you use, Photoshop displays a light-gray histogram in the Properties panel, as shown in *Figure 9-15*.

Refresh histogram

Shadows   Midtones   Highlights   Clip to layer below   Reset panel

FIGURE 9-15

The simplest way to use a Levels adjustment is by dragging the Input Levels sliders circled here. You'll also find a slew of options in the Preset drop-down menu at the very top of the panel; feel free to give them a spin to see what they do to your image and how they change your histogram.

As you drag each Input Levels slider, press and hold the backslash key (\) to see what your image looked like previously. To apply the adjustment to just one layer below (instead of all layers below), click the "Clip to layer below" button labeled here (right).

(Golden Lane, Castle Hill, Prague.)

TIP When you add a Levels Adjustment layer, you'll spot an Auto button near the top right of the resulting Properties panel. Back in CS6, Adobe changed the math that Photoshop uses when you click this button: Instead of the Enhance Per Channel Contrast method (wherein Photoshop adjusted the red, green, and blue channels individually, so the highlights got a little lighter and the shadows got a little darker—whether they needed it or not), it now uses the "Enhance Brightness and Contrast" method, wherein Photoshop analyzes your image and then adjusts the brightness and contrast accordingly. So feel free to go give this button a good, swift click.

As shown in *Figure 9-15*, the black slider at the far left of the histogram represents the shadows in your image. It starts out at 0, the numeric value for pure black. The white slider on the far right, which represents highlights, starts out at 255—pure white. To give your image the greatest possible tonal range and contrast, move the shadows and highlights sliders so they point to wherever your histogram's values begin to slope upward (at the foot of the mountains, so to speak). In other words, if there's a gap between the shadows slider and the bars on the left end of the histogram, drag that slider to the right. And if there's a gap between the highlights slider and the bars on the right end of the histogram, drag the slider to the left, as shown in *Figure 9-15*, right.

When you move the sliders, Photoshop adjusts the tonal values in your image accordingly. For example, if you drag the highlights slider left to 190, Photoshop changes all the pixels in the image that were originally at 190 or higher to 255 (white). (Translation: They get brighter.) Similarly, if you move the shadows slider right to 14, Photoshop darkens all the pixels with a brightness level of 14 or lower to 0 (black). The pixel levels in between 14 and 190 get redistributed, too, boosting the image's overall contrast by increasing its tonal range (widening the histogram's mountain range). *Figure 9-15* shows what a difference this can make.

The gray midtones slider in the middle lets you brighten or darken an image by changing the intensity of the middle range of grays (the box on page 389 explains why you're dealing with grays instead of color). Drag it left to lighten your image (or decrease contrast), or right to darken it (or increase contrast), as shown in *Figure 9-16*. Because this slider focuses on the image's midtones, it won't make the highlights too light or the shadows too dark—unless you go hog wild and drag it *all* the way left or right!

■ OUTPUT LEVELS

To help you—or the person you're handing the image off to—differentiate between an adjustment made to *correct* an image and an adjustment made only to suit a particular *printing* method (say, newsprint), the Properties panel includes *Output* Levels settings: the black-and-white bar and two fields near the bottom of the panel, shown in *Figure 9-15* (you may need to increase the height of your Properties panel to see 'em). The black-and-white bar includes a couple of sliders you can use to control the darkness of dark pixels and the lightness of light pixels in your image. Drag the black slider to the right to lighten the pure-black pixels or the white slider to the left to dim the pure-white pixels. These adjustments used to be crucial if you were sending grayscale images to a commercial press because the printing process was notorious for making highlights too light and shadows too dark (mainly due to the absorbency of the paper).

Four histograms are accessible
within the Properties panel

RGB histogram after adjusting
individual channels

FIGURE 9-16

Left: In the Properties panel, the unlabeled drop-down menu perched above the histogram is the Channel menu, which lets you view and adjust the composite channel (page 187) or individual channels. If each channel's histogram differs greatly, it's worth adjusting each one separately; but if their histograms are similar, you can get away with adjusting only the composite channel. Here you see the composite and individual color channel histograms for an RGB image. Since the gaps on the right side vary quite a bit, you should adjust each channel separately.

Right: Here are the before (top) and after (bottom) versions of this image of Matthias Church in Budapest, along with the new composite channel histogram. The histogram's mountain range is a little flatter and wider overall; that means the tonal range has expanded. (You can tell this image has been adjusted because its histogram looks like a comb.)

Nowadays, if you use good-quality color profiles (page 675), these settings aren't such a big deal, but knowing how to change the way your blacks and whites will print is still useful if you can't trust your printer to properly reproduce shadows and highlights. (For more on preparing images for newsprint, see the box on page 314.)

The Levels Eyedroppers

Another way to apply a Levels adjustment is to use the eyedroppers on the left side of the Properties panel's histogram (shown back in *Figure 9-15*). Instead of dragging the sliders below the histogram, you use the eyedroppers to sample pixels that should be black (the darkest shadows that contain details), white (the lightest highlights that contain details), or neutral gray (midtones), and Photoshop adjusts the sliders for you. The only problem with this method is that it can be darn tough to figure out *which* pixels to sample, though there's a trick you can use to solve this problem, as you'll learn shortly. Open an image, and then follow these steps:

1. **Grab the Eyedropper tool and change the Options bar's Sample Size drop-down menu to "3 by 3 Average."**

   Press I to activate the Eyedropper tool. Because you're about to use eyedroppers in a Levels adjustment to reset black and white points, you need to change the way the tool measures color (the eyedroppers in both Levels and Curves use the main Eyedropper tool's settings). In the Options bar, you'll see that the Sample Size menu is set to Point Sample, which means the Eyedropper samples exactly *one* pixel when you click with it. By changing the sample size to "3 by 3 Average," you tell Photoshop to average several pixels around the spot where you click, which is much better for color-correcting.

POWER USERS' CLINIC

Histogram Statistics

If you choose Expanded View or All Channels View from the Histogram panel's menu, you'll see a bunch of cryptic info below the histogram. The most useful thing there is the Source drop-down menu, which lets you choose whether the histogram represents the whole image, the active layer, or an *adjustment composite*. If your document contains Adjustment layers, that last option displays a histogram that's based on the active Adjustment layer and all the layers below it.

The other stuff below the Source menu is pretty heady, but here's the gist of what each item means:

- **Mean** represents the average intensity value of the pixels in the image.
- **Std Dev** (standard deviation) indicates how widely the image's intensity values vary.
- **Median** is the midpoint of the intensity values.
- **Pixels** tells you how many pixels Photoshop analyzed to generate the histogram.

- **Cache Level** shows the current image cache Photoshop used to make the histogram. When this number is higher than 1, Photoshop is basing the histogram on a representative sampling of pixels in the image rather than on all of them. You can click the Uncached Refresh button (shown in *Figure 9-13*) to make the program redraw the histogram based on the current version of the image.

If you position your cursor over the histogram, you also see values for the following:

- **Level** displays the intensity level of the area beneath the cursor.
- **Count** shows the total number of pixels that are at the intensity level beneath the cursor.
- **Percentile** indicates the number of pixels at or below the intensity level beneath the cursor, expressed as a percentage of all the pixels in the image.

Math geeks, bless their hearts, love this kind of stuff.

TIP If you have the Eyedropper or Color Sampler tool (see Appendix C) activated, you can also pick a new sample size by Control-clicking (right-clicking) anywhere in your image. If you're working with extremely high-resolution files, the pixels are so tiny and tightly packed that you may want to increase the sample size to, say, 51 x 51 or higher. (See page 233 for more on resolution.)

2. **Create a Levels Adjustment layer.**

   Click the half-black/half-white circle at the bottom of the Layers panel and choose Levels from the menu that appears. Photoshop adds an Adjustment layer to your image and opens the Properties panel.

3. **In the Properties panel, click the black eyedropper to the left of the histogram.**

   The left side of the panel sports three eyedroppers. The black one resets the image's black point (shadows), the gray one resets its gray point (midtones), and the white one resets its white point (highlights). Simple enough!

4. **Mouse over to your image and click an area near your focal point that should be black.**

   In most cases it's fairly obvious which parts of an image should be black, though sometimes it's hard to tell. If you need help figuring out where the darkest pixels in your image live, make sure the black eyedropper is active, and then hold down the Option key (Alt on a PC) as you drag the Properties panel's shadows slider to the right (see *Figure 9-17*). At first, your image turns completely white, but as you continue to drag, Photoshop displays neon colors in some areas; the first colored area that appears is the darkest spot in your image. While still holding down the Option (Alt) key, mouse over to your image and then click that spot with the black eyedropper. When you mouse away from the Properties panel, your image goes back to its regular colors, but as soon as the cursor is over your image in the document window, it'll go back to funky neons (if it *doesn't*, you forgot to activate the black eyedropper first).

   When you click, the colors in your image will probably shift a bit. If you don't like the results, click somewhere else to set a *new* black point, or undo your click by pressing ⌘-Z (Ctrl+Z on a PC).

5. **In the Properties panel, click the white eyedropper and then click an area in your image that should be white.**

   The same rules apply when it comes to choosing a new white point as choosing a black one: Try to pick an area that's close to the focal point and not pure white (because a pure white one doesn't have any details). You also don't want to pick a reflection from a light source as your white point because it's not a *true* white. You can use the same Option-drag (Alt-drag on a PC) trick to find the image's lightest highlights, though this time you'll need to click to activate the *white* eyedropper, and the image turns black rather than white. As you drag the highlight slider to the left, the first area that appears in color is the lightest. While still holding the Option (Alt) key, mouse over to your image and click that spot (your image temporarily changes to full color when you mouse away from the Properties panel, but it reverts to neon once your cursor reaches your image).

FIGURE 9-17

Top: It's tough to spot the darkest and lightest pixels in this image, so try this trick: In the Properties panel, Option-drag (Alt-drag) the shadows slider to the right (see the circle with an arrow on the right here). Your image turns white and the first areas to appear in color are the darkest ones. Mouse over to the image and click the darkest spot (circled at left).

Middle: Likewise, when you Option-drag (Alt-drag) the highlights slider to the left, your image turns black and the first colors to appear are the lightest. Mouse over to the image and click the lightest spot (circled, left).

Bottom: See the box on page 382 to learn a trick for finding a neutral gray, or just click the gray eyedropper and then find a spot in your image that looks gray and give it a click (both are circled here). As you can see, a little Levels adjusting can go a long way toward improving an image's color and contrast!

If you'd like to play around with the image shown here, download Manhole.jpg from this book's Missing CD page at www.missingmanuals. com/cds.

(Prague Castle, Prague.)

6. **Activate the gray eyedropper and then click an area that should be neutral gray.**

   Unfortunately, the Option-drag (Alt-drag) trick doesn't work here, but if you're willing to jump through a few hoops, you can track down a neutral gray. (The box below has the details.) If you don't have time for that, simply click gray areas until the image's color looks good to you.

7. **To see before and after versions of your image, turn off the Levels Adjustment layer's visibility.**

   In the Layers panel, click the visibility eye to the left of the Levels Adjustment layer to see whether the adjustment made a difference.

WORKAROUND WORKSHOP

Good Gray Hunting

Alas, if you're looking for a neutral gray to click with the gray Levels or Curves eyedropper and nothing in your image is gray, there's no quick trick for finding a good gray. Some images don't even *have* any neutral grays.

One way to look for them is to open the Info panel (*Figure 9-18*) and activate the Eyedropper tool by pressing I. Then, keep an eye on the Info panel's R, G, and B, values as you put your cursor over areas in the image that appear gray. When you find a spot with nearly equal RGB values (like R: 222, G: 222, B: 224, for example), you've found a neutral gray—so click it.

The Info panel method works just fine if you've got a few extra hours to spend mousing around an image checking pixel values. But if you're pressed for time, here's a foolproof way to hunt down neutral grays—if they actually exist in your image. With an image open, follow these steps:

1. Add a new layer by clicking the "Create a new layer" button at the bottom of the Layers panel. Make sure this layer sits *above* the Image layer.

2. Fill the new layer with gray by choosing Edit→Fill, picking 50% Gray from the Use drop-down menu, and then clicking OK.

3. Use the drop-down menu near the top of the Layers panel to switch the gray layer's blend mode from Normal to Difference. Your photo now looks really funky, but don't panic; this layer won't live long.

4. Create a Threshold Adjustment layer by choosing Layer→ New Adjustment Layer→Threshold.

5. In the resulting Properties panel, drag the Threshold slider all the way to the left until the image turns solid white, and then slowly drag the slider back to the right. The first areas that appear black are your neutral grays. As soon as you see a good-sized black spot, stop dragging.

6. Remember that spot or mark it with the Color Sampler tool (see Appendix C online): Press Shift-I repeatedly to activate the tool (it looks like an eyedropper with a tiny circle above it), and then click once in the black spot. A tiny circle with the number 1 next to it appears where you clicked. (Feel free to mark more than one spot if you'd like; the Color Sampler tool lets you place up to four markers.)

7. Delete both the Threshold Adjustment layer and the gray layer (you don't need 'em anymore). Shift-click to activate them both in the Layers panel, and then press Delete (Backspace on a PC).

That's it! With the neutral gray point marked, you don't have to wonder where to click with the gray eyedropper in a Levels or Curves adjustment. To delete the marker once you've set your gray point, grab the Color Sampler tool, mouse over the marker, and then Option-click (Alt-click) it. Your cursor turns into the tiniest, *cutest* pair of scissors you've ever seen.

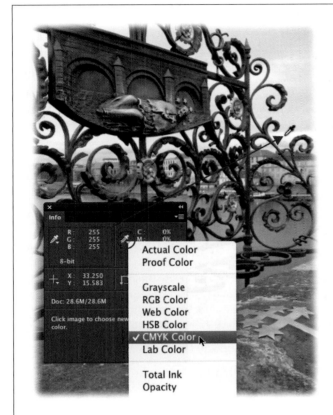

FIGURE 9-18

The Info panel displays various bits of info about your image. The top two sections show before and after color values (once you've made an adjustment). Here you can see that the white cloud is pure white (255,255,255) so this wouldn't be a good spot to click when resetting your white point, as described earlier (page 363). If you happen upon a gray area with (nearly) equal RGB values, congratulations—you've found a neutral gray!

Click one of the little eyedroppers (circled) in the panel's top two sections to summon this menu, and then choose the info you want displayed in that section. To change the info displayed in the panel's other sections, choose Panel Options from the Info panel's menu.

(Charles Bridge, Prague.)

Correcting by the Numbers

Ever heard the phrase, "Numbers don't lie"? That old adage applies to color correcting in Photoshop, too: Using numbers helps you take the guesswork out of it. Instead of relying on what looks good to your naked—and possibly tired—eye, you can use color values to balance an image's color perfectly.

To see pixels' color values, open the Info panel by choosing Window→Info. Once you do that, you can mouse over your image with any tool and the panel displays a numeric value for the particular pixel your cursor is over (see *Figure 9-18*). For RGB images, you'll see values for R, G, and B. If you're in CMYK mode, you see C, M, Y, and K values instead; in Lab mode you get L, a, b; and so on. (You also see C, M, Y, and K values in the Info panel when you're in RGB mode, which is useful if you need to keep an eye on the values of one mode while you're working in another.)

In RGB mode (which is where you spend the majority of your time), these values correspond to the 0–255 scale you learned about earlier in this chapter. Depending on the color your cursor is over, the numbers may lean more toward one channel than the others. For example, when it's over a pixel in a sky, the B (blue) value spikes higher than the R or G (red or green) values. When it's over reddish skin, the R value is higher than the B or G values. This info is useful in several situations:

- **You can use it to figure out what's causing a color cast**. For example, if your cursor is over a white cat and the B value is really high, you have a problem in the blue channel. If the G value is off the charts, then that's where the problem is.

- **It can help you find the darkest and lightest pixels when you're making a Levels or Curves adjustment**. If you put your cursor over the area you're considering using to reset the black or white points, you can see if it's really pure black (0, 0, 0) or pure white (255, 255, 255).

TIP If you're mousing around a shadowy area and the Info panel's numeric values keep changing, that means there are details lurking in that spot; if you lighten the image's shadows using the techniques in this section, you may be able to bring 'em out.

- **Monitoring these values can keep you from over-adjusting the image and losing details**. For example, since you know that three 0s means pure black and three 255s means pure white, you can take care that pixels in the important parts of your image don't reach those values when you're making an adjustment. You can use the Color Sampler tool with the Info panel to monitor the original and adjusted values of up to four sample points by following the steps below.

Here's how to correct an image in RGB mode by the numbers:

1. **Open the Info panel by choosing Window→Info.**

   As you move your cursor over various parts of your image, watch how the Info panel's numbers change to reflect the pixel underneath the cursor.

2. **Grab the Color Sampler tool and make sure its Sample Size is set to "3 by 3 Average."**

   Press I to activate the Eyedropper tool and then press Shift-I until you see the Color Sampler tool (it lives in the same toolset). Take a peek in the Options bar and make sure the Sample Size menu is set to "3 by 3 Average."

3. **Create a Levels Adjustment layer.**

   Click the half-black/half-white circle at the bottom of the Layers panel and choose Levels, or click the Levels button in the Adjustments panel. Technically, you don't *have* to create this layer just yet, but if you've already got a Levels adjustment open, you can use the Option-drag (Alt-drag on a PC) trick (described in the Tip at the top of page 367) to help you find the highlights and shadows points in the next two steps—just don't forget to drag the sliders *back* to their original positions when you're done performing the trick!

4. Mark the darkest shadow and lightest highlight in the image.

Following the guidelines explained in the previous section (starting on page 380), locate the darkest shadow that's not pure black (0) and click it once with the Color Sampler tool; Photoshop adds a marker like the ones circled in *Figure 9-19*. Then find the lightest highlight that's not pure white (255) and mark it, too (you'll see a little 2 next to the marker). Photoshop adds two sections to the Info panel—one for each of the markers you added (they're boxed in *Figure 9-19*).

FIGURE 9-19

Top: When you place sample-point markers (circled), the Info panel sprouts new sections that correspond to each of the markers. These new sections let you monitor the marked pixels' values before and during an adjustment (the two values are separated by a slash). As explained in steps 5 and 6, your goal is to make the highlight's color values 245 and the shadow's color values 10. You may not be able to get your numbers to match these exactly because they change as you adjust individual channels, but if the image has a halfway decent exposure, you should be able to get pretty close.

Bottom: As you can see, making adjustments based on the Info panel's data took care of this image's yellow color cast and improved its contrast.

TIP Strictly speaking, you don't have to activate the Color Sampler tool to place sample-point markers. If you're using the Eyedropper tool, you can Shift-click to place a marker, and Option-Shift-click (Alt+Shift-click on a PC) a marker to delete it.

5. **In the Properties panel, use the histogram to adjust each channel's highlight value.**

Your goal in fixing the highlights is to make all three channels' color values match the *optimal* highlight value, which is about 245 (close to—but not quite—pure white). To balance the channels' highlight values, you have to adjust the highlight in *each* channel. To do that, head over to the Properties panel and pick a channel from the unlabeled drop-down menu near the top of the panel. Then, while watching the numbers in the Info panel (undock it from its panel group if necessary), drag the Properties panel's highlights slider (*Figure 9-15*) left until it reaches 245, or just type *245* into the text field below the slider. Repeat this step for the other two channels. When all three channels' highlight values are nearly (or exactly) equal, you've got yourself a balanced image (well, in the highlights at least!).

6. **Adjust each channel's shadow value.**

Use the same process to balance the shadows: Choose each channel from the menu near the top of the Properties panel, and then drag the shadows slider to the right until it reaches 10 (close to—but not quite—pure black), or type *10* into the slider's text field.

7. **Adjust the image's midtones, if necessary.**

You don't always have to adjust midtones—the image may look just fine the way it is (though you may not realize how much better it *could* look!). In the Properties panel, pick the composite channel (RGB) and then drag the gray slider left to lighten the image, or right to darken it.

8. **Take a peek at the "before" version of the image by turning off the Levels Adjustment layer's visibility.**

In the Layers panel, click the layer's visibility eye so you can see what a difference your changes have made.

If you need to go back and make further adjustments, just double-click the Levels Adjustment layer to reopen its settings in the Properties panel. As you can see back in *Figure 9-19*, this technique makes a big difference.

TIP When you're using the Info panel, it can help to rearrange the various panels in your workspace. For example, if you really dig having the Info and Properties panels open—and you will once you get used to using 'em—you can create a custom workspace so they automatically open and appear wherever you'd like. Flip back to page 10 to find out how.

Color-Correcting Skin

You're not limited to monitoring the Info panel's values of highlights and shadows; you can slap sample points anywhere you want. If you're correcting a people picture, you most certainly want to monitor the values of skin tones. While you won't find any magic target values that work for *every* skin type, here are a few tips that can help you make sure skin tones at least look human, which is (hopefully!) your goal:

- When color-correcting photos of women, try to place sample points on your subjects' necks. Women don't typically put makeup on their necks, so you get a more accurate reading of the woman's *real* skin tone based on her neck than you would on, say, her cheek.

- Skin tones should have red values greater than their green values and green values greater than their blue values. This rule is easy to remember because that's the order of the letters in RGB.

- The difference between the red and green values in skin should be about double the difference between the green and blue values. For example, if the difference between the red and green values is 60, the difference between the green and blue values should be around 30.

- The fairer a person's complexion, the closer the RGB values should be to one another.

- The darker a person's complexion, the lower the blue value in her skin should be.

By following these guidelines, you should end up with nicely balanced skin colors in your images. And if you'd like to use a color swatch as a reference, you can find skin tone color charts lurking on the Web. An oldie but goodie is Bruce Beard's skin tone and hair color chart, available at *www.lesa.in/brucebeard*.

> **TIP** Photoshop provides yet another way to select the skin tones in an image. This method involves the Color Range command—flip back to page 151 to learn all about it.

■ Working with Curves

The last stop on the Color Correction Express is Curves, the most powerful—and fear-inducing—adjustment in all of Photoshop. The basic idea is that, by curving a diagonal line on a grid, you change the brightness of the pixels in an image. Instead of the three main adjustment sliders you get with Levels (shadows, highlights, and midtones), Curves gives you up to *16* adjustments. But that's not as scary as it sounds. If you survived the section on Levels relatively unscathed, you already know a *ton* about Curves. For example:

- You can use Curves as an Adjustment layer so that it's nondestructive, which means you can also use the included layer mask to restrict the adjustment to certain areas of an image. The Curves grid shows up in the Properties panel, just like Levels.

- A Curves adjustment uses a histogram and the same 256 shades of gray you saw in Levels. It also has the same shadows and highlights sliders (though no midtones slider), and it harbors the same trio of eyedroppers for resetting the black, white, and midtone points (page 379). So far so good!

- You can Option-drag (Alt-drag on a PC) the shadows and highlights sliders to find the darkest and lightest areas of your image, like you learned on page 367.

- You can use Curves to correct an image using the Info panel and the Color Sampler tool, and you can type target values into the Properties panel's Input field. To summon the Input field (shown in *Figure 9-20*), click a point on the curve (you may need to resize the panel—or scroll down in it—to see the field). If you haven't added any points yet (which you'll learn how to do shortly), click either the shadows or highlights slider beneath the grid to activate the corresponding *curve point* at the tip of the diagonal line to summon the Input Field.

Pick a channel to adjust

Panel menu

Drag edge to resize panel

Targeted Adjustment tool

Output bar (new value of point)

Curve

Adjustment point added to the curve

Input bar (original value of point)

Input: 113   Output: 90

Drag to resize panel

FIGURE 9-20

Top: Photoshop's Curves adjustment is incredibly flexible—and that's what scares most folks: They don't know when, how, or why to add adjustment points or in which direction to move them. Fear not: You'll learn everything you need to know about this powerful feature in the following pages.

Once you add points to the curve—here, they were added by clicking the Auto button—you can use the grayscale bars on the left and bottom of the grid to figure out which direction you need to drag each point. You can follow a point down the grid to see its original brightness value (on the input bar) and follow it to the left to see its new brightness value (on the output bar). After you click a point on the curve, those numeric values also appear in the Input and Output fields below the grid.

Bottom: Clicking the Auto button makes Photoshop analyze your image and adjust brightness and contrast all by itself. As you can see here, the new math the program began using back in CS6 makes a big difference and, in some cases, may be all your image needs.

(Holocaust Memorial, Great Synagogue, Budapest.)

NOTE You can make the Curves grid bigger (to a point) by dragging the left edge of the Properties panel, or *any* side if you've undocked the panel.

- You can use the unlabeled drop-down menu near the top of the Properties panel (to the left of the Auto button) to pick individual channels to adjust with Curves, just like with Levels.

- The Presets drop-down menu at the top of the Properties panel has some settings that are quite useful. It's worth taking them for a spin just to see how they affect both the curve and your image.

FREQUENTLY ASKED QUESTION

There Is No Color

What's all this talk about black, white, and gray? I'm trying to fix color!

Consider this concept: There *is* no color in Photoshop, so you can't use the program to *fix* color.

After you clean up the coffee you just splurted onto your screen, take a moment to think about the channel information you learned about in Chapter 5. Remember how Photoshop displays it all in grayscale (page 189)? That's because the information really *is* grayscale in each channel that's captured by your camera or scanner: red, green, and blue. The color you see is actually created by output devices like your monitor, printer, and professional printing presses (which you'll learn more about in Chapter 16); they convert the grayscale info your camera captured into colors they can reproduce.

Your computer (and the programs on it, like Photoshop), your digital camera, and your scanner are all digital devices; all they really understand are *bits*, which represent either zero or one (see the box on page 36). When you send these bits to an output device, the device assigns color values to that information.

If you can wrap your brain around this mind-bending concept, a few things start to make sense. For example:

- **Why it's so hard to match what you see onscreen with what you print**. When you realize that output devices are responsible for how the grayscale info is translated into

color, you understand why it's such a nightmare getting colors to match across devices that work differently (like LCD and CRT monitors) or that use different inks (like inkjet printers and printing presses). Chapter 16 has more on *color management*, the science behind matching colors.

- **Why color-correction tools like Levels and Curves focus on white, gray, and black values**. Since you're working with grayscale info, it makes sense that, to change a grayscale image, you have to change what Photoshop *thinks* should be black, neutral gray, or white (or change their intensity or brightness values) to alter the image. Shades of gray are all that matter when you're correcting in Photoshop.

- **Why the histogram measures color intensity (brightness) on a scale from 0 to 255**. A typical RGB image has 256 shades of gray, which correspond to brightness values of 0 percent to 100 percent gray. You see this 0–255 scale in the Info panel when you put your cursor over pixels in an RGB image. Each pixel has a value ranging from 0–255 for each channel.

All this talk of grayscale can sound pretty abstract since we see in color. But what it boils down to is that your *real* goal in color-correcting images is to get the *grayscale* information right. Once you do, your output device has a much better chance of getting the colors right. Now go refill that coffee cup!

To create a Curves Adjustment layer, choose Layer→New Adjustment Layer→Curves. You can also click the Curves button in the Adjustments panel (it looks like a grid with an S curve on it), or click the half-black/half-white circle at the bottom of the Layers panel and choose Curves. No matter which route you choose, the Properties panel pops open to reveal a grid with a diagonal line running from the bottom left to the top right (see *Figure 9-20*). This diagonal line—which is the actual *curve* even though it starts out straight—represents the original brightness values (tonal range) of your image. To adjust these values, you can place up to 14 points along the diagonal line. (You can't delete the points at either end of the curve, but you can adjust them like any other point.)

NOTE To try your hand at the Curves adjustments described in this section, download *Lisbon.jpg* (shown in *Figure 9-21*) from this book's Missing CD page at *www.missingmanuals.com/cds*.

To add a point to the curve, simply click the diagonal line, or make Photoshop add it by clicking the Auto button or activating the Targeted Adjustment tool and then clicking your image (*Figure 9-21* explains how that maneuver works). Each point on the line corresponds to a brightness value in the horizontal black-to-white gradient bar below the grid (called the *input bar*). The direction you drag a point determines whether the brightness of pixels in that tonal range increases or decreases: Drag *upward* to *increase* brightness or *downward* to *decrease* it. (Even if nothing else about Curves makes sense, that part certainly does!)

Ben Willmore (*www.digitalmastery.com*) compares Curves adjustment points to a row of dimmer switches, which makes perfect sense. Just as turning up a dimmer switch gradually turns up the light, raising a point on the curve gradually makes your image brighter and lighter. Likewise, just as lowering a dimmer switch gradually turns down the light, lowering a point on the curve makes your image darker. It's a great analogy because the adjustments you make with Curves are as gradual as using a dimmer switch, though Curves is more *sensitive* than a dimmer switch; you generally don't have to move a point very far to introduce a big change. As you move a point, the diagonal line curves in the direction you drag, and you can see its new brightness level represented on the *output bar* (the vertical gradient bar on the grid's left side), as shown in *Figure 9-21*, bottom.

TIP Instead of dragging the adjustment points around, you can nudge them with the up and down arrow keys on your keyboard. It's easier to make precise adjustments this way, and it keeps you from accidentally changing contrast (discussed in the next section) by dragging the point left or right. Simply click a point on the curve and then use the up arrow to brighten your image or the down arrow to darken it.

Point your cursor at a certain spot and a preview (hollow) point appears on curve

Bar on bottom
shows original
brightness
value of point

Clicking sets adjustment point on curve; drag down to darken

Bar on left
shows new
brightness
value of point

Click to set another adjustment point; drag up to lighten

FIGURE 9-21

Top: Curves is a lot easier to use than it used to be thanks to the Targeted Adjustment tool, which lets you add and move adjustment points by clicking and dragging in your image. Just click the button that looks like a pointing hand (circled, top) to activate this tool and then put your cursor over the area you want to darken (your cursor turns into an eyedropper). A white preview circle appears on the curve (circled, right) that corresponds to the tonal value of the pixels your cursor is over.

Middle: When you're ready to add an adjustment point to the curve, click once in your image and then—while still holding down your mouse button—drag downward to darken those pixels (your cursor turns into a hand with an up-and-down arrow [circled, left]). As you drag, the curve bends in the direction you're dragging, as shown here.

Bottom: Release your mouse button and click in your image to add another point. This time, pick an area you want to lighten and then drag upward, as shown here.

(Vasco da Gama monument, Lisbon.)

The grid behind the curve is merely a visual aid to help you move points around and determine which part of the tonal range you're affecting. It's set to a 25 percent, quarter-tone grid wherein shadows, midtones, and highlights are split into four parts: The left-hand column represents the darkest shadows, the middle two columns represent the midtones, and the right-hand column represents the lightest highlights. You can change it to a 10 percent grid that displays 10 rows and columns by Option-clicking (Alt-clicking on a PC) the grid in the Properties panel or by opening the Curves Display Options dialog box, shown in *Figure 9-22*.

FIGURE 9-22

You can open this dialog box by choosing Curves Display Options from the Properties panel's menu. To switch from a 25 percent grid to a 10 percent grid, just click the buttons shown here that look like tiny grids.

If you change your mind and want to go back to the 25 percent grid, you don't have to reopen this dialog box: Just Option-click (Alt-click) the grid in the Properties panel.

Here's a rundown of the other settings in the Curves Display Options dialog box:

- **Show Amount of**. Unless you change it, the Light radio button is turned on, which means your image's shadows correspond to the bottom-left corner of the Curves grid and its highlights to the top-right corner. You can turn on the "Pigment/Ink %" option instead to show ink percentages on the input and output bars instead of the 0–255 brightness scale. Usually, though, you'll want to leave this set to Light.

- **Show**. This setting has several options that are all turned on to start with:

  — **Channel Overlays** lets you see a separate curve for each channel in your document. If you're new to Curves and find a panel riddled with colorful diagonal lines both distracting and alarming, turn this checkbox off.

  — **Histogram** determines whether Photoshop displays a light-gray version of your image's histogram behind the grid. If you find the histogram distracting, turn this setting off.

  — **Baseline** tells Photoshop to display the original curve as a straight diagonal line, which is a great way to know at a glance just how much you've adjusted the image.

— **Intersection Line** makes Photoshop display horizontal and vertical "helper" lines when you drag a point to help you align it properly (which isn't really necessary if you use arrow keys to nudge points instead of dragging them).

Changing Contrast

The angle of the curve in the Properties panel controls contrast. If you steepen it, you increase the image's contrast; if you flatten it, you decrease the image's contrast. Just select an adjustment point by clicking it and then use the left or right arrow key to nudge it one way or the other.

Another way to increase contrast is to make a subtle S curve, as shown in *Figure 9-23* (middle). Here's how: Darken the image's shadows slightly by clicking to add an adjustment point to the lower-left grid intersection and then use the down arrow to nudge it 2-3 notches for a low-resolution image or more for a high-resolution image (you can also use the Targeted Adjustment tool as described earlier). Next, lighten the image's highlights by adding a point to the top-right grid intersection, and then nudge it up the same amount. Finally, adjust the midtones by adding a point to the very center of the grid and then nudge it slightly upward to lighten or downward to darken.

If the effect of the Curves Adjustment layer is a little too strong, just lower the Opacity setting at the top of the Layers panel. If you inadvertently intensify a certain color while making a Curves adjustment, just tweak that particular channel: In the Properties panel, choose the appropriate channel from the drop-down menu directly above the grid and then click the panel's Targeted Adjustment button. Then click the color in your image that you want to adjust and press the down arrow key to neutralize it, as shown in *Figure 9-23* (bottom).

TIP Remember, you can also change any Adjustment layer's blend mode (see the box on page 342). For example, to preserve the image's color, you can change a Curves Adjustment layer's blend mode to Luminosity so the adjustment affects only the image's lightness values and not its color balance—a great way to avoid color shifts.

Getting good at using Curves takes practice. But as long as you use an Adjustment layer, you'll never harm your original image. Heck, if you're feeling really frisky, you can click the pencil icon on the Properties panel's left and then draw your *own* curve by hand. (If you go that route, click the "Smooth the curve values" button just beneath the pencil to smooth the line you drew.) To add points to adjust the curve, click the "Edit points to modify the curve" button just above the pencil. And when you're ready to learn more about Curves, check out Ben Willmore's DVD *Mastering Curves* (*www.lesa.in/benscurves*).

TIP If you create a really useful or incredibly funky Curve, you can save it for use later by choosing Save Curves Preset from the Properties panel's menu. (You can save a favorite Levels adjustment in the same way.) From then on, it'll show up in the Preset menu at the top of the panel.

FIGURE 9-23

Top: Here's a flat and rather uninspiring image, though you can use a couple of well-placed Curves Adjustment layers to fix it fast.

Middle: After you adjust the shadows and highlights, you can add a point in the center of the grid (circled) to create a magic contrast-inducing S curve. It doesn't take much of an adjustment to make a major change in an image, so try using the arrow keys to nudge adjustment points up or down.

Bottom: You can add as many Curves Adjustment layers as you want to a document. For example, you can create one to fix shadows, highlights, and midtones, and another to neutralize the suddenly too-blue sky. If you choose Blue from the Channel menu (circled), you can use the Targeted Adjustment tool to select the super-bright blue and then use your down arrow key to nudge it back down to Earth.

(Vasco da Gama monument, Lisbon.)

Creating High Dynamic Range Images

Once you get used to peeking at the histogram, you'll notice that very few images exploit the full range of brightness values from light to dark. More often than not, you'll have more info on one end of the histogram than the other, meaning the highlights *or* shadows look really good, but rarely both. That's because digital cameras can collect only so much data in a single shot. If you've got a scene with both light and dark areas—like a black cat on a light background—you have to choose which area to expose for: the cat or the background. To capture more info, you can shoot multiple versions of the same shot at different *exposure values* (called *EV*) by varying your camera's shutter speed, aperture, or ISO, and then combine 'em later in Photoshop into what's known as a *high dynamic range* (HDR) image.

Adobe has put a lot of effort into making it easy for mere mortals to create HDR images. But before you get started, you need to dig out your camera's manual and hunt for a feature called *auto bracketing*, which makes the camera take a series of shots with different exposure settings (you can also set the exposure differences up yourself *manually*—see your camera's manual to learn how). Bracketing lets you tell the camera how many shots to take (use a minimum of three, though more is better) and how much of an exposure difference you want between each one (pick one or two EV steps if you have the choice). For example, for three shots, you'd have one at normal exposure, one that's one or two EV steps *lighter* than normal, and one that's one or two EV steps *darker* than normal. After you've taken a few series shots with these settings, transfer them to your computer (see Chapter 22 to learn how to import images using Bridge).

POWER USERS' CLINIC

Keyboard Curves

If you're a fan of keyboard shortcuts and keyboard/mouse combinations, dog-ear this page—or better yet, print a copy of the shortcuts included on this book's Missing CD page at *www.missingmanuals.com/cds*—because there are a slew of 'em that you can use with Curves:

- To cycle through a document's channels (starting with the composite channel), press ⌘-2, 3, 4, 5, 6 (Ctrl+2, 3, 4, 5, 6 on a PC). To cycle through a document's channels in the Properties panel, press Option (Alt on a PC)+2, 3, 4, 5 (and 6, if you're in CMYK mode).

- To show clipped shadows and highlights, Option-drag (Alt-drag) the Properties panel's shadows or highlights sliders, or click the shadows or highlights eyedropper and then press and hold Option (Alt) as you move your cursor over the image.

- To switch between the 25 percent to 10 percent grid (page 392), or vice versa, Option-click (Alt-click) the grid.

- To cycle forward (left to right) through curve points, press =.

- To cycle backward through curve points, press – (that's the minus sign).

- To deselect the selected point(s), press ⌘-D (Ctrl+D).

- To select multiple points, Shift-click them.

- To delete a single point, select it and then press Delete (Backspace), drag it off the grid, or ⌘-click (Ctrl-click) it.

- To nudge the selected point two units in the Properties panel, press one of the arrow keys.

- To nudge the selected point 16 units in the Properties panel, press and hold Shift and then use the arrow keys.

NOTE As far as file formats and HDR, using raw files is the best approach since they contain more info than JPEGs. Also, be sure to use a tripod so your camera doesn't move between shots!

Here's how to merge several exposures of the same shot into one:

1. **In Photoshop, choose File→Automate→"Merge to HDR Pro."**

   In the resulting dialog box (*Figure 9-24*) navigate to where the images (or folder) live on your hard drive and then click OK. Photoshop combines the images into one document and auto-aligns them on separate layers. Depending on your computer, this process might take a while. When it's finished, you see the resulting image in the "Merge to HDR Pro" dialog box (*Figure 9-25*).

NOTE Want to follow along? Visit this book's Missing CD page at *www.missingmanuals.com/cds* and download the practice file *Mini.zip*.

FIGURE 9-24

This dialog box lets you choose individual images or an entire folder. When it comes to HDR, the more exposures you use, the more realistic your final image will be.

You can also summon this dialog box in Bridge: Just Shift-click to activate the images you want to merge, and then choose Tools→Photoshop→"Merge to HDR Pro." For more on installing and using Bridge, see Chapter 22.

2. **In the full-size "Merge to HDR Pro" dialog box (*Figure 9-25*), turn on the "Remove ghosts" checkbox if the subject of your images moved between shots or has a lot of soft edges.**

   Even if you used a tripod, this setting is likely to improve the final image. When you turn it on, Photoshop compares all the images and tries to ignore content that doesn't match throughout the majority of the shots.

3. **From the Mode menu near the top of the "Merge to HDR Pro" dialog box, choose a final bit depth for your image.**

   Choosing 32-bit makes Photoshop keep all the dynamic range information captured in the original images. However, 32-bit images contain far more info than your monitor can display (plus they take up a ton of your computer's memory), so you'll see only a portion of the images' tonal range. To compress the information into something you can actually use, you need to convert the images to 16- or 8-bit, as explained in the next step. (For more on bit depth, see the box on page 36.) This conversion process is called *tone mapping*: mapping one set of colors to another.

NOTE   In Photoshop CC, you can use Camera Raw to tone your 32-bit HDR image. Once you choose 32-bit from the "Merge to HDR Pro" dialog box's Mode menu, you'll spot a new checkbox called "Complete Toning in Adobe Camera Raw" (it's turned on by default). Click the "Tone in ACR" button at the bottom right of the dialog box. When you do, Photoshop makes a Smart Object out of the images you've merged, and then opens the Camera Raw filter. When you're finished tweaking the image in Camera Raw, click OK to return to Photoshop.

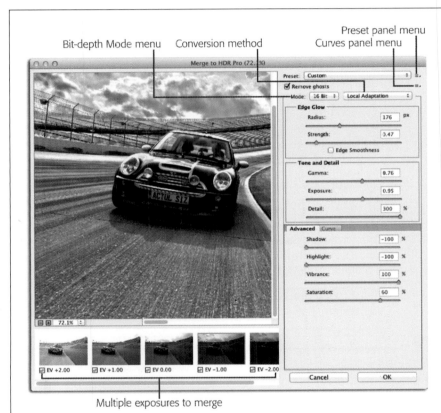

Bit-depth Mode menu   Conversion method

Preset panel menu
Curves panel menu

Multiple exposures to merge

FIGURE 9-25

At the bottom of the "Merge to HDR Pro" dialog box are the five shots used to create this image (photos by Karen Nace Willmore, www.karennace. com). As the thumbnails show, the sky is brighter than the car. If you first expose for the car and then shoot the same shot with your EV a step apart, and then change it again by another step, you eventually have a series of images that span a broad tonal range, even though it's spread out across several images. Experiment with the recipes in the Preset menu shown here. Once you've got your settings just right, save 'em by clicking the dialog box's Preset panel menu (labeled) and choosing Save Preset. Using its Curves panel menu (also labeled), you can load and save Curves presets, too.

NOTE Just because you *can* do tone-mapping in Photoshop doesn't mean you *should*. Even though the process improved back in CS5, you may still find third-party plug-ins—like Photomatix (*www.hdrsoft.com*) or HDR Efex Pro (*www.niksoftware.com*)—faster and easier to use. Both programs work on Macs and PCs and are relatively inexpensive.

4. **If you picked 8- or 16-bit in the previous step, choose a conversion method from the drop-down menu to the right of the Mode menu.**

This whole HDR business is purely subjective—there's no right or wrong way to do it—so you'll want to spend some time experimenting with the various settings to figure out what makes the image look good to you:

- **Local Adaptation** gives you a slew of additional options (shown in *Figure 9-25*) and even lets you apply a Curves adjustment to your image right there in the "Merge to HDR Pro" dialog box. Choose this option if you've mastered Curves and then tweak the settings in the following sections of the dialog box:

  — **Edge Glow** behaves much like the Clarity slider in Camera Raw (page 367). Use the Radius slider to control the size of the hazy glow around soft-edged items where there's little or no contrast; drag it left to make the edge glow smaller, or right to make it larger. Use the Strength slider to control the glow's contrast (drag it right to increase contrast, or left to decrease it).

  — **Tone and Detail** has controls much like those in Camera Raw's Basic tab (page 365) with the addition of Gamma, which modifies the overall flatness and brightness of the image.

  — **The Advanced panel** lets you tweak the image's Vibrance and Saturation to alter the intensity of its colors, as well as its Shadow and Highlight brightness values.

  — **The Curve panel** (click its tab to display it) lets you make a Curves adjustment. Flip back to page 387 for the scoop on using Curves.

NOTE If you've opened Photoshop in 64-bit mode (see the box on page xxviii), you'll see an HDR Toning option in the Image→Adjustments menu. If you choose it, Photoshop opens a dialog box with the same options discussed here, but you can apply them to *normal* images—ones that weren't shot with multiple exposures—including TIFFs. If you go this route, expect some rather unusual results!

- **Equalize Histogram** compresses the dynamic range of your HDR image while trying to maintain contrast (it gives you a peek at what your blended image looks like). This method doesn't work quite as well as the others because it doesn't have as many options, and it tends to make the darkest shadows black.

- **Exposure and Gamma** lets you adjust the image's exposure to make the highlights brighter or the shadows darker, or both. Drag the Exposure slider right to brighten the highlights, and use the Gamma slider to set the comparative brightness difference (across the series of shots) between shadows and highlights (drag it left to darken the shadows or right to brighten them).

- **Highlight Compression** compresses the highlights in your image in order preserve detail. Pick this method if you want to see details in your image's highlights without changing its overall contrast.

5. **Click OK to create the HDR image.**

   Photoshop applies your tone-mapping settings and makes the final HDR image (see *Figure 9-26*).

Be warned: Once you go HDR, you may not come back. The conversion process takes time, but it can produce amazing (though sometimes unrealistic) images. Once you've recovered from poring over this section, check out *Practical HDR* by David Nightingale (*www.lesa.in/practicalhdrbook*) to learn more about HDR photography.

■ Making Colors Pop

Once you've corrected an image's color and lighting, you can have some serious fun by boosting or intensifying its colors. You've already learned how to do that in Camera Raw with the Clarity, Vibrance, and Saturation adjustments; this section focuses on what you can do in Photoshop.

> **TIP** New in Photoshop CC, you can use the Adobe Camera Raw *filter* to make your colors pop. To learn how, flip back to the box on page 366.

Intensifying Colors

After you've got an image's colors just right using what you've learned in this chapter, you can boost 'em so they pop off the page. One of the simplest ways to emphasize colors is with a Vibrance Adjustment layer (see *Figure 9-26*), which has less of an effect on intense colors (because they're already highly saturated) than on lighter tones—yet it manages to leave skin tones relatively unchanged. You can also use a Vibrance Adjustment layer to tweak an image's saturation (it includes a regular Saturation slider, too), but when you do, Photoshop applies that change evenly to the whole image no matter how intense the colors already are and with no regard for skin tones. So if your picture includes people, stay away from the Saturation slider and stick to Vibrance instead...unless you *like* hot-pink skin.

To create a Vibrance Adjustment layer, choose Layer→New Adjustment Layer→ Vibrance. You can also click its icon in the Adjustments panel (it looks like a triangle) or click the half-black/half-white circle at the bottom of the Layers panel and choose Vibrance.

FIGURE 9-26

Unlike a regular saturation adjustment, a big boost of Vibrance (top) won't completely destroy your image, even if it contains skin tones.

However, you can easily hide its effects from part of the image—like the bottom right of this photo— by painting with black in the Vibrance Adjustment layer's mask (bottom).

To give this technique a spin, visit this book's Missing CD page at www.missingmanuals.com/cds *and download the practice file* Sintra.jpg.

(National Palace of Sintra, Portugal.)

> **TIP** You can also use the Layers panel's Opacity field to lower the Adjustment layer's opacity and, therefore, lessen its effect.

Adjusting Hue/Saturation

If you want to make a *specific* color pop, you can use a Hue/Saturation Adjustment layer to boost one color channel's contrast. It's a simple and nondestructive way to accentuate a certain range of colors.

To create a Hue/Saturation Adjustment layer, choose Layer→New Adjustment Layer→Hue/Saturation. You can also click its icon in the Adjustments panel (it looks like two horizontal gradient bars) or click the half-black/half-white circle at the bottom of the Layers panel and choose Hue/Saturation. Next, choose the color you want to intensify from the unlabeled drop-down menu near the top of the Properties panel—which is set to Master until you change it—and then drag the Saturation slider to the right. Be careful not to go hog wild or your image's colors will enter the dreaded Neon Realm. You should be fine with a 10–15 percent saturation increase. Good times!

Adding Lab Pop

Another way to make colors leap out of an image is to creatively blend color channels in Lab mode. It's incredibly easy and the results can be amazing, as shown in *Figure 9-27*. With an image open, follow these steps:

1. **Pop into Lab mode by choosing Image→Mode→Lab Color.**

2. **Duplicate the original layer by pressing ⌘-J (Ctrl+J).**

3. **Choose Image→Apply Image.**

4. **In the Apply Image dialog box, choose the layer you just created from (you guessed it) the Layer drop-down menu, and set the Blending drop-down menu to Soft Light.**

   As you learned on page 285, this blend mode makes bright areas brighter and dark areas a little darker; it also helps make colors pop off the page.

5. **In the Channel menu, pick the channel that makes your image look best.**

   As you choose different channels, take a peek at your image to see how it changes. Remember, this kind of color adjustment is purely subjective; there's no right or wrong channel to pick, and the channel that looks the best to you in *this* image may not look best in another image. *Figure 9-27* shows how the channels can differ.

6. **Lower the channel's opacity (if necessary), and then click OK.**

   If the effect is too intense, lower the channel's opacity by entering a new number in the Opacity field. Then click OK to close the Apply Image dialog box.

7. **Switch back to RGB mode.**

   Choose Image→Mode→RGB. If Photoshop asks whether you want to merge layers, say no.

You're done! Put your sunglasses on and smile as you enjoy your image's brilliant new colors. You can toggle the duplicate layer's visibility eye off and on to see before and after views. If you need to tone down the extra color, just lower the duplicate layer's opacity.

FIGURE 9-27

You can create some super-colorful images using this Lab Pop technique. The hardest part is picking which channel looks best! The Lightness version, for example, has a retro look thanks to its slight orange-greenish tinge.

To follow along, visit www.missingmanuals.com/cds and download Prague.jpg.

(Photo taken in the Mála Strana district of Prague.)

Original   Lab (composite)   Lightness

a   b

■ Rescuing the Unfixables

Sadly, even with all the tricks you've learned in this chapter, you can't fix *every* image. If you run into what seems to be a truly unfixable photo and you're desperate to salvage it (if the scene or subject just can't be reshot, say), try one of these techniques:

- Use the Lab Pop technique described on page 401 and use the Lightness channel to create unique, retro-style color.

- Create an overexposed, high-key version (see page 193).

- Convert it to black and white (the whole thing or just part of it) using one of the methods in Chapter 8. By draining the color from the image, its color problems vanish.

- Add a color tint using a Black & White or Photo Filter Adjustment layer (page 308 or page 336, respectively).

- Turn it into a duotone (page 323).

- Use a Threshold adjustment to create a pure black-and-white image (page 320).

- Use a combination of filters to turn it into a pencil sketch (page 666) or painting (page 640).

POWER USERS' CLINIC

Processing Multiple Files

By now, you've probably realized how time-consuming all this image-correction business can be. That's why it's important to know how to save time by correcting more than one image with a single adjustment. Happily, there are several ways to do that:

- **Open multiple files in Camera Raw**. If you're using Camera Raw, you can adjust several files at once by selecting 'em, and then Control-clicking (right-clicking) one and choosing "Open in Camera Raw." In the upper left of the window that appears, click the Select All button. From then on, Camera Raw applies anything you do to one image to all the others, too.

- **Drag and drop Adjustment layers**. If you've (wisely) corrected an image using Adjustment layers, you can drag and drop them into other open documents (use the Window→Arrange menu to position your documents so you can see 'em both at the same time; page 56 explains how). That way, you can quickly fix a bunch of images from the same shoot that have similar lighting. Even if you have to tweak the adjustment a tiny bit, it's faster than hunting for highlights, shadows, and midtones in *each* photo.

- **Record repetitive tasks with actions**. While you can't record *every* aspect of color-correcting because it's unique

to each image (or at most applies only to images taken during a single photo shoot), you *can* automate the little things you do over and over—like duplicating the original layer and adding an Adjustment layer—using *actions*. Creating an action that performs those two steps can save you a couple of clicks. You can also automate finishing touches like making colors pop (see the previous section), record an action for the sharpening techniques in Chapter 11, and so on. See Chapter 18 to learn all about actions.

- **Use Adobe Bridge to copy and paste Camera Raw settings**. If you're working on photos from the same shoot that have similar lighting, you can adjust one using Camera Raw and then copy and paste the Camera Raw settings using Bridge. See page 860 for the lowdown.

- **Use Adobe Bridge to rename a bunch of files**. OK, so this one has nothing to do with correcting images, but it can still save you some time! If you like renaming your processed files—before correcting them—and then saving them in a different location than the originals (a wise move), you can have Bridge do that for you for an entire folder of images. Page 861 explains how.

Changing Reality: Removing and Repositioning

I t's no secret that the beautiful models gracing the covers of magazines have been Photoshopped to within an inch of their lives. They've had the digital equivalent of every plastic surgery you can imagine, and then some: skin smoothing, blemish banishing, tummy tucking—they get it all.

This chapter shows you all those tricks and more, but that doesn't mean you should use every technique on every photo. It's easy to get carried away with this kind of stuff, and with great editing skills comes great responsibility. The challenge is to retouch your subjects enough to *enhance* their appearance without making them look fake. For example, if you're tempted to remove wrinkles completely, soften 'em instead. If you'd like to hack off 30 pounds, be content with 5 or 10.

All that aside, there's nothing wrong with a little vanity, and it's darn comforting to know you can zap a zit, whiten teeth, and fix red-eye whenever you need to (and you'll never want to let photos of yourself out into the wild until you've spent some quality time with them). When you're finished with this chapter, you'll be able to fix shiny spots, remove unsightly bulges, and enhance eyes with the best of 'em. In other words, you're about to become the most popular picture-fixer-upper in your entire social network.

> **NOTE**   For a fascinating profile of one of today's leading Photoshop-using, model-enhancing gurus, check out this older (yet still informative) *New Yorker* article: *www.lesa.in/nyretouching*.

But these kinds of changes aren't limited to pictures of people. You can also use Photoshop to remove objects from photos and scoot stuff from one spot to another using the Content-Aware tools, as well as twist and turn objects any which way you want using Puppet Warp.

This chapter explains everything you need to know about turning the photos you *have* into the photos you *want*.

The Great Healers

Some of the simplest retouching you can do is to remove dark circles and bags under eyes, as well as other blemishes. In the old days, you were stuck with cloning (copying) skin from one area to another, which never *really* looked quite right; texture and tonal (color) differences always made the fix stick out like a sore thumb. These days, Photoshop has a set of tools specifically for retouching skin. Instead of grafting skin by cloning, these tools blend two patches of skin together so the texture and tones actually match (see *Figure 10-1*).

FIGURE 10-1

Top: Photoshop's magical healing tools, including the Content-Aware Move tool (discussed on page 443).

Bottom: A lot of moles—and an eyebrow ring—have completely disappeared from this guy's face. With a few clicks here and a few drags there, you can clean up a photo without making it look obviously retouched. Some of the guy's lighter freckles are still hanging around, and the bags under his eyes aren't completely gone; they're just lightened so they're not distracting.

The Spot Healing Brush

This tool's cursor is a round brush—perfect for fixing round problem areas like pimples, moles, and so on. It's literally a one-click fixer-upper—you don't even have to drag, though you can if you want. When you click a spot with this tool, Photoshop looks at the pixels just *outside* the cursor's edge and blends them with the pixels *inside* the cursor. It's great for retouching people, fixing dust and specks in old photos, and removing anything that's roundish in shape. You can also drag with this tool to remove, say, power lines on a relatively solid background (like a sky) or to fix scratches in old photos. And with the Content-Aware Fill option (explained in a moment), the Spot Healing Brush does an amazing job at zapping unwanted stuff in images.

To use the Spot Healing Brush, grab it from the Tools panel by pressing J (its icon looks like a Band-Aid with a circle behind it). Then put your cursor over the offending blemish and adjust the cursor's size so it's slightly larger than the area you want to fix (see *Figure 10-2*).

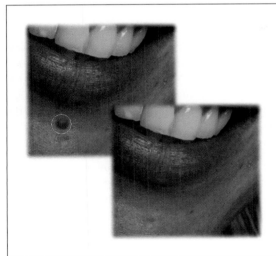

FIGURE 10-2

The key to success with the Spot Healing Brush is to make your cursor a little bit bigger than the area you want to fix.

You can change the cursor's size using the Brush preset picker at the left of the Options bar, the Brush Presets panel (page 499), or the bracket keys on your keyboard: Press [to make the cursor smaller, or] to make it bigger. Alternatively, you can also resize it by Control-Option-dragging (Alt+right-click+dragging on a PC) to the left or right.

The Options bar's settings let you control exactly how the Spot Healing Brush works:

- **Mode**. This menu lists some of the blend modes discussed back in Chapter 7: Replace, Multiply, Screen, Darken, Lighten, Color, and Luminosity. Unique to the Healing brushes (Spot and Healing), Replace mode is handy if you're using a soft-edged brush because it preserves some of the texture and details around the brush's edges. However, Normal mode usually works just fine.

- **Type**. This setting controls which pixels Photoshop looks at when it's healing. You've got three options:

  — **Proximity Match**. This option tells Photoshop to use pixels just outside the edge of the cursor to fix the blemish.

  — **Create Texture**. Choose this option if the area you want to fix is surrounded by tons of details. Instead of looking at pixels outside the cursor's edge, Photoshop tries to recreate the texture by looking at the pixels *inside* the cursor.

  — **Content-Aware Fill**. This option is pure magic, and Photoshop comes from the factory set to use it. It's great for removing objects from photos such as power lines, a Texas Longhorn in a pasture, an ex-boyfriend, and so on. You can either single-click or simply drag to remove the item and Photoshop fills in the area with surrounding pixels. Amazingly, the behind-the-scenes code can recreate complex structures like brick walls. You've got to use it to believe it, as *Figure 10-3* shows. It works with both the Spot Healing Brush and the Fill command, as the next section explains.

TIP   Want to give the new Content-Aware Fill option a spin? Skip on over to this book's Missing CD page at *www.missingmanuals.com/cds* and download *Fence.jpg*.

- **Sample All Layers**. Turn on this option to have Photoshop sample pixel info from *all layers* instead of just the active one. This setting also lets you do the healing on another layer instead of on the original image: Just create a new layer *above* the photo layer and make sure the new layer is active; when you click to fix a spot, the fix happens on the new layer. This technique builds a *ton* of flexibility into your document because, if you decide you've done too much healing, you can erase specific areas from the new healing layer or lower the opacity of that layer to soften the effect.

- **Always Use Pressure for Size**. This option, which looks like a pen drawing tiny circles, is for folks using graphics tablets (page 517). It lets you control the size of the Spot Healing Brush's cursor by applying pressure with your stylus (the pressure-sensitive pen that comes with a graphics tablet). Press harder to increase the size of the brush, or lighter to decrease it.

Using Content-Aware Fill

If you've got plenty of good pixels on either side of the ones you want to delete, the Spot Healing brush's Content-Aware feature works well. However, if you want to be more *precise* with your pixel zapping—say, if the item you want to delete is super close to something you want to keep—create a selection first and then use the Content-Aware version of the Fill command instead. For example, here's how to zap one of the cows in *Figure 10-4*:

FIGURE 10-3

Top: You need some space on either side of the soon-to-be-zapped object for this truck to work well, and this fence has plenty of extra snow around it. By turning on the Spot Healing Brush's Content-Aware option as well as Sample All Layers (circled), you can nondestructively delete this fence.

Bottom: As you paint across the fence, Photoshop marks your brushstrokes in dark gray (circled, left). When you release your mouse button, Photoshop copies surrounding pixels to make the fence disappear. In the Layers panel (right), you can see that the fence-zapping happened on its very own layer, leaving you plenty of room to add text.

TIP The Fill command's Content-Aware option works best if there's plenty of background on either side of the object you want to remove. So if you plan to use the Fill command for some quality pixel-zapping, it's best to do that *before* you crop the image.

---

1. **Open an image and duplicate the Background layer by pressing ⌘-J (Ctrl+J).**

   Since the Fill command can't sample all layers (bummer!), it won't work on an empty layer. You could use it on a locked Background layer, but that wouldn't protect your original image.

FIGURE 10-4

Top: There's precious little background space between these two cows, so it's best to create a selection of the cow you want to delete. In order for Photoshop to remove the object completely (instead of leaving a funky outline of what used to be there), you need to include a bit of the background in your selection by using the Expand command.

Middle: Once you've created a selection and expanded it, you can use the Fill command set to use Content-Aware to replace the selected pixels with those nearby.

Bottom: As you can see here, it does an amazing job! And by duplicating the Image layer first, the original remains unchanged.

Want to follow along? Then trot on over to this book's Missing CD page at www. missingmanuals.com/cds and download Cows.jpg.

2. **Use the selection tool of your choice to select the cow on the left.**

   Because there's a decent amount of contrast between the cow and the grassy meadow, the Quick Selection tool does a great job. Grab it from the Tools panel by pressing Shift-W until you see its icon. Next, mouse over to the image, and then click and drag to paint a selection onto it. (For more on using this tool, flip back to page 146.)

3. **Expand your selection to include some of the background by choosing Select→Modify→Expand.**

   If you're working with a low-resolution image, try entering a number between 5 and 10 pixels into the Expand Selection dialog box; you'll need to use a higher number on high-resolution images (see page 233 for more on resolution). When you click OK, the selection expands outward.

4. **Choose Edit→Fill and then, from the Use menu, choose Content Aware.**

   As soon as you click OK, Photoshop fills the selection with pixels from the surrounding area.

The voodoo Photoshop uses to fill your selection is random and changes each time you use the command. In other words, if at first you don't succeed, try choosing Edit→Fill again—you'll likely get different results! Until you can actually *wish* an object out of a photo, using the Fill command's Content-Aware option ought to suit you just fine.

The Healing Brush

Like the Spot Healing Brush, this tool also blends two areas of skin together, but you have to tell it *where* to find the skin that looks good (which makes it handy for fixing things that aren't round). This process, called *setting a sample point*, is how you let Photoshop know which portion of skin—or fur, or whatever—you want it to *sample* (blend the offending spot with).

Start by adding a new, empty layer; this is the layer on which you'll perform the healing. To set a point sample, activate the Healing Brush by pressing J (or press Shift-J to cycle through the healing tools) and then Option-click (Alt-click on a PC) an unblemished area of skin. Then mouse over to the bad skin and brush it away. This tool works really well on wrinkles, scratches, and so on, plus you can make the healing happen on its *own* layer, as explained in *Figure 10-5*. You also get a live preview of the sample point right inside your brush cursor (*Figure 10-5*, bottom left).

> **TIP** When you set a sample point, try choosing a spot that's as near to the problem spot as possible so the texture and color match better. For example, you wouldn't want to repair skin on Aunt Edna's nose with skin from her neck.

When you activate the Healing Brush tool, the Options bar includes the following options:

- **Mode**. You get the same set of blend modes for the Healing Brush as you do with the Spot Healing Brush. Both tools work really well in Normal mode, so you probably don't need to change this setting.

- **Source**. You can use a sample (which you choose by Option-clicking [Alt-clicking on a PC]) or a pattern as your source. Photoshop assumes you want to use a sample, but if you turn on the Pattern option instead, you can choose an option from the Pattern Preset picker to its right. Healing from a pattern is useful if you don't have enough area in your image to heal *from*. For example, if you're using the Healing Brush to remove graffiti from a wall, you can create a pattern from part of the wall's texture and save it as a reusable pattern (page 85).

> **TIP** You can also sample from another open document as long as both images are in the same color mode. Just hop over to the other document, Option-click (Alt-click) to set a sample point, and then click back in your original document to do the healing (use the Window→Arrange submenu to position both document windows so you can see them [see page 56]). This technique is handy when you want to snatch texture from one image and apply it to another; the Healing Brush does the heavy lifting of blending the texture with existing pixels.

POWER USERS' CLINIC

Fixing Spots in Camera Raw

If you find yourself using the Spot Healing Brush repeatedly to fix a pesky speck that appears in the *exact* same place in every photo you take, there's dust on your camera's sensor. Take the camera to a trustworthy shop and have them clean it, or do it yourself with a bit of bravery and the right tools. But fixing the camera doesn't fix the photos you've already taken with it. Fortunately, you can make Camera Raw zap those spots automatically. Here's how:

1. Open all the problem images in Camera Raw (see page 48).

2. Press B to grab Camera Raw's Spot Removal tool and then resize your cursor (a blue-and-white dashed circle) so it's *slightly* bigger than the spot itself. You can use the Size slider on the right side of the window or the bracket keys on your keyboard: The left bracket key ([) makes the brush smaller and the right bracket key (]) makes it bigger.

3. Click the offending spot to set your sample point. When you release your mouse button, Camera Raw displays a green-and-white circle near where you clicked, and the pesky spot should vanish. (New in Camera Raw 8 is the ability to click and *drag* with the Spot Removal brush, which lets you fix non-circular areas.) The green-and-white circle (which is connected to the red-and-white circle by a black-and-white line) marks the *sample point*

Camera Raw is using to remove the spot. Camera Raw usually does a good job of picking a sample point, but if you want to move it to another area that better matches the problem spot, put your cursor inside the green-and-white circle and drag to move the circle somewhere else (a four-headed arrow appears next to your cursor). If you need to fix several specks, repeat this step for each one until they're all gone. Now you're ready to apply the fix to the other open images.

4. Activate all the open images and then click the Synchronize button to apply the changes you just made to them, too. In the Camera Raw window's top-left corner, click the Select All button and then click the Synchronize button below it. In the resulting dialog box, choose Spot Removal from the Synchronize menu.

5. Click OK to close the Synchronize dialog box, and then click the Done button at the bottom of the Camera Raw window to save your changes. Clicking the Open Image button instead would pop 'em *all* open in Photoshop, which could send both your computer and Photoshop into a deep freeze (eek!).

In Camera Raw 8, you can click and drag with the Spot Removal tool to fix problem areas that aren't round. Nice!

Ignore Adjustment layers

Problem area (setting sample point)

Fix in progress

Final result with lowered opacity

FIGURE 10-5

Top: Set the Options bar's Sample drop-down menu to Current & Below so the healing happens on the new layer you've created (just be sure to position it above the Image layer). If you want the tool to sample from all the layers in the document, choose All Layers from the drop-down menu instead. Like the Spot Healing Brush, this tool also has a tablet-pressure option.

Bottom left: When you press the Option key (Alt on a PC), your cursor turns into a target; simply click to set a sample point (top). As you start painting over the bad skin, you see a little crosshairs cursor marking your sample point (bottom) that moves along with your brush.

Bottom right: By healing on another layer, you can lessen the effect of the healing by lowering that layer's opacity. Here it's set to 40 percent.

- **Aligned**. Turn on this checkbox to keep the sample point aligned with your cursor, even if you release your mouse button and move to another area. When this setting is *off*, Photoshop uses the original sample point each time you start to paint even if you move your cursor far away. If your healing requires several brushstrokes, it's helpful to turn this setting on.

- **Sample**. This menu lets you choose which layers you want to sample *from*. To make the healing happen on a separate layer, create a new layer above the one you want to fix and then choose Current & Below. To sample from all visible layers, choose All Layers instead; if you do that, you can make Photoshop ignore Adjustment layers by clicking the button to the right of this menu, which is labeled in *Figure 10-5*, top, and explained next.

- **Ignore Adjustment Layers**. If you added Adjustment layers to alter the color or lighting in the image, you can have Photoshop ignore them by clicking this "slashed" half-black/half-white circle.

- **Always use Pressure for Size**. If you have a graphics tablets (page 517), clicking this button lets you control the size of the Healing Brush's cursor by applying pressure with your stylus (the pressure-sensitive pen that comes with a graphics tablet). Just like with the Spot Healing brush, pressing harder increases brush size and pressing lighter decreases it.

Here's how to use the Healing Brush:

1. **Add a new layer above the one you want to fix.**

   Click the "Create a new layer" button at the bottom of the Layers panel, and name the new layer something like *Healing*. Make sure that it's above the layer you're fixing and that it's active.

2. **Choose the Healing Brush from the Tools panel.**

   Press J to activate this brush, whose icon is an itty-bitty Band-Aid.

3. **In the Options bar, set the Sample menu to Current & Below.**

   This setting tells Photoshop, "Create a sample from the current layer and any other layers that lie below it, but make the fixes happen on the layer I'm currently on." This process gives you a ton of flexibility: You can lower the layer's opacity to lessen the strength of the fix, change the layer's blend mode, or toss it in the trash if you decide you don't like it.

4. **Mouse over to your document and set a sample point by Option-clicking (Alt-clicking on a PC).**

   Photoshop has no clue where the good skin is, so you have to tell it. Option-click (Alt-click) an area of good skin that's similar in texture to the bad skin. (It's OK if the good skin is on the opposite cheek from the bad skin, for example, so long as the texture is the same.) Now you're ready to start healing.

5. **Click (or drag across) the area you want to fix.**

   Mouse over to the problem area and click it, or click and drag to paint it away. You'll see tiny crosshairs marking the sample point as you drag, and a *preview* of the sample area inside your cursor. If you're fixing a small area, like the bags beneath the guy's eyes in *Figure 10-5*, you're probably OK with setting just one sample point. If you're fixing a larger area, you may need to set a new sample point every few brushstrokes to match the tone and texture of what you're fixing.

TIP If you accidentally introduce a repeating pattern when using the Healing Brush, it's easy to fix. Just set another sample point and then paint the error away, or switch to the Spot Healing Brush and then click the problem area.

The Patch Tool

The Patch tool may become one of your favorite Photoshop tools because it's so easy to use and does an amazing job. It works like the Healing Brush in that you set a sample point, but it's often *better* than the Healing Brush for fixing big areas like dark circles or bags beneath tired eyes. It's also handy for removing piercings, tattoos, and with its Content-Aware option, even entire objects.

To use the Patch tool, grab it from the Tools panel (it lives in the same toolset as the Healing and Spot Healing brushes), mouse over to your image, and then drag to draw an outline around the area you want to fix (marching ants appear when you let go of your mouse). Next, click anywhere inside the selected area and hold down your mouse button as you drag to reposition the selection outline so it's over a *good* patch of skin (see *Figure 10-6*, top right). (To move the selection perfectly vertically or horizontally, hold down Shift as you drag.) A live preview of the good skin appears inside the selection as you drag. When you let go of your mouse, Photoshop blends the two areas together.

FIGURE 10-6

If you need to get rid of a new piercing before the parents see it, the Patch tool can get that done fast.

Top: First, draw an outline of the offending area freehand (left). Once you see marching ants, click inside the selection and drag it to a good patch of skin and then release your mouse button (right).

Bottom: Problem solved! The Patch tool can help you keep that piercing secret for a little while longer. And by doing the patching on an empty layer, the original image remains intact.

TIP If you need to adjust the selection while you're drawing it, use the buttons near the left end of the Options bar to add to or subtract from the selection or to create one from two intersecting areas. Better yet, use these keyboard shortcuts: Shift-drag to add to the selection, Option-drag (Alt-drag on a PC) to subtract from it, and Option-Shift-drag (Alt+Shift-drag) to select an intersecting area.

In addition to the "Add to selection," "Subtract from selection," and "Intersect with selection" buttons you're used to from working with the selection tools, the Options bar includes several settings for the Patch tool. The main choice you need to make is what to set the Patch to:

- **Normal**. Straight from the factory, the Patch tool is set to use this mode, and you see the following settings to the right of the Patch menu:

    — **Source**. With this setting, Photoshop takes the texture from the good skin and tries to match it with the color and lighting of the area just outside your original selection. To produce convincing patches, leave this radio button turned on.

    — **Destination**. If you'd rather select the good skin first and *then* drag it atop the bad skin, turn on this radio button.

    — **Transparent**. Turn on this checkbox if you want to copy an area's texture but not its content. For example, if you're working on a photo of a brick wall, you could use this option to copy the texture of the super grungy bricks onto those that look newer, without duplicating the grungy bricks in their entirety. This setting works best in conjunction with the Use Pattern setting, explained next.

    — **Use Pattern**. To apply a pattern to the area you've selected with the Patch tool, click this button and then choose a pattern from the menu next to it. However, you'll rarely use this option because, instead of merely making Photoshop copy and blend pixels from one area to another, it adds the pattern you picked from the menu to the selected area. That said, it's useful if you're trying to add texture to an area that doesn't have any.

TIP It's a little-known fact that you can actually select the area you want to patch *before* activating the Patch tool. That way, you can use any selection method you want—including Quick Mask mode (page 176)—instead of drawing the selection freehand (Chapter 4 has the lowdown on creating selections). You can also draw straight lines with the Patch tool by holding down the Option key (Alt on a PC).

- **Content-Aware**. The Patch tool sports a Content-Aware option (circled in *Figure 10-7*), which greatly improves its ability to remove objects in a realistic way by modifying the pixels *inside* the selected area. When you choose this mode from the Patch menu, you see the following settings instead of the ones described above:

    — **Adaptation**. This menu lets you determine how much blending Photoshop does inside the selected area, and contains five options ranging from Very

Strict to Very Loose. Set the menu to Very Strict for only a slight amount of blending or Very Loose for lots of blending. The other options—Strict, Medium, and Loose—fall somewhere in between. You'll need to experiment with this setting, as the best option varies from image to image depending on what you're trying to remove. You can make a choice from this menu either before or after you use the Patch tool.

— **Sample All Layers**. This option (also circled in *Figure 10-7*) makes Photoshop sample pixel info from *all* layers instead of just the currently active layer. This lets you use the Patch tool on an *empty* layer instead of a duplicate of your Image layer, resulting in a slightly smaller file size.

FIGURE 10-7

Top: By setting the Patch menu to Content-Aware (circled), Photoshop performs a little extra blending to make any lines or patterns inside the selected area match up with its surroundings. This feature is handy if your image contains a horizon line, buildings, or man-made objects.

Middle: After creating a selection, click and drag it to a new area in your image. Here, the selection was moved to the right and positioned so that the horizon lines remain parallel.

Bottom: As you can see, Photoshop did a remarkable job of removing this little guy from the beach scene. (Hey, even bands of superheroes break up!)

Try this technique yourself by visiting this book's Missing CD page at www.missingmanuals.com/cds and downloading the practice file Heroes.jpg.

Zapping Shines and Shadows

Shiny spots (or *hot spots*, as some folks call them) are truly evil. They can ruin a perfectly good photo by making your subject look like a big ol' sweat ball. That's OK if the person just finished a marathon—glistening skin is *expected* then—but not if she's sitting for a portrait. Fortunately, the Clone Stamp tool can get rid of shiny spots and unsightly shadows in a hurry. It works by copying pixels from one area of an image to another (see *Figure 10-8*).

NOTE Take these steps for a spin by visiting this book's Missing CD page at *www.missingmanuals.com/cds* and downloading the practice file *Shine.jpg*

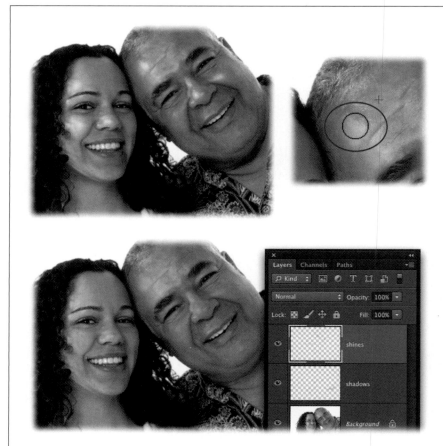

FIGURE 10-8

Top: This sweet photo would be worth framing if the subjects weren't so shiny. To fix it, grab the Clone Stamp tool and set your sample point as close to the shiny area as possible to match tone and texture (right). Be careful not to let the sample point (the crosshairs) go into the shiny area, or you'll replicate the shine.

Bottom: No more shiny spots! The shadows on the subjects' faces and necks have also been lightened. Setting the Options bar's Sample menu (not shown) to All Layers lets you clone on empty layers, keeping your original image safe and sound. Toggle the visibility of the layers you just added off and on for a quick before-and-after comparison.

TIP Be careful not to completely erase *all* the shine and shadows from your images; you want to leave a little bit hanging around so the photos look real. The goal is to remove just enough shines and shadows that viewers aren't *distracted* by 'em.

Here's how to reduce shine and shadows with the Clone Stamp tool:

1. **Open a photo and then add a new layer named** *Shines*.

   Click the "Create a new layer" button at the bottom of the Layers panel, name the layer in the resulting dialog box, and then click OK. Make sure this layer is active and is *above* the Image layer you want to fix. By doing your skin-fixing on this layer, you protect the original image and give yourself the option of reducing the strength of the fix by reducing the layer's opacity.

2. **Grab the Clone Stamp tool from the Tools panel.**

   Press S to activate this tool, which looks like a rubber stamp (in fact, it used to be called the Rubber Stamp tool).

3. **In the Options bar, choose a soft-edged brush and set the Opacity to 20–30 percent.**

   Using a soft-edged brush makes the retouching blend better with the surrounding skin. If you leave the tool's opacity at 100 percent, you'll perform a full-on skin graft and the retouching will be painfully obvious. Lowering the opacity lets you fix the area little by little; the more you paint, the more skin gets cloned (or copied).

   TIP If you're using the Clone Stamp tool to completely *remove* an object from your image or if you're *duplicating* something (you're giving a monster a third eye, say), leave the Opacity set to 100 percent.

   ---

4. **Set the Sample menu to All Layers.**

   To make the cloning (copying) happen on its own layer, you have to tell Photoshop to sample other layers. Now you're all set to start cloning.

5. **Create a sample point for the first shiny part.**

   Mouse over to your image and Option-click (Alt-click on a PC) some non-shiny skin. Make sure this sample point is close to the shiny skin so it'll match.

6. **Click and drag across the shiny area to paint away the shine.**

   As you drag, you see little crosshairs representing the sample point. Keep a close eye on it because if it heads into a shiny patch, you'll paint a shine with a shine. If that happens, don't panic; just set another sample point by performing step 5 again. When you've fixed one shiny spot, mouse over to another and repeat steps 5 and 6.

7. **When all the shiny spots are fixed, add another new layer and name it** *Shadows*.

   Not surprisingly, you'll use this layer to lighten shadowy areas.

8. **Set a new sample point and paint across the shadows.**

   Option-click (Alt-click) to set a sample point as close to the shadowy area as possible, and then drag across the shadows to make 'em lighter. This technique works *wonders* for decreasing double chins, deep crevices, and pretty much any problem area that's too dark (even if it's merely underexposed). Repeat this step until you've taken care of all the shadow problems.

9. **Save the document as a PSD file.**

   That way, you can go back and change your fixes later.

Print that baby out and slap it into the nearest frame!

■ Whitening Teeth

If you've ever enjoyed a big cup of coffee or a Texas-sized goblet of red wine and then had your picture taken, you'll want to bookmark this page. Stained teeth are even more embarrassing than shiny spots, but they're super easy to fix (see *Figure 10-9*). You *could* start by selecting the teeth—the Quick Selection tool works well—and then feather the selection, though it's *much* easier to apply the lightening to the entire image, hide it with a layer mask, and then *reveal* the lightening atop the teeth using the Brush tool.

Here's how to make those pearly whites, well, *white*:

1. **Open an image and zoom in so you can see the subject's teeth.**

   Press ⌘-+ (Ctrl-+ on a PC) to zoom in.

2. **Add a Hue/Saturation Adjustment layer.**

   Click the half-black/half-white circle at the bottom of the Layers panel and choose Hue/Saturation.

3. **Lower the Adjustment layer's saturation and increase its lightness.**

   In the Properties panel, drag the Saturation slider to the left and the Lightness slider to the right. Keep an eye on your image to make sure you don't make the person's teeth unnaturally white. The whole image lightens as you drag the sliders, but don't worry, you'll fix that in the next step.

4. **Fill the Hue/Saturation Adjustment layer's mask with black.**

   Since you'll reveal this adjustment only on your subject's teeth, it's faster to *fill* the mask with black than to *paint* with black to hide the adjustment from the rest of the image. So activate the mask and then press ⌘-I (Ctrl+I) to *invert* the mask. Photoshop fills the mask with black, which hides the adjustment from the entire photo (you'll reveal the lightening on the teeth in the next steps).

FIGURE 10-9

You can easily whiten teeth with a Hue/Saturation Adjustment layer, as shown here. That way, the fixing happens on its own layer so you don't harm the original image, plus you can lower the Adjustment layer's opacity to keep the teeth from looking too white.

Because the teeth are so small, it's easiest to lighten the whole photo and then reveal the lightening only on the teeth using the included layer mask.

You can use the same technique to whiten eyes, too, but you don't have to reduce the Adjustment layer's saturation; just increasing the lightness should do the trick. Page 434 explains another way to accentuate eyes, which also works on teeth. (You can't say Photoshop doesn't give you enough options!)

5. **Activate the Brush tool and choose a soft-edged brush set to paint with white.**

   Press B to grab the Brush tool and, in the Options bar, use the Brush Preset picker to choose a soft-edge brush. Then set your foreground color chip to white by pressing X to flip-flop the color chips.

6. **Click and drag to paint across your subject's teeth.**

   As you paint, Photoshop reveals the lightening in that area. If you mess up and reveal too much, just press X to flip-flop your color chips so that black is on top, and then paint across the area you didn't mean to lighten.

7. **Save the document as a PSD file.**

If you decide to tweak the teeth later, just open the file again, double-click the Hue/Saturation Adjustment layer, and then fiddle with the sliders to your heart's content.

This method will whip most teeth into shape, but if you encounter a set with a *serious* yellow cast, there's one extra step you can take: Click the Hue/Saturation Adjustment layer's thumbnail in the Layers panel; then, in the Properties panel, choose *Yellows* from the unlabeled drop-down menu near the top of the panel and then drag the Saturation slider slightly to the left. Sweet!

■ Super Slimmers

Photoshop has a slew of tools you can use to do some serious slimming like fixing flabby chins, shrinking paunchy waistlines, and instantly shaving off pounds. Tools of the body-sculpting trade include the Pinch and Liquify filters, the Free Transform command, and more, all explained in this section. Read on!

Fixing Flabby Chins

You can suck the life out of a flabby chin with the Pinch filter. Sure it sounds gross, but it makes a *huge* difference and takes mere seconds. All you have to do is duplicate the Image layer and then make a rough selection—the Lasso tool works well—that includes the flab and some of the surrounding details, as shown in *Figure 10-10* (bottom left). Next, choose Filter→Distort→Pinch. In the resulting dialog box, enter *100* in the Amount field, and then click OK. If you need to pinch it a little more, press ⌘-F (Ctrl+F) to run the filter again. Easy, huh?

Liquifying Bulges

Drastic bulges call for drastic action, and the Liquify filter is as drastic as it gets in Photoshop. This filter lets you push, pull, and pucker pixels any which way. You can use it to get a waistline under control, add a smile, enlarge lips, and so on (see *Figure 10-11*).

> **NOTE** In CC, the Liquify filter uses your graphics card's processing power, so it works much faster than it did in previous versions (up to *16 times* faster on large files). It also works with Smart Filters, which lets you use it non-destructively on *any* kind of layer including Shape, Type, and Video. To reopen the Liquify filter for more editing, simply double-click its name in the Layers panel.

FIGURE 10-10

Top: If you click in the Pinch dialog box's preview window and hold down your mouse button, Photoshop shows you the pre-pinched version of the image. You can drag to move the image around (your cursor turns into a little hand, which is circled here). Use the + and – buttons below the preview window to zoom into or out of your image.

Bottom: If you duplicate the Image layer by pressing ⌘-J (Ctrl+J) before running the filter, you won't harm the original image. (Alternatively, you can convert the image for Smart Filters, as explained on page 632).

A fix like this one will earn you loyal clients for life!

Here's how to do some serious bulge busting:

1. **Pop open a photo and convert it into a Smart Object.**

   Happily, the Liquify filter now works with Smart Filters. If your document consists of a single layer, choose Filter→"Convert for Smart Filters" to create a Smart Object. If your document consists of *multiple* layers, activate 'em, and then Control-click (right-click) near one of the layer's names in the Layers panel, and then choose "Convert to Smart Object." Alternatively, you can *start* with a Smart Object by choosing File→"Open As Smart Object."

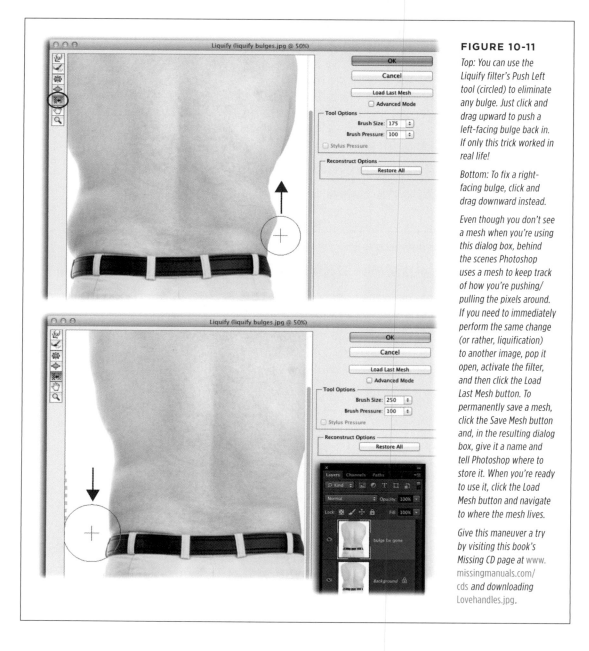

FIGURE 10-11

Top: You can use the Liquify filter's Push Left tool (circled) to eliminate any bulge. Just click and drag upward to push a left-facing bulge back in. If only this trick worked in real life!

Bottom: To fix a right-facing bulge, click and drag downward instead.

Even though you don't see a mesh when you're using this dialog box, behind the scenes Photoshop uses a mesh to keep track of how you're pushing/pulling the pixels around. If you need to immediately perform the same change (or rather, liquification) to another image, pop it open, activate the filter, and then click the Load Last Mesh button. To permanently save a mesh, click the Save Mesh button and, in the resulting dialog box, give it a name and tell Photoshop where to store it. When you're ready to use it, click the Load Mesh button and navigate to where the mesh lives.

Give this maneuver a try by visiting this book's Missing CD page at www. missingmanuals.com/ cds and downloading Lovehandles.jpg.

2. **Choose Filter→Liquify.**

Photoshop opens the humongous Liquify dialog box, which may take over your whole screen (you can resize it by dragging its bottom-right corner).

3. **Grab the Push Left tool and increase the brush size.**

The Liquify dialog box has a small toolbar on its left side. Grab the Push Left tool by pressing O (that's the letter O, not the number zero) or clicking its icon in the toolbar—it's active in *Figure 10-11*). You can use the Tool Options section on the right side of the dialog box to pick a bigger brush, but it's simpler to press the right bracket key (]) to increase the brush size or the left bracket key ([) to decrease it. You can also Control-Option-drag (Alt+right-click+drag on a PC) to change brush size.

4. **Mouse over to the bulge on the right side of the body and drag upward.**

If you need to, move your image around in the dialog box's preview area by pressing the space bar while dragging. Once you've got a good view of the bulge, position your cursor so the crosshairs touch the background and the edge of the brush touches the bulge where it starts down at the waistband. Then push the bulge back toward the torso by dragging *upward*. If you think that's weird, you're not alone; nobody knows why this process scoots pixels to the left, but it does.

5. **Move to the left side of the body and drag downward.**

Press the space bar and drag to move to the other side of the image. This time, position your cursor at the *top* of the bulge and then drag *down* to nudge the pixels to the right. Again, why this tool works this way is a mystery.

6. **Click OK when you're finished.**

> **TIP** To undo a single nudge, press ⌘-Z (Ctrl+Z). To undo *everything* you've done with the Liquify filter *without* closing its dialog box, press Option (Alt) and the dialog box's Cancel button changes to read "Reset"; click it to get the original image back. You can also use the Reconstruct tool discussed below.

You make all the tools in the Liquify dialog box work by holding down your mouse button or by dragging. Here's a rundown of the other tools (*Figure 10-12* gives you an idea of what you can do with 'em):

- **Forward Warp**. The most practical of all the Liquify tools, you can use it to push pixels forward (ahead of your cursor in the direction you're dragging) or Shift-drag with it to push pixels in a straight line. This is another great bulge-buster, waist-nipper, and arm-slimmer, plus you can use it to make your subjects smile whether they want to or not, as *Figure 10-12* shows. Its keyboard shortcut is W.

- **Reconstruct**. Think of this one as a customizable undo brush. If you alter pixels with any of the Liquify dialog box's other tools and then change your mind, you can paint over that area with this tool to restore the pixels to their original state.

If you turn on the Advanced Mode checkbox and then click the Reconstruct button (both shown in *Figure 10-13*, though the Reconstruct button is grayed out), you get a slider that you can use to lower the tool's strength. (If you want to zap *all* of your changes without painting across 'em, click the Restore All button.) Keyboard shortcut: R.

Original   Forward warp   Twirl

Pucker   Bloat

FIGURE 10-12

Here's a sampling of what the Liquify tools can do for you...or to you. (The Mirror and Turbulence tools available in older versions weren't very useful, so they disappeared back in CS6.)

- **Pucker**. This tool collapses pixels in on themselves like the Pinch filter (page 422). You can use it to make a tummy or thigh look smaller, or to shrink a flabby chin, a large nose, and so on. To make it have the opposite effect, press Option (Alt) so that it acts like the Bloat tool. Keyboard shortcut: S.

- **Bloat**. Use this tool to enlarge pixels from the center out. If you're considering collagen injections to fluff up your lips, try this tool first. It's also useful for opening squinty eyes. Keyboard shortcut: B.

- **Hand**. This Hand tool is the same one that you get by pressing the space bar or clicking the hand icon in the Tools panel. You can use it to move the image around when you're zoomed in. Keyboard shortcut: H.

- **Zoom**. This tool lets you zoom in and out of the document, but it's quicker to press ⌘ (Ctrl on a PC) and the + or – key instead. Keyboard shortcut: Z.

By turning on the Advanced Mode checkbox (circled in *Figure 10-13*), you get two more incredibly helpful tools (as well as oodles of controls that appear on the right side of the Liquify dialog box and are explained in *Figure 10-13*):

- **Smooth**. New in Photoshop CC, you can use this tool to smooth an area that you've tweaked, which is helpful in making your changes look more realistic.

When you use this tool, Photoshop applies a very a slight Gaussian Blur to areas of your image that you drag across. Keyboard shortcut: E.

- **Twirl Clockwise.** To spin pixels clockwise as if they were going down a drain, grab this tool. You can click and hold or drag with this tool. Option-drag (Alt-drag on a PC) to make the pixels rotate counterclockwise. Keyboard shortcut: C.

TIP   Aside from freezing body parts that you want to remain unchanged, be sure to freeze any horizontal or vertical lines and patterns that are near the area you're changing. Otherwise, the resulting distortion in those areas will be a dead giveaway that you used the Liquify filter.

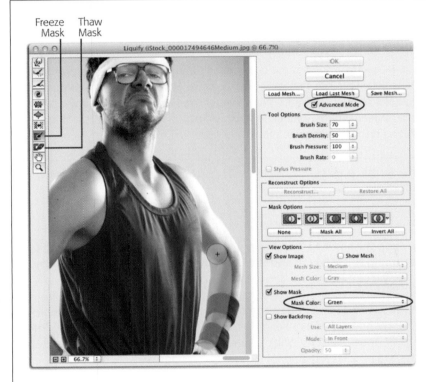

FIGURE 10-13

To slim this guy's waist without messing up his left arm, paint across the arm with the Freeze Mask tool. If you need to mask a large area, click the Mask All button in the Mask Options section, and then use the Thaw Mask tool to paint across the areas you don't want frozen. To flip-flop the mask so the areas that weren't frozen are and vice-versa, click the Invert All button. Click None to thaw the whole image.

To see the mesh described in Figure 10-11 or to change its color from gray to something else, use the controls in the View Options section. The controls in the Backdrop section let you view the contents of another layer (one that you're not editing), which is handy if you're distorting one image to look like it's part of another (say, if you're adding art to an image of a waving flag).

NOTE   From the factory, Photoshop marks frozen areas with a red overlay, though you can change it using the Mask Color drop-down menu (circled in *Figure 10-13*). If you create a selection or layer mask before choosing Filter→Liquify, or if the active layer has transparent areas, that info is accessible via the five drop-down menus in the Mask Options section, shown in *Figure 10-13*. From left to right, the icons are Replace Selection, Add To Selection, Subtract From Selection, Intersect With Selection, and Invert Selection. Click each icon to reveal its menu then choose between Selection, Transparency, and Layer Mask.

- **Freeze Mask**. If the area you want to change is close to an area that you *don't* want changed, you can use this tool to tell Photoshop what to leave alone. As you drag, Photoshop marks the frozen bits with a red overlay, though you can change that color by using the Mask Color drop-down menu circled in *Figure 10-13*. Keyboard shortcut: F.

- **Thaw Mask**. Use this tool to unfreeze any frozen areas, say, if you froze a little too much of the image or you're ready to perform a different kind of edit on that particular spot. As you drag with this tool, Photoshop removes the mask overlay. Keyboard shortcut: D.

> **TIP** While the Liquify filter is great for retouching people pictures, you can also use it to create all manner of special effects including a melting clock that would do Salvador Dali proud!

Slimming with Free Transform

Years ago, Hewlett-Packard came out with a "slimming camera" that promised to make you look five pounds skinner in every picture. Behind the scenes, the camera's software was squishing the sides of the images inward (reducing their width), making people appear slightly thinner. In Photoshop, you can do the *exact* same thing with the Free Transform tool, as shown in *Figure 10-14*.

> **NOTE** Follow along by visiting this book's Missing CD page at *www.missingmanuals.com/cds* and downloading the practice file *Belly.jpg*.

Here's how to lose five pounds instantly:

1. **Pop open the soon-to-be-slimmer photo, duplicate the Background layer by pressing ⌘-J (Ctrl+J), and then turn off the original layer's visibility.**

2. **Summon Free Transform.**

   Press ⌘-T (Ctrl+T) and Photoshop puts a bounding box around the whole image. Grab the little square handle in the middle of the right or left edge of the photo (it doesn't matter which), and then drag the handle toward the center of the image while keeping an eye on the Options bar's W field. You want to make the image 5–8 percent narrower (so the W value is 92–95 percent); if you narrow it any more than that, it'll look stretched out. (You can also type a new width into the W field, which is easier but not as much fun.) When you've got the width just right, release the mouse button and press Return (Enter) to accept the transformation.

FIGURE 10-14

Top: If you do this kind of retouching while you're working in public, be sure to look over both shoulders first—you don't want to reveal this secret to just anyone! Once you've summoned the Free Transform bounding box, you can simply type 95 into the Width field, circled here.

Bottom: By duplicating the Image layer first, you don't mess up your original. Just be sure to turn off the original layer's visibility eye so you can see the newer, slightly slimmer version.

3. **Trim the image to get rid of the newly transparent area.**

Choose Image→Trim and in the resulting dialog box, choose Transparent Areas and then click OK. Photoshop deletes the transparent bits.

This simple retouch is absolutely impossible to spot—*if* you keep it between 5 and 8 percent, that is. Anything more than that and your subject will look decidedly smushed.

■ SELECTIVE SLIMMING

Instead of using Free Transform to squish a whole image, you can use it to squish only a certain part. Just create a selection and *then* summon Free Transform by pressing ⌘-T (Ctrl+T). *Figure 10-15* has the details.

FIGURE 10-15

Top: If you select an area before activating Free Transform, you can use it to shrink just the selected area. (You may need to go back and use the Healing Brush or Clone Stamp tool to blend certain areas after you're finished.)

Bottom: This before-and-after shot shows quite a difference, no?

■ Skin Softeners

Skin is the body's largest organ, but not everyone gives it the respect it deserves. Folks sometimes forget to use sunblock, moisturizer, and so on. This section explains how to make anyone's skin look like it's *really* well cared for. You'll learn how to make it appear soft and glowing, and even how to reduce lines and wrinkles, all without spending tons of money on anti-aging creams.

Selective Blur

One of the fastest ways to smooth skin is to give it a good dose of the Gaussian Blur filter (named for the gentleman who invented this blur method, Carl Gauss). This filter is often the only skin fixer you need, and it's faster than the Healing brushes you learned about earlier in this chapter. The beauty of this filter is that you can run it on a separate layer, lower that layer's opacity, and then use a layer mask to apply it only where you need it (see *Figure 10-16*).

FIGURE 10-16

Just like Robitussin and duct tape, the Gaussian Blur filter can fix darn near anything. It made this woman's skin look nice and smooth by lessening the intensity of her freckles without removing them completely.

And by using Smart Filters, you can use the automatic layer mask that comes along with the filter to hide the effects from her hair, eyes, nostrils, and mouth.

To soften skin, follow these steps:

1. **Open a photo and convert it for Smart Filters.**

   Activate the layer you want to blur and then choose Filter→"Convert for Smart Filters." If your image consists of multiple layers, activate 'em all and then Control-click (right-click) near one of their names and in the Layers panel, choose "Convert for Smart Object."

2. **With the Smart Object activated, choose Filter→Blur→Gaussian Blur.**

   In the resulting dialog box, adjust the Radius slider until the image is severely blurred (a radius of 8 was used to create *Figure 10-16*). Don't worry if you start to lose details; you can tweak the layer's opacity to lessen the effect in a minute. Click OK to close the dialog box and blur the layer.

3. **Fill the Smart Filter's mask with black.**

As you've learned, when it comes to layer masks, black conceals and white reveals. Since you need to keep the majority of the image unblurred so folks can tell it's a face, save yourself some time by starting out with a black mask. To do so, activate the Smart Filter mask (the big white thumbnail beneath the Smart Object) and then press ⌘-I (Ctrl+I) to invert the mask. Photoshop fills the mask with black, hiding all the blurring.

4. **Press B to grab the Brush tool, and then set your foreground color chip to white.**

Peek at the color chips at the bottom of your Tools panel. Press D to set the chips to black and white, and then press X so white hops on top.

5. **With a fairly large, soft-edged brush, paint part of the skin you want to blur.**

Painting with white reveals the blurry layer. Be sure to avoid your subject's eyes, lips, nostrils, and hair. (If you reveal too much of the blur layer, press X to flip-flop color chips and paint that area with black.)

6. **Lower the Gaussian Blur filter's opacity to around 60 percent.**

In the Layers panel, double-click the icon to the right of the words "Gaussian Blur" to open the filter's Blending Options dialog box. There, lower the Opacity field's setting to about 60 percent so the skin looks more natural, and then click OK.

Easy Glamour Glow

Running the Diffuse Glow filter is a quick way to add an ethereal glow to skin. As with Gaussian Blur, you want to create a Smart Object to run this filter on.

Perform the skin-softening technique described in the previous section, and then activate the Smart Object and turn it into *another* Smart Object by Control-clicking (right-clicking) near its layer name and choosing "Convert to Smart Object." It's a good idea to rename the new Smart Object *diffuse glow* so you remember which filter you're about to run. Next, press D to set your color chips to factory-fresh black and white, and then press X until black is on top. Then choose Filter→Filter Gallery and up pops the giant dialog box shown in *Figure 10-17*, top; click the flippy triangle next to the Distort category to expand it, and then click Diffuse Glow. (If you've turned on all the Filter menu's categories as explained on page 635, choose Filter→Distort→Diffuse Glow instead.) *Figure 10-17* explains what to do after all that.

Softening Wrinkles with Faux Dodge and Burn

You've already seen a couple of tools that can reduce wrinkles: the Healing Brush and the Clone Stamp tool. Another option is to slightly lighten or darken the wrinkled area so the wrinkling isn't so severe.

FIGURE 10-17

Top: This filter adds a serious amount of grain, so grab the Graininess slider and drag it all the way left. Set the Glow Amount to about 5 and leave the Clear Amount set to 15. Click OK when you're finished.

Bottom: Back in the Layers panel, double-click the tiny icon to the right of the filter's name and, in the resulting Blending Options dialog box, change the Mode drop-down menu to Luminosity so Photoshop shifts lightness values, not colors. Finally, reduce the Opacity setting to between 40 and 70 percent (50 was used here), and then click OK to close the Blending Options dialog box.

You could reach for the Dodge and Burn tools to perform this task—after all, they're designed to lighten and darken pixels (respectively). These tools hail from the days when photographers developed their own film, disappearing mysteriously into a broom closet with an amber light and emerging hours later with dilated pupils and clothes reeking of pungent chemicals.

Without diving too deeply into what goes on in darkrooms, a photo is created by projecting an image onto special paper. During this process, if you block some of the light by holding an object in front of the light source, the resulting image will be lightened or *dodged* in the area that was exposed to less light. If you *increase* the amount of light that hits a certain area, that part of the image will be darkened or *burned*.

NOTE The Dodge tool's icon looks like a lollipop because you could theoretically block light from hitting your developing image by holding something in front of it that looks like a circle on a stick. The Burn tool's icon looks like a hand because you could use your hand to cover the areas that you want to keep lighter while letting light through your curled fingers. The icons are a bit of a stretch, but they make more sense when you know the techniques they're based on.

In Photoshop, you've got a fair amount of control over how the Dodge and Burn tools work. They each have a Range setting that lets you choose which pixels get altered—shadows, midtones, or highlights. You can also control the strength of the tools' effects by adjusting the Exposure setting, which works kind of like opacity. But it's important to remember that these tools are darn destructive. You have to use them on your original Image layer (or a duplicate of it), and they can both change the color of pixels, which might make the image look worse than it did before you started messing with it. Finally, it's a pain to keep trotting up to the Options bar to adjust the Range and Exposure settings. That said, these tools can certainly lighten and darken parts of an image. Just be sure to duplicate the Image layer first so you're not affecting the original, and lower the Exposure setting in the Options bar before you use 'em.

A *better* solution is to use the Brush tool so it *behaves* like the Dodge and Burn tools. By filling a layer with 50 percent gray and changing its blend mode to Soft Light, you do exactly that (see *Figure 10-18*).

Here's how to do some faux dodging and burning:

1. **Open an image and then, in the Layers panel, Option-click (Alt-click on a PC) the "Create a new layer" button.**

   In the resulting dialog box, name the new layer *Dodge Burn*, choose Soft Light from the Mode menu, turn on the "Fill with Soft-Light-neutral color (50% gray)" checkbox, and then click OK. (Sure, you *could* create a new layer, use the Edit→Fill command to fill it with gray, and then change its Mode setting, but this way is faster.)

2. **Press B to grab the Brush tool and set its opacity to 10–20 percent.**

   To retouch the image gradually, you need to lower the brush's opacity. Yes, the process takes longer this way, but you can dodge and burn little by little, which is better than doing too much at once.

3. **Set your foreground color chip to white for dodging.**

   Take a peek at the color chips at the bottom of your Tools panel. Press D to set them to black and white, and then press X to flip-flop them so white is on top.

4. **Mouse over to your image and paint across the dark wrinkles.**

   Use a small brush to lighten just the shadowy parts of the wrinkles, or else you'll lighten areas that don't need it. It's helpful to zoom *way* in on the image when you're doing detailed work like this by pressing ⌘ (Ctrl on a PC) and the + key. Photoshop switches to a pixel-grid view when you zoom in more than 500 percent (see page 51).

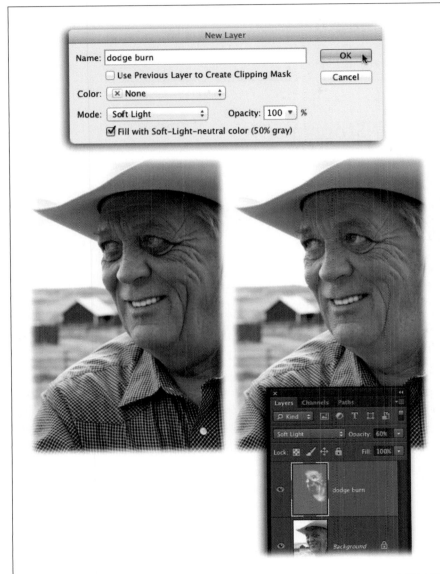

FIGURE 10-18

Top: The New Layer dialog box is a quick way to create a layer to use for faux dodging and burning; press Shift-⌘-N (Shift+Ctrl+N) to call it up. Set the Mode menu to Soft Light, turn on the "Fill with Soft-Light-neutral color (50% gray)" checkbox, and then click OK.

Bottom: When you faux dodge and burn, your subject retains his character but his wrinkles become less distracting. Notice how much brighter his eyes are, too. The whites were dodged and the darker rim of color around the outer edge of each iris was burned.

This technique isn't just good for softening wrinkles; it's also a great way to lighten or darken any part of an image, though it's especially helpful on portraits.

5. **Press X to swap color chips so black is your foreground color and then paint light areas that you need to burn (darken).**

   For example, if the wrinkles are so deep that they cause highlights, you can darken those a little. In *Figure 10-18* the edge of each iris was also darkened to make the man's eyes look brighter.

6. **Lower the Dodge Burn layer's opacity slightly.**

   If you've overdone the changes a bit, you can lower the layer's opacity.

7. **Save the document as a PSD file in case you ever need to go back and alter it.**

TIP For maximum flexibility, you can do your faux dodging on one layer and faux burning on *another* layer. That way, you can lower the opacity of the lightening and darkening layers separately.

▉ Show-Stopping Eyes

One of the simplest yet most impressive eye-enhancing techniques is waiting for you over in Chapter 11 (page 468), which explains how to use sharpening to make eyes stand out. Here in this section, you'll learn how to enhance and whiten eyes, fix red-eye a bazillion different ways, and even how to fix your furry friends' eyes.

Enhancing Eyes

A quick and painless way to make eyes stand out and look sultry is to lighten them by changing their blend mode to Screen. This technique enhances the iris *and* brightens the white bits, as *Figure 10-19* shows. To achieve this effect without duplicating the original layer (which increases your file's size), just use an empty Adjustment layer.

Here's what you do:

1. **Pop open a photo and add an empty Adjustment layer.**

   Click the half-black/half-white circle at the bottom of the Layers panel and choose Levels from the menu. When the Properties panel opens, single-click its tab to close it (you don't need to actually make a Levels adjustment; you're just adding an Adjustment layer that doesn't automatically change your image).

2. **Set the Adjustment layer's blend mode to Screen.**

   Near the top left of the Layers panel, change the drop-down menu from Normal to Screen. When you do, Photoshop makes your whole photo *way* too light, but don't worry—you'll fix it in the next step.

3. **Fill the Adjustment layer's mask with black.**

   Peek at your Layers panel and make sure the Adjustment layer's mask is active (it should have a tiny outline around it). Then, to hide the over-lightening that happened in the previous step, choose Edit→Fill, pick Black from the Use popup menu, and then click OK.

FIGURE 10-19

By using an empty Adjustment layer set to Screen mode, you can add a whole new dimension to your subject's eyes. (The original image is at left, and the adjusted image is on the right.)

The cool thing about this technique is that you can use it to enhance the iris and the white part simultaneously. That said, you could lighten the irises on one layer and the whites of the eyes on another layer in order to control their opacity separately.

4. **Grab the Brush tool and set your foreground color chip to white.**

   Press B to grab the Brush tool and then check the color chips at the bottom of the Tools panel. If white is on top, you're good to go; if it's not, press D to set the chips to black and white and then press X to put white on top. Now you're ready to paint a hole through the mask so the lightening will show through only on your subject's eyes.

5. **Paint the eye area.**

   Mouse over to your image and paint each iris and, if they need lightening, the whites of their eyes. If you mess up, just press X to flip-flop the color chips and paint with black. Be careful not to paint across the dark rim of the iris or you'll lighten it, too.

> **TIP** Sometimes it's helpful to brighten the *entire* eye area including the upper and lower lids, eyeballs, and the area beneath each eye (it's actually faster because you don't have to be so careful with your brushstrokes). If you go that route, click to activate the mask and then run the Gaussian Blur filter (Filter→Blur→Gaussian Blur) set to a small Radius to blur the effect so it looks real, and then continue on with steps 6 and 7.

6. **If you want to enhance the effect further, duplicate the Adjustment layer and then lower its opacity.**

   Once you've got the mask just right, you can intensify the effect by duplicating the Adjustment layer. Press ⌘-J (Ctrl+J) to duplicate the layer and then lower the duplicate's opacity to around 25 percent.

7. **Save the image as a PSD file.**

Ta-da! This technique makes a galactic difference, and your subject's eyes will pop off the page (well, not literally).

Fixing Red-Eye

One of the most annoying things about taking photos with a flash is the creepy red eyes it can give your subjects. Photoshop's Red Eye tool does a good job of fixing most cases of red-eye, though sometimes you'll encounter a really stubborn case that just refuses to go away. That's why it's good to have a few other tricks up your sleeve, including using the Color Replacement tool, using a Hue/Saturation Adjustment layer, or fixing 'em in Camera Raw. This section covers all those techniques.

■ THE RED EYE TOOL

Oh, man, if only *all* of Photoshop's tools were as easy to use as this one! The Red Eye tool is part of the Healing Brush toolset (it looks like an eye with a plus sign next to it). Just grab the tool, mouse over to your image, and then drag to draw a box around the offending eye, as shown in *Figure 10-20*, top. As soon as you let go of your mouse button, Photoshop hunts for the red inside the box and makes it black. That's all there is to it!

> **TIP** If this tool doesn't zap the red-eye completely on the first attempt, press ⌘-Z (Ctrl+Z) to undo the change. Then increase the Pupil Size and Darken Amount settings in the Options bar and have another go at it.

■ THE COLOR REPLACEMENT TOOL

Another option for getting rid of super-stubborn red-eye is the Color Replacement tool. If you set your foreground color chip to black, you can use this tool to replace the red with black. But because this tool is destructive (and there's no way of knowing what kind of job it'll do), it's best to select the eyes and jump them onto their own layer first. Here's how:

FIGURE 10-20

Top: Contrary to what you might think, it's better to draw a box around the whole eyeball rather than just the pupil. For some odd reason, the smaller the box, the less effective the Red Eye tool is.

Bottom: The original image is on the left, and the less evil-looking version is on the right.

1. **Select the eyes and copy them onto another layer.**

   Using the Lasso tool, draw a rough selection around both eyes (grab the whole eye, not just the pupil) and then press ⌘-J (Ctrl+J) to jump them onto their own layer. That way, if this technique goes south, you can toss this layer and start over. (Alternatively you can duplicate the whole Image layer.)

2. **Grab the Color Replacement tool from the Tools panel.**

   It's hiding in the Brush toolset, and it looks like a brush with a tiny curved arrow and a square (the square is supposed to represent the foreground color chip). You can press Shift-B repeatedly to cycle through this toolset.

3. **Set your foreground color to black.**

   Press D to set your color chips to black and white, and then press X until black hops on top. Alternatively, you can set the foreground color by Option-clicking (Alt-clicking on a PC) an eyelash or other black part of the eye.

4. **In the Options bar, set the Mode menu to Hue, the Limits menu to Contiguous, and the Tolerance field to around 30 percent.**

   Choosing the Hue blend mode makes the tool replace color without altering its brightness. The Contiguous setting tells Photoshop to replace only the red pixels that are clustered in one spot and not separated by other colors. And the Tolerance setting determines how picky the tool is: Lower numbers make it pickier; higher numbers result in a color-replacing free-for-all.

5. **Paint the red away.**

   You'll want to use a small brush for this maneuver. Press the left bracket key ([) to cycle down in brush size (the right bracket key cycles up), or Control-Option-drag (Alt-right-click-drag on a PC) to the left or right to decrease or increase your brush size, respectively. When you've got a size that looks good, mouse over to the pupils and paint over the red, being careful to touch *only* the red with the cursor's crosshairs.

6. **When you're done painting, use the Eraser tool or a layer mask to clean up the area just outside the pupil, if necessary.**

   If you end up with a little black outside the pupil, use the Eraser tool to fix it because the tool erases to the original layer below. Press E to activate the Eraser and carefully paint away any extra black pixels. Alternatively, you can add a layer mask to the eye layer and then paint with black to hide the excess black.

7. **Save the document as a PSD file and call it a day.**

You won't need to use this technique very often, but at least you know it just in case!

■ **FIXING RED-EYE IN CAMERA RAW**

Camera Raw's Red Eye Removal tool looks and works similar to Photoshop's. It's handy to have this option in Camera Raw because, if you're shooting in raw format and you don't need to do any other editing in Photoshop, you don't have to switch programs just to fix red eyes. After you open the image in Camera Raw (page 48), press E to grab the Red Eye Removal tool. Then simply drag to draw a box around the eyeball, as shown in *Figure 10-21*, and let go of your mouse button.

Fixing Animal White-Eye

OK, *technically* animals aren't people—though to some folks (your author included) they might as well be. Our furry friends also have a version of red-eye; it's called *white-eye*, and it can ruin their photos, too. White-eye is actually more challenging to fix than red-eye because there aren't any pixels in the eye left to work with—the pupils turn white, gold, or green. The Red Eye tool won't work because the pupils aren't red, and the Color Replacement tool won't work because there's no color to replace. The solution is to select the pupil and fill it with black, and then add a couple of well-placed glints (tiny light reflections) to make the new pupils look real (see *Figure 10-22*).

Here's how to fix your furry friend's eyes:

1. **Open the image and select the colored pupils.**

   Since you're selecting by color, you can use either the Magic Wand or the Quick Selection tool; just click one pupil and then Shift-click the other.

FIGURE 10-21

If drawing a box around the offending red-eye doesn't zap it completely, you can use the Pupil Size and Darken sliders on the right side of the Camera Raw window (not shown here). New in Camera Raw 8, the sliders give you a live preview as you drag 'em (it's hard to believe that wasn't always the case!).

When you're finished, a black-and-white circle appears around the pupil, letting you know that Camera Raw made the fix. To get rid of the box, turn off the Show Overlay checkbox or press V. Click Done to save your changes and close the Camera Raw window.

2. **Feather the selection with Refine Edge.**

   Once you've got marching ants around the pupils, click the Refine Edge button in the Options bar. In the resulting dialog box, set the Feather field to 1 pixel and the Smooth field to 1. To make sure you get *all* the white or gold bits, you might want to expand the selection 10–20 percent or so by dragging the Shift Edge slider to the right. When you're finished tweaking the sliders, click OK.

   NOTE Remember, the settings in the Refine Edge dialog box are sticky—they reflect the last settings you used. So take a second to make sure *all* the sliders are set to zero, save for the ones mentioned here.

3. **Add a new layer named *Pupils*.**

   Click the "Create a new layer" button at the bottom of the Layers panel, name the layer, and make sure it's at the top of the layer stack.

FIGURE 10-22

Selecting the blown-out pupils (top), adding some black paint, and topping it off with two flicks of a white brush to add a glint transforms this kitty from creepy to cute in minutes.

4. **Fill the selection with black.**

   To recreate the lost pupil, press D to set your color chips to black and white and then press X until black is on top. Next, press Option-Delete (Alt+Backspace on a PC) to fill the selection with black. If the color doesn't seem to reach the edges of the selection (which can happen if you feathered or smoothed the edges a little too much in step 2), fill it again by pressing Option-Delete (Alt+Backspace). Once the pupils are filled with black, get rid of the marching ants by pressing ⌘-D (Ctrl+D).

5. **Add another new layer and name it *Glint*.**

   You'll want to soften the glints you're about to create by lowering their opacity, so you need to put them on their own layer.

6. **Grab the Brush tool, set your foreground color to white, and then add the glints.**

Press X to flip-flop color chips and, with a very small brush (10 pixels or so), click once in the left eye to add a glint to mimic the way light reflects off eyes (every eye has one). Next, click in the *exact* same spot in the right eye to add a sister glint. Then lower the glint layer's opacity to about 75 percent.

7. **Save the document as a PSD file.**

Pat yourself on the back for salvaging such a great shot of your pet.

◼ Other Creative Madness

The retouching techniques you've learned thus far are relatively benign. Save for the Liquify filter, you haven't really done anything *drastic* to your images…until now. In this section, you'll learn how to use Photoshop's new Content-Aware Move tool to make objects (even buildings!) bigger, smaller, taller, or shorter, or to move objects around within in an image. You'll also find out how to reshape pixels using the Puppet Warp command. Read on for some serious image-changing voodoo!

Repositioning and Recomposing with Content-Aware Move

The Content-Aware Move tool lets you ever so slightly change the height, width, and position of a selected object. It uses Photoshop's Content-Aware technology to match up any lines or patterns in your selection so the changes look realistic.

To scoot an object around, pop open an image and create a new, empty layer (this is where you'll do the actual pixel moving). Then activate the Content-Aware Move tool by choosing it from the Tools panel—it lives in the Healing toolset—or by pressing Shift-J until you see its icon appear (it looks like two arrows overlapping to form an X). In the Options bar, set the Mode menu to *Move* and turn on Sample All Layers. Then, mouse over to your image and drag to create a selection around an object, like the left-hand soapbox racer in *Figure 10-23*, and then drag it elsewhere in the image.

> **NOTE** Follow along by visiting this book's Missing CD page at *www.missingmanuals.com/cds* and downloading the practice file *Racers.jpg*.

The Content-Aware Move tool also lets you change the height and width of an object to, for example, make a building taller, wider, shorter, or thinner. To do so, create a new Image layer, activate the Content-Aware Move tool, and then choose *Extend* from the Options bar's Mode drop-down menu. Then simply select the object you want to change and drag it up to increase its height, or drag left/right to increase its width. This feature works only if you make *very* small changes, and even then you'll probably need to use the Spot Healing Brush or the Clone Stamp tool (on empty layers, of course) to make the edit look real.

New selection   Intersect with selection

Add to selection   Subtract from selection

FIGURE 10-23

Top: Use the new, add, subtract, and intersect buttons labeled here to alter your selection. The Mode menu lets you tell Photoshop what you want to do: Move or Extend. The Adaptation menu lets you determine how much blending Photoshop does in the selected area, from a lot (Very Loose) to not very much (Very Strict). (These options are explained back on pages 416–417.)

Middle: Once you've selected the object, drag it to another position. As you drag, you see an overlay that includes position info.

Bottom: If you've got a good-sized chunk of background around the item you're moving and you're not moving it very far, this tool does a good job. That said, you'll need to use the Spot Healing Brush (set to Content-Aware) or the Clone Stamp tool to clean up areas that went astray (just be sure to perform the cleanup on new empty layers, positioned above the Content-Aware Move layer).

TIP   Just as with the Patch tool, you can also create a selection *before* activating the Content-Aware Move tool. If you've already created an empty layer where you'll do the aforementioned scooting, go ahead and grab the Quick Selection tool and, in the Options bar, turn on the Sample All Layers checkbox to make the tool look *through* the empty layer to where the pixels live below. Once you've made the selection, switch back to the Content-Aware Move tool and scoot to your heart's content.

Reshaping Objects with Puppet Warp

The Puppet Warp command made its debut back in Photoshop CS5, and most folks are *still* trying to figure out how and when to use it. It lets you distort individual objects while leaving the rest of the image unscathed (though it can warp whole images, too, if you like). You can use it to make subtle changes such as repositioning your subject's hair, or do more drastic stuff like repositioning an arm, leg, tail, or trunk.

It's a complicated process that puts *all* of your Photoshop skills to work. To warp an item, you select it, copy it onto another layer, remove it from the original layer, and then drop a series of markers (called *pins*) onto the copied object to let Photoshop know what you want to change. Photoshop places a grid-like mesh atop the object that contains handles you can drag to distort it. Once you finish moving the handles, Photoshop tries to adjust the *rest* of the image so it matches, making your alteration look real. While you certainly won't use this command daily, it can come in handy for moving your subject's arm or leg into a more visually pleasing or amusing position, as shown in *Figure 10-24*.

> **NOTE** You can use Puppet Warp on darned near everything: Image layers, Smart Objects (a good choice because you can distort 'em nondestructively); Shape and Type layers (provided you've converted them into Smart Objects first, or else you have to rasterize 'em); as well as pixel- and vector-based layer masks.

The Puppet Warp command doesn't work on locked Background layers, so either duplicate that layer or, better yet, use Puppet Warp on a Smart Object to protect your original, as described in the steps starting on page 447. Once you choose Edit→Puppet Warp, you see the following settings in the Options bar:

- The **Mode** menu lets you tell Photoshop how *elastic* (stretchable) you want the mesh to be. Your choices are Rigid (handy for more precise warping of objects you've marked with pins), Normal (the general-purpose mode), and Distort (great for warping an image shot with a wide-angle lens or creating an interesting texture for mapping onto another image [page 303]).

- **Density** controls the spacing of the mesh's points. Adding more points makes your change more accurate, but it'll take Photoshop longer to process. Fewer points speed up the process, though depending on the object you're warping, it might not look as real.

- **Expansion** lets you expand or contract the outer edge of the mesh by a pixel value. Higher numbers expand the outer edge (even beyond your document's edges), and lower values shrink it. Entering a negative value shrinks the mesh so it's inside your document's edges but also shrinks the image.

- **Show Mesh** turns the mesh on or off. If you turn this setting off, you'll see only the pins you dropped on the image. A better method is to *temporarily* hide the mesh by pressing ⌘-H (Ctrl+H); use the same keyboard shortcut to turn it back on.

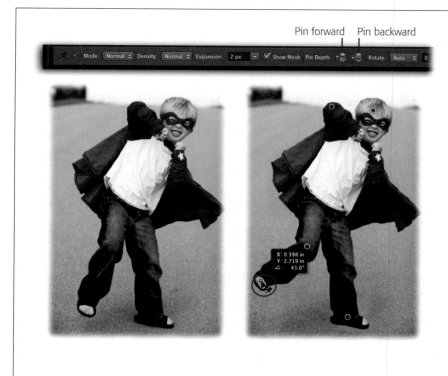

Pin forward   Pin backward

FIGURE 10-24

Top: Here are the Puppet Warp command's Options bar settings.

Bottom: Once you've prepared your subject or object for use with Puppet Warp as described in the steps on page 447, you can start dropping pins. To move this boy's leg and exaggerate the kick, drop pins onto the parts you want to move (his left foot) as well as the parts you want to remain in place (his left knee, arm, head, and right foot). (The original karate kid is shown on the left.)

If everything seems to go to heck in a handbasket and you want to start over, click the Options bar's Remove All Pins button (not shown—its icon is a curved arrow over a line).

- The **Set Pin Forward/Backward** buttons (labeled in *Figure 10-24*) let you determine how the objects you've warped overlap each other. Once you start setting pins, Photoshop treats the pinned areas like layers, which means you can change their stacking order. For example, if you set pins on your subject's hand and elbow and then drag the pinned hand atop his chest, the hand appears in front of his chest. However, if you then click the Set Pin Backward button once, Photoshop moves the pinned hand *behind* his chest instead. Depending upon how many pins you've set and how you've warped the object(s), you may have to click these buttons several times to arrange the object(s) to your liking.

- **Rotate** lets you turn the item you've dropped pins onto while you're dragging it into a new shape or position. Straight from the factory, this menu is set to Auto, which means the mesh around a pin automatically rotates as you drag the pin. If you want the mesh to rotate a fixed number of degrees instead, click to activate the pin and then press and hold the Option (Alt on a PC) key, and Photoshop displays a light gray circle around the pin representing rotation angle; then just click and drag around the circle to rotate the mesh (when you do, this menu changes to Fixed). When you're finished, release the Option/Alt key. *Figure 10-25* (top) shows this maneuver in action.

It's next to *impossible* to grasp how this command works until you try it. Go to this book's Missing CD page at *www.missingmanuals.com/cds* and download the practice file *Karate.jpg,* and then follow these steps to change the position of your subject's limbs:

1. **Open an image, duplicate the Background layer, and then turn off the visibility of the original layer.**

   Puppet Warp won't work on a locked Background layer, plus this command is about as destructive as it gets! So press ⌘-J (Ctrl+J on a PC) to duplicate the Background layer and then turn off the visibility of the original. (Using a Smart Object won't work either because you'll use the Edit→Fill command in step 4.)

2. **Create a selection of the object you want to change (like the kid in *Figure 10-24*, bottom left), jump it onto a new layer named *karate kid*, and then turn off the visibility of that new layer.**

   Select the item you want to warp using the techniques you learned back in Chapter 4 (the Quick Selection tool was used here). If necessary, click the Refine Edge button in the Options bar to fine-tune your selection. Once you have the selection just right, press ⌘-Option-J (Ctrl+Alt+J) to put the object on a new layer.

3. **Activate the duplicate Background layer you created in step 1, load a selection of the *karate kid* layer's contents, and then expand the selection to include more of the background.**

   To keep from creating another instance of the object you're warping, you have to remove that object from the original image (or rather, the copy you made in step 1), which is easy to do by expanding the selection and then using the Fill command's Content-Aware option. Click to activate the copy of the Background layer and then ⌘-click (Ctrl-click on a PC) the *karate kid* layer's thumbnail to load it as a selection. Next, expand the selection to include a little of the image's background by choosing Select→Modify→Expand. In the resulting dialog box, enter 10 pixels if you're working with a low-resolution image (use a higher number for a high-resolution image) and then click OK. Photoshop expands the selection by the amount your entered.

4. **Use the Fill command's Content-Aware option to delete the object from the image, and then deselect.**

   Because you expanded the selection to include more of the background in the previous step, Photoshop has an easier time removing the object from the image. Simply choose Edit→Fill and, in the resulting dialog box, make sure the Use menu is set to Content-Aware; then click OK. (If some of the original item is still visible, create a new, empty layer, and then use the Spot Healing Brush, Healing Brush, or Clone Stamp tool to fix it.) When the object is history, press ⌘-D (Ctrl+D) to deselect everything.

5. **Activate the *karate kid* layer, turn its visibility on, and then Control-click (right-click) near the layer's name in the Layers panel and choose "Convert to Smart Object" from the shortcut menu that appears.**

Using Puppet Warp on a Smart Object lets you come back and edit your warping later on, provided you save the document as a PSD file (which of course you will!). Now you're *finally* ready to start warping the object.

6. **Choose Edit→Puppet Warp and then, in the Options bar, turn off the Show Mesh checkbox.**

As soon as you summon Puppet Warp, Photoshop plops a mesh on top of the layer's contents (the kid), which keeps you from seeing anything useful. Turn off the Show Mesh checkbox so you can see what you're doing.

7. **Click in the image to drop pins on the object you want to move *and* on the items you want to remain in place.**

You can think of dropping pins as placing control handles that you can then click and drag to move or spin to rotate the object underneath them. Not only do these pins let you tell Photoshop which parts of the image you want to warp or move, but they also anchor areas in place—if you don't drag or spin a pin, the area where you placed it stays perfectly still. To move this little boy's left leg, drop a pin on his left foot and knee. Next, lock the rest of his body in place by dropping pins on his left elbow, head, and right foot. (If you don't, his whole body will rotate as you drag the pin on his left foot.)

TIP If you try to add a pin too close to an existing one, Photoshop displays an error message to let you know. The fix is to either set the Options bar's Density drop-down menu to More Points, or just press ⌘-Z (Ctrl+Z) to remove the pin and then click to place it a little farther away from the others.

---

8. **Click to activate the pin on his left foot and then drag it slightly up and to the left (as shown in *Figure 10-24*, bottom right).**

As you drag the pin, the pixels beneath it move, stretch, or contract depending on how far you drag and in what direction. To make the change look realistic, don't drag the pins very far (you don't have to move 'em much to create seriously cartoonish results). Once you start moving pins, you can change the stacking order of the pixels underneath them by using the Pin Depth buttons in the Options bar (labeled back in *Figure 10-24*, top). For example, if you swing the kid's foot to the *right* instead of left, his foot moves *behind* his right leg. Click the "Set pin depth forward" button to bring his foot forward in front of his leg.

To *rotate* the pixels beneath a pin rather than moving them, click to activate the pin (*Figure 10-25*, top left) and then press and hold Option (Alt) and put your cursor *near* the pin (but not directly over it); when a circle appears around the pin, drag clockwise or counterclockwise around it to rotate those pixels (you'll see the degree of rotation appear next to your cursor, as shown in *Figure 10-25*, top right).

9. **When you're finished, press Return (Enter) and then save the document as a PSD file.**

Photoshop adds a new layer named Puppet Warp beneath the Smart Object's mask (*Figure 10-25*, bottom) and your pins disappear. Saving the file as a PSD lets you edit the pins any time you want; simply double-click the Puppet Warp layer in the Layers panel and they reappear.

As you might imagine, using Pupped Warp involves a *lot* of trial and error, but isn't that what Photoshop is all about? (Just imagine what this command could let you do to photos of your ex!) A more *practical* use for Puppet Warp is to twist and turn ordinary objects into something extraordinary. For example, you could contort a piece of rope or barbed wire into letters or shapes. The possibilities are limited only by the amount of time you've got to experiment.

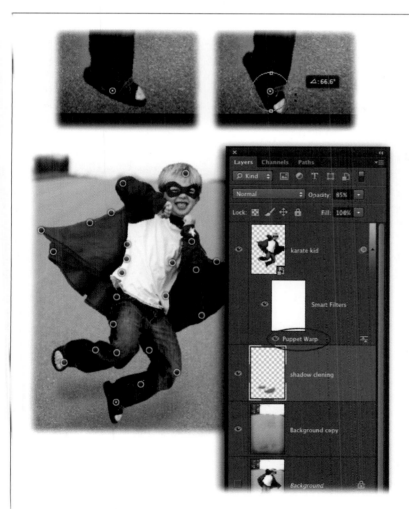

FIGURE 10-25

Top: To spin the pixels beneath a pin, click to activate the pin (left), and then press and hold Option (Alt) to reveal this handy circle (right); just click and drag around the circle when it appears. Photoshop displays the rotation angle as you drag.

Bottom: Here you can see all the pins needed to expand his cape and move his legs so it appears that he's jumping and kicking at the same time. To edit the pins later, just double-click the Puppet Warp layer in the Layers panel (circled).

Compare this image to the original photo shown back in Figure 10-24 and you'll really appreciate the power of Puppet Warp!

TIP If you want to move several pins at once, you can activate more than one pin by Shift-clicking them, or by Control-clicking (right-clicking) one pin and then choosing Select All Pins from the resulting shortcut menu. To delete a pin, Option-click (Alt-click) it (your cursor turns into a tiny pair of scissors); to delete *multiple* pins, activate them and then press Delete (Backspace).

The Art of Sharpening

You know the saying "last but not least"? Well, that definitely applies to *sharpening*—a digital attempt to improve an image's focus. Because it's such a destructive process, it's generally the last thing you do before sending images off to the printer or posting on the Web. Sharpening is *muy importante* because it brings out details and makes images pop, but it's also one of the least understood processes in Photoshop. In addition to teaching you *how* to sharpen, this chapter also gives you some guidelines about *when* and *how much* to sharpen, so you're not just guessing.

In case you're wondering which of your photos need sharpening, the answer is all of 'em. If your image came from a digital camera or a scanner, it needs sharpening. Why? In their comprehensive book on sharpening, *Real World Image Sharpening, Second Edition* (*www.lesa.in/rwsharpen*), Jeff Schewe and the late Bruce Fraser explain that images get softened (their pixels lose their hard edges) when cameras and scanners capture light and turn it into pixels. Then, those images get softened even more when they're printed. (Even if you create an image from scratch in Photoshop, the same deterioration occurs if you shrink it.)

While Photoshop is pretty darned good at this sharpening business, it's not magic—it can't take an out-of-focus image and make it *tack sharp* (photographer slang for super-duper sharp, derived from the phrase "sharp as a tack"). One of the few ways you can produce well-focused photos is to shoot using a tripod (to keep the camera stable) and a remote (so you don't move the camera when you press the shutter button), and use a lens (or camera body) that includes an image stabilizer. The program doesn't have a magical "make my blurry picture sharp" button, though CC's new Shake Reduction filter gets you closer to that reality. What Photoshop *can* do is take an in-focus image and make it nice and crisp. But before you start sharpening, it's important to understand exactly how the whole process works. Read on.

NOTE You can also save a *slightly* blurry image by using the Emboss filter. Flip to page 668 for the scoop.

What Is Sharpening?

Sharpening an image is similar to sharpening a kitchen knife. In both instances, you're emphasizing edges. On a knife, it's easy to identify the edge. In a digital image, it's a little more challenging: The edges are the areas where vastly different colored pixels meet (areas of high-contrast), as shown in *Figure 11-1*.

Unsharpened

Oversharpened

FIGURE 11-1

Left: It's easy to spot the edges in this image because its contrast is pretty high, especially between the antlers and the light background.

Right: In this before-and-after close-up of the Chihuahua's antlers—who does that to their pet?—see how the edges are emphasized after some overzealous sharpening (bottom)? The weird white glow around the antlers is the dreaded sharpening halo.

When you sharpen an image—whether in Photoshop, Camera Raw, or a darkroom—you exaggerate the edges in the image by increasing their contrast: Where two colors meet, you make the light pixels a little lighter and the dark pixels a little darker. Though it may sound similar to increasing the overall contrast of the image, it's not.

When you run one of Photoshop's sharpen filters, the program analyzes your image and increases the contrast *only* in areas it thinks are edges (and, as you'll learn in a bit, you have some control over what it considers an edge).

Sharpening is a bit of an art: If you don't sharpen enough (or at all), your image will look unnaturally soft and slightly blurred; if you sharpen too much, you'll get a *sharpening halo*, a nasty white or light-colored gap between light and dark pixels (*Figure 11-1*, bottom right). But if you sharpen just the right amount, no one will notice the sharpening—they'll just know that the image looks really good.

One of the downsides to sharpening is that it also emphasizes any kind of *noise*— graininess or color specks—in your image. One way around that problem is to get rid of the noise *before* you sharpen, or at least have a go at reducing it (see the box on page 455 for tips).

Now that you know what sharpening does, you're ready to give it a whirl. The next few pages focus on basic sharpening techniques; more advanced methods are discussed later in this chapter.

◾ Basic Sharpening

If you've ever peeked inside the Filter menu at the top of Photoshop's screen, you've probably noticed a whole category of filters devoted just to sharpening. They include the following:

- **Shake Reduction.** New in Photoshop CC, this filter attempts to fix the blurriness introduced by camera movement (called *camera shake*) when using slow shutter speeds and a long focal length (meaning you're zoomed in to shoot something far away). If you're not shooting with a tripod and a remote shutter release, it's impossible *not* to move the camera a little bit when you breathe or press the shutter button. This filter works best on images with decent lighting, very little noise or specular highlights (geometric shapes caused by reflections of light), and *without* moving subjects. You can also use this filter to make blurry text easier to read, which should make forensic scientists jump for joy.

- **Sharpen, Sharpen Edges, Sharpen More**. When you run any of these filters, you leave the sharpening up to Photoshop (scary!). Each filter analyzes your image, tries to find the edges, and creates a relatively narrow sharpening halo (*Figure 11-1*, bottom). However, none of these filters gives you any control, which is why you should forget they're even there and stick with the next two filters instead.

- **Smart Sharpen**. When you see three little dots (...) next to a menu item (like there are next to this filter's name in the Filter→Sharpen submenu), it means there's a dialog box headed your way—and when it comes to sharpening, that's good! Smart Sharpen lets you control how much sharpening happens in your image's shadows and highlights, and it lets you pick which kind of mathematical voodoo Photoshop uses to do the sharpening. This filter has been redesigned in CC, as you'll discover on page 459.

- **Unsharp Mask**. This filter has been the gold standard sharpening method for years because, until the Smart Sharpen filter came along in CS2, it was the only one that gave you dialog box–level control over how it worked. Most folks still prefer this filter because it's easy to use and quick (it runs faster than the Smart Sharpen filter). Page 456 has the lowdown.

> **NOTE** Though it doesn't live inside the Filter→Sharpen submenu, the High Pass filter is a popular sharpening tool because it does a great job and it's simpler to use than Unsharp Mask—it has just one setting to tweak instead of three. You can give it a spin on page 462.

No matter which filter you choose, sharpening is a destructive process, so it's a good idea to protect your image by following these guidelines:

- **Resize the image first**. Make sharpening your last step before you print the image or post it on the Web—in other words, after you've resized and retouched it. Because pixel size depends on an image's resolution and sharpening has different effects on different-sized pixels, it's important to sharpen the image after you make it the size you want.

- **Get rid of any noise first**. If you see any funky color specks or grains that shouldn't be in the image, get rid of them *before* you sharpen or they'll look even worse. The box on page 455 tells you how.

- **Sharpen the image on a duplicate layer or run it as a Smart Filter**. Before you run a sharpening filter, activate the Image layer and duplicate it by pressing ⌘-J (Ctrl+J). That way, you can toggle the sharpened layer's visibility on and off to see before and after versions of the image. You can also restrict the sharpening to certain areas by adding a layer mask to the sharpened layer, and reduce the sharpened layer's opacity if the effect is too strong (page 466 has tips for sharpening a multilayered file). Better yet, convert your Image layer for Smart Filters so Photoshop does the sharpening on its own layer *and* includes a layer mask automatically; page 468 has the details.

- **Change the sharpening layer's blend mode to Luminosity**. Because you're about to make Photoshop lighten and darken a whole lot of pixels, you risk having the colors in your image shift. However, if you change the sharpening layer's blend mode to Luminosity, the sharpening affects only the brightness of the pixels, not their color. (If you use the Smart Filter method described on page 468, change the *filter's* blend mode to Luminosity instead, using the Blending Options dialog box.) This trick does virtually the same thing as changing the color mode to Lab and then sharpening the Lightness channel, but it's a whole lot faster.

- **Sharpen the whole image and the details separately**. As you learned at the beginning of this chapter, every image needs sharpening, but what if you want certain parts of the image, like eyes and hair, to really stand out? If you sharpen enough for those details, then the rest of your image can look too sharp. The fix is to apply two rounds of sharpening: one for the entire image and another round for the details. Pages 468–471 explains how to do this without harming your original.

In the following pages, you'll learn various ways to sharpen, starting with the most popular method to date: the Unsharp Mask filter.

Keeping the Noise Down

Shooting in low-light conditions can introduce noise—black-and-white or colored speckles—into your images. This is especially true if you've increased your camera's ISO (it's light sensitivity setting). If that happens, be sure to reduce or get rid of the noise before you sharpen the image, or you'll end up sharpening the noise along with the edges (though CC's revamped Smart Sharpen filter now sports a Reduce Noise slider).

Photoshop gives you a variety of noise-reducing filters that are discussed on page 525. All of 'em work by *reducing* the amount of contrast between different-colored pixels—a process that's the exact opposite of sharpening, which is why removing noise also reduces sharpness!

(Because all filters run on the currently active layer—meaning they affect your original image—be sure to convert your image to a Smart Object before running a noise-reducing filter so the filter runs non-destructively, or run it on a duplicate Image layer.)

The aptly named Reduce Noise filter is the best of the bunch because it gives you more control than the others. To use it, choose Filter→Noise→Reduce Noise and, in the resulting dialog box, adjust the following settings:

- **Strength**. If you've got a lot of *grayscale noise*—luminance or brightness noise that looks like grain or splotches—or *color noise* that looks like little specks of color, increase this setting to make Photoshop reduce the noise in each color channel. This setting ranges from 1 to 10 (it's set to 6 unless you change it).

- **Preserve Details**. You can increase this setting to protect the detailed areas of your image, but if you do, Photoshop can't reduce as much grayscale noise. For best results, tweak this setting along with the Strength setting and find a balance between the two.

- **Reduce Color Noise**. If there are colored specks in your image, try increasing this setting so Photoshop zaps 'em.

- **Sharpen Details**. Because every noise-reducing filter blurs your overall image, this option lets you bring back some of the sharpness. However, resist the urge to use this option and set it to 0%; it's better to go with one of the other sharpening methods described in this chapter instead.

- **Remove JPEG Artifact**. If you're dealing with an image that's gotten blocky because it was saved as a low-quality JPEG—or because it was saved as a JPEG over and over again—turn on this checkbox and Photoshop tries to reduce that Lego look.

- **Advanced**. This setting lets you tweak each color channel individually (for more on channels, see Chapter 5). If the noise lives in one or two color channels—it's usually notoriously bad in the blue channel—turn on this radio button and adjust each channel's settings individually. (Because Reduce Noise can make images blurry, it's better to adjust as few channels as possible.)

Once you're finished modifying these settings, click OK to run the filter and then toggle the filter's (or duplicate layer's) visibility off and on to see how much effect the filter had. (You can preview the effect on your image by pressing P while the filter's dialog box is open.) You can also use the Smart Filter's included layer mask to restrict the noise reduction to certain parts of the image (handy if the noise is only in the shadows, for example).

And if you determine that the filter didn't help one darn bit, run—don't walk!—over to page 778 to find a third-party, noise-reduction plug-in that can. Or, if buying a plug-in isn't in your budget, flip to page 211 to learn how to sharpen individual channels, which lets you bypass the noise-riddled channel altogether.

You may now proceed with sharpening your image.

Sharpening with Unsharp Mask

This filter is many people's favored sharpening method, but its name is confusing—it sounds like it does just the opposite of sharpen. The odd name came from a technique used in darkrooms, which involves using a *blurred* (or "unsharp") version of an image to produce a *sharper* one. In Photoshop, the Unsharp Mask filter studies each pixel, looks at the contrast of nearby pixels, and decides whether they're different enough to be considered an edge (you control how picky the filter is using the Threshold setting, discussed below). If the answer is yes, Photoshop increases the contrast of those pixels by lightening the light pixels and darkening the dark pixels.

> **TIP** Any time you see a preview in a dialog box (like the one in *Figure 11-2*), you can click the preview and hold your mouse button down to see a before version of the image (in this case, the unsharpened version). You can also drag to move the preview around or click the little + and − buttons below the preview to zoom in or out. You can also use keyboard shortcuts: ⌘-click (Ctrl-click) to zoom in, and Option-click (Alt-click) to zoom out.

FIGURE 11-2

Before the Smart Sharpen filter came along, Unsharp Mask was the only sharpening method in Photoshop that gave you any level of control.

It's OK if your image looks a little too sharp onscreen. The onscreen pixels are much bigger than the ones your printer prints and, as mentioned earlier, the printing process itself softens the pixels a little. So to get a printed image that's nice and crisp, make the onscreen image look a little over-sharpened.

To bail out of the Unsharp Mask dialog box without doing anything, click the Cancel button or press Esc.

Here are the settings you can adjust in the Unsharp Mask dialog box:

- **Amount**. This setting, which controls the sharpening *intensity*, ranges from 1 percent to 500 percent. The higher the setting, the lighter Photoshop makes the light pixels and the darker it makes the dark pixels. If you set it to 500 percent, Photoshop makes all the light pixels along the edges white and all the dark ones black, giving your image a sharpening halo that's visible from outer space. For best results, keep this setting between 50 percent and 150 percent (you can find other magic numbers on page 458).

- **Radius**. This setting controls the *width* of the sharpening halo by telling Photoshop how many pixels on either side of the edge pixels it should analyze and therefore lighten or darken. When you increase this setting, you may need to reduce the Amount setting to avoid creating a Grand Canyon–sized sharpening halo. For best results, don't set the Radius higher than 4.

- **Threshold**. This setting lets you control how different neighboring pixels have to be from each other before Photoshop considers them an *edge*. Oddly enough, Threshold works the opposite of how you might expect: Setting it to 0 sharpens *every* pixel in your image! For best results, keep this setting between 3 and 20 (it ranges from 0 to 255).

Here's how to use the Unsharp Mask filter nondestructively using Smart Filters:

1. **Convert your image to a Smart Object.**

   Choose Filter→"Convert for Smart Filters" and Photoshop displays a dialog box letting you know that the Image layer will be converted into a Smart Object. Click OK and you'll see a tiny Smart Object badge appear at the bottom right of the image's layer thumbnail.

TIP If your document contains multiple layers, activate 'em all *and then* choose Filter→"Convert for Smart Filters." That way, Photoshop creates a single Smart Object out of the layers, primed and ready for filter action.

---

2. **Choose Filter→Sharpen→Unsharp Mask.**

   In the resulting dialog box (*Figure 11-2*), tweak the settings to your liking. In the next few pages, you'll find some recommended values that you can memorize, but for now, adjust the settings until the image in the preview looks good. Click OK when you're finished to close the dialog box; when you do, an item named Unsharp Mask appears in the Layers panel (*Figure 11-3*, left).

3. **Change the filter's blend mode to Luminosity.**

   Double-click the tiny icon to the right of the Unsharp Mask item (labeled in *Figure 11-3*, left) to view the filter's blending options. In the resulting dialog box, set the Mode menu to Luminosity and then click OK.

Sit back and marvel at your new, nondestructive Photoshop sharpening prowess. You'll learn more about using Smart Filters (and their masks) in Chapter 15, though you've gotten a nice head start here!

■ HOW MUCH TO SHARPEN?

Some images need more sharpening than others. For example, you don't need to sharpen a portrait as much as you do a photo of Times Square because they have different amounts of detail (the Times Square photo has lots of angles and hard lines). If you sharpen the portrait too much, you'll see pores and blemishes with enough details to haunt your next power nap.

FIGURE 11-3

Left: The Unsharp Mask filter is destructive—unless you run it as a Smart Filter. When you do that, you'll see a brand-new item in the Layers panel called Unsharp Mask. If necessary, use the Smart Filter's mask (labeled) to hide the sharpening from areas that don't need it. To adjust the filter's blending options, double-click its icon.

Right: This dialog box lets you change the filter's blend mode and reduce the opacity (strength) of the sharpening.

Smart Filter mask   Double-click to open filter blending options

Photoshop guru Scott Kelby came up with some especially effective values to use in the Unsharp Mask dialog box and published them in *The Adobe Photoshop CS6 Book for Digital Photographers* (*www.lesa.in/skcs6*). With his blessing, here they are:

- **Sharpening soft stuff:** If you're sharpening images of flowers, puppies, babies, and other soft, fluffy subjects (stuff that often blends into its background), you don't want to apply much sharpening at all. For extremely soft sharpening, try setting the Amount to 150 percent, the Radius to 1, and the Threshold to 10.

- **Sharpening portraits:** While close-up portraits need a bit more sharpening than the items mentioned above, you don't want to sharpen them as much as something hard like a building with lots of straight lines and angles. To sharpen portraits enough to make their subjects' eyes stand out, try setting the Amount to 75 percent, the Radius to 2, and the Threshold to 3.

- **Sharpening objects, landscapes, and animals:** This stuff tends to be a little harder and contain more details (sharp angles, fur, and so on) than portraits, so it needs a moderate amount of sharpening. Try setting the Amount to 120 percent, the Radius to 1, and the Threshold to 3.

- **Maximum sharpening:** For photos of cars or of buildings (which are chock full of hard lines, angles, and details) and photos that are a little out of focus, try entering an Amount of 65 percent, a Radius of 4, and a Threshold of 3.

- **Sharpening anything:** For everyday sharpening, regardless of what's in your image, enter an Amount of 85 percent, a Radius of 1, and a Threshold of 4, and then call it a day.

- **Sharpening for the Web:** If you've resized an image so it's small enough to post on the Web (see page 242), it needs more sharpening because downsizing often makes an image appear softer. Set the Amount to 200 percent, the Radius to 0.3, and the Threshold to 0.

NOTE These numbers are merely guidelines—they're not absolute rules. The most important variable is image resolution: Small pixels require *more* sharpening than big ones (and as you know from page 233, the higher the resolution, the smaller the pixels). Be sure to experiment with your own images and printer to see which settings give you the best results.

The Smart Sharpen Filter

The Smart Sharpen filter gives you a *lot* more options than Unsharp Mask. It lets you specify how much sharpening happens in the shadows and highlights *separately*, so if you like maximum control over your images, then this is the sharpening filter for you.

In Photoshop CC, the Smart Sharpen filter has been redesigned to work better *and* be easier to use, as *Figure 11-4* explains. It also lets you save your favorite sharpening settings as presets, which is nice, and its dialog box is (finally!) resizable. The downside? It's not quite as easy to use as Unsharp Mask, and it takes a little longer to run. Like Unsharp Mask, this filter is destructive, so be sure to run it as a Smart Filter (as described in the previous section) or make a copy of the layer you're sharpening first. When you're ready, run this filter by choosing Filter→Sharpen→Smart Sharpen.

TIP When it comes to sharpening, the ability to *see* what's happening to the edges in your image is crucial. That's why it's a good idea to set the document's zoom level to 100 percent and the dialog box's preview zoom level to a higher level to see the details, no matter *which* sharpening filter you use (they've all got little + and – zoom controls beneath their image previews).

In the resulting dialog box, you'll see a Preview checkbox, a Preset menu, and the (now familiar) Amount and Radius sliders (discussed in the previous section). You'll also find the following settings:

- **Reduce Noise**. New in CC, this slider lets you lessen any noise that might be loitering in your image; drag it to the right for more noise reduction (it's automatically set to 10 percent and goes up to 100).

- **Remove**. This menu is where you pick what kind of blur you want Photoshop to remove—or, more accurately, *reduce*. Your choices are:

  — **Gaussian Blur**. Think of this as the basic mode; it's the one that the Unsharp Mask filter uses.

FIGURE 11-4

In CC, the Smart Sharpen filter uses a new and improved sharpening method that keeps it from introducing planet-sized halos around edges that are super high in contrast.

Adobe also simplified the filter's dialog box (you can resize it now, too!). Instead of radio buttons and tabs, you now see all its controls as soon as you open it, including a new Reduce Noise slider, which is just the ticket for sharpening photos taken in low-light conditions with a high ISO setting.

If you want to save your settings to use again later, click the Preset menu and choose Save Preset. (The same menu also lets you load and delete presets.)

— **Lens Blur**. This setting attempts to detect the detail or edges in an image and then make the sharpening halos *smaller*. Pick this setting if your image has a lot of details and/or noise.

— **Motion Blur**. If your image is blurry because the camera or subject moved, you can use this setting to make Photoshop *try* to fix it, though it doesn't do a very good job. You're better off using CC's new Shake Reduction filter (page 462) or the Emboss filter technique described on page 668.

Since choosing Gaussian Blur basically makes this filter work like Unsharp Mask (in which case you could just *use* Unsharp Mask instead) and you use Motion Blur only when your picture is blurry, go with Lens Blur for most photos.

• **Angle**. If you choose Motion Blur from the Remove menu, use this dial to set the angle of the blur currently marring your image. For example, if you have a square image and the subject is moving diagonally across the shot from the lower-left corner to the upper-right corner, set this field to 45 degrees.

The Shadows and Highlights sections both contain the exact same settings, which let you control the following:

- **Fade Amount** lets you reduce the sharpening Photoshop applies to your image's shadows or highlights, depending on which section you're in. So, for example, if you enter *100* in the dialog box's Amount field but want Photoshop to do a bit *less* sharpening in the shadows, click the Shadows flippy triangle and enter a Fade Amount of 25 percent or so. If you want *no* sharpening to happen in the shadows, enter 100 percent. (This setting is similar to the Fade command described in the box below.)

- **Tonal Width** lets you control which shadows and highlights Photoshop sharpens. These settings start out at 50 percent, meaning the shadows and highlights get sharpened evenly throughout their tonal range. If you enter a lower number, Photoshop sharpens only the lightest highlights or the darkest shadows (depending on which section you're in); if you enter a higher number, Photoshop sharpens *all* the highlights or shadows. But unless you've increased the Fade Amount, this setting doesn't do a darn thing.

- **Radius** lets you control how many pixels Photoshop analyzes to figure out whether it thinks a pixel is in a shadow or a highlight. In other words, this setting controls how wide an area Photoshop sharpens in either shadows or highlights (depending on which section you're in). Like the Tonal Width setting, Radius doesn't do squat unless you increase the Fade Amount beyond 0 first.

POWER USERS' CLINIC

Fading Filters

You may feel that this chapter is jumping the gun a little by covering sharpening filters because there's a *whole chapter* on filters headed your way (Chapter 15). However, some of the things you can do with filters—like fading a filter you've applied—are too dad-gummed useful to wait until then, especially if, for whatever reason, you need to run a filter on your *original* Image layer.

If you run a filter (or an image adjustment, for that matter) and the effect is a little too strong, you can lower its opacity to lessen the effect and/or change its blend mode. However, Photoshop only lets you do this *immediately* after running the filter, so it's real easy to miss your chance. If you didn't duplicate the original layer before running the filter or if you didn't use it as a Smart Filter, this fix is your *only* saving grace.

After you run the filter and before you do or click *anything* else, head up to the Edit menu and choose "Fade [name of the last filter you ran]." In the resulting Fade dialog box, enter a percentage in the Opacity field to let Photoshop know how much you want to fade the filter. For example, if you think the filter is twice as strong as you need, enter *50* to reduce its effect by half. (If you click OK and then change your mind, you can choose Edit→"Fade [name of filter]" again and enter a new number.) The Edit menu's Fade option remains clickable until you run another command or use another tool.

The Fade dialog box also has a Mode menu that lets you change the filter's blend mode to adjust how the sharpened pixels blend with the original pixels. Changing this setting to Luminosity has the same effect as running the filter on a duplicate layer and setting that layer's blend mode to Luminosity. When you click OK, Photoshop lessens the filter's effect by the percentage you entered.

Of course, you can forget the Fade command ever existed by—you guessed it—getting into the habit of using Smart Filters or running your filters on duplicate Image layers.

Sharpening with the High Pass Filter

When you want foolproof sharpening that you can *see* before applying it *and* that doesn't require messing with a swarm of sliders, give this method a spin. It's quick and lets you add a bit more depth to an image by increasing contrast in the midtones (the colors in the image that fall between the lightest and darkest). It involves using the High Pass filter, which essentially exaggerates the highest-contrast edges in the image (the ones with the biggest difference between colors) and makes everything else in the image *gray* (see *Figure 11-5*).

To use the High Pass filter, create a duplicate layer for sharpening by pressing ⌘-J (Ctrl+J), or use Smart Filters as described in the section on using Unsharp Mask (page 457). Then change the duplicate layer's blend mode to Overlay, as shown in *Figure 11-6*. Next, choose Filter→Other→High Pass and enter a Radius between 0.5 and 4. (As page 284 explains, the neutral color in Overlay mode is gray, meaning that color will completely disappear, leaving behind the exaggerated high-contrast edges mentioned above and making the image look sharper.) That's it! Check out your image to see if you like it, and turn off the sharpening layer's visibility to see what the original image looked like for a quick comparison.

FIGURE 11-5

The beauty of using the High Pass filter is that you can see exactly which parts of your image will be sharpened in this handy preview; anything that isn't gray will get sharpened.

For more sharpening, increase the Radius setting, though try not to go above 4 or you'll introduce a sharpening halo.

To follow along, visit this book's Missing CD page at www.missing-manuals.com/cds *and download the practice file* Frida.jpg.

The Shake Reduction Filter

This filter is brand-spankin'-new in CC, and its special power is sharpening images that are slightly blurred due to movement of the camera itself (known as *camera shake*). When you run it, Photoshop analyzes the image from the center outward to locate the blurry bits, and then tries to discern a *pattern* from the blur by tracing it (creating what's called a *blur trace*). For example, if your camera moved in a straight line or in multiple directions during the shot, the blur pattern might be linear or zig-zagged. If you moved your camera in an arc or you rotated it slightly, then the blur pattern might be curved instead. Miraculously, you can use this filter to detect *all* these various blur patterns, even if there's *more* than one in your image (though the latter requires entering Advanced mode, described later in this section).

This filter works best on images that don't have a lot of noise (though it applies some noise reduction automatically) or any specular highlights or moving subjects. You'll also get better results if only a *portion* of the image is blurry, instead of the whole thing. That said, the results are pretty darned amazing.

To use Shake Reduction (be sure to run it on a duplicate Image layer or as a Smart Filter as described back on page 457), choose Filter→Sharpen→Shake Reduction, and the dialog box shown in *Figure 11-7* commandeers your screen. When you first open the filter, Photoshop analyzes a small, square portion of your image to detect a blur pattern (you see a light gray status bar in the Detail section at the bottom right of the dialog box while Photoshop is thinking). Once it's done analyzing (it takes a few seconds), lift your jaw up *off* the floor and evaluate the image.

TIP   After the Shake Reduction filter completes its automatic analysis of your image, you can click anywhere within the big preview area on the left to see it at 100 percent zoom level in the Detail section at the bottom right of the dialog box.

Blur Estimation tool
Blur Direction tool
Blur trace
in progress
Drag pin to move
blur trace

Add
auto
blur
trace

Delete
blur
trace

Lock/
Unlock
Detail

Enhance At Loupe Location   Zoom level   Float

FIGURE 11-7

By expanding the Advanced section (just click its flippy triangle), you can see which part of your image Photoshop scrutinized. When you do, a bounding box appears; drag the pin in the middle of the box to a different spot in your image to have Photoshop analyze it instead. Once you enter Advanced mode, you stay there until you click the flippy triangle angle to collapse the Advanced section.

You can use the Blur Estimation tool to draw another bounding box to make Photoshop analyze that area, too, and create another blur trace (circled). While Photoshop is thinking, a small gray status bar appears inside the bounding box and the blur trace icon. To stop the analysis, click the microscopic cancel button inside the bounding box.

Photoshop displays the area it analyzed at 100 percent zoom level in the Detail section at the bottom right; use the zoom controls labeled here to change the zoom level. To have a floating, undocked version of the Detail section, click the Float icon. From the factory, the Detail section's preview changes according to where you click in the large preview; click the Lock/ Unlock Detail button to keep it focused on a particular spot.

TIP You can press Q to undock the Detail section (it's called the *detail loupe* when it's undocked). When the detail loupe is visible, you can press Q or click the tiny X at its top left to dock it in the Detail section. You can also single-click a blur trace icon to make it bigger so you can see the blur pattern that Photoshop traced. The blur pattern looks like a whitish-gray area in a sea of black.

On the left side of the dialog box you'll spot the Blur Estimation and Blur Direction tools (labeled in *Figure 11-7*), as well as the familiar Hand and Zoom tools. On the right side are several settings; here's what they do:

- **Blur Trace Settings**. Straight from the factory, the Shake Reduction filter opens in basic mode (though there's no label telling you that). In this mode,

Photoshop analyzes your image to find a blurry area and then creates a blur trace to remove the blur. Evaluate the big honkin' image preview to see if your image needs further tweaking. If it does, here's what this section's settings do:

— **Blur Trace Bounds**. This slider lets you tell Photoshop how wide the blur is (in pixels)—in other words, how much you moved your camera during the shot. Drag this slider to the right to increase width (if you moved your camera a lot), or to the left to decrease it (if you didn't move your camera much).

— **Source Noise**. Use this slider to tell Photoshop how much noise is in your image. From the factory it's set to Auto, though you can also choose Low, Medium, or High.

— **Smoothing** and **Artifact Suppression**. These two sliders let you fine-tune how Photoshop handles *sharpening artifacts*, problems that are introduced or exaggerated as a result of sharpening (told ya this process was destructive!). They include such nasties as noise, halos, exaggerated texture, detail loss in shadows and highlights, and so on. Drag the Smoothing slider to the right to blur noise in areas of fine detail (also called *high-frequency sharpening noise*). Use the Artifact Suppression slider to lessen the number of larger artifacts that are introduced (alas, some artifacts are unavoidable). Unless you change 'em, both sliders are set to 30 percent.

• **Advanced**. In order to make Photoshop analyze and create blur traces of *multiple* areas, you need to enter Advanced mode by clicking the flippy triangle next to the word "Advanced" to display more options. When you do, Photoshop adds a pin to your image, surrounds it with a small (resizable) bounding box, and creates a *new* blur trace of that region (two blur traces are shown in *Figure 11-7*). To move the bounding box, click and drag its pin.

> **NOTE**   Once you enter Advanced mode, the filter will always open in Advanced mode until you close that section by clicking its flippy triangle.

To create *additional* blur traces, click and drag with the Blur Estimation tool to draw another box (its keyboard shortcut is E, though unless you switched to another, it's already active).

Once you're in Advanced mode, you can *manually* tell Photoshop the direction and width of the blur, grab the Blur Direction tool and then zoom *way* into your image so you can try to see a blur pattern. Then, drag across it in the direction the blur is headed and keep dragging to mark the blur's width (which likely won't be very far). When you're finished dragging, use the bracket keys to nudge the direction of the blur to the left ([) or right (]). To nudge the width, press ⌘-[or] (Ctrl+[or]). In the Advanced section, you'll spot a new blur trace with a red M on it (which stands for manual).

The Advanced section also includes the following settings:

- **Show Blur Estimation Region**. When this checkbox is turned on, you can click anywhere in your image to see that area in the Detail section.

- **Add Blur Trace**. Click this button to make Photoshop add an *automatically generated* blur trace (as opposed to one you draw yourself using the Blur Estimation tool).

- **Delete Blur Trace**. Clicking this button deletes the active blur trace (you can tell which one is active by the blue outline around it its icon).

When you've adjusted all the settings to your liking, click OK to close the dialog box and admire your less-blurry image.

> **TIP** While the Shake Reduction filter works wonders, don't depend on it to save every photo. To capture sharper images *without* schlepping a tripod around, try putting your camera in *burst mode* (consult your owner's manual to figure out how). This makes the camera fire off three to five shots (depending on the make and model) each time you press the shutter button. The image in the *middle* will usually be the sharpest, because it was taken while the shutter button was depressed. Sweet!

Sharpening Layered Files

When you run a sharpening filter, it affects only the *currently active layer*—there's no way to make it affect *all* the layers in a document. So what happens if your image is made from more than one layer because, say, you've combined several images and/or used Adjustment layers? The solution is to *merge* all those layers into a brand-new layer you can sharpen. The "sharpenable" layer can be either an Image layer or a Smart Object. Since the jury is out regarding which method is more efficient, this section covers both.

> **NOTE** Whether the Smart Object method is really faster or better is anyone's guess. Depending on how many and what kind of layers are in your document, the Smart Object method can produce slightly larger file sizes (though a much shorter Layers panel). Nevertheless, one of the techniques covered in this section will likely feel more comfortable to you than the other, so just choose the one you prefer. The important thing is that you do the sharpening somewhere *other* than on your original imager layer.

■ COMBINING LAYERS INTO A NEW IMAGE LAYER

Perhaps the most straightforward method of sharpening a layered document is to simply merge all the existing layers into a *new* Image layer. With this method (called *stamping*), your original layers remain gloriously visible in the Layers panel for further tweaking, should they need it.

> **TIP** When you have a multilayered file, it's a good idea to name the layers so you know what's what. Just double-click the new layer's name and type a descriptive name like *sharpen*. Organizing layers into groups is another great option, as explained on page 100.

Here's how to create a new Image layer from multiple layers:

1. **Open a layered file and, in the Layers panel, click the topmost layer to activate it.**

   Since the sharpening layer needs to be *on top of* your layer stack, activate the topmost layer; that way, the new sharpening layer will appear above it (*Figure 11-8*, left).

2. **Make sure you've turned on the visibility eyes of all the layers you want to merge.**

3. **Open the Layers panel's menu by clicking the upper-right part of the panel (circled in *Figure 11-8*, left) and then Option-click the Merge Visible menu item (Alt-click on a PC).**

   If you simply *click* Merge Visible, Photoshop compresses all your layers into one layer, flattening your document into an un-editable mess. Option-clicking (Alt-clicking) the Merge Visible option instead makes Photoshop compress your layers onto a completely *new* layer, perched atop your layer stack (circled in *Figure 11-8*, right). You can also press Shift-Option-⌘-E (Shift+Alt+Ctrl+E) to do the same thing.

FIGURE 11-8

If you need to sharpen a multi-layered document—especially one riddled with Adjustment layers—first you'll want to combine all the layers into a new Image layer by Option-clicking (Alt-clicking) Merge Visible on the menu shown here. Otherwise, you'll drive yourself crazy trying to figure out exactly which layer needs sharpening!

Now you can sharpen the new stamped layer using any of the methods described in the previous pages. To hide the sharpening from areas of your image that don't need it, add a layer mask by clicking the circle-within-a-square-icon at the bottom of the Layers panel (see page 108 for more on layer masks). To decrease sharpening intensity, lower the layer's opacity setting.

◼ COMBINING LAYERS INTO A SMART OBJECT

Another option for sharpening a multilayered document is to store the *content* of those layers in a Smart Object. The benefit to this approach is twofold. First, when you run a filter on a Smart Object, you automatically get a layer mask, saving you the step of adding one if you need to hide the sharpening from a certain spot. Second, creating a single Smart Object from multiple layers shortens a long Layers panel; you can always get back to the individual layers if you need to, say, tweak an Adjustment layer, but they don't remain visible in your Layers panel.

With this method, your original layers are stored inside the Smart Object (like a sandwich) and hidden from view. Tell Photoshop which layers to include in your new Smart Object by Shift- or ⌘-clicking (Ctrl-clicking on a PC) them in the Layers panel to activate them. Then, choose Filter→"Convert for Smart Filters" or, from the Layers panel's menu, choose "Convert to Smart Object." If you need to get back to those layers for more editing, you can expand the Smart Object by double-clicking its layer thumbnail. When you do, Photoshop displays the message shown in *Figure 11-9*.

This technique is also handy when you want to add more sharpening to specific areas (called *localized* or *selective* sharpening, and discussed in the next section). For example, you could apply sharpening to the whole image (called *global* sharpening), and then create a Smart Object out of the layer you used to do the sharpening—whether it's a stamped layer or a Smart Object—and then add *another* round of sharpening that you only reveal in certain spots (using the included layer mask, of course).

FIGURE 11-9

When you expand a Smart Object to edit its contents, the original layers open in a temporary *Photoshop document. When you're finished making changes, be sure to choose File→Save so your edits are stored in the same location as the original document. Then close the temporary document and your changes appear back in the original document. Amazing!*

Sharpening Part of an Image

To make certain parts of an image *really* stand out—such as areas that have interesting texture—you can add additional sharpening to those areas. For example, one of the most useful portrait-retouching techniques you'll ever learn is to accentuate your subject's eyes and lips, as shown in *Figure 11-10*.

If you've followed the advice in the previous section about sharpening a Smart Object or merging several layers into a stamped layer specifically *for* sharpening, then you're more than halfway there. If you went the Smart Object (or Smart Filter) route, you automatically got a layer mask (shown back in *Figure 11-3*). If you merged several layers into one, you need to add the mask yourself by clicking the circle-within-a-square icon at the bottom of the Layers panel.

NOTE You can follow along by visiting this book's Missing CD page at *www.missingmanuals.com/cds* and downloading the practice file *Puppy.jpg*.

FIGURE 11-10

When you sharpen a duplicate or stamped layer, you can add a layer mask and then use it to reveal the extra sharpening only in certain parts of the image. Here you can see what a difference an extra dose of sharpening makes in the details in the girl's eyes, lips, and green jacket, and the fur near the dog's face.

You can also lessen the intensity of the sharpening by lowering the sharpening layer's opacity (as shown in the right-hand image here) or adjusting the filter's blending options if you've gone the Smart Object route.

Here's how to apply extra sharpening to certain parts of an image:

1. **Create a duplicate layer or stamped layer to use for sharpening and change its blend mode to Luminosity.**

   If you're dealing with a single-layer file, activate the original layer and then press ⌘-J (Ctrl+J) to duplicate it. If you've got a multilayered file, combine all the layers into a single sharpening layer as explained in the previous section (and if you've already added one round of sharpening but want to add more, duplicate the layer you *previously* used for sharpening). Then use the crop-down menu at the top of the Layers panel to change the new layer's blend mode to Luminosity and, if you'd like, double-click its name and rename it *extra sharpening*.

If you're working with a Smart Object, change the blend mode of the *sharpening filter*, not the Smart Object. In other words, wait and switch modes only *after* you run the sharpening filter.

2. **With the new layer active, choose Filter→Sharpen→Unsharp Mask.**

   Enter an Amount of 120 percent, a Radius of 2, and a Threshold of 3. These numbers are rather arbitrary; the goal is to severely over-sharpen your image so you can then scale back the effect.

3. **Run the Unsharp Mask filter one or two more times.**

   Have a little faith, will ya? You'll reduce this extreme oversharpening in a minute. To run the filter again, press ⌘-F (Ctrl+F) or choose Filter→Unsharp Mask (the last filter you ran always appears at the top of the Filter menu).

   If you're in Smart Object Land, you'll see two or three Unsharp Mask layers appear in the Layers panel (one for each time you run the filter). To change their blend modes, double-click the tiny icon to the right of each one to open its blending options. In the resulting dialog box, set the Mode menu to Luminosity and then click OK.

> **NOTE** As mentioned at the start of this chapter, sharpening affects different-sized pixels in different ways. If you're performing this technique on a high-resolution image (wherein the pixels are tiny), you'll need *more* sharpening, so either increase the Amount value listed in step 2 or run the filter a few more times.

4. **Add a solid black layer mask to the sharpened layer.**

   At the bottom of the Layers panel, Option-click (Alt-click on a PC) the circle-within-a-square icon to add a layer mask filled with black, hiding the sharpened layer. (Recall that, in the realm of layer masks, black *conceals*.)

   If you're using a Smart Object, click to activate its mask—the big white thumbnail beneath the Image layer—and press ⌘-I (Ctrl+I) to invert the mask.

5. **Grab the Brush tool and set your foreground color chip to white.**

   Press B to activate the Brush tool and take a peek at the bottom of the Tools panel. If the foreground color chip is white, you're good to go (white *reveals*). If it's not, press D to return the color chips to the factory setting of black and white and then press X to flip-flop the chips. To reveal the sharpening in differing amounts across your image, switch to painting with gray (black conceals and white reveals, so gray does a little of *both*).

6. **With the mask active, mouse over to the image and paint your subject's irises.**

   When you're doing detail work like this, it's helpful to zoom in on the image by pressing ⌘-+ (Ctrl-+) a few times. You also need to adjust your brush's size:

Press the left bracket key ([) to make it smaller and the right bracket key (]) to make it bigger. Be sure to paint only the iris of each eye. If you mess up and reveal too much of the sharpening layer, don't panic; just press X to flip-flop color chips so you're painting with black, and then paint over that area again to hide the sharpening.

TIP   You can also drag to change your brush size by holding Control-Option as you drag left or right (on a PC, Alt+right-click+drag instead).

---

7. **When you're finished painting the eyes and you're still zoomed in, hold the space bar and drag to move the image so you can see your subject's lips, and then reveal the sharpening in that area, as well.**

   Painting over your subject's lips is like adding a bit of digital lip gloss. You'll probably want to increase your brush size a bit for this step.

8. **Lower the sharpened layer's opacity until you get a realistic effect.**

   At the top of the Layers panel, change the Opacity setting to lessen the effect of the sharpening you applied in step 3. (Eighty percent opacity was used in *Figure 11-10*.)

   Smart Object folks need to open the filter's blending options by clicking the tiny icon to the right of the filter's name in the Layers panel, and then lower the Opacity setting in the resulting Blending Options dialog box.

9. **Save the image as a PSD file.**

With this method, you're not harming the original pixels, and you can alter the sharpened layer's opacity to lessen the effect and make it look real instead of otherworldly. Saving the document as a PSD file lets you go back and edit the layer mask or change the sharpened layer's opacity, which is a great option if you print the image and then think, "If only it was just a *hair* sharper..."

■ Advanced Sharpening Techniques

Now that you understand the basics of sharpening, it's time to delve into the realm of advanced sharpening. Consider yourself warned that this is pro-level stuff and not for the faint of heart. (Basically, these methods involve many more steps than the techniques you've learned so far.) In this section, you'll learn how to create a detailed edge mask and make a new high-contrast channel. Read on, brave warrior!

NOTE   This book doesn't cover *every* Photoshop sharpening technique; if it did, it'd be too heavy to lift! Instead, it covers the most practical and frequently used methods. If you want to learn more, pick up a copy of *Real World Image Sharpening, Second Edition* by Jeff Schewe and Bruce Fraser (*www.lesa.in/rwsharpen*). That book is a few years old, but it teaches you more than you ever wanted to know about the art of sharpening.

Creating an Edge Mask

An *edge mask* is simply a layer mask that accentuates the edges in an image. (Pop back to page 452 if you need a refresher on what "edge" means in this context.) The mask itself, which you apply to the layer you want to sharpen, is black except for a white outline of your image. Because black conceals and white reveals in the Land of Layer Masks, this makes the sharpening show only on those edges. However, instead of drawing such a complicated mask yourself—that would take days!—you can have Photoshop create one for you by using the (rather lengthy) method described in this section. It takes some time, but it can be worth the effort (*especially* if other sharpening methods introduce too many artifacts [page 465]):

The Sharpen Tool

What's all this talk about sharpening with filters? Why can't I use the Sharpen tool instead?

While it seems like a no-brainer that the Sharpen tool would be your best bet for sharpening (it's specifically designed for that, right?), you can actually get better results using other methods. However, if you're sharpening a few image *details* instead of the whole enchilada, this tool can be useful. Here's how it works:

The Sharpen tool is part of the blur toolset. When you click its icon (which looks like a triangle) and mouse over to your image, you see a familiar brush cursor. You can then paint areas you want to sharpen and, well, that's it. (You don't get nearly as much control with this tool as you do with the sharpen filters discussed so far in this chapter.) Up in the Options bar, you can adjust the following settings:

- **Brush.** This menu lets you pick brush size and type (big or small, hard or soft).

- **Mode.** Use this menu to change the tool's blend mode from Normal to Darken, Lighten, Hue, Saturation, Color, or Luminosity.

- **Strength.** This field is automatically set to 50 percent. But unless you want to over-sharpen your image, lower this setting to 25 percent or less before you use the Sharpen tool. That way, you apply reasonable amounts

of sharpening and can brush over areas repeatedly to apply more.

- **Sample All Layers.** Photoshop assumes you want to sharpen only the active layer. If you want to sharpen *all* the layers in your document (or rather, the ones that you can see through the current layer, if it's partially transparent), turn on this checkbox. This setting is also your ticket to sharpening on an empty Image layer, thereby *protecting* your original.

- **Protect Detail.** This option prompts Photoshop to be extra careful about what it sharpens (technically, it triggers a set of sharpening instructions called an *algorithm*). Added in CS5, this setting is a definite improvement, and it can be handy if you need to sharpen a small area quickly without fussing with Smart Filters or a duplicate (or merged) layer. But the extra thinking Photoshop has to do to accomplish this means it'll run like molasses on large images (or slow computers).

As you might imagine, using this tool can be a time-suck of epic proportions because you're sharpening with a brush *by hand*, so it's best to use it only on small areas. And be sure to do your sharpening on a new, empty Image layer so you're not harming the original (just make sure to turn on the Sample All Layers checkbox or Photoshop will squawk at ya).

1. **Find the channel with the greatest contrast and duplicate it.**

As you learned back in Chapter 5, an image's color info is stored in individual containers called channels. To create an edge mask, you need to find the channel with the greatest contrast (which channel that is depends on your image). To do that, open the Channels panel and cycle through 'em—if you're in RGB mode—by pressing ⌘-3, 4, and 5 (Ctrl+3, 4, and 5 on a PC). (If you're in CMYK mode, you've got one more channel to look at, so add ⌘-6 [Ctrl+6] to that list.)

To leave your original image intact, you need to keep your channels intact, too, so that means creating an edge mask on a *duplicate* of the highest-contrast channel. So once you find the channel with the most contrast, activate it in the Channels panel, Control-click (right-click) it, and then choose Duplicate from the resulting shortcut menu. In the dialog box that appears, name the channel *mask*. (Another option is to create a brand-new, even *higher*-contrast channel by using the Calculations adjustment or Channel Mixer. See the box on page 478 for the scoop.)

2. **With the mask channel active in the Channels panel, choose Filter→Stylize →Find Edges.**

You don't get a dialog box when you run this filter; it's an all-or-nothing kind of deal. Photoshop instantly makes your image look like a drawing, with the edges shown in dark gray and black. This is the exact *opposite* of what you want, but you'll fix that in the next step.

3. **Invert the mask channel by choosing Image→Adjustments→Invert.**

Photoshop flip-flops the info in the mask channel so the image's edges are white instead of black (see *Figure 11-11*). That way, when you copy the mask channel and paste it into a layer mask on the sharpened layer, the sharpening will be revealed *only* along the edges (because, in the realm of layer masks, black conceals and white reveals).

NOTE If you'd like to work with the image used in this example, download *Building.jpg* from this book's Missing CD page at *www.missingmanuals.com/cds*.

4. **Tweak the mask channel's contrast with a Levels or Curves adjustment.**

To control how much of the image gets sharpened, you can change the mask channel's contrast with a Levels adjustment: Choose Image→Adjustments→Levels, and then move the gray slider to the left for more sharpening or to the right for less. (Normally you create an Adjustment layer when you use Levels or Curves, but in this case you need to *apply* the adjustment to the mask channel, so a trip up to the Image→Adjustments menu is in order.) Remember, the sharpening won't show in the black areas of the mask channel, only the light gray and white areas. Click OK when you're finished to close the dialog box. (See page 373 for more on using Levels.)

FIGURE 11-11

Left: When you first run the Find Edges filter, your image looks like a pencil sketch, as shown here. (To see the original photo, check out Figure 11-12, left.) The edges in the image are black, which is the opposite of what you want.

Right: After you invert the mask channel, the edges turn white and everything else turns black. Now, when you paste this channel into a layer mask, the sharpening will show through only in the white areas.

5. **Blur the mask channel slightly with the Gaussian Blur filter.**

   To avoid harsh sharpening halos, blur the mask channel a little by choosing Filter→Blur→Gaussian Blur. Enter a radius between 0.5 and 4 to soften the mask's edges (use a lower number for low-resolution images and a higher number for high-resolution ones).

6. **Load the mask channel as a selection, and then turn on the composite channel.**

   Since you're already in the Channels panel, go ahead and load the mask channel as a selection by clicking the tiny dotted circle at the bottom left of the Channels panel; you'll see marching ants appear. (You don't need this selection just yet, but you will in a minute; with an active selection, Photoshop will automatically fill in the layer mask you create in the next step.)

   In order to see your full-color image, turn on the composite channel: Scroll back up to the top of the Channels panel and click the composite channel—either RGB or CMYK, depending on your document's color mode—to simultaneously turn the composite channel *on* and the mask channel *off*.

7. **Back in the Layers panel, duplicate the layer you want to sharpen (or combine several layers to create a new one, as described on page 466), name it *sharpening*, and add a layer mask to it.**

Activate the layer you want to sharpen and duplicate it by choosing Duplicate Layer from the Layers panel's menu (the usual ⌘-J [Ctrl+J] trick won't work because it'll only duplicate the *selected* parts). In the resulting Duplicate Layer dialog box, type *sharpening* into the As field, and then click OK. Next, add a layer mask to the sharpening layer by clicking the circle-within-a-square-icon at the bottom of the Layers panel.

8. **Run the Unsharp Mask filter on the sharpening layer.**

   Click the sharpening layer's thumbnail and then choose Filter→Sharpen→Unsharp Mask. In the resulting dialog box, adjust the settings as described on pages 456–457, and then click OK to make Photoshop run the filter.

9. **Change the sharpened layer's blend mode to Luminosity and lower its opacity, if necessary.**

   To avoid weird color shifts that can be caused by sharpening, use the drop-down menu in the Layers panel to change the sharpened layer's blend mode to Luminosity (*Figure 11-12*, right). If the sharpening looks too strong, you can also lower the layer's opacity (you may not need to, but it's sure nice to have the option).

Whew! That was a lot of work, but your image should look light-years better, as shown in *Figure 11-12*. You can toggle the sharpened layer's visibility off and on to see what a difference the edge sharpening made. Thanks to the edge mask, only the building's details got sharpened, leaving areas like the sky untouched (which all but eliminates sharpening-induced noise).

■ Sharpening in Camera Raw

Camera Raw's sharpening capabilities are incredible. Sharpening in Camera Raw affects your image's *luminosity* (lightness or brightness values) but leaves the color alone so you shouldn't see any unexpected color shifts.

But *should* you use Camera Raw for sharpening? The answer is yes—*if* you're not going to edit the image much in Photoshop. If you *are* going to do a lot of editing in Photoshop, you should make sharpening the very last step (after resizing and retouching) and then use one of the methods described earlier in this chapter instead.

You *don't* want to sharpen in both programs—at least, not the whole image. Sharpening in Camera Raw is a global process, meaning it affects the entire image (though you can wield a little control using Camera Raw's Adjustment Brush, discussed later in this section). It's also a somewhat automatic process: The image gets sharpened the minute you open it in Camera Raw (unless you turn off automatic sharpening as described in the next section). If you let Camera Raw sharpen your image, you'll need to practice local or selective sharpening (page 468) once the image is in Photoshop to avoid over-sharpening it and introducing artifacts (page 465).

FIGURE 11-12

Left: The original, unsharp-ened photo of the Chrysler Building in New York City looks pretty soft and lacks detail.

Right: Sharpening the same photo with an edge mask (visible in the Layers panel) confines the sharpening to the image's details.

Global Sharpening

You can sharpen in Camera Raw by first opening an image and then clicking the tiny Detail icon circled in *Figure 11-13*. If you don't want any global sharpening, drag the Amount slider to zero (from the factory, it's set to 25). If you *do* want to sharpen the image, mosey on down to the lower-left corner of the Camera Raw window and change the view percentage to 100 so you can see the effect of the changes you'll make to the Detail settings (otherwise it'll look like your sharpening isn't having any effect and boy howdy that's frustrating). Then, tweak the following settings to your liking:

- **Amount**. This setting works just like Unsharp Mask dialog box's Amount slider (page 456); it controls the sharpening's intensity. Setting it to 0 means no sharpening, no how; setting it to 150 means tons of sharpening (way too much).

Try setting it to 40 and toggling the Preview checkbox at the top of the Camera Raw window off and on to see if it makes a difference (be sure you're zoomed in to 100 percent, though!).

FIGURE 11-13

If you don't want Camera Raw to sharpen your images automatically, you can make it stop. Click the Detail icon (circled, top) and then drag the Amount slider to zero (circled, left). Then open the Camera Raw panel menu (circled, right) and choose Save New Camera Raw Defaults, as shown here.

- **Radius**. This slider controls the size of the details that Camera Raw sharpens. If you're sharpening a photo with lots of fine details, leave this set to 1. If your photo doesn't have many details, you can pump it up to 1.5, or if you're feeling wild and crazy, *maybe* 2.

- **Detail**. This slider lets you control the level of detail Camera Raw brings out (how much it emphasizes the edges). Crank this setting way up (to 90 or so) if you've got an image with tons of details and textures (like a rocky landscape, a close-up of a tree, or a fancy-schmancy building). This slider ranges from 0 to 100; for most images, keep it around 40 (but be sure to experiment to see what looks good).

- **Masking**. If you increase this setting, Camera Raw reduces the amount of sharpening it applies to areas that aren't edges. It's sort of like using a layer mask on a sharpened layer in Photoshop, except that it's automatic, so you can't really control where the sharpening is hidden. Nevertheless, it's worth experimenting with. If you set Masking to 0, Camera Raw sharpens everything; at 100, it sharpens only edges.

- **Luminance**. This setting controls the amount of grayscale noise (see the box on page 455) that Camera Raw tries to decrease in your image by *smoothing* the pixels (similar to blurring). Make sure you're zoomed in to at least 100 percent and then drag this slider to the right to reduce the grains or splotches in your image. For example, a setting of 25 should provide a reasonable balance of noise reduction and image detail, though you'll need to experiment with your own images.

- **Luminance Detail**. This slider controls the *luminance noise threshold*—how much smoothing Camera Raw performs on grayscale noise in detailed parts of the image. Drag it to the right to preserve more details and apply less noise reduction in those areas. On really noisy images, drag it to the left to produce a smoother image and apply more noise reduction (though low numbers can zap detail, so keep an eye on that). Straight from the factory, it's set to 50.

- **Luminance Contrast**. This setting lets you safeguard the image's contrast. Drag it right to preserve contrast and texture, or left to throw caution to the wind and produce a smoother, less noisy image. From the factory, this slider is set to 0.

> **NOTE** The Luminance Detail and Luminance Contrast sliders are *dependent* on the Luminance slider—if it's set to 0, they'll both be grayed out. The fix is to increase the Luminance slider in order to activate the other two.

POWER USERS' CLINIC

Creating a High-Contrast Edge Mask

If you're trying to create an edge mask (page 472) but your color channels don't have much contrast, you can always create a *new* channel with contrast aplenty. If creating a new channel sounds hard, don't panic; it's easier than you think. There are two ways to go about it:

- **The Calculations adjustment** can combine two channels for you. After strolling through your channels to see which ones have the most contrast (let's say they're the red and green channels), head up to the Image menu and choose Calculations. In the resulting dialog box, tell Photoshop which channels you want to combine by choosing Red from the Channel drop-down menu in the Source 1 section and Green from the Channel drop-down menu in the Source 2 section. From the Blending menu near the bottom of the dialog box, pick one of the blend modes in the Overlay category like Soft Light (Chapter 7 describes all these blend modes in detail). When you click OK, Photoshop creates a brand-new channel you

can tweak into a high-contrast edge mask. *Now* you're ready to proceed with step 2 back on page 473. (Since this channel is totally new, you don't have to duplicate it like you did in step 1 on that page.) To learn more about the Calculations adjustment, flip to page 211.

- **The Channel Mixer** doesn't really create another channel; instead, it lets you create a black-and-white version of your image that you can use as if it *were* a channel. Duplicate your Image layer by pressing ⌘-J (Ctrl+J), and then choose Image→Adjustments→Channel Mixer. In the dialog box that appears, turn on the Monochrome checkbox and then tweak the various sliders. When you get some really good contrast, click OK. Next, start with step 2 on page 473 but run the Find Edges filter in the Layers panel instead of the Channels panel (the steps are exactly the same). For more on using the Channel Mixer, head to this book's Missing CD page at *www.missingmanuals.com/cds*.

- **Color**. If your image has a lot of color noise (funky specks of color), which can happen if you shoot in really low light or at a high ISO (your camera's light-sensitivity setting), move this slider to the right to make Camera Raw try to remove the specks. A value of 25 produces a decent amount of speck zapping.

- **Color Detail**. This slider controls the image's *color noise threshold*. Drag it left to remove more color specks, though that may cause color to bleed into other areas. If you've got a lot of thin, detailed high-contrast areas of color (edges) in your image, drag the slider to the right for less noise reduction.

TIP   To see what's *really* going on with any of Camera Raw's sharpening options, zoom in to 100 percent or more and then hold the Option key (Alt on a PC) as you drag the individual sliders. Your image goes grayscale, letting you see which areas Camera Raw is adjusting (though it's tough to see *anything* when you're tweaking the Radius setting). The most useful setting is Masking—if you hold the Option (Alt) key while you tweak it, you see what looks like an edge mask that shows exactly which parts of your image are being sharpened and which parts are being hidden by the mask.

Local Sharpening

As you learned in Chapter 9, Camera Raw sports an Adjustment Brush that lets you paint slider-based adjustments directly onto an image. Behind the scenes, Camera Raw builds a mask to hide the adjustments from the rest of the image. Great, but how does that relate to sharpening, you ask? The Sharpness slider in the Adjustment Brush panel lets you selectively increase or decrease the amount of global sharpening you set in the Detail tab by painting certain areas with the Adjustment Brush. Sure, the global sharpening still affects your whole image, but by using the Adjustment Brush, you can turn the volume of that global sharpening up or down in specific areas, as shown in *Figure 11-14*. The Sharpness slider ranges from –100 to +100.

FIGURE 11-14

If you've applied a round of sharpening to your whole image by adjusting the Detail tab's settings, you can apply more sharpening to specific areas like the edges of this Hawaiian flower (for the curious, it's a Heliconia). Press K to grab the Adjustment Brush, increase the Sharpness slider (circled), and then paint the edges.

To decrease the sharpening in a specific area, drag the Sharpness slider to the left instead.

TIP To better see the area you're adjusting, turn on the Show Mask option near the bottom of the Adjustment Brush panel (not shown—you may have to scroll down to see it) or press Y, and Photoshop highlights your brushstrokes with a white overlay.

Painting in Photoshop

Many artists who learned to sketch and paint using pencils, oils, and brushes
have come to *love* the creativity that the digital realm affords. The biggest
advantage is that there aren't any brushes to clean or paints to mix! And you
can't beat the infinitely forgiving Undo command. Most important, as you can see
in *Figure 12-1*, there's no limit to the kind of artwork you can create in Photoshop.

If you're a traditional artist, the techniques covered in this chapter will set you on
the path of *electronic* creativity. You'll learn how to use Photoshop's color tools and
built-in brushes to create a painting from start to finish, in full step-by-step detail.
Happily, the program's brushes behave more realistically than ever before! You'll also
discover how to load additional brushes, customize the ones Photoshop provides,
and create new ones of your very own.

If you're a graphic designer or a photographer, there's a ton of info here for you,
too. Just think about how much time you spend with brushes when you're working
in Photoshop. Whether you're retouching an image with one of the healing brushes,
painting on a layer mask to hide an adjustment, or removing objects with the Clone
Stamp tool—all of those techniques (and more) involve either the Brush tool itself
or a tool that uses a brush *cursor*. For that reason, learning how to work with and
customize brushes is extremely important. Plus you'll learn all kinds of other fun
and useful stuff like the basics of color theory, how to use Photoshop's various tools
to choose the colors you work with—including the Kuler panel from which you can
snatch whole color schemes!—and how to give your photos a painted edge.

Since painting is all about using color, that's where your journey begins.

FIGURE 12-1

This beautiful painting by Deborah Fox of her daughter, Jordan, was created entirely in Photoshop.

You can see more of Deborah's artwork at www.deborahfoxart.com.

■ Color Theory: The Basics

Color can evoke emotion, capture attention, and send a message. That's why choosing the *right* color is so important. It may also explain why picking colors that go well together can be an exercise in frustration. Some colors pair up nicely, some don't, and who the heck knows why.

The great thing about using Photoshop is that you don't actually need to know *why* certain colors go together. Instead, thanks to a circular diagram called a *color wheel*, you can easily identify which colors live in sweet visual harmony. A color wheel won't turn you into the next Matisse, but for most mortals it's the tool of choice for deciding which colors to use in a project.

Before you take the color wheel for a spin, you need to understand a few basic color concepts. Consider this section *Color Theory: The Missing Manual*:

- **A color scheme** (or color palette) refers to the group of colors you use in a project or painting. Just take a look at any book cover, magazine ad, or website and you'll see that it's made from a certain set of colors (usually between three and five colors, plus white or black). The designer usually picks a main color (like blue) and then chooses the other colors according to how they look together and the feeling they evoke when they're viewed as a group. There's a whole science behind picking colors based on what they mean to us humans and how they make us feel. For example, hospitals are typically bathed in pale blue or green because researchers have found that those colors have a soothing effect. If this type of thing interests you, pick up a copy of *Pantone's Guide to Communicating with Color* by Leatrice Eiseman (*www.lesa.in/leatricecolorbook*).

- **A color wheel** is a tool that helps you pick colors that look good together. Without diving too deeply into the science of color relationships, let's just say that all colors are related because they're derivatives of one another. The color wheel, which dates back to the 17th century, arranges visible colors on a round diagram according to their relationships. It's based on the three basic colors: yellow, blue, and red—the *primary colors*—from which all other colors spring. By mixing equal amounts of the primary colors, you get a second set of colors called—surprise—*secondary colors*. As you might suspect, mixing equal parts of the secondary colors gives you a third set of colors called *tertiary colors*. Together, all these colors form the color wheel shown in *Figure 12-2*.

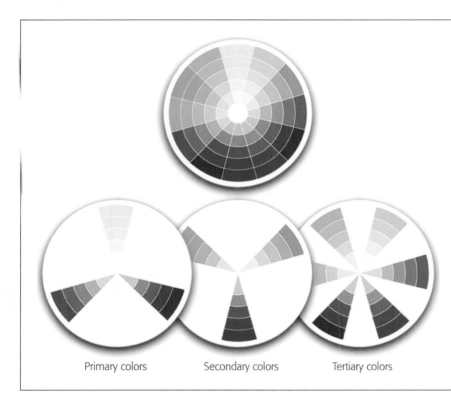

Primary colors   Secondary colors   Tertiary colors

FIGURE 12-2

*Top: You can pick up a color wheel at your local art-supply store or order one from Amazon (*www.lesa.in/colorwheel*). It may not look exactly like the one shown here (it might have more colors), but it'll be similar. Once you learn a few rules about which colors go best together (described in the next section), you can easily use a color wheel to pick visually pleasing color schemes.*

Bottom: Here's the same color wheel with a few of the color wedges hidden so you can see the primary, secondary, and tertiary colors.

NOTE Photoshop has a built-in color wheel in the Kuler panel, a color scheme generator discussed later in this chapter on page 487.

You'll also run into three different terms used to describe color: hue, saturation, and brightness (you've seen 'em here and there throughout this book). Together, they form all the glorious colors the human eye can perceive:

- **Hue** is a term for pure color, before it's had any white or black mixed with it. For the purposes of this discussion, think of hue as another word for "color," as in red, blue, lime green, or cotton-candy pink. So when you see it in a Photoshop dialog box, just substitute the word *color* in your mind.

- **Saturation** describes a color's strength or intensity. For example, a highly saturated hue has a vivid, intense color. A less saturated hue looks dull and gray. Think "vibrancy" and you'll have this one down pat.

- **Brightness** (or lightness), which is usually measured in terms of percent, determines how light or dark a color appears. You can think of brightness as the amount of light shining on an object, ranging from white (100 percent) to black (0 percent). For example, if you shine an incredibly powerful flashlight on an apple, the apple looks almost white (100 percent lightness). When the flashlight is off, you've got no light, so the apple appears almost black (0 percent lightness).

■ Choosing a Color Scheme

As mentioned earlier, if you're picking a color scheme for your project, you usually begin by choosing a main (or *base*) color. This color can come from a piece of art that you're starting with (like a logo or photo) or it can be a color that you want to build your design around. Once you know the main color, you can use a few simple rules to find other colors that go well with it. In this section, you'll learn how to use a color wheel to pick a color scheme based on four popular *color scheme harmonies* (color combinations proven by color experts to go well together). But don't worry: You'll also learn where to find tools to automate this process in case picking colors *manually* isn't your cup of tea.

NOTE The rule of thirds you learned about back on page 216 applies to colors, too. Imagine splitting the colors in your painting or design into two categories: dominant and accent. You can think of the *dominant* color as the color of the environment in the image (like white in a photo of a field of snow); it sets the mood of your piece. The *accent* color is the color of the focal point (like a brown tree in the field of snow). If you shoot for using 2/3 dominant color and 1/3 accent color, you can't go wrong!

Using a Color Wheel

Let's say you've gotten your hot little hands on a color wheel. Great! Now, what the heck do you do with it? For starters, you need to pick the main color you want the color scheme to revolve around and then find it on the color wheel. Then you can use one of the following color scheme harmonies to help pick other colors that go well with it (to see what these color schemes look like, skip ahead to *Figure 12-4*):

- **Monochromatic** schemes use colors from the same wedge of colors on the color wheel.

- **Analogous** schemes use colors from the wedges on both sides of the main color.

- **Complementary** schemes use colors from the wedge directly across from the main color.

- **Split complementary** schemes use colors from the wedges on either side of the main color's complement.

NOTE For more on choosing colors and mastering graphic design, check out your author's online workshop *Graphic Design for Everyone* (*www.lesa.in/clvideos*).

To use a color wheel to pick a color scheme, follow these steps:

1. **Open an image and choose a main color.**

   Every project starts with something, whether it's a photo, a company logo, or a piece of art. Give it a good long stare and decide on a main color to use for the color scheme. Let's say you want to add color to the design shown in *Figure 12-3*. Since there's quite a bit of blue in the image, you could easily start there and designate one of the blues as your main color.

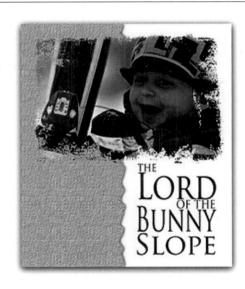

FIGURE 12-3

Instead of racking your brain trying to pick colors for the text and background of this greeting card, it's much easier to start with a color that's already in the design.

In this case, you could start with one of the blues in the photo.

2. **Once you've picked a color, find its general location on the color wheel.**

   If you've got an actual color wheel in your hand, you can do this simply by looking at the wheel.

3. **Locate other colors that go with the main color by using one of the color scheme harmonies described earlier in this section and shown in *Figure 12-4*.**

   If you choose your other colors from the related color wedges, you can be sure they'll look good when you use them together.

FIGURE 12-4

There are tons of color scheme harmonies out there (you'll need to study up on color theory to learn about 'em all), but you can think of these ones as the Fantastic Four. Here you can see what the design looks like using monochromatic (top left), analogous (top right), complementary (bottom left), and split complementary (bottom right) color schemes.

The red box marks the main color's location on the wheel, and each color wedge used in the color schemes is highlighted (the other wedges are faded out).

These are only the four most common color scheme harmonies. To learn others, grab a copy of Color Index, Revised Edition by Jim Krause (www.lesa.in/colorindex).

Using the Kuler Panel

Kuler is an amazingly useful, community-driven color scheme generator that debuted back in Photoshop CS4, though before that it was a Web application. If you're not a fan of color wheels, don't have one handy, or just need some fresh new color schemes, you can choose from many *themes*—Kuler's name for color schemes—that folks in the Kuler community have created. To pop open the panel, choose Window→Extensions→Kuler (see *Figure 12-5*).

NOTE In order for the Kuler panel to download the latest and greatest themes from the Kuler online community, you need to be connected to the Internet. Kuler is also available as an iPhone app that lets you take a photo of an object; the app then extracts the color info from the photo and—if you're a Creative Cloud subscriber (page xxvii)—imports it into Adobe Illustrator's Swatches panel. Ain't technology grand?

FIGURE 12-5

Left: Use the Browse tab to check out themes created by members of the Kuler online community.

Right: The color wheel on the Create tab lets you make your own themes.

At the very top of the Kuler panel are these three buttons:

- **About**. If you want to get to know—or get involved with—the online Kuler community, clicking this button tells you more about it. If you create a free account at *www.lesa.in/kuleronline*, you can upload your own themes, rate other people's themes, post to the forums, and so on.

- **Browse**. To browse themes that other people have created, click this button. On the tab that appears (shown in *Figure 12-5*, left), enter a descriptive word ("rustic," "nature," "corporate," and so on), creator, theme name, or *hex number* in the search field near the top of the panel (see the box on page 731 to learn about hex numbers). Or just use the scroll bar to see what's there. The drop-down menus near the top of the panel let you sort themes by their ratings, when they were uploaded, and so on.

  To use a particular theme—that is, to import its colors into Photoshop—activate it in the panel and then click the "Add selected theme to swatches" button labeled in *Figure 12-5* (the Swatches panel is discussed on page 492). You can also click the little triangle that appears to the right of the scheme's name and choose "Add to Swatches Panel" from the drop-down menu (see *Figure 12-5*, left).

- **Create**. Click this button to see the tab shown in *Figure 12-5*, right, which lets you cook up your *own* themes. Start by picking a color scheme type (page 484) from the Select Rule menu—choices include analogous, monochromatic, triad, complementary, and so on—and then click the white-rimmed circle on the color wheel and drag it to the color you want to base the theme on (your main color, in other words). You'll see little bars sprout from your original color choice that follow the rule you picked. The other colors will move around, too, as you move the base color. Drag the white-rimmed circle inward or outward, left or right, up or down until you find the main color you want. The middle, square color swatch beneath the wheel shows the resulting base color.

  Once you find the right color, you can change its lightness value by using the slider to the right of the color wheel (drag it up to lighten the base color or down to darken it). To change another color in your theme, activate it by clicking its square swatch below the color wheel. You'll see the corresponding circle on the wheel highlighted in white (you can also just click the circle itself to highlight it). Once the circle is highlighted, drag it to another area on the wheel to change it or use the slider on the right to adjust its brightness. When you're happy with your colors, click the Save Theme button at the panel's bottom left to save it and then click the button to its right to load it into the Swatches panel. If you want to share your theme with the world, click the Upload button and Photoshop sends you to the Kuler website.

TIP For easier access to the Kuler panel, drag its tab into the Color and Swatches panel group so you don't have to trot up to the Window menu every time you want to use it. If your Color and Swatches panel group looks too crowded, drag the Styles tab out of the group—you won't use it much unless you're creating your *own* Styles. See page 7 for more on working with panels.

Other Color Scheme–Generating Tools

If this whole color-picking business feels overwhelming, never fear—helper applications aplenty are lurking around the Web, and most work just like Kuler: You pick a base color and a color-scheme rule, and the program generates the rest of the scheme based on the rule you chose. Helpful websites include:

- **Color Scheme Designer 2**. Free, Web-based version only (*www.colorscheme designer.com*).

- **Color Schemer**. Free, Web-based and iPad/iPhone version, or $50 download-able versions for both Mac and Windows (*www.colorschemer.com*).

- **GenoPal**. $25 downloadable Mac and Windows versions (*www.genopal.com*).

■ Choosing Individual Colors

Once you decide on the colors you want to use, the next step is to summon 'em in Photoshop. As you learned in Chapter 1, you can use the color chips at the bottom of the Tools panel to choose colors quickly. But, as with most things in Photoshop, you've got plenty of other options, including the Color Picker, the Eyedropper tool, and the Color and Swatches panels, which are all discussed in this section.

The Color Picker

To choose the color you want to paint with, click the foreground color chip at the bottom of the Tools panel to open the *Color Picker* (*Figure 12-6*). The Color Picker is a fine tool for choosing colors, and it's the one you'll use most often because so many dialog boxes call it into action. If you're not trying to summon a specific color value, simply pick a color by clicking it in the big, square *color field* on the left side of the dialog box; use the color slider to the right of the field to choose a different range of colors. The color you pick shows up in the smaller square swatch at the upper right of the box. Click OK to close the Color Picker, and your foreground color chip changes to the color you chose.

NOTE You can also summon a heads-up version of the Color Picker while you're painting: Just ⌘-Control-Option-click (Alt+Shift+right-click on a PC) your image. Flip ahead to page 502 to see it in action!

As you learned back in Chapter 2, each color mode identifies colors with specific numeric values. When you click within the color field on the left side of the dialog box, you'll see the values on the right side change to reflect the currently selected color. If you need to pick a *specific* color, enter its color values in the HSB (hue, saturation, brightness), RGB (red, green, blue), hex number, Lab, or CMYK (cyan, magenta, yellow, black) fields. Or, if you want to use a color that already exists in your Photoshop document, just mouse away from the Color Picker and your cursor turns into an eyedropper. When you click the color you want to snatch, it appears in the color swatch in the Color Picker. Sweet!

Click within the spectrum to choose a color

FIGURE 12-6

Use the Color Picker to tell Photo-shop which color you want to use with a particular tool. Here you can see the difference between viewing all possible colors in a given color space (top) and only those that are considered web safe (bottom).

If you see a tiny gray triangle with an exclamation point (shown in Figure 12-8 beside one of the color swatches), it means the color can't be reproduced with CMYK ink (see Chapter 16 for more info on printing images). A little 3D cube beside the swatch (circled) means the color isn't web safe (the box on page 724 explains what that means and why it's not such a big deal anymore).

Once you get used to working with colors and seeing their numeric values, you may begin to visualize the color from the values alone. But to really understand how colors mix to make other colors, you need to study color theory.

In Photoshop CC, the Color Picker's hex field (the numeric value used on the Web) is automatically highlighted when you open the dialog box (provided you're in RGB mode), making it super easy to copy and paste that number to use elsewhere in Photoshop or in another program.

TIP Photoshop even lets you mix your own colors by using the Mixer Brush. Skip to page 498 to learn how!

The Eyedropper Tool

When you're developing a color scheme, it's helpful to start by grabbing colors that are already in your image. The Eyedropper tool is perfect for that job, and it includes a handy *sampling ring* that lets you more accurately snatch the *exact* color you're after (see *Figure 12-7*). Grab the tool by pressing I, mouse over to your image, and then click once to make your foreground color chip match the color your cursor is over. If you want to hunt around for a good color, press your mouse button and drag around your image until you find just the right hue, and then let go of your mouse to choose it. To use the Eyedropper tool to set your *background* color chip, Option-click (Alt-click on a PC) your image instead.

> **TIP** In older versions of Photoshop, you could use the Eyedropper tool's Sample menu (in the Options bar) to grab color from all layers or the currently active layer...and that was it. But back in CS6, that menu expanded to include Current & Below (which samples the current layer and any layers below it), "All Layers no Adjustments" (samples all layers except Adjustment layers), and "Current & Below no Adjustments" (samples the current layer and any layers below *except* Adjustment layers).

FIGURE 12-7

The Eyedropper tool's sampling ring displays the current foreground color on the bottom and the new color (the one your cursor is pointing at) on the top. To help isolate those colors from the rest of the colors in your image so you can actually see 'em, Photoshop places a neutral gray ring around them. If you're unimpressed by the sampling ring, you can turn it off by clicking the Show Sampling Ring checkbox in the Options bar (circled).

Author caricature by Richard and Tanya Horie.

> **TIP** When you're painting with the Brush tool and want to pick up a color from your image, you can Option-click (Alt-click) to temporarily switch to the Eyedropper tool. See the box on page 731 to learn how to snatch color from a document or web page *outside* Photoshop.

Loading Color Libraries

Sometimes, you need to be very precise when picking colors. Maybe a client has given you specific colors to match or you're creating a piece of art that needs to mesh with another designer's work. Enter Photoshop's built-in *color libraries*, which feature specialized color collections. *Figure 12-8* shows you how to get started with them.

The most popular library is the Pantone Matching System (PMS), which lets designers keep colors consistent across projects. Each PMS color has a number corresponding to a very specific ink mixture that lets professional printers reproduce the color with the same results every time. That said, to use *true* PMS colors you have to create a spot channel (see page 699). If you pick a color from a color library without using spot channels, Photoshop picks the nearest RGB or CMYK equivalent (depending on which color mode you're in).

FIGURE 12-8

Click the Color Libraries button on the right side of the Color Picker to open this dialog box (you can also load libraries using the Swatches panel, discussed in the next section). Choose a library from the Book drop-down menu and then use the slider (or your up and down arrow keys) to move through the list. Once you've found the color you want, click it once to make it your foreground color. Then click OK to close the Color Libraries dialog box or click the Picker button to go back to the Color Picker.

TIP If the Color Libraries dialog box is open and you know the name of the color you want (for example, Pantone 375), you can choose it by entering a shorthand version of its name with your keyboard; simply type the color's number. This feels weird because there's no text field to enter it in, but you must trust in the Force! Type *375*, for example, and you'll see a lovely light-green swatch appear in the dialog box's list.

The Swatches Panel

The built-in color libraries are actually just collections of swatches. If you want to save a certain group of colors that you've created yourself—or snatched from the Kuler panel—you can store them in the Swatches panel for easy access (see *Figure 12-9*). Think of this panel as a holding pen for frequently used colors, each of which you can summon with a quick click. To open the panel, choose Windows→Swatches. To use a swatch as your foreground color, just click it.

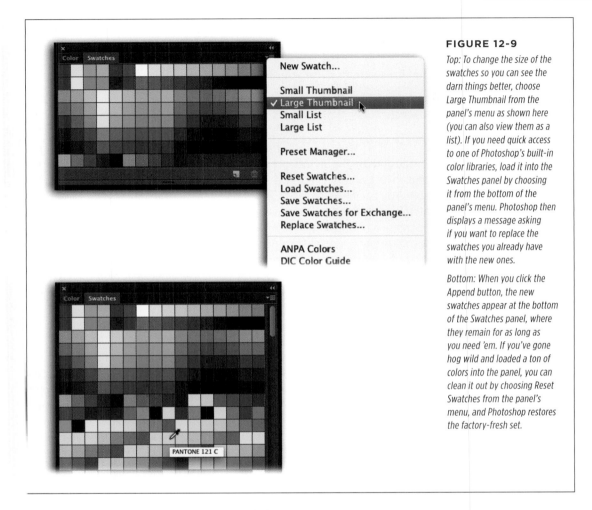

FIGURE 12-9

Top: To change the size of the swatches so you can see the darn things better, choose Large Thumbnail from the panel's menu as shown here (you can also view them as a list). If you need quick access to one of Photoshop's built-in color libraries, load it into the Swatches panel by choosing it from the bottom of the panel's menu. Photoshop then displays a message asking if you want to replace the swatches you already have with the new ones.

Bottom: When you click the Append button, the new swatches appear at the bottom of the Swatches panel, where they remain for as long as you need 'em. If you've gone hog wild and loaded a ton of colors into the panel, you can clean it out by choosing Reset Swatches from the panel's menu, and Photoshop restores the factory-fresh set.

Here's how to manage the Swatches panel like a pro:

- **To add a new swatch that matches your current foreground color**, point your cursor at an empty area of the panel. When the cursor turns into a little paint bucket, click to add the swatch. Photoshop displays a dialog box where you can give the new swatch a meaningful name.

- **Use the Preset Manager to arrange your swatches**. Since Photoshop lets you load additional swatches only at the end of the list, you may want to use the Preset Manager to rearrange them by project, client, and so on. Flip to page 28 for the details.

TIP Photoshop CC can automatically create swatches from colors specified in an HTML, CSS, or SVG file, though you'd *never* know it because there's no menu item for it. To get it done, choose either Load or Replace from the Swatches panel menu and then, in the resulting dialog box, navigate to one of those file types. When you do, Photoshop creates swatches from *all* the colors it finds in the file. This kind of thing is *insanely* handy when you're creating Web graphics!

- **To make a swatch's color your foreground color**, click the swatch.
- **To make a swatch's color your background color**, ⌘-click (Ctrl-click on a PC) the swatch.
- **To delete a swatch**, Option-click (Alt-click) it.

The downside of using the Swatches panel is that there's no way to open a certain set of swatches *in its own panel*—they're always intermingled with the other swatches in the panel. You can keep 'em all together using the Preset Manager, or make your own swatch layer in the document where you're using those colors. To accomplish the latter, create a new layer and then use the Brush tool to add little blobs of color to it from your project or color scheme (you can even place these blobs just outside the margins of your design and then crop 'em out when you're ready to save your masterpiece). Lock the layer so you can't accidentally paint on it, and then use the Eyedropper tool to sample colors from it when you need them. You can keep the swatch layer out of the way by turning off its visibility.

The Color Panel

Photoshop has yet *another* place where you can choose colors: the Color panel (*Figure 12-10*). It's a lot smaller than the Color Picker and, since it's a panel, it won't pop open a dialog box that covers up your image. To open it, choose Window→Color. You'll see the color values of your foreground or background color chip on the right side of the panel (just click the appropriate swatch in the panel to pick it). The sliders let you adjust the color of the current color chip. To pick a new color, click within the spectrum bar at the bottom of the panel (your cursor turns into an eyedropper).

TIP You can capture any color's hex value after you've chosen the color; simply open the Color panel's menu and choose Copy Color's Hex Code. For more on what you can *do* with that info, skip ahead to the box on page 731.

■ (Re)Introducing the Brush Tool

You've already used the Brush tool for all *kinds* of things in previous chapters: editing layer masks, creating selections, colorizing grayscale images, and so on. In this section you'll learn how to *paint* with it, and these days it's a more realistic experience than ever before. But first you need to understand a bit more about how this tool works. Grab the Brush tool by pressing B or clicking its icon in the Tools panel (see *Figure 12-11*).

FIGURE 12-10

Though the Color panel stays nicely tucked out of the way in the panel dock, it's much smaller than the Color Picker, making it a little tough to see. If your eyesight is really good, you'll probably enjoy using it because it takes up so much less space.

This panel is also customizable; you can use its menu to control what it displays. Here, the sliders are set to RGB, and the spectrum bar at the bottom is set to Grayscale.

TIP You can control brush size and hardness with a keyboard shortcut: Control-Option-drag (Alt+right-click+drag on a PC) *left or right* to change the size, or *up or down* to change the hardness. When you use this trick, you'll see brush diameter, hardness, and opacity info appear next to your cursor.

FIGURE 12-11

As you can see, the Brush tool has a slew of options. They let you adjust the brush's size (up to a whopping 5000 pixels!), choose the kind of tip you want, and adjust opacity, among other things.

New in CC is the brush tip preview in the Preset picker, labeled here. You can also open the Brush Preset picker by Control-clicking (right-clicking) atop your image with the Brush tool.

If you peek at the Options bar, you'll see a slew of settings:

- **Tool presets**. Use this drop-down menu at the left end of the Options bar to access brush settings you've previously saved.

- **Brush Preset picker**. Photoshop has a ton of built-in brushes, and this drop-down menu lets you access and manage them, control brush size and edge hardness, *and* save your settings as a preset. Think of it as a mini version of the full-fledged Brush panel (described next). New in CC, you also see a preview of your brush tip, as *Figure 12-11* shows.

- **Brush panel**. This tiny icon gives you one-click access to the Brush panel discussed starting on page 514, which lets you customize brushes in ways you've never imagined.

- **Mode**. This menu contains all the blend modes you've seen so far, along with two others: Behind and Clear. Behind mode acts like the pixels you're painting are *behind* the pixels already on that layer (which is essentially the same, though not quite as safe, as painting on a new layer below it)—if there are transparent pixels on that layer, then your brushstrokes are visible (if there aren't, nothing happens). Clear mode mimics the Eraser tool and makes the pixels you paint over transparent.

- **Opacity**. This setting controls how transparent your brushstrokes are; you'll use it a lot since it lets you change the appearance of the paint you're applying. For example, you can start by painting with bright green at 100 percent opacity and then keep lowering the opacity to produce lighter and lighter shades of green.

- **Tablet pressure controls opacity**. If you use a graphics tablet, click this icon to make the Brush tool's opacity vary when you change the amount of pressure you're applying to the tablet. Press harder to increase opacity or more lightly to decrease it.

- **Flow**. To control the flow of paint to the brush (the rate at which the color is applied to your image), adjust this setting. Use a low number for less paint and a high number for more paint. When you paint by dragging across an area multiple times, the paint builds up in that spot.

- **Airbrush**. Click this button to make your brush work like an artist's airbrush, which sprays paint onto the canvas with compressed air (see *Figure 12-12*). Photoshop includes several airbrush brush tips, too, that behave like a professional airbrush system.

- **Tablet pressure controls size**. If you have a graphics tablet, click this icon to control brush size with your stylus.

Once you've adjusted these settings, you can paint with the brush by mousing over to your image and dragging. Your cursor reflects the size and shape of the brush you picked. Most of the time, the cursor is round like in *Figure 12-12*, top, unless you've chosen one of the textured or more creative brushes discussed later. When you mouse over a dark part of your image, the ring representing your cursor turns white; when you mouse over a light area, it turns black.

FIGURE 12-12

Top: In Airbrush mode, the Brush tool "sprays" paint onto your canvas with (fictitious) compressed air. If you drag or continue to hold down your mouse button, it keeps applying more paint (left) than you get with a single click (right) or when you're using the Brush tool not in Airbrush mode. Several of the tool's airbrush brush tips also trigger this spray-paint behavior.

Middle: Here you can see the difference between a soft-edged brush (top), which has very soft, semitransparent pixels around the edge, and a hard-edged brush (bottom).

Bottom: Photoshop's Bristle Tips work like their real-world counterparts, letting you create more natural strokes. If you're using a graphics tablet, pressing down with the stylus makes the bristles splay, just like a real brush (the Round Blunt Medium Stiff brush was used here). You can also use these tips with other tools that employ a brush cursor, such as the Mixer Brush (see the next section), Eraser, and Clone Stamp tools.

TIP To paint a straight horizontal or vertical line (or one that's at a 45-degree angle) with the Brush tool, click once where you want the line to start and then Shift-click where you want it to end. Who knew?

Controlling the Brush Cursor's Appearance

Straight from the factory, your brush cursor reflects the size and shape of whatever brush you've chosen, but you can change the cursor using Photoshop's preferences. Choose Photoshop→Preferences→Cursors (Edit→Preferences→Cursors on a PC) to control how the program displays your brush's cursor (*Figure 12-13*).

Most of the time, you'll want to stick with either the Normal Brush Tip or the Full Size Brush Tip setting because they give you the most natural painting experience (the Normal Brush Tip is slightly smaller than your actual brushstroke). The Precise version of the cursor has crosshairs so small they're nearly *impossible* to see; the Standard option is even less useful because it makes the cursor look like the Brush tool's icon, and neither option gives you any indication of the brush size. The "Show only Crosshair While Painting" option came along back in CS5, but again, the crosshairs icon gives you no indication of size, and is so darn small you'd probably use it for painting only the tiniest of details when you're zoomed in.

TIP If the brush cursor suddenly turns into a microscopic dot inside the crosshairs, check your keyboard to see if Caps Lock is turned on. Pressing Caps Lock lets you switch between the precise cursor (the crosshairs) and the cursor you're currently using, which can be useful when you're zoomed in and painting tiny details. (Turning on Caps Lock is a *fantastic* trick to play on your coworkers; just make sure you 'fess up before they reinstall Photoshop! Other good tricks include setting the Crop tool's width to 1 pixel and then setting the Brush tool's mode to Behind.)

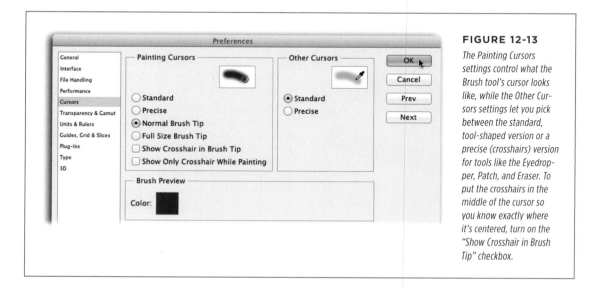

FIGURE 12-13

The Painting Cursors settings control what the Brush tool's cursor looks like, while the Other Cursors settings let you pick between the standard, tool-shaped version or a precise (crosshairs) version for tools like the Eyedropper, Patch, and Eraser. To put the crosshairs in the middle of the cursor so you know exactly where it's centered, turn on the "Show Crosshair in Brush Tip" checkbox.

TIP The color swatch in the Brush Preview section shown in *Figure 12-13* indicates which color you see when you use the drag-to-resize keyboard shortcut (see the Tip on page 113).

Meet the Mixer Brush

Back in CS5, Photoshop's brush engine—the electronic brains behind its Brush tool—got a major overhaul, and Adobe also added a brand-new tool: the Mixer Brush. As the name implies, you can use it to mix colors just like you can mix paints in real life, as well as load multiple colors onto its tip.

You can use this tool on a blank canvas or with a photograph to create realistic, "painterly" effects, as shown in *Figure 12-14*. The Options bar lets you control the "wetness" of the canvas, the amount of paint you're mixing from canvas to brush, and whether Photoshop *cleans* or *refills* the brush after each stroke. (If you're feeling extremely creative, you can paint with a *dirty* brush!)

To turn a photo into a painting, follow these steps:

1. **Open a photo and add a new layer at the top of the layer stack.**

   Click the "Create a new layer" icon at the bottom of the Layers panel, and then position the new layer above your Image layer. (This new layer is where the new paint will go, as shown in *Figure 12-14*.) If you like, name the new layer something clever, like *Paint*.

2. **With the Paint layer active, grab the Mixer Brush by pressing Shift-B repeatedly until you see its icon appear in the Tools panel.**

   The Mixer Brush lives in the Brush toolset and looks like a brush with a drop of paint above it.

Brush preview   Brush cursor

Delete brush preset
New brush preset
Open Preset Manager
Show/hide brush preview

FIGURE 12-14

With a few well-placed strokes of the Mixer Brush, you can turn a photo into a painting. Unless you're an experienced painter or have a background in fine art, mastering this tool will require some experimentation, though it's a lot of fun to use. (Photoshop also includes a filter that can turn a photo into a painting in no time flat. It's called Oil Paint and you can see it in action on page 642.)

On the right you can see the Brush Presets panel that gives you the ability to turn on/off a handy brush preview that appears in your document (shown at top left).

You can follow along by visiting this book's Missing CD page at www.missingmanuals.com/cds and downloading the practice file Railroad.jpg.

3. **In the Options bar, turn on Sample All Layers.**

   Turning on this checkbox makes Photoshop sample colors from the Image layer *below* the active layer, though the paint itself will appear on the active layer. This keeps you from completely destroying the original image.

4. **In the Options bar, click the Brush panel icon (see *Figure 12-15*) to open the Brush panel, and then click the Brush Presets button.**

   In the Brush panel's top-left corner, click the Brush Presets button (*Figure 12-14*) to open another panel—within the same panel group—that includes a list of built-in brushes.

5. **In the Brush Presets panel, scroll down the list of brushes until you see the Round Fan and then give it a click to activate it.**

   If your computer can run OpenGL (see the box on page 58), you'll see a preview of the bristle near the top left of your document window, as *Figure 12-14* shows. If not, well—you won't. You can turn this preview off and on using the button at the bottom of the Brush Presets panel (labeled in *Figure 12-14*).

6. **Adjust the brush's size.**

   Use the Brush Preset picker in the Options bar, or—better yet—Control-Option-drag (Alt+right-click+drag on a PC) to the right to increase the brush's size, or to the left to decrease it. (If that's one too many keys to remember, you can also decrease/increase brush size by tapping the left/right square bracket keys.)

   NOTE You can also change the *regular* Brush tool's hardness (opacity) by pressing Control-Option (Alt+right-clicking on a PC) and then dragging *up* to make the brush softer or *down* to make it harder, but that doesn't work on the Mixer Brush.

7. **From the Brush Combinations menu in the Options bar, choose "Wet, Light Mix."**

   This menu lets you tell Photoshop how you want the brush to behave. After you make a choice from this menu, you can fine-tune it using the Wet, Load, and Mix settings shown in *Figure 12-15*.

   NOTE If you're using a graphics tablet, try assigning the scroll button on your stylus (pen) to resize brushes. (To find out how, you'll need to dig out your graphics tablet's manual.)

8. **Mouse over to your image and start painting.**

   Photoshop begins applying paint to the layer you created in step 1. As you brush across the image, the Mixer Brush samples color from the image and mixes it with the color shown in the color swatch in the Options bar (which comes from your foreground color chip). You can vary your brushstrokes by tweaking the Bristle Tip settings in the Brush panel (page 514), or switch brush tips by picking a new one in the Brush Presets panel.

Open Brush panel | Load brush after stroke | Brush setting combinations | Airbrush mode

Loaded color | Clean brush after stroke | Tablet controls brush size

FIGURE 12-15

The Options bar's color swatch displays the color loaded on the brush tip. By clicking the down-pointing triangle to its right, you can load another color, clean your brush, or have Photoshop load solid *colors only instead of grabbing a* mix *of colors each time you Option-click (Alt-click on a PC). The drop-down menu to the left of the Wet field contains useful setting combos; choosing one populates all the fields to the menu's right.*

9. **Change the Options bar's Mix setting to 70 percent and then Option-click (Alt-click) a color in your image to load it onto the brush tip.**

You can change the Mix setting by double-clicking its field in the Options bar and typing a new percentage, or by clicking its down-pointing triangle and dragging the resulting slider to the right. Option-clicking (Alt–clicking) your image lets you add more colors to your brush tip to create a different painting effect. To switch to a completely different color, summon the *heads-up display* (HUD) Color Picker by Control-Option-⌘-clicking (Shift+Alt-right-clicking on a PC). *Figure 12-16* has the scoop.

> **TIP** Ee careful not to load *too* many colors onto the Mixer Brush, as the paint can quickly turn to a yucky muddy-brown. If that happens, turn on the "Clean brush after each stroke" setting in the Options bar.

10. **Continue painting until you've covered the whole image with brushstrokes.**

If you like the results, save the image as a PSD file. If you don't, delete the paint layer by activating it and pressing the Delete key (Backspace on a PC).

Whew! Painting a photo is a lot of work, but it's also lots of fun (if you like painting, that is). And you don't have to start with a photo—you can use a blank canvas instead. In fact, that's what the next section is all about.

TIP Photoshop includes a set of *actions* (see Chapter 18) created by painting wizard John Derry that automatically prepares all the layers you'll need for painting. Pop open a photo and then choose Window→Actions. In the Actions panel that appears, scroll down to near the bottom of the list and double-click the Mixer Brush Cloning Paint Setup action to run it. Photoshop instantly creates a *slew* of layers, complete with proper opacity and blend modes, primed and ready for your next masterpiece.

FIGURE 12-16

Top: To summon the HUD Color Picker (shown here in Hue Strip mode), Control-Option-⌘-click (Shift+Alt-right-click on a PC) your image. This handy feature lets you swap paint colors while *you're painting. When it's onscreen, you can mouse over to the Hue selector bar on the right until your cursor is over the color range you want (purples, for example), and then press your space bar to pick that range. Next, mouse over to the Lightness and Saturation selector on the left to pick the exact color you want to paint with (just point at it with your cursor). Release your mouse button and the HUD Color Picker disappears. This process takes some getting used to, as any additional clicks—or releasing your mouse button—will close the HUD Color Picker. Oy!*

Bottom: You can also change the HUD Color Picker to this groovy Hue Wheel by opening Photoshop's Preferences (Photoshop→Preferences→General on a Mac; Edit→Preferences→General on a PC). Then, from the HUD Color Picker menu near the top of the Preferences dialog box, choose Hue Wheel. The Hue Wheel works the same way as the Hue Strip. You also get small, medium, and large choices for both the Hue Strip and Hue Wheel.

Painting from Scratch

Now you're ready for the really good stuff: actually *painting* in Photoshop. Not only is it fun, but it's a fabulous way to get used to the Brush tool.

One thing to remember about painting is that different people use different techniques. Some folks start by drawing a sketch, while others dive right into painting. People even have different ways of creating *sketches*: Some draw pencil sketches on paper, scan them into their computers, and then paint over them, while others sketch right in Photoshop. And some folks use a graphics tablet, which makes painting a *lot* easier and more natural, while others fare quite well with a mouse or trackpad. The following steps are very basic and explain how most folks paint from scratch, but, in the end, it's all about what works for you, so feel free to adapt these steps to suit your style.

> **TIP** You can rotate the canvas so it's at a more natural angle while you paint. Just press R to grab the Rotate View tool, and then click and drag your canvas to spin it. See page 55 for more details.

Turn on some music, think about what you want to draw, and then follow these steps:

1. **Create a new document by pressing ⌘-N (Ctrl+N), give it a white background, and then save it.**

   Which canvas size and resolution to use depends on what you want to do with your painting. If you've got a new computer with a lot of memory, you may as well make it big enough to print just in case it turns out really well; 3600x5400 pixels at a resolution of 300 ppi is a good choice. If you have a slow computer and/or you're going to post it on the Web or view it only onscreen, make it 1200x1800 at a resolution of 72 ppi instead. It's a good idea to make your document at least 1200 pixels wide or high (it doesn't matter which); that way, you'll have enough pixel info to show details when you zoom in to work on tiny stuff. (If it's less than 1200 pixels in one direction, it'll look really blocky when you zoom in.) And since the steps ahead are a bit long and involved, protect your hard work by saving the document as a PSD file now by choosing File→Save.

2. **Create a new layer and name it *Sketch*.**

   It's usually best to start with a rough sketch, though you certainly don't have to. You can draw the sketch on paper and scan it into Photoshop (see the box below for the scoop on isolating a sketch onto its own layer) or sketch it with the Brush tool, as explained in the following steps. (If you're starting with a photo, skip ahead to page 686 for tips on quickly creating a pencil sketch from a photo.) To add a layer to the document so you can draw the sketch in Photoshop, click the "Create a new layer" button at the bottom of the Layers panel (see Chapter 3 for more on layers) or press Shift-⌘-N (Shift+Ctrl+N).

FREQUENTLY ASKED QUESTION

Isolating a Scanned Sketch

Help! I scanned my sketch, but it's got a white background! How do I get rid of it?

If you go the pencil-and-paper route rather than drawing a sketch in Photoshop, you'll end up with a white background when you bring the scanned image into Photoshop. Luckily, you can get rid of it quickly using channels.

Flip back to page 202 for the scoop on using channels to create a selection. Once you've got marching ants around the sketch, open the Layers panel and create a new layer for the sketch. Fill the selection with the color of your choice by choosing Edit→Fill. Poof! That's all there is to it. Now you've got an inked outline of the sketch, ready for you to fill with paint.

---

3. **Press B to grab the Brush tool, choose a brush, and pick a color.**

   Hop up to the Options bar and pick a fairly small, round, hard-edged brush using the Brush picker or the Brush Presets panel (*Figure 12-14*, right). Then set your foreground color chip to a dark gray (the color of pencil lead).

4. **Draw your sketch.**

   With the Sketch layer active, mouse over to your document and draw a rough sketch of what you want to paint, like the one shown in *Figure 12-17*. Don't worry about fine lines or getting things perfect; you can add details later.

FIGURE 12-17

Here's the original sketch (left) and the more detailed, refined drawing (right). If you set the Refined Drawing layer's blend mode to Multiply, it appears much darker, which helps you paint over it later.

Technically, you could use the Pencil tool to draw your sketch, but the Brush tool is far more flexible and produces nice, soft-edged lines instead of the Pencil tool's hard, jagged edges. The only redeeming feature of the Pencil tool is its Auto Erase option that lets you erase previous strokes by drawing over them again (which is mainly just cool to watch!).

To follow along, download the file Angel.psd from this book's Missing CD page at www.missingmanuals.com/cds.

5. **Lower the Sketch layer's opacity to about 40 percent.**

   At the top of the Layers panel, lower the opacity of the sketch until it looks kind of ghostly. You'll create a more detailed drawing in the next step.

6. **Create a new layer named *Refined Drawing* and set its blend mode to Multiply.**

   Press Shift-⌘-N (Shift+Ctrl+N) to add another new layer, name it, set the New Layer dialog box's Mode menu to Multiply, and then click OK. Swapping blend modes makes this layer's content appear darker so it's easier to paint over later.

This new layer helps you fine-tune your sketch—think of it as a piece of tracing paper you've placed on top of the original sketch. The Sketch layer underneath acts like a guide to help you draw more precise and intricate details on the Refined Drawing layer.

7. **Using the Brush tool, refine the drawing until you're happy with it.**

By refining your sketch on another layer, you're protecting the original. If you need to erase some of your brushstrokes, hold the E key to switch temporarily to the Eraser tool. Once you're satisfied with the refined drawing, hide the original sketch layer by clicking its visibility eye.

8. **Create another new layer named *Blue Background* and drag it below the Refined Drawing layer.**

Adding the background before you paint gives you a strong color foundation on which to build the painting. That way, you can bind the painting together using the background color(s).

9. **Fill the background layer with whatever you want the dominant background color to be.**

Over in the Tools panel, click the foreground color chip and choose a fairly dark blue from the Color Picker, and then fill the Blue Background layer with that color by pressing Option-Delete (Alt-Backspace on a PC). Alternatively, you can choose Edit→Fill and then pick Other from the Use drop-down menu to open the Color Picker; then click OK twice to fill the layer—once to close the Color Picker and again to close the Fill dialog box. (Because you'll *paint* on this layer in the next step, using a Fill layer won't work.)

10. **In the Options bar, grab a large, round, textured brush, lower its opacity to 25 percent, and start painting over the background.**

Why add even *more* paint to the Blue Background layer? To add texture and keep the angel from looking flat. Choose a textured brush or one with rough edges (like the speckled spatter brushes). Once you pick a brush, lower its opacity to 25 percent in the Options bar. Then mouse over to your document and start painting over the dominant background color until you get the look you want, varying brushes, brush sizes, color, and opacity as you go (see *Figure 12-18*, top).

TIP To paint with a color that's already in your document, Option-click (Alt-click on a PC) to temporarily turn the brush cursor into an eyedropper. This lets you click a color to make it your foreground color without switching tools. You can also use the HUD Color Picker described back on page 502.

FIGURE 12-18

Top left: A variety of grainy, textured brushes were used at varying sizes and opacities to create this chalky pastel look. To give the background depth, use darker versions of similar colors for shadows and lighter versions of similar colors for highlights. (A newbie mistake is to use pure white for highlights and pure black for shadows, which makes paintings look flat. However, experienced painters can use white or black sparingly with reduced brush opacity, then build the highlight or shadow by repeatedly brushing over the same area.)

Top right: While you'd normally keep the background turned on when you're filling a sketch with color, it's turned off here so you can see the blocked colors. Though the areas of dark shading may look black, they're really purple and red.

Bottom: Here's how the colors and refined drawing look on top of the background.

11. **Create a new layer named** *Blocked Colors* **and drag it between the Blue Background and Refined Drawing layers (***Figure 12-18***, bottom).**

    You'll use this layer to add colors to your drawing (also referred to as "blocking with color" or "roughing in" because you'll add more details later).

> **TIP** If all this color-picking business feels overwhelming, you can always create a painting with black, white, and shades of gray—which, in fact, is a great way to learn!

12. **Use a big, round brush with an opacity of 25 percent to colorize the drawing.**

     For this step, pretend you're a kid with a coloring book; you don't have to worry much about staying within the lines. Start with the big stuff first—painting works best when you work from the general (larger areas) to the specific (tiny details). Using a big brush at a low opacity lets you build up color with multiple strokes (see *Figure 12-18*, top right). For a smooth look, paint with a soft-edge brush. To add more character, use one of the textured or spatter brushes. Use the foreground color chip or any of the other color-picking tools you learned about earlier in this chapter when you need to change colors.

13. **Create a new layer named *Refining & Detailing* and drag it above the Blocked Colors layer.**

     You'll use this layer to add fine details like lined edges and other embellishments. That being said, if the lined edges on your Refined Drawing layer are good enough (as is the case in the angel painting), you don't need to add more lines, so concentrate on adding other color details to the Refining & Detailing layer instead.

14. **Using a variety of brush sizes, add details to your painting.**

     Use a big, soft brush set to 65 percent opacity for large areas of color and blend them by painting over them again and again, changing colors as necessary. Switch to a small (about 5-pixel), textured brush at 100 percent opacity for finer details (see *Figure 12-19*, top).

> **TIP** If you're having trouble getting certain colors to blend with others, try the Mixer Brush or the Spot Healing Brush—both can do wonders for blending stubborn areas. Steer clear of the Smudge tool (see Appendix C, online at *www.missingmanuals.com/cds*) because all it does is smear the paint and move it around, creating a truly *awful* effect.

15. **Create a new layer named *Effects* and drag it to the top of your layer stack.**

     If your painting needs a bit more punch, add some special lighting effects. *Figure 12-19* (right) shows blue-tinted shadows around the edges of the angel's face and in her hair. If you change this layer's mode to Multiply, the blue paint acts like a double coat of ink, although lowering the layer's opacity to about 75 percent makes the effect subtle.

FIGURE 12-19

Left: The painting really starts to take shape when you add details. Brushes from the Dry Media set work really well in this situation (see page 509 for the scoop on loading 'em), though the Rough Round Bristle brush from the Assorted Brush Set at 100 pixels was used here. You'd normally leave the background turned on so you can pick up color from it, but it's turned off here so you can see what the colorized drawing looks like by itself.

Right: For a bit of extra polish, add some blue highlights using a new, separate layer. Remember to experiment with different layer blend modes and opacities to get just the right effect. (Flip back to Chapter 7 for a refresher on blend modes.)

16. **Add some texture.**

    To keep the painting from looking too perfect and, well, *digital*, mess it up a bit with additional texture. You can use *anything* to create texture, including grainy, funky-edged brushes or a photo set to Overlay blend mode. *Figure 12-20* describes one texture-inducing maneuver—adding, get this, a photo of a piece of tile.

17. **Save your painting one last time by pressing ⌘-S (Ctrl+S).**

    Congratulations for sticking through a *ton* of steps to create your first digital painting from scratch!

As you can see, Photoshop paintings are a lot of work, but they can be very rewarding. Putting every aspect of the painting on a separate layer lets you build the image gradually so you don't destroy the whole thing if you mess up. OK, who needs a nap?

FIGURE 12-20

Texture can give a painting life and keep it from looking plastic because it's too perfect (left). In this example, a photo of a slate tile was added at the top of the layer stack. Changing the photo layer's blend mode to Overlay gives the painting a little depth and makes it look more believable (right).

This image, created by Deborah Fox (www. deborahfoxart.com), was recognized for creative excellence in advertising with an ADDY award.

TIP To learn more about digital painting techniques, pick up a copy of *ImagineFX* magazine (*www.imaginefx. com*) or visit these websites: Computer Graphics Society (*www.cgsociety.crg*), Concept Art (*www.conceptart.org*), and Epilogue (*www.epilogue.net*). You'll be glad you did!

Loading More Built-in Brushes

For all the built-in brushes you see in the Brush Preset picker and the Brush Presets panel, there are hundreds more lying in wait right inside Photoshop—you just have to load 'em. More brushes mean more creativity at your fingertips for stuff like digital paintings, applying a painted edge to a photo (discussed in the following list), adding a sparkle (page 513), or aging a photo so it looks torn and tattered (page 530).

Here's how to load more brushes *and* give your photo a painted edge (if you want to skip the technique and go straight to loading brushes, hop to step 6):

1. **Open a photo and double-click its Background layer to unlock it.**

   This technique involves adding a layer beneath the Background layer, which Photoshop won't let you do. The fix is to unlock the Background layer first by double-clicking it. In the resulting dialog box, give the layer a new name (if you like), and then click OK.

POWER USERS' CLINIC

Shading an Object by Hand

Way back in Chapter 7 you learned that the Dissolve blend mode turns semi-transparent pixels into a spray of dots. While that's not very useful on a daily basis, it turns out that when you set the Brush tool to Dissolve mode you get a brush that's absolutely *perfect* for hand-shading an object you've drawn in Photoshop.

For example, let's say you used the Custom Shape tool—set to Shape mode so it creates a new layer—to draw a heart (one of Photoshop's built-in shapes). And then you used the Fill setting in the Options bar to fill the heart with red. To give it some depth, you can add some soft shading around its edges

Once you've drawn the shape, load it as a selection by ⌘-clicking (Ctrl-clicking on a PC) its layer thumbnail. Then add a

new, empty layer on which you'll perform the aforementioned shading. Grab the Brush tool and, in the Options bar, choose a big, soft-edge brush from the Brush Preset picker and then set the Mode menu to Dissolve. Next, set your foreground color chip to black, and then mouse over to your image and paint all the way around the edges of the heart. Since you wisely selected that area that you wanted to paint, your brushstrokes only affect the area *inside* the selection, keeping you from painting outside the lines.

To soften the shading, you can lower its layer opacity and/or run a Gaussian Blur filter. That's all there is to it!

2. **Add a solid white Fill layer to the bottom of your layer stack.**

In a few steps, you're going to hide the edges of the image with a layer mask. If you don't fill the new layer with color, then when you hide the image's edges, you'll see through the new layer to the transparent checkerboard pattern, which makes it tough to see the creative edges you're about to add. A white background (or other solid color) works much better. Choose Layer→New Fill Layer→Solid Color and, in the resulting Color Picker, choose white and then click OK. Drag this layer to the bottom of your layer stack.

3. **Press M to grab the Rectangular Marquee tool and draw a selection box about a quarter of an inch inside the edges of your image.**

You'll paint the edges outside this box in step 9.

4. **Activate the Image layer and add a layer mask to it.**

In the Layers panel, activate the Image layer (the one you opened in step 1) and then click the circle-within-a-square icon to add a layer mask. When you do, Photoshop hides the part of the photo that's outside the selection you made in the previous step.

5. **Press B to grab the Brush tool, and then click to open the Brush Preset picker in the Options bar.**

Head up to the Options bar and click the down-pointing triangle to the right of the brush preview to see all the brush presets (it's labeled in *Figure 12-21*).

Click to open Brush Preset picker   Click to load more brushes

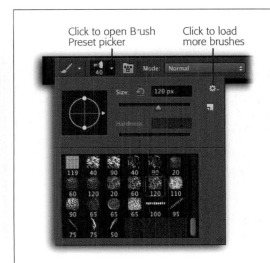

FIGURE 12-21

Once you open the Brush Preset picker, you can click the tiny gear to open a long list of options that let you load, save, and reset brushes, as well as control the size of your brush previews. At the bottom of the list are a variety of brush categories.

Once you've picked a new category of brushes (like Faux Finish Brushes) and clicked Append, they'll appear at the bottom of the Brush Preset picker as shown here. For this particular technique, the Rolled Rag brush (circled) works quite well.

The number below the brush preview indicates the size of the brush preset, though you can make it any size you want using the Size slider shown here, or the keyboard shortcuts scattered throughout this chapter.

---

6. **Click the gear icon in the Brush Preset picker and choose Faux Finish Brushes.**

Click the tiny gear at the top right of the Brush Preset picker (labeled in *Figure 12-21*) to see options for the size of your brush previews, loading and saving brushes, and so on. (You can find these same options in the Brush Presets panel's menu.) At the bottom of the list are lots of brushes organized into categories like Assorted Brushes, Basic Brushes, and so on. Click Faux Finish Brushes; when you do, Photoshop asks if you want to replace your current brushes with the new ones. Instead of clicking OK, click Append so Photoshop adds them to the bottom of the list (below the ones that are already there).

7. **Pick one of the new brushes.**

Scroll down the list of brushes until you see "Rolled Rag – Terry 120 pixels" (circled in *Figure 12-21*) and click it. Then mouse over to your document and you'll see the funky, squarish brush cursor circled in *Figure 12-22*.

8. **With black as your foreground color and the layer mask active, paint along the edges of the image to create a unique border.**

Peek at the color chips at the bottom of the Tools panel and press D to set them to black and white, and then press X until black hops on top. With the layer mask activated, paint over the edges of the photo as shown in *Figure 12-22*. If you paint too much of the image, press X to swap color chips so that white is on top, and then paint the areas you want to reveal.

FIGURE 12-22

Top: Be sure to use short brushstrokes or you'll create an edge that looks like a repeating pattern of your brush cursor's shape. Just keep brushing back and forth until you get an interesting look (Alternatively, skip ahead to page 518 to learn how to adjust Angle Jitter in the Brush panel.)

Bottom: By using a layer mask to create this effect, the original image remains unharmed, as shown in this Layers panel. If you like this edge effect, you can create something similar by using the Refine Edge dialog box. Flip back to page 172 for more info.

9. **Save your image as a PSD file.**

If you decide to go back and edit the painted edges, just activate the layer mask, grab the Brush tool, and have a ball.

◼ MAKING AN OBJECT SPARKLE

Another fun use for interesting brushes is to make an object look like it's *sparkling*. Just perform steps 6 and 7 of the previous list, but instead of loading the Faux Finish Brushes, load the Assorted Brushes. Once the new brushes are in your Brush Preset menu, scroll down the list of brush previews and you'll spot a couple of crosshatch brushes that make a perfect sparkle if you rotate them (see *Figure 12-23*). Click one of the crosshatches to activate it, click your foreground color chip at the bottom of the Tools panel, and then pick a nice gold from the resulting Color Picker. Over in the Layers panel, create a new layer for each sparkle, so you can rotate 'em individually.

FIGURE 12-23

Top: The Assorted category's crosshatch brushes, like the one circled here, are perfect for making an object look like it's sparkling.

Bottom: The beauty of putting each sparkle on its own layer is that you can move them around, spin 'em, and control their intensity with the layers' opacity settings.

If you load a new set of brushes and then want to get back to the set you had when you first started using Photoshop CC, click the gear icon labeled back in Figure 12-21 and then choose Reset Brushes.

With the first new layer active (it should be at the top of the Layers panel), click once in your image to add a sparkle. Add another new layer and then click again to add another sparkle. Finally, rotate the sparkle using Free Transform by pressing ⌘-T (Ctrl+T); page 257 has the lowdown on Free Transform. Press Return (Enter) when you're finished rotating and then Shift-click both sparkle layers in the Layers panel to activate them. Then press V to grab the Move tool and drag the sparkles into place.

TIP You can press the V key to switch temporarily to the Move tool. When you let go of the key, you switch back to whatever tool you were using before.

Painted photo edges and sparkles are just two of an infinite number of visually interesting effects you can create using the extra brushes that come with Photoshop. Look through the various brush sets and see if some of the unusual shapes inspire you to try another technique!

Customizing Brushes

Once you get comfortable with the Brush tool, you can experiment with changing the way it behaves. Maybe you'd like to adjust the spacing between brush marks in a single stroke, have the brush apply a texture, or whatever. The Brush panel (*Figure 12-24*) gives you an amazing amount of control over brushes. To open it, choose Window→Brush.

Panel menu

Create new brush from current settings   Delete brush

FIGURE 12-24

The Brush panel gives you a gaggle of options for changing the way brushes behave. By mastering these controls, you can create some super-cool brushes that make your brushstrokes look real (not too perfect). Start by choosing one of the brush tips in the upper-right part of the panel (the number beneath each tip represents its default size in pixels). If you don't see any brush tips, click the Brush Tip Shape category on the panel's left side. And if the panel's settings are all grayed out, simply switch to a tool that uses a brush cursor, like the Brush tool (obviously) or even the Eraser tool.

Here, one of Photoshop's Erodible brush tips is active. All of these tips wear down as you use 'em just like real chalk or graphite (pencil lead), though you can use the Softness slider shown here to control how fast the tip melts away (a setting of 100 percent prevents the tip from wearing down at all). To restore the tip to its original shape after using it, click the Sharpen Tip button (circled). To gain easier access to this command, assign it a keyboard shortcut by choosing Edit→Keyboard Shortcuts; set the Shortcuts For drop-down menu to Tools, and then scroll down until you see the Sharpen Erodible Tip command (see page 27 for details).

The following sections explain in detail the various settings you can tweak in the Brush panel, but here's the basic procedure for customizing brushes:

1. **Pick a brush tip preset from the upper-right part of the Brush panel or by clicking the Brush Preset button at its top left to open the Brush Presets panel (you choose a brush tip by simply clicking its icon).**

2. **In the Brush panel, click a category on the panel's left side to activate it, and then tweak the various settings that appear on the right.**

As you adjust settings, the preview area at the bottom of the panel shows how those changes affect the brush. Once you've got the brush's settings just right, click the little padlock icon to the right of that setting's name to lock those options.

The next few sections explain the various ways to customize brushes—Photoshop gives you a *ton* of choices, including options that you let you alter the individual *brush marks* (the look of pixels created by a single dab of the brush tip) that comprise a *brushstroke*.

> **NOTE** In the following pages you'll learn a million ways to customize brushes (OK, maybe not quite that many, but a whole lot). It'd be great to list an example of what each customization is best suited for, but there's just not enough room in this book. You can use a brush to paint nearly anything in Photoshop, so how you use the following options depends more on your personal preferences and experimentation than on a specific formula. The majority of these settings are geared toward introducing randomness into brushstrokes so they don't look too perfect and computery.

Brush Tip Shape

These options, not surprisingly, affect how the *tip* of the brush is shaped, which determines how your brushstrokes look. Once you pick a brush tip from the list of presets on the upper-right part of the Brush panel, you can control the following characteristics:

> **NOTE** The options in this category differ depending on which brush tip you picked. For example, if you choose a Soft Round brush tip, you see the options in the following list. If you choose a Round Fan brush tip instead, you get a *different* set of options including bristle shape, length, thickness, and so on. This list covers some of the most common settings.

- **Size**. This setting controls how big the brush is. You can also change size by going to the Options bar and clicking the down-pointing triangle to the open Brush picker and then adjusting the Size slider. Another option is Control-Option-dragging (Alt-right-click-dragging on a PC): Drag left to decrease the brush size or right to increase it. (When you drag, a handy info overlay appears next to your cursor that shows the brush's diameter, hardness, and opacity.)

- **Flip X**. Turning on this checkbox flips the brush tip horizontally. For example, if the brush is shaped like a curved line that points to the right, turning on this checkbox will make it point left instead. If the brush is symmetrical, you won't notice any change.

- **Flip Y**. This checkbox flips the brush vertically. If your brush tip is a leaf that points up, for example, this setting will make it point down.

- **Angle**. If you're working with an irregular-shaped or elliptical brush, this setting lets you change its angle, which is great for making a chiseled stroke (imagine an ellipse tilted to one side, similar to calligraphy). You can either enter a number in the Angle box or drag the right-facing arrow in the crosshairs diagram to the right of the box.

- **Roundness**. This setting controls the shape of the brush, from perfectly round to elliptical. You can enter a percentage or click one of the white dots on the crosshairs image and drag up or down to change this setting.

- **Hardness**. This slider controls the edges of the brush, from 0 percent (very soft) to 100 percent (hard). The harder the brush's edges, the cleaner your lines; softer edges create an airbrushed look. Unfortunately, you can't adjust this setting on custom brushes you've made from images. Bummer!

- **Spacing**. This slider lets you adjust the amount of space between brush marks when you make a stroke. The lower the percentage, the closer together they are, creating a more solid, cleaner line. Higher percentages cause gaps between the brush marks, which is excellent if you've also tweaked the Scattering settings (page 518). If you turn off the Spacing checkbox, Photoshop bases the spacing on how quickly you move the mouse while you paint: Drag slowly for narrow spacing and quickly for wider spacing.

Shape Dynamics

These options let you create brushes that make natural, realistic-looking brushstrokes that are made up of a series of brush marks rather than solid, perfect-looking brushstrokes.

- **Size Jitter** and **Control**. These settings determine how much the size of the brush marks varies (see *Figure 12-25*). When you paint with a real brush, the strokes aren't perfectly uniform (you'd be hard-pressed to make two identical strokes). With this setting, you can specify how much jitter you want by entering a percentage or dragging the slider, or turn it off altogether by choosing Off from this Control menu. The Control menu's Fade setting makes each stroke taper off (like it ran out of paint) within the number of steps you enter in the text box that appears. Setting the Control menu to Pen Pressure makes the stroke taper off at the beginning and end of the mark *if* you're using a graphics tablet. If you have a high-end tablet like an Intuos or Cintiq (*www.wacom.com*), you can choose the Stylus Wheel or Pen Tilt setting for other variations (like being able to tilt the brush by tilting your pen).

FIGURE 12-25

The jitter controls let you introduce a bit of randomness into the brush marks in your stroke. Here's an example of a brushstroke with no jitter (left) and one with size and angle jitter turned on (right).

Some of the settings in the Shape Dynamics category may not work for you. For example, Pen Pressure doesn't work with a mouse, so if you choose it from the Control menu and you don't have a graphics tablet attached to your computer, you'll see a tiny triangular warning symbol next to the menu.

POWER USERS' CLINIC

The Joy of Painter

If you got a charge out of creating a painting from scratch (page 502), you may enjoy using a program called Painter (*www.corel.com/painter*) as a companion to Photoshop. For years, Painter has been revered by fine artists, commercial designers, and entertainment artists who work on everything from special effects to character and set design.

Painter is designed *by* artists *for* artists: It's the digital equivalent of a traditional art studio. It works on both Macs and PCs, and it costs $60 for the junior version (called *Essentials*) and $300 for the full version. If you want to get really *serious* about digital painting, it's a must-have. Here's a sampling of what you can do with it:

- See the bristles of each brush and how they splay on your canvas, just like brushes in the real world.
- Control how fast the paint dries, where the wind is coming from, and how many bristles are in the brush.
- Create color swatches from an image, layer, or from a mixer pad, letting you have custom swatch sets for different projects.
- Blend paints using a mixer pad just as if you were mixing two colors of wet paint together.
- Specify the kind of (virtual) paper you're drawing on and whether your brush picks up that texture. You can also create custom brush- and paper-texture palettes (the equivalent of Photoshop's panels).
- Automatically save the settings you use for individual brushes so you don't have to keep resetting them. For example, if you tweak one brush, switch to another brush, and then go back to the *first* one, Painter remembers the settings you used for it (unlike Photoshop, which *resets* the original brush completely unless you save it as a preset).

You can save Painter projects as layered PSD files that you can open in Photoshop for more fine-tuning like color-correcting (Chapter 9) and sharpening (Chapter 11). You can also work the other way around and open PSD files directly in Painter.

For true bliss, invest in a Wacom graphics tablet while you're at it (*www.wacom.com*) and then you may *never* leave your studio again. A graphics tablet is an electronic pad that you draw on using a special pen called a *stylus*. You can control brush size and opacity by varying the amount of pressure you apply to the tablet with the stylus. Combined with the Rotate View tool (page 55), a tablet gives you a truly natural painting experience—without all the mess!

- **Minimum Diameter**. This setting controls how small the brush can get. It's helpful on custom brushes when you don't want them to get too small, and on round or elliptical brushes when you don't want them to get too thin.

- **Tilt Scale**. This setting is available only if you have a graphics tablet (otherwise it's grayed out); it lets you resize the brush by tilting your stylus.

- **Angle Jitter** and **Control**. These settings determine how much the angle of the brush marks vary within a single stroke. It's automatically set to 0 percent, but if you want a lot of variation in the angle of your brushstrokes, set it higher. Use this Control drop-down menu to choose from settings like Off, Fade, Pen Pressure, Pen Tilt, Stylus Wheel, and Rotation, discussed earlier in the Size Jitter bullet. The other options are Rotation, which rotates the brush marks; Initial Direction, which bases the brush-mark angle on the way you *initially* drag the mouse when you start the brushstroke; and Direction, which bases the brush-mark angle on the direction of the brushstroke. Adjusting the Angle Jitter of sampled brushes (custom brushes you've made from images—see page 526) can turn a flat, repetitive brushstroke into a richly textured one.

- **Roundness Jitter** and **Control**. These settings control how much the roundness of your brushstrokes varies. This Control menu includes Off, Fade, Pen Pressure, Pen Tilt, Stylus Wheel, and Rotation options. If you've turned on Brush Projection (see the last bullet in this list), these settings are grayed out.

- **Flip X Jitter** and **Flip Y Jitter**. These checkboxes let you flip the jitter on its x- or y-axis (or both), much like you can flip the shape of the brush.

- **Brush Projection**. If you're using a graphics tablet, this option lets you apply tilt and rotation settings to the brush tip. For example, if you're using a brush tip that has a shape to it (say, a fan brush), the brush marks inside the brushstroke curve, stretch, and rotate as you tilt and rotate your stylus to behave more like a real brush. Turning on this checkbox overrides the Roundness Jitter and Control settings mentioned above.

Scattering

Head to this category when you want to make the spacing between brush marks a bit random as if your brushstroke were splattered onto the canvas instead of applied evenly (see *Figure 12-26*). You can adjust the following settings:

- **Scatter** and **Control**. Unless you change this setting, all your brush marks will follow the line of your stroke. The Scatter slider distributes the brush marks above and below the center of the stroke line, giving them a random look. Turn on the Both Axes checkbox to make Photoshop scatter to the right and left, too. This Control menu's options are described in the previous section.

- **Count**. This setting controls the number of marks Photoshop applies at each spacing interval, which you set using the Spacing setting in the Brush Tip Shape category (page 516). Increasing this setting makes the program create more marks; lowering it means fewer marks.

FIGURE 12-26

When you use a scatter brush inside a layer mask, you can break a photo into pieces as shown here.

To create this effect, pick a brush from the Square Brushes category, turn on Scatter and set it to 60 percent, and then—in the Brush Tip Shape category—set the Spacing to 25 percent.

- **Count Jitter** and **Control**. These settings control how random the number (quantity) of brush marks is. If you're using a graphics tablet, set this Control menu to Pen Pressure to make the brush marks thin out at the beginning and end of the stroke but be dense in the middle.

Texture

These options let you apply a repeating pattern to your brushstrokes, which makes them look textured. Photoshop comes with a ton of ready-to-use patterns—although you have to load most of 'em as explained in *Figure 12-27*—and you can create your own by choosing Edit→Define Pattern (see page 85).

- **Invert**. Since texture in Photoshop doesn't literally mean that some parts of your image stick up farther than others, the program bases texture on the colors in a pattern. It considers dark areas "lower" than lighter ones, which makes sense because, in the real world, more light reaches the parts of a textured surface that protrude than lower areas, which are darker because they're filled with shadows. Also as in real life, when you paint over a textured part of a document, the lighter (higher) areas get more paint than darker (lower) ones since the hairs on your brush have a hard time reaching down into those low areas. If you turn on this checkbox, Photoshop reverses the high and low points of the texture, so light areas are low points that don't get very much paint and dark areas are the high points that get lots of paint.

- **Scale**. This slider lets you adjust the size of the pattern. Drag it left to make the pattern smaller or right to make it bigger.

- **Brightness** and **Contrast**. These two sliders let you tweak the brightness and contrast of the texture within a brushstroke. Before CS6, there was no way to do this; you had to create different *versions* of the texture to produce lighter, darker, or higher-contrast brushstrokes.

- **Texture Each Tip**. This checkbox makes Photoshop apply the texture to each brush mark *within* the stroke, rather than the *whole* stroke, creating a more textured look (and slightly less chance of a painfully obvious repeating pattern). You have to turn this setting on to use the Depth setting discussed later in this list.

- **Mode**. Here's where you pick the blend mode Photoshop uses to apply the pattern to the brushstroke (see Chapter 7 for the lowdown on blend modes).

- **Depth**. This slider controls how deeply the paint "seeps into" the texture by increasing the contrast of the colors in the texture. Changing this to a high percentage means the "low" points of the texture won't get any paint, and entering a low percentage means all the areas get the same amount of paint—which reduces the contrast so much you can't see the texture.

- **Minimum Depth**. This slider lets you set the minimum depth that paint can seep into the texture.

- **Depth Jitter** and **Control**. These settings let you introduce randomness into how the depth varies when the Texture Each Tip checkbox is turned on. Drag this slider left to decrease the amount of depth jitter, or right to increase it. In this Control menu, you can choose from Off, Fade, Pen Pressure, Pen Tilt, Stylus Wheel, and Rotation (discussed on page 516).

Click to open preset menu

Click to load more presets

FIGURE 12-27

Left: Click the down arrow beside the texture preview (labeled, top) to open the Texture preset menu. You can click the gear icon in the menu's upper-right corner (labeled, bottom) to load even more textures.

Right: Here's the difference between a brushstroke with no texture (left) and one with the texture applied (right). The only drawback to using a pattern texture is that you risk introducing an identifiable repeating pattern into your image. If that happens, try using a Dual Brush tip instead.

Dual Brush

These options let you combine two brush tips to introduce more texture and randomness into a brushstroke or to give texture to a brush that doesn't have any. Photoshop applies the second brush's texture to the first brush's brushstrokes wherever the two strokes overlap, as shown in *Figure 12-28* (brush tips of differing shapes will overlap in different places). To choose two brushes, pick your first brush from the Brush Tip Shape category by clicking one of the presets and then adjusting its options. Then click the Dual Brush category and follow the same process to choose a second brush.

The Dual Brush category includes these options (they all apply to the *second* brush):

- **Mode** lets you set the blend mode Photoshop uses to combine your brush marks into a brushstroke. (This drop-down menu is at the top of the Brush panel, above the list of presets.)

- **Flip** introduces a bit of randomness into the frequency with which each brush tip is used within a brushstroke.

- **Size** controls the size of the second brush tip.

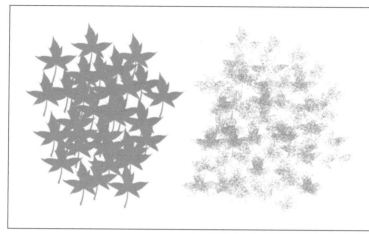

FIGURE 12-28

To introduce texture to a brush that doesn't have any, like the leaf brush shown here (left), head to the Dual Brush category and choose a textured brush tip as your second brush.

The image on the right shows what such a combination looks like.

- **Spacing** controls the distance between each tip's brush marks in a stroke.

- **Scatter** controls how the brush marks are distributed throughout the stroke.

- **Count** lets you specify the number of brush marks at each spacing interval.

Color Dynamics

These settings control how the paint color varies throughout a brushstroke—another way to introduce a bit of variety into your strokes so they don't look uniform (see *Figure 12-29*).

FIGURE 12-29

The Color Dynamics settings can make a single brushstroke look like it's made from more than one color. With your foreground color chip set to green and Color Dynamics turned off, your brushstroke will look like the one on the left. But if you turn on Color Dynamics and set your background color to yellow, you can use the Foreground/Background Jitter slider to create a brushstroke that randomly combines those two colors (middle). And if you turn on the Hue Jitter setting, Photoshop introduces all kinds of funky colors to your brushstrokes (right).

- **Apply Per Tip**. Turn this checkbox on to apply variations to every brush mark that appears in a brushstroke (rather than varying the brush mark *once* per brushstroke). This option lives at the top of the Brush panel, to the right of the Brush Presets button.

- **Foreground/Background Jitter** and **Control**. These settings let you control how the paint alternates between the foreground and background colors throughout a stroke. In this Control menu, you can choose from Off, Fade, Pen Pressure, Pen Tilt, Stylus Wheel, and Rotation (all described on page 516).

- **Hue Jitter**. Lets you control color variation in your brushstroke; a higher setting introduces all kinds of funky colors. Drag the slider to the right to shift the color farther away from the original color, or drag it left to shift the color less. If you have Apply Per Tip turned on, the color will vary within the stroke, as shown in *Figure 12-29* (right).

- **Saturation Jitter**. Increasing this setting makes Photoshop vary the color saturation once per stroke. If you turn on the Apply Per Tip checkbox, then it varies the saturation for each brush mark inside the stroke.

- **Brightness Jitter**. Use this setting to vary the brightness of the color once per stroke, or for each brush mark *inside* a stroke if you turn on the Apply Per Tip checkbox. A setting of 0 represents 100 percent of the color you're using, and dragging this slider to the right darkens the color's brightness.

- **Purity**. This setting controls how far the color varies from its original saturation value once you've tweaked Saturation Jitter. Adjust this setting to a positive percentage for more variation, or to a negative percentage for less variation.

Transfer

This category lets you adjust how much paint Photoshop transfers to the "paper" (your document) with each brushstroke (see *Figure 12-30*). The Opacity and Flow settings here override the ones in the Options bar, so if you tweak them, you may find that the Options bar's settings don't seem to work. For example, if you set your Opacity Jitter to 60 percent, that's the most opaque your brush can be, even if you set Opacity to 100 percent in the Options bar. (You've been warned!) Here are your options:

- **Opacity Jitter** and **Control**. These settings control how transparent the paint is throughout the brushstroke. Setting Opacity Jitter to a higher percentage makes the stroke more see-through (see *Figure 12-30*, bottom). In this Control menu, your choices are Off, Fade, Pen Pressure, Pen Tilt, and Stylus Wheel (see page 516).

- **Flow Jitter** and **Control**. This lets you specify how much paint the brush lays down throughout the brushstroke. A higher percentage means the flow varies more, and a lower percentage means the flow varies less. This Control menu gives you the same options as the Opacity Jitter Control menu.

FIGURE 12-30

To make your brushstroke's opacity vary randomly, increase the Opacity Jitter setting.

Here you see the difference between a brushstroke with no opacity jitter (top) and one with the opacity jitter set to 100 percent (bottom).

- **Wetness Jitter** and **Control**. You can use this setting to make Photoshop vary how wet (liquidy) your brushstrokes are when you're painting with the Mixer Brush.

- **Mix Jitter** and **Control**. Also available when you're using the Mixer Brush, these settings let you vary how much paint you're mixing from the canvas onto your brush.

- **Minimum**. Once you make a choice from the Control drop-down menus for the Opacity, Flow, Wetness, and Mix Jitter settings, you can use these sliders to set their minimum values.

Brush Pose

You can use the settings in this category to control brush tilt, rotation, and pressure with a graphics tablet or mouse. If you're using a graphics tablet, you can override its input by turning on the Override checkboxes beneath each slider, which can be handy when you need to create exactly the same brushstroke over and over and over again. If you don't have a graphics tablet, these settings let you make your mouse behave more like a stylus.

Noise

Turn on this checkbox to make Photoshop apply a dose of random, grainy texture to the semi-transparent edges of a soft brush tip (if you're using a dual brush tip, the noise applies to both tips; if you're using a hard-edged brush, nothing happens). You can use this setting to introduce more texture and randomness into brushstrokes you make with soft-edges brushes.

Wet Edges

Turning on this checkbox makes the center of your brushstrokes transparent, so the paint looks like it's building up along the edges of the stroke (similar to painting with watercolors).

Build-up

Turn on this checkbox to make your brush behave like a professional artist's airbrush rig). This setting has the same effect as clicking the Airbrush button in the Options bar (page 496). Basically, Photoshop adds brush marks as long as you hold down your mouse button, and extends the brush marks past your cursor to create a real-world spray effect.

Smoothing

To make your brushstrokes look smoother than they were when you painted them, turn this checkbox on. It's especially helpful if you don't have a very steady hand, which can make for jagged brushstrokes.

Protect Texture

This checkbox lets you apply the same texture, pattern, and size to all the built-in brush presets that have a texture. So, for example, you could use this option to make it look like you're painting on the same surface with a variety of brushes without actually having to turn on the Texture category for each brush. You can think of this as a global texture option.

Suggested Brush Customizations

With so many settings, it can be confusing to figure out which brushes really need changing. You'll find that the built-in presets are really handy, and with just a few tweaks here and there, they can become indispensable. *Figure 12-31* shows a sample of some extremely useful yet simple customizations. If you like what you see, check out Table 12-1 to learn about specific settings.

FIGURE 12-31

There's no limit to the number of brushes you can customize or create, so feel free to go hog wild.

Here are a few brushes digital artists can't live without. The first column shows what a single dab of paint looks like using each brush so you can get an idea of the brush's shape. The second column shows a single brushstroke, and the third column shows multiple brushstrokes using three different colors of paint (green, yellow, and blue).

If any of these brushes strike your fancy, see Table 12-1 to learn the specific settings used to create each one.

■ Defining a New Brush

For some seriously creative fun, try making your own brushes. You can make them out of anything—a stroke that you've drawn with another brush, your logo, even an image that you've scanned into your computer to use as texture (like a leaf). Some folks call brushes that you create yourself *sampled brushes* because you *sample* part of a pattern, object, or image to create them; in other words, you have to select the pattern, object, or image you want to base the brush on.

TABLE 12-1 *Suggested brush customizations*

BRUSH NUMBER IN FIGURE 12-31	DESCRIPTION	OPACITY[1]	SPACING[2]	SHAPE DYNAMICS	OTHER DYNAMICS	USES
1	Round, hard-edged brush	25%	0%	Size Jitter = Pen Pressure	None	Shading, blocking in color, sketching
2, 3	Rough-edged brush	25%	0%	None	With (2) or without (3) Flow Jitter = Pen Pressure	Shading, adding texture, making hair
4	Rough brush (custom)[3]	30%	0%	Angle Jitter = 20%; Control = Off	None	Adding texture, shading
5	Small dot brush (custom)[3]	30%	0%	Size Jitter = Pen Pressure	Opacity Jitter = Pen Pressure	Making hair, shading
6	Round, rough-edged brush	100%	20–25%	Size Jitter = Pen Pressure	Opacity Jitter and Flow Jitter = Pen Pressure	Shading, blocking in color
7	Textured round brush	30%	0%	None	Flow Jitter = Pen Pressure	Adding texture, shading
8	Textured round brush	100%	0%	Size Jitter = Pen Pressure	Flow Jitter = Pen Pressure	Sketching, creating line art, adding fine details in small areas
9	Scattered spot brush (custom)[3]	70%	25%	Scatter = 20%; Size Jitter = Pen Pressure	Opacity Jitter and Flow Jitter = Pen Pressure	Adding texture

[1] Adjust this setting in the Options bar.
[2] Set this in the Brush panel's Brush Tip Shape category (page 516).
[3] Meaning a custom brush you make from scratch as described in the next section.

The first step is to create the *paint dab*—a dab of paint that will form the shape of the new custom brush tip (see *Figure 12-32*, left). You can create a paint dab in a variety of ways, which range from quick to incredibly involved. The basic premise is to create a 300x300–pixel document and then use a variety of brushes at various opacity settings to create the dab. You can even add texture to it—the more irregular and messy the dab, the more interesting your brush will be. To turn the dab into a brush that you can use to apply color, you *have* to create it using black and gray paint at 100 percent opacity (that's the *Options bar's* opacity setting). When you paint with the brush later, the 100 percent black areas will create opaque color and the gray areas will be semitransparent.

FIGURE 12-32

Left: You can create this paint dab by starting with one of the small, soft-edged brush presets. Set your foreground color chip to black, paint a few dots, and then switch to some shade of gray and paint a few more. Just make sure that the Options bar's Opacity field is set to 100 percent.

Right: If you tweak a few settings in the Brush panel, you can create an extremely useful texture and shading brush.

NOTE To practice making a custom brush using the paint dab shown in *Figure 12-32*, download *DotsBrush.psd* from this book's Missing CD page at *www.missingmanuals.com/cds*.

Once you've created a paint dab, follow these steps to turn it into a brush:

1. **Use the Rectangular Marquee tool to select the dab.**

   To define a brush, you have to select the image first. Press M (or Shift-M) to grab the Rectangular Marquee and draw a selection around the dab (*Figure 12-32*, left).

2. **Choose Edit→Define Brush Preset.**

   In the resulting dialog box (*Figure 12-32*, left), give your brush a name and then click OK.

3. **Create a new document (it can be any size) and then press B to grab the Brush tool.**

   Press ⌘-N (Ctrl+N) to open a new document so you can test drive your new brush.

4. **In the Options bar, choose your new brush from the Brush Preset picker and then open the Brush panel.**

   Once you've activated your new brush, click the button to the right of the Brush Preset picker (or choose Window→Brush) to open the Brush panel. Alternatively, you can open the Brush panel first: Just click the Brush Presets button at the top of the Brush panel (or the Brush Presets tab, if you've already opened that panel) and then choose your new brush from there.

5. **In the Brush panel, click the Brush Tip Shape category.**

   To create a brush similar to number 4 in *Figure 12-31*, set the size to 100 pixels, the angle to 70 degrees, and the spacing to 1 percent. If you have a graphics tablet, click the Other Dynamics option and then set the Opacity Jitter and Flow Jitter options' Control menus to Pen Pressure.

6. **Click the Shape Dynamics category.**

   If you have a graphics tablet, set Size Jitter to Pen Pressure and Minimum Diameter to 30 percent. If you don't have a graphics tablet, try entering a Size Jitter of 25 percent instead (you just won't be able to change it by applying more or less pressure with your pen).

7. **Turn on the Smoothing checkbox.**

   As explained on page 525, this setting makes your brushstrokes less jagged.

8. **Save your brush again.**

   Click the "Create new brush" button at the bottom right of the Brush panel (it looks like a piece of paper with a folded corner). If you don't save the brush again, you lose the settings you just changed. In the resulting dialog box, give it the same name that you did in step 2.

Not only have you created a brush that's great for adding textures to digital paintings, but you can also use it to create some interesting grunge effects when you're editing photos. The ability to make your own brushes gives you a ton of control when you're applying textures.

TIP If you want to share your new brush with the masses, choose Save Brushes from the Brush Preset panel's menu (the Brush panel's menu doesn't have this option). Give the brush a name and then hop on over to the Adobe Photoshop Marketplace (*www.lesa.in/custompsbrushes*) and upload your file to achieve Photoshop fame! You can also use the new Adobe Exchange panel to share custom brushes (as well as actions, patterns, and so on). Choose Window→Extensions→Adobe Exchange to give it a spin.

Installing New Brushes

You're not alone when it comes to creating new brushes. Folks love sharing their creations, and once they've made a really cool brush, they're usually happy to share it with the masses. That's why all manner of free brushes are available on the Web.

One of the best resources is the Adobe Studio Exchange website. Going to *www. lesa.in/custompsbrushes* leads you straight to the Brushes category, though you can use the list on the right side of that web page to find all manner of actions, custom shapes, gradients, and so on there, too. You can even download a brush set that'll make your image look like it was printed on torn paper as shown in *Figure 12-33*. Once you've downloaded the brush set to your hard drive, head to the Options bar and choose Load Brushes from the Brush Preset picker's menu (see *Figure 12-21*)—or choose it from the Brush Preset panel's menu instead—and then navigate to where the brush set lives (look for a file whose name ends in ".abr," such as *Paper_Damage. abr*) and then click Load (you can also double-click the .abr file on your hard drive and Photoshop will put it in the right spot). The new brushes appear in the Brush Preset picker, ready for you to use.

TIP In Photohop CC, you can access the Adobe Studio Exchange website by choosing Window→Extensions →Adobe Exchange. This handy new panel lets you browse, purchase, and install all kinds of brushes, actions, plug-ins, and so on from within Photoshop!

The streaks shown in *Figure 12-33* (bottom) were made by setting the foreground and background chips to white and brown (respectively) and then choosing Filter→Render→Cloud, followed by Filter→Blur→Motion Blur. Next, the streak layer's blend mode was changed to Hard Light. With a few clicks of the funky Paper Damage brushes, the photo looks ancient!

FIGURE 12-33

At the Adobe Studio Exchange site (top left), you can download some amazing brushes and share your own creations. For example, after you download and install the Paper Damage brush set (top right), you can use its brushes to age a photo (bottom). You can go straight to this brush set by visiting www.lesa.in/ pspaperdamage.

In the bottom image, each damaging brush-stroke was painted in white on its own layer to control the layer's opacity and protect the original image.

The Art History Brush

Adobe would have you believe that you can use the Art History Brush to turn a photo into a painting, but the darn thing doesn't work very well (as is painfully clear in the figure below). It's similar to the more useful History Brush in that you can choose a snapshot of your image (a previous version saved at a particular time) to work from, which is why it's in the same toolset. That said, take this tool for a spin and decide for yourself whether it deserves a spot in your regular tool rotation. Here's how:

1. **Grab the Art History Brush by pressing Y.** (If pressing Y activates the History Brush, simply press Shift-Y to snag the Art History Brush instead.)

2. **In the History panel, pick a snapshot or history state.** Open the History panel by choosing Window→History, and then choose a state by clicking the left column beside the state or snapshot you want to work with.

3. **Pick a small, soft-edged brush from the Options bar's Brush menu.** You can set the tool's blend mode and opacity in the Options bar just like you can with the Brush tool, and use the Control-Option-drag (Alt+right-click+drag on a PC) keyboard shortcut to resize your brush cursor on the fly—drag left to make it smaller or right to make it bigger.

4. **In the Options bar's Style menu, choose Tight Short.** You'll find 10 different painting styles in this drop-down menu, including Tight Short, Loose Medium, Loose Long, and so on. Any option with the word "tight" in its name works a little better than the others because it keeps the brushstrokes close together.

5. **Change the Options bar's Area field to 50 pixels.** This setting controls the area covered by the artsy (and totally destructive) brushstrokes you create as you brush across the image. Enter a large number for more strokes or a smaller number for fewer strokes. If you have any hope of recognizing the object you're painting, keep this number relatively low (less than 40 pixels).

6. **Make sure the Tolerance field is set to 0 percent.** A low tolerance lets you paint strokes anywhere you want. A high tolerance limits them to areas that differ from the color in the snapshot or history state you picked in step 2.

7. **Mouse over to your image and paint it.** As you paint, your clear, recognizable photo will be replaced with random, supposedly artistic swaths of paint, transforming it into madness and mayhem. Undo command, anyone?

Drawing with the Vector Tools

I f your first thought when someone mentions drawing is, "But I can't even draw a straight line!" don't worry: You *can* draw in Photoshop. To draw a straight line, just grab the Line tool (it's one of the shape tools—see page 547) and drag from one spot to another. Or, as you learned in the previous chapter, grab the Brush tool, click in one spot, and then Shift-click another spot; it's that simple. The program also includes all kinds of built-in shapes like circles, rectangles, and rounded rectangles that are incredibly easy to use (see page 555).

But what about creating more sophisticated drawings and illustrations? The good news is you don't have to worry about drawing *anything* freehand, whether it's a line or a curvy shape. Instead, the vector drawing tools you'll learn about in this chapter let you create a series of *points*; Photoshop then adds a *path* between those points to form the outline of the shape. Unlike the things you draw by hand with the Brush tool or a real-world pencil, these vector objects are infinitely tweakable: You can move points and adjust the paths to create any shape you want, letting you make complex yet flexible works of art from scratch, as *Figure 13-1* shows.

If you're tempted to bail from this chapter because you're not an artist, hold your horses—you can use the vector drawing tools in a variety of other ways. For example:

- Once you get the hang of these tools, you can use them to add elements to images that don't exist and can't be photographed, like the ornamental shapes and embellishments shown on page 300.

- You can use the drawing tools to create precise selections that you can't make any other way. In fact, the Pen tool is a favorite of seasoned Photoshop jockeys because of its selection prowess (see page 565).

- You can use the shape tools to mask (hide) parts of an image (see page 565). Because those masks are vector based, they're a lot more flexible than regular ol' layer masks.

Learning to draw with Photoshop's vector tools takes time and patience because they work *very* differently from any other tool you've used so far. But taking the time to master them sets you on the path (pun intended) to becoming a true Photoshop guru.

Before you dive into using the tools themselves, though, you need a quick tour of the different drawing modes you can use. Take a deep breath and read on!

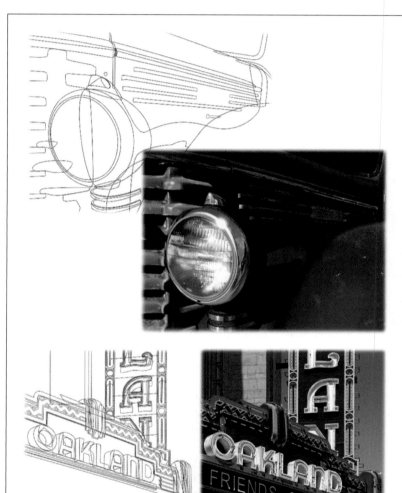

FIGURE 13-1

Top: Here you can see the paths that make up the basic shapes of this digital painting by Bert Monroy called "Red Truck." You read that correctly: It's not a photograph—Bert drew every detail by hand. He created the basic shapes using the Pen tool, and then filled in the details with the Brush tool. Instead of a mouse, he used a Wacom interactive pen display (a monitor you can draw directly on; see www.wacom.com/cintiq).

Bottom: This wire-frame drawing (called "Oakland" and also by Bert) is even more complex. If you look closely, you can make out the shapes he created with the Pen tool to make the neon tubes and the sockets that the tubes go into. Now that's something to aspire to!

You can see more of Bert's amazing work at www.bertmonroy.com.

■ Photoshop's Drawing Modes

In the real world, the word *drawing* implies that you're sketching lines and shapes by hand. But in Photoshop and in this book, drawing refers to creating objects using Photoshop's vector tools: the Pen tool and the various shape tools. Drawing with these tools is more like drafting (think technical illustrations such as blueprints) because you're creating precise *outlines* of shapes instead of the varying lines of a sketch or painting.

> **NOTE** Here's a way to make sense of the difference between Photoshop's painting tools and its vector drawing tools: If Van Gogh or Michelangelo had used Photoshop, they would have liked the Brush tool because of its similarity to real-world paintbrushes. However, artists like Matisse, Mondrian, and Picasso would have favored the vector drawing tools because their painting styles are more precise and angular and depend on creating smooth, clean geometric shapes and lines.

Photoshop has three different drawing modes, accessible in the Options bar (see *Figure 13-2*), that determine exactly what happens when you use the Pen and shape tools. Here's what each mode does:

Drawing modes   Path operations   Path options

Tool presets   Path alignment   Path arrangement

FIGURE 13-2

When you press P to grab the Pen tool, you see a drop-down menu for different drawing modes near the left end of the Options bar. The buttons to the right of the Make label let you tell Photoshop what you want to create out of the shape you've drawn: a selection (marching ants), a vector mask, or a Shape layer.

- **Shape**. When you're in this mode and you make your first click with any vector drawing tool, Photoshop creates a new Shape layer for you to work on. When you finish drawing the shape, Photoshop automatically fills it with black, though you can use the Fill and Stroke settings in the Options bar to change fill color as well as add a solid, dashed, or dotted outline (skip ahead to page 552 for more on this fabulous feature). Drawing in this mode is similar to using a pair of scissors to cut shapes out of a piece of construction paper—these shapes can *hide* content on any layers below 'em, where the layers overlap.

> **NOTE** In Photoshop CC, the Shape layer thumbnails in the Layers panel display the contents of your *entire document*, not just the shape itself.

Shape mode works with the Pen tool and the shape tools. It's great for creating geometric shapes filled with color that you can use in designs or overlay onto images (like the embellishments shown on page 300). You can also use this mode to add a symbol or a logo to a product in an image (see page 548). Photoshop comes with a slew of built-in shapes to choose from, but you can also create your own (page 557) and download shapes created by other folks on the Internet. As you learned back in Chapter 4, you can also use the shape tools to create selections.

- **Path**. As you learned earlier, paths are lines and curves between *points*, which you'll find out more about in the next section. Path mode doesn't create a new Shape layer or fill the path with color; instead, when you're in this mode, Photoshop turns whatever you draw into an empty outline. Use this mode when you want to use the Pen tool to make selections (page 565) or create a clipping path (page 568), or when you want to create a vector mask that you may need to resize (see page 565). You can also fill paths with color (page 563) and give them a stroke (page 562), but Photoshop doesn't automatically create a new layer when you use the Pen tool or a shape tool in Paths mode; you have to create a new layer first *and then* add the fill or stroke. The paths you create in this mode live in the Paths panel, which you'll learn about on page 546.

- **Pixels**. This mode works only with the shape tools. Normally when you use one of these tools, Photoshop plops you into Shape mode and fills the vector-based shape with your foreground color on a new Shape layer. But in Pixels mode, Photoshop creates a *pixel*-based shape on the currently active pixel-based layer instead (it still fills the shape with your foreground color). This is handy if you need to edit the shape using tools that don't work with vectors, like filters, painting tools, and so on. That said, you could just as easily rasterize a Shape layer and then use those tools, or you could convert the vector layer for Smart Filters. So unless you know *for sure* that you'll never need to change the shape of the object you're drawing, use Shape mode instead of Pixel mode.

The basic drawing process is the same no matter which mode you choose: You pick the Pen tool or one of the shape tools, choose a drawing mode, draw the shape, edit the shape, and then—if you went the Path mode route—save it for future use. In the following sections, you'll learn how to do all that and more.

Now that you have a bird's-eye view of the process, it's time to dig into drawing with the Pen tool.

■ Drawing Paths with the Pen Tool

The Pen tool made its debut in Adobe Illustrator way back in the late '80s, and offered people precision and control the likes of which they'd never seen. The only problem was that the tool was (and still is) *darn* hard to use. It was met with all kinds of resistance from the artistic community because it didn't conform to the way folks were used to working with digital graphics (not to mention pens and pencils). Instead of dragging to draw a line, with the Pen tool you create *anchor points* and *control handles*, which are collectively referred to as *vector paths* or *Bézier curves* (named for their inventor). The handles aren't actually part of the line; they're little levers you use to control each line segment's curvature (see *Figure 13-3*).

As you learned back in Chapter 2, you can edit and resize vectors without losing quality. For example, you can adjust an object's points and paths (see *Figure 13-3*, bottom) to tweak its shape and then use Free Transform to resize, rotate, distort, warp, or flip the object. When it's just right, you can fill the shape with color, trace its outline with one of the painting tools, or use it to create a mask.

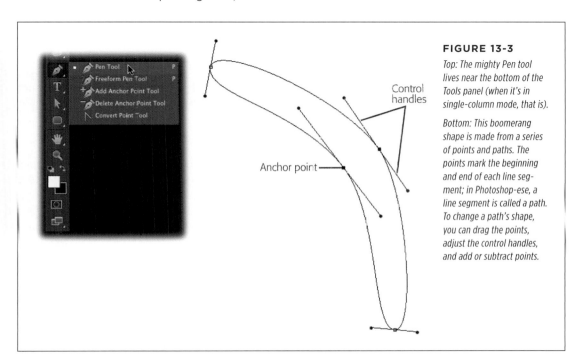

FIGURE 13-3

Top: The mighty Pen tool lives near the bottom of the Tools panel (when it's in single-column mode, that is).

Bottom: This boomerang shape is made from a series of points and paths. The points mark the beginning and end of each line segment; in Photoshop-ese, a line segment is called a path. To change a path's shape, you can drag the points, adjust the control handles, and add or subtract points.

To create a line with the Pen tool, you have to click *twice*: The first click creates the line's starting anchor point, the second click adds the ending anchor point, and then Photoshop *automatically* adds the path in between. It's kind of like digital connect-the-dots: Each time you add a new anchor point, a path appears connecting it to the previous point.

You use two different kinds of anchor points to tell Photoshop whether you want a curved or straight path:

- **Smooth**. Use these anchor points when you want the path to curve. If you click to set an anchor point and then drag in any direction—before releasing your mouse button—the Pen tool creates a *control handle* that you can drag to make the next path curve. (The direction you drag is extremely important, as you're about to learn.) When you click to make the second anchor point, Photoshop creates the actual path—a curved line between the two points.

- **Corner**. Use these anchor points when you want to draw a straight line. Simply click *without* dragging to set a point, and you don't get any control handles; instead, the Pen tool creates points connected by straight paths. To draw perfectly horizontal or vertical lines, press and hold the Shift key while you click to set more points. This limits the Pen tool to drawing straight lines at angles that are multiples of 45 degrees (45, 90, and so on), which is great when you want to draw geometric shapes.

Once you have, well, a *handle* on points and handles, you can make any shape you want. In the following pages you'll learn how to create both straight and curved paths.

Drawing Straight Paths

The easiest thing you'll ever do with the Pen tool is to make a straight path. To give the tool a spin, create a new document by choosing File→New, and then follow these steps:

1. **Press P to grab the Pen tool.**

   The Pen tool lives near the big T in the Tools panel, and its icon looks like a fountain pen nib.

2. **Choose Path mode in the Options bar.**

   From the mode drop-down menu near the left end of the Options bar, choose Path (shown in *Figure 13-2*). You could use Shape mode for this exercise, but in that mode, Photoshop starts filling the path with color as soon as you start drawing it, which gets visually confusing (and these techniques are hard enough as it is!). So to see only the path itself—with no fill color—work in Path mode instead.

3. **Mouse over to your document and click once to create an anchor point.**

   Photoshop puts a tiny black square where you clicked (*Figure 13-4*, top).

First click

Second click

FIGURE 13-4

Each time you click, Photoshop adds another anchor point, and connects each point with a path that forms your shape.

If you want to start a new path instead of adding to an existing one, just tap the Esc key and then click somewhere else in the document.

4. **Move your cursor to the right of the first anchor point and click to create a second anchor point.**

   Photoshop adds a straight line that connects the two points.

5. **Move your cursor down an inch or so, and click to create another anchor point.**

   Photoshop continues to connect the points with paths after you create each point. If you want to create a perfectly horizontal or vertical line, press and hold the Shift key as you click to add another anchor point (you can also use this trick to create lines at 45-degree angles).

6. **When you're finished drawing lines, press the Esc key or ⌘-click (Ctrl-click on a PC) elsewhere in the document.**

   The anchor points you created disappear, and you see a thin gray line representing the path you just drew.

7. **If you want to move an anchor point to change the angle of the line, grab the Direct Selection tool by pressing Shift-A until a white arrow appears in the Tools panel (see *Figure 13-4*, bottom).**

   You'll learn more about this tool when you start editing paths on page 557.

8. **Click to activate one of the line's anchor points, and then drag it somewhere else.**

   As long as you hold your mouse button down, you can move the point wherever you want. When you get it positioned just right, release the mouse button.

Congratulations! You've just drawn your first path with the Pen tool. Savor your success because it gets a *lot* harder from here on out.

Drawing Curved Paths

Drawing curves with the Pen tool is more complicated than drawing straight paths because you have to use the control handles mentioned on page 537 to tell Photoshop how *big* you want the curves to be and in what *direction* you want them to go. Here's what you do:

1. **With the Pen tool active, click within the document to set an anchor point and then—without letting go of your mouse button—drag to the left or right to make the point's control handles appear.**

   The control handles pop out from the point you created, and one of the handles sticks to your cursor. These handles indicate the direction the path will take; if you drag to the right, the path curves right when you add the next anchor point; if you drag left, the path curves left. For this exercise, drag upward and to the right about half an inch, and then release your mouse button (see *Figure 13-5*, top).

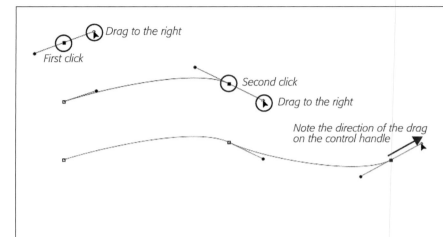

FIGURE 13-5

The direction you drag the control handle determines the direction of the next path you draw; you can watch the path between two points twist and bend as you drag the handle. And notice that the two opposing handles are connected and move in tandem. If you drag a handle to make it longer, the curve gets bigger.

NOTE It's next to *impossible* to get a sense of how the control handles work by reading about 'em. So if you're near a computer, fire up Photoshop so you can follow along. Better yet, visit this book's Missing CD page at *www.missingmanuals.com/cds* and download the file *Curve.tif* so you can practice drawing the curves shown in *Figure 13-5*.

2. **About two inches to the right of the first point, click to add a second point and, while still holding your mouse button down, drag the new handle downward and to the right half an inch, and then release your mouse button.**

   In step 1, you pulled the first handle upward and the curve obediently bent upward. By dragging this second control handle downward, your next curve will head downward (see *Figure 13-5*, middle).

3. **Create a third point by clicking and dragging upward and to the right.**

   The path that appears when you click to add this third point curves downward because you pulled the control handle downward in the previous step. Drag the third point's control handle upward and slightly to the right to make the curve shown in *Figure 13-5*, bottom.

4. **When you're finished, press the Esc key to let Photoshop know you're done drawing the path.**

   You can also ⌘-click (Ctrl-click) elsewhere in the document.

You've just drawn your first curved path! With practice, you'll get the hang of using the control handles to determine the direction and size of the curves. And as you may have guessed, the drawing process gets even more complicated from here.

TIP New in Photoshop CC, you can press and hold the space bar to reposition an anchor point *while* you're drawing a path.

Converting Anchor Points

As you learned on page 537, there are two kinds of anchor points in Photoshop: smooth and corner. To draw complicated paths, you need to know how to *switch* between these point types so you can create curves within a single path that go the same direction. (Take a peek ahead at *Figure 13-7*, bottom, to see what this looks like.) To do that, you start by creating a series of curves, and then convert some of the smooth points to corner points. Here's how:

1. **With the Pen tool active, click and hold with your mouse button to create a point, and then drag the control handle up and away from the anchor point to set the direction of the next curve (*Figure 13-6*, top left).**

   Release your mouse button when you're ready to set the next anchor point.

2. **Move your cursor an inch or so to the right, and then click to set a second point to the right of the first and drag downward (*Figure 13-6*, top right).**

   When the path has the curve you want, release your mouse button.

3. **Move your cursor another inch to the right and then click and drag downward to create a third point (*Figure 13-6*, middle).**

4. **Hop right another inch and then click and drag downward once again to create a fourth point (*Figure 13-6*, bottom).**

5. **Head over to the Tools panel and grab the Convert Point tool (*Figure 13-3*).**

   This tool is tucked away inside the Pen toolset (its icon looks like an upside-down V). Just click and hold on the Pen tool's icon to see the rest of the toolset, and then give it a click (for unknown reasons, the Shift-P trick doesn't work for the Add Anchor Point, Delete Anchor Point, or Convert Point tools).

6. **Drag the bottom control handle that's attached to the third anchor point (see *Figure 13-7*, top) up so it's close to the opposite control handle on the same anchor point.**

   The Convert Point tool "breaks" the bottom half of the control handle away from the top half so it can move independently. This nifty little maneuver converts the anchor point from a smooth point to a corner point and changes the path from a smooth curve to a sharp angle. Once you break control handles apart, they behave much like the hands of a clock and you can move them independently to adjust the angle and curve of the path.

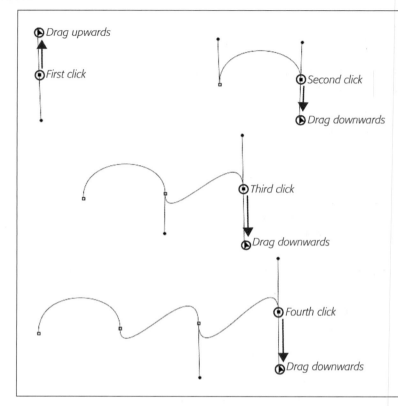

FIGURE 13-6

Here's how to draw a series of curves using smooth anchor points (the kind you get by dragging as you set an anchor point).

With smooth anchor points, the paths curve in the direction you dragged the control handle of the preceding anchor point.

To practice drawing these paths yourself, visit this book's Missing CD page at www.missingmanuals.com/cds *and download the file* ComboPath.tif.

7. **Use the Direct Selection tool to grab the path's second point from the left.**

   Unfortunately, you can't activate points with the Convert Point tool, so to see the second anchor point's control handles, you have to use the Direct Selection tool. As soon as you activate the anchor point, its control handles appear.

   TIP Holding down the ⌘ key (Ctrl on a PC) changes the Convert Point tool to the Direct Selection tool temporarily, saving you a trip to the Tools panel.

8. **Grab the Convert Point tool, click the bottom control handle that just appeared, and drag it upward next to its partner (see *Figure 13-7*, middle).**

   When you're finished, you should have a series of curves that all bend in the same direction (*Figure 13-7*, bottom).

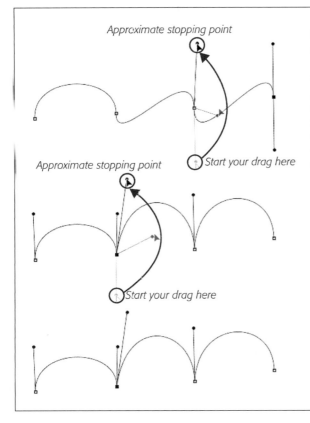

Approximate stopping point

Start your drag here

Approximate stopping point

Start your drag here

FIGURE 13-7

Once you convert smooth anchor points into corner anchor points, you can adjust each control handle separately to create a series of curves that bend in the same direction, as shown here.

If you move both parts of the control handle so they're on top of each other, you see only one handle (like the third anchor point shown at the middle and bottom), just as you see only one hand of a clock at noon, when the hour and minute hands overlap. If that happens, grab the Direct Selection tool and drag one of the handles out of the way so you can see them both.

Path Drawing Tips

Here are some things to keep in mind when you're drawing curved paths with the Pen tool:

- **Exaggerating curves**. If you want to create an exaggerated curve or one that curves back on itself, you need to drag one side of the control handle in the opposite direction from the way you drew the path (see *Figure 13-8*, left). Also, keep in mind that it's the *length* of the handle that determines the height or depth of the curve. (You lengthen a control handle by dragging it farther in any direction.) *Figure 13-8*, right, shows the effect of different-length handles on two similar paths.

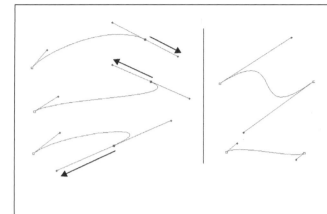

FIGURE 13-8

Left: Here's what happens when you drag the control handles in different directions. In all of these examples, the path was drawn from left to right. The top one shows what happens when you drag the control handle in the same direction as the path is traveling (left to right), the middle one shows what happens when you drag the handle up and to the left, and the bottom one shows what happens when you drag the control handle down and to the left.

Right: The farther you drag control handles, the longer they get and the more curved the path becomes. In the upper example, long control handles make for a really deep curve. In the lower example, short controls handles result in a shallow curve.

UP TO SPEED

Drawing with a French Curve

This Bezier curve business is darn tough to wrap your brain around. But if you've taken any kind of art class—even if it was as far back as middle school—there's a real-world counterpart that makes the curved paths you draw with the Pen tool a *little* easier to understand.

Drawing with Photoshop's Pen tool is similar to using a brush, pencil, or art knife with a set of *French curves*—plastic stencils that folks use as guides to create flowing, curved lines. French curves have some of the same limitations as the Pen tool. For example, the main challenge when using French curves is picking the stencil that will give you the longest sweep (or

arc) possible. You often have to switch stencils or change its position to follow a particular sweep.

With the Pen tool, you can take a similar approach: Try creating the longest possible distance between two points to keep your paths as simple—that is, with as few anchor points—as possible. The more points in a path, the less smooth the curves will be (using fewer points also makes your paths a little easier to edit). If you want to *print* what you've drawn, the printer itself has to translate and draw the path, so keeping it as simple as possible helps avoid problems.

- **Closing a path**. The paths you've seen so far have all been left open, meaning the starting and ending anchor points aren't connected. If your goal is to draw an arc, you *want* to leave the path open. To make an open path, after you create the last anchor point, just press the Esc key, ⌘-click (Ctrl-click) somewhere else in the document, or activate another tool in the Tools panel. But if you want to fill the path with color, you need to close it to create a *closed shape*, where the path's two ends are connected. To create a closed path, add the last anchor point and then point your cursor at the path's starting anchor point until a tiny circle (like a degree symbol) appears next to your cursor. Once you see the tiny circle, click the starting anchor point and Photoshop adds a straight path that joins the two points and closes the shape.

> **TIP** If you Option-click (Alt-click on a PC) to close a path, Photoshop adds *smooth* anchor point handles to it automatically.

- **Adding control handles**. If you want to add a control handle to an anchor point that doesn't have one—like the starting or ending anchor point of a straight line—grab the Pen tool and Option-click (Alt-click on a PC) the anchor point. You'll see a tiny, upside-down V (called a *caret*) appear next to your cursor. Keep holding the mouse button down and drag outward to create a *new* control handle that you can adjust to any angle you want, as shown in *Figure 13-9*. (If you Option-click [Alt-click] an anchor point that already has handles, you'll just grab that point's existing handles instead of creating a new one.)

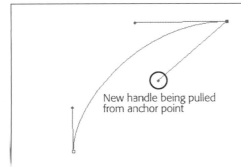

New handle being pulled
from anchor point

FIGURE 13-9

If you need to change the direction of a curve, you have to create a control handle, as shown here. When you drag the new control handle away from the path, you get a curve that heads in the direction you're dragging. But if you Option-click (Alt-click on a PC) the control handle and drag toward the path, you'll create a corner point that changes the direction of the curve. This gives you independent control over each of the point's control handles.

> **TIP** You can adjust the length of a path's control handles by ⌘-dragging (Alt-dragging on a PC) the path. This trick changes the depth of the curve as you drag. If the anchor point at the other end of the path segment doesn't have control handles, you'll end up with an angled corner at the far end of the path segment. You can move anchor points that don't have control handles by ⌘-dragging (Ctrl-dragging on a PC). These tricks make it easier to edit paths while you're drawing 'em.

Saving Paths

After all your hard work creating a path, it's a good idea to save it so you can edit it (as explained later in this chapter) and use it again later. Or you might want to use the path to make a vector mask, as explained on page 565. Since paths are vector-based, they don't take up much memory and won't increase a file's size much at all, so feel free to save as many of 'em as you want.

As you're drawing a path, Photoshop stores it in the Paths panel as a temporary *work path* (see *Figure 13-10*) and displays it in your document as a thin gray line. If you want to hide the gray line—so it's not a visual distraction—just press Return (Enter on a PC). To create multiple paths in a single document, click the "Create new path" icon at the bottom of the Paths panel (otherwise you have to save each path before starting on the next one to keep Photoshop from adding the subsequent path to the previous one). To work with your paths, open the Paths panel by choosing Window→Paths (see *Figure 13-10*).

NOTE Miraculously, Photoshop keeps an unsaved work path in your document even if you close the file and don't open it for a *year*. The catch is you can have only *one* unsaved work path in a document at a time. If you want to add to that work path, activate it in the Paths panel and start drawing. Don't forget to activate the path in your document, too, because if you start drawing *without* activating the work path first, the original path goes the way of the dodo bird. To be safe, you're better off saving a path if you think you'll want to reuse it.

Panel menu

Fill path with foreground color
Stroke path with brush
Load path as selection
Make work path from selection
Add layer mask
New path
Delete path

FIGURE 13-10

The Paths panel works pretty much like any other panel. When you're working with a particular path, Photoshop highlights it in the panel. If you want to delete a path, activate it and then press Delete (Backspace on a PC) or drag it onto the trash can at the bottom of the panel.

As with layers, you can change paths' stacking order, double-click to rename them, and so on. Changing the stacking order is a good way to keep related paths together; unfortunately, you can't organize paths into groups like you can with layers.

New in Photoshop CC is the ability to activate multiple paths by Shift- or ⌘-clicking (Ctrl-clicking) 'em in the Paths panel. This lets you delete, duplicate, or change their stacking order en masse.

Photoshop gives you several ways to save a path:

- **Choose Shape mode** (page 535) from the Options bar before you start drawing and Photoshop stores the path on its own layer. Don't forget to name the layer so you can keep track of the different paths you make.

- **Save the path before you draw it** (or rather, create a *placeholder* for it) by clicking the "Create new path" button at the bottom of the Paths panel (it looks like a piece of paper with a folded corner). Photoshop names the currently empty placeholder *Path 1*, but you can double-click its name later to change it.

- **Save the path after you draw it** by choosing Save Path from the Paths panel's menu.

- **Save the path as a custom shape** (page 546) that you can access through the Options bar's Custom Shape menu. You can save as many paths as you want (they won't bloat the file's size), so go ahead and have a path-saving party so you can reuse 'em again later.

- **Save the path as a clipping path** (see page 568) that you can use to *isolate* an object (hide its background) in a page-layout program like QuarkXpress or InDesign. If you plan on working with the image in older versions of these programs—which don't understand layered Photoshop documents—this method is your best bet.

Drawing with the Shape Tools

Photoshop has a pretty good stockpile of built-in, vector-based shapes, which are perfect for adding artistic embellishments or using as vector masks (discussed later in this chapter). They include a rectangle, a rounded rectangle (great for making round-edged selections; see page 143), an ellipse (handy for romantic, soft-edge vignette collages; see page 140), a polygon, a line, and a gazillion custom shapes (page 556). These preset goodies are huge timesavers because they keep you from having to draw something that already exists. And since these preset shapes are made from paths, you can also use the techniques described later in this chapter to morph them into anything you want.

The shape tools work in all three drawing modes (see page 535). This section focuses on the first mode: Shape. Just like any other kind of layer, you can stroke, fill, and add layer styles to Shape layers, as well as load 'em as selections.

Say you want to create a starburst shape to draw a viewer's attention to some important text in an ad (*Figure 13-11*); there's no sense in drawing the starburst from scratch because Photoshop *comes* with one. And since the shapes are all vector-based, they're resizable, rotatable, and colorable. If you need to make the shape bigger, for example, just activate the Shape layer, press ⌘-T (Ctrl+T) to summon Free Transform, and then use the little handles to make it as big as you want with no fear of quality loss.

FIGURE 13-11

You can save time and energy by using Photoshop's built-in shapes. Unless you tell the program otherwise (page 555), it puts each shape on its own Shape layer (circled). You can resize and rotate the shape using Free Transform (both the Shape and Type layers are active here so they rotate together; a handy info overlay appears showing the rotation angle).

You can change the shape's color by double-clicking its layer thumbnail to open the Color Picker, or gussy it up even more by adding a layer style like the drop shadow shown here.

The next section explains even more shape-formatting options.

Using the Shape Tools

The shape tools couldn't be easier to use: If you can move your mouse diagonally, you can draw a shape. Each shape—rectangle, rounded rectangle, and so on—has its own Options bar settings; *Figure 13-12* shows the Line tool's settings (Photoshop considers a line a shape). These settings let you create shapes that are certain sizes or have certain proportions, specify the number of sides in a polygon, indent the sides to make a star, and so on. You also get a bunch of *formatting* options that let you change the Shape layer's fill, stroke, stroke style (solid, dashed, or dotted), width, height, and so on.

Drawing with the Freeform Pen Tool

Lurking in the Pen toolset is the *Freeform Pen* tool, which lets you draw simply by dragging (kind of like how you draw with a real pen) instead of clicking to add points and tugging on control handles. Once you've used it to draw a path, you can edit that path using any of the techniques discussed in this chapter. If you're comfortable working with a graphics tablet (see the box on page 517), the Freeform Pen tool may be the way to go. For precise shapes, however, you're better off sticking with the Pen tool.

When using the Freeform Pen tool, you can turn on the Magnetic checkbox in the Options bar to switch to *Magnetic Pen* mode, which lets you create a path by clicking and then moving your cursor around the edge of the shape you want to select, trace, or mask (like you do with the Magnetic Lasso tool). When you turn on the Magnetic checkbox, Photoshop puts a tiny horseshoe magnet next to your cursor. The downside to this mode is that this tool sometimes produces more points than you can shake a stick at, which means you have to go back and do some point pruning, as explained in a moment.

To change the Magnetic Pen tool's settings, in the Options bar, click the gear icon to the left of the Magnetic checkbox. The resulting menu includes the following settings:

- **Curve Fit** lets you control the error tolerance when Photoshop fits Bezier curves along the path you're

making. Straight from the factory it's set to 2 pixels.

- **Width** determines how close to an edge your cursor has to be before Photoshop puts down a point, like the Magic Wand's tolerance setting. You can enter a value from 1 to 256 pixels.

- **Contrast** tells the tool how much contrast there has to be between pixels before it considers an area an edge and plunks down points. You can enter a percentage between 1 and 100; use a higher value for objects that don't have much contrast.

- **Frequency** lets you control how many points the Magnetic Pen tool adds. Enter a value between 0 and 100; the higher the number, the more points it adds.

- **Pen pressure**. If you're using a graphics tablet and pressure-sensitive stylus, turn on this checkbox.

When you're ready to start drawing, click once to set the starting point and then simply trace the outline of the object with your cursor. If the tool starts to go astray and adds points in the wrong spot, just click to add a point of your own. If you want to delete a point the tool created, move your cursor over the point and then press Delete (Backspace on a PC). When you've got an outline around the object, move your cursor over the starting point (a little circle appears next to your cursor) and then click once. That's it—the point is gone!

NOTE Remember, in Photoshop, the term "stroke" means "outline."

FIGURE 13-12

Top: One of the most commonly used shapes is the Line tool.

Bottom: When you activate it, you can use the settings in the Options bar to control fill and stroke color, stroke options (solid, dashed, or dotted lines), as well as add arrowheads to either end of the line— or both ends. Click the icons circled here to open the corresponding panels underneath for even more formatting goodness (you can't open 'em all at once though).

As you can see here, fills and strokes can be set to none, a solid color, gradient, or even a pattern.

Labels in figure: Gradient fill / Solid fill / No fill · Stroke width · Shape width & height · Line weight · Pattern fill · Click to open Color Picker

TIP Need to copy a shape's exact size, color, and position on the page for use with a website that uses CSS (cascading style sheets) to control its formatting? No problem. In CC you can grab *all* that info in one fell swoop by Control-clicking (right-clicking) near a Shape layer's name in the Layers panel and choosing Copy CSS. Photoshop copies the info to your computer's memory so you can hop over to a text editor or web-design program (Adobe Muse or Dreamweaver, say) and paste it right in. Nice!

All the shape tools work pretty much the same way, though they have slightly different settings in the Options bar. Here's how to use the Line tool:

1. **Grab the Line tool from the Tools panel.**

   The Line tool lives in the shape toolset near the bottom of the Tools panel (see *Figure 13-12*, top). If you've never used the shape tools before, the Rectangle tool is probably on top. Click it and hold down your mouse button to choose the Line tool from the resulting menu, or cycle through the various shape tools by pressing Shift-U repeatedly.

2. **In the Options bar, set the tool's drawing mode to Shape (page 535).**

   If you've used any other drawing mode, the Options bar will still be set to that previous mode.

3. **In the Options bar, choose fill and stroke colors, set the stroke width to 5 points, and then choose a solid line from the Stroke options menu.**

You can use the Options bar to set the line's fill and stroke color, as well as its style. Just click the Fill menu that's circled in *Figure 13-12* (bottom), and then pick a color from the resulting panel to create a solid color fill (if you don't pick a color, Photoshop uses your foreground color). Click the Stroke menu (also circled *Figure 13-12* and slightly redesigned in CC) and choose the same color as you did for the fill (the Stroke panel is identical to the Fill panel). Enter 5 points in the stroke width field, and then click the Stroke Options menu (it's circled in *Figure 13-12*, too) and click the solid line preset at the top of the resulting panel.

4. **Add an arrowhead.**

Click the gear icon that's circled in *Figure 13-12* (bottom) to open the Arrowheads menu, and then turn on the Start or End checkbox (or both). If you like, specify a size for the arrowhead(s) by entering percentages in the Width and Length fields (the factory setting of 500 percent of the line weight usually works fine). To curve the sides of the arrowhead inward, enter a percentage in the Concavity field.

TIP Using Photoshop's shape tools are also helpful when making custom *patterns*. For example, to create a diamond-shaped pattern, simply draw a shape using the Rectangle tool, adjust its fill and stroke as discussed in the next section, and then rotate the shape using Free Transform (page 257). Next, use the Rectangular Marquee tool to create a selection of the shape—be sure to include a little empty space around the shape so the repeating pattern won't be solid—and then follow the instructions on page 85 to define the pattern. To fill your document with the new pattern, use a Pattern Fill layer (which also gives you the ability to adjust the size of the pattern).

---

5. **Enter a weight for the line.**

In the Options bar's Weight field, enter a thickness for the line in pixels.

6. **Mouse over to the document and click where you want the line to start, drag, and then release your mouse button where you want the line to end.**

Photoshop creates a new Shape layer in the Layers panel that has a large colored box and a mask area. If the line isn't quite at the angle you wanted or it's not long enough, summon Free Transform by pressing ⌘-T (Ctrl+T) and then use the resizing handles to rotate the line or make it longer (be careful, though: The arrowhead might get squished or stretched in the process). Alternatively, you can enter a width and height for the line (or shape, if you're using a different tool) in the Options bar's W and H fields.

7. **Just for fun, change the line's fill color by double-clicking the Shape layer's thumbnail in the Layers panel and choosing a different color from the resulting Color Picker.**

Click OK when you're finished and the arrowhead turns the new color. (Changing the color in this way affects the shape's *fill*, not its *stroke*.)

NOTE If you don't like how the line turned out, you don't have to start over. Instead, with the Shape layer active, grab the Direct Selection tool and click the line you drew to reveal its anchor points; then, move 'em around until you get the look you want. To adjust the Options bar's line weight and arrowheads, switch back to the Line tool.

For practice, you can try performing the steps listed above using the Rectangle or Ellipse tool instead. And remember, once you've created a shape you can modify it in several ways:

- Grab the Direct Selection tool and move the shape's anchor points or alter the points' control handles.

TIP To activate several points at once, click and drag with the Direct Selection tool to encompass the points you want to edit. However, in Photoshop CC, this maneuver *also* activates anchor points of any overlapping shapes on other layers. To keep that from happening, first activate the layer(s) you want to edit in your Layers panel, and then choose Selected from the Layers panel's filtering drop-down menu (page 71).

- Use the Pen tool to add or subtract points. You'll learn more about editing paths on page 557.
- Change the shape's color by double-clicking the Shape layer's thumbnail or by clicking the Fill swatch in the Options bar to open the Fill panel, shown in *Figure 13-12* (bottom).
- Use Free Transform to resize, distort, or rotate the shape.
- Use layer styles to add special effects to the Shape layer.

TIP To draw a symmetrical shape (like a perfect square or circle), press and hold the Shift key as you drag with a shape tool; Photoshop keeps the shape's sides the same size. To draw a shape from the center out, press and hold Option (Alt on a PC) as you drag.

You can do all kinds of wonderful things with Shape layers, so it's worth taking the time to experiment with all the different shape tools and their various settings.

TIP You can also Shift-click within your document with a shape tool to summon a dialog box where you can enter the shape's dimensions (be sure to enter the unit of measurement, such as *px* for pixels or *in* for inches). Click OK and Photoshop creates the shape *for* you. Alas, this trick doesn't work with the Line or Pen tools.

■ CUSTOMIZING STROKE OPTIONS

There's no end to the different kinds of strokes you can add to shapes and paths in Photoshop. By clicking the More Options button at the bottom of the Stroke Options panel (shown back in *Figure 13-12*), you get the dialog box shown in *Figure 13-13* (right).

FIGURE 13-13

Left: You can create many different line styles in Photoshop including arrowheads and even dashed and dotted lines. Clicking the More Options button at the bottom of the Stroke options panel (visible back in Figure 13-12) opens the Stroke dialog box shown here, which lets you customize exactly how the stroke looks (some of these settings are available in the Stroke options panel, too). For example, a dashed line set to 0 length and a gap setting of 4 was used to create the dotted line you see here at top left.

Right: Shape layers have a special badge on their layer thumbnails; it looks like a square with clear corner points (circled).

Photoshop's Stroke dialog box lets you customize the stroke in the following ways:

- **Presets**. Use this menu to access Photoshop's stroke presets, which, initially, are a solid, dashed, or dotted line. Once you customize a stroke, you can save it as a preset by clicking the Save button to this menu's right. When you do, Photoshop adds the new preset to this menu, as well as to the Stroke options menu in the Options bar. You can't name your preset: Photoshop shows you a preview of what the line *looks* like instead.

- **Align**. This menu controls the alignment of the stroke itself (not the shape the stroke is attached to). From the factory, it's set to Inside, meaning the stroke appears on the inside of the shape you've attached it to. Your other choices are Center and Outside.

- **Caps**. You can use this menu to control stroke's the line cap style. Your choices are Butt, Round (the factory setting), and Square.

- **Corners**. Use this menu to choose a *join* type for the stroke, which controls the way a straight line changes direction or turns a corner. Your choices are Miter (creates pointed corners), Round (creates rounded corners), and Bevel (creates squared corners that are ever so slightly rounded).

- **Dashed Line, Dash, Gap**. Turn on the Dashed Line checkbox to create a dashed or dotted line. To increase dash length, enter a number in the Dash fields (a dot is just a dash set to 0 length). To increase the space between dashes or dots, enter a number in the Gap field. You can use the other Dash and Gap fields to vary individual dashes within the *same* stroke.

As you adjust these settings, Photoshop displays a preview in the Preset field that changes to match your choices. Once you've formatted a stroke to your liking, you can copy and paste it onto other shapes. Just click the little gear icon at the top right of the Stroke Options panel (see *Figure 13-12*) and choose Copy Stroke Details. Then click to activate another shape (or a different Shape layer), pop open the Stroke Options panel, and choose Paste Stroke Details from its panel menu. This same menu also lets you save your customizations as a preset you can use again later, though that's not necessary for simply copying and pasting stroke settings.

■ USING LIVE SHAPE PROPERTIES

New in Photoshop CC is the ability to change formatting options of shapes you've drawn with the Rectangle, Rounded Rectangle, and Ellipse tools using the Properties panel. You get nearly the same settings that are in the Options bar—with the addition of X and Y fields that let you *reposition* the shape on your document horizontally and vertically (respectively)—though if you keep your Properties panel floating near your image window, they're a bit easier to get to there (rather than *way* up in the Options bar).

The big honkin' deal about these new *Live Shape Properties*, as Adobe calls 'em, is the ability to change the radius of the corners drawn with the Rounded Rectangle tool—set to *Shape* mode (page 535)—*after* you've drawn it, as *Figure 13-14* explains. This handy bit o' magic also works with the Rectangle tool, so if you draw a rectangle and then decide you'd rather have rounded corners, you don't have to start over; just activate that layer and pop open the Properties panel (it doesn't matter what tool is active when you do so). Live Shape Properties also work on multiple rectangles (rounded or not), provided they were all drawn in Photoshop CC and not a previous version of the program.

NOTE As of this writing, CC's new Live Shape Properties are not available for use with actions (Chapter 18).

FIGURE 13-14

The Rounded Rectangle tool is incredibly handy, though when you use it, it's tough to get the radius (roundness) of the rectangle's corners just right. To alleviate the Radius-setting guessing game, Photoshop now lets you change it after you've drawn the shape by using the new Live Shape Properties in the Properties panel.

To adjust each corner's roundness after you've created a Shape layer with the Rounded Rectangle tool, make sure that layer is active, and then open the Properties panel to summon the settings shown here (Window→Properties). To adjust the radius, enter a new value into the Radius fields labeled here (you can adjust each corner separately, which lets you create some nifty looks). Alas, these options aren't available when you've used the tool in Path drawing mode.

Fill, Stroke options

Radius

Path operations

Drawing Multiple Shapes on One Layer

Each time you draw with a shape tool in Shape mode (page 535), Photoshop adds a new Shape layer to your document. If you want to keep drawing on the *same* Shape layer instead of creating new ones, use the Options bar's Add, Subtract, Intersect, and Exclude buttons (they're nestled in the Path operations menu labeled in *Figure 13-2* and *Figure 13-14*; flip ahead to page 560 for details on how these options work). Rather than hunting for those menus, you can press and hold the Shift key to add shapes to the active Shape layer; just release the Shift key once you've clicked to start drawing the shape to keep from constraining it to be perfectly square, elliptical, and so on.

> **TIP** You can move shapes independently of one another even if they live on the same Shape layer. To do that, grab the Path Selection tool from the Tools panel (the black arrow—see page 558), click within your document to activate the shape, and then drag it wherever you want. Or, instead of dragging, use the arrow keys on your keyboard to nudge the shape one pixel at a time (add the Shift key to nudge it 10 pixels at a time).

Using Custom Shapes

To find the *really* useful shapes that come with Photoshop, you have to do a bit of foraging. Grab the Custom Shape tool (which looks vaguely like a starfish) from the Tools panel—it's in the same toolset as all the other shape tools (see *Figure 13-12*, top). Then head up to the Options bar and open the Custom Shape picker by clicking the field labeled in *Figure 13-15*.

TIP   Technically, you don't have to trot all the way up to the Options bar to access Photoshop's Custom Shapes; just Control-click (right-click on a PC) within your document and the Custom Shape picker menu appears next to your cursor. Who knew?

When the menu opens, click the little gear icon circled in *Figure 13-15*. In the resulting menu, choose All. A dialog box appears asking if you want to replace the current shapes; click OK. Now you can see a preview of *all* the built-in shapes right there in the Custom Shape picker (why Photoshop doesn't load these shapes automatically is a mystery). You can also use this menu to change the size of the previews or to display them as a text-only list.

Click to open Custom Shape picker

FIGURE 13-15

If you create a shape with the Pen tool, you can save it by choosing Save Shapes from the menu shown here (click the circled gear icon to open it). Give your shape a name and it appears in the list of presets.

You can also do the same thing by creating a shape, activating its layer in the Layers panel, and then choosing Edit→Define Custom Shape.

You draw with these shapes just as you do with the Line tool (page 550), except that instead of dragging horizontally or vertically, drag *diagonally* to create the shape (or Shift-click within your document to summon a dialog box where you can enter a width and height for the shape). You can also press and hold the Shift key to make the shape perfectly proportional so it looks like the little icon you picked in the Shape picker. You can modify the shape by using the Options bar's Fill and Stroke settings, applying layer styles, or customizing their shapes by using the Direct Selection tool to tweak their anchor points and control handles.

TIP   Skip ahead to page 747 to see how to add a *watermark* (custom copyright info) to your images using the Custom Shape tool. This is a great way to protect your images from online theft.

The *real* power of using custom shapes, however, lies in defining your own, which can save you tons of time. For example, if you have a piece of vector art that you need to use over and over, you can save it as a custom shape. Choose File→Place to import the art into Photoshop, and then load it as a selection by ⌘-clicking (Ctrl-clicking) its layer thumbnail. Next, save it as a path by opening the Paths panel and choosing Make Work Path from the Paths panel's menu. Finally, choose Edit→Define Custom Shape; in the resulting dialog box, give the new shape a memorable name, and then press OK. From then on, your custom shape appears in the Options bar's Custom Shapes picker any time you're using the Custom Shape tool. To draw the shape you added, just choose it from the menu and then drag in your document.

Editing Paths

All this talk about setting points, dragging handles, and creating shapes can sound a bit intimidating. But it's important to remember that the Pen and shape tools are *very* forgiving—if you don't get the path right the first time, you can always edit it by adding, deleting, and repositioning points and dragging their control handles (yes, this applies to shapes drawn on Shape layers, too). The trick lies in knowing *which* tool to use to make the changes you want. This section explains all your options.

Adding, Deleting, and Converting Points

At first, you may have a wee bit of trouble drawing paths—*especially* with the Pen tool—that look exactly like you want (surprise!). But don't stress; just add more points, move them around, and adjust the curves until you get the shape you want. You'll need fewer and fewer points as you get more comfortable using the vector drawing tools. And if you've had yourself a point party, you can delete the extra ones.

Adding and deleting points is really easy since the Pen tool figures out what you want to do depending upon what your cursor is pointed at. For example:

- **To add a point**, grab the Add Anchor Point tool (shown on page 537) from the pen toolset (it looks like the Pen tool's icon with a plus sign next to it). When you see a tiny plus sign appear next to the cursor, you can click an existing path to create a new point. You can also just grab the Pen tool, point your cursor at an existing path (but avoid pointing it at anchor points) and the cursor turns into the Add Anchor Point tool automatically. Click anywhere on the path to set new anchor points.

- **To delete a point**, open the Pen toolset and grab the Delete Anchor Point tool (it looks like the Pen tool with a tiny minus sign). Or grab the Pen tool and then place your cursor over an existing point; a tiny minus sign appears next to the cursor to let you know that the Delete Anchor Point tool (shown on page 537) is active. Either way, click once to get rid of that point.

- **To convert a point from a smooth point to a corner point (or vice versa)**, use the Convert Point tool nested in the Pen toolset (see the exercise on page 541). To quickly change to this tool while using the Pen tool, press the Option key (Alt on a PC) and place your cursor over an anchor point. (Photoshop puts a tiny, upside-down V next to the cursor to let you know that it's swapped to the Convert Point tool.) Click to make Photoshop change the anchor point from one type to the other.

> **NOTE** Prior to CS6, there was a bug involving the Convert Point tool when it was used to introduce a break in a curved path (dragging the resulting path segment ignored the break). Happily, that problem has been fixed. Now when you use the tool to break a curved path, dragging in the middle of a resulting path segment affects just that segment. If you click on a segment closer to an anchor point, the anchor still moves, but it doesn't straighten out the segment on the other side of it.

- **To add a segment to a path**, put your cursor over the ending anchor point of an open path and then click or simply drag to continue drawing. (A tiny forward slash appears next to the cursor.)
- **To join the ends of two open path segments**, grab the Pen tool, click one segment's endpoint and then put your cursor over one of the other segment's endpoints. When a tiny circle with a line on either side of it appears next to the cursor (it looks almost like a chain link), click to connect the two.

Activating and Moving Paths

Because Photoshop's paths are made from multiple line segments or individual shapes, you can activate, move, reshape, copy, or delete parts of a path—or the whole thing—using the Path Selection and Direct Selection tools, which share a toolset near the middle of the Tools panel (their icons look like arrows). To activate 'em, click the arrow icon in the Tools panel or press A (or Shift-A to switch between the two).

> **TIP** New in Photoshop CC is the ability to activate multiple paths in your document by Shift-clicking them. And if you're editing an object drawn with one of Photoshop's shape tools, you can ⌘-click (Ctrl-click on a PC) outside the shape to deactivate a path whenever a shape tool is active.

The Direct Selection tool turns your cursor into a *white* arrow and lets you activate specific points in a path or individual line segments and apply changes only to them, leaving the rest of the path alone (see *Figure 13-16*, bottom left). The Path Selection tool turns your cursor into a *black* arrow and lets you activate a whole path (*Figure 13-16*, bottom right) so you can do things like move, resize, or rotate the whole thing.

Once you've activated a path(s) or part of a path, you can do the following:

- **Copy it** by Option-dragging (Alt-dragging on a PC) it to another location. This is handy if you're making a pattern or want to add a bunch of objects to your document. Add the Shift key to copy in a straight line (the copies are all part of the same work path or saved path).

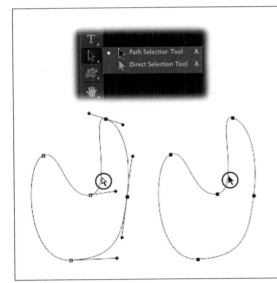

FIGURE 13-16

Top: To move points and paths around, grab 'em with the Direct Selection and Path Selection tools, respectively.

Bottom left: Use the Direct Selection tool to choose specific points. You can tell which points are active because they turn black (here, two points are active).

Bottom right: Use the Path Selection tool to activate a whole path (notice how all the points are black).

You can make the Direct Selection tool act like the Path Selection tool by pressing Option (Alt on a PC). You can also activate multiple points by drawing a box around them by dragging with either the Direct Selection or the Path Selection tool.

TIP You can also use the Paths panel (page 456) to activate, copy, and delete paths. New in Photoshop CC is the ability to activate multiple paths in the Paths panel by Shift- or ⌘-clicking (Ctrl-clicking) them. CC also lets you *duplicate* a path by Option-dragging it (Alt-dragging on a PC) within the Paths panel.

- **Delete a segment** by pressing Delete (Backspace on a PC). If you've got a point activated, you can delete the *whole* path by pressing Delete (Backspace) twice.

- **Align it** using Photoshop's alignment tools (page 562). Use the Path Selection tool to activate two or more paths and Photoshop displays alignment tools in the Options bar.

- **Combine it** with another path by activating both paths and then clicking the Options bar's Combine button.

- **Resize it**. Summon Free Transform by pressing ⌘-T (Ctrl+T) and Photoshop adds a bounding box around the path you activated, complete with resizing handles.

- **Change its intersect mode**. Lurking in the Path operations menu—it's to the right of the W and H fields when the Path Selection or Direct Selection tools are active—are four options that let you intersect overlapping shapes (closed paths) in a variety of ways. These modes, which are described in the next section, let you combine paths to make new shapes.

- **Change it** (by filling it with color or adding a stroke to it, for example) without affecting the whole path. As shown in *Figure 13-17,* by activating certain segments, you can fill them with color or give them a stroke (you'll learn how on page 563 and page 562, respectively).

FIGURE 13-17

Top: Here's a close-up of the painting shown in Figure 13-1, bottom, with certain paths activated (notice the black anchor points around the active shapes).

Bottom: By activating specific paths, you tell Photoshop to apply any changes you make only to those paths. Here, the active paths were filled with dark blue.

To temporarily hide a path's outline, press Shift-⌘-H (Shift+Ctrl+H).

Making Paths Intersect

You can use the Options bar's Path operations menu to change the *intersect mode* of two or more overlapping paths (*Figure 13-18*, top). These modes let you combine overlapping shapes in a variety of ways. Here are your options:

> **TIP** In Photoshop CC, you can also access the Path operations menu in the Properties panel when you've created a Shape layer using the Rectangle, Rounded Rectangle, or Ellipse tools.

- **Combine Shapes**. Use this mode to add one shape to another. The combined shapes merge into one, and Photoshop deletes the paths in the shapes' overlapping areas (*Figure 13-18*, middle left). Its icon is two overlapping squares that blend together in the middle. Keyboard shortcut: Shift.

- **Subtract Front Shape**. This mode cuts out the area where two shapes overlap (*Figure 13-18*, bottom left). Its icon is a white square overlapping a gray square. Keyboard shortcut: Option (Alt).

FIGURE 13-18

Top: The tools for making paths intersect live in the Path operations menu, shown here.

Middle left: The first piece in this flower was drawn in Shape mode, but the rest of the parts were drawn in Combine Shapes mode so everything stayed on one layer. (Drawing all your shapes on a single layer lets you combine the parts together into a single shape.) Use the Path Selection tool to grab all the shapes in the flower, and then choose Merge Shape Components. Photoshop joins the active paths together into a single shape.

Bottom left: While you're in Combine Shapes mode, draw a circle in the flower's center. With the new circle active, choose Subtract Front Shape and Photoshop knocks the center out of the flower.

Middle right: To hide the top and bottom of the flower, grab the Pen tool, and then choose Intersect Shape Areas. Next, grab the Rectangle tool and drag over the flower to hide everything that falls outside the square's edges.

Bottom right: You can hide the whole flower save for its tips by choosing Exclude Overlapping Shapes. Then grab the Rounded Rectangle tool and drag over the flower to hide the parts that overlap the rectangle. (Since the circle in the center of the flower was already hidden, it flips back to its original color.)

Combine Shapes

Merge Shape Components

Intersect Shape Areas

Subtract Front Shape

Exclude Overlapping Shapes

TIP Want to see your work without lines and handles? You can hide the shape outlines and handles by pressing Shift-⌘-H (Shift+Ctrl+H); press those same keys again to bring 'em back.

- **Intersect Shape Areas**. Use this mode to get rid of the parts of your shapes that *don't* overlap (*Figure 13-18*, middle right). Its icon is two hollow squares with a dark area where they overlap. Keyboard shortcut: Shift-Option (Shift+Alt).

- **Exclude Overlapping Shapes**. This mode hides the areas where shapes overlap (*Figure 13-18*, bottom right). Its icon is two overlapping gray squares that are transparent where they intersect.

- **Merge Shape Components**. This mode combines the active shapes into a single shape.

■ ALIGNING AND REARRANGING PATHS

Photoshop also includes a few more helpful settings for arranging paths just the way you want 'em. The following settings live in the Options bar to the right of the Path operations menu and are active any time more than one path or Shape layer is active:

- **Path alignment**. This menu gives you all the same alignment tools that you get with layers (page 93). Once you've activated more than one path, you can choose to align their left edges, horizontal centers, right edges, top edges, vertical centers, bottom edges, as well as distribute their widths and heights. From the factory, this menu is set to Align To Selection, which aligns the right-most *path* edges. The last option is Align To Canvas, which aligns all the paths to the edge of the *canvas* instead.

- **Path arrangement**. Use this menu to control the stacking order of your paths. Your options are Bring Shape To Front, Bring Shape Forward, Send Shape Backward, and Send Shape To Back.

- **Align Edges**. This checkbox lets you align the edges of a path's stroke (if you've added one) to the pixel grid, ensuring sharper strokes.

- **Constrain Path Dragging**. This option is only available for the Path Selection or Direct Selection tools. You can use this checkbox to adjust a single path contained *within* a shape instead of altering the *entire* shape.

Adding a Stroke to a Path

After you create a path with the Pen tool, you can add a *stroke* (outline) to it using the Options bar's Fill setting (shown in *Figure 13-12* on page 550); however, you can also stroke a path with Photoshop's painting tools. This is handy when you're trying to draw a long, smooth, flowing line like the one in *Figure 13-19* (right). Try drawing that Z freehand using the Brush tool—it's *really* hard to create such a perfect Z shape. But with the Pen tool, you can draw the path first, edit it (if necessary) using the techniques described in the previous sections, and then add the fancy red stroke using your favorite brush (see Chapter 12 for more on brushes).

NOTE When you add color to a path with either a fill or a stroke, the color appears on the currently active layer. So it's a good idea to take a peek in the Layers panel and make sure you're on the *right* layer first.

Once you've created a path, open the Layers panel and add a new layer by clicking the "Create a new layer" button at the bottom of the panel. With the new layer active, you can add a stroke to a path in a couple of ways:

- **Choose Stroke Path from the Paths panel's menu**. In the resulting dialog box (*Figure 13-19*, left), pick the tool you want to use for the stroke. The drawback to this method is that the stroke picks up whatever settings you last applied to that tool (you don't get a chance to change them). For example, if you set the Brush tool to a certain blend mode or lowered its opacity, the stroke uses that blend mode or opacity.

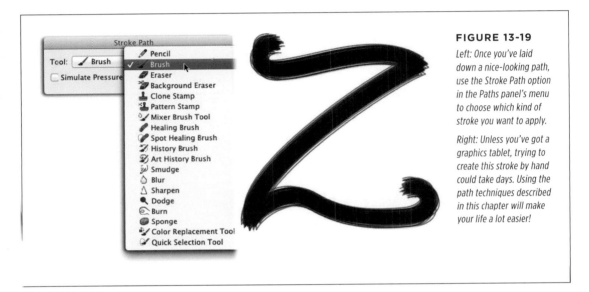

FIGURE 13-19

Left: Once you've laid down a nice-looking path, use the Stroke Path option in the Paths panel's menu to choose which kind of stroke you want to apply.

Right: Unless you've got a graphics tablet, trying to create this stroke by hand could take days. Using the path techniques described in this chapter will make your life a lot easier!

TIP You can open the Stroke Path dialog box by Option-clicking (Alt-clicking on a PC) the Stroke Path button at the bottom of the Paths panel (it looks like a hollow circle), or by Option-dragging (Alt-dragging) the path in the Paths panel onto the Stroke Path button.

- **Activate the tool you want to use to stroke the path**. Adjust its settings in the Options bar, and then click the Stroke Path button at the bottom of the Paths panel. This method helps you avoid having to undo the stroke because the tool's settings are all screwy.

Filling a Path

Before you fill a path, take a moment to consider whether it's an open or closed path. As described earlier, the starting and ending anchor points of an open path don't meet. Since you can't really fill a shape that's not closed, if you try to fill an open shape, Photoshop *imagines* a straight line that connects the starting point to the ending point, and then fills all the closed areas created by that imaginary line. This can lead to some rather strange results, as shown in *Figure 13-20*, top. When you fill a closed path—one where the starting and ending points *do* meet—Photoshop fills the whole shape just like you'd expect (*Figure 13-20*, bottom).

FIGURE 13-20

Top: When you fill an open path, Photoshop creates areas to fill by pretending there's a straight line connecting the start and end points.

Bottom: Not surprisingly, filling a closed path stocks the shape with color.

After you draw a path, choose from the following fill methods:

- **Use the Fill setting in the Options bar**. When you click this icon, Photoshop opens the Fill panel shown back in *Figure 13-12*, which lets you fill the path with a solid color, gradient, or pattern. It's discussed earlier in this chapter on page 551.

- **Choose Fill Path from the Paths panel's menu**. Photoshop opens the Fill Path dialog box, where you can choose what you want to fill the shape with (see *Figure 13-21*). This is handy if you want to use a pattern or a specific blend mode.

- **Click the "Fill path with foreground color" button** at the bottom left of the Paths panel (it looks like a gray circle) and Photoshop uses your foreground color as the fill color (you don't get a dialog box with this method). Activating the path in the Paths panel and then dragging it onto this button does the same thing.

- **Option-click (Alt-click on a PC) the "Fill path with foreground color" button** to summon the Fill Path dialog box (*Figure 13-21*). You can do the same thing by activating the path in the Paths panel and then Option-dragging (Alt-dragging) it onto this button.

FIGURE 13-21

This dialog box let you tell Photoshop exactly what you want to fill the path with and change the fill's blend mode or feather its edges.

To open the Color Picker, choose Color from the Use drop-down menu.

The Fill Path dialog box (*Figure 13-21*) is divided into three sections:

- **Contents**. The Use drop-down menu lets you decide whether to fill the path with your foreground or background color, Content-Aware (see page 408), or a pattern (you pick the pattern from the Custom Pattern drop-down menu). Choose Color to summon the Color Picker so you can choose any color you want. If you choose History, Photoshop fills the path with the currently active History state or a snapshot of the document in a previously saved state.

- **Blending**. Use the Mode drop-down menu to change the fill's blend mode and the Opacity field to change its opacity. Turn on the Preserve Transparency checkbox if you're filling a path on a layer that's partially transparent so Photoshop fills only the part that's *not* transparent.

- **Rendering**. If you want to make the fill's edges soft and slightly transparent, enter a number in the Feather Radius field (this setting works like the Refine Edge dialog box's Feather slider; see page 170). The higher the number, the softer the edge. Leave the Anti-alias checkbox turned on to make Photoshop smooth the fill's edges by adding a slight blur; if you turn it off, the fill's edges will be hard and look blocky in curved areas.

Making Selections and Masks with Paths

As you learned in Chapter 4, Photoshop is loaded with selection tools. However, when you're trying to select something *really* detailed, like the column section shown in

Figure 13-22, none of the regular selection tools can help. That's because the shape is complex and there's very little contrast between the area being selected and the surrounding pixels.

Luckily, you can use the Pen tool to draw a path that follows the contours of any shape you want to select (*Figure 13-22*, bottom), no matter how intricate it is. The beauty of this method is that the Pen tool is so forgiving—if you don't get it right the first time, you can edit the path. When you've got the path in place, you can load it as a selection and proceed merrily on your way, doing whatever you want with the selected object.

FIGURE 13-22

The lack of contrast in this image makes it nearly impossible to select just part of the façade (top).

However, you can use the Pen tool to draw a path around the section you want by hand (bottom).

To load a path as a selection, first create the path with the Pen tool and then choose one of these methods:

- **Click the Selection button in the Options bar**. This summons the dialog box shown in *Figure 13-23*, where you can adjust settings like the selection's feather amount and whether you want Photoshop to apply anti-aliasing. In the Operation section, you can choose to create a new selection, add to or subtract from an existing one, or create a selection from the intersection of this one and an existing one.

FIGURE 13-23

The Make Selection dialog box lets you feather the selection, apply anti-aliasing to its edges, or combine it with an existing selection (discussed on the next page).

- **Choose Make Selection from the Paths panel's menu** and Photoshop opens the Make Selection dialog box.

- **Click the "Load path as a selection" button** at the bottom of the Paths panel (it looks like a tiny dotted circle). This method lets you bypass the Make Selection dialog box. Photoshop applies the settings you used the *last* time you used the Make Selection dialog box (like the feather radius). If you haven't yet used that dialog box, Photoshop sets the feather radius to zero, leaves anti-aliasing turned on, and—if a selection tool is active—creates a brand-new selection.

- **Option-click (Alt-click on a PC) the "Load path as a selection" button** at the bottom of the Paths panel. When you do, Photoshop opens the Make Selection dialog box.

- **In the Paths panel, drag the path's thumbnail onto the "Load path as a selection" button**. This method bypasses the Make Selection dialog box and applies the settings you used last time.

- **Then ⌘-click (Ctrl-click) the path's thumbnail in the Paths panel**. You won't get a Make Selection dialog box this way, either; the program simply applies the last settings you used.

TIP If you're a fan of keyboard shortcuts, you can load your path as a *new* selection by pressing ⌘-Return (Ctrl-Enter on a PC); add the path to the active selection by pressing Shift-⌘-Return (Shift+Ctrl+Enter); *subtract* the path from an active selection by pressing Option-⌘-Return (Alt+Ctrl+Enter); or *intersect* the path with an active selection by pressing Shift-Option-⌘-Return (Shift+Alt+Ctrl+Enter).

At the bottom of the Make Selection dialog box lies a section labeled Operation (*Figure 13-23*). If you don't have any active selections, Photoshop assumes you want to make a new selection and doesn't let you choose any of the other options.

But if you already have an active selection, you can make the selected path interact with it in different ways:

- **Add to Selection** adds the path's shape and attributes (like feather radius, fill color, stroke thickness, and so on) to the active selection.
- **Subtract from Selection** subtracts the path's shape and attributes from the active selection.
- **Intersect with Selection** selects only the area where the path and the active selection overlap.

Making a Path from a Selection

You can also do the opposite and create a path from an existing selection. This is helpful if you need to alter a selection you made with another tool. For example, you can start out with a selection you created with the Rectangular Marquee tool, turn it into a path, and then tweak it with the Pen tool. Here's how: Create a selection, and then click the "Make work path from selection" button at the bottom of the Paths panel (it looks like a circle with lines extending from either side). Then, using the path-editing techniques you learned earlier in this chapter, edit away. To transform the path back into a selection, just use one of the options listed in the previous section.

TIP The paths that Photoshop creates when you turn a selection into a path aren't always terribly sharp. Pixel selections—especially ones you make with the Magic Wand—can create bumpy paths that have too many points. If you select an area that needs to be smoothed, open the Paths panel's menu and choose Make Work Path. In the resulting dialog box, you can adjust the Tolerance setting to smooth out the pixels. The higher the tolerance, the smoother the resulting path will be. But if you set the tolerance *too* high (anything over 5), you'll start to lose details. (This dialog box doesn't appear when you click the Make Work Path button at the bottom of the Paths panel.)

Making a Clipping Path

If you want to isolate an object from its background to use it in an *older* version of a page-layout program like QuarkXPress or Adobe InDesign, you can create a *clipping path* (newer versions of both programs prefer PSD files). A clipping path is like a written description of your selection that those programs can understand even if they can't handle PSD files, layers, and transparency. You still send the whole document to the page layout-program, but the clipping path specifies which *portion* of the image to display.

For example, *Figure 13-24* shows a cup that's been isolated from its background in Photoshop using a clipping path and then placed on a blue background in a page-layout program. The page-layout program understands the clipping path that travels along with the file, and uses it to hide the cup's original background.

FIGURE 13-24

Top: You can use a clipping path to isolate this cup from its background in a way that older page-layout programs understand.

Bottom: Here's the cup after it was placed on a totally different background in a page-layout program.

Both Adobe InDesign CS4 and later and QuarkXPress 8 can read layered Photoshop files with transparency and recognize paths saved in TIFF files. So if you're using the latest versions of those programs, you don't need to worry about clipping paths. But if you're dealing with an older version, mastering clipping paths can make you the office hero.

To create a clipping path around an image like the cup in *Figure 13-24*, follow these steps:

1. **Draw a closed path around the cup with the Pen tool.**

   Press P to grab the Pen tool and draw a path around the outside edge of the cup using the techniques discussed earlier in this chapter. (Zoom in nice and close when drawing the path; see *Figure 13-25*, top.) When you're done, make sure to click the starting point to close the path.

2. **Draw a second path inside the cup's handle.**

   To knock out the area inside the handle, click the Options bar's Path operations menu and choose Exclude Overlapping Shapes so the second path cuts a hole through the first (see *Figure 13-25*, bottom). Be sure to close this second path by clicking its starting point.

3. **Save the paths.**

   Photoshop won't let you make a clipping path until you save the path. Over in the Paths panel, activate the work path (page 546) and drag it onto the "Create new path" button at the bottom of the panel, or choose Save Path from the Paths panel's menu. In the dialog box that appears, give the path a descriptive name like *Cup outline*.

FIGURE 13-25

You can see the path as it travels along the edge of the cup (top left), and continues until the entire cup is surrounded (top right).

To omit the space inside the handle, draw a second path around the inside of the handle (bottom).

When you're trying to isolate an object from its background, it's a good idea to draw the path about 1 or 2 pixels inside the object's edge just to make sure that none of the background sticks around. This way, you're more likely to avoid jagged edges where bits of the background show through the selection.

4. **Turn the path into a clipping path.**

   From the Paths panel's menu, choose Clipping Path. In the resulting dialog box (*Figure 13-26*, top), choose the path's name from the Path menu. The Flatness field controls how accurately printers will follow the path. A lower number means the printer pays attention to more points on the path (so the print is more accurate), and a higher number means it pays attention to fewer points (so the print is less accurate). Some printers can't handle paths with lots of points, so setting this field to a higher number reduces the path's complexity and helps make things easier on your printer. For now, though, just leave this field blank and click OK. In the Paths panel, the path's name now looks like a hollow outline to let you know that it's a clipping path (*Figure 13-26*, bottom).

5. **Save the document as an EPS or TIFF file.**

   Choose File→Save As, and then pick EPS or TIFF from the format drop-down menu. If you're paranoid about print quality, pick EPS to ensure the best results; because this format is based on the same language PostScript printers use, it tends to print a little more crisply.

FIGURE 13-26

Top: Pick your path from the drop-down menu at the top of this dialog box.

Bottom: Once Photoshop has converted the path into a clipping path, it displays the path thumbnail's name in hard-to-read hollow text in the Paths panel.

If you get a call from your printing company complaining that your file caused a printing error, you may need to redo the clipping path and increase the Flatness setting to 4 or 5. This cuts the printer a little slack as far as how precisely it has to follow the clipping path.

You've now got yourself a perfectly selected and isolated cup, ready to be beamed up into the nearest page-layout program.

TIP Some stock photography comes with clipping paths, which save you a *ton* of work if you need to place that object on another background. The next time you download a stock image, open it in Photoshop and then take a peek in the Paths panel to see if the file contains a clipping path. If so, you can activate the path's thumbnail and then add a layer mask by clicking the "Add layer mask" button at the bottom of the Paths panel (it looks like a circle inside a square). Sweet!

Using Vector Masks

Photoshop gives you two ways to create *vector masks* with paths: using a path made with a shape tool in Path mode, or by using a path drawn with the Pen tool. These masking methods are quick and easy, and you're absolutely gonna love their flexibility (vectors are infinitely resizable and editable, remember?). That said, it's worth noting a few things about vector masks. First, they work just like the pixel-based masks you learned about in Chapter 3: They can hide any underlying layer content that's *beyond* the shape's edges. Second, because vector masks are made from vector-based paths, they give you much smoother edges than pixel masks. Third, you can feather them nondestructively on the fly by using the Feather slider in the Properties panel. Woo-hoo!

■ MASKING WITH PATHS

You can easily create a vector mask from a path outline made by any shape tool or the Pen tool, as shown in *Figure 13-27*. A mask created in this way works just like the regular ol' layer masks you learned about back in Chapter 3 and adds a mask thumbnail to the currently active layer, though the mask is filled with gray instead of black. (If the Background layer is locked, you'll need to double-click it before adding the vector mask.) The difference is that, since the mask is vector-based, you can resize it all you want and its edges stay nice and sharp.

FIGURE 13-27

Top: Here's an oval drawn with the Ellipse tool in Path mode (the Ellipse shape tool, not the Elliptical Marquee tool).

Bottom: After creating a vector mask from the path, the photo is only visible through the oval mask. If you decide to resize the mask later on, simply activate it and summon the Free Transform tool (page 257).

Once you've combined two images into the same document and you've double-clicked the Background layer to unlock it, follow these few steps to make a vector mask from a path:

1. **Grab the Ellipse tool by pressing Shift-U repeatedly and then, in the Options bar, choose Path mode.**

   You can also use any of the other shape tools, or the Pen tool, set to Path mode (page 535).

2. **Draw a path using the method described on page 539.**

3. **Over in the Layers panel, activate the layer you want to add the mask to and then create the mask by ⌘-clicking (Ctrl-clicking on a PC) the "Add a layer mask" button at the bottom of the panel.**

Photoshop adds an infinitely resizable vector mask to the layer and pops open the Properties panel.

4. **In the Properties panel, drag the Feather slider to the right to soften the mask's edges.**

Photoshop softens the edges of the mask in real time. The beauty of feathering the mask in this way is that you can always change it later by simply double-clicking the mask to reopen the Properties panel, and then adjust the Feather slider.

5. **Save the document as a PSD file so you can edit it again later if you need to.**

That's all there is to it! It's a super-fast and super-flexible technique.

If you decide you need to edit the vector mask later on, pop open the document and activate the mask thumbnail in the Layers panel and then use the Path Selection tool to activate its anchor points and control handles. Alternatively, to resize the vector mask, simply summon the Free Transform tool (page 257).

Creating Artistic Text

Text has the power to make or break a design, and Photoshop CC has a veritable *smorgasbord* of text-creation and formatting options—heck, it even has its own Type menu! But just because you *can* do something doesn't mean you *should*: The act of creating text is something of an art form (called *typography*), though it's all too easy to get carried away with *decorating* rather than creating legible prose.

Keep in mind that Photoshop isn't always the right place to be wordsmithing in the first place. (The box on page 577 gives you some pointers to help decide whether to hunt and peck in another program.) Nevertheless, Photoshop has plenty of tools that, when used tastefully, can help you create beautiful text. Some of these tools are easy to find, while others are hidden so deep in the program that you'd need a treasure map to find 'em. This chapter guides you in the right direction, and more importantly, teaches you when and how to use each tool. You'll also learn quite a lot about the art of type in the process.

Typography 101

People have been creating and arranging symbols for thousands of years. In the early days of print, text and symbol wrangling was handled by exacting craftsmen called typesetters, who lovingly hammered letterforms into metal plates that were then physically set onto printing presses (hence the phrase, *setting type*). With the advent of desktop publishing, however, everyone *and* their cocker spaniel started creating text. This has been both good and bad: It's great that you can whip up your own yard sale signs, invitations, and posters; but, as you might suspect, the quality of typography has suffered since most folks lack professional training. *Figure 14-1* shows examples of good and bad typography.

FIGURE 14-1

Left: When formatted well, text can be a beautiful and powerful form of art.

Right: Done badly, text can be garish and difficult to read. The combination of Comic Sans (a truly horrible font) and multiple layer styles makes this innocent text hideous. (For more on layer styles, see page 124.)

Some of the most frequent typographic offenses include:

- **Overusing decorative fonts and using too many fonts per design**. Just because you have a ton of wacky fonts doesn't mean you should *use* them—especially not all in one document.

- **Setting whole sentences in capital letters**. All-capped text takes folks longer to read because they're not used to it, but even worse is that it tends to imply that you're YELLING. That said, with the right formatting, small portions of all-capped text can look classy (flip to page 605 for a quick peek).

- **Underlining text that isn't a hyperlink**. Thanks to the Internet, when folks see an underlined word, they assume it's a hyperlink. Find another way to make your text stand out, such as bolding or italicizing it.

- **Centering large bodies of text**. It's best to reserve centered text for formal announcements; you'll learn why on page 612.

- **Misusing straight and smart (curly) quotation marks and apostrophes**. Use the straight ones to indicate units of measurement (feet and inches) and curly ones for everything else. You can switch between 'em using Photoshop's preferences: choose Photoshop→Preferences→Type (Edit→Preferences→Type on a PC) and turn Use Smart Quotes on or off.

- **Misusing (or not using) hyphens, en dashes, and em dashes**:

  — **Hyphens** are for combining two words (like "pixel-jockey") and for line breaks (when a word gets split across two lines of text).

  — **En dashes** are slightly longer than hyphens and are a good substitute for the word "to," as in "Chapters 1–4" or "8:00 a.m.–5:00 p.m." On a Mac, you can create an en dash by typing Option-Hyphen (on a PC, press and hold Alt while typing *0150* on the numeric keypad).

— **Em dashes** are the longest of the bunch and imply an abrupt change—like this!—or a halt in thought or speech. Use them instead of a comma or period when the former is too weak and the latter too strong. To create an em dash on a Mac, press Shift-Option-Hyphen (on a PC, press and hold Alt while typing *0151* on the numeric keypad).

- **Improperly spaced ellipses (…)**. An ellipsis indicates an omission, interruption, or hesitation in thought, as in, "But…but…you promised!" Instead of typing three periods (which can get broken across lines), let your computer create the dots for you. On a Mac, it's Option-; (on a PC, press Alt and type *0133* on the numeric keypad).

There are more offenses, to be sure—such as putting *two* spaces after each period instead of *one*—though this isn't *Typography: The Missing Manual* (now there's an idea!). Nonetheless, the guidelines listed above will serve you well throughout the rest of this chapter, if not your entire career.

UP TO SPEED

Printing Photoshop Text

There's a time and a place for everything, and that includes Photoshop text. Although each new version of the program boasts new and improved text formatting capabilities, it's just not made for handling big hunks of text. This book, for instance, was written in Microsoft Word, *not* Photoshop.

If your document includes a lot of text, it's much better to use a page-layout program like Adobe InDesign or QuarkXPress because they produce *vector* text (each character is described mathematically as a series of curves and lines—see Chapter 13 for details), which looks nice and crisp in print. Though Photoshop text starts out as editable vectors, it can get *rasterized* (converted to dots) when the file is flattened (page 108) and exported in TIFF or JPEG format, which can make it look fuzzy when it's printed, especially if you've resized the resulting TIFF or JPEG (take a peek at the ads in the back of any magazine,

and you'll spot some examples). If you're printing a Photoshop document (PSD), you don't have anything to worry about; your text will print just fine.

If you *have* to use Photoshop—because it's the only program you've got or the text is part of the image itself (if you've pushed a photo through text [page 626], say, or given it an artistic treatment like texture [page 622])—then be sure to save the file in either EPS or PDF format. With EPS, the file still gets flattened and rasterized, but the letterforms remain vectors; however, the text is no longer editable (the only advantage to using EPS is that it works with older workflows so some print shops may require it). With PDF, you can turn on the Preserve Photoshop Editing Capabilities option in the Save Adobe PDF dialog box so your layers remain intact and the text stays editable. So if you have a choice, go with PDF format.

The Face of Type

At the heart of typography lies the *glyph*, a unique graphical representation of a letter, number, punctuation mark, or pictographic symbol. In the digital realm, a collection of glyphs is called a *typeface* or *font*. Technically, a typeface is the overall shape or design of the glyphs and a font is the specific size, style, and weight, but people use the terms interchangeably. For example, Times is a typeface, while Times 14-point bold is a font—the latter being more descriptive. (For the purpose of this book—and your sanity—they'll both be referred to as fonts from here on out.) You may also encounter the term *font family*, a collection of various weights and widths of the same design. An example of a font family is Futura Book, Futura Semibold, Futura Heavy, Futura Sumo (kidding!), Futura Bold, Futura Extra Bold, and so on.

■ COMMON FONT FORMATS

Fonts come in various formats that determine how and what kind of information gets stored in each font file and ultimately, how they print. There are only three formats you need to worry about in Photoshop: PostScript, TrueType, and OpenType. If you've already created some Photoshop text, you can discover what format it's in by taking a peek at the font family menu—the unlabeled drop-down menu showing the font's name—in the Options bar or Character panel, as explained in *Figure 14-2*.

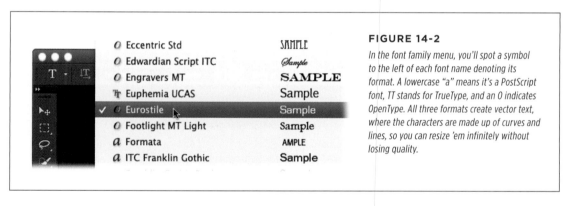

FIGURE 14-2

In the font family menu, you'll spot a symbol to the left of each font name denoting its format. A lowercase "a" means it's a PostScript font, TT stands for TrueType, and an O indicates OpenType. All three formats create vector text, where the characters are made up of curves and lines, so you can resize 'em infinitely without losing quality.

These days font format isn't such a big deal—any printer with equipment less than 15 years old can print any format you throw at 'em. But in case you're curious, here's how the formats differ:

- **PostScript**. Most graphic design pros consider this format the safest and most reliable for printing because it's been around for years (it comes in both Mac and Windows flavors). Each PostScript font consists of two files: one that contains the shapes that get displayed onscreen (called the *screen* or *bitmap* file because monitors display bits or dots) along with font family and spacing info, and another that contains outline drawings of each glyph for the printer (commonly referred to as the *printer* file). This format produces high-quality text when printed on PostScript devices like laser printers and professional printing presses. The downside is that the two files can get separated or lost, which may make the font unusable (though, these days, most computers ignore the screen file and use the printer file for everything, but you shouldn't count on that). Folks who install and manage fonts manually (see the box on page 581) occasionally run into these kinds of problems.

- **TrueType**. Developed jointly by Apple and Microsoft, TrueType is the most common font format, and it's what you'll find in both the Mac and Windows operating systems (though they're likely different versions so they may not look the same). Both the screen and outline information are stored in a single file, so they can't be separated or lost. Though these fonts rival the quality of PostScript and their usage in the design community has increased, many professional printers still prefer PostScript out of habit. TrueType fonts for Windows can be used on Macs, but not vice versa.

- **OpenType**. This format, created by Microsoft and Adobe, is the new standard. Like TrueType, OpenType fonts store the screen and outline information together in one file. They work well and look the same on both Macs and Windows computers, plus they can store more than 65,000 different glyphs in one font file. This makes them ideal for decorative and pictorial languages like Asian and Middle-Eastern ones, and for other fancy typographic goodness like ligatures and stylistic alternates (page 609). As an added bonus, the same OpenType font can be used on both Mac and Windows machines. As with most things, change takes time, so a lot of printers don't yet support this format. But because it's so versatile, someday OpenType will rule the typographic world!

> **NOTE** If you're designing a graphic that'll be posted online, font format doesn't matter because the text isn't headed for a printer. And if you're printing to a non-PostScript device like an inkjet printer, *anti-aliasing* matters more than font format—see page 600 for details.

■ FONT CATEGORIES

Font foundries, the purveyors of fonts, crank out new fonts daily. Depending who you ask, there are between 50,000 and 150,000 known fonts in the wild. No wonder it's tough to pick one! Luckily, there are a few basic principles for choosing a font that's appropriate to your message—one that will reinforce it rather than distract from it. *Figure 14-3* shows examples of the following font categories:

- **Serif**. These fonts have little lines (*serifs*) extending from their letters' main strokes that resemble tiny feet. The main strokes vary from thick to thin, and the serifs help lead the eye from one character to the next. Serifs are great for large bodies of text like books, newspapers, or magazines where legibility is paramount. However, they're not so good for large bodies of *online* text (the next bullet point explains why). Examples include Times New Roman, Garamond, and Minion.

- **Sans serif**. Fonts lacking the aforementioned feet are called *sans serif* ("sans" means "without"). They're perfect for headlines, subheads, and surprisingly enough, online body copy. (You're reading a sans-serif font now.) Because their main strokes are uniform—they don't vary from thick to thin—they display well at small sizes, so they're ideal for Web use. Examples include Arial, Helvetica, and Futura.

- **Slab serif**. These guys have uniform main strokes, thick serifs, and often appear bolded. Use them when you want to attract attention, or when printing body copy under less-than-optimal conditions (cheap paper, cheap printer, or fax machine). Examples include Bookman, Courier, and Rockwell.

- **Decorative, Display**. This group includes all kinds of distinctive, eye-catching fonts, from the big and bold, to the swirly, to letters made out of bunnies. Though gloriously unusual, they're harder to read due to the extra ornamentation or stroke thickness. Use them sparingly and on small blocks of text (perhaps a single word). Examples include Impact, Party, and Stencil.

FIGURE 14-3

Different situations call for different fonts. It would be silly to print a newspaper in a decorative font—it'd be nearly impossible to read.

And no one will come to your tea party if they're put off by the big, bold letterforms of a display font, which seem to say, "Come to my party or else!"

- **Scripts**. Casual scripts are designed to look as though they were drawn (quickly) by hand. Formal scripts have carefully crafted strokes that actually join the letters together, like cursive handwriting. Use casual scripts for small blocks of text (because they can be hard to read), and reserve formal scripts for fancy announcements (weddings, graduations, and so on). Examples include Brush Script, Freestyle, and Edwardian.

■ FONT STYLES

Most fonts include several *styles* (variations) like bold, semibold, italic, condensed, and so on. When these styles are included in the font itself (meaning they were designed by the font's creator), they're called *native* or *built-in styles*. To view all native styles for a particular font, use the font styles drop-down menu (which sits to the right of the font family menu) in the Options bar or Character panel. Just click a style to apply it to highlighted text (page 585) or the next thing you type.

If the font doesn't include a bold or italic version, Photoshop can fake it for you. Just choose a font from the font family menu and then head over to the Character panel (choose Window→Character to open it) and click the bold or italic button (the bold button has a capital T on it, and the italic button has a slanted *T*). Photoshop will then do its best to make the characters thicker or tilt them, creating what's known as a *simulated* or *faux style*. These faux styles often look fine onscreen but terrible when printed, as the printer has no outline file (drawing) to go by. Whether it's font styles, shoes, or handbags, real is *always* better than fake.

> **TIP** If you subscribe to the full Creative Cloud package, you get access to the entire Adobe web font collection. To use 'em, open the Creative Cloud app (more on that in a sec), and then click the Fonts button at the top. Once they're installed, the fonts are available to any program on your machine that has a font menu—that is, as long as your Creative Cloud subscription is current. For more about using the Creative Cloud app, check out online Appendix A available from this book's Missing CD page at *www.missingmanuals.com/cds*.

POWER USERS' CLINIC

Managing Fonts

Everybody adds new fonts to their computers; in fact, Adobe's Creative Suite adds new fonts when you install it. That's great, but because fonts are actually little programs that are accessed by other programs, it's easy for problems to crop up.

You may run into font conflicts—when you have two or more fonts with the same name—or worse, damaged fonts (fonts that get corrupted and don't work properly). Either scenario can wreak havoc on the performance of both your computer and Photoshop, and can make them crash. If you think this is scary, you're right; and, if you've got a ton of fonts, it's a matter of *when* you'll run into a conflict, not if.

The solution, Grasshopper, is to invest in font-management software. These programs serve as a repository for all your fonts so they're not scattered across your hard drive. They can let you turn fonts on or off (so you don't have to scroll through a mile-long font list), manage duplicate fonts for you, and organize fonts in a multitude of ways, such as by favorites, font style, manufacturer, project, client, and so on.

There are some free font-management programs flitting around on the Web, and Mac OS X includes the Font Book program, but when it comes to working with professional design programs such as Adobe Creative Suite, it's worth spending a few bucks on a professional font manager. Extensis (*www.extensis.com*), Insider Software (*www.insidersoftware.com*),

and Linotype (*www.linotype.com*) have useful cross-platform font managers that are loaded with features designed to make your font life easier and more importantly, headache free.

Available for both Mac and Windows for about $100, Extensis's Suitcase Fusion and Insider Software's FontAgent Pro have similar features: They track and manage the fonts you add to your computer as well as system fonts (the ones that came with your computer), which is helpful if you have third-party fonts with the same names as your system fonts. They also let you activate fonts as you need them—in fact, if Photoshop encounters a missing font when opening a document, they'll activate it on the fly (assuming you have the font). (See the box on page 592 for more on missing fonts.) They also perform basic checks when you add new fonts to make sure they're not damaged. This alone could save your hide because damaged fonts are notorious for causing Photoshop crashes and printing problems.

But the best of the bunch is Linotype's FontExplorer X Pro for Macs and PCs. It performs all the tasks mentioned above but runs rings around the other two programs because of its friendly design, easier access to advanced features, excellent font sample printing feature, and much more. Plus, it costs just $80.

■ PREVIEWING FONTS

Choosing a font is 100 times easier if you can actually *see* what it looks like. Photoshop shows you an example of each font in the font family menu shown back in *Figure 14-2*. And if these previews are hard to see, you can use the Type menu to make those previews bigger: Choose Type→Font Preview Size and pick one of the six options ranging from None to Huge (Large is a good choice).

■ Creating and Editing Text

You can create all kinds of text in Photoshop, from plain ol' horizontal to up-and-down vertical. You can even make text flow around or inside a shape. No matter what kind of text you create, it lives on a special layer called a *Type layer*. You can do anything to a Type layer that you can with any other layer (see Chapter 3): adjust its opacity, change its blend mode, apply layer styles, and so on. Type layers are labeled with a big fat T in the Layers panel so they're easy to spot. Photoshop automatically names each new Type layer with the first few words you type, though like any other layer, you can double-click its name in the Layers panel to rename it.

To create a Type layer, grab either the Horizontal or Vertical Type tool from the Tools panel, as shown in *Figure 14-4*. Click once in the document where you want the text to start and let the hunting and pecking begin. When you're finished typing, press Enter on your computer's numeric keypad (not Return!) or click the checkmark on the right side of the Options bar to let Photoshop know you're done; this is technically called *committing* text. (You can also just pick another tool from the Tools panel).

Horizontal

V
e
r
t
i
c
a
l

FIGURE 14-4

Left: Click the big T in the Tools panel to reveal all your type tool options: the Horizontal and Vertical Type tools, and the Horizontal and Vertical Type Mask tools (discussed on page 589).

Right: Use the Horizontal Type tool to create text that flows from left to right in a straight line. Use the Vertical Type tool to create text that flows down the page from top to bottom in a column (and which absolutely no one can read).

You can change the orientation of text—whether it flows from left to right or top to bottom—anytime by clicking the Text Orientation button in the Options bar (it looks like a capital T with tiny downward and right-facing arrows). To create text that flows backward (from right to left or bottom to top), see page 588.

TIP To edit several Type layers at once, first activate 'em in the Layers panel and make sure the Type tool is also active. Then make your changes using either the Options bar or Character panel, and they'll apply to *all* the active layers in one fell swoop—a huge timesaver. (Find and Replace is another great tool for multilayer changes—see page 597.)

You can locate multiple Type layers fast by using the layer filtering options in the Layers panel: From the drop-down menu in the panel's upper left, choose Kind, and then, to the right of the menu, click the T button, and Photoshop instantly shows you only the Type layers—even if they're nestled within a group (page 100). Then choose Select→All Layers and format 'em to your heart's desire. To see all your layers once more, click the T button again. (For more on filtering layers, see page 70.)

Point Text vs. Paragraph Text

Chances are, most of the text you'll create in Photoshop will be *point text*, which starts at a certain spot (or *point*) and continues along a single line. To create point text, just activate the Type tool, click in your document, and start typing. If you type a bunch of text and want it to wrap to the next line, press Return (Enter on a PC) to force the line to break—otherwise, Photoshop is quite content to let text dangle off the edge of your document. To make Photoshop *automatically* wrap text to the next line, you have to create *paragraph text* instead.

NOTE Photoshop refers to these two kinds of text as point and paragraph, but you might hear people call them *character* and *area text*, respectively. (Adobe Illustrator calls it area text, too.)

GEM IN THE ROUGH

Scrolling for Fonts

Have you ever grown weary of scrolling through all your available fonts? Even with font previews, you'll still probably try out several fonts before you find one that's just right. The process usually goes like this: Highlight the text, mouse over to the Options bar or Character panel's font family menu and choose a font, and then *hide* the text highlighting by pressing ⌘-H (Ctrl+H) to see how it looks in your document. If you don't like that font, you trot back to the font family menu and pick another one, and so on. A font-management program lets you preview fonts quickly and easily (see the box on page 581),

but if you don't have one, this kind of manual font trolling is a royal pain.

Here's a better method: The next time you need to pick a font, highlight the text in your document, and then click the font family menu in the Options bar or Character panel. Next, click the name of a font, and then use the up and down arrows on your keyboard to cycle through the list. The highlighted text changes as you do so, saving you loads of mouse-travel time. Nice!

Paragraph text is text that lives inside a box, and when you create this kind of text, Photoshop makes your prose flow from line to line all by itself. To create paragraph text, activate the Type tool and then either drag in your document to draw a box or Option-click (Alt-click on a PC) your document and then enter the desired width and height into the resulting dialog box, shown in *Figure 14-5*, left. (From the factory, Photoshop assumes these measurements are in points, though you can type another unit of measurement such as *in* for inches or *px* for pixels.) Click OK to dismiss the dialog box, and Photoshop places a dashed box in your document, with the upper-left corner in the spot where you clicked. If the box isn't the right size, press Esc and have another go at it, or simply adjust the box's size by dragging the tiny white resizing handles strategically placed around its edges (see *Figure 14-5*, right).

Instead of clicking to create point text, drag with the the Type tool to draw a text box.

FIGURE 14-5

Left: To create a multiline text box, Option-click (Alt-click on a PC) in your document and enter the dimensions you want. (You can also drag with the Vertical or Horizontal Type tools to draw the box manually.)

Right: To resize a text box, activate the Type layer, click within the text box, and then drag any of the resulting square white handles, like the one circled here.

TIP If you're designing an ad and the copy for it isn't ready yet, Photoshop can create placeholder text for you *automatically*. Grab the Type tool, click and drag within your document to create a text box, and then choose Type→Paste Lorem Ipsum. Photoshop instantly fills the box with a big ol' chunk of temporary gibberish that reads, "This is Photoshop's version of Lorem Ipsum. Proin gravida..." (You can do the same thing with point text, too, though if you do, the text will continue off the edge of your screen for *miles*.)

Better-Looking Text in CC

For years, folks—mostly web designers—have claimed that text created in Photoshop looks a little too big or thick when anti-aliasing is turned on, especially at small point sizes like those used on the Web. (*Anti-aliasing* is when Photoshop slightly blurs the edges of letters so they don't look jagged; see page 600.) To fix that, Adobe tweaked the way Photoshop blends the colors on Type layers with colors on other layers, which makes for more balanced anti-aliasing and thus text that displays more accurately. (In technical terms, Photoshop uses linear gamma 1.0 blending instead of non-linear tone reproduction curve encoding—don't ask.) And in CC, Adobe added two *new* anti-aliasing methods that help web designers see what the text will look like in popular web browsers (you'll learn about 'em on page 600).

The bottom line is that Photoshop text looks a bit cleaner and clearer than it used to. The improvement is more noticeable on smaller text sizes (12 points or less) where the anti-aliasing blur makes up a bigger portion of each letter's pixels. Also, dark text on a light background looks thinner, while light text on a dark background looks thicker.

When the text box is all set, just start typing. When your text hits the edge of the box, Photoshop adds line breaks and hyphenates words. You can still resize the text box after you type in it—just make sure the Type layer is active in the Layers panel, and then click in the text box and drag any of the resulting handles. The size of the *text* doesn't change, but the size of the text box does, and Photoshop automatically reflows the text to fit inside the newly sized box. (If you want to change the size of the text itself, flip to page 587.) As explained on page 583, using paragraph text instead of point text gives you some extra formatting options such as alignment, hyphenation, and so on.

TIP Photoshop can convert point text to paragraph text (or vice versa) on the fly. Just activate the appropriate Type layer in the Layers panel and then choose Type→"Convert to Point Text" or "Convert to Paragraph Text." You can also Control-click (right-click) a Type layer in the Layers panel while the Type tool is active and then choose the same items from the resulting shortcut menu (there's no need to highlight or click within the text first; if you do, this menu item doesn't appear).

Moving Text

If you start typing and then decide the text isn't in the right spot, no problem—moving it is easy. Just grab your mouse and move the cursor *away* from the text box (about a half inch) until the cursor turns into a tiny arrow with four arrows beneath it. Then simply click and drag the Type layer to a new position in your document and continue typing.

Another way to move text while typing is to press and hold ⌘ (Ctrl on a PC), place your cursor inside the resulting box, and then drag the text to a new spot. If you've already finished typing, you can still move the text. Just make sure the appropriate Type layer is active in the Layers panel—but don't click within the text—press V to grab the Move tool, and then drag the Type layer to a new position in your document. If dragging isn't your thing, grab the Move tool and then nudge the layer by tapping the arrow keys on your keyboard.

Highlighting Text

Chances are, the text you create won't be perfect right off the bat; it'll need to be massaged, manipulated, and played with (and honestly, that's half the fun). To tweak your text, activate the appropriate Type layer in the Layers panel (it'll be highlighted, as shown in *Figure 14-6*, left), and then highlight the text you want to change (you'll learn how in a sec). When text is highlighted, you see a black background behind the characters (which are now white), as shown in *Figure 14-6*, right.

NOTE The color you see when you highlight text is actually a contrasting opposite of the color *underneath* the text (whether it's an image or a solid color). For example, if your text is on a white background, the highlight color is black; if it's on a blue background, the highlight color is orange. Neat, huh?

Click to see only Type layers

FIGURE 14-6

Left: To alter text in Photoshop, you've got to activate the Type layer it's on and then highlight the portion you want to change, as shown here. To highlight all the text on a Type layer, simply give its layer thumbnail a quick double-click.

Right: When you highlight text, a colored background appears behind it and Photoshop temporarily makes the text a contrasting color so you can see it, as shown in the upper sentence here. And why does the lower sentence look so blurry? Because it's been loaded as a selection so each letter is surrounded by marching ants.

TIP The background that appears behind text when it's highlighted makes it nearly impossible to see any formatting changes you make. Fortunately, you can toggle this background off and on by pressing ⌘-H (Ctrl+H)—that is, unless you've reassigned that keyboard shortcut to hide Photoshop on a Mac, as explained in the box on page 4.

TROUBLESHOOTING MOMENT

Adding Type Layers

There are lots of benefits to putting different pieces of text on their own Type layers. As you learned in Chapter 3, you can edit anything that lives on its own layer independently of everything else, letting you position it precisely within the document, change its blend mode and opacity, and so on, without messing with other layers. So, if you're creating a poster publicizing Woodstock IV, for example, it's a good idea to put the (obligatory) psychedelic heading on one layer and the details of the concert on layers of their own.

Creating your first Type layer is easy: Simply click the big T in the Tools panel to activate the Type tool and then click in your document to add the new Type layer. However, it can be

challenging to create *additional* Type layers near the existing ones while the Type tool is active because when you click in your document, Photoshop insists on activating the *existing* Type layer nearest to where you clicked. Likewise, if you put your cursor close to an existing path, Photoshop assumes you want to create text on that path (see page 593) and promptly attaches the text to it.

The fix for both situations is to press the Shift key while you click somewhere within the document, which forces Photoshop to create a brand-new, bright and shiny Type layer. Now, take back all those bad things you said about the Type tool.

Highlighting text—which most folks erroneously call "selecting text"—is totally different from *loading text as a selection*, which puts marching ants around each character as shown in *Figure 14-6*, bottom right. To load text as a selection, simply ⌘-click (Ctrl-click on a PC) the Type layer's thumbnail. What's the difference, you ask? Highlighting text lets you edit the characters (to fix a typo, for example), whereas loading text as a selection lets you apply effects to the *shape* of characters, such as adding a stroke (page 618), altering other images in the shape of the characters (page 626), or creating another piece of art out of 'em altogether.

Like most tasks, Photoshop gives you several ways to highlight text (you need to have the Type tool active to use any of them):

- **To highlight a character**, click within the text and, once your cursor turns into a blinking I-beam, drag across the character(s).

- **To highlight a word**, click within the text and then double-click the word.

- **To highlight a whole line**, click within the text and then triple-click anywhere in the line you want to highlight.

- **To highlight a paragraph**, click within the paragraph and then quadruple-click (that's four quick clicks).

- **To highlight all the text on a single Type layer**, in the Layers panel, double-click the layer's thumbnail or, in your document, click within the text and then click five times really fast.

- **To activate multiple Type layers**, mouse over to the Layers panel and Shift- or ⌘-click (Ctrl-click on a PC) the name—*not* the thumbnail—of each layer you want to activate.

- **To activate all the Type layers in a document**, mosey over to the Layers panel and choose Kind from the drop-down menu at the top left, and then click the button with a T on it (labeled in *Figure 14-6*, left). Photoshop instantly hides everything but the Type layers in that document. To activate all of 'em, choose Select→All Layers.

> **TIP**   When you've got a single Type layer activated and the Type tool is *also* active (but no text is highlighted and you haven't clicked *within* the text), you can Control-click (right-click) anywhere in your document to summon a shortcut menu with all kinds of useful options for working with text. These include Check Spelling, Find and Replace Text, Rasterize, Create Work Path, and more. (You get a similar menu when you've highlighted some text, but it offers fewer options.)

Resizing Text

Photoshop lets you create everything from nano-sized text that you'd need an electron microscope to read to ginormous letters fit for the side of a building. You can resize text by highlighting it using any of the methods described earlier, and then altering the point size in either the Options bar or Character panel. But where's the fun in that?

Unless you know the *exact* size your text needs to be, you're better off resizing it visually, either while typing or afterward. To resize visually, activate a Type layer in the Layers panel and then click within the line of text (or the text box) so you see an I-beam cursor blinking within the text (if you're typing, you should already see this cursor). Next, press and hold ⌘ (Ctrl on a PC) to make Photoshop display resizing handles around the text (the handles around a *text box* resize the box itself). While keeping the ⌘ (Ctrl) key down, press and hold the Shift key, and then drag any handle to resize the text, as shown in *Figure 14-7*, left (adding the Shift key makes Photoshop resize the text proportionately so it doesn't get squished or squashed). The point size displayed in both the Options bar and Character panel changes as you drag.

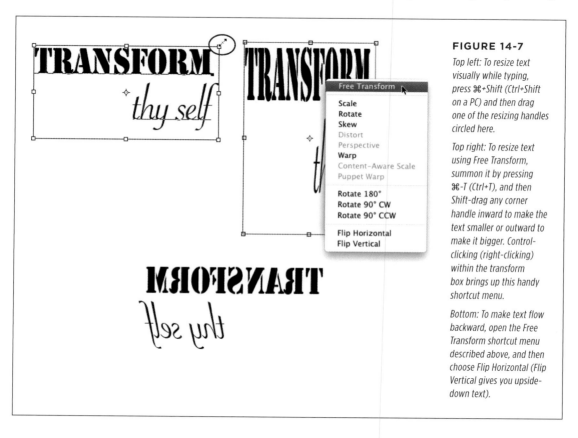

FIGURE 14-7

Top left: To resize text visually while typing, press ⌘+Shift (Ctrl+Shift on a PC) and then drag one of the resizing handles circled here.

Top right: To resize text using Free Transform, summon it by pressing ⌘-T (Ctrl+T), and then Shift-drag any corner handle inward to make the text smaller or outward to make it bigger. Control-clicking (right-clicking) within the transform box brings up this handy shortcut menu.

Bottom: To make text flow backward, open the Free Transform shortcut menu described above, and then choose Flip Horizontal (Flip Vertical gives you upside-down text).

TIP If you're a keyboard shortcut fan, you can increase the font size of highlighted text in 1-point increments by pressing Shift-⌘-> (Shift+Ctrl+>), and decrease it by pressing Shift-⌘-< (Shift+Ctrl+<). To increase or decrease in *5-point* increments, add the Option key (Alt on a PC) to those key combinations. These are *great* keyboard shortcuts to memorize if you want to format text quickly.

You can also use Free Transform to resize text. With a Type layer active—not the *text* itself, just the layer it's on—summon the Free Transform tool by pressing ⌘-T (Ctrl+T). A resizing box (complete with little white handles) appears around the text; simply

Shift-drag one of these handles in any direction to resize the text proportionately. (You won't see the point size change as you drag because that happens only when the Type tool is active.) For even more resizing options, Control-click (right-click) within the transform box for a handy shortcut menu (see *Figure 14-7*, right).

Creating a Hollow Text Selection

Sometimes you don't really need letters *themselves* to create the effect you're after, you just need a *selection* of them—in other words, their outline. Enter the Type Mask tool, which is hidden in the type toolset (shown on page 582). Instead of creating a Type layer, this wonderful tool creates an empty text *selection*, which you can use on other layers, like one that contains an image.

When you use the Type Mask tool, it'll look like you're creating normal text, but once you're finished typing, marching ants will surround the edges of the characters, creating a hollow selection in the *shape* of that text, and Photoshop won't create a new Type layer. Think of a type mask as one of those plastic stencils you used as a kid to draw perfectly formed letters and numbers—the letters are hollow so you can see through 'em to the layer below.

WORD TO THE WISE

Beware of Rasterizing Text

Most of the text you create in Photoshop—whether it's horizontal, upside down, inside a shape, or what have you—begins life as *vector* text. (The exception is text you create with the Type Mask tool.) With vector type, each character is made up of curves and lines, rather than pixels. (See the box on page 43 for a detailed discussion of raster vs. vector files.)

This is great news because it means the text is editable and fully *scalable*, so you can make it bigger or smaller without worrying that it'll be blurry when printed. However, some cool effects require you to rasterize the text (convert it to pixels), like running filters (though there is a workaround—see page 626), distorting, and applying perspective, to name a few. If you try to do any of these things to a Type layer, you'll be met with an error message asking your permission to rasterize.

The bad news is that some things in Photoshop *automatically* rasterize text so that it becomes completely un-vectored, uneditable, and pretty much un-resizable. (You can *shrink* raster text without much quality loss, but enlarging it will give you disastrously jagged results.) Photoshop automatically rasterizes text—without asking for permission—when you do any of the following:

- Merge a Type layer with one or more other layers (page 106).

- Flatten a file (page 108).
- Save a file in any format *other* than PSD, EPS, PDF, or DCS.
- Send a file to a non-PostScript (inkjet) printer (Chapter 16).

If you save a file in EPS or DCS format, Photoshop preserves the text by converting it to vector outlines, which is pretty much the same thing as converting it to a shape (page 627). You won't be able to edit the text anymore, but it'll look nice and crisp when printed. Watch out, though: If you open *either* of these file types again in Photoshop, the program automatically rasterizes the text. However, you can preserve the text by importing the file into your document as a Smart Object instead; to do that, choose File→Place. (This method doesn't let you edit the text, though.) If you save the file as a PDF, you can turn on the Preserve Photoshop Editing Capabilities option in the Save Adobe PDF dialog box (page 683) to keep the text editable.

All that being said, if you truly wish to rasterize text, it's a good idea to duplicate the Type layer first (by pressing ⌘-J or Ctrl+J) just in case you want to edit it later. Once you've duplicated the layer, you can rasterize either the copy or the original by choosing Type→Rasterize Type Layer, or by Control-clicking (right-clicking) the Type layer and choosing Rasterize Type.

NOTE   Sure, you could just use the regular type tools to create text and then load it as a selection by
⌘-clicking (Ctrl-clicking) the Type layer's thumbnail. But the Type Mask tool *creates the selection for you*,
sparing you that extra step.

The Type Mask tool opens a boatload of graphic design possibilities because it lets you affect other graphical elements (meaning other layers) through the shape of the text, as shown in *Figure 14-8*. Like the regular Type tool, the Type Mask tool comes in two flavors: one for creating horizontal text and one for creating vertical text. They both merely create a selection of whatever you type without creating a new layer. You can then treat the text selection as you would any other selection: Move it around, use it to create a layer mask (page 176), wear it as a hat (kidding!), save it to use later (see page 179), or turn it into an editable path (page 568).

One of the many neat effects you can create with the Type Mask tool is a text-shaped photo fade, a unique look that can make an eye-catching magazine ad, for example. Here's how:

1. **Open a photo and grab the Horizontal Type Mask tool.**

   To activate the tool, click the big T in the Tools panel, hold down your mouse button, and then click the Horizontal Type Mask tool in the toolset's menu (you can also press Shift-T repeatedly to cycle through all the tools in the type toolset). You don't need to bother duplicating the background layer, because this technique is 100% nondestructive, meaning the original pixels will remain untouched.

2. **In the Options bar or Character panel, choose a font from the font family menu.**

   Be sure to choose a thick font so the selection area will be fairly big (thin or script fonts won't work). Arial Black and Impact are good ones to use for this technique.

3. **Click anywhere in the document and then type your text.**

   You'll notice that the text appears hollow (you can see through it to the photo, as shown in *Figure 14-8*, top), while the background takes on the red cast of Quick Mask mode, though you can't use other tools or filters like you *normally* can in Quick Mask mode.

4. **Format the text to your liking.**

   If you don't like the font, change it by highlighting the text (page 585) and choosing something else from the font family menu. You can reposition the text by moving your cursor away from it about half an inch, and then dragging with the resulting arrow cursor. You can also move the text by pressing ⌘ (Ctrl on a PC), clicking inside the resulting box, and then dragging it or nudging it with your keyboard's arrow keys. Shift-drag any of the square handles to resize the text (holding the Shift key resizes it proportionately).

FIGURE 14-8

*Top: When the Type Mask tool is active, clicking in a
document causes a red overlay or mask to appear
(see page 176 for more on this particular mask). As
you type, the letters are revealed through the mask.
The text remains editable (and resizable) until you
accept the mask by clicking the Options bar's checkmark button or pressing Enter on your computer's
numeric keypad (not Return).*

*Middle: Once you accept the mask, you'll see a selec-
tion of the text appear, indicated by the little army
of marching ants surrounding the characters, as
shown here (in real life, they actually move).*

*Bottom: After you inverse (flip-flop) the selection,
the area behind the text gets selected, letting you
change the background of your design in the shape
of the text. Here, the text selection was used in
conjunction with an adjustment layer on a photo
of pizza.*

*As you can see, all manner of graphic design good-
ness is possible with this technique.*

5. **Convert the mask to a selection.**

   When the text looks just right, click the checkmark in the Options bar or press
   the Enter key on your numeric keypad (*not* Return) to accept the mask. This
   creates a selection of the text (so you see marching ants) and gets rid of the
   red overlay, as shown in *Figure 14-8*, middle.

NOTE   If you decide to edit or reformat the text after accepting the mask, you have to start over. Just grab
the Type Mask tool and retype the text (you don't have to deselect first).

6. **Inverse the selection.**

   In order to fade the area of the photo around the letters, you need to flip-flop
   the selection. Choose Select→Inverse to select everything *except* the letters.
   Now you can adjust the photo's background while leaving the letter area alone.

7. **Create a Hue/Saturation Adjustment layer and use it to desaturate and
   lighten the part of the photo in the selection area.**

   Over in the Layers panel, click the half-black/half-white circle and choose Hue/
   Saturation from the resulting menu. (Using an Adjustment layer lets you do
   the desaturating and lightening on a separate layer, instead of on the original
   image.) In the Properties panel that opens, drain most of the photo's color by
   lowering the Saturation setting to –65. Next, drag the Lightness slider to +60
   to lighten the photo, making the text more legible.

FREQUENTLY ASKED QUESTION

Type Warnings

*Sometimes when I open a document, I see a little triangle
on the Type layer in the Layers panel. What the heck does
that mean?*

One day you're bound to open a Photoshop document only
to be met with a *type warning*. They come in two flavors and
show up in the Layers panel as a tiny yellow or gray triangle
on the Type layer's thumbnail:

- **A yellow warning symbol** means you're missing a font.
  You'll see this icon if you open a document that uses a font
  that's not installed on your machine (you'll also likely see
  an error message *before* the document actually opens that
  lets you either cancel opening the document or proceed).
  If you don't need to edit the text, you've got nothing to
  worry about—just do what you need to do and then save
  the file. If you *do* edit the text, Photoshop will substitute
  another font for the missing one the moment you double-
  click the Type layer, and this substitution is permanent,
  even if you send the file back to its creator who *has* the
  original font. So if it's important to keep the original

font, you'll have to close the document, quit Photoshop
(unless you're running font-management software—see
the box on page 581), install or activate the font, relaunch
Photoshop, and then reopen the document.

- **A gray warning symbol** means that the document you've
  opened was created in a different version of Photoshop
  and that the text *may* get reflowed if you edit it (but
  that doesn't necessarily mean it *will* get reflowed).
  Because each new version of Photoshop contains new
  type features, text created in an earlier version might
  get spaced or hyphenated differently in the new version.

Happily, Photoshop lets you take action on *both* kinds of warnings swiftly and easily. To replace missing fonts with something
else so you can edit the text, choose Type→Replace All Missing
Fonts, and Photoshop opens a dialog box kindly asking which
font you'd like to use as the replacement. To update all the text
in a document created in a previous version of the program,
choose Type→Update All Text Layers instead.

You're done! *Figure 14-8* (bottom) shows the final result: clear, photo-filled text with a faded background.

Creating Text on a Path

Photoshop lets you bend text to your every whim, and one of the coolest tricks is to make text march around a shape. The key is to use the Type tool on a preexisting path (either open or closed—see page 545) that was drawn with the Pen tool or created with a vector shape such as one made by the Rectangle, Rounded Rectangle, Ellipse, Polygon, or Custom Shape tools (*Figure 14-9*). (See Chapter 13 for a detailed discussion of paths and shape tools.) When you attach text to a path, both the text and the path remain editable, so you can reformat the text or reshape the path anytime.

TIP Heck, you can even turn text *into* a path (think outline) or shape—a nifty trick that lets you rotate individual letters and create cool intersecting effects. Head on over to page 627 for the details.

Here's how to attach text to a custom shape:

1. **Create a path.**

   Using either the Pen tool or one of the vector-shape tools mentioned above, create a path for the text to follow. *Figure 14-9* shows a snail drawn with the Custom Shape tool (see page 555 to learn how to load other built-in shapes).

   NOTE The direction you draw the shape (or path) determines the direction the text flows. For example, draw the shape from left to right and the text will flow normally; draw it from right to left and the text will appear backward and upside down.

2. **Attach text to the path.**

   Grab the Horizontal Type tool (click the big T in the Tools panel) and then point your cursor just above the path or the shape's edge. You'll see a wavy line appear across the I-beam cursor (see *Figure 14-9*, top). This is the Type tool's way of telling you that it recognizes the path you're about to attach the text to. Click once and then start typing.

3. **Align or reposition the text on the path.**

   You can use any of the alignment buttons in the Options bar or Character panel to align the text on the path.

FIGURE 14-9

Top: With the Type tool active, put your cursor above any path and a little wavy line appears at the bottom of the cursor. That's Photoshop's way of saying "permission granted" for creating type on a path.

Middle: Slide the type along the path by dragging with the Path Selection tool (the black arrow that lives below the type toolset in the Tools panel in single-column mode). A tiny black arrow appears next to the cursor facing either left or right, depending on which end of the text your cursor is near (here it's facing right). The starting point of the text is marked with a tiny X, and the end point is marked with a dot (both circled).

Bottom: To give your text a little breathing room, adjust the baseline shift (page 606) over in the Character panel. This scoots the text away from the path it's attached to. You can also increase tracking (page 605) if the letters start crashing into each other.

You can also slide the text back and forth along the path, or flip it from the top of the path to the bottom, using the Path Selection tool—just click the black arrow below the Type tool in the Tools panel to activate it (see page 558 for more on this tool). Put your I-beam cursor over the starting point of the text (which is marked with an x—see *Figure 14-9*, middle). When a tiny, right-facing arrow appears next to the cursor, drag to the left or right to move the text. (The little arrow points to the left if you put your cursor over the end of the text, which is marked with a black dot.) To flip the text to the opposite side of the path—in this example, that means putting it *inside* the snail shell rather than on top—drag your cursor below the path (toward the bottom of the shape).

What's *really* happening here is that Photoshop is adjusting the start and end points of the text. You can move the start point by clicking the path with the right-arrowed cursor. Likewise, you can move the end point by putting your cursor at the end of the text and then clicking with the left-arrowed cursor. (If the text is center aligned, you'll likely see a double-arrowed cursor.)

NOTE If your text disappears, that means the space between the start and end points is too small to house the text. In that case, adjust one of the points or reformat the text to make it fit.

You can format type on a path like any other text. Just switch back to the Type tool and then highlight it using one of the techniques described on page 585. (To highlight all the text on a layer *and* activate the Type tool at the same time, give the Type layer a quick double-click in the Layers panel.)

Filling a Shape with Text

Placing text inside a shape is even simpler than placing t on an object's edge, and it's a fun little exercise in type design. First, create a closed shape with the Pen tool or one of the shape tools as discussed above, and then grab the Horizontal Type tool. Put your cursor inside the shape and, when it turns into an I-beam surrounded by tiny dots (shown in *Figure 14-10*, top), just click and type your text. Easy, huh?

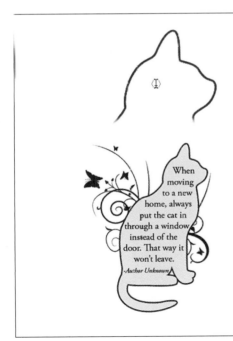

FIGURE 14-10

Top: Once your cursor is surrounded by tiny dots, click inside the object and start typing to add your text.

Bottom: When you're finished typing, you can format the text using any of the options discussed on page 598 and beyond. Centered align-ment is especially useful for this technique, because it pushes the text away from the edges of the object, as shown here. Or, you can give the text a little more space using the Paragraph panel's Indent Left Margin and Indent Right Margin controls (page 611).

Warping Text

Another way to create text that follows a shape is to use the Create Warped Text command. Be forewarned, though, that this option distorts the *shape* of the letters (so they might not be very legible when you're done), whereas type on a path alters only the baseline and orientation (direction) of the text.

The Create Warped Text button appears in the Options bar whenever a type tool is active (it looks like a T with a curved line under it). If you're using any other tool, choose Type→Warp Text to access its dialog box (*Figure 14-11*). Unlike placing type on a path or inside an object, to warp text, you have to create the text first and *then* click the Warp button (or choose the menu command). Next, pick one of the 15 canned settings in the Warp Text dialog box's Style menu, and then customize the style by tweaking the Bend, Horizontal Distortion, and Vertical Distortion sliders (you may have to move the dialog box aside so you can see how the text is changing.)

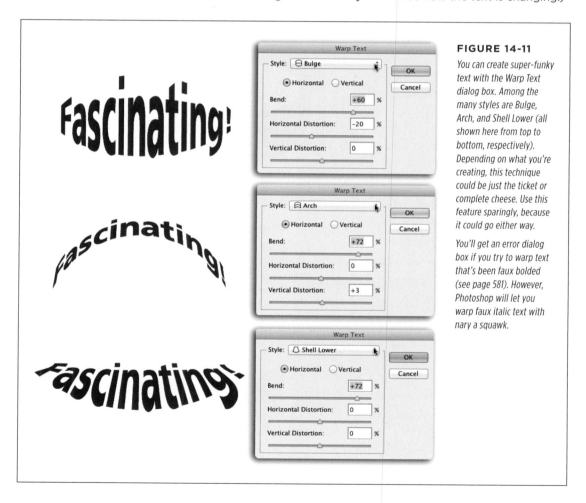

FIGURE 14-11

You can create super-funky text with the Warp Text dialog box. Among the many styles are Bulge, Arch, and Shell Lower (all shown here from top to bottom, respectively). Depending on what you're creating, this technique could be just the ticket or complete cheese. Use this feature sparingly, because it could go either way.

You'll get an error dialog box if you try to warp text that's been faux bolded (see page 581). However, Photoshop will let you warp faux italic text with nary a squawk.

If you don't like the result, just press Option (Alt on a PC) and the Warp Text dialog box's Cancel button changes to a Reset button. Click it to snuff out any changes you've made so far (or click Cancel to exit the dialog box completely). Once you've got your text looking good, click OK.

As long as you don't rasterize the Type layer and turn it into pixels (see the box on page 589), you can change the warp settings at any time. Just activate the Type layer and then choose Type→Warp Text to see the warp settings you used previously.

Using Find and Replace

No matter what kind of text you work with, at some point you might need to exchange a word, phrase, or character for something else. It's usually easy enough to make such fixes manually, but if there's a fair amount of text in your document, reach for the Find and Replace command instead.

For example, suppose you're working on a full-page ad for a sports-drink company and they've just changed the name of their flagship product from Dr. Bob's Thirst Remedy to Quenchtastic 4000. In that situation, you can save yourself lots of time by using the Find and Replace feature. Photoshop will seek out the offending word or phrase and replace it with whatever you want.

Choose Edit→"Find and Replace Text" to summon the dialog box shown in *Figure 14-12* (you don't even need to have the Type tool or a Type layer active). Enter the offending word or phrase in the Find What field and its replacement in the Change To field. Use the checkboxes to tell Photoshop whether you want it to search through all the Type layers in your document; look only for instances that match the case (capitalization) of what you've typed; search from a specific point in a Type layer forward (this one's only available if you have the Type tool active and the cursor blinking at a point within the text); look for whole words only; ignore accent marks; or any combination of these options.

FIGURE 14-12

Hopefully you'll never set enough text in Photoshop to need the Find and Replace Text feature, but it can come in handy in a pinch. You also have the option to ignore accents, handy when you're working with languages other than English.

Formatting Text

Now that you've learned all about the different *kinds* of Photoshop text, it's time to dig in to how to format it. Photoshop lets you control text to within an inch of its life. Beyond the basics of font, size, and color, you can adjust the softness of the letters' edges, the space between each letter, the space between lines of text, and so on.

The most commonly used settings live in the Options bar, while the more advanced typographic goodies are nestled inside the Type menu, as well as the Character and Paragraph panels. No matter where the settings live, if they control text, you'll learn about them in the following pages. Read on!

> **TIP** If you're designing a website in Photoshop, you can make Photoshop copy all the text's formatting, as well as its position on the page, for use in the program you'll use for actually *building* the site (say, Adobe Dreamweaver). Once you've got the text formatted just right, Control-click (right-click) near a Type layer's name in the Layers panel, and then choose Copy CSS (short for "cascading style sheets"). Photoshop grabs all the pertinent info, which you can then paste into another program. Sweet!

Formatting with the Options Bar

When you have the Type tool active, the Options bar (*Figure 14-13*) offers basic text-tweakers such as font family, style, size, anti-aliasing (see page 600), alignment, and color. (The Character panel, discussed on page 601, offers all these settings and more.)

> **NOTE** Remember, any changes you make in the Options bar *remain* until you change 'em back. So if you suddenly find that your text isn't behaving like you expect, chances are there's a setting in the Options bar that needs changing.

WORD TO THE WISE

Thou Shalt Spell Check

Few mistakes are as embarrassing (or avoidable) for a graphic artist as a misspelled word. Most software comes with a built-in spellchecker, and Photoshop is no exception, so there's little excuse for typos (on the other hand, *wordos*—real words in the wrong place—are another story). And let's face it: The people who create copy can rarely spot their own mistakes, either because they've been staring at it for too long or because they're rushing to meet a deadline. In those situations, using a spellchecker is essential.

To check spelling in Photoshop, choose Edit→Check Spelling. Photoshop scours your document's Type layers and, in the resulting dialog box, alerts you to words it considers suspect. It dutifully offers a list of suggestions that you can ignore or accept, changing just one instance or all of them. If it encounters an unknown word that is oft used and correctly spelled, just click the Add button and Photoshop assimilates the word into its dictionary.

Whether you're typing five words or five paragraphs, take time to run the spellchecker—you'll be glad you did.

FIGURE 14-13

These formatting choices appear in the Options bar when the Type tool is active. A handy way to change any numeric setting (like font size) is to point your cursor at the field's label until you see a double-arrowed scrubby cursor (circled). Then simply drag left or right to decrease or increase that setting (respectively).

You can apply formatting either before or after you create text:

- **Before you type**. If you know exactly what font, style, and size you want to use before you start hammering out text, applying formatting beforehand is the way to go. Press T to grab the Type tool and then head to the Options bar or the Character panel to pick your settings.

- **After you type**. This is the more common method, since it's easier to see how formatting choices affect *existing* text than try to imagine how it might look. With the Type tool active, highlight the text you want to format using one of the methods described on page 585, and then use the Options bar or Character panel to change the formatting however you wish.

From left to right, the Options bar gives you control over the following:

- **Type Tool Preset picker**. From the factory, this setting performs the fairly useless service of letting you quickly summon horizontal 24-point type in the Myriad font. Thankfully, with just a little bit of work, you can create your own presets—a fantastic idea if you use the same formatting over and over again. Start by formatting some text exactly the way you want it and then make sure its Type layer is active (you don't have to highlight the text itself). Next, click the triangle next to the Type Tool Preset picker, and then, in the menu that appears, click the gear icon and choose New Tool Preset. Enter a meaningful name in the resulting box, and then click OK. Photoshop memorizes how you formatted the text so it can apply that formatting automatically the next time around. Just grab the Type tool, pick your style from the Type Tool Preset picker, and then click in your document and start typing.

TIP Photoshop also lets you create *character* and *paragraph styles,* detailed text formatting recipes that you can apply on the fly. See the box on page 613 for details.

- **Text orientation**. There's no need to decide whether you want horizontal (left to right) or vertical (top to bottom) text before you type: Clicking this little button will flip the whole Type layer on the fly. You don't even have to highlight any text first.

- **Font family**. This menu lists every font that's active on your machine and includes a preview of what each one looks like. (If you want to turn off this preview, page 582 tells you how.)

- **Font style**. Here's where you can choose a native style (page 580) for the font you picked, such as light, bold, or condensed.

- **Font size**. Enter a point size for the text in this field, or point your cursor at the field's label and then use the scrubby cursor shown in *Figure 14-13* to change the size. Though text size is typically stated in points, you can change the unit of measurement to pixels or millimeters by choosing Photoshop→Preferences→Units & Rulers (Edit→Preferences→Units & Rulers on a PC).

TIP If you need to create *super* large text, Photoshop will put up a fight. When you type a number greater than 1296 into the Font size field, you'll see an error message asking you to enter a number between 1 and 1296. This is an odd little quirk of Photoshop's, but if you're sneaky, you can work around this limitation by resizing your text with the Free Transform command (page 257): Enter *1296* into the size field and then choose Edit→Transform→Scale. Drag the resulting resizing handles outward to make the text really honkin' big, and then press Return (Enter on a PC) to accept the transformation.

- **Anti-aliasing**. Anti-aliasing was mentioned way back in Chapter 4 as a method for smoothing the edges of a selection. Similarly, this option smooths text by blurring its edges ever so slightly, helping you avoid the dreaded jagged edges so common when printing to a low-resolution inkjet printer or posting on the Web.

  Your choices here include None, Sharp, Crisp, Strong, and Smooth. Each setting has a different effect on various text sizes, so you might have to do a little experimenting. Use None on extremely small text to make it clean and sharp (especially if it's destined for the Web), and Strong or Smooth for larger text to keep it from looking jagged when it's printed (especially if it's headed for an older inkjet printer).

  In Photoshop CC, you'll spot two *new* options at the bottom of the menu that help make text look like it will when it's displayed onscreen in popular web browsers or other programs on your computer, which is good news for mobile and web designers. The first option, Mac LCD (Windows LCD on a PC) makes your text look like it would look in Safari (on a Mac) or Internet Explorer (in Windows). The second option, named simply Mac (Windows on a PC) makes your text look like it would in any other program (say, Microsoft Word). By choosing one of these new options, you're turning *off* the Adobe type engine and turning *on* your operating system's type engine for slightly different-looking text.

- **Alignment**. These three buttons make text flush left, centered, or flush right (respectively) within a single line of text or a text box. Unless you specifically apply a different alignment, Photoshop automatically left-aligns text. To align a single line of text on a Type layer that contains several paragraphs, press T to activate the Type tool, click anywhere within the line or paragraph, and then click one of these buttons. To center everything on a Type layer, double-click the Type layer's thumbnail in the Layers panel, and then click an alignment button.

TIP You can also use keyboard shortcuts to align text. For left alignment, highlight some text and then press Shift-⌘-L (Shift+Ctrl+L). For center alignment, press Shift-⌘-C (Shift+Ctrl+C), and for right alignment, press Shift-⌘-R (Shift+Ctrl+R).

- **Text color**. You can set text's color by highlighting the text (page 585) and then clicking this little colored swatch in the Options bar, which shows the current text color. (There's a similar button in the Character panel that does the same thing.) You can also set text color before you type by clicking the foreground or background color chip. To recolor some text to your foreground color, highlight the text, and then press Option-Delete (Alt+Backspace on a PC). To use the background color instead, press ⌘-Delete (Ctrl+Backspace).

NOTE When choosing a text color, resist the urge to go hog wild. Bear in mind that black text on a white background is easy to read, as is dark-colored text on a light background. The key is contrast—it's really hard to read text that's similar in color to its background. However, if you're adding text to a *dark* background, you risk the danger of introducing *too* much contrast. For example, a single line of pure white text on a black background is quite legible, but a large block of white text on a black background—especially on the Web—is eye-numbing. In that situation, you'd be better off using light-gray text instead so the contrast won't be quite so high.

- **Create warped text**. You can use this option to curve and distort text in all manner of exciting ways, as explained on page 596. This button is easy to spot: Its icon is a capital T perched atop a curved line.
- **Character and Paragraph panels**. Click this button to pop open the Character and Paragraph panels for even more text formatting goodness, as explained in the next two sections. (Click it again to hide the panels.)

The Character Panel

If you've ever clicked the Options bar's rightmost button when the Type tool is active (see *Figure 14-13*), then the Character and Paragraph panels' icons are probably lurking near the right side of your screen in the panel dock—they look like a capital A and a paragraph symbol (¶), respectively. If you don't see 'em, choose Type→Panels→Character Panel (or Type→Panels→Paragraph Panel) and Photoshop adds them both to the dock for you (you can also open both panels by using the

Window menu). It assumes that if you're using one, you'll soon be using the other, which is a pretty safe bet.

The Character panel, shown in *Figure 14-14*, has enough formatting options to please even the most discerning typesetter. It includes all the settings found in the Options bar when you're using the Type tool, plus it lets you control the space in and around individual characters, where they sit on a line, the height of the line, and more. It also holds the key to unlocking the amazing OpenType features discussed on pages 609–610. Mastering this panel can help you turn ordinary text into a work of art.

NOTE Like the Options bar, any changes you make in the Character panel remain in effect until you change them back. So if you play with leading (explained below) on Monday and then add text to a brand-new document on Tuesday, the leading may look a bit off. Either use the leading drop-down menu to change it back to Auto or go to the Character panel's menu (see *Figure 14-14*) and choose Reset Character, which reverts *all* the panel's settings back to normal.

FIGURE 14-14

Behold the mighty option-riddled Character panel!

Here you'll find controls for tracking, kerning, adjusting text's baseline, and OpenType options. Point your cursor at numeric field's label to summon the ever-handy scrubby cursor (circled in Figure 14-13*), and then drag left or right to decrease or increase the field's value, respectively. If you (understandably) forget what some of these settings do, put your cursor over any of the field's labels to make Photoshop display a handy tooltip that explains what that setting does.*

■ A LESSON IN LEADING

Adding extra returns (by pressing Return [Enter]) between lines of text to create space or wondering how designers make lines of text appear all squashed together means you've encountered *leading* (rhymes with "bedding"). Leading controls the amount of blank space between lines of text. The term originated back in the days when type was set by hand onto printing presses, and strips of lead in various thicknesses were used to create space between lines. Learning to adjust leading is a useful design skill, and Photoshop gives you complete control over it, as shown in *Figure 14-15*.

FIGURE 14-15

Attention Goldilocks: The leading on the left is too little, the leading on the right is too much, but the leading in the middle—set to Auto—is just right (for this situation, anyway; auto leading isn't perfect for every project). As you can see, leading can make a design statement.

Leading is measured in points just like text, though it *includes* the point size of the text itself. Leading that's equal to the point size of text is called *solid leading*, which creates lines of text that almost touch (resulting in spacing that's somewhere between what's shown in the left and middle of *Figure 14-15*). Unless you change it, Photoshop's leading is set to Auto, which is approximately 120 percent of the text's point size (see *Figure 14-15*, middle). For example, 10-point type has an auto leading of 12 points.

The Character panel's leading control is labeled with two A's stacked on top of each other. You can adjust the leading of several lines of text at once or one line at a time. To adjust the leading of all the lines of text that are on the same layer, double-click the offending Type layer in the Layers panel so all its text is highlighted, and then choose a point size from the Character panel's leading menu, or type directly into the text field. (Better yet, put your cursor above the field's label and then use the handy scrubby cursor.) To adjust the leading of a *single* line of text on a Type layer that contains many lines, highlight the line of text first and then change its leading.

> **TIP** You can also use keyboard shortcuts to change leading: Highlight the text and then press and hold Option (Alt on a PC) and tap the up or down arrow keys to change the leading in increments of 1 points; add ⌘ (Ctrl) to change it in increments of 5 points. To set leading back to Auto, press Shift-Option-⌘-A (Shift+Alt+Ctrl+A). This shortcut works on vertical text, too!

■ LEARNING TO KERN

Kerning means adjusting the amount of space between pairs of letters. Poorly kerned (or unkerned) text looks funky and can be distracting to the reader, as you can see in *Figure 14-16*, top. A lack of kerning is one of the *biggest* clues that text has been set nonprofessionally (nothing exposes a typographical novice faster!). Admittedly, the problem is more noticeable with less expensive—or free—fonts (think Frolicking

Ferrets), scripts, and decoratives (*especially* fonts that mimic handwriting, like the one in the figure).

FIGURE 14-16

Top: Here's some text borrowed from a BMW motorcycle ad in a pitiful, unkerned state. Notice how several of the letters appear too close together? The punctuation is even worse—it's practically in a different Zip code.

Bottom: After a little kerning, the text looks normal instead of helter-skelter, so readers can focus on what the copy says instead of the weird spacing.

Get it? My hairstylist is my motorcycle helmet? Oh, never mind.

Over in the Character panel, the kerning button is marked by the letters VA and a left-pointing arrow. The numbers in the kerning menu range from positive to negative; positive values increase space, and negative values decrease space. Kerning values are measured in 1/1000 *em*. An em is a relative measurement that's based on the point size of the text. For example, if the text size is 12-point, 1 em equals 12 points. Since you can create text of various sizes, this measurement ensures that your kerning is always based on the size you're currently working with.

> **NOTE** Though Photoshop tries to kern text automatically, it's best to do it manually as described here. The box on page 605 has more on auto vs. manual kerning.

Because the amount of space each letter needs on either side differs according to which letter comes next—an *A* can tuck in closer to a *V* than it can to an *M*, for example—you'll want to kern each space individually. Press T to grab the Type tool and position the cursor in the first problem area you spot. To widen the space, pick a positive value from the kerning menu, drag the scrubby cursor gently to the right, or type a value into the kerning field. To narrow the space, pick a negative value or drag the scrubby cursor to the left.

> **TIP** There's a keyboard shortcut for changing kerning, but you need to place your cursor *between* the letters you want to adjust first. Press and hold Option (Alt on a PC) while tapping the left or right arrow key to change the kerning in increments of 20. Add the ⌘ key (Ctrl) to change it in increments of 100.

■ TRACK IT OUT

To change the spacing between *all* letters in a word by the same amount, you need to adjust *tracking*. This adjustment is great when you're trying to make text fit into a small area. Also, vast amounts of tracking, as shown in the word "conference" in *Figure 14-17*, can be a useful design trick. Like kerning, tracking is measured in 1/1000 em. To make an adjustment, first highlight the word(s) you want to track and then trot over to the Character panel and look for the setting marked with the VA with a double-headed arrow beneath it. Pick a value from the drop-down menu, enter one manually, or use the scrubby cursor you get by putting your cursor over the VA.

FIGURE 14-17

Tracking is a great way to make a word fit in a small space or fill a big space. In this example, the word "conference" has been tracked out to stretch from the G in "digital" to the last A in "camera." Because the large amount of space between the letters is uniform and obviously deliberate, it becomes a useful design element. (This is also one of the few ways all-caps text looks good—the extra space makes it seem less like screaming.)

UP TO SPEED

Auto vs. Manual Kerning

Ever helpful, Photoshop tries to kern text for you. Perched at the top of the kerning menu in the Character panel are two auto-kerning methods: Metrics and Optical.

Metrics kerning is the most common method. It tells Photoshop to adjust the space between letters according to their *kern pairs*—the amount of spacing between pairs of letters (like *Tr, To, Ta*, and so on) that the designer specified when creating the font. Photoshop applies metrics kerning automatically any time you create or import text (unless you've changed this menu's setting).

However, some fonts contain little or no info about kern pairs, but you won't know that until you start typing. So, if the kerning looks really bad, Adobe recommends that you manually switch to optical kerning, where Photoshop adjusts the space according to characters' shapes instead. Optical kerning is also helpful when you use more than one font (or font size) in a single word.

Using automatic kerning is fine for large blocks of text—imagine hand-kerning this book!—but for standalone text, the best method is to kern it manually as described on page 603. It takes more time, but the results are *well* worth it.

TIP　As you might suspect, there's a keyboard shortcut for this one too. To adjust tracking in increments of 20, highlight some text and then press and hold Option (Alt on a PC) while tapping the left or right arrow key. Add the ⌘ key (Ctrl) to change tracking in increments of 100.

■ DOIN' THE BASELINE SHIFT

The invisible line onto which text sits is called its *baseline*. Changing this line can make a character appear higher or lower than other characters on the same line (see *Figure 14-18*). This is called *baseline shift*, and you can think of it as an exaggerated super- or subscript control (as in degree and trademark symbols). Remember the section on page 593 about text on a path? Baseline shift was used to scoot the text above the path in that example. It's also helpful when you want to create fractions, use initial caps (shown in *Figure 14-18*), or manually adjust characters in a decorative font. Basically, this setting keeps you from having to put the character on its own Type layer in order to manually position it with the Move tool.

FIGURE 14-18

The big, fancy D is lower than the rest of the word "domestic" because its baseline shift has been decreased to –30 points.

To shift the baseline in increments of 1 points, highlight some text, and then press Shift-Option (Shift+Alt on a PC) while tapping the up or down arrow on your keyboard. Add the ⌘ key (Ctrl) to shift it in increments of 5 points.

To adjust the baseline of a character, word, or phrase, highlight the text you want to tweak and then head to the Character panel (if you don't highlight anything, the adjustment gets applied to the next thing you type). Use the baseline shift setting (it's marked with a big A, a little A, and an up arrow) to move the text up or down by picking a positive or negative value (respectively) from the menu, entering a value manually, or using the scrubby cursor.

■ OTHER CHARACTER OPTIONS

The Character panel is chock-full of other formatting controls. Just remember that, to apply any of the formatting discussed in this section, you first have to highlight some text.

As shown back in *Figure 14-14*, the Character panel has a whole row of buttons that let you apply faux styles, like bold and italic (meaning they're not built into the font, but faked by Photoshop instead). Feel free to use faux styles if you're creating a piece for online use or at-home printing, but if the project is bound for a professional printer, it's best to stay away from the faux stuff as it can cause unexpected results. Problems include jagged text (due to rasterization); characters that refuse to print (which will cause Photoshop to substitute another font); or a PostScript error, which can halt printing altogether.

Among the other styles offered by the Character panel for your formatting pleasure are underline (which places a line under the text), and strikethrough (which places a line *through* the text).

TIP The keyboard shortcut for faux-bolding text (after it's highlighted) is Shift-⌘-B (Shift+Ctrl+B); for faux-italicizing, it's Shift-⌘-I (Shift+Ctrl+I); for underlining, it's Shift-⌘-U (Shift+Ctrl+U); and for adding a strikethrough, it's Shift-⌘-/ (Shift+Ctrl+/). Whew!

The other options in the Character panel are:

- **Vertical** and **Horizontal Scale**. These two settings (which stretch or shrink text vertically or horizontally) have the power to squish, cram, and spread type to within an inch of its life, rendering it utterly unreadable and unrecognizable, so use these options at your own risk. If you're trying to save space, a better solution is to adjust kerning or tracking (or both). If you're trying to fill space, increase the type size or tracking instead.

TIP If you've played around with your text's scale, you can instantly get it back to normal with the flick of a keyboard shortcut. Reset the vertical scale to 100 percent by highlighting the text and then pressing Shift-Option-⌘-X (Shift+Alt+Ctrl+X), or reset the horizontal scale to 100 percent by pressing Shift-⌘-X (Shift+Ctrl+X).

- **All Caps** and **Small Caps**. To switch lowercase text to uppercase, just highlight the text and then click the All Caps button (marked with TT). But keep in mind that, unless you're creating a small amount of text and perhaps tracking it out as shown in *Figure 14-17*, using all caps is a bad idea. It makes text extremely hard to read because the words all take on the same blocky shape. Besides, they tend to insinuate screaming (LIKE THIS), and that's not very reader friendly. The Small Caps button (marked with a big T and a smaller T) isn't much better, as it simply creates a smaller version of hard-to-read all caps. The keyboard shortcut for all caps is Shift-⌘-K (Shift+Ctrl+K); for small caps, it's Shift-⌘-H (Shift+Ctrl+H).

- **Superscript** and **Subscript**. These buttons cause the baseline and point size of the highlighted character(s) to change. (If you don't have any text highlighted, the next character you type will be superscript or subscript.) Superscript increases the baseline shift so the character sits above other text in the same line (great for trademark symbols such as ™ and ®), while subscript decreases the baseline shift so the character sits below other text (perfect for footnotes and scientific or mathematical text).

- **Language**. The language menu at the bottom of the Character panel won't translate text for you; it merely means that Photoshop will adjust its spell checking and hyphenation to suit the language you picked. The 40 or so choices include everything from Bulgarian to Ukrainian. (The box on page 598 has info on spell checking.)

- **Anti-Aliasing**. The Character panel's anti-aliasing setting (in the lower-right corner of the panel) works just like the anti-aliasing setting on the Options bar (page 600), and slightly blurs the edges of text so they don't look jagged.

The following goodies—which used to live in the Character panel's *menu* but now have their own buttons in the panel—are reserved for OpenType fonts only, so they're grayed out if you're using a PostScript or TrueType font. As discussed on pages 609–610, OpenType format lets font designers include alternative character designs and all manner of glyphs. Some have alternate *ligatures* (two or more characters that have been combined into one for better flow—like an *fi* or *fl* combo), fancy flourishes (see *Figure 14-19*), a whole set of ornaments, and more. These embellishments are perfect for creating fancy initial caps, formatting numbers, and adding a bit of typographic pizzazz:

- **Standard Ligatures** are alternate character designs for certain letter combinations that tend to touch—like *fi, fl, ff, ffi,* and *ffl*.

- **Contextual Alternates** substitutes certain letterforms for others that join together more fluidly. This option is common in script fonts because it makes the letters look like cursive handwriting.

- **Discretionary Ligatures** are replacements for letter pairs like *ct, st,* and *ft*. They tend to have a bit more flourish than their standard ligature counterparts.

- **Swash** substitutes a standard character for one with an exaggerated stroke (think calligraphy).

FIGURE 14-19

The top line of text here is in standard Adios Script Pro, a truly gorgeous OpenType font. The middle line was created using Contextual Alternates, which summons different letter designs depending upon where the letter falls within a word. The last line was created using the extra-flourishy Swash option, which is best reserved for single letters and not words.

Keep in mind that some OpenType fonts have extras and some don't; if one of the Open-Type buttons near the bottom of the Character panel is grayed out, it means the feature doesn't exist in that particular font.

Fancy

Fancier

Fanciest

- **Stylistic Alternates** are characters that have extra bits of decoration here and there, as shown at the bottom of *Figure 14-19*. They're for your visual pleasure only (and, of course, that of the font designer).

- **Titling Alternates** calls to action a special set of all-caps characters designed to be used at large sizes, for things like titles (hence the name).

- **Ordinals** decreases the size of letters appearing next to numbers and increases their baseline shift so they look like this: 2nd, 3rd, 4th, and so on.

- **Fractions** converts a number-slash-number combination (like this: 1/2) into a real fraction (like this: ½).

But wait—that's not all! The Character panel has *even more* settings hidden in its menu, which lives in the panel's upper-right corner (it's labeled back in *Figure 14-14*):

- **Change Text Orientation**. This menu item lets you switch horizontally aligned text to vertical, and vice versa. Just activate the Type layer you want to change, not the text itself, and then choose this option.

- **Standard Vertical Roman Alignment**. This is a fun one, though it works only on vertical type. Instead of the letters flowing from top to bottom, perched atop one another, they'll flow from left to right as if they were turned on their sides. (Picture the word "Vertical" back in *Figure 14-4* [page 582] laid down on its side.) Another way to create this effect is to use the Free Transform tool to spin the text 90 degrees.

- **OpenType**. As you just learned, the majority of Photoshop's OpenType formatting goodies have their own buttons near the bottom of the Character panel.

They also live in the panel menu's OpenType submenu, along with a couple of extra options (though not all OpenType fonts include these options):

— **Oldstyle** prompts Photoshop to use smaller numerals than normal; some even sit below the baseline so they blend more smoothly into the flow of text. Use this option when you want numbers to appear more elegant, but *not* when you need them to line up in a stack, as in an annual report.

— **Ornaments** are symbols or pictographs. Typically this option is available only for symbol-based fonts (like Wingdings). When you choose this option, Photoshop replaces the original symbols with an alternate set.

- **Fractional Widths**. This setting rounds character widths to the nearest *part* of a pixel instead of a whole pixel. This setting is automatically turned on because it usually tightens text spacing, making it more visually pleasing (like kerning, discussed on page 603). However, Adobe recommends turning this option *off* if you're working with anything smaller than 20-point text because the tighter spacing can make it hard to read. When this setting is off, Photoshop uses whole-pixel spacing, which gives characters a bit more breathing room and keeps them from running into each other.

NOTE   You can't apply the Fractional Widths setting to individual characters—it's an all-or-nothing, everything-on-the-Type-layer-is-affected kind of thing. To use whole-pixel increments for the entire document, choose System Layout (explained next) from the Character panel's menu.

- **System Layout**. This option reverts text to the way your particular operating system displays it—similar to what you might see in TextEdit on a Mac or in WordPad on a PC. It switches character widths to whole pixels (as discussed in the previous bullet) and turns off anti-aliasing. This can be a good option to use when designing text for the Web, because the extra space and letter sharpness makes super small text a little easier to read. That said, the two new anti-aliasing methods in CC do pretty much the same thing (see page 600).

- **No Break**. When it comes to hyphenation, some words are meant to be broken and some aren't (as shown in *Figure 14-20*). To prevent such typographical gaffes, highlight the word(s) you want to keep together and then choose No Break from the Character panel's menu. This forces Photoshop to reflow the text so the word doesn't end up sliced in two. For more on hyphenation, see page 612.

- **Reset Character**. If you've gone a bit overboard with formatting and want to return some text to its original glory, highlight it and then choose Reset Character from the Character panel's menu. (If you don't have any text highlighted, the newly restored character settings will affect the next thing you type.)

In MotoGP, Rossi is a leg- end.

Angry wife is jailed for mans- laughter.

FIGURE 14-20

This is what happens when good hyphenation goes bad. The fix is to highlight the offending word and then choose No Break from the Character panel's menu.

The Paragraph Panel

The Paragraph panel, shown in *Figure 14-21*, doesn't have anywhere *near* the number of options as the Character panel, though that doesn't make it any less important. Paragraph formatting controls alignment, hyphenation, justification, indentation, and spacing. Read on for a full discussion of each.

FIGURE 14-21

You can apply the Paragraph panel's formatting options to one or more paragraphs of text. If you don't highlight any text before adjusting these settings, Photoshop changes all the text on the active Type layer. But if the Type layer contains two lines of text separated by a carriage return, you can highlight one line and left-align it, and then highlight the other and right-align it, for example.

■ ALIGNING TEXT

Alignment gives readers' eyes a hard edge to follow as they read through text, with the edge itself forming an invisible line that connects items on a page. The basic alignment types are left, center, and right, and picking the correct one for your document can make it look stronger, cleaner, and more dramatic. So which alignment should you choose? It depends on what you're going for. Here are a few guidelines:

- **Use left alignment for big blocks of text**. Newspapers, books, and magazines (which should not be created in Photoshop, mind you) usually stick with left alignment because it's the easiest to read. Unless you tell it otherwise, Photoshop will left-align everything.

- **Use centered alignment for formal situations**. There's a reason the copy in every graduation and wedding announcement you've ever seen is centered—it conveys a feeling of formality and elegance. So unless you live on Pennsylvania Avenue, resist the urge to center the copy on your next yard sale flyer.

- **Use right alignment for small blocks of text or numbers**. Right alignment can make text stand out because it's unusual and therefore draws attention. But it's harder to read than left alignment, meaning you'll want to save it for relatively small chunks of text (so don't right align your next novel). However, it's great for lists of numbers because it makes the decimals points (or commas) line up.

> **TIP** With vertical type, these options align the text based on a vertical line instead of a horizontal one. So instead of left, center, and right alignment, your options are top, center, and bottom.

You can align text on a single layer (or even a single line on a layer) or across multiple Type layers:

- **Aligning text on a single Type layer or on multiple Type layers**. Feel free to use different alignments on lines of text that live on the same Type layer, so long as there's a carriage return after each line. First, activate the Type tool and the Type layer you want to work on. To align a single line of text, click anywhere within that line and then click the appropriate alignment button in the Options bar or the Paragraph panel. To align *all* the text on that layer, highlight it using one of the methods described on page 585, and then click an alignment button.

  To align the text on several Type layers, activate the layers by Shift- or ⌘-clicking (Ctrl-clicking on a PC) to the right of their thumbnails in the Layers panel, and then click an alignment button. (You can also use Photoshop's layer-filtering feature to isolate all the Type layers, as described on page 70.)

- **Aligning Type layers themselves**. To align the left edge of text across several layers, you use a whole different set of alignment tools. Activate the offending layers as described in the previous bullet point, and then press V to grab the Move tool and poof!—a whole flock of alignment options appear in the Options bar. Click the one you want to apply, and the active layers dutifully jump to the left, right, or center. These incredibly useful alignment options are covered more fully on page 93.

■ HYPHENATION AND JUSTIFICATION

Known to page-layout pros as H&J, these controls work together to spread paragraph text so that both the left and right edges are perfectly straight, or *justified*. (The text in most magazines, newspapers, and books—including this one—is justified.) They also determine how the words are sliced and diced (*hyphenated*) in order to make them fit within a text box or to make the margins perfectly straight.

> **NOTE** Hyphenation and justification work only on paragraph text, not point text. Page 583 explains the difference between these two.

Character and Paragraph Styles

Back in Photoshop CS6, Adobe introduced character and paragraph styles to give you the option of saving your hand-crafted text formatting to use on *other* text later on. Think of these features as quick text recipes you can use any time you want—a nice way to ensure consistent formatting across several documents.

To use character styles, format some text exactly the way you want using any of the Character panel options mentioned in the previous pages. When you get it just right, choose Type→Panels→Character Styles Panel. In the Character Styles panel, choose New Character Style from the panel's menu, and then double-click the style's name (Character Style 1) and give it a meaningful name like *callout*. The next time you want to apply the exact same formatting, activate the Type layer in the Layers panel, highlight the text using one of the techniques described on page 585, and then pop open the Character Styles panel and apply the style by clicking it in the list.

Paragraph styles work the same way, but they let you save both character *and* paragraph formatting. They're useful when you're formatting text like headlines, subheads, and body copy where things like spacing, alignment, indentation, and so on, come into play. (You'll learn all about paragraph formatting in the next section.) To open it, choose Type→Panels→Paragraph Styles Panel. It works the exactly the same way as the Character Styles panel.

If you apply additional formatting to an existing style, a tiny + appears next to its name in the relevant panel. To get rid of the extra formatting and revert back to the original style, click the Clear Override button at the bottom of the panel (it looks like a curved arrow). Or, to add the extra formatting to the style, click the checkmark. To edit or rename a style, simply double-click its name in the panel and then rename it in the dialog box that opens, which contains the myriad options available in both the Character and Paragraph panels. If you copy text that has a style applied to it and then paste it in another Photoshop document, the style comes along for the ride.

New in CC is the ability to save character and paragraph styles so they're automatically added to each new document you create and to existing documents that don't yet contain any styles. To do so, choose Save Default Type Styles from the Character Styles or Paragraph Styles panel menu (circled), or choose the same command from the Type menu. Also new is the ability to activate multiple styles in either panel and then delete 'em en masse. Unfortunately, you can't import styles from other programs (not even InDesign), nor can you export the ones you create here in Photoshop for use in *other* programs, though you *can* export a style from Photoshop and then load it onto someone else's machine for use in Photoshop using the menu shown here.

While Adobe considers these styles great timesavers—and they may be in small doses, especially for photographers—it's doubtful you'll create enough Photoshop text to use 'em very often. And if you do, that's a darn good indicator that you should be using a page-layout program such as InDesign or QuarkXPress instead.

Close panel | Double-click tab collapse vertically | Collapse panel horizontally

New Paragraph Style
Style Options...

Rename Style
Duplicate Style
Delete Style
Redefine Style
Load Paragraph Styles...

Clear Override

Load Default Type Styles
Save Default Type Styles

Clear override
Redefine by merging overrides
New style
Delete style

Photoshop's hyphenation feature is automatically turned on, but you can turn it off by clicking the checkbox at the bottom of the Paragraph panel, or by highlighting the text and then pressing Shift-Option-⌘-H (Shift+Alt+Ctrl+H). However, you have to turn justification on manually by picking one of the following options (just click the appropriate button near the top of the Paragraph panel):

- **Justify last left**. This setting spreads text so that the left and right edges are perfectly straight, with the last line of the paragraph left aligned (meaning it doesn't reach across to the right margin), like the text in this book. The keyboard shortcut for this kind of justification is to highlight your text and then press Shift-⌘-J (Shift+Ctrl+J).

TIP Justification is affected by which *composition method* you've chosen. See the box on page 617 for more info on this.

- **Justify last centered**. This is the same as the previous setting, but with the last line center aligned instead.

- **Justify last right**. Same again, but with the last line right aligned.

NOTE When working with vertical text, your justification options are Justify last top, centered, and bottom.

- **Justify all**. With this setting turned on, the left and right edges of text are perfectly straight, but the last line is spread out to span the entire width of the paragraph. The results usually don't look very good (the last line tends to be really sprawled out), but once in a while some rebellious designer manages to pull it off, as shown in *Figure 14-22*.

FIGURE 14-22

To truly tax your text, use "Justify all." This forces all the lines of text to line up vertically, even the last one. (Thank goodness newspapers and magazines are beginning to shift toward more reader-friendly left alignment instead.)

It's really hard to make blocked text look good, though the folks at QuotableCards.com managed it quite nicely in this magnet design.

It's unlikely you'll ever need to adjust the H&J options, and if you do, that's a sign you should be creating text in another program (see the box on page 577). Nevertheless, you *can* customize hyphenation and justification via the Paragraph panel's menu. *Figure 14-23* has the scoop on adjusting these settings.

FIGURE 14-23

Top: To get to this dialog box, choose Hyphenation from the Paragraph panel's menu. Here you can specify the minimum length of words that Photoshop can break across lines, where it can break them (after how many letters), and how many consecutive lines can have hyphenated words at the end (for the best results, leave this set to 2). The Hyphenation Zone field controls how close to the right margin text can get before Photoshop hyphenates it. Turn off the Hyphenate Capitalized Words checkbox to make sure names and proper nouns stay intact.

Bottom: Access this dialog box by choosing Justification from the Paragraph panel's menu. This is where you control how far apart words and letters get spread when Photoshop makes the margins perfectly straight. You can also adjust how far the program stretches glyphs (page 578), and specify leading (page 602).

TIP To prevent Photoshop from hyphenating a word or phrase, use the No Break option over in the Character panel's menu, as described on page 610.

■ INDENTING TEXT

It should be clear by now that Photoshop is no word processor, so don't go rooting around expecting any serious margin controls. However, you do have *some* say in how much space Photoshop puts between the text and the left or right edge of a single line (for point text) or the boundaries of a text box (for paragraph text). You can find the following options in the middle of the Paragraph panel (shown back in *Figure 14-21*):

- **Indent Left Margin** and **Indent Right Margin**. These settings scoot a line of text left or right, respectively, by the number of points you enter.

- **Indent First Line**. This option indents only the first line of the paragraph. If you need to create a *hanging indent*—where all lines of a paragraph are indented *except* the first—you can do that here by entering a positive number (like 10) for the left indent and a negative number (like –10) for the first-line indent.

- **Roman Hanging Punctuation**. This totally awesome feature is actually tucked away in the Paragraph panel's menu. You can use it to make the punctuation sit *outside* the text margin, while the letters themselves remain perfectly aligned, as shown in *Figure 14-24*. (You don't need to highlight any text before applying this setting.)

"To enjoy the flavor of life **take big bites.**"

Robert Heinlein

FIGURE 14-24

The Roman Hanging Punctuation setting moves punctuation (in this case, the initial quotation mark) outside the margin, leaving the text perfectly aligned.

Savvy graphic designers love this option!

■ SPACE BEFORE AND AFTER

Take a peek at the headers and subheads in this book. Notice how there's more space above them than below? This kind of spacing makes it easy for you to tell—even at a glance—that the paragraph following the header is related to it. That's because the spacing itself is a visual clue: Information that *is* related should appear closer together than information that's *not* related. (In design circles, this is known as the rule of *proximity*.) Proper spacing makes it a lot easier for people to read or scan a document quickly and understand how it's organized.

To adjust the spacing in your document, you could take the easy way out and add a few extra carriage returns, though chances are good that you'll introduce too much—or too little—space. Instead, use the Paragraph panel's Space Before and Space After options, which let you control spacing right down to the point. To do that, activate a Type layer and grab the Type tool by pressing T. Then click anywhere in the offending line (don't highlight it, just click it), and then head to the Paragraph panel and enter an amount (in points) into the Space Before or Space After field, or both (you can also use the scrubby cursor).

■ Special Text Effects

You can spice up Photoshop text in a variety of ways by adding fades, strokes, drop shadows, textures, and more. You can even take a photo and place it *inside* of text.

The great thing is that you can perform all these techniques without rasterizing the text, so it remains fully and gloriously editable. Read on to learn all kinds of neat ways to add a little something special to your text.

> **TIP** Perhaps the easiest special effect of all is creating partially opaque or *ghosted* text. All you have to do is lower the Type layer's opacity in the Layers panel, as explained on page 90. That's it!

Faded Text

It's easy to make text look like it fades into an image, as shown in *Figure 14-25*. This technique is useful when you're creating a photo-centric advertisement or postcard announcement, or want to showcase a collection of photos on your website. Here's what you do:

1. **Open a photo and add some text.**

   Press T to grab the Type tool and type a single word. Be sure to pick a thick font such as Helvetica Bold or Black, Arial Black (used here), or Impact from the Options bar or Character panel.

> **TIP** Instead of straining your brain to choose a color for the text, you can snatch one from the photo instead; that way, it'll match. Simply highlight the text and then click the color square in the Options bar (or the Character panel) to open the Color Picker. Next, mouse away from the dialog box and, when your cursor turns into an eyedropper, click a spot in your image to grab that color; the text changes color instantly. Then simply click OK to close the Color Picker.

POWER USERS' CLINIC

Photoshop's Composition Methods

"Great artists steal," or at least that's what Picasso and Steve Jobs supposedly said, and the folks at Adobe clearly agree: Deep within the Paragraph panel's menu, you'll find a couple of options snatched unabashedly from InDesign, Adobe's page-layout program.

Displaying text is a complicated matter. To determine how it displays paragraph text, Photoshop takes into consideration word spacing, letter spacing, glyph spacing, *and* any hyphenation options you've set. With that information, it uses a complex formula to determine how to space lines of text (and break them, if necessary) in order to fit them within the text box you created. This is called *composition*, and you have two composition methods to choose from:

- Use **Single-line Composer** if you're dealing with just one line of text, or if you want to handcraft the spacing between letters and lines with kerning or by inserting manual line breaks (carriage returns). With this method, Photoshop composes each line individually, no matter how many lines the paragraph contains.

- Go with **Every-line Composer** if you've got more than one line of text. (Photoshop uses this method automatically unless you tell it otherwise.) Choosing this method tells Photoshop to compose the paragraph as a whole. The program tries to arrange lines in such a way that it avoids nasty line breaks. This method generally creates more visually pleasing text, in part because it makes Photoshop avoid hyphenation whenever possible.

FIGURE 14-25

Text that looks like it fades into an image is eye catching. The best thing about this technique is that the text remains fully editable so you can experiment with formatting to get just the right effect.

2. **Add a layer mask to the Type layer.**

   This mask will let you make the text look like it fades into your photo. With the Type layer active, click the circle-within-a-square icon at the bottom of the Layers panel to add the mask.

3. **Use the Gradient tool to fill the mask with a black-to-white, linear gradient.**

   Press G to grab the Gradient tool and, near the left end of the Options bar, click the down-pointing triangle to the right of the gradient preview to open the Gradient picker. From the resulting preset menu, choose the black-to-white gradient (it's the third one in the first row). Then take a peek at the little Gradient Type buttons to the right of the Gradient picker and make sure the first one is active so you're creating a linear gradient. Next, mouse over to your image and, with the mask active, click and drag from the bottom of the text to the top of the text (or a little past it). When you let go of your mouse, Photoshop automatically fills the mask with the gradient, hiding your text in such a way that it looks like it fades into the photo.

4. **If necessary, use the Move tool to reposition the text.**

   That's it! Save the file as a Photoshop document and the text will remain editable until the end of time (well, until the end of *Photoshop*, at least!).

Stroked Text

One of the easiest ways to enhance headline text—meaning text that's fairly big—is to give it an outline, making it really stand out. Photoshop calls this outline a *stroke*, and it's simple to add one using the Layer Styles menu. The following steps explain how to add a plain black stroke, as shown at the top of *Figure 14-26*.

FIGURE 14-26

Here are a few ways of stroking text with a layer style. No matter what kind of stroke you create, you can edit it by double-clicking the stroke style layer in the Layers panel.

Top: A classic thick, black, outside stroke.

Middle: By changing the stroke Fill Type to Gradient and picking Shape Burst from the gradient Style menu, you can introduce more than one color into the stroke. This gradient stroke was made with the Silver preset from the Metal set (see page 346 for more on loading gradients).

Bottom: By using the Gradient Editor (page 347) to create a custom solid gradient, you can make multi-stroked text like this, as explained in the next section.

1. **Add some text and commit it.**

   Press T to grab the Type tool and type a word. Be sure to choose a fairly weighty font like Futura bold or Cooper (the latter was used in *Figure 14-26*); if the letterforms are too thin, the stroke can overpower them. Then, when you're finished editing the text, tell Photoshop you're done by pressing Enter on your numeric keypad or by clicking the checkmark button in the Options bar.

   > **TIP**   You might be tempted to choose Edit→Stroke instead of following the steps below. Don't. To use the Edit menu's Stroke command, you have to rasterize the text first (in fact, the Stroke menu item will be grayed out if you've activated a Type layer, since it's vector-based). Using layer styles is a much more flexible way to outline text, because the text remains *editable*.

2. **From the Layer Style menu at the bottom of the Layers panel (the fx button), choose Stroke.**

   Photoshop pops open the Layer Style dialog box and displays the many options for adding a stroke.

3. **Enter a stroke width.**

   In the Size field, enter a pixel width (or drag the slider). Use a lower number for a thin stroke and a larger number for something more substantial (in *Figure 14-26*, top, the size was set to 8).

4. **Make sure the Position menu is set to Outside.**

Using Outside works well for text because it tells Photoshop to put the stroke on the *outside* of the character (as opposed to the inside, where it takes up more space, or straddling the character's edge, as is the case with a Center position). Leave the blend mode set to Normal and the opacity at 100 percent.

5. **From the Fill Type menu, choose Color.**

Photoshop assumes you want to fill the stroke with color (as opposed to a gradient, as explained in the next section) and it automatically chooses black. To create a standard black stroke, as shown at the top of *Figure 14-26*, leave this setting alone. To pick something else, click the color swatch and then choose something from the resulting Color Picker.

6. **When you're finished, click OK to close the Layer Style dialog box and admire your newly stroked text.**

You can edit the new stroke anytime by double-clicking the stroke style in the Layers panel.

> **TIP** To produce *hollow* text, apply a Stroke layer style and then lower the Type layer's Fill setting to 0% using the field near the top of the Layers panel. The stroke will still be visible, but everything *inside* it will vanish.

■ THE RARE MULTI-STROKED TEXT EFFECT

If you *really* want to make text stand out—like in a comic book—try giving it more than one stroke, like the "Shazam" at the bottom of *Figure 14-26*. This technique is rewarding, but it requires a few more steps than the plain ol' single-stroked method in the previous section. Begin with steps 1 and 2 for creating stroked text, and then proceed as follows:

1. **In the Layer Style dialog box, set the Fill Type field to Gradient and the Style menu to Shape Burst, as shown in *Figure 14-27*, top.**

Using a gradient lets you add a multicolored stroke to the text, though you'll need to do some gradient editing first. Choosing Shape Burst as the gradient style makes the gradient stroke appear on the *outside* of the text only. You don't *have* to pick a gradient style before editing the gradient; doing so just lets you see what you're creating.

2. **Open the Gradient Editor and choose a new a gradient.**

To open the Gradient Editor shown in *Figure 14-27* (bottom), click the rectangular gradient preview in the Layer Style dialog box. In the resulting dialog box, click once to use one of the handy preset swatches. If you want to get really creative, proceed to the next step. If not, skip to step 4.

Click to open Gradient Editor

Two stacked color stops · Color well · Controls location of color stop

FIGURE 14-27

Here are the settings that were to create the multicolored strokes around "Shazam" back in Figure 14-26.

Top: Once you get the hang of editing gradients, you can simulate space between the color strokes by creating a solid gradient that goes from black to white (or whatever your document's background color is) to green and then back to white. Note that the color that's closest to the text (white, in this case) is the last color in the gradient preview shown here.

Bottom: To make your gradient match this one, you'll need to create six color stops. Place two stops at the 25% mark and stack them directly atop each other so the white stop covers the black one. Next, add two stacked stops at 50% and arrange them so the green stop covers the white one. Then add two more stacked stops at 75% and make the white stop cover the green one. As shown here, you'll see just three color stops when you're finished because the other three are hidden directly underneath 'em.

3. **Choose Solid as the Gradient Type and edit the color stops.**

   To edit one of the gradient's colors, double-click one of the tiny color stops (circled in *Figure 14-27*) to summon the Color Picker. Move the color stops around by dragging them or by entering a number in the Location field. You can create the illusion of space between the strokes by including white in the gradient, as shown in *Figure 14-27*.

4. **When the preview looks good, click OK in the Gradient Editor, and then click OK again to close the Layer Style dialog box.**

Pretty nifty, eh? Once again, if you want to edit the stroke, just double-click the stroke style layer in the Layers panel.

> **NOTE** To learn how to create text that looks like it's made out of shiny metal—a technique you're allowed to use but once a year!—head to this book's Missing CD page at *www.missingmanuals.com/cds*.

Texturizing Text

Design trends come and go, but the distressed, tattered look has been popular for a long time. You can spot it everywhere: movie posters, magazine ads, and book and album covers. Admittedly, it looks pretty darn good when applied to text. After all, text doesn't always have to look new, does it?

As with most effects, Photoshop gives you all kinds of ways to create a textured look. You can swipe the texture from a photo, run a filter (or several) on the text, or hide portions of the text using a layer mask and then paint it back with an artistic brush. Depending on your situation, one of these methods will work better for you than the rest (or at least be faster). They're all covered in the following pages.

■ TEXTURE FROM A PHOTO

You can come up with some unique effects by grabbing texture from a photo and applying it to text through a layer mask. And the great thing about this technique is that it's completely nondestructive: The Type layer remains editable. Start with an extremely busy photo—one with lots of hard lines and angles, like a picture of wood, leaves, or an interesting piece of architecture. In the steps below, you'll use the Threshold adjustment to morph that photo into a high-contrast texture primed for plopping into the nearest layer mask, as shown in *Figure 14-28*.

Here's how to texturize text using a photo:

1. **Add some hefty text to your document.**

   Use a thick font (like Impact), and set its font size to something high (try 107 point). This will ensure you have plenty of surface area to texturize.

2. **Open a photo and then convert it to a high-contrast, black-and-white image using a Threshold adjustment.**

   Choose Image→Adjustments→Threshold. Drag the slider in the Threshold dialog box almost all the way to the left to make the highlights in the image completely white, and the shadows black. The black areas will become the texture, so bear in mind that too much texture (black) will render the text unreadable. Click OK when it looks good.

3. **Copy the new and contrast-riddled image.**

   Choose Select→All to surround your image with marching ants, and then copy the selection by pressing ⌘-C (Ctrl+C).

FIGURE 14-28

*Top: You can create a texture
from any photo using a
Threshold adjustment;
the more lines the photo
contains, the better. Areas in
shadow will become black
and the highlights become
white. For this technique to
work, you need to apply the
adjustment to your image instead of using an Adjustment
layer (just be careful not to
save over your original file
with this adjusted version).*

*Bottom: Here's what the
wood texture looks like after
it's been copied into a Type
layer's layer mask. Imagine
the possibilities!*

*Want to follow along? Visit
this book's Missing CD page
at www.missingmanuals.
com/cds and download the
practice file Wood.jpg.*

4. **Switch back to your text document, add a layer mask to the Type layer, and
   then open the mask.**

   Give the Type layer a layer mask by clicking the circle-within-a-square icon at
   the bottom of the Layers panel. Next, open the mask by Option-clicking (Alt-
   clicking on a PC) its thumbnail in the Layers panel. Your document should go
   completely white because the mask is empty.

5. **Paste the texture into the mask and, if necessary, reposition the text, mask,
   or both with the Move tool.**

   Once you're in the layer mask, press ⌘-V (Ctrl+V) to paste the new texture into
   the mask. Feel free to move it around with the Move tool.

6. **Exit the layer mask to reveal the newly textured text.**

   To get out of the layer mask and see the newly textured results, single-click the Type layer's thumbnail to the left of the layer mask, and marvel at your creativity.

> **NOTE** Photoshop assumes that if you want to move a layer mask, you'll want to move whatever it's attached to as well, though this may not always be the case. For example, if you want to move the text independently of the mask, or vice versa, you have to unlink them first. Just click the little chain icon that lives between the Type layer and layer mask thumbnails in the Layers panel, and the chain vanishes. Next, activate the Move tool and then click the thumbnail of whatever you want to reposition—either the image or its mask—and drag it into place. To lock them back together, click between their thumbnails in the Layers panel and the chain icon reappears. (You can unlink Adjustment layer masks, too!)

■ TEXTURE FROM A BRUSH

Another way to texturize text is by painting on a layer mask with the Brush tool. Photoshop has some amazingly funky-shaped brushes, so you might as well make good use of them! With this method, you can be a little more particular about exactly where the texture goes since you paint it by hand, as shown in *Figure 14-29*.

To get started, add some big, thick text to your document, and then do the following:

1. **Add a layer mask to the Type layer.**

   Activate the Type layer and add a layer mask to it by clicking the circle-within-a-square icon at the bottom of the Layers panel. This mask will let you *hide* bits of the text instead of deleting it.

2. **Grab the Brush tool and choose one of its more artistic manifestations, like Spatter or Chalk.**

   Press B to activate the Brush tool and then open the Brush Preset picker in the Options bar. Scroll through the brush previews and pick one of the more irregular, splotchy brushes. Photoshop has a *ton* of super-cool brushes built right in; page 509 explains how to load 'em.

3. **Increase the brush size to 100 pixels or so.**

   Making the brush fairly big will help you see its edges more clearly when you paint, so you'll know exactly what kind of texture you're painting where. While the Brush tool is active, you can press the right bracket key (]) repeatedly to increase brush size, or the left bracket key ([) to decrease it. This is an important keyboard shortcut to memorize, because this particular technique looks better if you vary the brush size quite a bit. (There are other, more complicated shortcuts for resizing brushes, but this one has been around forever—plus it's easy to remember!).

FIGURE 14-29

By using some of Photoshop's more creative brushes, you can paint a unique texture onto text using a layer mask (circled here). The cursor even takes on the shape of the brush, as you can see on the left side (it looks like a bunch of black squiggles).

As with most text effects, you'll want to start out with a weighty font so you can actually see the texture you've so painstakingly applied (Poplar Std at 134 and 236 points was used here).

4. **Make sure your foreground color chip is set to black and the mask is active, and then mouse over to your document and start clicking the text to apply the texture (clicking works better than dragging).**

As you've learned, painting with black within a layer mask conceals (hides) whatever is on that layer, while painting with white reveals. To hide portions of the text in the shape of the brush, you need to paint with black, so take a peek at the color chips at the bottom of the Tools panel and make sure black is on top. If it's not, press D to set the color chips to the factory setting of black and white, and press X to flip-flop the chips until black is on top.

If you hide too much of the text, press X to swap color chips so that white is on top, and then click to paint that area back in. (You'll do a lot of swapping color chips when editing masks.)

The best part of this technique is that, by using a layer mask, you haven't harmed the text. If you don't like the effect, just delete the layer mask and you're back where you started.

■ TEXTURE FROM FILTERS

Running a filter on text is one of the fastest ways to give it extra character. Like the previous two techniques, this method involves using a layer mask, though this time you need to create a selection of the text *before* adding the mask.

Add some chunky text to your document and then, in the Layers panel, ⌘-click (Ctrl-click) the Type layer's thumbnail to load the text as a selection. Once you see marching ants, add a layer mask to the Type layer as described in step 1 in the previous section. Then head to the Filter menu and choose Distort→Ocean Ripple. In the resulting dialog box, tweak the filter's settings so that the text's edges look fairly tattered in the handy preview window. *Figure 14-30* shows the results of changing the Ripple Size to 8 and Ripple Magnitude to 4, and then running the filter three times. Click OK to dismiss the Filter dialog box and admire your newly distressed text.

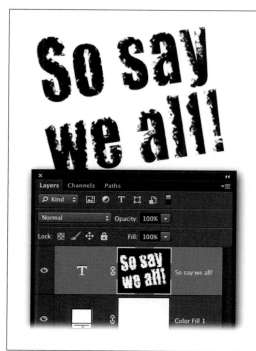

FIGURE 14-30

Top: By loading the text as a selection before adding the layer mask, the mask takes on the shape of the letters, giving you a safe place to run the filter (otherwise, you'd have to rasterize the Type layer before running it).

Bottom: As you can see in this Layers panel, the Type layer remains unscathed after applying this technique, so you can still change the text's color or size. To change the color, double-click the Type layer and then click the color swatch in either the Options bar or Character panel. Page 587 explains how to resize text.

Other filters that work well with this technique include the Artistic and Distort sets, along with Torn Edges, all found in the Filter Gallery. To rerun the last filter you used, just press ⌘-F (Ctrl+F), and Photoshop will use the exact same settings you used last time (don't expect a dialog box, though). This trick works until you quit Photoshop.

Placing a Photo Inside Text

Ever wonder how designers place an image inside text? It takes *years* of practice. (Just kidding!) They do it by creating a *clipping mask* (see the box on page 119), which takes about 5 seconds. All you need is a photo, a Type layer, and the secret layer stacking order. To create the effect shown in *Figure 14-31*, follow these steps:

1. **Open a photo and unlock the Background layer.**

   Since the text you'll create in the next steps needs to be positioned *beneath* the Image layer, you need to double-click the Background layer in the Layers panel to unlock it. In the resulting dialog box, give the layer a new name (if you'd like), and then click OK.

2. **Create some text.**

   Press T to grab the Type tool and add some text to your document. It doesn't matter what color the text is (as long as you're able to see it while you're typing); what matters is that you pick a really big, thick font. *Figure 14-31* was made using Impact—a display font—at 95 points. Short words work better than longer ones (they're easier to read), and you may want to use all caps so more of the photo shows through.

3. **Over in the Layers panel, drag the Type layer** *below* **the Image layer.**

   If the Type layer is *above* the photo layer, this technique won't work.

4. **Clip the photo layer to the Type layer.**

   With the photo layer active, choose Layer→Create Clipping Mask, or press and hold Option (Alt on a PC) while pointing your cursor at the dividing line between the two layers in the Layers panel and, when the cursor turns into a square with a down-pointing arrow, click once. Either way, the thumbnail of the photo layer scoots to the right and a tiny downward-pointing arrow appears to let you know that it's clipped (masked) to the Type layer directly below it. You should now see the photo peeking through the text.

5. **Add a new Fill layer at the bottom of the layer stack.**

   Rather than stare into the checkerboard of a transparent document, add a colorful background (in *Figure 14-31*, the background is sage green). Choose Layer→New Fill Layer→Solid Color and the Color Picker opens. Choose a color, click OK to close the dialog box, and then drag the new Fill layer to the bottom of your layer stack. To make sure the background goes well with the photo, double-click the Fill layer's thumbnail to reopen the Color Picker, mouse over to your image and click within the photo to snatch a color, and then click OK.

6. **Use the Move tool to reposition either the photo or the text (see the box on page 116 to learn how to move the layer independently of its mask, or vice versa).**

You're basically done at this point, but feel free to play around with text formatting, layer styles, and different fonts, or just sit back and admire your handiwork.

Converting Text to a Shape

Last but certainly not least, Photoshop lets you do all kinds of cool things with text that's been converted into a vector shape (for more on shapes, see Chapter 13). Though you can't edit the converted text, what used to be the Type layer turns into a resizable, distortable piece of art or editable path that you can do all kinds of interesting things to.

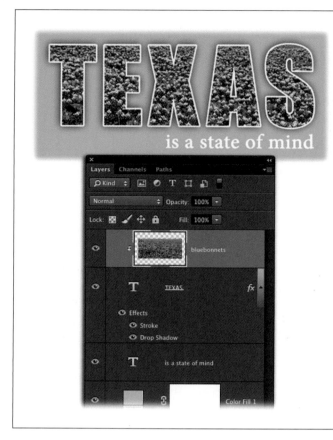

FIGURE 14-31

Placing a photo inside text is one of the easiest Photoshop text tricks, even though it looks complicated. Be sure to pick a nice, thick font like Impact (used here) so you can see a good chunk of the photo through the letters.

For even more fun, use layer styles to add a stroke and drop shadow to the Type layer, as shown here. Another neat Photoshop trick is to place text behind an object. This technique, in all its step-by-step glory, is detailed on page 111.

To convert text into a path or shape, just activate the Type layer in the Layers panel and then choose Type→"Convert to Shape." That's it! This miraculous transformation lets you do any of the following:

- **Edit the letterforms**. Want to add an extra flourish here or a swoosh there? Convert the text into a shape and then use the Path Selection tool to twist and pull the letters any which way you like.

- **Apply distort and perspective with Free Transform**. You may have noticed that the Free Transform tool's Distort and Perspective options are grayed out when a Type layer is active, but they're ready for action on a Shape layer. If you've ever wanted to create text that fades into the distance in proper perspective, here's your chance.

- **Rotate individual letters**. Instead of creating each letter on its own layer and rotating them individually, you can convert the word into a vector Shape layer first, and then use the Path Selection tool to grab one letter at a time and rotate them with Free Transform, as shown in *Figure 14-32*. Graphic designers *love* doing this kind of thing.

- **Creating intersecting or intertwining text**. Once you've converted text to a vector Shape layer, you have the full arsenal of drawing tools at your disposal, including the ever-useful Exclude Overlapping Shape Areas button, whose effect is shown in *Figure 14-32*. (For more on using Photoshop's drawing tools, see Chapter 13.)

- **Scale to infinity—and beyond!** Because the letter shapes are vectors, you don't have to worry about jagged edges. So after you've performed one of the techniques in this list, feel free to resize the text using Free Transform without fear of losing quality.

- **Enjoy stress-free printing**. That's right: You can send the file off to a professional printer (or to an inkjet printer, for that matter) without a care in the world. By converting text to a shape, you don't have to worry about including the original fonts or about how the text will print.

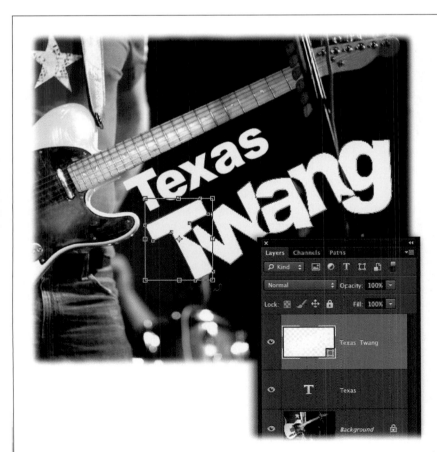

FIGURE 14-32

This effect was created by converting the text (Arial Black) into a shape and then spinning each letter individually using Free Transform. Don't forget to press Return—Enter on a PC—when you're done rotating each letter.

For added fun, you can use the Path Selection tool to move each letter so they overlap just a touch. Next, use the same tool to activate all the letters and then click the Path Operations icon in the Options bar (it looks like two overlapping squares) and choose Exclude Overlapping Shape Areas. This makes the color disappear from the overlapping areas, letting the image show through. To tweak the text's color, double-click the Shape layer's thumbnail to open the Color Picker.

■ More Typographic Resources

This book is by no means the be-all and end-all on typography and fonts. To learn more about finding, identifying, and buying fonts, crack open a nice bottle of wine and check out some of the following resources:

- *www.lesa.in/clvideos*. Your humble author records a slew of online video workshops. For more on typography, including how to create typographic logos, check out *Graphic Design for Everyone.* You can also download a handy typographic cheat sheet by visiting *www.facebook.com/photolesa* and clicking the Like button.

- *www.DesignToolsMonthly.com.* The executive summary for graphic designers, this 12-page publication has been around for over 20 years and it's chock-full of design tips and features a bunch of fonts each month. (You can even download a free sample issue.)

- *The Non-Designer's Type Book, Second Edition,* by Robin Williams (*www.lesa. in/robinnddb*). This book is an easy read and well worth the time; you'll learn more than you ever wanted to know about typography.

- *Fonts & Encodings* by Yannis Haralambous (*www.lesa.in/fontsencoding*) is a priceless resource. If you've ever wondered how our current font situation came to be or how and why fonts work the way they do, you'll enjoy this tome.

- *www.Helveticafilm.com.* Visit this site for a feature-length film about typography and graphic design made in celebration of the Helvetica font's 50th birthday in 2007. It's fascinating!

- *www.fonts.com.* Hands down the Internet's number one resource for all things font related.

- *www.myfonts.com.* Another great site, which features a font-identification service called WhatTheFont. Just send them an image of some text and they'll tell you the closest matching font. How cool is that?

- *www.fontsite.com.* To get professional fonts at a fraction of their usual price, this is the place to go.

- *www.lesa.in/jaymacworld.* Jay Nelson, who's the founder and publisher of DesignToolsMonthly.com, writes a column for *Macworld* magazine wherein he discusses all manner of font features and type-related news (full disclosure: he's married to yours truly). Visit this web address to see all the columns he's written.

The Wide World of Filters

Photoshop's filters let you create a *multitude* of special effects that you can apply to images or use to conjure interesting backgrounds. You can run filters on Image layers, masks, channels, Smart Objects, Shape layers, and even Type layers (provided you convert them into Smart Objects or rasterize 'em first). The list of special effects you can create by applying filters once, twice, or even *10* times is a mile long. There are a bunch of the little critters too, each with its own special brand of pixel wrangling. These days, Photoshop's Filter menu *appears* to have fewer items than in older versions of the program—the result of a menu reorganization that happened in CS6—but it actually has tons. The program also includes two *new* filters that are sure to delight photographers, and possibly a few designers too (especially those who are called upon routinely to fix blurry photos!).

You've already seen a few filters in action, like the ones for sharpening, blurring, adding texture to text, mapping one image to the contours of another, and so on. But that's just a tiny sliver of what's available. In this chapter, you'll be *immersed* in the realm of filters and discover how you can use 'em to do all kinds of fun and useful stuff. But before you start plowing through the Filter menu, you need to know how to use filters in ways that won't harm your original images. That means learning to use Smart Filters. Onward, ho!

NOTE If you like learning by watching videos, check out your author's online workshop, *Photoshop Deep Dive: Filters*, at *www.lesa.in/clvideos*.

■ The Joy of Smart Filters

Filters, by their very nature, are destructive—they move, mangle, distress, and distort pixels like you wouldn't believe, and they *always* run on the currently active layer, mask, or selection. Before Photoshop CS3, the only way to protect your image—and retain *any* level of editing flexibility—was to *duplicate* the Image layer first and then run the filter on the copy. That way, you could lessen the filter's effect by reducing the duplicate layer's opacity or hide the filter from parts of the image using a layer mask. However, as you know from Chapter 3, duplicating layers can bloat your Layers panel, and then there's the *extra* step of adding a layer mask. Yuck.

Then along came Photoshop CS3 with its nifty *Smart Filters*. If you convert a layer—or multiple layers—into a Smart Object *before* applying a filter, you can make the filter run in its *own* special spot in the Layers panel (similar to layer styles), complete with blend mode and opacity controls. It even comes with a layer mask.

Smart Filters are the best thing since sliced bread, and in Photoshop CC, more filters take advantage of that capability than ever before; new to the Smart Filter family are the Liquify, Field, Iris, and Tilt-Shift Blur filters. That said, Vanishing Point and Lens Blur work only on regular *Image* layers (ones that haven't been converted to Smart Objects); to use one of *these* filters, just do things the old-fashioned way: Duplicate your Image layer and then run the filter on the copy. Smart Filters are also picky about which color mode your image is in; for instance, not all of 'em work in CMYK or Lab mode, but since you spend most of your time in RGB mode, anyway, that isn't a huge deal.

> **TIP** If you can't use a Smart Filter and you forgot to duplicate your Image layer before running a filter, you can lessen the filter's strength and change its blend mode by choosing Edit→Fade—but you have to run this command before you do *anything* else, or it won't be available. Flip back to the box on page 461 for the skinny on using the Fade command.

When Smart Filters *are* an option, they're the only way to roll, and using them couldn't be easier: All you do is open an image, activate the layer you want to work on, and then choose Filter→"Convert for Smart Filters." You'll get a friendly message letting you know that Photoshop is about to turn the active layer into a Smart Object, to which you should reply with a resounding OK. (You'll probably want to turn on the "Don't show again" checkbox to keep Photoshop from displaying this message in the future.) Alternatively, you can choose File→"Open as Smart Object," and you're ready to rock filters nondestructively.

> **TIP** If you convert your layer(s) for Smart Filters and then create a *selection* before running a filter, Photoshop fills in the Smart Filter mask *for* you so the filter's effects are hidden from the rest of your image. Sweet!

Once you convert a layer for smart filters (or open a file as a Smart Object), over in the Layers panel, the Image layer now carries the special Smart Object badge at the bottom right of its thumbnail, and the next filter you run will appear *beneath* the

Smart Object as if it were a layer of its own (see *Figure 15-1*). You can run as many filters as you want; they'll just continue to stack up in the Layers panel, much like layer styles. If you need to rearrange their stacking order—say, to keep one from covering up the effect of another—just drag 'em up or down in the Layers panel. To collapse the layer, temporarily hiding any filters you've run and shortening the Layers panel, click the triangle at the far right of the Smart Object; click it again to expand the layer (it's labeled in *Figure 15-1*).

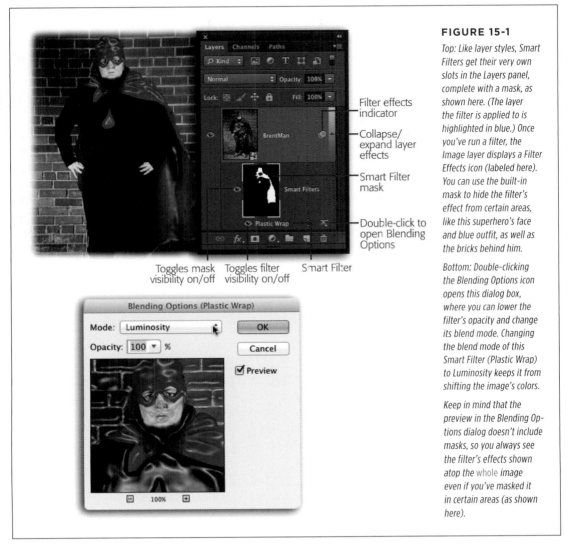

FIGURE 15-1

Top: Like layer styles, Smart Filters get their very own slots in the Layers panel, complete with a mask, as shown here. (The layer the filter is applied to is highlighted in blue.) Once you've run a filter, the Image layer displays a Filter Effects icon (labeled here). You can use the built-in mask to hide the filter's effect from certain areas, like this superhero's face and blue outfit, as well as the bricks behind him.

Bottom: Double-clicking the Blending Options icon opens this dialog box, where you can lower the filter's opacity and change its blend mode. Changing the blend mode of this Smart Filter (Plastic Wrap) to Luminosity keeps it from shifting the image's colors.

Keep in mind that the preview in the Blending Options dialog doesn't include masks, so you always see the filter's effects shown atop the whole image even if you've masked it in certain areas (as shown here).

NOTE While it's fine to run multiple filters on a single Smart Object, you only get *one* mask per Smart Object. So if you need to mask the effects of filters *differently*, so they affect different parts of your image, you'll need to create *another* Smart Object out of the first in order to get another mask.

To apply the same Smart Filter to another layer, copy it from one layer to another by Option-dragging (Alt-dragging on a PC) the Smart Filter itself (say, Plastic Wrap [*Figure 15-1*]); you see a ghosted image of the Filter Effects icon beneath your cursor as you drag.

NOTE You can delete a garden-variety layer by activating it and then pressing Delete (Backspace on a PC), but that doesn't work for Smart Filters (or layer styles, for that matter). You have to Control-click (right-click) the Smart Filter in the Layers panel (say, Plastic Wrap), and then choose Delete Smart Filter from the resulting shortcut menu. Alternatively, you can drag the Smart Filter to the trash or activate the layer, click the trash can icon, and then click OK in the resulting "Are you sure?" dialog box.

A Filters Tour

With so many filters to choose from, it can be tough to get a handle on what they all do. That's why several filters—those in the Artistic, Brush Strokes, Distort, Sketch, Stylize, and Texture categories—summon a large window called the Filter Gallery (*Figure 15-2*) when you choose 'em from the Filter menu (if you don't see some of these categories in the Filter menu, the box on page 635 explains how to display them). It has a nice big preview of your image on the left (you can zoom in or out by clicking the + and – buttons below it), a list of *all* the filters in these categories in the middle (with cute little preview thumbnails), and the specific settings associated with each filter on the right. Sweet!

NOTE Several filters automatically open the Filter Gallery, and while you *can* open it manually by choosing Filter→Filter Gallery, *don't*. If you do, any filter you run gets the generic name of *Filter Gallery* in the Layers panel. To make Photoshop name the filter properly, choose its name from the Filter menu and let *it* open the Filter Gallery instead. For more on this filter-naming conundrum, see the box on page 635.

Once the Filter Gallery opens, you can test drive a filter by clicking its name and then tweaking its settings; Photoshop updates your image preview accordingly. You can even run additional filters *while* you're in the Filter Gallery by clicking the "New effect layer" button at the window's bottom right (Photoshop includes each filter in the list above this button). You can also delete individual filters you've added by clicking the tiny trash can icon.

NOTE Not *all* of Photoshop's filters are listed in the Filter Gallery, so don't let that throw you; you can choose the others straight from the Filter menu. If the Filter has three dots after its name in the Filter menu, it summons a dialog box that lets you tweak various settings; if it doesn't have dots, that sucker just *runs*.

FIGURE 15-2

*The Filter Gallery makes it easy to zip
through most filters to get a quick idea
of what they do. (Heck, with the right
music and snacks, filter browsing can
make for an entertaining evening!)*

*Here you can see what the Film Grain
filter looks like on a superhero wannabe.*

Choose preview zoom percentage
Zoom in/out of preview

Create new effect layer
Delete effect layer

Throughout this chapter, you'll learn how to use at least one filter in each category
(they're listed in the order they appear in the *long* version of the Filter menu—see
the box on page 635 to learn how to repopulate it). You can think of this as a Filter's
Greatest Hits Tour; a *complete* listing of an example of every filter would swell this
book to *War and Peace* proportions. So grab your favorite beverage, sit back, and
read on to discover the wide world of filters.

WORKAROUND WORKSHOP

Repopulating the Filter Menu

Back in Photoshop CS6, Adobe pruned the Filter menu by
removing some categories that also live in the Filter Gallery.
While this makes for a *much* shorter Filter menu, it also makes
keeping track of which filters you've run in a document a
nightmare. For example, if you choose Filter→Filter Gallery
and then run any filter on a Smart Object, instead of listing the
specific name of the filter in the Layers panel (Plastic Wrap,
say), Photoshop just lists its name as "Filter Gallery." This is the
exact *opposite* of helpful. (That said, if you apply *more* than one
filter to your image while you've got the Filter Gallery open,
such a generic naming scheme is to be expected as Photoshop
can't give the Smart Filter *multiple* names in the Layers panel.)

Since you can't double-click a Smart Filter's name in the
Layers panel to rename it, the only solution is to make
Photoshop list *all* its filters in the Filter menu by changing
its Plug-Ins preferences (technically, filters are plug-ins).
To do that, choose Photoshop→Preferences→Plug-Ins
(Edit→Preferences→Plug-Ins on a PC), turn on the "Show
all Filter Gallery groups and names" checkbox, and then click
OK. After that, the Filter menu will be longer and you'll see
accurate filter names in the Layers panel. This chapter describes
filters in the order they appear in the *long* version of the Filter
menu, so go ahead and turn this option on.

Adaptive Wide Angle

This filter fixes distortion problems commonly found in photos shot with a wide-angle or fish-eye lens, as well as panoramas. For example, some lenses distort images so that tall buildings appear to *bend* toward a vanishing point in the sky (called *pincushion distortion*, where lines bend inward), or make people, objects, and horizon lines look bowed, as shown in *Figure 15-3* (called *barrel distortion*, where lines bend outward). And sometimes the problem isn't the lens but your sense of balance—maybe you accidentally tilted the camera vertically or horizontally, making a lake or ocean look like it's running downhill instead of staying level (called *perspective distortion*).

Photoshop's Adaptive Wide Angle filter can fix all of these problems quickly and easily, and you don't have to spend a ton of time tweaking settings to use it. If Photoshop can figure out which lens you used to take the shot (it probably can if you're using fairly recent equipment), all you have to do is draw a line across the part of the image that needs fixing and Photoshop takes care of the rest.

> **NOTE** You can use this filter on Smart Objects *and* when you're recording actions, which is handy if you've got several photos distorted in the same way. (See Chapter 18 for more on actions.)

To use it, open an image and duplicate your Image layer or choose Filter→"Convert for Smart Filters." Then choose Filter→Adaptive Wide Angle and Photoshop opens the giant Adaptive Wide Angle dialog box and tries to find a *lens profile*—a detailed set of info about common lenses—for your camera (it knows what kind of equipment you used because of the image's *metadata*). If it locates one, it sets the Correction menu on the right side of the dialog box to Auto. (The chances of Photoshop finding your lens profile are good because its database is updated constantly; if it *can't* find one, the next paragraph explains what to do.) Next, mouse over to the area that needs fixing and click once to mark the point where the distortion begins. (For example, in *Figure 15-3*, top, the horizon is bowed, so you'll want to click the horizon's far left edge.) Then move your cursor to the *end* of the distortion and click again to set an end point (the horizon's far right edge, in this example). The thin blue line that appears between the points is called a *constraint*. As soon as you click to set the end point, Photoshop adjusts the image according to the curvature of the constraint (*Figure 15-3*, bottom). Click OK to apply the changes to your image and close the dialog box.

> **NOTE** You can give this filter a try by downloading the practice file *Horseshoe.jpg* from this book's Missing CD page at *www.missingmanuals.com/cds*.

If Photoshop *can't* find a lens profile, pick the type of lens you used from the Adaptive Wide Angle dialog box's Correction menu. Your choices are Fisheye, Perspective, and Full Spherical (think 360-degree panoramas). Photoshop then analyzes the metadata embedded in the image and tries to figure out the image's *focal length* (which determines the angle of view and how much the subject is magnified in relation to your camera's location) and *crop factor* (the level of magnification of your digital camera's sensor in relation to a 35 mm full-frame sensor). If it can't, Focal Length and Crop Factor sliders appear on the right side of the dialog box so you can adjust them manually.

Tools   Constraint   Panel menu

Start point   Click & drag to rotate constraint   End point

FIGURE 15-3

Top: Wide-angle and fish-eye lenses are great for exaggerating the depth and relative size of an object or scene, though you usually end up with some straight areas that look curved.

Bottom: If Photoshop can find your lens profile, it can fix an image like this in just two quick clicks. If you've clicked to set a start point and then decide to delete it, just press the Esc key. If you've already created a constraint and you press Esc, Photoshop asks if you're sure you want to close the dialog box without saving your changes. Click the Don't Save button to close the dialog box without applying any changes, click Cancel to return to the Adaptive Wide Angle dialog box for more editing, or click Save to close the dialog box and apply your changes.

Photo of Horseshoe Bend by Karen Nace Willmore (www.karennace.com).

Straight from the factory, the Adaptive Wide Angle filter produces irregularly shaped images that are smaller than the original and scaled to fit the area where you placed constraints (see *Figure 15-3*, bottom). To change the image's size to, say, end up with a *larger* image so there's less transparency to fill in or crop out, drag the Scale slider to the right or enter a percentage in the Scale field (drag the slider left to make the image smaller).

In the upper-left corner of the Adaptive Wide Angle dialog box, you'll find the following tools:

- **Constraint tool**. Photoshop activates this tool automatically when you first open the dialog box. Use this tool to set as many constraints as you need to in order to correct your image. For example, click where the distortion begins and then mouse over to where the distortion ends and click again, and Photoshop adjusts the distortion along the constraint to straighten your image.

  To create a *new* constraint with a start point near or atop an existing one, press and hold ⌘ (Ctrl) while you click. To create a horizontal or vertical constraint, press and hold the Shift key after you set a start point (when you go past 45-degrees, the resulting line is yellow for horizontal or magenta for vertical). To *delete* a constraint, click one of its points and press Delete (Backspace on a PC), or Option-click (Alt-click) the point itself. To move a constraint, point your cursor at the start or end point (it turns into little crosshairs) and then drag it to a new location. Keyboard shortcut: C.

> **TIP** To change the color of the constraints or mesh, choose Preferences from the Adaptive Wide Angle dialog box's panel menu, and then click the colored swatches in the resulting dialog box.

- **Polygon Constraint tool**. Use this tool to create a polygonal constraint instead of a straight or curved one (useful when fixing 360-degree panoramas). Click once to set a start point, and keep adding additional points as needed. To close the polygon, click the start point. Keyboard shortcut: Y.

> **TIP** To save a constraint so you can use it again later (if you've got more photos from the same shoot that need fixing, say), choose Save Constraint from the Adaptive Wide Angle dialog box's panel menu, and then give the constraint a meaningful name in the resulting Save dialog box (Photoshop gives it the file extension .wac). You can also import a constraint (perhaps one you created on another machine or one made by a colleague) by choosing Load Constraint from the same menu. In the resulting Load Constraints dialog box, navigate to where the .wac file lives on your hard drive, and then click Open.

- **Move tool**. If you increase the dialog box's Scale setting, part of your image will extend past the edges of the preview area so they won't get fixed. If that happens, you can use this tool to click and drag the important bits of your image back into the preview area so Photoshop can fix them. Keyboard shortcut: M.

- **Hand tool**. This tool lets you move around within the image after you've zoomed in using the Zoom tool (discussed next). Just drag within the preview area to view another part of the image. Keyboard shortcut: H.

- **Zoom tool**. As you might suspect, you can use this tool to change your view of the image (it's completely unrelated to image scale, discussed earlier). Simply click the image to zoom in on it, or click and drag to draw a box around part of the image to zoom in on just that area; then Option-click (Alt-click on a PC) to zoom back out. You can also use the zoom controls at the bottom left of the dialog box to do the same thing (they're shown in *Figure 15-3*, top), or press ⌘

(Ctrl) and the + or – key. Once you zoom in past 100 percent, you can press and hold the X key to temporarily double the zoom percentage. Keyboard shortcut: Z.

You're not finished yet! These additional options live at the *bottom* of the dialog box:

- **Preview**. This checkbox is on from the factory, so you see a preview of the results using your current settings and constraints in real time. To see your original image instead, simply turn this setting off. Keyboard shortcut: P.

- **Show Constraints**. This setting is turned on automatically whenever the Constraint tool is active. Turn it off to temporarily hide the constraints so you can better see your image.

- **Show Mesh**. This checkbox places a green mesh atop your image preview and shows you exactly how Photoshop will warp, twist, and turn the image in order to fix it according to the constraints you've set.

Camera Raw Filter

As you know from Chapter 9, Camera Raw is an incredibly powerful plug-in that you can use to correct the color and lighting in images shot in raw format, though it also works—minus the color temperature controls—on other file formats such as JPEGs and TIFFs. Happily, new in Photoshop CC, you can access a *version* of this plug-in from the Filter menu, meaning you can use it on *any* kind of layer. To learn more, and to see which tools are missing from the filter version, flip back to the box on page 367.

Heck, this new filter is quite possibly worth the price of upgrading to CC all by itself!

Lens Correction

Back in Photoshop CS5, the Lens Correction filter got a *major* overhaul. Not only can you use this filter to fix all kinds of weirdness that can be caused by camera lenses (see the box on page 641), but you can also use it to add a dark-edge vignette effect that can beautifully frame a portrait (see *Figure 15-4*). Here's how:

1. **Pop open a portrait and then choose Filter→"Convert for Smart Filters."**

   Alternatively, you can open the image as a Smart Object by choosing File→"Open as Smart Object."

2. **Choose Filter→Lens Correction.**

   Photoshop opens the petite (ha!) Lens Correction dialog box.

3. **Click the Custom tab and adjust the Vignette amount.**

   Near the top right of the dialog box are two tabs: Auto Correction and Custom. Click the Custom tab and then, near the middle of the tab, grab the Vignette section's Amount slider and drag it all the way left; Photoshop softly darkens the edges of the image. Then, to widen the darkening, drag the Midpoint slider left to about 30, as shown in *Figure 15-4*.

4. **Click OK and then save the document as a PSD file so you can edit it again later.**

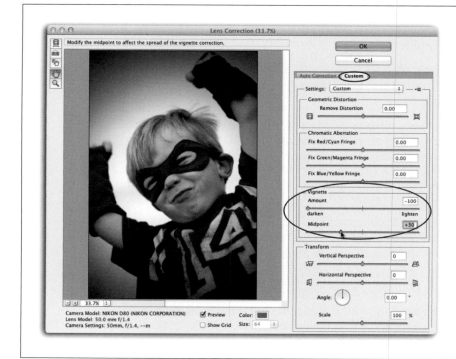

FIGURE 15-4

Even a little thing like softly darkening an image's edges can make a huge difference, especially in portraits. Notice how the dark edges draw your eyes to the pint-sized superhero.

This technique is also handy to use with a sepia tone (page 275) to produce an aged-photo look.

See how fast that was? If, after admiring your handiwork, you decide the effect is a little too dark, mouse over to the Layers panel, double-click the icon to the right of the words "Lens Correction" to open the Blending Options dialog box, and then lower the Opacity setting slightly. In most cases, though, full strength looks just fine. If the edge vignette affects part of your subject's face, you can always use the Smart Filter mask to hide it from that area.

Liquify

The amazingly powerful and, in Photoshop CC, smokin' fast Liquify filter lets you push, pull, stretch, bloat, and pinch pixels manually. It's mainly good for reshaping facial features or entire bodies in order to change reality, and that's why it's covered in Chapter 10 beginning on page 422. Happily, this filter now works with Smart Filters. Hooray for progress!

Oil Paint

If you've ever wanted to *quickly* turn a photo into a painting, you can use the Oil Paint filter to create a fairly realistic piece of art incredibly fast. (This filter used to be part of the optional Pixel Bender plug-in, but it officially migrated to the Filter menu back in CS6.) This filter is fun to use and does a *surprisingly* good job of making photos look painted *without* you having to make a single brushstroke, or spending hours running *multiple* filters to try and produce a similar effect.

Once you've duplicated the Image layer or converted the original layer for Smart Filters, choose Filter→Oil Paint and the dialog box in *Figure 15-5* appears. The sliders in the Brush section let you adjust the stylization, cleanliness, and scale of your brushstrokes, along with the level of detail in the brush's bristles (a higher number increases bristle stiffness for deeper-looking brushstrokes). The sliders in the Lighting section let you adjust the direction of the light and control how shiny the reflections are. Each change you make is instantly reflected in the large preview area on the left.

> **TIP** If you run the Oil Paint filter on a portrait, your subject's face and skin can become completely obscured. The fix is to hide the paint effect from those areas by adding a mask to the duplicate Image layer or by using the Smart Filter mask. However, you don't want to hide *all* of the brushstrokes or the image would look pretty weird. Instead, once you're finished editing the mask, double-click its thumbnail in the Layers panel to open the Properties panel, and then drag the Density slider slightly leftward to make the mask somewhat see-through. That way, *some* of the brushstrokes show through the mask, but not all of 'em.

UP TO SPEED

Fixing Lens Distortion

No matter what kind of image-editing voodoo you've got up your sleeve, you can't hide the quality of your camera's lens. Some potential problems include a darkening in the corners of images called *vignetting*, or a weird color fringe along an object's edges called *chromatic aberration*. Luckily, the Lens Correction filter can fix these problems (that is, if your image is 8- or 16-bit and in RGB or Grayscale mode only).

Choose Filter→Lens Correction and Photoshop updates its database of lens profiles and then opens the Lens Correction dialog box with the Auto Correction tab activated. This tab is where you tell Photoshop what kind of problem you have. If the program figures out what camera and lens you used, just turn on the checkbox for the kind of problem your image has: Geometric Distortion (a deformation of the image in a uniform manner), Chromatic Aberration, or Vignette. If it *can't* find your camera and lens, then these checkboxes boxes are grayed out.

In that case, use the tab's Search Criteria section to tell Photoshop what equipment you used to capture the image. Pick your camera's make, model (this one doesn't have to match exactly), and lens model from the drop-down menus. If Photoshop finds a matching profile, it appears in the Lens Profiles section below. To see all the profiles for a specific brand, choose the brand from the Camera Make menu, and then set the other two menus

to All. If Photoshop doesn't find a match, click the Search Online button at the bottom of the tab. You can also click the Lens Profiles section's panel menu and then choose Browse Adobe Lens Profile Creator Online, which also lets you create custom profiles. To snag an online profile so you can use it when you don't have an Internet connection, choose Save Online Profile Locally from the panel menu.

Once you find the right (or close-enough) lens profile, give it a click and then use the checkboxes near the top of the tab to let Photoshop know what kind of problem(s) your image has (you can turn on multiple checkboxes). Photoshop uses the info in the lens profile to fix the problem the moment you click a checkbox. (To learn how to create your *own* lens profile, visit *www.lesa.in/createlensprofile* and then scroll down to the Resources section to find info on the Adobe Lens Profile Creator.)

If fixing the image will cause it to expand or shrink beyond its original size (and you may not know until you try to fix it), leave the Auto Scale Image checkbox turned on and then use the Edge menu to tell Photoshop what to do with any resulting blank edges: It can fill the empty spots with transparency or black or white pixels, or enlarge the image to fill the edges (choose Edge Extension).

When you're finished, click OK and then save the document as a PSD file so you can go back and edit the filter's settings later. (This is serious editing flexibility that you just can't get in the real world.) Be sure to give this filter a spin on inanimate objects like flowers, rocks, and landscapes, too; you'll be amazed at the results. And if you produce something frame-worthy, hop online and use a service such as *www. mpix.com* to have it printed on a real canvas and stretched onto a wooden frame for hanging (which, by the way, is a *great* product to offer your photography clients).

TIP To rerun the last filter you used with the same settings, press ⌘-F (Ctrl+F). (To summon the filter's dialog box so you can adjust its settings *before* running it, press Option-⌘-F [Alt+Ctrl+F] instead). You can also click the Filter menu, where the last filter shows up as the first item in the list.

Vanishing Point

During your illustrious Photoshop career, there will be times when you need to edit an object so it appears in proper perspective (meaning it seems to get smaller as it disappears into the distance). Here are a few situations where you'll likely run into perspective problems:

- If you need to affix a graphic or text to any surface that's not flat, like an image of a book cover, cereal box, or DVD case that's positioned at an angle to the camera (Chapter 21 explains how to do this using Photoshop CC's 3D tools).

- If you need to clone an object that's on a wall or on top of a table.

- If you want to make a building or other structure look taller than it really is (you can do this with the Content-Aware Move tool set to Extend mode [page 443]).

This kind of editing is a real challenge because Photoshop sees everything as flat, with no perspective at all (that is, unless you're using the new 3D tools covered in Chapter 21). The fix is to use the Vanishing Point filter to draw *perspective* planes—a mesh grid that automatically conforms your edits to the perspective of the planes you create—*before* you start painting or cloning. After you draw the grid in the Vanishing Point dialog box (*Figure 15-6*, top), you can do your editing on the grid inside the dialog box, too. While you're there, you can create a selection, copy and paste an image or text, or use the Clone Stamp or Brush tool, all in perfect perspective.

Here's how to paste one image on top of another in proper perspective:

1. **Select and copy the object you want to paste (for example, the cartoon superhero in *Figure 15-6*, bottom).**

   Open the image, select the object using one of the techniques covered in Chapter 4, and then press ⌘-C (Ctrl+C) to copy it. (If you intend to add a layer mask to the image to make its background transparent, you need to apply the mask *before you copy the object*. Since this maneuver deletes the mask, duplicate that layer first by pressing ⌘-J [Ctrl+J] to keep the mask intact in case you need to edit it later. Then, on the duplicate layer, Control-click [right-click] the mask thumbnail and choose Apply Mask.)

2. **Open the image you want to add the copied image *to* and create a new layer.**

   You can't run Vanishing Point as a Smart Filter, so it runs on the currently active layer. To run it nondestructively, you either have to duplicate the Image layer or add a *new* layer, depending on what you want to do. For example, if you're going to use the Brush or Clone Stamp tool, duplicate the Image layer by pressing ⌘-J (Ctrl+J) so you don't harm the original. If, on the other hand, you're pasting another object *into* this document—as in this exercise—you need to create a new layer for the pasted object to land on (because the pasting happens *inside* the filter's dialog box, and not in the Photoshop document), so click the "Create a new layer" button at the bottom of the Layers panel (in *Figure 15-7*, this new layer is named "perspective hero"). Since the new layer is transparent, you can see through it to the layer below—the original Image layer—that you'll use as a guide when you draw the perspective plane in step 4.

Edit plane
Create plane
Marquee
Stamp
Brush
Transform
Eyedropper
Measure
Hand
Zoom

Vanishing Point

Grid Size: 100   Angle: 0

Click+drag to adjust the plane. Line up the grid with perspective content in the image.

FIGURE 15-6

When you get the grid placed and sized in the proper perspective, it turns blue; if it turns red or yellow, there's more work to be done.

A red grid means you've drawn an impossible perspective, so grab the Edit Plane tool labeled here and then resize the grid by dragging one or more of its corner points to another position. A yellow grid means the perspective is possible but unlikely; you can continue to edit the plane or keep it as is.

You can also use the Grid Size setting at the top of the dialog box to resize the grid to fit your object.

3. **Choose Filter→Vanishing Point or press Option-⌘-V (Alt+Ctrl+V).**

   Photoshop opens the *huge* Vanishing Point dialog box.

4. **Use the Create Plane tool to draw your perspective plane.**

   Happily, Photoshop automatically activates the Create Plane tool when you open the Vanishing Point dialog box. Just click once in the image to set the first corner point of your plane (in this example, the building). Next, mouse over to the next corner point and click it, and then mouse to the third corner point and click it; when you do, Photoshop places a blue grid over the area as shown in *Figure 15-6* (top). If you have trouble seeing where to click to add corner points, zoom into your image by holding the X key.

5. **Use the Edit Plane tool to position and tweak the grid.**

   Once you've drawn the grid, Photoshop automatically activates the Edit Plane tool so you can resize the grid and/or reposition its corner points by dragging the white square handles that appear. To extend the bottom of the grid to make it larger, grab the white square handle at the bottom center of the grid and drag it downward. To move the *whole* grid, click inside it and then drag it to another position.

> **TIP**   If you need to draw *more* than one perspective plane in your image (if you have two similar buildings to work on, say), you can copy a plane to another area by Option-dragging (Alt-dragging on a PC) it. If you're working with an object that has more than one side and you need to make the grid wrap around it (like a book cover and its spine), you can ⌘-drag (Ctrl-drag) one of the grid points (it doesn't matter which one) to tear off another plane that you can position at an angle.

6. **Paste the object you copied back in step 1 and drag it on top of the plane.**

   Press ⌘-V (Ctrl+V) to paste the object into the Vanishing Point dialog box. At first, the object appears flat (not in perspective) and is surrounded by marching ants, but when you click and drag it on top of the plane, it twists and distorts to conform to the perspective you've drawn. (If you're working with an image that includes a layer mask and you forgot to *apply* it back in step 1, the pasted object won't be transparent. If that happens, press the Esc key to close the Vanishing Point dialog box and, unfortunately, start over.)

7. **If you need to resize the object you just pasted, press T to summon a resizable bounding box.**

   Photoshop puts a bounding box around the object. To resize it proportionately, hold the Shift key as you drag one of the box's corner handles. (If the object is bigger than the plane, you can't *see* the handles because they're beyond the edges of the grid. In that case, click the object and drag it in one direction or another until you can see one of the handles, and then drag the handle inward to make the object smaller.) If you need to move the pasted image, click inside it and then drag it to another position. When you're finished, click OK to close the dialog box; Photoshop adds the image to the layer you created in step 2.

> **TIP**   Interestingly, you're allowed to perform *multiple* undos when you're in the Vanishing Point dialog box—just keep pressing ⌘-Z (Ctrl+Z) and Photoshop keeps undoing the last thing you did. To *redo* the last thing you did, press Shift-Z instead.

8. **In the Layers panel, change the blend mode of the pasted Image layer to Soft Light.**

   This blend mode makes the superhero's colors blend better with the colors in the building, as shown in *Figure 15-7*.

FIGURE 15-7

As you learned back on page 285, the Soft Light blend mode is great for creating reflections.

At the top of the Layers panel, you see two layers with their visibility turned off. Since the hero image had a white background, a layer mask was used to hide it; however, the Vanishing Point dialog box doesn't understand masks, so you have to apply it to the layer it's attached to first (here, that layer is named "hero mask applied"). By duplicating the layer with the mask (here, that's the "hero mask" layer) before you apply the mask, you keep the mask intact in case you need to edit it later. Turning off the visibility of those extra layers keeps them from getting in your way. Whew!

Here's what the other tools on the left side of the Vanishing Point dialog box are for:

- The **Marquee tool** lets you draw a selection (in perspective) to duplicate an area inside the plane. For example, if you want to make a building taller, you can use this tool to select and then duplicate the top few floors (though you could also try using the Content-Aware Move tool set to Extend mode [page 443]). Or, more practically, you can use the Marquee tool to restrict the effect of the Stamp and Brush tools (discussed later in this list) to a specific spot in your image. You can use the options at the top of the dialog box to feather the selection so its edges are soft, or change the opacity of the object inside your selection (handy if you're moving an object from one area of an image to another). Keyboard shortcut: M.

> **TIP** To activate the entire plane, simply double-click the grid with the Marquee tool.

If you're copying the selection to another area, use the Heal drop-down menu (it appears when the Marquee tool is active) to determine how the selection blends with the area you're dragging it to. Your options are Off (no blending), Luminance (Photoshop blends the selected pixels with the lightness values of *surrounding* pixels), and On (it blends the selected pixels with the color values of the pixels you're dragging the selection *onto*).

The Move Mode drop-down menu lets you specify how the selection *behaves*. Choose Source to make Photoshop *fill* the selection with the pixels you move your mouse over (you can also ⌘-drag [Ctrl-drag] the selection to do the same thing). The selection itself won't move; it'll just get filled with the pixels you put your cursor over. Use this option when you want to remove an object like a window or a door by copying other pixels on top of it. The Destination option makes Photoshop *select* the area you move the selection to; the selection moves, but Photoshop doesn't copy any pixels. Choose this option when you want to copy a selection so you can resize it using the Transform tool (discussed below) to make it *float*. For example, if you've removed a window using Destination mode, you can copy the selection and then move it to remove even *more* windows. You can also press Shift-⌘-T (Shift+Ctrl+T) to repeat your last duplicating move (helpful when you've got a bunch of windows to zap).

- The **Stamp tool** works just like the Clone Stamp tool. It lets you copy pixels from one area to another by painting while you use the perspective of the plane you've drawn. This tool comes in handy when you're extending an object or adding height to a building. Keyboard shortcut: S.

- The **Brush tool** lets you apply paint *and* puts your brushstrokes into proper perspective. If you activate this tool and then choose Luminance from the Heal menu, the new paint takes on the lightness values of the underlying pixels. To pick the brush's color, click the color well at the top of the dialog box. Keyboard shortcut: B.

- You can use the **Transform tool** to resize a selection that you've pasted. Don't press Return (Enter) when you finish resizing or you'll close the Vanishing Point dialog box. Turn on the Flip checkbox at the top of the dialog box to flip your selection horizontally, or the Flop checkbox to flip it vertically. Keyboard shortcut: T.

- Activate the **Eyedropper tool** to snatch a color from the image so you can use it with the Brush tool. Keyboard shortcut: I.

- The **Measure tool** lets you measure the distance and angle of items in a plane. Architects, interior designers, and scientists love this option. (Until CC, this tool was available only in Photoshop Extended.) Keyboard shortcut: R.

- Activate the **Hand tool** to move around your image by dragging. Keyboard shortcut: H.

- The familiar **Zoom tool** lets you zoom in and out of the image. Pressing ⌘ (Ctrl) and the + or – key or picking a magnification percentage at the bottom left of the dialog box works, too. Keyboard shortcut: Z.

Artistic

To make an image resemble a painting or a cartoon, turn to the filters in this category. Their special purpose is to mimic real-world artistic effects created with brushes, pencils, and palette knives, though they can also give images a very artsy look. If you're just looking for a quick artistic touch, these filters can get the job done.

> **NOTE** If you don't see this category in the Filter menu, you need to tweak your Plug-In preferences to display it. The box on page 635 tells you how.

For example, to soften an image and make it look like it's painted, try running the Paint Daubs filter to introduce brushstrokes, and then the Underpainting filter to give the image a little texture (as if it were painted on a real canvas). But if you *really* want to make an image look like a painting, you need to use these filters along with the painting techniques covered in Chapter 12 (or paint the image from scratch). Another good option is to run the Oil Paint filter (page 640).

You've already seen two filters from the Artistic category in action. *Figure 15-1* shows the effects of Plastic Wrap, which makes an image look shiny (as if it were covered in plastic); it's also great for making objects look glossy or slimy. And the Poster Edges filter makes the edges of an image black and reduces the whole thing to primary colors, which creates a cartoonish look (see *Figure 8-21* on page 338).

Blur

You've seen one of Photoshop's blur filters in action already—Gaussian Blur was used to smooth skin back on page 431. The program includes a slew of 'em, including three gems that let you change an image's depth of field to create a camera-realistic blurry background (discussed in a sec). Blur filters are worth their weight in gold when you need to soften pixels for better blending or to simulate motion, as shown in *Figure 15-8*.

> **NOTE** In Photoshop CC, the Field Blur, Iris Blur, and Tilt-Shift filters *all* work with Smart Filters (though, for reasons known only to Adobe, you *don't* get access to filter blending options). And, thanks to OpenCL (see the box on page 58), you'll enjoy faster performance and previews than you did back in CS6. Sweet!

To get your subject moving, open an image and then choose Filter→"Convert for Smart Filters." Next, trot back up to the Filter menu and choose Blur→Motion Blur. In the resulting dialog box, adjust the Angle setting to make the blur go in the direction you want. For example, to create the vertical blur shown in *Figure 15-8*, the angle was set to 90 degrees. To adjust the strength of the blur, drag the Radius slider right for more blurring or left for less. Click OK when you're finished and then save the document as a PSD file so you can go back and tweak the blur later by double-clicking the Motion Blur filter in the Layers panel.

FIGURE 15-8

Applying a Motion Blur to this super family makes it look like they're taking flight. To keep their heads in focus, a stroke of the Brush tool (set to paint with black) was added to the Smart Filter mask.

To try this yourself, download the file Superfamily.jpg *from this book's Missing CD page at* www.missingmanuals.com/cds.

■ **FIXING COLOR FRINGE**

You can also use Photoshop's blur filters to eliminate *color fringe*—that slight blue or purple haze loitering around the edges of near-black objects (*Figure 15-9*, bottom left). This problem is especially common when you shoot something really dark on a light background (like black numbers on a white clock face). The image may look OK at a glance, but a closer inspection often reveals some serious bluish or purplish fringing (also called *artifacts*) around the dark objects. If you're preparing to submit such an image to a stock image company, it's sure to be rejected.

TIP You can also remove color fringe with the Lens Correction Filter (see the box on page 641 to learn how) or in Camera Raw (either the plug-in or filter version). In Camera Raw, open the Lens Corrections panel (the sixth button), and then click the Color tab. Turn on the Remove Chromatic Aberration checkbox and then, if necessary, adjust the Defringe sliders until it's gone.

FIGURE 15-9

At first glance, there doesn't appear to be anything wrong with this image of a clock. However, at a zoom level of 200 percent, you can see the weird color fringe around this 8 (bottom left).

Happily, running the Gaussian Blur filter (top) and changing the filter's blend mode to Color removes the fringe completely (bottom right). That said, the Tip above has info on how to fix color fringe using the Lens Correction filter or Camera Raw.

Try this technique yourself by downloading Clock.jpg from this book's Missing CD page.

Here's how to fix color fringe with a dose of the Gaussian Blur filter:

1. **Open the problem image and activate the layer you want to work with.**

2. **Choose Filter→"Convert to Smart Filters."**

3. **Choose Filter→Blur→Gaussian Blur, and then adjust the filter's settings.**

   In the resulting dialog box, enter a Radius of 5–7 pixels (this setting controls how much blurring Photoshop applies to the image), and then click OK. Depending on the image's pixel dimensions, you may need to experiment with this value; increase it for larger images and reduce it for smaller ones.

4. **Change the filter's blend mode to Color and its Opacity to 96 percent.**

   In the Layers panel, double-click the Blending Options icon next to the Gaussian Blur layer, and then change the Mode drop-down menu to Color. (The Color blend mode affects only hue, and since your goal is to blur the *colored* pixels—as opposed to the black ones—this mode works perfectly.) Then adjust the Opacity setting to 96 percent to keep the blur from being noticeable.

5. **Click OK when you're finished, and then save the document as a PSD file.**

   A quick zoom-in reveals that the pesky color fringe has left the building, as shown in *Figure 15-9*. Saving the document in PSD format ensures that you can edit the image again later if you need to.

FIELD BLUR

This incredibly handy filter is perfect for creating beautifully blurred backgrounds *after* you've taken a photo (images like this are said to have a *shallow depth of field*). It's a million times easier to use than the Lens Blur filter, and you don't have to select anything before you run it (though you can if you want). Instead, you create the blur by dragging over the image itself, as shown in *Figure 15-10*.

Inactive pin   Active pin & blur ring   Remove all pins   Collapse panels

FIGURE 15-10

You can add pins to control exactly which parts of the image are in focus and which parts are blurry. When you add two pins, Photoshop essentially uses a linear gradient mask (page 274) to fade the blur between them. If you add three or more pins, Photoshop constrains the blur so that it affects the vicinity around each pin and extends to about half the distance to the next neighboring pin.

To temporarily hide the blur ring and pins, press and hold the H key.

Try this technique yourself by heading to this book's Missing CD page and downloading the file Kryptonite.jpg.

Here's how to make an image look like it was shot with a shallow depth of field:

1. **Open an image and convert it for Smart Filters.**

   In Photoshop CC, this filter works on Smart Objects, so instead of duplicating your Image layer to make the filter run safely, simply activate the layer and then choose Filter→"Convert for Smart Filters." If the image is made up of *multiple* layers, activate 'em all first and *then* choose this command.

   NOTE While the Field Blur, Iris Blur, and Tilt-Shift filters work as Smart Filters in Photoshop CC, for some reason you don't get access to the Blending Options dialog box like you do with every *other* Smart Filter. That means there's no way to adjust the filter's blend mode or opacity. So if you need that extra flexibility, duplicate your Image layer first and then run the filter on *that* instead.

   ---

2. **Choose Filter→Blur→Field Blur, and then adjust the filter's strength.**

   Your Photoshop window changes to include a big image preview on the left and a set of collapsible controls on the right (*Figure 15-10*). In the image preview, you see a single *pin* (it looks like a dot inside a circle) with a black-and-white *blur ring* around it. The pin controls which part of the image is blurred—one pin makes the whole image blurry—and the blur ring lets you adjust the blur's strength; you see the ring any time a pin is active (Photoshop activates the initial pin automatically when you run the filter). To *increase* the blur, drag the black part of the ring clockwise (so there's more white than black; solid white is 100 percent blur strength); to *decrease* the blur, drag the black part of the ring *counterclockwise* (so there's more black than white; solid black is a blur strength of 0 pixels). As you drag, a handy overlay appears showing the blur's strength from 0 to 500 pixels. Alternatively, you can drag the Blur slider on the right side of the window.

3. **Click the image's focal point to add another pin, and then reduce its blur strength to 0 pixels.**

   As you mouse around your image, your cursor looks like a pushpin with a tiny plus sign next to it, indicating that clicking will add a pin. To keep part of your image in focus (like, say, your subject's face), click to add another pin. If you don't get the pin in quite the right spot, just drag it somewhere else. Then use the blur ring (or Blur slider) to reduce the blur's strength to 0 pixels so there's no blurring in that spot.

   TIP To delete a pin, click it and then press Delete (Backspace on a PC). To zap *all* the pins in one fell swoop, click the Options bar's "Remove all pins" button (labeled in *Figure 15-10*).

   ---

4. **Adjust the settings in the Blur Effects panel to your liking.**

   In the Blur Effects panel on the right side of the window is a group of settings labeled *Bokeh*, which is a Japanese term used to describe the aesthetic qualities of out-of-focus highlights (also known as *specular* highlights). Use the Light

Bokeh slider to increase the brightness of the out-of-focus areas to make them sparkle (see *Figure 15-11*, bottom). The Bokeh Color slider changes the highlights from no color or white (0 percent) to colorful (100 percent), wherein they begin to pick up the colors of surrounding pixels. And the Light Range slider lets you pick *which* lightness values are impacted by the Bokeh settings; just drag the black and white triangular sliders to set a range of colors (a fairly small range of the lighter highlights usually works well). To make Photoshop display a more accurate preview of your changes to the Bokeh settings, turn on the High Quality checkbox in the Options bar.

FIGURE 15-11

As you can see in this before (top) and after example (bottom), the Field Blur filter can produce nice results. By adjusting the Bokeh settings, you can really make the highlights in these crystals sparkle! It takes some experimenting to get the filter's pins placed correctly and the blur strength just right, but the controls are easy to use.

To bail out of using Field Blur without applying it to the image, click the Options bar's Cancel button or tap the Esc key on your keyboard.

5. **In the Options bar, turn on the "Save Mask to Channels" checkbox.**

   Once you start adding pins, Photoshop creates a temporary mask that shows/ hides the blur as you've specified by placing pins (you don't see or have access to the mask). Turning on the "Save Mask to Channels" setting makes Photoshop save the temporary blur mask as an alpha channel. This is handy when you want to adjust your image or add another effect to it using the exact same mask as you did for blurring (say, to add a bit of noise or grain to make the image look less perfect).

6. **Click OK in the Options bar to apply the filter.**

   As soon as you click OK (or press Return/Enter), the program applies the blur to the Smart Object or duplicate image layer, and switches you back to the regular Photoshop window.

■ IRIS BLUR

For even *more* control over the shape and size of the blur Photoshop applies, reach for the Iris Blur filter. You get the same large preview and panels that you do with Field Blur, and the same kind of on-image controls (though more of 'em). To use it, open an image, duplicate the Image layer or convert it for Smart Filters, and then choose Filter→Blur→Iris Blur. (If you're already *in* the Field Blur filter's window, simply head over to the Blur Tools panel on the right side of your screen and click the checkbox next to Field Blur to turn it *off*, and then click the checkbox next to Iris Blur to turn it *on*. Then click the flippy triangle to its left to expand its options.)

NOTE As mentioned in the Note on page 652, if you run Iris Blur as a Smart Filter, you can't adjust its blend mode or opacity. The Note above explains what the filter's layer is named if you go the Smart Object route.

Photoshop places a pin in the center of your image inside an elliptical-shaped blur with a white outline. To move the blur, drag anywhere inside the blur's outline. To change the blur's strength, use the blur ring as described in the previous section or adjust the Blur slider in the Blur Tools panel. In the Options bar, the Focus setting lets you determine how blurry the area inside the outline is (from the factory, it's set to 100 percent, which means no blur). *Figure 15-12* explains how to use the filter's various controls to customize the blur's size and shape.

TIP When you drag one feather handle, they *all* move. If you want to move 'em independently of one another, Option-drag (Alt-drag on a PC) instead.

■ TILT-SHIFT

The Tilt-Shift filter mimics the effects of a popular tilt lens called Lensbaby (*www.lensbaby.com*), a bendable lens—if you can imagine—that lets you control which part of the picture is in focus. It's a great way to draw the viewer's eye to your subject, but at $150 or more, it's not quite an impulse buy. Fortunately, the Tilt-Shift filter doesn't cost extra. Adding a tilt-shift blur to a bird's-eye view of a cityscape makes the city look miniature. You won't want to use this kind of effect on *every* image, but it can certainly enhance some, especially those with distracting backgrounds.

TIP The Tilt-Shift filter can produce interesting effects when used on video clips, as explained on page 817. And remember that, as the Note above explains, you can't adjust this filter's blend mode or opacity if you run it as a Smart Filter.

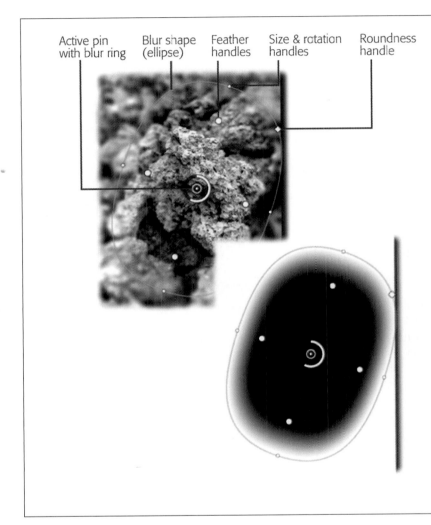

Active pin with blur ring

Blur shape (ellipse)

Feather handles

Size & rotation handles

Roundness handle

FIGURE 15-12

Left: The Iris Blur filter includes four size handles (they look like tiny dots on the blur outline) that you can drag to change the blur's size and therefore blur the area around this Hawaiian lava rock. If you position your cursor just outside the blur outline near one of these handles, your cursor turns into a curved, double-sided arrow that you can use to rotate the blur. To adjust the shape of the blur, drag the roundness handle to make the outline rounder or squarer. To adjust the feather of the blur's edges, drag one of the four circles inside the blur outline; drag it toward the pin to increase the feather amount, or away from the pin to decrease it.

Right: To temporarily see the mask Photoshop's created in the background, press and hold the M key. (This trick works on the Field and Tilt-Shift Blur filters, too.)

The Tilt-Shift filter works just like Field Blur and Iris Blur filters, though you get (you guessed it) even *more* controls. Give this filter a spin by converting your Image layer(s) for Smart Filters (page 632), by duplicating your Image layer, or by creating a stamped layer (page 107) first, and then choosing Fi ter→Blur→Tilt-Shift. (If you go the Smart Filter route, see the Note at the top of page 654 for info about how this filter is named in the Layers panel.) Whichever method you choose, Photoshop places an active pin and blur ring in the middle of the image and surrounds 'em with a series of solid and dashed lines that you can use to adjust the size of the in-focus and blurry areas (see *Figure 15-13*). The Options bar's Focus setting controls how in focus the non-blurry area is; you'll probably want to leave it set to 100 percent for no blur.

Focus lines

Focus zone
(no blur)

Transition zones
(blur)

Feather lines

Size & rotation handles   Active pin with blur ring

Before

After (with Bokeh applied)

FIGURE 15-13

The various lines that appear when you summon the Tilt-Shift filter control different things. The area between the two solid lines is in focus (though you can change that by adjusting the Options bar's Focus setting); the area between a solid line and a dashed line is partially blurred; and the area beyond the dashed lines is completely blurred. Drag any of these lines to adjust an area's size by dragging up or down.

To rotate the blur, point your cursor at one of the two solid white dots and then drag. When you do, Photoshop displays the rotation's angle (circled).

The Distortion slider in the Blur Tools panel on the right side of the window lets you change the shape of the lower blur zone (here, that's the blur zone on the left). Turn on the Symmetric Distortion checkbox to make Photoshop adjust the blur zones on both sides.

NOTE Give the Tilt-Shift filter a spin by downloading *Dubai.jpg* from this book's Missing CD page at *www.missingmanuals.com/cds*.

TIP For serious fun, try applying a combination of the Field Blur, Iris Blur, and Tilt-Shift filters to the *same* image. While you're applying one of the three filters, you can turn on the others using the checkboxes next to their names in the Blur Tools panel on the right side of your screen.

■ LENS BLUR

The Lens Blur filter is another super useful one, though it's been around for several versions of Photoshop. You can use it to produce effects similar to the ones you get with the Field Blur and Iris Blur filters, though with *far* more effort. But because it lets you create a blur mask (in the form of an alpha channel) by *hand*, this filter gives you maximum control and lets you produce extremely accurate and photo-realistic blurring. These days, the Lens Blur filter works faster than it used to because it takes advantage of multi-core processors (provided your computer *has* more than one). Here's how to use it:

1. **Open an image and the Channels panel.**

   To tell Photoshop which part of the image to blur and which part should stay in focus, you need to create a selection that the Lens Blur filter can use. An easy way to do that is by adding an alpha channel, which you'll do in the next step. To get started, open the Channels panel by clicking its tab in the Layers panel's group or by choosing Window→Channels.

2. **Create a new alpha channel.**

   Click the New Channel icon at the bottom of the Channels panel. Then, at the top of the panel, click the visibility eye next to the RGB channel (a.k.a. the composite channel). Your entire image takes on the Quick Mask mode's red overlay so you can create your selection. Don't worry: The red overlay is temporary—your image won't end up pink.

3. **Grab the Brush tool and set your foreground color chip to white.**

   Your goal here is to edit the mask so that the area you want to keep in focus doesn't have any red on it (the red areas will become blurry once you finish this technique). Make sure your color chips are set to black and white (press D if they're not), and press X until white is on top.

4. **Choose a big, soft brush and lower its opacity to 50 percent.**

   Hop up to the Options bar and, from the Brush Preset picker, choose a soft brush (one with fuzzy edges) that's fairly big (around 200 pixels). To create a subtle transition from in-focus pixels to blurry ones, lower the brush's opacity to 50 percent (and, while you're up there, make sure Flow is set to 100 percent).

TIP You can resize the brush by Option-Control-dragging (Alt+right-click+dragging on a PC) left to make it smaller or right to make it bigger. To adjust the brush's hardness, use the same keyboard shortcut but drag *vertically* instead. Photoshop places brush size, hardness, and opacity info next to your cursor as you drag.

5. **Paint across the areas you want to keep in focus.**

In *Figure 15-14*, top, for example, paint over the boy's face. As you paint, the photo starts to show through just a little, but since you lowered the brush's opacity, you need to keep painting over an area to achieve 100 percent focus. Remember: Anything that's red will be blurry when you're done, and the rest of the image will remain sharp. To create a perfectly sharp area, lower your brush size and paint over that area until all the red is gone. If you mess up and bring back too much of the photo, press X to flip-flop the color chips and paint that area with black to make it red (blurry) again.

6. **Turn off the alpha channel's visibility eye and activate the RGB channel.**

There's no need to leave the alpha channel turned on, so go ahead and hide it by clicking its visibility eye in the Channels panel. Next, click the RGB channel so you can see the full-color version of the image again.

7. **Open the Layers panel and duplicate the original layer.**

Since Lens Blur isn't available as a Smart Filter, the only way to protect your original image is to copy the layer and then run the filter on the copy. Click the Image layer to activate it, and then duplicate it by pressing ⌘-J (Ctrl+J).

8. **With the duplicate layer active, choose Filter→Blur→Lens Blur.**

Don't worry that the parts of the image that you want to be blurry are in focus and vice versa; you'll fix that in step 10.

9. **In the Lens Blur dialog box, set the Depth Map section's Source menu to Alpha 1.**

Tell the filter about the alpha channel you created by selecting it from the Depth Map section's Source menu. Unless you gave it a different name, the channel goes by Alpha 1.

10. **Turn on the Invert setting.**

Turning on the Invert checkbox flip-flops the blurry and sharp areas, as shown in *Figure 15-14* (bottom).

11. **Adjust the Shape menu and Radius slider until you get the blur just right.**

The Shape menu lets you change the blur's shape, and the Radius slider lets you determine just *how* blurry the background is. Be sure to release your mouse button so Photoshop can generate a new preview.

> **TIP** To make the image look less perfect, you can add a little noise to the blurry bits. At the bottom right of the Lens Blur dialog box, adjust the Noise Amount slider and turn on both the Gaussian radio button and the Monochromatic checkbox.

12. **Click OK when you're finished, and save the document as a PSD file.**

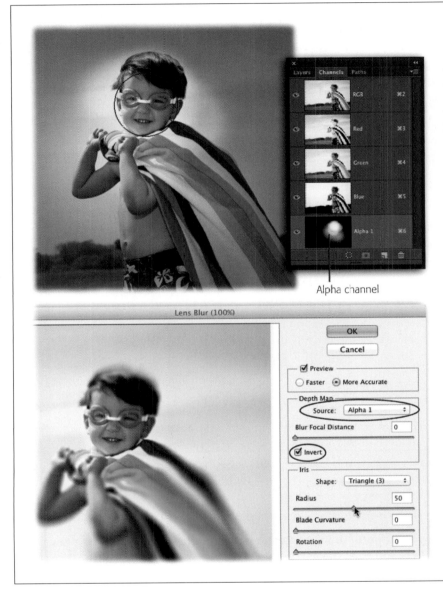

Alpha channel

FIGURE 15-14

Top: Since you used an alpha channel to create this effect, you can change the results. If you don't like how the image looks, just toss the duplicate Image layer, pop open the Channels panel, grab the Brush tool, and edit the alpha channel. Then repeat steps 6–12 to run the filter again.

Bottom: When you first run the Lens Blur filter, it does the exact opposite of what you want—it blurs what's supposed to be sharp, and vice versa. To fix that, just turn on the Invert checkbox, circled here.

Brush Strokes

There are a slew of filters in this category and, like the Artistic set, they're geared toward creating traditional fine-art effects. If you want to add interesting edge treatments to your images, these filters work especially well when used with layer masks (see *Figure 15-15*). Among the most useful for these kinds of edge effects are Spatter and Sprayed Strokes (Filter→Brush Strokes→Spatter or Sprayed Strokes).

FIGURE 15-15

By drawing a selection around the image (left) and then adding a layer mask (right), you can run the filter on the mask, which makes for some really nice edge effects—without harming the original image. Tack on a well-placed inner shadow for an even more interesting look!

A few other filters that work well for this technique are Glass, Ocean Ripple, Twirl (all found under Filter→Distort), and Torn Edges (Filter→Sketch→Torn Edges).

You can also use the Refine Edge dialog box to give a photo interesting edges. Flip back to page 172 for the scoop.

NOTE If you don't see this category in the Filter menu, flip to the box on page 635 to learn how to adjust your preferences so that it appears.

When you're ready to spice up an image's edges, take this technique for a spin:

1. **Open a photo, grab the Rectangular Marquee tool, and then draw a box where you want the new edges to be.**

   Since you'll run the filter on a layer mask, you don't need to use Smart Filters. For best results, draw the box at least a quarter of an inch in from the edges of your photo as shown in *Figure 15-15*, left. The filter will run *outside* this selection, on the edges of the image.

NOTE To give this technique a spin, trot on over to this book's Missing CD page at *www.missingmanuals. com/cds* and download *Superchick.jpg*.

2. **Add a layer mask.**

At the bottom of the Layers panel, click the circle-within-a-square icon to add a layer mask to the part of the image where you'll apply the filter.

3. **With the layer mask active, choose Filter→Brush Strokes→Spatter.**

In the resulting Filter Gallery dialog box, increase the Spray Radius to 20 and the Smoothness to 8. (These numbers are purely subjective, so adjust them until they look good to you.)

4. **Click OK to make Photoshop run the filter.**

For even funkier edges, run the filter *again* by pressing ⌘-F (Ctrl+F). And if you want to soften the new edges just a bit, you can run an additional filter: Choose Filter→Blur→Gaussian Blur, adjust the blur radius until you get the look you want, and then click OK.

Because the layer mask hides the image's edges, you'll see the checkerboard transparency pattern there. To create a new background, add a colored layer *beneath* the Image layer by choosing Layer→New Fill Layer→Solid Color, and then dragging it below the Image layer. Choose a color from the resulting Color Picker, click OK, and Photoshop adds the new layer. As a final touch, add an inner shadow or a drop shadow to the image by clicking the *fx* at the bottom of the Layers panel. (For more on layer styles, see page 124.)

TIP To reposition either the photo or the frame in your document, you have to unlink the layer from the mask by heading to the Layers panel and clicking the little chain icon between the layer and mask thumbnails. Then click the thumbnail of the layer or mask and reposition it with the Move tool. To link them together again, just click between the two thumbnails and the chain icon reappears.

Distort

The filters in this category, not surprisingly, distort and reshape images. It includes all kinds of goodies like the Displace filter, which lets you apply one image to the contours of another (page 303); the Pinch filter, which is great for shrinking double chins (page 422); and the Glass, Ocean Ripple, and Twirl filters, which work well as edge effects, as you learned in the previous section.

Noise

These filters let you add or remove *noise* (graininess or color speckles). If you're working on an extremely noisy image or restoring an old photo, these filters can come in really handy. For example, if you've scanned an old photo that has scratches in it, run the Dust & Scratches filter to make Photoshop scour the image for irregular pixels and blur them to smooth 'em out. Of the filters in this category, you'll likely use the Reduce Noise filter most often; it helps lessen noise in the dark areas of images shot in low light (a good idea before sharpening). The box on page 455 has the scoop.

Sometimes, you may need to *add* noise to an image, as odd as that sounds. For example, if you're working with a portrait that's been corrected to within an inch of its life so that it looks *too* perfect (as if it were airbrushed), run the Add Noise filter to introduce some random speckles and make the image look more realistic.

Pixelate

You probably won't use these filters often, but once in a while they're useful for applying funky blurs and textures to images. For example, the Crystallize filter makes an image look like it's behind a textured shower door. And if you're aiming for a newspaper-image look (think lots of tiny, visible dots) try the Halftone filter.

Render

These filters can generate cloud patterns, introduce lens flare, and add lighting to images. Two in particular—Clouds and Difference Clouds—are great for creating all kinds of backgrounds, such as the splotchy-colored ones you see in studio portraits. These filters mix your foreground and background colors into what look like soft, fluffy clouds. The more times you apply each filter, the more clouds you get (Difference Clouds gives you clouds with higher contrast). If you run the Motion Blur filter after the Cloud filter, you can create some *terrific* streaks that make an image look old (see page 530).

> **TIP** A little-known fact about the Lens Flare filter is that Option-clicking (Alt-clicking on a PC) in the dialog box's preview lets you reposition the flare and/or enter precise coordinates for it. Who knew?

Another useful filter in this category is Lighting Effects, which was *completely* redesigned back in CS6 so it's easier to use and works in 64-bit mode (page xxviii). This filter, which works only on 8-bit RGB images, gives you a window with a big preview on the left and a Properties panel on the right (*Figure 15-16*) where you choose among three kinds of light sources: Point (shines in all directions like a light bulb), Spot (shines in a beam like a flashlight), and Infinite (shines from a distance and is slightly diffused, like sunlight through a cloud).

Once you choose a kind of light from the unlabeled drop-down menu near the top of the Properties panel, you can adjust its strength with the Intensity field or the slider below it (drag it left to weaken the light or right to strengthen it). To change the light's color, click the colored box to the left of the Intensity field and choose a new color from the resulting Color Picker. For example, instead of adding a stark white light to a portrait, you could change it to light peach or yellow to give the subject a slight warm glow. If you've chosen Spot, you can also adjust the angle of its *hot spot* (the brightest point of light) with the Hotspot slider; drag it left to make the light small and narrow or right to make it tall and wide (*Figure 15-16* shows a fairly wide hot spot).

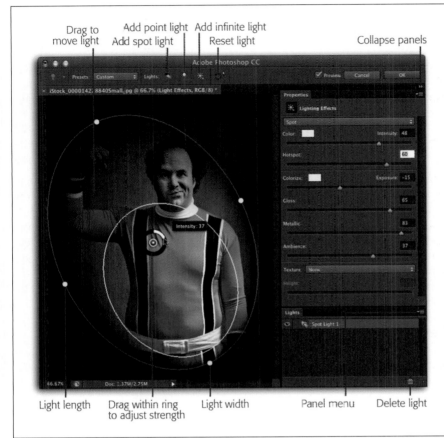

Drag to
move light
Add spot light
Add point light
Reset light
Add infinite light
Collapse panels

Light length
Drag within ring
to adjust strength
Light width
Panel menu
Delete light

FIGURE 15-16

If you didn't get your sub-ject lit right in the studio, there's a good chance you can fix it here. Click the little light icons in the Op-tions bar (labeled) to add additional light sources. To delete a light, activate its icon in the Lights panel, and then click the trash can icon at the bottom right of that panel.

To save a light source as a preset so you can use it again later, choose Save from the Preset menu near the top left of the Photoshop window. Give your custom light source a memorable name, and then click OK to add it to the Option bar's Presets menu.

You can find some excellent presets for the Lighting Effects filter in the Options bar's Presets menu. Once you choose one, you can pick a different type of light (Point, Spot, or Infinite) as mentioned earlier, and adjust the following settings:

- **Exposure**. You can control the total amount of available light with this setting. Drag the slider left to decrease the amount of light or right to increase it. To change the color of the exposure (or color of light), click the colored box to the left of this field, and then choose another color from the resulting Color Picker.

- **Gloss**. This setting controls how reflective the surface in the image is. For ex-ample, if you shine light onto a plain old piece of paper, it doesn't reflect very much. But if you shine light onto a *glossy* piece of paper, the reflection is much greater. Drag this slider left for less reflection or right for more.

- **Metallic**. This setting lets you change the surface the light is reflecting off of. For example, a plastic surface reflects the light's color, while a metallic surface reflects your subject's color. Drag the slider left to make the surface more plastic or right to make it more metallic (anything in between reflects both your light's color *and* your subject's color).

- **Ambience**. This setting lets you tone down the light source you've been painstakingly creating by mixing in more light from *another* source (as if the sun were also shining in the room or you turned on an overhead light). Drag this slider left to remove the additional light source or right to mix in more light from it.

- **Texture**. You may need to scroll down in the Properties panel to see this dropdown menu, which lets you tell Photoshop to shine the light through your image's red, green, or blue channel information to give your lighting some depth (referred to as a *bump map*). Once you've made a choice in the menu, use the Height slider below it to intensify the effect by dragging it right, or decrease the effect by dragging it left.

Sharpen

The filters in this category let you exaggerate areas of high contrast in an image (called *edges*) to make them appear sharper. Since resizing and editing an image can make its pixels a little soft, it's a good idea to sharpen each and every image you open in Photoshop. Sharpening is incredibly important and it has the power to make or break an image. That's why you'll find *full* coverage of these filters—including the new Shake Reduction filter for fixing blurry images—back in Chapter 11.

Sketch

To add a bit of texture to an image, reach for this category. It includes a variety of filter-driven pens, crayons, paper, and so on that give images a hand-drawn look. The Graphic Pen filter is perfect for adding realistic snow, as shown in *Figure 15-17*.

> **NOTE** If your Filter menu is missing the Sketch category, the box on page 635 tells you how to make it appear.

Here's how to use the Graphic Pen filter to add some realistic-looking flurries:

1. **Open a snowless photo and add a new layer filled with black.**

   As you learned back in Chapter 7, blend modes have various neutral colors that disappear when a particular blend mode is used. If you run the Graphic Pen filter on a solid black layer, you can use a blend mode to make the black disappear, leaving just the streaks made by the filter (which, in this case, look like snow). To add the black layer, click the "Create a new layer" icon at the bottom of the Layers panel. To fill it with black, choose Edit→Fill, pick Black from the Use menu, and then click OK. If this new layer isn't at the top of the layer stack, drag it upward so it is.

2. **With the black layer active, choose Filter→"Convert for Smart Filters."**

   To make the Graphic Pen filter run safely on this layer, you need to convert it for Smart Filters.

3. **In the Layers panel, change the black layer's blend mode to Screen (see** *Figure 15-17*, **right).**

As you learned on page 282, the Screen blend mode lightens the underlying photo and completely ignores black, so the snow-like streaks you create in the next step will lighten the photo and the black will disappear.

4. **Choose Filter→Sketch→Graphic Pen.**

Photoshop opens the Filter Gallery dialog box set to the Graphic Pen filter.

5. **On the right side of the dialog box, set the Stroke Direction menu to Vertical.**

This setting makes the snowflakes fall straight down.

6. **Set the Stroke Length to 5 and the Light/Dark Balance to 90.**

Think of Stroke Length as flake size; lowering it to around 5 creates fairly small flakes. And think of Light/Dark Balance as the amount of snowfall: Set it to 60 for a blizzard or to a higher number (like 90) for light snow (on your own image, you may have to experiment with different settings). When you're done, click OK to close the Filter Gallery dialog box.

FIGURE 15-17

Meet the Graphic Pen filter, which generates random streaks in the direction and length you choose, so it's perfect for making fake snow.

To create a visually pleasing snowfall that doesn't completely bury your subject, lower the filter's Stroke Length setting to around 5 and increase the Light/ Dark Balance setting to about 90. (If the Stroke Length is too high and the Light/Dark Balance is too low, your subject will look like he's stuck in a blizzard of sleet.)

7. **Choose Filter→Blur→Gaussian Blur and, in the resulting dialog box, enter a Radius of 1.5.**

This filter softens the snowflakes so they don't have hard edges.

8. **Click OK when you're finished, and save the document as a PSD file.**

The beauty of creating artificial snow using a Smart Filter is that you can control the snow's opacity—if the effect is too strong, just trot over to the Layers panel and double-click the icon to the right of the Graphic Pen Smart Filter and then, in the Blending Options dialog box, lower the Opacity setting. If the snow looks terrible, you can trash the filter and start over. It's lots of fun to add snow to *completely* inappropriate photos, too!

Stylize

This category is also artistic, but its filters let you create looks with more contrast than you can get with the Artistic filters. One filter in this category (Emboss, discussed later in this section) can save out-of-focus images. Several of the filters found here enhance the edges in images, and Find Edges does such a good job of locating edges that you can use it to create a pencil-sketch effect. It's a great technique to have in your bag of tricks because it can single-handedly save an image with color problems that can't be fixed with any of the techniques you learned back in Chapter 9. As a bonus, you create an image with a totally different look and feel from the original, as shown in *Figure 15-18*.

Here's how to use Find Edges to convert a photo into a pencil sketch:

1. **Pop open a photo and add a Black & White Adjustment layer.**

   The first step toward a pencil sketch is to get rid of the image's color, which you can do easily with a Black & White Adjustment layer. Click the half-black/half-white circle at the bottom of the Layers panel and choose Black & White. In the Properties panel that appears, adjust the various sliders until you're happy with the image's contrast.

2. **Activate the Image layer(s), and then choose Filter→"Convert for Smart Filters."**

   To make the filter run safely, you have to convert the image for Smart Filters first. In addition to protecting the original image, Smart Filters let you change the filter's blend mode and opacity (which you'll do in a couple of steps).

3. **Choose Filter→Stylize→Find Edges.**

   You won't get a dialog box with this filter—it just runs. Don't panic when your image turns into a freaky-looking outline; you'll reduce the filter's strength in a second.

4. **In the Blending Options dialog box, change the Mode to Hard Mix and lower the Opacity to about 85 percent.**

   In the Layers panel, double-click the little icon to the right of the Find Edges filter to open the Blending Options dialog box. As you change the dialog box's settings, keep an eye on your image (you may need to move the dialog box out of the way). As you learned in Chapter 7, the blend modes in the Lighting category increase an image's contrast, which is great when you're trying to create a pencil sketch. You may need to experiment with other Lighting blend modes for this technique because some will work better than others depending on the colors in your image. The best Opacity setting also varies according to how much contrast the original image has, though a setting between 75 and 85 percent usually works well. Click OK to close the Blending Options dialog box. Your image should start resembling a pencil sketch at this point, though you'll want to soften it by blurring it slightly in the next step.

5. **Choose Filter→Blur→Gaussian Blur and, in the resulting dialog box, enter a Radius of 2.**

   This Radius setting works well for most photos, but, again, you'll have to experiment. Click OK to close the Gaussian Blur dialog box.

FIGURE 15-18

As you can see, the Find Edges filter can help you completely change a photo's feel, and it can do wonders to rescue an image with lousy color. The lighter color of the pencil sketch brings out tons of details that you couldn't see before because the original photo was so dark and saturated.

For more fun effects involving blend modes, check out your author's video, Photoshop Deep Dive: Blend Modes, *at* www.lesa.in/clvideos.

6. **Open the Gaussian Blur layer's Blending Options dialog box, change the blend mode to Lighten, and then click OK.**

   In the Layers panel, double-click the icon to the right of the Gaussian Blur layer to open the dialog box, and then change the Mode setting. When you choose Lighten, the Gaussian Blur filter blurs only the light pixels in the image, preserving the darker pixels' details (the edges you accentuated with the Find Edges filter).

You're finished, but if the sketch is too dark, try placing it atop a white background and then lowering its opacity: Click the half-black/half-white circle at the bottom of the Layers panel, choose Solid Color, and then pick white from the resulting Color Picker. If the original Image layer is a locked Background layer, double-click it to unlock it (Photoshop won't let you place any layers beneath it if it's locked). Drag the white layer *below* the original Image layer, and then activate the original Image layer and lower its opacity to about 85 percent. That oughta soften your sketch right up!

> **TIP** To create a watercolor look, activate the Black & White Adjustment layer and then lower its opacity slightly to let some of the original color show through. If you do this, you'll definitely need to add a white Solid Color Fill layer below the Image layer, as described in the previous paragraph.

■ EMBOSS

Although no magic fixer-upper can make an out-of-focus image look like it's perfectly in focus, the Emboss filter comes close. (So does the new Shake Reduction filter, described in detail on page 462.) Technically, it doesn't really *fix* the image and make it sharp, it merely brings out the edges that are already there, making the image *look* sharper (see *Figure 15-19*). Here's how to use it:

1. **Open the out-of-focus image and choose Filter→"Convert for Smart Filters."**

2. **Choose Filter→Stylize→Emboss.**

   In the resulting dialog box, leave the Angle, Height, and Amount settings as they are. Your image will be mostly gray, and the edges of your subject will be brightly colored (see *Figure 15-19*, top), but that's exactly what you want, so click OK to close the Emboss dialog box. In the next step, you'll change the blend mode to make the gray parts disappear.

3. **Open the Emboss filter's Blending Options dialog box and change the Mode setting to Hard Light.**

   Over in the Layers panel, double-click the tiny icon to the right of the Emboss layer. As you learned on page 284, the blend modes in the Lighting category add contrast to images and ignore gray. Since the Emboss filter turned your image gray and gave it brightly colored edges, changing the blend mode to Hard Light makes the gray vanish, leaving only the edges visible so they stand out more and appear sharper than before. Nice, eh?

4. **Click OK to close the Blending Options dialog box, and save your document as a PSD file.**

That's all there is to it—well, aside from grinning triumphantly because you fixed the image.

FIGURE 15-19

*The Emboss filter can't
save a* completely *out-
of-focus image, but it
can sure take one that's
slightly blurry and make
it look much sharper.
(Another option for fixing
blurry photos is to use
the new Shake Reduction
filter, described back on
page 462.)*

*By the way, Samantha and
Sylvester say hello! (Sadly,
Sylvester passed during
the writing of the CS6
version of this book at the
ripe old age of 16.)*

Texture

As you'd expect, the filters in this category add texture to images, which can help
add depth and visual interest, as shown in *Figure 15-20.* For example, to spice up
an image's background, you can add a texture to just that area by selecting it and
then running one of these filters.

> **NOTE** Initially, the Texture category isn't included in the Filter menu. Happily, there's an easy fix—hop back
> to the box on page 635 to learn what to do.

FIGURE 15-20

If you select the dark-green rays in this image's background with the Quick Selection tool before running the Craquelure filter (Filter→Texture→Craquelure), the filter's effect is visible in just those areas.

As you can see here, Photoshop filled in the Smart Filter mask for you. Remember that, when you're dealing with layer masks, black conceals and white reveals.

The technique is super simple: Just open an image and choose Filter→"Convert for Smart Filters." Then select the area behind your subject using any of the techniques described in Chapter 4. Next, choose Filter→Texture and pick one of the six options: Craquelure, Grain, Mosaic Tiles, Patchwork, Stained Glass, or Texturizer. (The Texturizer filter lets you load your *own* images and use them as a texture; see page 622 for an example of how you can snatch texture from a photo and use it on text.) Adjust the various sliders in the Filter Gallery dialog box, and then click OK.

Video

As the name suggests, the two filters in this category deal strictly with individual frames extracted from videos. De-Interlace smooths moving images, and NTSC Colors restricts the image's color palette to colors that TVs can display. For more on working with video in Photoshop, head to Chapter 20.

Other

Since these filters don't really fit into any *other* category, they get their own. Custom, for example, lets you design your own filters to manipulate images' brightness.

As you learned on page 462, you can use the High Pass filter to sharpen images. Maximum and Minimum have more practical uses—you can use 'em to enlarge or shrink a layer mask, respectively. For example, if you select an object, add a layer mask, and then place it atop *another* image, you may find some stray pixels around the object's edges from the original background. To eliminate those strays, use the Minimum filter to shrink the mask (*Figure 15-21*, bottom right).

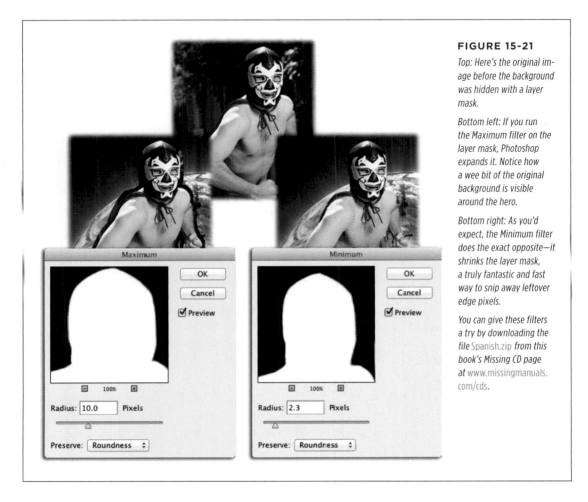

FIGURE 15-21

Top: Here's the original image before the background was hidden with a layer mask.

Bottom left: If you run the Maximum filter on the layer mask, Photoshop expands it. Notice how a wee bit of the original background is visible around the hero.

Bottom right: As you'd expect, the Minimum filter does the exact opposite—it shrinks the layer mask, a truly fantastic and fast way to snip away leftover edge pixels.

You can give these filters a try by downloading the file Spanish.zip *from this book's Missing CD page at* www.missingmanuals. com/cds.

NOTE The Maximum and Mininum filters have a nasty habit of making round things in your image look square. To fix that, Adobe added a new Preserve drop-down menu, which lets you tell Photoshop CC to preserve the squareness or roundness of pixels in your image. When you choose Roundness from this menu, you can enter decimals into both filters' Radius fields for more precise control (yay!), which is incredibly handy when you're using 'em to edit layer masks.

The last filter in this category is Offset, which you can use to shift a selected object horizontally or vertically a precise amount in pixels. Since *moving* a selection creates a hole in its original location, you get to tell Photoshop what to do with the empty spot. Your choices are "Set to Transparent," Repeat Edge Pixels, and Wrap Around.

Digimarc

This filter lets you add a nearly invisible watermark to your images to protect them from being stolen and used without your permission (a problem inherent in posting images online). Page 747 has the scoop.

Browse Filters Online

Since filters are basically little programs that run inside Photoshop, they're easy to install (see page 776 for instructions). When you choose Filter→Browse Filters Online, you'll be transported to Adobe's website, where you can choose from loads of filters.

Photoshop and Print

Getting your prints to match what you see onscreen is one of the biggest challenges you'll face when dealing with digital images. Unless you prepare your monitor and files properly, it's *impossible* to make them match. As you learned before, image files are actually filled with grayscale information—it's the monitor and printer's job to give them color. And with the sheer volume of monitors, printers, inks, and papers out there, producing consistent color can be a *nightmare*.

Thankfully, there's a solution, but it lies in understanding *why* this stuff happens to begin with. Unfortunately, that means learning about things like color modes, gamuts, and color profiles. These are heady topics, to be sure, but it's not rocket science. The main concepts are (fairly) straightforward, and if you can make it through this chapter (an energy drink will help), you'll know how to create consistent, predictable, high-quality prints.

■ The Challenge of WYSIWYG Printing

WYSIWYG (pronounced "wiz-e-wig") is an acronym for "What you see is what you get." For image-editing buffs, it describes the elusive goal of getting prints to match what's onscreen. When you think about the different ways colors are produced by monitors versus printers, the problem starts to make sense.

A monitor's surface is made from glass or some other transparent material, and, as you learned in Chapter 5, it produces colors with phosphors, LCD elements, or other light-emitting doodads. In contrast, printers use a combination of paper, reflected light, and cyan, magenta, yellow, and black inks. To add even *more* excitement, some printers use additional colors like light cyan, light magenta, several varieties of black, and so on. Given these two completely different approaches to creating colors, it's a miracle that the images on your monitor look *remotely* similar to the ones you print. And because there are a bazillion different monitors and printers on the market—each using different technologies—you'll see a big difference in how your images look depending on the monitor or printer you use. Heck, even changing the *paper* in your printer makes a big difference in how your images print.

The only way to achieve consistent printing results is to have a calibrated and profiled monitor of decent quality (you'll learn about that stuff shortly), to know which printer your image is headed for, which color mode that printer wants the image to be in, which range of colors that printer can reproduce, *and* exactly what type of paper you're using. Whew! Once you have all that info, you need to communicate it to Photoshop. This section describes how to do that.

Understanding Color Gamuts and Profiles

As a first step toward WYSIWYG printing, remember from Chapter 5 that, in most cases, your image starts life in RGB color mode and eventually ends up being converted to some version of CMYK when it's printed (as you'll learn later, either the printer can convert the image's mode or you can do it manually). So the next step is to understand a little more about how those two color modes differ. Enter *color gamuts*.

A color gamut is the range of colors a given device can reproduce (flip back to Chapter 5 for more on how color works). An RGB monitor, for example, can reproduce one range of colors, and a CMYK printer can reproduce another (and no monitor or printer can produce a color range as wide as your eyes can see). While the color ranges of monitors and printers frequently overlap, they're never identical. Your printer's color gamut depends on the specific combination of printing technologies you're using, which include the following:

- **Colorants (color-producing substances)**. The printers you're likely to encounter include inkjet and laser printers, commercial offset presses, and digital presses. Some printers, like commercial offset presses, use pigment-based inks to produce color. Others, like inkjets, often use dye-based inks, and still others, like laser printers and digital presses (which are like fancy laser printers), use powdered toners.

- **Dot pattern**. All the printers mentioned above use a pattern of dots to reproduce images. Commercial offset presses typically use *halftone dots* that are commonly made from ellipses and diamonds.

- **Paper type**. Each printer can also use a wide range of paper, from plain paper to matte or super high-quality glossy paper. (Quick tip: You'll usually get *much* higher-quality prints using glossy paper.) If you want your inkjet printer to reproduce its full gamut of color, you need to use a specially coated paper made to work with specific dye-based inks.

To account for all these variations, you can use *color profiles* to tell Photoshop exactly which colorants and papers you want to print with. Color profiles contain detailed info about the printer's color gamut and, in some cases, the paper you're using, though usually that info lives in a separate file called a *paper profile*. Photoshop comes with a variety of all-purpose, generic profiles, but you can also get profiles from the printer and paper manufacturers. Throughout this chapter, you'll learn how to use profiles both to *proof* (check and review) images and to print them on commonly used printers like inkjets, commercial printing presses, and digital presses.

> **NOTE** Manufacturers are inventing new printers all the time, and this book can't possibly cover them all. That said, if you're going to use a professional print shop, you'll want to work *very* closely with them to ensure an accurate print.

■ FINDING AND INSTALLING DRIVERS AND COLOR PROFILES

Most of the time, you can download *printer drivers*—the software that lets Photoshop communicate with your printer—right from the printer manufacturer's website, although you might have to poke around a bit to find 'em. It's *always* best to get printer drivers straight from the company that made the device. The manufacturer's site should explain how to install the driver.

You can typically download color profiles from the website of the company that made the paper (be sure to get the one that's made for *your* printer), though you can also get custom color profiles from professional printing companies, too (they're usually happy to share 'em with you if you ask). Luckily, the profiles you get from larger companies, such as Epson, come with an installer program. If yours doesn't, ask the company it came from where you should put it on your computer (it depends on your operating system). The box on page 676 has more about color profiles.

> **TIP** For high-quality ICC profiles, visit the International Color Consortium Registry at *www.lesa.in/iccregistry*.

Every printer and paper manufacturer's website is different, but they all have similar options (though you may have to hunt for 'em!). Typically, drivers and profiles live in the download or support section of the manufacturer's website, but it's usually much easier to go Google your printer's name plus the item you're after, such as *Epson R3000 driver* or *Epson R3000 color profile*.

Once you've installed the appropriate printer driver and color profile, you can access them via Photoshop's Print and Custom Proof dialog boxes, explained later in this chapter.

Calibrating Your Display

To ensure accurate prints, it's also important to make sure your display is showing colors accurately. Both the Mac and Windows operating systems come with a built-in calibration program, but for best results, use an external measuring device like a *colorimeter* or *spectrophotometer* (hand-sized gadgets that clamp onto your monitor and measure the color it displays) instead. The calibration process involves adjusting your monitor so that it displays a series of colors and images consistently. Having a calibrated monitor also lets you more accurately preview how images and colors will print (a process called *soft-proofing*, discussed later in this chapter).

You can buy a profiling device for your display for around $100 (USD), although the more sophisticated ones cost a little more. There's no harm in starting with an affordable model like Pantone's ColorMunki Smile (*www.lesa.in/colormunkismile*) or DataColor's Spyder4Express (*www.lesa.in/spyderexpress*), but to be able to *truly* trust the colors your display is showing you, you'll need to spend more. Options include the SpyderPro (*www.lesa.in/spyderpro*), which runs about $170, or the Pantone i1 Display Pro (*www.lesa.in/i1display*), which is around $270. However, a simpler and perhaps more accurate solution is to buy a display that comes with its *own* calibration software and colorimeter, such as an NEC model with SpectraView; you can pick up a 24″ model for around $1000 (*www.lesa.in/necspectraview*).

Another step toward making your display show your images the way they'll look when printed is telling Photoshop which color profile your *display* should use while you're working on the image (also called your *color workspace*). Choose Edit→Color Settings and, in the Working Spaces section of the Color Settings dialog box, choose a profile from the RGB menu. These color workspaces differ greatly in color gamut, as shown in *Figure 16-1*.

Profiles Aren't All Equal

It's shocking but true: Some profiles are just plain wrong.

Photoshop comes with many built-in profiles—like Adobe RGB (1998) and sRGB—that include general color mode info for displaying images, as well as slightly more specific (though still generic) profiles—like US Sheetfed Coated v2—that contain gamut information for printing on a typical sheetfed press using standard inks and coated paper. If your printing conditions are indeed standard, you may get decent results by using one of these built-in profiles.

You can also use printer-and-paper-specific profiles, commonly referred to as *paper* or *output profiles*, created by manufacturers like Epson, who make profiles to match almost every kind of paper they sell: glossy, luster, matte, and so on. The more closely a profile matches your printing conditions, the more

accurate and useful it is. You'll find that high-quality paper profiles like the Epson ones provide invaluable help with proofing and printing.

When you're out paper shopping, it's wise to confirm that the paper manufacturer does indeed have paper profiles that match your printer and ink (and be wary of buying paper from companies that don't!).

You'll also want to test the profiles by actually printing with them. If you've been printing with other paper and profiles, print some test images using the same image for both sets of papers and profiles and then compare the results. You'll probably find that some paper manufacturer's profiles are better than others.

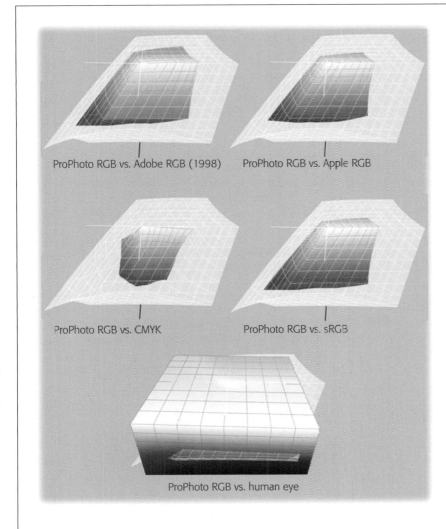

FIGURE 16-1

Here you can see how the gamut (range of colors) differs from one color workspace to the next. In each of these examples, ProPhoto RGB, the largest digital color workspace currently in use, is shown in white with the other workspaces displayed in color on top of it. Notice how small the CMYK gamut is in comparison to the others, due to the smaller number of colors that are reproducible with ink vs. those that are reproducible with light.

The bottom image shows the ProPhoto RGB workspace in comparison to the color gamut of the human eye.

ProPhoto RGB vs. Adobe RGB (1998)   ProPhoto RGB vs. Apple RGB

ProPhoto RGB vs. CMYK   ProPhoto RGB vs. sRGB

ProPhoto RGB vs. human eye

Here's what you need to know about choosing the color workspace that's right for you:

- **Adobe RGB (1998)**. This is the most popular color workspace to date. It includes a *wide* range of colors, so it's perfect for designers and photographers alike. It's also great for printing on inkjet printers as well as commercial presses.

- **Apple RGB**. This workspace was designed for use on small Apple monitors. It's *slightly* smaller than Adobe RGB (1998), meaning it contains a narrower range of colors. So unless you're rockin' a vintage 13-inch display, don't use this workspace.

- **ColorMatch RGB**. Designed to match the color space of the old Radius Pressview monitors, this workspace has a slightly smaller gamut than Adobe RGB (1998). If you've got one of those Radius monitors, this workspace is a good choice.

- **ProPhoto RGB**. Currently the *largest* color workspace in use, ProPhoto RGB is used by software that processes raw images (those shot in the super-high quality raw format—see page 48). It's the native workspace of Camera Raw (page 361) and Photoshop Lightroom (Adobe's professional-grade photo organizing and editing program). Choose this mode if you're a pro photographer shooting in raw format *and* you're working with 16-bit files in Photoshop.

- **sRGB**. Also slightly smaller than Adobe RGB (1998), this workspace is great for preparing images for use on the Web, in presentation programs, in videos, and submitting to an online source for printing (a lab like *www.mpix.com*, say). This is the RGB workspace Photoshop uses unless you pick another one.

If you routinely edit CMYK images, pick a profile from the CMYK menu in the Color Settings dialog box that most closely describes the kind of press your images will be printed on. If you don't know, ask your print shop.

TIP You can also change your *digital camera's* color profile to match what you use in Photoshop. For example, most cameras are set to sRGB mode right out of the box, but you can change it to Adobe RGB instead. Alas, you'll have to dig out your owner's manual to learn how, but the increased range of colors and monitor consistency is well worth it!

◼ Resizing and Formatting Files

Besides making sure your images are in the right color mode, installing the right color profiles for your printer and paper, and calibrating your monitor—are you exhausted yet?—you also need to make sure your image's size matches the size you want to print. For example, to print an image at 5"×7", it should really *be* 5"×7" (as opposed to, say, taking a 6"×8" image and cramming it into that smaller format). You also need to make sure the image has sufficient resolution (see the table on page 239 for resolution guidelines). Finally, you need to save the image in a file format that works well with your printer. This section walks you through all those steps.

Printer-Friendly File Formats

Printers can accept a wide range of file formats, including PSD (Photoshop), TIFF, EPS, PDF, and even JPEG. Don't worry: Choosing a format isn't as hard as you might think. Once you've saved the master file in PSD format, choose File→Save As and then pick one of the following formats:

- **TIFF**. This format (whose name is short for "tagged image file format") has long been considered the print-safe gold standard, and for that reason, almost any program can work with TIFF files. Saving a file in this format doesn't compress it, so the quality remains as good as that of the original. And if the image will be used in another program but you don't know which one—for example, you're sending the image off to someone else to use in a book or magazine—saving it as a TIFF is a safe bet.

TIP   If you have to email or upload a TIFF, be sure to create and send a .zip archive of the file first, because TIFFs are notorious for getting corrupted in transit. To do that on a Mac, Control-click the file's icon, and then choose "Compress [file name]" from the resulting shortcut menu. On a PC running Windows, right-click the file and then choose Send to→"Compressed (zipped) folder," or use a program like WinZip (*www.winzip.com*).

- **PDF**. This format (short for "portable document format") is hugely popular. While it *can* compress files, it doesn't do so automatically, which makes it perfect for images you plan to print, plus it preserves the smooth edges of vectors. And if you need to email the file or upload it to an online print company, PDF is a better choice than TIFF because its file size will be smaller and it's a more modern format.

- **EPS**. If you've created a multitonal image (page 232) or one with spot colors (page 697), you can use this format (whose name stands for Encapsulated PostScript), which has long been the native format for vectors. However, PDF files can *also* handle multitonal images and ones with spot colors, and you'll find that saving an image in PDF format is simpler than saving it in EPS format (plus it usually results in a much smaller file size). For that reason, go with PDF format unless someone—like a prepress manager at your printing company—specifically requests an EPS file. (And if she does, ask her tactfully if she's heard about PDFs—and then duck!)

Resizing and Saving as a TIFF

Here's how to prepare an image for a high-quality print even if you don't know exactly what resolution you need *or* which program will be used to print the image:

1. **With the image open, summon the Image Size dialog box.**

   Choose Image→Image Size or press Option-⌘-I (Alt+Ctrl+I). See page 234 for a full description of this important dialog box.

2. **Near the bottom of the dialog box, turn off the Resample checkbox.**

   This prevents you from changing the image's pixel count—and therefore changing its quality.

3. **Set the Width and Height fields to the size you want to print (for example, 10"×10").**

   Photoshop preserves your image's original aspect ratio (the relationship between its width and height), so if you can't get the dimensions just right, you can always crop the image first. And don't worry about changing the resolution—Photoshop changes it automatically as soon as you enter the width or height, and you'll save the file at its maximum resolution. If you're sending the file to a professional printer and the resolution is between 300 and 450 ppi, you can sleep well knowing it'll print nicely. (If the resolution is lower than that, see the box on page 238 for a workaround.) Click OK to close the Image Size dialog box.

4. **Save the file in TIFF format.**

   Choose File→Save As or press Shift-⌘-S (Shift+Ctrl+S) and, in the resulting dialog box, choose TIFF from the format drop-down menu.

5. **At the bottom of the dialog box, turn off the Layers and Alpha Channels checkboxes, if they're on.**

   Turning these options off forces Photoshop to save a new, flattened version of your image that's good for printing.

6. **In the upper part of the dialog box, name the new file and tell Photoshop where to save it; then click Save.**

   You may want to develop your own naming system for print files. A name like AlaskaLight_10x10_Print_CMYK.tif specifies the file's dimensions and color mode, and indicates that it's a file designed for printing (see *Figure 16-2*, left). Click Save to close the Save As dialog box. Photoshop opens the TIFF Options dialog box.

7. **Adjust the TIFF Options dialog box's settings (see *Figure 16-2*, right).**

   In the dialog box's Image Compression section, choose None to keep the file more compatible with other programs (though its file size increases). Leave the Pixel Order section set to Interleaved, and in the Byte Order section, turn on the IBM PC radio button to make the file compatible with Windows computers (Macs can read either byte order). That said, all modern programs support the compression options you see here and both Byte Order settings.

8. **Click OK and Photoshop saves the image as a TIFF file.**

Following these steps lets you create an uncompressed, single-layer, print-ready copy of the image at the right size for printing without harming your original file. You can now print the TIFF image straight from Photoshop or hand it off to a page-layout program like InDesign or QuarkXPress (though these days both programs are happier with PSD or PDF files).

Resizing and Saving as a PDF

Another high-quality format option is PDF. You can use PDF format to save some of the most complex images you'll ever create like those with spot colors (page 697) or multitonal images (page 323) that historically required EPS format or its print-specific variation, DCS (Desktop Color Separations) format (page 701).

FIGURE 16-2

Left: Adopting a naming scheme like this one can help you keep images organized.

Right: As soon as you click Save in the Save As dialog box, you see the big ol' TIFF Options dialog box shown here.

Photo by Taz Tally (www.taztal-lyphotography.com).

As mentioned earlier, creating a PDF file is usually easier than making an EPS file, and PDFs are safer to transfer over the Internet. Here's how to resize an image and save it as a PDF:

1. **Open your Photoshop document and duplicate it.**

   Since this technique involves lowering the resolution, it's safer to work with a *copy* of your image rather than the original. Choose Image→Duplicate and name the new file something like AlaskaLight_5x5_300, which includes info about the resulting file's size and resolution.

2. **Open the Image Size dialog box, turn off the Resample checkbox, and then resize the image.**

   Choose Image→Image Size or press Option-⌘-I (Alt+Ctrl+I) and then turn off the Resample option near the bottom of the dialog box. Then change the document's width and height if you need to. For example, the image in *Figure 16-3* started at 9″×9″, but is now 5″×5″. This change caused the resolution to balloon from 384 ppi to 691 ppi, but you'll lower that number to a more reasonable level in the next step (see page 239 for a discussion of resolution overkill).

3. **Near the bottom of the Image Size dialog box, turn the Resample checkbox back *on* and then lower the resolution to 300 ppi.**

   The Resample checkbox has to be on for you to change the resolution. After you turn it on, enter *300* in the Resolution field.

FIGURE 16-3

Anything over 450 ppi resolution is usually overkill, so aim for something closer to 300 ppi (between 120 and 200 for newsprint). Notice that when this file was resized, its pixel dimensions shrank from 3456x3456 to 1500x1500 and its size decreased from 34.2 MB to 6.44 MB, a much more manageable size.

Now if you need to email the file, it'll transfer much faster—heck, it'll even print faster thanks to its new svelte size.

4. **Choose Automatic from the Resample menu.**

Setting this menu to Automatic makes Photoshop picks the best method *for* you. Alternatively, you can use "Bicubic Sharper (reduction)," which makes Photoshop reduce the softening (blurring) that results from making the image smaller (See page 235 for more about resampling.) Click OK to close the Image Size dialog box.

> **TIP** You may want to apply a round of sharpening after you resize and resample an image to help maintain its crispness (an amount between 50 percent and 75 percent should do the trick). See Chapter 11 for serious sharpening enlightenment.

5. **Summon the Save As dialog box by choosing File→Save As or pressing ⌘-S (Ctrl+S).**

Since you're working on a copy that you haven't saved yet, you need to tell Photoshop where to save it and in what format.

6. **In the format drop-down menu, choose Photoshop PDF and then turn off the Layers and Alpha Channels checkboxes, if they're on.**

Turning off these checkboxes forces Photoshop to create a single-layer PDF for printing.

7. **Name your file and tell Photoshop where to save it, and then click Save.**

When you do, Photoshop alerts you that, "The settings you choose in the Save Adobe PDF dialog can override your current settings in the Save As dialog box." Click OK and the Save Adobe PDF dialog box appears.

8. **On the left side of the Save Adobe PDF dialog box, choose General and then make sure the Compatibility menu on the right side is set to Acrobat 5 (PDF 1.4) as shown in *Figure 16-4*, top.**

If you think you'll want to edit this PDF in Photoshop later, make sure the Preserve Photoshop Editing Capabilities checkbox is turned on (though you're better off editing the PSD you made the PDF *from* instead).

9. **Click the Compression category on the left and, from the first drop-down menu in the Options section of the dialog box, choose Do Not Downsample, and then set the Compression menu to None (see *Figure 16-4*, bottom).**

These options let you retain all the original pixel info so you can create a high-quality print. However, if you want to reduce the file's size without losing too much image quality, choose Zip and "8 bit," or JPEG and Maximum, from the Compression and Image Quality menus (respectively). A maximum-quality JPEG is a great choice when you're sending an image to a print company that lets you upload files to its website, or to a stock image service.

FIGURE 16-4

The Save Adobe PDF dialog box has a slew of options. To go through them, choose a category on the left (General, Compression, and so on) and then adjust the settings that appear on the right.

10. **Click the Output category and then pick No Conversion from the Color Conversion menu.**

    This option makes Photoshop retain all the image's color info.

11. **Optionally, save these settings as a preset so you can use them again later.**

    Think about whether you'll ever want to use these settings again. If the answer is yes (and it probably is), click the Save Preset button in the lower-left corner of the dialog box (*Figure 16-5*). Give your preset a descriptive name like *Print Image PDF*, and then click Save.

FIGURE 16-5

If you save your settings as a preset, you can access them via the Adobe PDF Preset drop-down menu at the top of the Save Adobe PDF dialog box. Photoshop lets you save as many presets as you want, which can be a huge timesaver.

You can also choose one of the built-in PDF presets listed in the Standard menu, shown here; when you make a choice from this menu, Photoshop sets all the other options for you. Ask your printer which standard they'd like you to use.

12. **Click the Save PDF button.**

    You can place your newly created PDF file in an InDesign document or send it to somebody via email or FTP site. Unlike TIFF and EPS files, which usually need to be encased in a protective .zip archive (a compressed document container—see the Tip on page 679), PDF files are Internet compatible and safe.

◼ Printing on an Inkjet Printer

If you're a photographer, you probably use an inkjet printer—most likely of the *expanded-gamut* variety that uses six to eight inks, rather than the standard four (they're technically dyes, but most folks call 'em inks). The most common combination of expanded-gamut ink includes the four standard *process colors*—cyan, magenta, yellow, and black (CMYK)—plus light cyan and light magenta. You may also have a choice of black inks, like glossy or photo black, matte black, light black, and even light *light* black (seriously!).

NOTE Inkjet printers are more common than dye-sublimation or color laser printers, so they're the focus of this section. But you can use printer and paper profiles as explained in this section no matter what kind of printer you use.

FREQUENTLY ASKED QUESTION

Why Not Print JPEGs?

Hey, what do you have against JPEGs? It seems like a decent enough file format.

You may be wondering why you shouldn't save and print images in JPEG format. That's a legitimate question because, after all, JPEG is the format supported by most digital cameras. There's certainly nothing wrong with printing a first generation JPEG (the one from your camera); the problem occurs once you start editing, resaving, and then printing *subsequent* JPEGs.

When you save images as JPEGs, Photoshop automatically shrinks 'em using a process known as *lossy compression*, which reduces the amount of color info in the image (mainly in areas of fine detail), lowering the image's quality. The amount of compression, and the resulting loss of info and quality, varies from one JPEG to another. (You can set the level of compression yourself, as discussed on page 723.) If you have no choice but to use JPEG—because you're sending the image to an online lab for printing, like your local camera store or *www.mpix.com*, for example—use the highest quality and lowest compression settings to preserve as much quality as possible.

However, when you *resave* a JPEG that you've edited without changing its format to something else like PSD or TIFF, you apply yet *another* round of compression, and *that's* when everything goes to heck in a handbasket. Here's what you should do instead:

- Save any JPEGs you receive in PSD format when you first open them for editing in Photoshop, and then create a JPEG *from* the PSD if you need to (say, for posting on the Web or emailing). To speed up this file conversion, you can use Photoshop actions (Chapter 18) and/or the Image Processor script (page 247) to quickly convert several images from one format to another.

- If your images are going to be edited extensively, set your digital camera to capture images in an uncompressed format like TIFF or raw to prevent any initial compression and resulting loss of info and quality. As you learned on page 48, raw is the most flexible format, so choose that option if possible (most cameras can save images in raw format; consult your owner's manual to see whether yours can).

Now you can relax knowing you're not *re*-compressing already compressed files. Whew!

Nearly all expanded-gamut inkjet printers can convert RGB images to CMYK (plus any additional inks they may have). For the brightest and most saturated colors, let the printer convert the colors for you (see the discussion in step 8 below). However, for the most *accurate* results, manage the conversion *yourself* in the Photoshop Print Settings dialog box. Here's how to do just that when printing a high-quality image on an expanded-gamut printer (also called CcMmYyK or, if it's an HP printer, CMYK-Plus):

1. **Prepare your image for printing by cropping, editing, and resizing it.**

   Make sure you've cropped, color-corrected (Chapter 9), and resized the image and set its resolution to between 200 ppi and 450 ppi (Chapter 6). If you don't crop the image to the exact dimensions you want, your printer may crop it for you (it's *far* better to do it yourself). It's also a good idea to double-check the Image Size dialog box to confirm that the document's dimensions and resolution are correct (open it by pressing Option-⌘-I or Alt+Ctrl+I on a PC).

2. **Choose File→Print or press ⌘-P (Ctrl+P) to summon the Photoshop Print Settings dialog box, shown in *Figure 16-6* (top).**

FIGURE 16-6

Top: Adobe redesigned and simplified Photoshop's Print dialog box back in CS6; it has a big preview area on the left and sports multiple sections on the right that are brimming with options. Click a section's name to collapse or expand it and use the scroll bar on the right to move down through the sections. (You can make the dialog box bigger by dragging any edge or its lower-right corner.) Click the Print Settings button near the top for more printer-specific options like paper and quality. If you're on a Mac and your printer offers a utility for nozzle cleaning and the like, you can summon it by clicking the icon to the right of the Printer menu that looks like a tiny printer (Windows users can usually click on the Print Settings button).

Bottom: If your printer can print to the edges of the paper (called a full-bleed or borderless print), head to the Paper Size menu in your printer's dialog box (the one that opens when you click Print Settings at the top of the Photoshop Print Settings dialog box) and choose an option that includes the word "borderless." Otherwise, your printer won't print all the way to the paper's edge, which creates a pesky white border.

3. **In the Printer menu at the top of the dialog box, pick your printer.**

   If your printer isn't listed, visit the manufacturer's website and download the latest driver for your printer (see page 275).

NOTE When you make changes in the Photoshop Print Settings dialog box and then click the Done or Print button, Photoshop saves those settings—in the document, as well as in its own *program* preferences—the moment you save the document. (If you *don't* save the document, your print settings fly out the window [unless you saved them as a preset]). This lets you print the same document with the same print settings quickly by choosing File→Print One Copy. In fact, *any* document you print will automatically use those same print settings unless you change them (at which point, Photoshop will use those *new* settings the next time you print—provided you saved the document after changing them).

To start fresh with all *new* print settings, press and hold down the space bar when choosing File→Print; this can help you troubleshoot printing weirdness. (The print settings in your operating system aren't affected by the print settings you choose in Photoshop.)

---

4. **Click the Print Settings button at the top of the dialog box.**

   Most folks miss this critical step. The dialog box that opens when you click this button belongs to your *printer*, not Photoshop, so the settings you see might be slightly different than what's described in steps 5 and 6 (which were written using an Epson model). In other words, you may have to hunt around a bit to find settings similar to the ones discussed here.

5. **In your printer's dialog box, from the Paper Size menu, choose your paper's dimensions.**

   If you're printing borderless, be sure to choose a borderless version of the paper dimension you picked (see *Figure 16-6*, bottom). If you *don't* pick an option that includes the word "borderless," your image will print with a pesky white border around it. (If you don't see an option that includes "borderless," that means your printer can't create borderless prints).

TIP If your printer driver isn't the latest version, it may have trouble communicating with Photoshop and you may not be able to print to the edges of the paper or change paper size. Trot on over to the manufacturer's website to make sure you have the current driver, and then you should be good to go.

---

6. **In your printer's dialog box, choose Print Settings (circled in *Figure 16-7*).**

   The wording of your printer's dialog box may vary slightly, or you may not have this option at all. Instead, you may see some or all of the following settings:

   • **Media Type**. Choose the paper you're printing on, like Ultra Premium Photo Paper Luster.

   • **Print Mode**. Your printer controls this menu, which chooses the appropriate mode for the Media Type you picked, so you don't need to adjust this setting.

- **Color Mode**. This setting is controlled by the Color Management section of Photoshop's Print dialog box. If you choose Photoshop Manages Colors (see step 8), this setting is turned off. That said, it's important to make *sure* it's turned off so your printer doesn't try to adjust the document's color, too.

- **Output Resolution**. You can think of this as a quality setting. Your printer automatically adjusts this setting based on the Media Type you chose earlier so, once again, you don't need to change this setting.

- **High Speed**. This option lets your printer's *print head* (the bit that applies the ink to the paper) print while it's moving in *both* directions instead of just one. If you turn it off, your image will print more slowly, but it might look a little better. (If you like, fire off a couple of test prints—one with this setting turned on and one with it off—and then look closely to see if you can spot any differences.)

FIGURE 16-7

Your printer's dialog box may look a little different from this one depending on your operating system and printer manufacturer, but you should be able to find similar settings lurking somewhere.

7. **Click Save (or OK, or the equivalent button) to close your printer's dialog box and return to the Photoshop Print Settings dialog box.**

   Back in Photoshop's dialog box, check the paper's orientation to make sure it's what you want; you can select portrait or landscape by clicking the Layout buttons (see *Figure 16-6*, top). Also, in the preview area on the left side of the dialog box, make sure your image fills the whole thing. If you wisely cropped the image to your exact print dimensions, it should fill the preview area perfectly.

8. **In the Color Management section's Color Handling menu (see *Figure 16-8*), choose Photoshop Manages Colors.**

   Color management is the process of making the colors produced by the devices you work with—your digital camera, monitor, and printer—match as closely as possible by referencing specific color profiles. This menu controls whether Photoshop or your printer driver converts the image's colors from RGB to the printer's colors. For the brightest and most vibrant colors, choose Printer Manages Color and then skip to step 10. For more *accurate* results, choose Photoshop Manages Colors. It's certainly worth experimenting with both options, though you'll likely find that letting Photoshop manage colors will give you higher quality and more consistent results *if* you're using paper-specific profiles.

   When you choose Photoshop Manages Colors, the program displays a warning that reads, "Remember to disable the printer's color management in the print settings dialog box." Most printers are configured to apply *some* kind of color management to your image, which can conflict with the color management you're trying to apply through Photoshop (usually with unsavory results).

   TIP To learn more about color management, check out Eddie Tapp's super affordable online video workshop at *www.lesa.in/eddietappcm*.

9. **From the Printer Profile menu in the Color Management section, choose the option that matches the paper and print settings you're using.**

   Click the Printer Profile menu and scroll through the long list of profiles (which gets longer each time you install new profiles) to find the appropriate one. For example, if you're using an Epson SPR3000 printer, look under E or S, and then pick the profile that matches your paper, such as Epson SPR3000 Premium Glossy.

   NOTE If you're letting Photoshop manage color (see step 8), Photoshop communicates with your printer and picks the best printer profile *all by itself*. It does this by reading the printer's JobOptimalDestinationColorProfile tag (don't ask). But don't jump for joy just yet: As of this writing, hardly any printer manufacturers included this info, though boy howdy it'll be cool when they do! (And at that point, you'll be able to skip step 9 entirely.)

10. **In the Rendering Intent menu, choose Perceptual and then make sure the Black Point Compensation checkbox is turned on.**

These options help maintain the color relationships in your image, and preserve contrast by making sure that the black shadows in your original RGB image are also black in the final print.

11. **In the "Position and Size" section, make sure the Center checkbox is turned on (see** *Figure 16-8*, **top).**

If you *didn't* crop your image before starting this process, this setting will make your image print from the center outward—as much of it as will fit on the paper size you picked—instead of aligning the upper-left corner of the image with the upper-left corner of the paper.

FIGURE 16-8

Top: The Color Management and "Position and Size" sections of the Photoshop Print Settings dialog box let you determine who controls your document's color conversion and how it prints on the page (respectively).

Bottom: Fans of the old "Print to Selection" option that was nixed in CS5 will be glad to see it's back at the bottom of the "Position and Size" section, though now it's called Print Selected Area. This option is helpful for printing (and thus proofing) a small portion of an image.

If you forget to make a selection before opening this dialog box, simply turn on the Print Selected Area checkbox and then use the gray triangles shown here to mark the area you want to print. You can drag each triangle individually; Option-drag (Alt-drag) to move two at a time; or ⌘-drag (Ctrl-drag) to move 'em all at once. As you drag, Photoshop helpfully displays height and width info (use the Units menu to the right of this checkbox to switch to pixels, inches, or whatever).

12. **In the Scaled Print Size area, make sure the Scale option is set to 100%.**

You can use this setting, along with the Position setting mentioned in the previous step, to control which part of your image prints if you didn't crop it first. However, just because you *can* scale (resize) an image while it's being printed doesn't mean you *should*. Besides preventing you from sharpening the image after you make it smaller, scaling it via the Print dialog box makes it take longer to print (and Photoshop doesn't perform any image resampling [see page 235 for more on resampling]). If you don't care about such things, you can turn on "Scale to Fit Media" and Photoshop adjusts the Scale, Height, and Width settings in this section to make the image fit the paper size you picked earlier.

> **TIP** You can drag within the preview area of the Photoshop Print Settings dialog box to scale and position your image on the page (though the "Scale to Fit Media" checkbox has to be turned *off* for this to work). Your cursor turns into a four-sided arrow when you mouse over the preview, and Photoshop displays height and width info as you drag: Just drag the corners or edges of the image to resize it. Just keep in mind that these adjustments cancel out any changes you've made in the "Position and Size" section.

13. **If you're using paper that's bigger than your image, take a peek at the options in the Printing Marks and Functions sections.**

These sections let you turn on different kinds of marks that can help you trim the image once it's printed, as well as control background and border colors (handy for making your print look like it has a matte behind it).

In the Printing Marks section, turn on Corner Crop Marks to make Photoshop place a small horizontal and vertical line just outside of each corner of the image. If you plan to fold the image in half (say, if you're creating a greeting card), turn on Center Crop Marks. Professional printers use registration marks for printing separations (page 706), but you can leave 'em turned off. The Description option instructs Photoshop to print the info you've entered into the Description field of the File Info dialog box (page 729) below the image, though you can also use the Edit button to its right to add a description here. The Labels option prints the document's name above the image.

The Functions section lets professional print shops—like those that use offset presses, discussed in the next section—do things like flip the image on the film (Emulsion Down) and reverse its colors (Negative); this film is then used to make plates for the printing press. Professional printing aside, you can click the Background button to summon the Color Picker and Photoshop prints the color of your choice around the outside of the image like a matte. Use the Border button to add an outline around the image. The Bleed button lets you tell Photoshop how far to move the corner crop marks *into* your image so there's a little sliver of the image hanging outside the trim lines. (That way you don't end up with a white strip around the edge of the image if your trim job isn't perfect.)

14. **If you picked Photoshop Manages Colors in step 8, take a peek below the preview area and make sure the Match Print Colors and Show Paper White settings are turned on so you can view an onscreen proof (also called a *soft proof*).**

    Photoshop displays a simulation of what your printed image will look like (see page 707 for more on proofing). Adobe improved Photoshop's soft-proofing accuracy back in CS4, so the preview should give you a good sense of what the print will look like—assuming you've calibrated your monitor (page 675), of course.

15. **Turn on the Gamut Warning checkbox to make Photoshop highlight any out-of-gamut pixels in gray.**

    You can ask Photoshop to show you a proof of any colors in the image that are *out of gamut* (meaning unprintable) for the printer and paper you've picked. When using an expanded-gamut printer, you'll encounter far fewer out-of-gamut colors than you would with a standard CMYK printing press. If the gray areas aren't important parts of your image, then don't worry about this warning (though the printed color in those spots won't match the color you see onscreen). If the gray areas *are* important, use the techniques discussed in Chapter 9 to adjust the image's colors, which usually means desaturating those spots slightly. Alternatively, try printing on different paper or, if possible, using a different printer.

16. **Glance over your choices in the Photoshop Print Settings dialog box one last time and, if they look OK, click the Print button.**

    After *all* that hard work, you see the fruit of your labors in the form of a gloriously accurate, high-quality print. Yippee!

TIP   You can save time by recording your print settings in an *action* (see Chapter 18). Bear in mind, though, that the program will memorize *everything* in the Photoshop Print Settings dialog box, including print size and positioning. So if you typically print both landscape and portrait images, you need to record two actions, one for each orientation. Then you can use Photoshop CC's new conditional actions to make the program pick the right action for the image all by itself. See page 768 for more info!

■ Printing on a Commercial Offset Press

If you prepare artwork for stuff that's printed using a commercial offset printing press (magazines, product packaging, newspapers, and so on), you've got *loads* more to worry about than if you're sending an image to an inkjet printer. Unlike printing to an inkjet printer, where your images get converted from RGB to CMYK during the printing process, a commercial offset press usually requires you to convert the image to CMYK *before* it's printed. This section explains the very specific steps you need to follow to preserve an image's color when you convert it to CMYK. But before you dive too deeply into color-mode conversion, you need to understand a bit more about how offset presses work.

Commercial offset presses are huge, noisy, ink-filled metal beasts. An inkjet printer sprays ink from a print head directly onto a page, whereas an offset press transfers, or *offsets*, ink from an image on a plate onto a rubber blanket and *then* onto a page. As you learned back in Chapter 5, offset presses split an image's four CMYK channels into individual color separations, which are loaded onto big cylinders aligned so that all four colors are printed, one on top of another, to form the final image. If these cylinders aren't aligned properly, you'll see faint traces of one or more colors peeking outside the edges of the image, making it look blurry (this blurriness is called being "out of registration").

Instead of the dyes used by inkjet printers, commercial offset presses use two types of ink: *process* and *spot*. Process inks include cyan, magenta, yellow, and black (CMYK), and they're printed as overlapping patterns of halftone dots (*Figure 16-9*, left) that can economically reproduce the wide range of colors found in *continuous-tone images* like photos (*Figure 16-9*, right).

FIGURE 16-9

Left: If you look closely at an image printed on a press, you can see the dots it's made from. (The next time you pick up a magazine or newspaper, stick it right up to your nose and you'll see 'em.) To keep the dots from printing on top of each other, they're printed at specific angles according to ink color.

Right: Images that contain a wide range of smooth colors are called continuous-tone images, like this beautiful photo by iStockphoto/Arild Heitmann.

Spot inks, on the other hand, are used to match very *specific* color requirements (like a color in a corporate logo, such as the official UPS brown), and they're printed using *additional* plates on the press. More spot colors mean more plates and therefore more separations, which translates into higher printing costs. Since it's easy to get hit with unexpected costs when you're sending out a print job, make *darn* sure you know exactly how many colors it'll take to print the image (most print jobs involving color photos use only the four process colors). You'll learn all about spot colors later in this chapter.

Finally, unlike sending an image straight from Photoshop to your inkjet printer, you'll *rarely* (if ever) send a single image to an offset press. Instead, you'll send the image over to a page-layout program like InDesign or QuarkXPress and put it in a document that contains other images, along with text (referred to as *copy*), and *that's* what you send to the printing company. So you need to make sure the image has the right print dimensions and resolution, and that it's in the right color mode *before* you place it in InDesign. The following pages explain how to do that as painlessly as possible.

Converting RGB Images to CMYK Using Built-In Profiles

First and foremost, you need to know who's handling the conversion from RGB to CMYK mode. Historically, printing companies have requested (or required!) you to convert images yourself, but this is *slowly* changing, particularly with the increased use of digital presses.

If you have no idea whether you're supposed to convert the RGB image to CMYK yourself or if you want to know whether the printing company has a custom profile you can use for the conversion, *pick up the phone*. Communication is crucial in situations like this, because if your print job hits the press at 2:00 a.m., it'll be *your* phone that rings if there's a problem. This is definitely a call you're better off making than receiving.

If you have to convert the image yourself, it's important to choose the proper printer and paper profiles. You can do that in a couple of ways, but the following steps will lead you down a simple and foolproof path:

1. **Open your RGB image and duplicate it.**

   Choose Image→Duplicate to create a copy of the image to *guarantee* that you won't accidentally save over your original.

2. **Name the new file and save it as a TIFF file.**

   Choose File→Save or press ⌘-S (Ctrl+S) and then give it a name. (It's a good idea to include the file's color mode in the name so you can see at a glance which mode it's in.) Choose TIFF from the format drop-down menu at the bottom of the Save dialog box and then click Save. In the TIFF Options dialog box that appears, choose None in the Image Compression section and leave the Pixel Order section set to Interleaved. In the Byte Order section, turn on the IBM PC radio button. Leave the "Discard Layers and Save a Copy" option turned on (it's grayed out if your image has just one layer), and then click OK.

3. **Choose Edit→"Convert to Profile."**

In the Conversion Options section of the dialog box that appears (see *Figure 16-10*), set the Engine menu to Adobe (ACE) and the Intent menu to Perceptual. Also, make sure Use Black Point Compensation is turned on.

4. **From the Profile menu (*Figure 16-10*), choose a profile that reflects the type of ink, press, and paper your printing company will use to print the image.**

You can think of this menu as a printer profile menu. If you can't find a custom profile (see the next section), hunt for the best match for your current print job. If the image is being printed in North America on a sheetfed printing press using coated paper stock, for example, you can pick the tried-and-true "U.S. Sheetfed Coated v2" profile. A newer commercial sheetfed profile that also might work is "Coated GRACoL 2006." But instead of guessing, *ask* your printing company what profile to use.

FIGURE 16-10

Don't panic when you open the Profile menu. These super funky names are simply the various color profiles you can use to convert RGB to CMYK.

As you learned at the beginning of this chapter, there are a bazillion printers, papers, and colorants (inks, dyes, toners) out there, so this long list merely reflects that diversity.

5. **Click OK to complete the color-conversion process, and then save the image.**

Press ⌘-S (Ctrl-S) to save the image in the new color mode.

After you save the new CMYK image, you're ready to place it in a page-layout document.

Custom RGB to CMYK Profile Conversions

If your printing company has painstakingly created its own custom color profile, you're much better off using it than one of Photoshop's built-in options. The process is similar to the one just described, but you need to *install* the custom profile (as explained on page 675) before you can use it. Once you've downloaded it, follow these steps to put it into play:

1. **Find where color profiles are stored on your hard drive.**

   Figuring out where to store the profile is the biggest challenge, since different operating systems *and* different versions of Photoshop store profiles in different places:

   - **On a Mac,** color profiles live in *Macintosh HD/Library/Application Support/Adobe/Color/Profiles*.

   - **On a PC running Windows,** simply right-click the ICC profile, and then choose Install Profile from the resulting shortcut menu. That said, profiles are stored in *C:\Windows\System32\Spool\Drivers\Color*. (If for some reason you don't see the Windows folder, you'll need to turn on hidden folders by going to Control Panel→"Appearance and Personalization"→Folder Options; in the dialog box that appears, click the View tab and then turn on the "Show hidden files, folders, and drives" radio button, and then click OK.)

   If you have trouble finding the right folder or just want to double-check that you've found the right spot, call your printing company and ask them where to store profiles on your particular operating system.

   NOTE If your computer uses Windows, you can use the Color Management Control Panel to add and remove profiles. Go to Start→Control Panel→Color Management.

2. **Copy the custom profile to the Profiles folder (the Color folder on a PC).**

   Printing companies that have embraced color management have CMYK color profiles for a *variety* of paper stocks, so be sure you load the one for the paper you're printing on by dragging the file into the folder.

3. **Open your image, duplicate it, and then save it as a TIFF file.**

   To duplicate the image, choose Image→Duplicate, and then choose File→Save or press ⌘-S (Ctrl+S) and give the copy a name. Pick TIFF from the format drop-down menu at the bottom of the Save dialog box and then click Save. In the TIFF Options dialog box that appears, choose None in the Image Compression section and leave the Pixel Order section set to Interleaved. In the Byte Order section, turn on the IBM PC radio button. Leave the "Discard Layers and Save a Copy" option turned on, and then click OK.

4. **Choose Edit→"Convert to Profile" and, in the resulting dialog box, choose the new profile from the Profile menu.**

   If you don't see the right profile in the list, try restarting Photoshop. Press ⌘-Q (Ctrl+Q) to quit, and then double-click the image file to relaunch the program.

5. **Change the file's Conversion Options settings, if necessary.**

Ask the printing company if you need to adjust any settings in the Conversion Options section of the "Convert to Profile" dialog box (Edit→"Convert to Profile").

6. **Click OK and then press ⌘-S (Ctrl+S) to save the image.**

You've just completed your first custom CMYK conversion!

Using Spot Color

As mentioned earlier, commercial printing presses sometimes use special premixed, custom inks called *spot colors*. If you're a graphic designer working in *prepress* (the department that preps files for printing), the info that lies ahead is really important. If you're a photographer or Web designer, save your brainpower and skip this section. Really.

Photoshop wizard Ben Willmore (*www.DigitalMastery.com*) has come up with a great analogy to explain spot colors. Remember the box of crayons you used as a kid? A small box had eight basic colors, like blue, orange, and yellow. And then there was the big box of 64—with a sharpener on the back!—that had special colors like cornflower, melon, and thistle. No matter how hard you tried, you couldn't reproduce those special colors with a box of eight crayons. In Photoshop, you can think of the box of eight crayons as CMYK color mode and those special colors as spot colors.

> **NOTE** The most popular brand of spot-color ink is Pantone (*www.pantone.com*). You'll also hear Pantone colors called *PMS* colors, which stands for "Pantone Matching System."

Because of the impurity and variety of CMYK inks, they can't produce all the colors you see in RGB mode (just like you can't reproduce, say, cornflower with those original eight crayons). If you're tooling around in the Color Picker and choose a color that *can't* be produced in CMYK, Photoshop places a little gray triangle next to it (see *Figure 16-11*). This triangle is known as an *out-of-gamut warning* (gamut, as you learned earlier, means the full range of colors possible within a color mode or workspace). If you click the triangle (or the tiny color swatch below it), Photoshop changes that color to the closest possible match that *can* be printed with CMYK inks.

In some cases, the closest color match is good enough, but spot-color ink comes in handy in certain situations, like when you need:

- **To reduce printing costs.** As you learned earlier, the more colors you use, the more cylinders and separations the printer needs and the more the job will cost. But if you print an image using black and just one or two spot colors, you can actually *reduce* printing costs because you'll use only two or three separations instead of four. This technique is common with line art (illustrations or outline drawings like those in a coloring book), though you can also use it for photos. (However, it's always best to discuss pricing with your printing company up front because CMYK printing can be cheaper than two-color printing in some situations.)

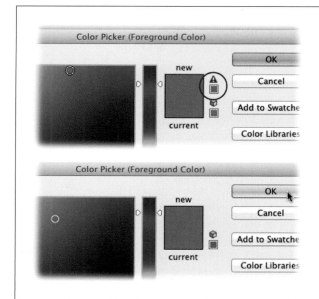

FIGURE 16-11

Top: If you pick a color that can't be produced with CMYK inks, a little warning triangle appears next to the color swatch. Click the triangle or the tiny square of color below it to make Photoshop pick the next best color.

Bottom: In most cases, you can't see much difference between the original color and the new one, but if you check your cursor's location in the color field, you can see that Photoshop has moved it slightly.

- **To ensure color accuracy**. If your paycheck depends on color accuracy, you *have* to use spot colors. For example, if UPS hires you to design a flyer for their company party, you need *your* version of brown to match their *official* brown. Unless you use a spot color (which is consistent because it's premixed), your brown will be printed using a mix of CMYK inks and may end up looking, say, maroon.

- **To use specialty inks**. To add a bit of pizzazz to a printed image, you can use specialty inks like metallics or a varnish that looks glossy when it's printed. You can also add a vibrant spot color to a particular area to make that part stand out. However, if you use specialty inks on a CMYK document, you're *adding* color separations to the job, which increases the cost.

Before you can use a spot color, you have to create a special channel for it called a *spot channel*. Each spot color you use needs its very own spot channel. (See Chapter 5 for more on channels.)

Let's say you're preparing the cover photo for the next issue of *Cutting Horse* magazine, and, to reduce printing costs, the magazine has decided to use a grayscale image with one spot color for visual interest. (That way, they're paying for two separations instead of four.) Your mission is to make the horse's bridle Pantone Red. No problemo! Just make a selection of the bridle and then create a spot channel for the special ink (see *Figure 16-12*).

NOTE To follow along, download the practice image *Bridle.jpg* from this book's Missing CD page at *www. missingmanuals.com/cds*.

Here's how to add a spot channel:

1. **Select the area you want to colorize and, if necessary, convert the image to grayscale.**

   If you're lucky enough to start with the full-color version of the photo, you can easily select the horse's bridle by using the Quick Selection tool. Then see page 307 for the scoop on converting a color image to black and white and page 314 for changing the image's color mode to Grayscale.

2. **From the Channels panel's menu, choose New Spot Channel (*Figure 16-12*, top).**

   You can also add a spot channel by ⌘-clicking (Ctrl-clicking on a PC) the New Channel icon at the bottom of the Channels panel. Either way, Photoshop opens a dialog box where you can name the new channel and pick its color.

FIGURE 16-12

Top: Once you've selected the area you need to colorize, add a new spot channel by choosing New Spot Channel from the Channels panel's menu (circled, top).

Bottom: Click the little color swatch (circled) in the New Spot Channel dialog box to open the Color Picker. There, click the Color Libraries button to see the oh-so-helpful list of Pantone presets shown here. Photoshop will automatically add the ink you choose here to your selection.

3. **In the New Spot Channel dialog box, click the color swatch to open the Color Picker, and then choose an ink color.**

To see a list of Pantone presets, click the Color Libraries button. In the Color Libraries dialog box (*Figure 16-12*, bottom), choose a color library from the Book menu. (For example, if you're preparing a photo for a magazine that prints on glossy paper, pick "PANTONE solid coated"; if you don't know which one to choose, ask your print shop.)

Next, pick a spot color. If you know the number or name of the ink you want (like *150* or *red*), type the number or name and Photoshop will flip to that color in the list. You can also drag the triangles along the vertical scroll bar to find the one you want, or use the arrow keys to move through the list of ink swatches. When you find the right color, click its swatch to choose it, and then click OK to close the Color Libraries dialog box.

> **NOTE** By picking a color from the Color Library, you don't have to worry about naming your new spot channel—Photoshop names it automatically.

4. **Back in the New Spot Channel dialog box, leave Solidity set to 0% and click OK to close the dialog box.**

You can think of solidity as ink opacity, though it affects only the onscreen image and not the printed version. Depending on the image you're working with, increasing the ink's opacity so it appears solid and not see-through may be helpful (it's a personal preference).

When you click OK, you'll see a new spot channel appear in the Channels panel (see *Figure 16-13*).

FIGURE 16-13

Here's the final cover shot for your magazine. As you can see, there are just two channels in the Channels panel (and thus this image can be printed with just two separations).

If you send this grayscale Photoshop document straight to InDesign, that program adds a color swatch for the spot color and makes sure that the new color prints on top of the black ink (a technique called overprinting*).*

■ EDITING SPOT CHANNELS

Once you've created a spot channel, you can change its ink color by double-clicking it in the Channels panel. You can also add or remove color from the spot channel by painting with the Brush tool, or by using any selection tool and filling the selection with color as described on page 181.

Since Photoshop shows channel information in grayscale, you can edit a spot channel just like a layer mask (page 114)—by painting with black, white, or shades of gray:

- **To add color at 100 percent opacity**, grab the Brush tool by pressing B and set your foreground color chip to black. Then mouse over to the image and paint where you want to add color.

- **To remove color at 100 percent opacity**, set your foreground color chip to white before you paint.

- **To add or remove color at any other opacity**, set your foreground color chip to a shade of gray before you paint.

■ SAVING A DOCUMENT WITH SPOT CHANNELS

To keep spot channels intact, you need to save the document in a format that understands them: DCS, PSD, or PDF. So which one do you pick? It depends on what you're going to do with the file.

If you're the hired Photoshop gun and you'll be handing the file off to someone else for further fluffing, save it as a PSD file, get your motor runnin', and head out on the highway (insert guitar riff here). If you're importing the image into InDesign or QuarkXPress 6.5 or later, you'll also want to save it as a PSD file.

If you're using the image in QuarkXPress 6 or earlier, you need to save it as a DCS 2.0 or a PDF file (see page 702). DCS (short for Desktop Color Separation) is a special format that pre-separates the image's color channels into plates for a printing press. To save a document as a DCS file, make sure it's in either Grayscale or CMYK color mode, and then choose File→Save As and pick Photoshop DCS 2.0 from the format drop-down menu. When you click Save, you'll see the DCS 2.0 Format dialog box (*Figure 16-14*) where you can fine-tune the following settings:

- **Preview**. This menu controls which kind of image preview you see in QuarkX-Press. Your choices include "TIFF (1 bit/pixel)" and "TIFF (8 bits/pixel)." Choose the latter if you want a nice, 256-color preview. If you don't need to see the image preview in QuarkXPress (because, say, you're building a catalog with hundreds of images and that many previews would slow down your vintage computer), choose None. (The box on page 36 explains what "8 bits" means.)

- **DCS**. Leave this menu set to "Single File DCS, No Composite" so Photoshop doesn't generate all kinds of files that only the printing press peeps know what to do with.

- **Encoding**. This menu controls how Photoshop *encodes* (represents and stores) the print information in the file. If you're on a Mac, choose Binary. If you're on a Windows computer, choose ASCII or (for a more compact file) ASCII85.

FIGURE 16-14

DCS 2.0 is one of three formats you can use to save spot channels intact. While most page-layout programs can read DCS files, you'll find that using a PDF is easier, as discussed below.

> **NOTE** *ASCII* stands for "American Standard Code for Information Interchange." ASCII was developed as a way to convert binary (computer) information into text, and ASCII85 is the newest version. (This stuff is *great* bar-bet trivia.)

Leave the checkboxes at the bottom of the dialog box (Include Halftone Screen, Include Transfer Function, Include Vector Data, and Image Interpolation) turned off and then click OK. You're now ready to import the DCS file into QuarkXPress 6 or earlier. Party on!

■ SAVING SPOT COLORS IN PDF FORMAT

DCS 2.0 has long been the standard format for saving documents with spot colors, but PDF format yields a smaller and more flexible file. To see for yourself, follow these steps:

1. **Open an image that contains a spot color and then choose File→Save As.**

2. **In the Save As dialog box, pick Photoshop PDF from the format drop-down menu.**

   If your document has layers, turn off the Layers checkbox to flatten the image.

3. **Turn on the Spot Colors checkbox.**

   This step ensures that Photoshop includes your spot colors in the PDF, along with process colors (CMYK).

4. **Rename the image to indicate that it harbors a spot color and then save it.**

   For example, call it "Autumn Art_CMYK_Spot" and then click Save. Photoshop warns you that the PDF settings you're about to make cancel out the settings in the Save As dialog box. Simply click OK and Photoshop opens the Save Adobe PDF dialog box.

5. **At the top of the Save Adobe PDF dialog box (shown back in *Figure 16-4*), choose Acrobat 5 (PDF 1.4) from the Compatibility menu.**

   This setting lets you specify the PDF version. As of this writing, version 1.4 is the safest and most widely accepted choice.

6. **Click Compression on the left side of the dialog box and adjust the settings so your images don't get compressed.**

   From the first drop-down menu in the Options section, choose Do Not Downsample. Then, from the Compression menu, pick None.

7. **Click Output on the left side of the dialog box and then make sure the Color Conversion menu is set to No Conversion.**

8. **Click Save PDF.**

That's it. You're now free to send the PDF file to the page-layout program of your choice.

If you save the settings you entered as a preset (see page 684), this method is much faster than saving a file in DCS 2.0 format. However, be sure to ask your printing company if it accepts PDFs with spot colors. Although almost everyone can take PDFs these days (and most places prefer them), some companies using older equipment may not, so be sure to ask—change is hard, you know!

Printing Duotone (Multitonal) Images

One advantage of using a commercial printer is that you can print duotones and other multitonal images by adding *additional* ink to grayscale images (see the box on page 707). You can add Pantone inks, additional gray inks, or even process inks—great news if you want to add an overall color tint to a grayscale image, add some tonal depth and richness, or both. These techniques let you create some amazingly beautiful effects, as discussed back in Chapter 8. However, it's really easy to add *too* much ink, which can make the image way too dark once it's printed. If that happens, you lose details in the shadows and the image's contrast goes down the tubes.

TIP   Photoshop includes a set of 38 gradient presets called *Photographic Toning*. When you use them with a Gradient Map Adjustment layer, you get the look of a multitonal image *without* having to use Duotone mode. See page 313 for more info.

To produce a truly amazing duotone or multitone image, you need to start with a good quality grayscale image—one that has high contrast and isn't overly dark. Once you've settled on an image and converted it to black and white (Chapter 8) and then switched it to Grayscale mode (page 314), follow these steps:

1. **Duplicate the image.**

   Choose Image→Duplicate and then give the copy a name. Consider incorporating the word "duotone" into the name, as in "Cowgirl_Duotone."

2. **Choose Image→Mode→Duotone.**

   If this option is grayed out, you're not in Grayscale mode. In that case, choose Grayscale mode first and *then* switch to Duotone mode. When the Duotone Options dialog box opens, it shows that the image is a monotone made from nothing but black ink.

3. **Click the Curve icon to the left of the black ink (see *Figure 16-15*).**

   Clicking this icon opens the Duotone Curve dialog box, where you can peek at how the ink will be applied in your image. For this particular ink, you have a straight 45-degree curve from the highlight to shadow areas, and it's being applied at 100 percent. Click OK to close the Duotone Curve dialog box.

4. **In the Duotone Options dialog box, choose Duotone from the Type menu.**

   This menu gives you a choice of various kinds of multitonal images. When you choose Duotone, Photoshop activates two inks in the dialog box (choosing Tritone activate three inks, and so on). However—and this is key—*both* inks have straight, 45-degree highlight-to-shadow curve lines, which means they print with the same amount of ink in the same color range. That's *not* good! Why? Because if you were to click the Ink 2 color swatch and choose a new color, you'd add too much of that ink for the image to print decently unless you edited the Duotone Curve, which is tricky to do. So instead, use one of the many presets as described in the next step.

5. **Click the Preset menu and choose one of the gazillion Duotone presets.**

   Feel free to experiment with the wide variety of choices in the Preset menu. Some items, like the true duotones, come in anywhere from one to four variations, which represent substitutions for the second ink ranging from stronger to weaker. (In other words, presets with a *1* in their names add the most color, and those with a *4* in their names add the least.) These are excellent starting points for your creations. There's nothing wrong with tweaking the Duotone Curves to fine-tune your results (see *Figure 16-16*), but you'll want to print some tests to make sure you're not adding too much ink.

   Testing duotones is tough because you *can't* proof them unless they're made from process colors (in which case they're really quadtones). If you pick a preset with inks not available on your printer, you won't get an accurate proof. The best you can do is contact your printing company and see if they'll print you a test on the paper they'll use for the final image. (If you don't need the proof right away, they may be able to hold onto it and slide it in with another job that uses a similar ink-and-paper combo.)

FIGURE 16-15

Duotone Curves are just like the Curves you learned about back in Chapter 9, except that here they let you know how much ink will be applied to the image's shadows, midtones, and highlights.

The percentages (circled) tell you how much ink is being added.

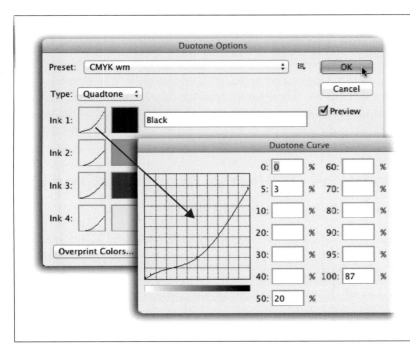

FIGURE 16-16

Once you pick a preset, take a peek at the individual curves for each ink color.

Notice how the curves shown here are all slightly reduced to make room for one another.

6. Save the document in EPS or PDF format.

Here's yet another opportunity to chat with your printing company! Give 'em a ring and ask whether they prefer EPS or PDF format for duotones or multitones. If they say EPS, ask them which settings to use. Then choose File→Save As and pick Photoshop EPS from the format drop-down menu. In the EPS Options dialog box (*Figure 16-17*, bottom), choose an 8-bit option from the Preview menu and pick Binary from the Encoding menu. Unless your printing company told you otherwise, leave the rest of the options turned off and then click OK.

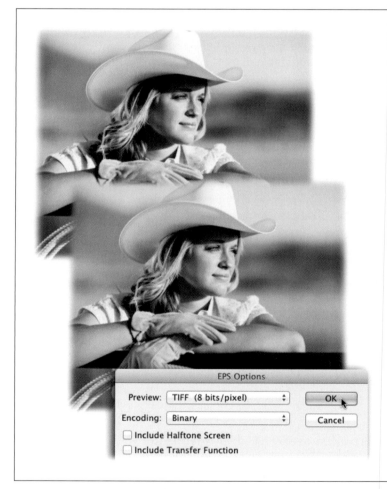

FIGURE 16-17

If you're working with a CMYK image and want to add a warm tone to it (like the one shown here, middle), try switching the document's color mode to Duotone. Then, in the Duotone Options dialog box, choose Quadtone from the Type menu and "CMYK wm" from the Preset menu.

As you can see, the difference between a grayscale image (top) and the quadtone preset "CMYK wm" (middle) can be impressive.

To save a duotone as a PDF file instead, you can use the same settings you used to save a spot-color image in the previous section (page 702).

Photo by iStockphoto/Andrew Rich.

Printing Color Separations

To avoid running into unexpected printing costs, it's a good idea to print separations (called *seps* around the water cooler) before sending your image to a print shop. That way, you can make sure an extra color hasn't snuck its way into the document—especially if you've toyed with some spot colors that you're not going to use.

However, you probably won't use Photoshop to print separations—in most cases, you'll place an RGB or CMYK image in a page-layout program along with text and other images, and then use *that* program to print the separations. But if you ever *do* need to print separations from Photoshop, visit this book's Missing CD page at *www.missingmanuals.com/cds* for step-by-step instructions.

Proofing Images Onscreen

When you're sending images out for printing, it'd be nice to peek into the future and see what they'll look like. Happily, Photoshop can create an onscreen proof simulation known as a *soft proof*, a straightforward process that involves the color profiles you learned about in the previous sections. Here's what you do:

1. **Calibrate your monitor using the tools described earlier (page 675).**

   If your monitor isn't calibrated, soft-proofing is a *galactic* waste of time.

2. **Open an RGB image you intend to print.**

   You can soft-proof either RGB or CMYK images, but it's especially cool to proof an RGB image and see what it will print like in CMYK without having to color-convert it first.

3. **Choose Window→Arrange→"New Window for [name of image file]" to open a second window containing a copy of your image.**

   Then position the two windows so they're side by side by choosing Window→ Arrange→2-up Vertical.

UP TO SPEED

Duotones Explained

The term *duotone* generally refers to a grayscale image that has had additional inks added to it. Technically, if you add one ink, it's a duotone; adding two inks make it a tritone; and adding three inks make it a quadtone. The correct *general* term that describes all these variations is "multitonal images." But most folks use the term "duotone" to describe all these alternatives, which can get confusing.

So why add other inks to grayscale images to begin with? A couple of reasons: Some folks use duotones to add color to an image inexpensively (as you learned earlier, reducing the number of colors in an image can mean a cheaper print job). However, duotone (or multitone) aficionados will tell you the additional inks add tonal range and depth to an image—and they're right! In fact, you can even add a second gray ink to enhance tonality without adding any color at all.

The two keys to creating quality duotones are:

- Start with a high-quality grayscale image with a good tonal range and lots of contrast. (See Chapter 8 for more black-and-white conversion methods than you can shake a stick at.)

- Substitute the second ink for part of the original black ink, rather than just adding it to the black (see page 703). This prevents the image from becoming too dark and flat because it's drowning in ink.

With a bit of practice, you'll gain confidence in creating duotones and enjoy doing it. However, it's always a good idea to plan extra time in your production schedule to print some tests. Since you can't trust your monitor or proof non-process duotones (see page 704), a test print is worth its weight in gold.

---

4. **Click the right-hand window to activate it and then choose View→Proof Setup→Custom.**

5. **In the resulting Customize Proof Condition dialog box, make sure the Preview checkbox is turned on (*Figure 16-18*, top).**

FIGURE 16-18

Top: Soft-proofing isn't 100 percent accurate, but it's better than nothing and you'll almost always find it useful. It's also a good way to help control your client's expectations, especially when the client is printing on cheap, low-quality paper.

Bottom: Notice that the image on the right is ever so slightly less saturated and has lower overall contrast than the original on the left. You can try choosing different printer profiles and see how they affect your soft-proofing results.

6. **From the "Device to Simulate" menu, choose the profile for your final printer.**

   If the image is headed to a printing press, for example, pick your old profile friend, U.S. Sheetfed Coated v2.

7. **Choose Perceptual from the Rendering Intent menu, and make sure the Black Point Compensation checkbox is turned on.**

   The Perceptual option takes into account how humans see color. The Black Point Compensation option helps preserve the contrast of your original.

8. **In the Display Options (On-Screen) section, turn on the Simulate Paper Color checkbox.**

You can watch your onscreen proof change if you turn this option on and off.

9. **Click OK and then sit back and examine the differences between the two windows.**

You can perform soft-proofing for other printers, too, like your inkjet printer or a digital press. All you need to achieve good results is a calibrated monitor, an accurate printer, and a paper-specific profile.

Printing Proofs

If you're working in a prepress environment—and especially if you're *not* printing on a digital press—you're often proofing on a different printer than the one that will print the final document. For example, you might print a proof using an inkjet, but the final image will print on a commercial offset printing press. In that situation, you can make the proof printer print a *simulation* of what will happen on the printing press.

Simulating an image involves reining in the proof printer's large color gamut to include only the colors that the printing press can reproduce. You can prepare a simulation in Photoshop using profiles and the proofing feature you learned about in the previous section. Here's how:

1. **Pop open an image and then choose File→Print.**

2. **At the top of the Photoshop Print Settings dialog box, pick your proofing printer from the Printer menu.**

3. **In the Color Management section, choose Photoshop Manages Colors from the Color Handling menu.**

> **NOTE** If you leave the Color Handling menu set to Printer Manages Color—which you might do if your color-conversion tool is a special *RIP* (page 712) set up for proofing—then Photoshop has zero effect on your color; all the color conversion occurs at the RIP. In that case, you can't soft-proof your image using the Photoshop Print Settings dialog box as discussed here, but you *can* use the soft-proofing tools discussed in the previous section.

4. **Click the Print Settings button and make *sure* your printer's color management is turned off.**

In the resulting dialog box, pick your paper size and then verify that the printer's color settings are turned off (they should be) to keep the printer driver from interfering with the color-management voodoo you've got going on in Photoshop. See step 8 on page 689 for help finding this setting.

5. **Click Save or OK to return to the Photoshop Print Settings dialog box.**

6. **From the Printer Profile menu, choose the setting that matches the printer, paper, and quality you'll use to print the proof.**

7. **In the next drop-down menu down (it doesn't have a label), choose Hard Proofing.**

   This setting lets Photoshop know you intend to simulate a proof on one printer as if it were *another* printer (see *Figure 16-19*).

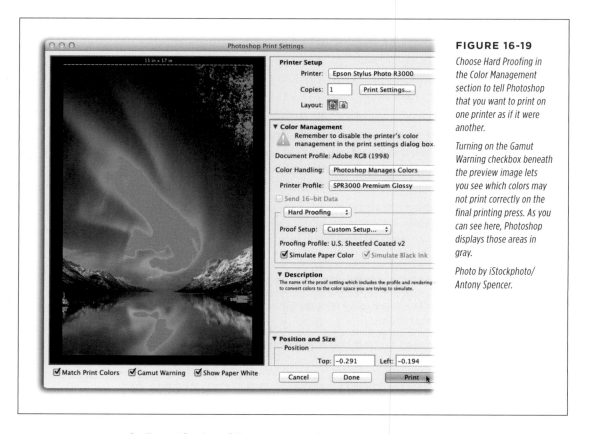

FIGURE 16-19

Choose Hard Proofing in the Color Management section to tell Photoshop that you want to print on one printer as if it were another.

Turning on the Gamut Warning checkbox beneath the preview image lets you see which colors may not print correctly on the final printing press. As you can see here, Photoshop displays those areas in gray.

Photo by iStockphoto/ Antony Spencer.

8. **From the Proof Setup menu, choose Custom Setup.**

   Straight from the factory, this menu is set to Working CMYK. By choosing Custom Setup, Photoshop opens the Customize Proof Condition dialog. Use the "Device to Simulate" menu to pick a profile that more closely matches your final output device, and then click OK.

9. **Back in Photoshop's Print dialog box, turn on Simulate Paper Color to get the best simulation.**

10. **Beneath the preview area on the left side of the dialog box, turn on all three checkboxes: Match Print Colors, Gamut Warning, and Show Paper White.**

    These options let you see an onscreen view of your image that indicates which, if any, colors might not print on the final printer because they're out of gamut (*Figure 16-19*). If the gray areas aren't important parts of the image, then don't worry about this warning (though the printed color in those spots won't match the color you see onscreen). If the gray areas *are* important, use the techniques described in Chapter 9 to adjust the image's colors (you'll likely want to desaturate those spots slightly).

For the fun of it, test the Gamut Warning results using both coated and uncoated paper to see how the paper affects the printed image. To do that, change the profile that you picked from the "Device to Simulate" menu in step 8.

11. **Click Print and wait eagerly to see what your proof looks like.**

Isn't it amazing what you can do with color profiles? Quick, go tell everyone you know how cool this stuff is—and watch their eyes glaze over. (See the box on page 711 for info on printing proofs of spot channels.)

Printing on a Digital Press

It used to be the case (and sometimes still is) that, when you prepared a document for a commercial printer, you would convert the images to the CMYK color mode *before* you inserted them into a page-layout document and certainly before you fired them off to the printing company. However, that process is changing because an increasing number of print shops now use *digital presses*.

Most digital presses work just like laser printers or copiers; they use electrostatic charges to transfer images from cylinders to the print surface. Like commercial offset presses, digital presses are primarily CMYK printers, but they use powdered toners instead of inks (which is why they can't print spot colors). Some digital presses, like the Kodak NexPress, actually do offer toner spot-color printing, but they're limited to very specific colors like red, green, or blue. And rather than being used for special objects like logos, these additional spot colors typically expand the gamut of the CMYK toners, much like light cyan and light magenta do in inkjet printers.

Because of these quirks, you have to perform some special steps if your project is headed for a digital printer. The following sections explain how to prepare various types of images for a run on a digital press.

WORKAROUND WORKSHOP

Printing Spot-Channel Proofs

Since spot channels are used only by commercial printing presses, getting them to print on your *own* printer for proofing can be...exciting. The solution is to pop into RGB mode temporarily and merge the spot channels. Here's how:

To safeguard your original document, save it and then create a copy by choosing Image→Duplicate. Next, choose Image→Mode→RGB Color and then, in the Channels panel, Shift-click to activate each spot channel in the document. Then open the Channels panel's menu and choose Merge Spot

Channels. When Photoshop asks if it's OK to flatten the layers, click OK. Each spot channel is instantly swallowed up by the closest matching RGB equivalent.

At this point, you can fire the document off to your printer without a fuss. The colors won't be *exact*, but you'll get a decent approximation of what the image will look like when you finish editing it. After you print the temporary RGB document, you can toss it and continue editing the original.

Printing RGB Images on a Digital Press

Digital presses handle images much the same way that expanded-gamut inkjet printers do (page 685), so feel free to send 'em an RGB file. Because the RGB-to-CMYK-Plus conversion occurs at the printing press's processing *RIP* (see the box below), you're dealing with RGB images the whole time instead of converting them to CMYK. That's great news because, as you learned at the beginning of this (exhausting!) chapter, RGB mode provides you with the widest range of printable colors. So if your image is already in RGB mode, you're good to go.

Printing CMYK Images on a Digital Press

If your images are already in CMYK mode, it's OK to leave 'em that way. Most digital presses recognize CMYK values and print them well enough. That said, you might want to confirm with your printing company that the press will use your current CMYK values rather than converting the image to another color mode and then back to CMYK on the press. (This type of color-shuffling can lead to unpredictable—and usually terrible—results.) Also, keep in mind that CMYK images will be darker and more saturated if they're printed on a digital press than if they're printed on a conventional, ink-based printing press.

Printing Spot Colors on a Digital Press

Toner-based digital presses are becoming more common, so it's important to know which kind of digital press your document will end up on. If it's destined for one that uses gamut-expanding digital spot toners, leave it in RGB mode to take full advantage of the press's expanded color gamut.

Since most digital presses don't print conventional spot color inks, if you send a file that contains any spot colors to a digital printing company, those colors will get converted into CMYK or CMYK-Plus colors (depending on the toners the press uses) before they're printed. The printing press automatically performs this conversion using a built-in spot-to-process *color lookup table* (also called a *color LUT*). Just be sure to use the name provided by Photoshop when you created the spot channel. (For example, PANTONE 810 C is a proper color name, but "Logo spot color" is *not*.) That's because the printer's RIP needs to identify the spot color properly in order to produce the best simulation of it.

Meet the RIP

I thought RIP meant "rest in peace." What the heck does it have to do with printing?

Quite a lot, actually—and it has nothing to do with funerals.

The acronym RIP refers to a device known as a Raster Image Processor. It's a term you'll often hear tossed around at com-mercial printing companies (also called *service bureaus*). RIPs convert raster images, vectors, text, and transparency info in page-layout documents into print-ready formats for specific printers, image-setters, sign-cutters, and other output devices. You can think of RIPs as super sophisticated printer drivers.

TIP Back in Photoshop CS6, Adobe added Color Lookup Adjustment layers, which are useful when you want to add a creative color treatment to your image. The box on page 337 has the scoop on using 'em (there are a few new ones in Photoshop CC).

■ Printing Multiple Images

Sometimes it's handy to print multiple images at one time. For example, you can combine images into a single document that prints across several pages—so you don't have to wade through the Print Settings dialog box 10 times—or gather several images onto a *single* page for comparison and/or client approval. Photoshop used to include three handy features that let you quickly and easily organize, format, and print multiple images: PDF Presentation, Picture Package, and Contact Sheet. They were wildly useful and folks squawked when Adobe removed them in CS4. Happily, two of 'em made their way *back* into Photoshop: PDF Presentation and Contact Sheet II.

TIP No matter which option you choose—PDF Presentation or Contact Sheet II—you can simplify things by gathering the images you want to use into a single folder *first*. That way, you can choose that folder instead of rooting through your hard drive for files scattered here and there.

PDF Presentation

To create a multipage PDF that contains one image per page, or a PDF that advances automatically like a slideshow, choose File→Automate→PDF Presentation. In the resulting dialog box (*Figure 16-20*), pick the images you want to include (by clicking Browse), what color background you want 'em displayed on (white, black, or gray), and which tidbits of info you want printed with them (such as file name, description, and so on).

When you get your settings just right, click Save and you'll see the Save dialog box. Choose where you'd like to put the new PDF, name it, and then click Save. Up pops the Save Adobe PDF dialog box you saw back on page 683. Click Save PDF and Photoshop does all the heavy lifting of combining those images into a single PDF faster than you could *ever* do it yourself.

Contact Sheet II

The Contact Sheet II plug-in works in the exact same way as it did in older versions of Photoshop, so if you've used it before, it'll feel familiar. Contact Sheet II lets you choose multiple images and then have Photoshop shrink them to fit on a single page (and if they won't fit on one page, Photoshop adds more pages). This kind of thing is incredibly handy when you need to compare and evaluate images for use in a project, or send images to a client so *she* can pick the one she likes best.

FIGURE 16-20

Choosing Presentation in the Output Options section (instead of Multi-Page Document) turns your images into a self-running PDF slideshow.

The Presentation Options at the bottom of this honkin' big dialog box let you control how long each image stays onscreen, whether the slideshow starts again after it finishes, and what kind of transition you'd like between slides, if any (Fade is always a good choice).

To create a contact sheet, choose File→Automate→Contact Sheet II. In the Source Images section at the top of the resulting dialog box (*Figure 16-21*, top), click Choose and then locate the images you want to include (or pick Open Documents if you've already got 'em open). In the Document section, enter the paper size you want use (for example, to print on U.S. letter-size paper, enter 8.5 in the Width field and 11 in the Height field). Leave the Resolution set to 300 for a nice, high-quality print, and then use the Thumbnails section to tell Photoshop how many columns and rows you want (these settings determine the *size* of the thumbnails). If you want each image's file name to appear beneath its thumbnail, leave the checkbox below "Use Filename as Caption" turned on, and then choose a font and size for the file names from the drop-down menus to the right of the checkbox. Click OK and Photoshop creates a sheet of beautiful miniatures like the one in *Figure 16-21*, bottom.

FIGURE 16-21

Having trouble deciding which image of the northern lights your client will like the best? No problem, just create a contact sheet you can print and send to her.

In the Thumbnails section, enter lower numbers in the Columns and Rows fields if you want larger thumbnail images. If you think you'll use the same settings again later, save them as a preset by clicking the Save button in the upper right.

■ Recap: Stress-Free Printing Tips

Congratulations! You've just waded through a ton of dense information. Some of it you'll remember and some of it you won't, but, no matter what, it's here whenever you need it. To recap, here are some of the most important tips:

- **Communicate with your printing company**. Find out at the beginning of your project *exactly* which file format and settings the company wants. Knowing this info ahead of time can help keep your project from going past its deadline and over its budget.

- **Calibrate your monitor with an external calibration tool**. This is the only way to accurately view and proof images onscreen.

- **Resize images to the print dimensions before you print**. This ensures that the image will print at the size you want, with no unexpected cropping. Besides, physically smaller images print faster.

- **Make sure your image has enough resolution**. After resizing the image, check that its resolution is between 240 and 300 ppi so it will produce a high-quality print.

- **Sharpen the image if you've made it substantially smaller**. Any time you change the number of pixels in an image, it gets softened (blurred) just a bit. A final round of sharpening (see Chapter 11) can help you get some focus back.

- **Save editable PSD files**. Saving your Photoshop document in its native format lets you go back and edit its layers, alpha channels, and so on. When you're creating a version for printing (described in the next bullet), duplicate the file or use File→Save As to make a copy so you don't overwrite the original.

- **Create a flattened version for printing**. Though this step isn't essential, flattening layers and removing alpha channels makes documents less complex, resulting in a smaller files that print faster and more reliably.

- **Proof, convert, and print with printer- and paper-specific profiles**. Now that you've seen how powerful profiles can be, take the time to download and use them (or make your own). Using proper profiles lets you proof, change color modes, and print images with the most reliable, most predictable, and highest-quality results.

- **Know your target color mode**. Be sure to choose the correct color mode for your image, whether it's RGB for expanded-gamut printers like inkjets and digital presses or CMYK for commercial printing presses.

- **Choose a high-quality file format**. Use compression-free, print-compatible formats like PSD, TIFF, PDF, and EPS for saving, sending, and printing your images.

- **Use real names for spot colors**. When you're printing spot colors, use the names listed in Photoshop's Color Libraries dialog box instead of custom names. This increases the chance that the colors will be recognized by other programs like InDesign, or by RIPs that may have to convert them to process colors during printing.

- **Use duotone or multitone presets**. When you're creating duotones or multitonal images, be sure to use Photoshop's presets rather than adding additional colors yourself (at least as a starting point). The presets ensure that your original black ink and any additional inks are properly controlled by Duotone Curves, which reduce the amount of ink used during printing. This keeps the image from losing details and contrast because it's dripping with ink.

Photoshop and the Web

P reparing graphics for a website is a journey into the unknown: You've got no idea what kind of monitor folks will use to view your images, how fast (or slow) their Internet connections are, or which web browsers they use. It's a proposition riddled with variables that you have zero control over; all you can do is prepare your graphics well and hope for the best.

The main challenge in preparing images for the Web is finding a balance between image quality and file size. Premium-quality, minimally compressed JPEGs look stunning under almost any condition—but if your site visitor has a pokey dial-up connection, she might decide to click elsewhere rather than wait for the darn thing to download. On the other hand, if you try to satisfy the slowest common denominator by making ultra-lightweight images, you'll deprive those with broadband (high-speed) connections from seeing the impressive details you've lovingly created.

Luckily, there are several tricks for keeping file sizes down *and* retaining quality. That's what this chapter is all about. You'll learn which size and file format to use when creating images destined for the Web. You'll also discover how to make animations; craft *favicons* (those tiny graphics you see in web browsers' address bars); mock up web pages; and publish professional-looking online photo galleries.

TIP If you're using one of Apple's new Retina displays (called HiDPI on Windows)—which sport *twice* as many pixels per inch as regular displays—then your web graphics will look *half* their normal size. To see 'em at the size they'll actually appear in a web browser, choose View→200%.

Creating Web- and Email-Friendly Images

Whether you're designing an image destined for life on the Web or creating an email-friendly version of a digital photo, you need to perform three very specific steps to create a high-quality image that people can download quickly. Consider the following a basic overview of the process; you'll learn detailed info about each step later in this section:

1. **Adjust the image's dimensions.**

   First, you need to decide how big the image should be. In some cases, someone else may give you the size (like when you're hired to create a web banner or an ad). Other times, you choose the size (like when you email a digital photo, send a sample design to a client, or post an image in an online discussion forum). Once you know the size you need, you can use the Image Size dialog box (page 234) to resize it, provided your image is already the correct aspect ratio. If your image needs a little pruning around the edges, grab the Crop tool and then choose "W × H × Resolution" from the Option bar's aspect-ratio-and-crop-size menu (page 220). Next, enter your desired dimensions in the width and height fields and *be sure* to include the unit of measurement, such as *800 px*. You can either leave the resolution field blank or enter *72*. (For more on resizing with the Crop tool, see Chapter 6.)

2. **Decide which file format you want to use.**

   The most common choices are JPEG, PNG, and GIF. See page 721 for the pros and cons of each Web-friendly format.

> **NOTE** As you learned in Chapter 2, you should always save your master file as a PSD file (Photoshop document) so you can open, edit, and resave it as often as you want without losing quality. (Each time you save a JPEG as *another* JPEG, Photoshop recompresses it, degrading the image's quality.) The PSD format also retains any layers you created during the editing process.

3. **Save and compress the file.**

   When you're finally ready to create the version that's going to live online, you can squeeze it down to the smallest size possible using the "Save for Web" dialog box, which you'll learn all about beginning on page 723.

If you follow each of these steps, you'll end up with images that match the dimensions you want, look great, and download quickly. The following pages explain how to do all those things.

Resizing an Image

As you learned in Chapter 6, resolution matters when you *print*, but it doesn't mean a hill of beans when you're preparing images for the Web, presentation software, or an email. In the online realm, it's the *pixel dimensions* that matter instead. If you reduce an image's pixel dimensions before posting or emailing it, you won't force unsuspecting folks to download an image that's so big it takes over their whole screen, and you'll end up with a smaller file that will download faster.

> **NOTE** If you're emailing an image to someone who needs to print it, send him a full-size version in one of the print-friendly formats discussed on page 678. Just be sure to compress the image into a .zip file before you send it so it transfers as fast as possible (the Tip on page 679 explains how).

If you're a designer, someone may give you the pixel dimensions for your project so you can create a new document at that size to start with. But if you're emailing a digital photo or a sample design, or posting an image to an online forum, *you* pick the size. In that case, here are a few all-purpose width-by-height pixel dimension guidelines:

- **800×600 (or 600×800)**. Use this size if you're sending a design or photo sample to a client and she doesn't need to print the image. This size image is almost big enough to fill a web browser window (unless your viewer has a 30-inch screen, that is), so she won't have to scroll much to see the whole thing.

- **640×480 (or 480×640)**. Use these dimensions if you're emailing a photo or posting it to an online forum. These dimensions produce an image big enough to see well and a file size of less than 1 megabyte (so it transfers nice and fast).

- **320×240 (or 240×320)**. These dimensions work well if you're emailing multiple photos or posting to an online forum that contains *a lot* of images. If your recipient has a slow Internet connection, she'll appreciate the smaller file size. And if you crop wisely, these dimensions produce a photo that's big enough for your subject to be identifiable.

- **100×133 (or 133×100)**. If you're creating headshots for the company website—a great way to humanize your firm—this size makes for a nice, small portrait. If you're building a catalog page with a ton of product thumbnails (small preview pictures), this size won't bog down the page. (Linking the thumbnails to full-sized versions lets visitors view enlargements if they want to.)

Once you pick a size, flip back to Chapter 6 for step-by-step instructions on how to resize images using the Crop tool or the Image Size dialog box.

> **TIP** You can also use the Fit Image command to resize images. With an image open, simply choose File→Automate→Fit Image, enter a maximum dimension in either field, and then click OK. Short and sweet!

■ RESIZING WEB IMAGES VISUALLY

Sometimes, it's easier just to choose the size you want for your resized image by *looking* at it. For example, you can use the Zoom tool to decrease the size of your image until it looks good onscreen, and then enter *that* zoom percentage in the Image Size dialog box. Here's how:

1. **Open the image you want to resize and zoom in or out until it looks like it's the right size on your screen.**

   Press Z to grab the Zoom tool and click within your image to zoom in, or Option-click (Alt-click on a PC) to zoom out. To use keyboard shortcuts instead, press ⌘ (Ctrl) and the + or – key to zoom in or out (respectively).

2. **Make a note of the zoom percentage.**

   You can find this percentage in several places: in the document's tab at the top of the screen, in its title bar if you're using floating windows (page 2), and in the status bar at the bottom left of the document window; the last two are circled in *Figure 17-1*, top.

3. **Open the Image Size dialog box by choosing Image→Image Size or pressing Option-⌘-I (Alt+Ctrl+I).**

   Near the bottom of the resulting dialog box (*Figure 17-1*, bottom), make sure the Resample checkbox is turned *on*.

4. **Set the Width or Height drop-down menu to Percent.**

   Photoshop automatically changes the second menu when you change the first.

5. **Enter the zoom percentage in the Width or Height field.**

   Photoshop automatically constrains the proportions of your image (so it doesn't get squished or squashed), so you only have to enter the percentage in *one* field.

6. **Make sure the Resample menu near the bottom of the dialog box is set to Automatic.**

   Happily, straight from the factory, the Image Size dialog box chooses the best resampling method *for* you, so you shouldn't have to adjust it. (If you're using a pre-CS6 version of the program, choose Bicubic Sharper instead; when you make an image smaller, you lose some details because the pixels become softer, but with this particular method, you get a little sharpening that helps make up for it).

7. **Click OK when you're finished to close the Image Size dialog box.**

Now you can upload the image to the Web (or fire it off in an email) knowing you did your part to be a respectful web citizen. Your mom would be proud.

TIP   To *really* make up for the tiny amount of softening that occurs when you make an image smaller, give it another round of sharpening (see Chapter 11).

FIGURE 17-1

Top: After you use the Zoom tool to resize your image onscreen, make a note of the zoom percentage shown in the title bar or status bar (both circled). If you're working with tabbed documents instead of the floating windows shown here, you still see the zoom percentage displayed in the tab itself.

Bottom: Then pop open the Image Size dialog box and enter the percentage in the Width or Height field. Take a peek at the top of this dialog box to see how much smaller the file size has become; instead of the original 5.49 MB, it's now a svelte 351.9 KB.

Choosing the Best File Format

Once you've resized an image, you need to save it in a format that's not only compatible with both the Web and email, but also reduces it to the smallest possible file size. As you learned back in Chapter 2, those formats include JPEG, PNG, GIF, and WBMP (see *Figure 17-2*). The one you should pick depends on how many colors are in the image and whether or not it has any transparent (empty) areas:

- **Use JPEG for photos**. This format supports millions of colors, although, as you learned in the box on page 685, it's a *lossy* format, meaning it throws away fine details in order to create a smaller file. However, you can choose the level of compression when saving a JPEG—whether you use the "Save As" or "Save for Web" dialog box (page 723)—by setting the amount of compression using the Quality drop-down menu (it ranges from Low to Maximum) or by entering a number between 0 and 100 in the Quality field (0 is the most compression and lowest quality; 100 is the least compression and highest quality).

> **TIP** No matter which file format you choose, be sure to crop the image as close to the artwork's edges as possible before you save it. That way, you shave off extra pixels you don't need. The Image→Trim command is especially handy for this particular job. In fact, that command was used on *every* figure in this book!

- **Use GIF for images with solid blocks of color**. If you're dealing with line art (black and white with no shades of gray) or images made from areas of solid color (logos, comic strips, and so on), GIF is the way to go (see *Figure 17-2*). It supports fewer colors than JPEGs, so it doesn't work very well on photos. GIFs can be lossy or not; it's up to you. If you want to make 'em lossy, use the "Save for Web" dialog box's 0–100 scale (it works just the *opposite* of JPEGs: 0 is lossless and 100 is full-on lossy). To make the files smaller without resorting to lossy compression, you can limit the number of colors included in the image to anywhere between 2 and 256 (fewer colors equal a smaller file). The latter options is available in the Indexed Color dialog box that you get when saving a GIF using the "Save As" dialog box.

FIGURE 17-2

Once you learn each file format's strengths and weaknesses, it's easy to decide which one to use when.

Here are prime examples of images suited for two of the best Web formats: Use JPEG for photos (top left) and GIF for solid blocks of colors (bottom left) and line art (right).

- **Use GIF or PNG for images with transparent backgrounds**. Use one of these formats when you want a graphic (a logo, say) to blend seamlessly into the background of a web page. If you've painstakingly deleted the background of your image, JPEG won't work since Photoshop *automatically* sticks a solid background behind any empty spaces in that kind of file. Only GIF and PNG lets you retain transparent regions.

  The newer PNG-8 format is *lossless* (meaning it doesn't throw away any details) and can create a higher-quality file at smaller file sizes than GIF. The PNG-24 format supports 256 levels of transparency so it produces the highest-quality transparent image of all—making it perfect for images containing transparency *and* a drop shadow—though the file size is substantially larger than a PNG-8 or GIF. The drawback to PNGs is that some older web browsers—Internet Explorer 6 in particular—don't display transparent PNGs properly and stick a white background behind 'em. PNG is still a relatively new kid on the file-format block, so hopefully this problem won't be around forever. If you know your Web audience will view your site on outdated browsers, then stick with GIF. But if you think they'll have the latest and greatest browsers, go with PNG.

- **Use PNG for super high-quality files**. If quality is more important than download speed, save your image as a PNG. For example, if you're a photographer trying to sell your images, use PNG-8 for the enlarged versions in your portfolio so potential clients can see every last detail in the images. (Resist the urge to use PNG-24 unless you need a super-high quality transparent image as mentioned above, because this format can create files that are *twice* as big as PNG-8.)

- **Use GIF for animations**. If you want to combine several images into an automatic slideshow, save it as an animated GIF. These are handy when you have too much ad copy to fit in a small space on a website; an animated GIF can cycle through the content automatically. You'll learn how to create animated GIFs starting on page 732.

- **Use WBMP (Wireless Bitmap) for black-and-white images headed for mobile devices**. If you're designing black-and-white images for handheld devices (cellphones, smart phones, and so on), choose WBMP. This format supports only black and white pixels and gives you crisp text and logos that are readable on those itty-bitty screens.

Saving and Compressing Files

The "Save for Web" dialog box can save an image *and* compress the heck out of it at the same time. It also gives you four big preview windows—one for your original image and three for other file type and compression levels of the same image—so you can monitor the image's quality while you're trying to squeeze it into a smaller file size (see *Figure 17-3*).

FIGURE 17-3

In this Texas-sized dialog box, you can see up to four previews of your image in various file formats at different levels of compression.

Below each preview, Photoshop lists the file format, size, and an estimate of how long the image will take to download at a given connection speed. You can use the tiny drop-down menu to the right of the estimate (labeled here) to choose a different speed.

A Farewell to Web-Safe Colors

Do I still have to use web-safe colors in my graphics? That feels so 1990.

Negative, good buddy. Computer monitors have come a long way over the years, and they can now display a much wider range of colors than they used to. Heck, today's iPods display more colors than the monitors of the early '90s! So there's no need to stick with the boring, 256-color web-safe palette anymore.

However, if you're convinced that the majority of your audience is afflicted with prehistoric monitors—ones that can display only 256 colors—you can find the web-safe color palette in the Color Picker by turning on the Only Web Colors checkbox at the bottom left of the dialog box. You can also convert other colors

to their web-safe equivalents by using the Color Table section of the "Save for Web" dialog box (see page 726).

These days, it's more important to make sure you have decent contrast in your images than to worry about web-safe colors. Sure, you can upload images and check their contrast on as many monitors or devices as you can get your hands on, but you can't possibly see how they look on *every monitor* (although the "Save for Web" dialog box can help with that). The cold, hard fact is that your images will look darker on some monitors and lighter on others—that's just the way it is. But as long as there's a decent amount of contrast between their darkest and lightest colors, your images will still look good.

You saw this dialog box in action when you resized a JPEG back in Chapter 6 (page 242). To explore even *more* of its settings, follow these steps:

1. **With an image open, choose File→"Save for Web" and then, in the resulting dialog box, click the 4-Up tab.**

   At the top of the dialog box, you'll notice four tabs that let you view the original image and up to three other versions so you can see what it looks like when you change its settings. The most useful tabs are 2-Up and 4-Up. Pick 2-Up if you already know the format you want to use and 4-Up if you want to make more comparisons. Optimize gives you no comparison at all and shows only the resized image, not your original.

2. **Click the preview window to the right of the original and then, at the top right of the dialog box, choose a file format from the Preset menu.**

   The Preset menu contains a list of frequently used file format/compression level combinations for the formats previously mentioned (all of which are discussed later in this section). When you choose one of these options, Photoshop changes the various quality and color settings on the right side of the dialog box for you and displays the file size and estimated download time below the preview. (You can change the connection speed Photoshop uses to calculate the download time by clicking the tiny icon to the right of the listed speed as shown in *Figure 17-3*.)

   If you don't want to go the preset route, pick a format from the unlabeled drop-down menu *below* the Preset menu, and then adjust the quality/color settings manually, as discussed in the next step.

TIP　If you've been experimenting with different file formats in your preview windows, you can have Photoshop return them all to the *same* format automatically. Click to activate the preview window with the file type you want (say, JPEG) and then head to the "Save for Web" dialog box's Optimize menu (labeled in *Figure 17-3*) and choose Repopulate Views. Photoshop looks at the active preview window's file format and then loads up the *other* windows with previews of the same format at different compression or color settings.

---

3. **On the right side of the "Save for Web" dialog box, adjust the quality and color settings for the format you picked.**

   Each item in the Preset menu has its own entourage of settings related to quality and color. Different settings appear in the upper-right part of the dialog box depending on the format you chose in the previous step. Here's the lowdown on what they all mean:

   - **JPEG.** This format is the one you'll probably use most often. When you choose one of the Preset menu's JPEG options, you see the following settings:

     — **Quality.** Right below the Format menu is an unlabeled drop-down menu that lets you set the image's compression level. This menu includes five settings that range from Low (highest compression, smallest file size) to

Maximum (least compression, largest file size). You can fine-tune the image's quality by using the numeric Quality field to its right; 0 is the highest compression/smallest file size, and 100 is the least compression/largest file size. (The Preset menu changes if you happen to choose a format and quality level combination that matches one of the presets.)

— **Progressive.** Normally, an image has to download completely before it appears in a web browser, but if you turn on this checkbox, the image loads a little bit at a time (row by row), sort of like a waterfall effect. If your audience is still on dial-up, turn this setting on.

— **Optimized.** This option creates a slightly smaller, though somewhat less compatible file. Turn it off if your audience is likely to use older browsers.

— **Embed Color Profile.** If you want the image's color profile to tag along with the file, turn on this checkbox. If the viewer's monitor can actually *read* the profile correctly (some can't), the colors will look more accurate. If the monitor can't read the profile, you've added a little file size for nothing. However, if color accuracy is really important (say, you're posting images of hair coloring or clothing online for sale), then go ahead and turn this checkbox on.

— **Blur.** Use this field to add a slight Gaussian Blur to the image to reduce its file size a little. For a decent-quality image, you can get away with a setting of 0.1 to 0.5 pixels, but anything higher looks terrible.

— **Matte.** This color swatch lets you pick a color to use in place of any transparent (or partially transparent) pixels in your image. Since JPEG doesn't support transparency, those pixels will turn white unless you pick another color here. (Transparency options are discussed on page 727.)

• **GIF** and **PNG.** You get similar options for both these formats:

— **Colors.** This menu is the most crucial setting. It controls the number of colors the image contains (they're shown in the Color Table a little lower in the panel). If you reduce the number of colors in the image, you greatly reduce its file size; the downside is that Photoshop substitutes the closest match for any missing colors, which can produce some weird-looking images. Both GIF and PNG-8 let you choose anywhere between 2 and 256 colors. You don't see this menu if you're using PNG-24, though, as that format gives you 16.8 *million* colors and you can't delete a single one of 'em.

— **Color reduction method.** This unlabeled drop-down menu lives below the Format menu (see *Figure 17-3*). If you've reduced the number of colors as described in the previous bullet, this menu lets you pick the method Photoshop uses when it tosses them out. From the factory, it's set to Selective, which makes Photoshop keep colors that your eyes are most sensitive to, although it favors colors in large areas (like a sky) and those that are safe for the Web. Selective usually produces the most visually pleasing palette, so feel free to leave this menu alone. But in case you're interested, here's what the other options do: The Perceptual method is similar to Selective but ignores large areas of color, and Adaptive creates a palette from the most dominant colors in the image (like greens and blues in landscape images and peachy colors in portraits). Restrictive uses only the web-safe palette (see the box on page 724), and Custom lets you modify the color palette yourself (eek!) using the Color Table section of the panel. Choose "Black – White," Grayscale, Mac OS, or Windows to use those respective color palettes.

— **Dither method and amount.** If your image contains colors that the viewer's monitor can't display, you can fake 'em with a process called *dithering*. Use the unlabeled drop-down menu to the *left* of the word "Dither" to choose a dither method (or to turn dithering on or off), and the numeric field to its *right* to set the amount. A high dither amount (percentage) produces more accurate colors; the tradeoff is larger file size (try a setting between 80 and 90 percent). If you're desperate to make the file smaller, lower the dither amount.

You can choose from three dither methods: Diffusion simulates missing colors with a random pattern that's not too noticeable, so it's usually the best choice. Pattern simulates missing colors with a square pattern (which can sometimes create a weird color seam), and Noise uses a random pattern that doesn't spread across nearby pixels (so you won't get a weird seam). If you choose No Dither, Photoshop won't fake any colors. As of this writing, only a tiny number of web users' monitors are still limited to 256 colors, so you can leave dither turned off (you'll end up with a smaller file size by doing so).

— **Transparency** and **Matte.** If you've deleted the image's background, turn on the Transparency checkbox. If you want to change partially transparent pixels (those around the edges; see *Figure 17-4*) to a certain color, click the Matte swatch and then pick a color from the resulting Color Picker. You can also choose a matte color from within your image by choosing Eyedropper Color from the Matte menu. Then grab the Eyedropper tool at the far left of the dialog box—*not* the one in Photoshop's main Tools panel—and then, in the dialog box, click the image; whatever color you clicked shows up on the left side of the dialog box in the color swatch beneath the Eyedropper tool's icon. Use the drop-down menu below the Transparency checkbox to turn dithering on or off for any partially transparent pixels around the matte color, and use the numeric field to its right to set that dither amount. You'll typically leave transparency dithering off.

NOTE If you've masked (hidden) your image's background using the Refine Edge dialog box's Color Decontamination feature, this whole Matte color business is less of an issue. Flip back to page 165 for the scoop on using the Refine Edge dialog box.

— **Interlaced, Web Snap, Lossy.** Turn on the Interlaced checkbox to make your image appear a little at a time in your visitor's web browser. If you want to convert the image's colors to the web-safe color palette (see the box on page 724), use the Web Snap setting (the higher the number, the more web-safe colors you get). The Lossy setting (which is available only for GIF format, not PNG) lets you lower the image's quality to make the file smaller. You'll typically leave these settings turned off or set to 0, but feel free to experiment with them if you're feeling frisky.

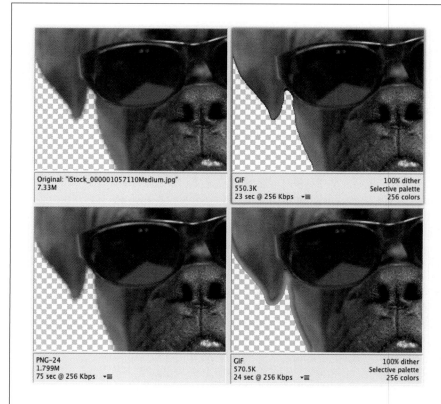

FIGURE 17-4

The edges of a transparent image with a drop shadow look much better as a PNG-24 (bottom left) than a GIF (top right) because the PNG-24 can display so many more colors. But, as the file sizes beneath each preview show, the PNG-24 is larger and takes longer to download. If file size is more important than download speed, use the Matte menu to change the shadow's partially transparent pixels to the color of your destination background (here that's blue, shown at bottom right). This trick makes the shadow look nice and soft again because Photoshop mixes the matte color with the shadow. It also keeps you from seeing edge halos—leftover pixels from the image's original background.

• **WBMP.** If you've made a black-and-white image that's destined for a cellphone or other handheld device with an itsy-bitsy screen, choose this format from the unlabeled drop-down menu below the Preset menu. Since you're dealing only with black and white pixels in this format, you just need to decide whether to turn on dithering (to fake colors the viewer's screen can't display with shades of gray) and, if so, the amount. For the best results, choose Diffusion as the dither method and then shoot for the lowest percentage possible that lets you maintain some detail in the image.

TIP If you're saving a graphic that has to weigh in at a certain size (like a Web banner ad), you can choose "Optimize to File Size" from the Optimize menu (labeled in *Figure 17-3*). In the resulting dialog box, enter the target size and pick a Start With option. Choose Current Settings to make Photoshop use the settings in the "Save for Web" dialog box. If you want Photoshop to pick a format, choose Auto Select GIF/JPEG instead. If you're dealing with an image that contains slices (page 738), you can choose to optimize the current slice, each slice, or all of 'em. When you click OK, Photoshop tries to make the image as close to your target size as possible. You may still have some tweaking to do afterward, but the program does most of the work for you.

4. **Make sure the "Convert to sRGB" checkbox is turned on.**

   With this option turned on, Photoshop converts the image to sRGB, a color space designed to mimic the characteristics of a Windows monitor. Since the majority of monitors are attached to Windows computers, that's what you want.

5. **Use the Preview drop-down menu to see what the image looks like on a Mac or Windows computer with no color management or with the document's current color profile.**

   This setting doesn't change your image; it just lets you see it through the eyes of someone with a different monitor. From the factory, this menu is set to Monitor Color, so you see the image exactly as your monitor sees it. Choose Legacy Macintosh (No Color Management) to check what it looks like on a Mac running OS X 10.5 (Leopard) or earlier, and Internet Standard RGB (No Color Management) to check what it looks like in Windows or on a Mac running OS X 10.6 (Snow Leopard) and later. (Windows monitors make images look darker than Macs due to a difference in *gamma* value. So if you're designing images for the Web on a Mac, it's worth choosing Internet Standard RGB here to see how dark they'll look.) If the image has a color profile attached to it, choose Use Document Profile to make the preview match.

6. **Set the Metadata menu to "Copyright and Contact Info."**

   This menu lets you include the information Photoshop captured from your camera (metadata) or the copyright and contact info you stored using the File Info dialog box (File→File Info). As you might suspect, including data in your document increases its file size a hair, but it's a good idea anyhow so your image includes info about where it came from; otherwise it can appear *orphaned* (visit Wikipedia.com and search for "orphan works" for more on this topic).

7. **Use the Color Table to edit the colors in your image, if necessary.**

   This chart of color swatches lets you change or delete colors in your image. If your viewers are certain to have super old monitors, use the tiny menu near the table's upper right to shift the colors in a GIF or PNG-8 image to web-safe colors. If you need to make the file even smaller, you can delete colors by clicking the swatch you want to zap and then clicking the little trash can icon below the Color Table (shown in *Figure 17-3*); the number at the bottom left of the table tells you how many colors the image includes. To make a certain color transparent, choose its swatch and then click the transparency button below the table (it looks like a white-and-gray checkerboard). To shift a color to its closest web-safe equivalent, click the little cube. And to prevent a color from being tossed, click the tiny lock.

8. **When you're finished, click Save.**

   Photoshop opens the Save dialog box so you can pick a name and location for the new file.

> **TIP** If you decide you've got some image editing left to do but you want Photoshop to remember your current settings, click Done instead.

The left side of the "Save for Web" dialog box contains these tools:

- **Hand**. This tool lets you move the image around within the dialog box's preview windows. You can also press the space bar (or H) to activate it and then move your mouse to see another part of the image.

- **Slice Select**. If you've mocked up a web page and sliced it accordingly (see page 738), use this tool to choose slices you want to save in specific formats. Keyboard shortcut: C.

- **Zoom**. You can use this tool to zoom in and out of your image, though it's faster to press ⌘-+ or – (Ctrl-+ or – on a PC). Alternatively, in the field at the bottom left of the dialog box, enter a zoom percentage or pick a preset from the drop-down menu. You can also Control-click (right-click) within the preview window, and then choose a zoom percentage from the shortcut menu. Keyboard shortcut: Z.

- **Eyedropper**. Use this tool to snatch colors from the image in the dialog box's preview area, which is helpful when you're creating a matte color for a transparent background as discussed on page 726. Keyboard shortcut: I.

- **Eyedropper Color**. This color swatch shows the Eyedropper's current color.

- **Toggle Slices Visibility**. To see the slices in your image, click this button. (Slicing is discussed starting on page 738.) Keyboard shortcut: Q.

And finally, here's what the buttons at the bottom of the dialog box do:

- **Preview**. To see what the image looks like in a web browser, click this button. Photoshop automatically uses the main browser on your computer, but you can choose a different browser by choosing Other from the drop-down menu to the Preview button's right. In the Preview In Other Browser dialog box, navigate to where that browser lives on your hard drive, and then click Open. The next time you click the Preview button, Photoshop uses the browser you just picked.

- **Save, Cancel, Done**. Once you have the dialog box's settings just right, click the Save button to save the image and give it a name. If you want to bail and do nothing, click the Cancel button. Clicking Done makes Photoshop remember the current settings and close the dialog box. Holding Option (Alt on a PC) changes the last two buttons to Reset and Remember, respectively. Click Reset to revert all the settings in this dialog box to the last ones you saved (in other words, what they were the last time you clicked the Save button). Clicking Remember makes Photoshop use your current settings the next time you open the "Save for Web" dialog box (whether you click Save or not).

POWER USERS' CLINIC

Matching and Snatching Colors on the Web

If you're designing an image destined for an existing web page, you may find yourself in a color-matching conundrum. If you need to match the color scheme or colors in a company logo, you can do that by finding out the colors' *hexadecimal* values.

Hex numbers, as they're affectionately called, are six-digit, alphanumeric programming codes for color values. The first two digits represent red, the next two represent green, and the last two represent blue (since your image will appear only onscreen, RGB values are the only ones that matter). You can find a color's hex number in several different ways:

- If you've gotten your hot little hands on an HTML, CSS, or SVG file from the website you're trying to match, Photoshop can automatically import color info for you as swatches. Choose Window→Swatches, and then choose Load Swatches or Replace Swatches from the Swatches panel's menu. In the resulting dialog box, navigate to where one of those files lives and click Open. Magically, Photoshop creates a swatch out of every hex number it finds in that file. (In case you're curious, those file formats stand for HyperText Markup Language, Cascading Style Sheets, and Scalable Vector Graphics, respectively.)

- Grab the Eyedropper tool by pressing I, and then click a color in an open Photoshop document to load it as your foreground color. Next, choose Window→Color to open the Color panel and then, from the panel's menu, choose Copy Color's Hex Code. You can also choose "Copy Color as HTML" from the same menu; it does the same thing except that it adds the HTML tag "Color" to what's copied to your computer's Clipboard.

- Using the Eyedropper tool, click a color in an open Photoshop document and then click your foreground chip to open the Color Picker. The color's hex number appears at the bottom of the dialog box in the field labeled #.

- Choose Window→Info and, from the Info panel's menu, choose Panel Options. In the dialog box that appears, set the Mode menu to Web Color, and then click OK. After that, when you mouse over a color in your Photoshop document, its hex number appears in the Info panel no matter which tool is currently active.

- Using the Eyedropper tool, Control-click (right-click) any color in an open Photoshop document. From the resulting shortcut menu, choose Copy Color's Hex Code.

- Snatch color from *anywhere* on your screen, whether it's on your desktop or in a web browser. In Photoshop, click your foreground color chip to open the Color Picker, mouse over to your document, and then click and hold your mouse button down *while you're in the Photoshop window* and keep it held down as you mouse *outside* Photoshop. Point to the color you want to snatch, *and then* release your mouse button. As long as you first click *within* Photoshop, your cursor remains an eyedropper no matter where you drag it. (You can do the same thing with the Eyedropper tool or by pressing and holding Option [Alt] while using the Brush tool.)

Once you've captured the hex number, you can enter in the field marked # at the bottom of the Color Picker dialog box, or use it in your favorite HTML editor when you're building the web page (just choose Edit→Paste).

■ Animating a GIF

You may think that creating an animation is a complicated process, but it's really not. In Photoshop, all you do is create a slideshow that plays automatically. You can control which images the program uses, how long it displays each one, whether it *loops* the slideshow (automatically starts over), and so on. This kind of control is really handy when you're making website ads. For example, say you're designing a 140×140-pixel ad for a costume shop, and you need to include a logo, a few costume samples, and a 10% off coupon. Since you'll *never* fit all that into a tiny space, you can make an animated GIF that *cycles* through several images automatically. Here's how:

1. **Create the images you want to string together, putting** *each image on its own layer* **within the same Photoshop document.**

2. **Open the Timeline panel by choosing Window→Timeline, and then create a frame animation.**

   At the bottom of Photoshop's Application Frame (or near the bottom of your screen if you've got the Application Frame turned off), a long horizontal Timeline panel appears. This panel also has controls for video editing (see Chapter 20), so you need to switch it to animation mode by clicking the downward-pointing triangle to the right of the Create Video Timeline button (*Figure 17-5*, top). Choose Create Frame Animation, and then click the Create Frame Animation button to the triangle's left. Photoshop then displays one frame representing what's currently visible in the Layers panel (each frame serves as a *placeholder* for the image you want to show onscreen).

3. **Add another frame.**

   At the bottom of the Timeline panel, click the "Duplicate selected frames" icon (it looks like a piece of paper with a folded corner) as shown in *Figure 17-5* (middle) to create a new placeholder for the next image in your animation. Initially, it contains the same image as the starter frame (don't worry; you'll fix that in the next step).

4. **In the Layers panel, use the visibility eyes to display only the layer containing the next image in your animation.**

   When you turn off the visibility of every layer *except* the one you want to show next, Photoshop displays the visible layer in the frame you created in step 3. That's all there is to it! There's no dragging or dropping, just showing and hiding using the layers' visibility eyes.

5. **Repeat steps 3 and 4 until you've made all the frames of your animation.**

6. **Click the Play button to see the slideshow.**

   Photoshop displays your animation in the main document window. The images flash by quickly, but don't worry—you'll learn how to make 'em stick around longer in the next section.

FIGURE 17-5

Top: The Timeline panel does double-duty for both video and animation, so you have to tell it which one you want to work with using the menu shown here. Click the button to its left to apply your choice, and Photoshop sets up the panel accordingly.

Middle: Use the playback buttons at the bottom of the panel to move through your animation frame by frame. Photoshop highlights the active frame, as shown here. You can click a different frame to activate it.

Bottom: Open this dialog box by clicking the Set Loop triangle (labeled in the middle image in this figure) and choosing Other. This dialog box lets you determine how many times the animation plays. If you want it to keep playing without stopping, choose Forever.

You just created your first animated GIF! There's still some work to do, but you're more than halfway there.

NOTE Photoshop lets you open animated GIF files and preserve the individual frames from which they're made. This is *extremely* helpful when you need to edit an existing animation and don't have the original files because it keeps you from having to start from scratch.

Editing Your Animation

Once you've created all the frames in your animation, you can edit it in the following ways:

- **Frame delay**. To control the length of time each image is visible, use the drop-down menus at the bottom of each frame (*Figure 17-5*, middle). These menus include options ranging from No Delay to 10 seconds. If you want to use a duration that's not listed, choose Other and then type a number in the Set Frame Delay dialog box. You can set the duration for each frame individually, or change several at once by Shift- or ⌘-clicking (Ctrl-clicking) to activate them, and then changing the duration of *one* of 'em.

- **Set loop count**. To make the animation play over and over, you can set it to loop a certain number of times. Click the down-pointing triangle at the bottom left of the Timeline panel and choose Once, 3 Times, Forever, or Other. If you choose Other, Photoshop opens the dialog box shown in *Figure 17-5* (bottom), where you can enter any number you want.

- **Rearrange frames**. To change the frames' order, simply drag them into place. Easy peasy!

- **Delete frames**. Just like most panels in Photoshop, this one has its own little trash can icon. To zap a frame, activate it and then click the trash can or drag it onto the trash can. To delete more than one frame, activate 'em by Shift- or ⌘-clicking (Ctrl-clicking) them, and then click the trash can. In the resulting "Are you sure?" dialog box, click Yes. Alternatively, choose Delete Frame from the Timeline panel's menu.

- **Tween frames**. At first, there isn't any transition between your frames; the animation works just like a regular slideshow, with one frame abruptly giving way to the next. To make the frames fade in and out, you can add *tweening* (short for "in-betweening"). Just tell Photoshop *which* frames to tween, along with how many frames of fading you want, and it adds the new frames for you. When you play the animation, the frames blend into one another. *Figure 17-6* has the details.

> **NOTE** Tweened frames take on the duration settings of the *first* frame, so once you start adding 'em, you may need to speed up the whole animation's frame duration so it doesn't take forever to play!

You can create all kinds of special effects using tweening, though you'll need to play around with it to learn what you can do. It's all about setting up a layer for each frame, creating the frames, and then adjusting what you want to happen *between* each frame. For example, if you move the contents of a layer in one frame, you can use tweening to make it look like the object is moving. You can also turn layer styles on or off, add solid-colored frames to make the animation look like it fades into that color, and so on. The creative possibilities are endless!

Saving Your Animation

When you've got the animation just right, you need to do a couple more things before you post it on the Web. Save it as a Photoshop (PSD) document so you can go back and edit it later, and then do the following:

FIGURE 17-6

Top: To fade the first frame into the second (see Figure 17-5), activate the first one and then click the Tween button (circled). In the Tween dialog box, choose Next Frame from the Tween With menu, enter 5 in the "Frames to Add" field, and then click OK.

Bottom: Here, Photoshop has added five additional frames (numbered 2–6) that gradually change opacity. When you play the animation, it'll look like the text and Chihuahua photos fade together. For a more gradual fade, enter 10 in the Tween dialog box's "Frames to Add" field.

- **Optimize it**. Choose Optimize Animation from the Timeline panel's menu to create a slightly smaller file, which makes the animation download faster and run more smoothly. The resulting Optimize Animation dialog box has two settings:

  — **Bounding Box** crops each changed frame to the part that's different from the previous frame. This is like running the Trim command on each frame, so that each one is cropped closely to the content.

  — **Redundant Pixel Removal** makes unchanged pixels transparent in subsequent frames, making the file a little smaller.

  Both settings are turned on straight from the factory, but Photoshop doesn't *apply* them until you choose Optimize Animation and then click OK.

- **Save it as an animated GIF**. Last but not least, choose File→"Save for Web" and, in the upper right of the resulting dialog box, choose GIF from the unlabeled format drop-down menu (below the Preset menu). When you do, Photoshop activates the Animation section at the bottom right of the dialog box, giving you one last chance to change the Looping Options setting and preview your handiwork. When you've finished, click Save and exclaim with gusto, "I'm an *animator*!"

■ Designing a Website Favicon

You know those tiny little icons on the left edge of your web browser's address bar (see *Figure 17-7*). They're called *favicons* (short for "favorites icons"), and they're great for adding a bit o' branding to web pages. They show up not only in web browsers, but also in news feeds (clickable headlines from your favorite websites that you can access through a newsreader program or your browser). Creating them in Photoshop is a snap, and you'll be designing them like a pro after you read this section.

The first step is to spend some quality time looking at other sites' favicons. Your goal is to brand your website with a graphic that's exactly 16×16 pixels—no more, no less. It's tough to design anything that small that's recognizable, but it *can* be done. For example, you might use a portion of your logo rather than the whole thing, or your company's initials rather than its full name.

FIGURE 17-7

Here are the favicons for a couple of websites (circled).

Designing favicons is a good way to test your design skills, since you're limited to 16 pixels square!

Next, you need to download a plug-in that lets Photoshop save the file in the Windows Icon (ICO) file format. The free plug-in ICO Format is a good option: *www. telegraphics.com.au/sw*. Just quit Photoshop and follow the instructions on page 776 to install this plug-in. When you relaunch Photoshop, you should see ICO appear in Save As dialog box's format menu.

Now you're ready to create your teeny-weeny work of art. Here's how:

1. **Create a new document that's 64×64 pixels with a resolution of 72.**

   Choose File→New or press ⌘-N (Ctrl+N) to start a new document. Your favicon will *ultimately* be 16×16 pixels, but that's too small a size to work with initially. To save yourself some eyestrain, start with a 64×64-pixel canvas; you'll reduce its size later.

2. **Create or place your artwork in the new document.**

   If you designed a logo using Adobe Illustrator, choose File→Place to add it as a Smart Object. If you're creating it in Photoshop, be sure to turn off the anti-alias setting of whatever tool(s) you used to create your design so the edges are nice and crisp (this is especially important when creating tiny text for the Web).

3. **If necessary, resize the artwork to fit the canvas.**

   If you added your artwork as a Smart Object, Photoshop automatically surrounds it with resizing handles. If you went another route, you can resize it by pressing ⌘-T (Ctrl+T) to summon Free Transform, and then dragging one of the corner handles. When you're happy with the size, press Return (Enter) to let Photoshop know you're done.

4. **Resize the document.**

   When your design is finished, choose Image→Image Size. In the middle of the dialog box, set the Width or Height field to 16 pixels (Photoshop automatically changes the other field to 16, too), make sure the Resample checkbox is turned on, and then click OK.

5. **Sharpen the image, if needed.**

   If your design looks a bit blurry, run a sharpening filter on it (see Chapter 11).

6. **Save the file in the ICO format and name it** *favicon*.

   Choose File→Save As and pick Windows Icon (ICO) from the format drop-down menu at the bottom of the dialog box, and then click Save.

That's it! You've created your very first favicon. If a client asked you to create the favicon and send it to her, email the *favicon.ico* file so she can add it to her website. If you created it for your own site, you're ready to upload the file to the root level of your website, where your index (home) page lives. (If you have no idea what that last sentence means, check out *Creating a Website: The Missing Manual, Third Edition* (*www.lesa.in/websitemm3*).

Be aware that not *all* web browsers support favicons, and some even want you to bury a link to the favicon in the code of each page. If you want to take that extra step, insert the following code somewhere within the <head> section of your web pages:

```
<link rel="SHORTCUT ICON" href="/favicon.ico">
```

If you've got a multi-page website, adding that line of code can be time consuming, so you may want to use the "Find and Replace" command found in most HTML editors, which lets you search for a piece of code that appears in every page, like the closing </title> tag. For example, you could search for </title> and Replace it with </title><link rel="SHORTCUT ICON" href="/favicon.ico">.

NOTE Another fun exercise is to design your own custom Twitter page. Since this book can only hold so many techniques, that tutorial lives on this book's Missing CD page at *www.missingmanuals.com/cds*.

■ Creating Web Page Mockups and Image Maps

As you've learned throughout this book, Photoshop is an amazingly powerful image editor, which means it's great for designing web pages. In fact, Photoshop has a tool that'll let you *slice* your design into web-friendly pieces that, when clicked, lead to whatever web address you link them to. Photoshop churns out the proper code that you can then paste into your own web page using your favorite HTML editor.

But does all that mean you *should* use Photoshop to build a website? Heck, no. Remember how back in Chapter 14 you learned that, even though Photoshop has a powerful text tool, you shouldn't use it to write a book? The same principle applies here. While you *could* use it to build real web pages, you shouldn't; you're much better off using a program designed for the job, like Adobe Muse or Dreamweaver. That said, Photoshop's Slice tool comes in really handy in these situations:

- **Building a website prototype**. If you've designed a website for a client in Photoshop and want to give him an *idea* of how the site will look and behave, you can use the Slice tool to get that done fast. If you slice up your design and assign different hyperlinks to navigation bars, you can give the client a good idea of how the navigation in the final website will *feel*.

TIP For an even *more* realistic mockup, create the website's text using Photoshop's new, "make it look exactly like it will in popular web browsers" anti-aliasing option: Mac LCD or Windows LCD (page 600).

- **Making an image map**. The Slice tool lets you add hyperlinks to certain portions of a single image.
- **Making an image-heavy page load a bit faster**. Chopping images into pieces makes them load a little at a time instead of in one big piece. However, this is becoming less of a problem as more people get faster Internet connections.

TIP An alternative to slicing images is to buy a plug-in called SiteGrinder, which can build a fully functional website from a layered Photoshop document. See page 786 in Chapter 19 for details or visit *www.medialab.com*.

Slicing an Existing Image

Once you've created an image or design that you want to chop up, you can use the Slice tool to draw the pieces by hand, or make *Photoshop* create slices from individual layers by choosing Layer→New Layer Based Slices. You can also make

Photoshop slice an image according to the guides you've drawn (as discussed later in this section).

Here's how to slice and dice a web-page mockup:

1. **Turn on Photoshop's rulers and draw guides around the areas you want to slice.**

   Instead of drawing each slice yourself, make Photoshop do the hard work by dragging a few well-placed guides around each slice you want to create. Turn on rulers by pressing ⌘-R (Ctrl+R), and then click within the horizontal ruler and drag downward to create a horizontal guide. Do the same thing in the vertical ruler (but drag rightward instead) to create vertical guides until you've placed a guide around every slice you want to make, as shown in *Figure 17-8*.

2. **Press C to grab the Slice tool.**

   This tool, which looks like a tiny X-Acto knife, hides in the crop toolset (it's circled in *Figure 17-8*).

FIGURE 17-8

Here, Photoshop created individual slices from the guides. A bounding box and a tiny number appear at the top-left corner of each slice; Photoshop numbers each slice beginning at the document's top left and working down to the bottom right. If you draw the slices yourself (to create what are called user slices), the number appears in a blue box. If you make Photoshop draw the slices for you (to create auto slices), the number appears in a gray box instead (not shown).

3. Trot up to the Options bar and click the Slices From Guides button.

In a split second, Photoshop draws slices around the areas you specified, following the guides you placed in the first step.

If you decided not to use guides, you can slice areas yourself by clicking where you want the slice to begin and then dragging diagonally to the right. (To draw a perfectly square slice, hold Shift as you drag.) When you let go of your mouse button, Photoshop puts a blue bounding box around the slice. This kind of slice is called a *user slice*. Alternatively, you can choose Layer→New Layer Based Slice to make Photoshop create a slice out of whatever is on the active layer (say, a button graphic). If you go that route, you get a (you guessed it) *layer-based slice*. To account for the rest of your image (the areas you haven't yet sliced), Photoshop draws other slices (called *auto slices*) automatically and marks them with gray bounding boxes. Auto slices are discussed in the next section.

> **TIP** If you've drawn a slice that's perfectly suited for another graphic, you can duplicate it by Option-dragging (Alt-dragging on a PC) the slice onto the other image.

Modifying Slices

Once you create a slice, you may need to move or change it. If so, activate it using the Slice Select tool. (Press Shift-C to activate the tool or, if the Slice tool is active, you can grab the Slice Select tool temporarily by pressing ⌘ [Ctrl]; when you let go of that key, Photoshop switches back to the regular Slice tool.) To activate a slice, just click it. Its bounding box turns brown and little resizing handles appear in the center of each side, as shown in *Figure 17-9*.

UP TO SPEED

The New Copy CSS Command

As you read on page 738, Photoshop really isn't the place to build a whole website. However, it's the *perfect* place to design all the text and graphics that are destined to live on a website. For example, you can use Type layers full of placeholder text (see the Tip on page 584) to figure out exactly how big the text should be, what font and colors work the best, and so on. Likewise, you can use Photoshop's Shape layers to create all manner of colored bars, buttons, background elements, and so on.

When you get everything designed just right in Photoshop, you can copy the formatting and page positioning of the content in any Type or Shape layer, and then paste it into the program you'll (wisely) use to build the site. Simply Control-click (right-click) near any Type or Shape layer's name in the Layers panel, and then choose Copy CSS. Photoshop analyzes the content of those layers and copies the info to your computer's memory and formats it for Cascading Style Sheets (CSS), programming code that's used to control the formatting and positioning of elements across web pages. What a huge time-saver!

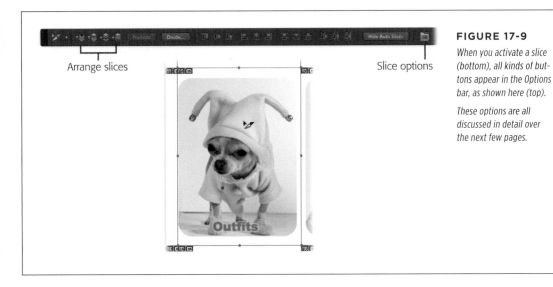

FIGURE 17-9

When you activate a slice (bottom), all kinds of buttons appear in the Options bar, as shown here (top).

These options are all discussed in detail over the next few pages.

Now you're ready to:

- **Resize the slice**. Once you activate a slice, you can drag any of its corner or center handles (they look like tiny solid squares) to make it bigger or smaller.

- **Move the slice**. Click within the slice and then drag it to another location. To make it so you can drag the slice only horizontally or vertically, hold the Shift key as you drag.

> **TIP** To make your slices to snap to guides, other slices, or objects, choose View→Snap To. (Unless you've previously turned it off, this option is already turned on.)

- **Promote slices**. You can change a layer-based or an auto slice into a user slice by clicking the Option bar's Promote button (*Figure 17-9*, top). This is useful because you can't edit auto slices. For example, if you placed guides and had Photoshop create the slices for you, as described in the previous section, you can't move or resize any of those slices until you promote 'em to user slices (as shown in *Figure 17-10*). Similarly, layer-based slices are tied to the pixel content of that layer. Before you can change the slice itself or the layer's contents, you have to promote t to a user slice.

- **Arrange slices**. Because the Slice tool draws only rectangles, you have to overlap slices to make other shapes. To do that, you may need to fiddle with their stacking order by first activating a slice with the Slice Select tool, and then clicking the arrange buttons labeled in *Figure 17-9*, top.

FIGURE 17-10

Notice that the auto slices around the document's edges are tagged with gray icons while the user slices are tagged with blue ones.

Promoting auto slices to user slices lets you do things like divide them, as was done in the pink navigation bar shown here.

- **Align slices**. Photoshop lets you align slices just like you can align layers. Using the Slice Select tool, Shift-click to activate *more* than one slice, and then click the appropriate alignment button in the Options bar. (If just one slice is active, these buttons are grayed out.)

> **TIP** To change the color of the slice lines, choose Photoshop→Preferences→"Guides, Grid & Slices" (Edit→ Preferences→"Guides, Grid & Slices" on a PC). In the Slices section at the bottom of the dialog box, use the Line Color menu to pick a new color. You can turn off the Show Slice Numbers checkbox here, too.

- **Divide slices**. If you need to slice a slice (oy!), activate it with the Slice Select tool and click the Options bar's Divide button. In the resulting Divide Slice dialog box, turn on either the Divide Horizontally Into or the Divide Vertically Into checkbox, enter the number of slices you want to create, and then click OK.

- **Combine slices**. Activate two or more slices by Shift-clicking with the Slice Select tool. Then Control-click (right-click) one and choose Combine Slices from the resulting shortcut menu. This technique is helpful when Photoshop creates too many auto slices and you want to combine 'em so they'll load as a single image.

- **Copy and paste slices**. You can copy and paste a slice by activating it and then pressing ⌘-C (Ctrl+C). Next, open the target document and press ⌘-V (Ctrl+V). The slice and graphics from the associated layers appear in your new document, but they're all on one layer, which means you can't edit 'em individually (you have to do that back in your original document).

- **Give it a URL**. To transport visitors to a particular web address when they click a slice, activate the slice, and then click the Slice Options button labeled in *Figure 17-9* or double-click the slice itself. In the resulting Slice Options dialog box, enter the *full* web address into the URL field (for example, *http://www. petstumes.com*). (The next section also discusses Slice Options.)

- **Delete it**. To delete a slice, activate it with the Slice Select tool, and then press Delete (Backspace on a PC).

- **Hide**. If you find all those slice borders and numbers distracting, you can hide 'em temporarily by pressing ⌘-H (Ctrl+H)—unless you've reassigned that keyboard shortcut to hide Photoshop on your Mac, as described in the box on page 4.

- **Lock**. To lock all your slices so they can't be changed, choose View→Lock Slices (you can't lock individual slices).

- **Clear**. To zap all your slices, choose View→Clear Slices.

To forget you ever *heard* of slices, hire a web designer (kidding...sort of!).

■ SLICE OPTIONS

Once you've drawn slices and put them in the right spots, you can start controlling how they behave in your web browser by setting Slice Options. The Slice Options dialog box (shown in *Figure 17-11*) lets you control the following:

- **Slice Type**. Most of your slices probably consist of an image, although they can also be solid blocks of color or plain text. If you want to create an empty space that you can fill with HTML color or HTML text later, choose No Image from this drop-down menu, and a "Text Displayed in Cell" field appears that lets you enter text that'll be—you guessed it—displayed in that cell (the empty space).

- **Name**. Photoshop automatically gives slices generic names that include the document name and a number. To use a name that's more descriptive (and useful), enter it here.

- **URL**. One of the big benefits of slicing an image is that you can make part of it act as a *hyperlink* that takes visitors to another web page. Enter the full web address here to make that happen. Photoshop doesn't actually embed this info into your image; instead, it stores it in a separate HTML file that you can copy and paste into your *own* web page.

> **NOTE** Assigning a hyperlink to part of an image is called *creating an image map*. Now if you hear image maps mentioned at the water cooler, you'll be in the know!

- **Target**. This field determines where the hyperlink opens. For example, to make the hyperlink open the URL in another browser window, enter _*blank* into this field (complete with underscore). If you want the page to load within the same window, then leave this field blank.

FIGURE 17-11

Click the Slice Options button on the right side of the Options bar (shown in Figure 17-9) to open this dialog box, which lets you assign each slice a descriptive name and URL.

You can also open this dialog box by double-clicking a slice with the Slice Select tool.

- **Message Text**. Almost every web browser has a status bar at the bottom of the window that let folks know what's going on in the background. For example, when you type a URL into your browser's address bar and then press Return (Enter on a PC), you'll see some kind of "loading" message. If you want to include messages in the status bar (like a love note to your visitors: "Dude—thanks for clicking!"), enter it in this field. But since few folks ever look down that far, your efforts may be in vain.

- **Alt Tag**. Because some folks surf the web with graphics turned *off* (to make sites load faster), you can use this field to give your image an alternate text description. Visually impaired people using *web readers*—special software that speaks the contents of web pages—will hear this text read to them. The text also pops up as a balloon or tooltip when visitors point to it with their cursors.

- **Dimensions**. This info lets you know the width and height of your slice, along with its X and Y coordinates.

- **Slice Background Type**. If you chose "No Image" in the Slice Type menu or if part of the image is transparent, you can use this menu to give that slice a color. Your choices include None, Matte (page 726), White, Black, and Other (which summons the almighty Color Picker).

Saving Slices

Once you've set all the options for your slices, it's time to save them to use on the Web (finally!). Use the File→"Save for Web" dialog box to set all those file-type, compression, and other options discussed earlier in this chapter. (If you use File→Save As, all your slice options will fly right out the window.)

On the left side of the "Save for Web" dialog box, click the Slice Select tool to grab each slice so you can apply different format and compression settings to each one (though if you're building a website prototype, choosing one file format for the whole thing works just fine). When you're finished, click Save and tell Photoshop where you want to store the files. If you've assigned URLs to the slices, be sure to choose "HTML and Images" from the Format drop-down menu at the bottom of the Save Optimized As dialog box, as shown in *Figure 17-12*. (Then make sure to change the Format menu *back* to Images the next time you use the Save Optimized As dialog box.)

FIGURE 17-12

Left: If you've chosen to save both HTML and images, as shown here, it's a good idea to create a folder to store 'em in first. That way, all the files are saved together in one place and not scattered across your computer's hard drive.

Right: Once you've saved the slices, you can open the folder and see the images, along with the HTML document containing code you can use in your very own web page.

Protecting Your Images Online

Being able to share images with the world via the Web is a glorious thing, but, in doing so, you risk having your images stolen (gasp!). It's frighteningly easy for thieves to snatch photos from your website to sell or use as their own, so it's important to take steps to protect them. You can deter evildoers in several different ways, including posting smaller versions of your images (640×480 pixels, for example), using photo galleries such as *www.smugmug.com* that *prevent* folks from Control-clicking (right-clicking) to copy images to their hard drives, embedding copyright info, adding watermarks, or using Zoomify (see the box on page 750). Keep reading for the scoop on each option.

Embedding Copyright Info

One of the first steps you can take toward protecting your work is to embed copyright and contact info into the image file by choosing File→File Info (see *Figure 17-13*). Sadly, this won't keep folks from stealing your image (heck, they won't even see it unless they open your file and peek at its title bar or choose File→File Info themselves), but they *might* think twice about taking it if they do find a name attached to it. Alternatively, you can declare that the image is in the public domain, granting anyone and everyone a license to use it.

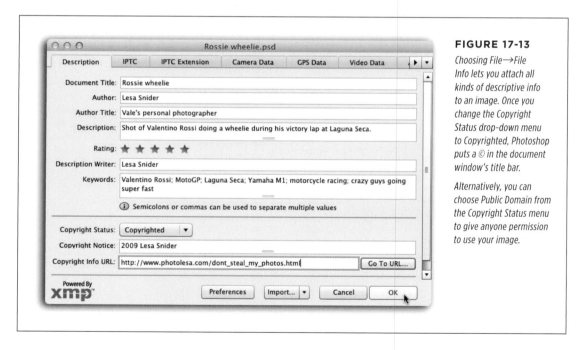

FIGURE 17-13

Choosing File→File Info lets you attach all kinds of descriptive info to an image. Once you change the Copyright Status drop-down menu to Copyrighted, Photoshop puts a © in the document window's title bar.

Alternatively, you can choose Public Domain from the Copyright Status menu to give anyone permission to use your image.

Watermarking Images

One of the best ways to protect images online is to add a *watermark* to them—a recognizable image or pattern that you either place atop the images (as shown in *Figure 17-14*, bottom) or embed into them invisibly. A watermark is a great deterrent because would-be thieves will have one *heck* of a time trying to get rid of it. You can add watermarks in Photoshop in a couple of ways:

- **Use custom shapes to add an opaque copyright symbol or logo**. The simplest way to watermark an image is to stick a big ol' copyright symbol (or your logo) on top of it. This process is called *visual watermarking*. If you make the logo partially see-through, folks can still see the image but won't, presumably, steal it because of the huge graphic stamped on top of it.

- **Use the Digimarc filter**. This paid service creates a nearly invisible watermark by adding noise to your image (called *digital watermarking*). It's not cheap, but you also get other features like image linking and tracking, online backups, as well as visual watermarking. The cost depends on the number of images you use it on and the type of service you pick. A basic account runs $50 per year for 1,000 images; a pro account (which includes an online image-tracking service) is $100 for 2,000 images; and so on. You can learn all about it by visiting *www. digimarc.com*.

Since you've already plunked down good money on both Photoshop *and* this book, here's how to watermark images for *free* using the Custom Shape tool:

1. **Open an image and grab the Custom Shape tool.**

   You can find this tool in the shape toolset, or grab it by pressing Shift-U repeatedly (the tool's icon looks like a rounded star).

2. **Set your foreground color chip to light gray.**

   Setting the foreground color now means you won't need to change the watermark's color later. At the bottom of the Tools panel, click the foreground color chip, choose a light gray from the resulting Color Picker, and then click OK.

3. **Open the Custom Shape menu and choose the copyright symbol.**

   In the right half of the Options bar, click the downward-pointing arrow to the right of the word "Shape" to open the menu of custom shape presets (see *Figure 17-14*, top). Scroll down until you see the copyright symbol (©), and then click it once to activate it.

4. **Draw the shape on top of your image.**

Mouse over to your image, click once where you want the shape to begin, and then Shift-drag diagonally to draw the shape. (Holding Shift keeps the symbol perfectly proportioned.) When you let go of the mouse, Photoshop adds a layer named Shape 1 to your document. If you want to tweak the shape's size, summon Free Transform by pressing ⌘-T (Ctrl+T).

FIGURE 17-14

Top: The Custom Shape tool makes creating your own watermark a snap.

Bottom: If you change the Shape and Type layers' blend modes to Hard Light and lower their opacity to about 50 percent, you can create a nice, professional-looking watermark that doesn't completely obscure your image.

5. **Add a Bevel & Emboss layer style.**

To give your watermark a little depth, tack on a layer style. Click the tiny *fx* at the bottom of the Layers panel and choose Bevel & Emboss. Feel free to fiddle with the settings (though they're probably fine the way they are), and then click OK to close the Layer Style dialog box.

TIP The shape's gray outline can make it darn difficult to see a preview of the layer style you're about to apply. Luckily, you can hide the outline by pressing ⌘-H (Ctrl+H). This trick works with paths, too!

---

6. **Grab the Type tool and type your name below the copyright symbol.**

   Press T to fetch the Type tool, mouse over to your image, and then click where you want the text to start (Photoshop adds a Type layer to your document). You can type whatever you want, but it's a good idea to include "Copyright" followed by the current year and your name or studio name. To change the font and text size, double-click the Type layer in the Layers panel and then tweak the Options bar's settings (Arial Black is a good choice). Flip back to Chapter 14 for more on formatting text.

7. **Copy the Shape layer's style to the Type layer to make the text look similar to the copyright symbol.**

   You can copy a layer style from one layer to another by Option-dragging (Alt-dragging on a PC) the layer effect to the new layer in the Layers panel (your cursor turns into a double-headed arrow, and you'll see a little *fx* icon behind it when you drag). In this example, Option-click (Alt-click) the layer named Bevel & Emboss, and then drag it to the new layer and release your mouse button. If you don't press Option (Alt) *before* you start to drag, you'll *move* the layer style instead; if that happens, just press ⌘-Z (Ctrl+Z) to undo and then try again.

8. **Change the Shape and Type layers' blend modes to Hard Light.**

   Doing this makes your watermark see-through. You can change the blend modes of *multiple* layers at the same time: Just Shift-click in the Layers panel to activate both the Shape and Type layers, and then change their blend modes to Hard Light using the drop-down menu at the top of the panel.

9. **Lower the Shape and Type layers' opacity to 40 percent.**

   While you've got the Shape and Type layers active, lower their opacity to 40 percent using the Opacity slider at the top of the Layers panel. This keeps the watermark from overpowering your image.

10. **Save the file and upload it to the Web.**

    Now you can enjoy peace of mind knowing that it'd take someone *weeks* to clone away your watermark.

Protecting your images takes a bit of effort, but it's well worth it. In fact, watermarking is *exactly* the kind of thing you should record as an action. Just follow the instructions in Chapter 18 for creating a new action (page 759) and then repeat the steps in this list (you can even include the bit about embedding copyright info in your file, as explained on page 746). Once you create the action, you can run it on a whole folder of files to save yourself tons of time.

> **NOTE** You can also use the Image Processor script (page 247) to resize images, run a watermarking action on them, and add copyright info to them all at the same time!

Building Online Photo Galleries

Once you've massaged and tweaked your images to perfection, why not have Photoshop prepare a web-ready photo gallery, complete with thumbnails and enlargements? Actually, Bridge *CS6*—yes, you read that right—can do all the work using something called the Adobe Output Module (AOM). However, as of this writing, Adobe has ripped that feature out of Bridge *CC*. Why? Adobe says it's because

---

POWER USERS' CLINIC

Zoomify Your Enlargements

It can be dangerous to post a full-sized image on the Web—you're practically giving thieves permission to steal it. But if you're a photographer and you want folks to see all the intricate details of your work, you can protect your images by using a Photoshop feature called Zoomify.

Instead of posting an image as one high-quality piece, Zoomify chops it into pieces and displays it in a Flash-based window with controls that visitors can use to zoom in on and move around within the image. (People who view the image need to have the Adobe Flash plug-in installed on their computers, but if they don't, their browser should prompt them to get it [it's free].) That way, instead of seeing the whole thing at full size, they see only one piece at a time, so they can't grab it by taking a screenshot or downloading the whole image. Plus, Zoomify exports to Flash *and* HTML5, which gives your image's admirers a few more viewing options. To see Zoomify in action, visit *www.bertmonroy.com/timessquare/timessquare.html*.

To use Zoomify, follow these steps:

1. Adjust the image's size using the techniques discussed in Chapter 6. (This step is optional; if you want to upload a full-size image from your camera, feel free, although Zoomify won't work on raw files).

2. Choose File→Export→Zoomify.

3. In the Zoomify Export dialog box, use the Output Location

section to name the file and tell Photoshop where to save it.

4. In the Image Tile Options section, choose an image quality. Use the Quality field, drop-down menu, or slider to set the quality of the individual pieces. (Behind the scenes, Zoomify chops your image into a bunch of pieces—called *tiles*—that it reassembles on the fly when your visitor looks at a given area.) Leave the Optimize Tables checkbox turned on so Photoshop optimizes the compression tables for each tile.

5. Enter a width and height (in pixels) for the Zoomify window to determine how large it is in your visitor's web browser.

6. Click OK, and Zoomify creates a block of code that you can paste into your web page. If you left the Open In Web Browser checkbox turned on, Photoshop opens your browser to show you what your Zoomify window looks like.

Now all you have to do is open the HTML document that Zoomify made, copy and paste the code into your web page, and then upload the page and image pieces that Zoomify created to your server. After that, folks who look at your image online can see all its exquisite details but *can't* swipe it and claim it as their own.

AOM hasn't been updated to work on Apple's Retina displays (known as HiDPI on Windows machines), which sport *twice* as many pixels per inch as regular displays. That said, a lot of folks depend on this feature, so keep your eyes peeled for a way to restore the AOM into Bridge CC via a separate installation. For the latest info, download online Appendix A from this book's Missing CD page at *www. missingmanuals.com/cds*.

Nevertheless, if you *have* a copy of Bridge CS6 lying around (say, you didn't uninstall it when you got Photoshop CC), you can still create beautiful web galleries without having to pay for yet *another* piece of software. Otherwise, try jAlbum, a $30 solution that lets you build and upload web galleries to any web server (*www.jalbum.net*).

Here's how to create a web gallery using Bridge CS6:

NOTE The following steps also work in Bridge CS4 and CS5, though in CS4 you don't have the option of saving your settings as a preset, as described in *Figure 17-15*.

FIGURE 17-15

Top: Bridge CS6 has both an Output menu (circled) and Output workspace that let you create a web gallery or PDF page.

Bottom: When you click the Web Gallery at the top of the Output panel, Bridge CS6 adds all kinds of options to the panel so you can customize your gallery. Once you've got the settings just right, click the tiny icon labeled here to save those settings as a preset style you can use again later.

1. **Place the images in a single folder.**

   It's a lot easier to grab all the images you want to include in your web gallery if you stick 'em all in a folder first.

2. **Fire up Adobe Bridge CS6.**

   You'll learn tons about Bridge in Chapter 22. For now, launch it by locating the program on your computer and double-clicking its icon. (If you use the File→"Browse in Bridge" command in Photoshop, Bridge *CC* will open instead; that is, if you installed it [page 848].)

3. **On the left side of the Bridge CS6 window, use the Folders panel to navigate to your images.**

   The images appear in the Content panel in the middle of the Bridge window.

4. **In the Content panel, arrange the images in the order you want them to appear in the gallery.**

   A vertical orange line appears as you drag an image around to show you where it will end up when you drop the image. When the line is in the right place, just let go of your mouse button.

5. **Activate the images you want to include in your gallery.**

   If you've taken the time to place your images in a single folder as described in step 1, press ⌘-A (Ctrl+A) to activate 'em all. If you've changed your mind about including some of the images, ⌘-click (Ctrl-click) to pick just the ones you want included in the gallery.

6. **At the top left of the Bridge CS6 window, click the Output button (which looks like a piece of paper with a folded corner) and choose "Output to Web or PDF" as shown in *Figure 17-15*, top.**

   On the right side of the Bridge CS6 window, the Output panel opens.

7. **Click the Web Gallery button at the top right of the Output panel.**

   Because Bridge CS6 can create either a PDF or a web gallery, you have to tell it which one you want.

8. **In the Output panel's Template menu, choose HTML Gallery.**

   For a basic photo gallery, this template is tough to beat.

9. **In the panel's Site Info section, add a title, caption, and description.**

   You can add all sorts of other stuff, too, if you want, including your name, email address, and copyright info. These extra tidbits appear at the top and bottom of your web page.

10. **Scroll down to the Output panel's Color Palette section and edit the background, text, and link colors.**

    Bridge CS6 has all kinds of settings that let you customize how your web gallery looks. To change one of the gallery's colors, just click one of the color swatches, and then choose something else from the Color Picker.

11. **In the Appearance section, set the photo size, quality, and number of columns and rows.**

    Unless you change these settings, your gallery will have three rows and columns, and the previews will be medium sized. (If necessary, Bridge CS6 automatically builds more pages to accommodate all your images.)

12. **Back near the top of the Output panel, click the "Preview in Browser" button to get a sneak peek at your web gallery.**

    This button lets you view your gallery in a real web browser. Depending on the number of images in the gallery, this process may take a few seconds.

13. **Head back to Bridge CS6 and, if you want to make changes to your gallery, scroll to the appropriate Output panel section and tweak the settings.**

    If necessary, preview your changes by clicking the "Preview in Browser" button again.

14. **When everything looks good, scroll down to the Create Gallery section of the Output panel to tell Bridge CS6 whether to save the gallery to your hard drive or upload it to the Web.**

    At the bottom of the Output panel, you can give your gallery a name and save it to your hard drive or upload it to your web server. If you upload it, you'll need to enter your website's *FTP* (file transfer protocol) settings, along with your login and password.

15. **Click Save (if the gallery is headed for your hard drive) or Upload (if it's bound for the Web).**

Creating web galleries using Bridge CS6 is incredibly painless and faster than it was in previous versions. And if you take the time to create a preset, as described in *Figure 17-15*, you won't have to fiddle with all the Output panel's settings the next time around.

Working Smarter with Actions

S ure it's fun to spend hours playing and working in Photoshop, but once you've used the program for a while, you'll start to notice that you repeat the same steps over and over on most of your images. At first, the repetition probably won't bother you—it's actually good while you're learning—but when a deadline approaches and the boss is eyeing you impatiently, you need a way to speed things up. It would also be great to automate tasks that you don't really enjoy doing yourself.

Luckily, Photoshop includes all manner of automated helpers (some of which you've already learned about), including these:

- The Image Processor script, which resizes images *and* converts them to different file formats (page 247).

- The Contact Sheet II script (page 713).

- Automated photo stitching with Photomerge (page 294).

- The Lens Correction filter (page 639), which fixes distortion problems caused by your camera's lens and/or sensor.

- Automated layer aligning and blending with the Auto-Align and Auto-Blend Layers commands (covered starting on page 291).

Some of the best timesavers of all, however, are *actions*—all-purpose, amazingly customizable systems for automating mundane tasks like adding or duplicating layers, running filters with specific settings, and so on. You can use actions to record nearly every keystroke and menu choice you make, and then play them back on another image or a whole *folder* of images. (Actions won't work on things that don't affect your image, such as zooming in or out, but page 764 has a workaround). Because

Photoshop doesn't need to press keys or move and click a mouse when it's running actions, it can *blast* through actions at warp speed. Photoshop can even record strokes you make with the Brush and Pen tools, so you can replay—and thereby recreate—a painting or drawing from start to finish. Just imagine the YouTube videos you can make!

This chapter explains how to use the built-in actions that come with Photoshop, and how to create, edit, and save your own. You'll also learn how to create drag-and-drop actions called *droplets*—icons you can drop files on to trigger an action—as well as how to find and load actions made by other folks. By the time you're finished reading, you'll be working 10 times smarter and not one bit harder.

■ The Actions Panel

You record, play, and edit keystrokes using the Actions panel (*Figure 18-1*). Choose Window→Actions to display the panel in the panel dock on the right side of your screen (its icon is a triangular "play" symbol).

FIGURE 18-1

You can rename, duplicate, and delete actions just like layers and channels. Shift-click or ⌘-click (Ctrl-click) to activate multiple actions so you can add them to an action set (see below) or delete them.

The Actions panel's menu (shown in Figure 18-2) is chock full of useful commands for working with actions.

To view each step inside an action, click the little flippy triangle next to the action's name.

The panel's controls are pretty straightforward. The Stop, Record, and Play buttons do what you'd expect: They stop, record, and play actions. The "Create new set" button at the bottom of the panel (it looks like a folder) lets you store actions in a set just like you can store layers in a group. You can create a brand-new action by clicking the "Create new action" button, and duplicate an action by dragging it onto that same button or Option-dragging (Alt-dragging on a PC) it up or down in the panel. Duplicating an action comes in handy when you want to run the same filter more than once within an action, or when you want to edit a *copy* of an action to make it do something slightly different (which is faster than rerecording the action from scratch).

The Actions panel has three unlabeled columns that let you do the following:

- **Turn steps on or off**. The leftmost column lets you turn individual steps in an action on or off via a checkmark next to each step, which is useful if you've created a fairly complex action and only want to run, say, half of it. For example, if you record an action that creates a Smart Object out of all visible layers (page 122), sharpens your image (Chapter 11), and then saves it as a high-quality JPEG file, you can turn off the "save" step and stop at sharpening instead. These checkmarks also come in handy when your action includes a step that will only work on *your* computer. For example, if you open a file while recording the action, Photoshop captures your hard drive name's, your user name, and so on. If someone else wants to use the action on his machine, you can turn that step off.

  To turn off a step, click the flippy triangle next to the action's name to expand it, and then click the checkmark to the left of that particular step. To turn off *all* the steps in an action or all the actions in a set, click the checkmark to the left of the action or set's name. To turn off all the steps in a particular action *except* one, Option-click (Alt-click on a PC) the checkmark next to the step you want to leave on.

> **TIP** In the Actions panel, a *gray* checkmark next to an action's name means Photoshop will run all the steps in that action; a *red* checkmark means that it'll skip some steps (the ones you've turned off). This handy visual clue lets you keep actions *collapsed* in the panel but still see that you've turned some steps off.

- **Show/hide dialog boxes**. The middle column is for showing or hiding any dialog boxes that are included in the action's steps. For example, if you create an action for sharpening an image, the settings you enter in the sharpening filter's dialog box may not work for *every* image you run the action on. If an image is bigger or smaller than the one you used to create the action, for example, having Photoshop show the dialog box when it's playing back the action lets you enter specific settings for that image.

  To have Photoshop show dialog boxes for a particular action (or a *step* in an action) just click within this column and a light gray icon appears (it's supposed to look like a tiny dialog box). If the column is empty, no dialog boxes will open during playback.

> **TIP** If the tiny dialog box icon to the left of an action's name has a dash in the middle of it, that means only some of the steps in that action need your input. If the icon doesn't include a dash, then *all* the steps in that action need your input

- **Expand or collapse an action**. The rightmost column in the Actions panel lists each action's name and keyboard shortcut (if you've assigned one). To see the individual steps within an action, expand the action by clicking the flippy triangle to the left of its name—handy when you want to turn off individual steps (as explained earlier) or explore the inner workings of an action (great for learning how to make your own or for troubleshooting the ones you created).

> **TIP** To expand or collapse all the actions in a set or all the steps in an action, Option-click (Alt-click on a PC) the action or step's flippy triangle.

Straight from the factory, Photoshop displays actions as a list (see *Figure 18-1*), though you can also display them as clickable *buttons* (see *Figure 18-2*); just open the Actions panel's menu and choose Button Mode. Unless you're in the process of creating or editing actions, this is a great way to roll!

FIGURE 18-2

Instead of triggering an action by choosing it in the panel and then clicking the Play button, you can just click the button with the action's name on it.

One drawback to using Button mode is that it doesn't let you edit actions or create new ones. You also can't turn individual steps within an action on or off. Darn!

Using Actions

Photoshop comes loaded with dozens of built-in actions, though only a smidgen initially appear in the Actions panel. *Nine* additional sets of built-in actions are tucked away in the panel's menu (shown in *Figure 18-2*): Commands, Frames, Image Effects, LAB - Black & White Technique, Production, Star Trails, Text Effects, Textures, and Video Actions. To load one of these sets, simply choose it from the menu and Photoshop adds it to the panel's main list.

NOTE Among Photoshop's built-in actions is the Mixer Brush Cloning Paint Setup by Photoshop painting pioneer John Derry (*www.pixlart.blogspot.com*). Give it a swift double-click, and Photoshop adds a slew of well-organized layers to the current document that you can then use to turn your photo into a painting. For more on this action, see the Tip on page 502.

Each set includes several actions that you can use as is or edit to your own personal taste. For example, if you think the Spatter Frame action (part of the Frames set) is a little lame with its 15-pixel spray radius, you can bump it up to 25 pixels instead. (Editing actions is discussed later in this chapter.) Or you can duplicate that particular step to make the Spatter filter run twice!

TIP An easy way to duplicate an action that you want to customize is to Option-drag (Alt-drag on a PC) it to a different set.

To use one of Photoshop's built-in actions, follow these steps:

1. **Open an image.**

   With most actions, you simply need to open an image and then you're ready to invoke the action's magic. You don't even have to unlock the Background layer because Photoshop duplicates it for you.

2. **If necessary, tell Photoshop which *part* of the image you want to work with by creating a selection.**

   Occasionally, you need to create a selection before you run some of the built-in actions (like the ones with "selection" in parentheses after their names, such as "Vignette (selection)" [see *Figure 18-3*]).

3. **Choose the action you want to run.**

   In the Actions panel, click an action to activate it. If you're in Button mode (page 758), simply clicking an action's name triggers that action, so you're done. If you're not in Button mode, continue with the next step.

4. **Click the Play button.**

   Click the little Play button at the bottom of the Actions panel to run the action. Before you can blink, Photoshop is finished and dusting off its hands. If the program displays a dialog box that requires your input, the action pauses while you enter settings. Once you click OK, it continues on its merry way.

Recording Actions

When you're trying to decide on an action to record, start by thinking of any repetitive tasks you often perform. For example, back in Chapter 4 you learned that a simple one-pixel black border adds a classy touch to an image destined for a magazine, newspaper, or newsletter (page 181). If you add those borders regularly, that process is an *excellent* candidate for an action.

FIGURE 18-3

Top: Photoshop's built-in actions include "Vignette (selection)," which creates images like this. As you can tell from its name, you have to create a selection before running it.

Bottom: Another useful built-in action, named "Sepia Toning (layer)," adds a sepia (brown) tone to images.

In both these examples, the action created all the layers you see here, except for the original Background layer (which shows you what the original images looked like).

Before you record an action, it's a good idea to create a new *set* (think folder or group) for it to live in. There's no limit to how many sets you can create or how many actions you can add to each set. If you forget to make a set before you record an action, you can drag and drop the action into a set later. You can also copy actions *between* sets by Option-dragging (Alt-dragging) 'em.

Oddly enough, Photoshop doesn't capture Undo commands when you're recording actions. For example, if you mess up during the recording process and you use the Undo command to fix the mistake and then continue recording the rest of the action, Photoshop records everything *except* the Undo command, so the action won't run as you expect. So if you mess up while recording an action, just click the Stop button. Delete the bad steps in the Actions panel by dragging them to the trash can icon, and then choose Edit→Step Backward to get your image back to the last good step. Make sure the good step is active in the Action's panel, and then click the Record button to continue.

Here's how to create an action that adds a thin black border around an image:

1. **Open an image.**

   To record the steps, you have to perform them, so you need an open image to play with.

2. **Open the Actions panel and create a new set.**

   Choose Window→Actions, and then click the folder icon at the bottom of the panel. In the resulting dialog box, enter a descriptive name for your new action set (see *Figure 18-4*, top), and then click OK.

3. **Click the panel's "Create new action" button.**

   The button looks like a piece of paper with a folded corner (just like the "Create new layer" and "Create new channel" buttons). In the resulting dialog box, give the action a short but meaningful name, like *Black border* (*Figure 18-4*, bottom). You can also assign it a keyboard shortcut and a color (you see these colors only in Button mode [page 758], but they're still handy). When everything looks good, click the Record button to close the dialog box and start recording your action.

FIGURE 18-4

Top: Keep your Actions panel organized by storing actions in sets. This also lets you keep the actions you've made (or downloaded—see page 771) separate from those that come with Photoshop, as well as group 'em together by task or project.

Bottom: This dialog box lets you name your action and assign it a keyboard shortcut for faster access. The shortcut can be a function key (the F keys at the top of your keyboard) and, if you want, a modifier key (Shift or ⌘ [Shift or Ctrl on a PC]). By combining F keys and modifiers, you can create as many as 60 custom shortcuts for your actions (depending on the number of function keys on your keyboard).

You can edit the settings you applied in the New Action dialog box *after* you record it by activating the action in the Actions panel and then choosing Action Options from the panel's menu, or by simply double-clicking to the *right* of the action's set or name in the panel.

4. **Click the Record button in the New Action dialog box, and then perform the steps you want to record.**

   Once you click Record in the dialog box, the Record button at the bottom of the Actions panel turns red to let you know Photoshop is recording nearly every keystroke and mouse click you make. To record the border action mentioned earlier, consider whether you'll always start out with a locked Background layer. If so, begin by double-clicking the layer to unlock it. If not, click the square Stop button at the bottom of the Actions panel, double-click the Background layer to unlock it *before* you start recording the action, and then click the Action panel's Record button.

   Another solution is to *duplicate* the Image layer using the keyboard shortcut ⌘-J (Ctrl+J) so Photoshop doesn't capture the layer's name. If you think the images you'll run this action on will be comprised of *multiple* layers, you can activate all the layers by pressing ⌘-Option-A (Ctrl+Alt+A) so Photoshop doesn't capture specific layer names, and then create a Smart Object (page 120) or stamped layer (page 107) out of 'em. (See? There are a *ton* of things to consider when you're recording actions!)

   Next, press ⌘-A (Ctrl+A) to select the whole image and then click the "Add a layer style" button at the bottom of the Layers panel (the tiny *fx*) and choose Stroke. In the Layer Style dialog box that appears, enter a pixel value in the Size field *even* if the correct pixel value is already there—you never know what you might change in this dialog box between now and when you run the action. (Since Photoshop's dialog box, Options bar, and panel settings are sticky, you need to make sure your action includes resetting anything that may have changed in those places.) Choose Inside from the Position drop-down menu—even if it's *already* set to Inside—set the Fill Type menu to Color, and then click the colored rectangle underneath. When the Color Picker opens, choose black, and then click OK *twice* to close the Color Picker and Layer Style dialog boxes.

5. **Click Stop.**

Once you're finished recording, click the Stop button at the bottom of the Actions panel (the panel's Record button turns light gray) or press the Esc key.

6. **Choose File→Revert and test your action on the open image.**

To make sure your action works, return your image to its original state, click the new action's name in the Actions panel, and then click the Play button. If you run into problems, you can delete the action by dragging it to the trash can icon at the bottom of the panel and then have another go at it, or edit the action using the techniques discussed later in this chapter.

Give yourself a big pat on the back for successfully recording your first action!

> **TIP** Photoshop lets you capture strokes made with the brush tools and paths drawn with the Pen or shape tools, though you have to turn that feature on *before* you start recording by choosing Allow Tool Recording from the Actions panel's menu. This is a great way to capture the creation of a painting from start to finish in order to replay it later. You can even create the action in a low-resolution document and then replay it in a higher-resolution document later! (Photoshop captures your *strokes* but not the tool's *settings*, so if you used a particular brush tip or size for the recording, set that up *before* playback or Photoshop will use the tool's current settings).

Running Actions on a Folder

When you trigger an action, Photoshop performs the action's steps on the document you're currently working on. However, to *really* make actions work for you, you can run them on *more* than one document (this technique is called *batch processing* or *batching*). It takes an extra step or two, but it's worth it. For example, you can run the black-border action you created in the previous section on all your open files or on a folder of files instead of running it on each image individually. Just imagine the time you'll save!

> **TIP** You can record actions that trigger *other* actions, which is *extremely* helpful when you're batch processing. That way, instead of running the actions on the files one after another, you can simply run the action that triggers the rest. To include another action inside the one you're recording, ⌘-double-click the other action (Ctrl-double-click on a PC) in the Actions panel.

Here's how to run an action on more than one file:

1. **Open all the files or place them in a single folder.**

Photoshop's Batch command works on all open files or a whole folder (unless you're using Bridge, as noted in step 3 below). So depending on how many files you want to work on, you'll probably want to stick 'em in a folder first.

2. **Choose File→Automate→Batch, and then pick the action you want to run.**

In the Batch dialog box (*Figure 18-5*), choose an action from the Actions menu.

FIGURE 18-5

To reap the full reward of using actions, use the Batch dialog box to run them on multiple files (called batches).

Turn on the Include All Subfolders checkbox if you want to process files in folders within a master folder. This setting is especially handy if you use nested folders to organize your images.

WORKAROUND WORKSHOP

Beware of Recording Layer Names

Using actions is typically a trial-and-error operation—it can be challenging to get 'em just right because there are so many variables to consider. If Photoshop encounters *any* condition that varies from what you recorded, it slings an error dialog box at you and comes to a full stop.

One of the most common errors is Layer Unavailable, because most folks don't realize that Photoshop captures *layer names* when you record an action. For instance, if you start an action by double-clicking the Background layer to unlock it, Photoshop searches for a layer named Background when you run that action on other images. If it doesn't find one, you'll be greeted with an error dialog box that says, "The object 'layer Background' is unavailable." At that point, you can either continue running the action (by clicking Continue) or stop right there (by clicking Stop). If you choose to proceed and Photoshop *can* finish the remaining steps, it will. If it can't, you get (surprise!) another error dialog box expressing Photoshop's regret.

Admittedly, having to click Continue once in a while is no biggie, but it brings your action to a screeching halt. To cut down on this type of error, use *keyboard shortcuts* to activate layers instead of clicking them in the Layers panel. That way, Photoshop records the *shortcuts* instead of specific layer names. (The box on page 76 has a honkin' big list of shortcuts for activating and moving layers.)

You also don't want to record the act of *double-clicking* a layer to rename it because Photoshop captures the *original* layer's name in the action. Instead, activate the layer you want to rename *using a keyboard shortcut* and then choose Layer→Rename Layer. Type the new name into the resulting dialog box and click OK. By doing it this way, Photoshop changes the name of the currently active layer instead of hunting for a layer with a specific name. Neat, huh?

3. **In the Batch dialog box, pick the files or folders you want to process.**

   Use the Source drop-down menu to tell Photoshop whether to run the action on all open files or on a folder. If you pick Folder, click the Choose button and navigate to the folder containing your images. You can also choose Import to snatch files parked in your scanner or on an attached digital camera or memory card.

   If you've picked a few files and/or folders in Adobe Bridge, you can run the action on them by choosing Tools→Photoshop→Batch in the Bridge window (see Chapter 22 for more on using Bridge). Likewise, if you've picked files in Photoshop's Mini Bridge panel, Control-click (right-click) one of the thumbnails and choose Photoshop→Batch from the shortcut menu that appears. (You have to install Bridge and the Mini Bridge panel separately from Photoshop CC, as described on page 848.)

4. **Adjust other settings, if needed.**

   Turn on the "Override Action 'Open' Commands" checkbox if there's a step in your action that opens a file. That way, Photoshop opens the files you've picked in the Source menu instead of hunting for the file name recorded in the action. However, leave this checkbox off if you recorded the action to open a *specific* file that's necessary for the action to work properly, like when you're adding a specific texture file to the images.

   If you've chosen Folder as your source and the folder you want to work with contains *other* folders of images that you want Photoshop to process, turn on the Include All Subfolders checkbox.

   If your action summons an Open dialog box and want to bypass it completely, turn on the Suppress File Open Options Dialogs checkbox. Doing so prevents the Open dialog box from opening, so you can open a group of images without seeing that dialog box for each one (handy if you batch process raw images from your digital camera).

   Finally, turn on the Suppress Color Profile Warnings checkbox if you want Photoshop to always use its own color profile (page 675) without asking if that's OK.

5. **Tell Photoshop where you want to save the processed files.**

   From the Destination drop-down menu, choose None to have Photoshop leave your files open *without* saving them (not a good idea if you're running the action on hundreds of files!). Pick "Save and Close" to overwrite the originals (scary!) and close the files. A better option is to preserve the originals by choosing Folder, and then clicking the Choose button to tell Photoshop where it should save the newly processed files.

   If your action includes any Save As steps, turn on the "Override Action 'Save As' Commands" checkbox to make Photoshop use the settings you've specified in this dialog box. If you don't turn on this checkbox, Photoshop saves your images *twice*: once where you specified in the action and a second time in the location you set in the Batch dialog box.

6. **If you want to rename the resulting files, enter a naming scheme in the File Naming section.**

   You can name the new files anything you want. Choose Document Name from the first drop-down menu to have Photoshop keep the original file names, or enter something else in the name field. You can also rename files with the current date (in several formats), using an alphabetical code or numeric serial number, and so on. Keep the second field in each row set to "extension" so you don't encounter any problems with incompatible file formats down the road.

7. **Turn on the appropriate Compatibility checkbox(es) based on where the files are headed.**

   If you know your images will be opened or stored on a computer that runs a different operating system than yours, then turn on the checkboxes for each system your file is likely to end up on (Photoshop automatically turns on the checkbox for the operating system you're using). For example, if you're using a Mac and your images are destined for a Unix- or Windows-based machine, check Mac and Unix or Windows. (It's OK to turn on all three compatibility checkboxes.)

8. **Choose an error-handling method from the Errors menu.**

   This is where you tell Photoshop what to do if it encounters a problem while it's running the action. Your options are "Stop for Errors" and "Log Errors to File." By choosing the latter, Photoshop writes down all the errors in a text file and continues to process your images (yay!); click the Save As button below this drop-down menu to tell the program where to save that text file.

9. **Click OK to run the action.**

   Sit back and smile smugly as Photoshop does all the work for you (and cross your fingers that you don't get any errors!).

TIP Yet *another* option for applying actions to a slew of files is to use the Image Processor (choose File→ Scripts→Image Processor; see page 247). The Image Processor dialog box has fewer options than the Batch dialog box, so it's a little easier to use, plus you get the option of changing file formats during the save process (say, from a PSD to a JPEG) without having to manually add the step of flattening the document in the action itself.

◼ Managing Actions

If you don't get your action quite right the first time (and most likely you won't, which is perfectly normal), you can go back and edit it, though it's *usually* easier to just start over from scratch. That said, the Actions panel's *menu* has a few commands that can help you whip misbehaving actions into shape:

- **Record Again**. When you choose this option, Photoshop runs through all the steps in the action and opens all the dialog boxes associated with them so you can adjust their settings, and then updates the action accordingly.

TIP   When you're troubleshooting an action, it can be helpful to run the action one step at a time; as you run each step, you can see it applied in the image and in your Layers panel, and therefore figure out where the action went astray. To run an action step by step, simply ⌘-double-click the step you want to start with in the Actions panel (Ctrl+double-click on a PC), or single-click a step and then ⌘-click (Ctrl-click on a PC) the panel's Play button. (Remember, you have to click the flippy triangle next to the action's name to see the individual steps within the action.) This maneuver also lets you nest an existing action *inside* a new action that you're currently recording, as explained in the second Tip on page 763.

- **Insert Menu Item**. For some unknown reason, when you're creating an action, you can't record any items in the View and Window menus (think zooming in or out of your document, fitting it onscreen [very helpful when sharpening], or arranging the document windows on your screen), but you can *insert* them—or any other menu item—using this command, either while you record the action or after. Simply activate the step above where you want the menu item to go, or, if you want to insert the menu item at the end of the action, activate the action's name. Then choose Insert Menu Item from the Actions panel's menu and, in the resulting dialog box, pick the item, and then click OK. If the menu item pops open a dialog box, Photoshop won't record any settings you enter, so you'll have to enter them manually when you run the action.

WORKAROUND WORKSHOP

Different Files, Different Results

When you're recording actions, it's important to realize that not only is Photoshop recording every step *exactly* as you perform it, but it's also memorizing info about your document. It remembers stuff like file size, color mode, layer names, and even what color your foreground color chip is set to.

For that reason, if you try to run an action on a file that's in a different color mode or is a different size than the document you used to record it, you may encounter errors or unexpected results. To fix that kind of thing, you've got several options:

- If you create an action that resizes a landscape-oriented image to 800 pixels in width using the Image Size dialog box and then you run it on a portrait-oriented image, you won't get the same results. The fix is to re-record the action using the File→Automate→Fit Image command instead, which lets you enter maximum dimensions for either width or height.

- If you use certain tools while you're recording an action, Photoshop remembers the tool's *position* within the image by snagging coordinates from the program's vertical and horizontal rulers. Among these are the Marquee, Slice, Gradient, Magic Wand, Lasso, Shape, Path, Eyedropper, and Notes tools. So if you run an action

involving these tools on files of varying pixel dimensions, you'll run into problems. For example, if you record an action that includes drawing an Elliptical Marquee in the center of a document and then run that action on a document with vastly different pixel dimensions, the document's center won't be in the same place. The fix is to change the unit of measurement for the rulers to *percentages* (page 25) before you record the action. That way, Photoshop records your cursor's location as a *relative* position instead of an absolute position.

- If you create an action that requires an image to be in a specific color mode (say, RGB), make the first step of your action choosing File→Automate→Conditional Mode Change. The dialog box that appears includes a series of checkboxes that you can use to take an image in any mode (say, Grayscale or CMYK) and convert it to RGB (or whatever you want).

The other option is to use Photoshop CC's new *conditional actions*, which are explained on page 768 (and they're easier to use than you might think!).

TIP There's no way for you or anyone else running an action to turn off a dialog box that you've added using the Insert Menu Item command (though you can turn off *other* action dialog boxes—see page 757), so this command is a good way to *force* whomever is running the action to enter a particular menu's settings.

- **Insert Stop**. Use this command to pause the action so you can give the person who's running it *instructions* on what to do next, or tell them to do something that you can't record, such as open a specific file (because Photoshop captures the path name of where the file lives) or edit a layer mask. To add a stop after a particular step (it's helpful to think of it as a *message*), activate the step in the Actions panel and then choose Insert Stop (see *Figure 18-6*). Photoshop displays a dialog box that you can type instructions into, such as, "Change the Brush tip to Charcoal Pencil," "Adjust the Radius setting until the image looks sharp enough to you," or "Use the layer mask to hide the texture from your subject's face." This kind of thing is especially helpful if you plan to give the action to someone else to run on a variety of images with different sizes and resolutions (because the settings would need to be tweaked for each image).

FIGURE 18-6

Top: When you insert a stop, you get to include instructions for the person running the action; you can type whatever you want. The message appears when that person triggers the action's stop point. If you want to let folks continue with the action after they've preformed the step described by the message, turn on the Allow Continue checkbox.

Bottom: Here's what you see when you run the action and hit the stop point. If you turned on the Allow Continue checkbox, you get a Continue button. If you didn't, your only choice is to click Stop. After you've performed the part of the action that couldn't be recorded, click the Actions panel's Play button to finish off the action—and if you go that route, be sure to include the text, "...and then click the Play button in the Actions panel" in your Stop message so folks know what action (ha!) to take.

- **Insert Conditional**. New in Photoshop CC, this option lets you record a *conditional* action that chooses among several *previously* recorded actions in order to meet criteria you set. To use this incredibly handy feature, start by recording *separate* actions for each eventuality you expect to encounter: different document sizes, color modes, bit depths (page 36); documents with and without selections, multiple layers, alpha channels, locked layers, Adjustment layers, and so on. Next, place those individual actions inside a set, and then record yet *another* action—in the same set—that riffles through 'em to find the right action to run. (Don't panic: it's not as time-consuming as it sounds. You'll likely have just 2 or 3 conditions to plan for.)

To do that, choose Insert Conditional from the Actions panel menu. In the resulting dialog box, use the If Current drop-down menu to pick a criteria, and then use the Then Play Action drop-down menu to pick the action that should play if that criteria *is* met. Finally, use the Else Play Action drop-down menu to tell Photoshop what action to run if that criteria *isn't* met.

- **Insert Path**. Photoshop can record the act of drawing a path (as explained in the last bullet in this list), though it can't record Pen tool *settings*, so you can use this command to insert a path you've *already* drawn. Just open the Paths panel, activate the one you want to insert, and then choose this command.

- **Action Options**. This command (which works on both custom and built-in actions) opens the Action Options dialog box so you can edit the action's name, keyboard shortcut, and color. You can also open this dialog box by Option-double-clicking (Alt-double-clicking on a PC) the action in the Actions panel. (To rename an action, simply double-click its name in the Actions panel.)

- **Playback Options**. If you can't figure out where an action has gone haywire, you can make Photoshop play the action more slowly by choosing this command. In the resulting dialog box, you can choose Accelerated (normal speed), "Step by Step" (Photoshop completes each step and refreshes the screen before going to the next step), or "Pause For _ seconds" (Photoshop pauses between each step for the number of seconds you specify).

- **Allow Tool Recording**. This option tells Photoshop to capture strokes you make with the brush tools and paths you draw with the Pen or shape tools (though it doesn't capture the tool's particular *settings,* such as brush tip, size, and so on). Be sure to turn this setting on *before* you begin recording the painting of your next masterpiece, and you'll be able to replay—and thus recreate—the painting any time you want.

Editing Actions

You can add, delete, or tweak actions' steps, and scoot 'em around within the Actions panel (just like layers). To rearrange your Actions panel, just drag an action to a new position in the panel; when you see a light-colored line where you want the action to go, release your mouse button. This lets you keep certain actions together so they're easier to spot (handy when you're in Button mode [page 758]). You can also drag and drop steps *within* an action to rearrange 'em (because there are *so* many things to consider when you're recording an action, some step rearranging will likely be in order). To change an action's *settings* (such as those found in a filter's dialog box), double-click the relevant step while an image is open, enter a new value in the resulting dialog box, and then click OK.

> **NOTE** By clicking OK in a dialog box while editing an action's settings, you'll actually *run* the command associated with that dialog box (sharpening an image, for example). The fix is to immediately undo it by pressing ⌘-Z (Ctrl+Z). Photoshop still remembers the new settings you entered and will simply use 'em the next time you run that action.

You can also add steps to an action. Simply activate the step that comes *before* the one you want to add, and then click the Record button; perform the new step(s), and then click the Stop button. Photoshop adds the new steps below the one you picked.

To get rid of a step, action, or set of actions, just activate what you want to delete and then drag it onto the trash can icon at the bottom of the Actions panel. (To bypass the "Are you sure?" dialog box Photoshop displays when you use that method, activate the items and then Option-click [Alt-click on a PC] the trash can button to delete 'em.) To do a *thorough* spring cleaning of the Actions panel, choose Clear All Actions from the Actions panel's menu and, when Photoshop asks if you *really* want to delete everything (including Photoshop's built-in Default Actions set), take a deep breath and click OK.

> **TIP** To get the Default Actions set back after using the Clear All Actions command, just choose Reset Actions from the Actions panel's menu. Whew!

Creating Droplets

Droplets are actions that you trigger by dragging and dropping files onto special icons, so they're great for running actions on images without actually *opening* the images. They can do things like change file formats, image size, convert images to black and white, or apply an overall color boost. As self-contained mini-applications, they can live outside Photoshop on your desktop, as *aliases* (pointer or shortcut files) in your Dock (taskbar on a PC), or on someone else's computer.

It's easy to create a droplet from an action; just follow these steps:

1. **Trot over to the Actions panel and choose an existing action.**

   You can't put the cart before the horse! To make a droplet, you've got to record the action first.

2. **Choose File→Automate→Create Droplet.**

   The resulting dialog box looks like the Batch dialog box shown back in *Figure 18-5* (page 764). Click the Choose button at the top to tell Photoshop where to save your droplet, and then set the other options according to the advice on pages 763–766.

3. **Click OK and you're finished.**

   Your droplet (which looks like the one shown in *Figure 18-7*, top) magically appears wherever you specified.

FIGURE 18-7

Top: A droplet looks like a big, fat, blue arrow.

Bottom: To use a droplet, simply drag and drop a file or folder onto its icon, and Photoshop performs the action on the file(s).

If Photoshop isn't currently running, it launches automatically.

Sharing Actions

When it comes to actions, folks love to share—there are tons of actions floating around on the Web. Most are free (though you'll probably have to register with the website you download them from), but you have to pay for the more useful and creative ones. Sharing your own actions is pretty easy; the only requirement is that you save your actions as a set (see below) before uploading them to a website. This section explains how to load actions that other people have created, and how to save your own actions as a set so you can share 'em.

> **NOTE** For easy access to actions others have shared with the Adobe Photoshop community, pop open the new Adobe Exchange panel by choosing Window→Extensions→Adobe Exchange. This handy panel lets you locate, purchase, and install all manner of actions, brushes, plug-ins, and so on right inside Photoshop.

Loading Actions

Downloading and analyzing actions made by other folks is a fantastic way to learn what's possible. That said, actions that are short and sweet—ones that expand your canvas, add a new layer and fill it with color, and so on—can be even more useful than more complex actions because you'll use 'em more often.

One of the best places to find useful actions is the Adobe Photoshop Marketplace (*www.lesa.in/psmarketactions*). Others include Action Central (*www.lesa.in/actioncentral*) and ActionFx (*www.lesa.in/actionfx*). (These sites are also great resources for brushes, textures, and so on.) Most of these sites arrange their goodies by category, so you'll probably have to choose Actions from a menu.

Here's how to load somebody else's action onto your computer:

1. **Download the action or action set.**

   What you're actually downloading is an ATN file (if the set is compressed, you'll end up with a Zip file that you need to double-click to expand). Save it somewhere you'll remember (like on your desktop or in your Downloads folder).

2. **Drag and drop the action into an empty Photoshop window (no documents open), as shown in *Figure 18-8*.**

   You can also load a new action by choosing Load Action from the Actions panel's menu, by double-clicking the ATN file, or by right-clicking the ATN file and choosing Open With→Adobe Photoshop CC. No matter which method you use, the new action appears in your Actions panel.

FIGURE 18-8

You can quickly load an action by dragging and dropping its ATN file into the Photoshop workspace. The new action appears in your Actions panel.

Alternatively, use the new Adobe Exchange panel to automatically install a downloaded action, as the Note on page 771 explains.

3. **Choose the action and give it a whirl.**

   Test drive your new action by opening an image, clicking the action's name in the Actions panel, and then clicking the Play button. That's the only way to find out whether it's lovely or lame.

Saving Actions as a Set

Photoshop temporarily stores the actions you create or load in a special spot on your hard drive. If you reinstall or upgrade the program—or if the program crashes—there's a decent chance your actions will get zapped in the process (though the Migrate Presets option helps a lot when you're upgrading; just choose Edit→Presets→Migrate Presets [see page 29 for details]). If you've grown fond of your actions, you can save 'em *outside* the Photoshop application folder for easy backup. That way, you can reload them if they accidentally get vaporized. As a bonus, once you save your actions as a set, you can share 'em with others by uploading them to sites like the Adobe Photoshop Marketplace, discussed in the previous section. Here's what to do:

1. **In the Actions panel, choose an action set.**

   You can save only actions that are part of a set—you can't save individual actions. (Page 756 explains how to create sets and add actions to 'em.)

2. **Choose Save Actions from the Actions panel's menu.**

   In the resulting dialog box, Photoshop prompts you to save the file in the Presets folder. To keep from losing your actions when you reinstall or upgrade Photoshop, save them somewhere else. No matter where you save them, if you add or edit the set later, be sure to pick the *same* spot or you'll end up with multiple versions of that action set.

3. **Click Save.**

   Photoshop creates an ATN file that you can move between computers, back up to an external hard drive, or share with the planet via the Internet.

TIP On Macs, Photoshop saves your actions in *Macintosh HD/Users/[your user name]/Library/Application Support/Adobe/Adobe Photoshop CC/Presets/Actions*. On computers running Windows 7, it saves them in *C:\ Users\[your user name]\AppData\Roaming\Adobe\Adobe Photoshop CC\Presets\Actions*. (If you use a different version of Windows, you can use the "Save in" drop-down menu in the Save dialog box to see where Photoshop puts your new action set.)

FREQUENTLY ASKED QUESTION

Sharing Droplets

I want to send my extra-special Mac droplet to a Windows computer. Is that legal?

Sure! It's within your Photoshop User Bill of Rights to share droplets between computers with different operating systems. However, the droplet won't work unless you know these secrets:

- Save the droplet with an .exe extension, which tells a Windows computer that it's an *executable file*—in other words, a program you can run (this extension isn't necessary on Macs).

- If you created the droplet on a Windows computer and want to move it to a Mac, drag it onto the Photoshop CC

icon on the Mac to make Photoshop update it so it works on Macs, too.

- Photoshop can't understand file name references between operating systems, so if your action includes an Open or Save As step that references a specific file, the action pauses and demands the file from the poor soul who's using the droplet. If that happens to you, use the error dialog box to find the file Photoshop is asking for so the droplet can resume its work.

Beyond Photoshop: Plug-Ins

With enough patience, practice, and keyboard shortcuts burned into your brain, you can get smokin' fast in Photoshop—but you'll *never* be as fast as a computer. As you've learned, some things—like creating complex selections, correcting colors, retouching skin extensively, and so on—are darned difficult, so they're going to take you a long time no matter how fast you get.

That's where plug-ins come in handy. Think of them as little helper programs that run inside Photoshop (though a few run outside Photoshop, too) and let you do the hard stuff faster. You can get plug-ins from all kinds of websites, and they range from free to pricey. The really good ones give you amazing results in seconds, rather than the hours it would take you to do the same thing manually (if you can do it at all). Plus, the newer ones do their thing on a separate layer and, in some cases, run as Smart Filters, so you don't even have to duplicate your original layer first. Nice!

In this chapter, you'll learn how to add and remove these little jewels, as well as how to store them somewhere other than your Photoshop CC folder (it's often safer that way). You'll also be introduced to some of the most amazing plug-ins on the market today—the crème de la crème—that run on Macs *and* PCs.

> **NOTE** Photoshop on the Mac is 64-bit mode only, so you can forget about using any 32-bit plug-ins that you might have hanging around. What's the workaround? Contact the folks who made the plug-in and see if they've *updated* it for 64-bit and install that instead.

Adding and Removing Plug-Ins

To install a plug-in on a Mac, download it or copy it from the installer disc it shipped with, and then drag it from wherever it's saved on your computer into the Plug-ins folder, which lives here: Adobe Photoshop CC→Plug-Ins (*Figure 19-1*, top). On a PC, download the plug-in or copy it from the installer disc and look for an .exe (execut-able) file; then simply double-click that file to run the installer.

FIGURE 19-1

On a Mac, you can install a plug-in manually by dragging it into Photoshop's Plug-Ins folder (top) or by using the installer provided by the folks who made the plug-in (bottom). You can also use the new Adobe Exchange panel to find and install plug-ins, as the Note on page 771 explains.

On a PC, simply double-click the plug-in's .exe file (if it doesn't include one, just drag the file into the Adobe Photoshop CC→Plug-Ins folder).

If you have trouble installing a plug-in, contact the person or company who cre-ated it for help.

Once you've installed the plug-in, you might have to dig through Photoshop's menus to find it. If a plug-in deals with batch processing (modifying multiple files at once), you may find it in the File→Automate menu instead of the Filter menu. And if it deals with selections or masking, you may find it lurking in the Select menu.

After you install the plug-in, quit Photoshop if it's running (File→Quit [File→Exit on a PC]) and then relaunch it. When Photoshop reopens, you should see the plug-in listed at the bottom of the Filter menu.

Some plug-ins, like the one shown in *Figure 19-1* (bottom), come with an installer and an *uninstaller*, which is handy if you want to get rid of it. That said, you can remove a plug-in manually by opening the Plug-Ins folder and dragging it to the Trash. (On a PC running Windows 8, go to Start by putting your cursor in the bottom-left of the screen, then find the program and right-click its icon; click Uninstall on the toolbar at the bottom of the screen, and then—in the Programs and Features window that appears—click Uninstall. In Windows 7, go to Start→Control Panel→Programs→"Uninstall a program." Choose the plug-in from the list of programs and then click Uninstall.) The next time you launch Photoshop, you'll see neither hide nor hair of the banished plug-in.

Photoshop CC runs in 64-bit mode (page xxviii) on both Macs and PCs, so you may find that some of your older 32-bit plug-ins are incompatible and are therefore missing from Photoshop's menus even *after* you install 'em. You can, however, launch Photoshop in 32-bit mode in order to make them work...*if* you're using a PC (CC for the Mac is 64-bit only). When you install Photoshop on a PC, you get two full versions of the program in two separate Plug-ins folders: one for 32-bit mode and another for 64-bit mode (located in *C:\Program Files\Adobe\Photoshop CC* and *C:\ Program Files (x86)\Adobe\Photoshop CC*, respectively).

■ Managing Plug-Ins

Unlike previous versions, Photoshop CC wants you to store plug-ins in its Plug-ins folder and the Required folder (see the box on page 781), so that's where it looks each time you launch the program. That's all well and good, but there's an *awfully* good chance your plug-ins will get zapped if the program crashes, or you upgrade to a new version of Photoshop or reinstall the current one. (The same is true of actions, brushes, and other presets, though the new Migrate Presets option helps if you're upgrading [see the Note on page 29].)

FREQUENTLY ASKED QUESTION

Dude, Where's My Plug-In?

Help! I don't see my plug-in in the Filter menu. Did it load or what?

Peace, Grasshopper. You can find out whether your plug-in loaded in a couple of ways.

When Photoshop encounters a plug-in that won't load, it presents you with a dialog box that says, "One or more plug-ins are currently not available on your system. For details, see Help→System Info." To find out why the plug-in didn't load, choose Help→System Info and scroll down in the resulting dialog box until you see the offending plug-in, along with Photoshop's oh-so-brief explanation of what went wrong. For example, if you try to learn why the Variations adjustment (see the Note on page 339) didn't load in 64-bit mode, you'll see the following line of text: "Variations NO VERSION - 32-bit plug-in not supported in 64-bit - next to the text: 'Variations.plugin.'"

In CC, if a plug-in doesn't load, it's likely that it works only in 32-bit mode. In that case, if you're on a PC, make sure that you're running the right version of the program. For a plug-in that works only in 32-bit mode, you have to launch the 32-bit version of the program, as explained on page xxviii. If you're on the Mac, you're out of luck: Photoshop runs in 64-bit mode only.

If you don't get the "plug-in didn't load" message and your plug-in is *still* missing, take a peek in other menus—such as Select or File→Automate—to see if it ended up in there. You can also look at the list of loaded plug-ins by choosing Photoshop→About Plug-In (Help→About Plug-In on a PC). If your plug-in is included in the list but isn't loading, about the only thing you can do is install a fresh copy of it or, better yet, see if a newer version is available from the developer's website. Keep in mind that some plug-ins continue to work with newer versions of Photoshop, but some don't.

To protect your precious plug-ins, you can store 'em elswhere, though you have to tell Photoshop *where* you put them by using the Load command in the respective panel's menu (say, the Actions panel if you're loading an action that's stored somewhere else on your hard drive or the Brush panel if you're loading custom brushes). In Photoshop CC, it's no longer possible to direct the program to look for another folder full of plug-ins using its Plug-Ins preferences.

In the following pages, you'll find brief descriptions of some of the most amazing plug-ins on the market. Each one performs its own special brand of magic, such as noise removal, color enhancement, or special effects—one even turns your Photoshop document into a fully functional web page! These plug-ins range in price from $50 to $500, but don't let that scare you; if a plug-in saves you valuable hours, you'll make that money back in no time flat. There are *gobs* of Photoshop plug-ins, so don't be alarmed if you don't see your favorite one in the following list—it's simply impossible to catalog 'em all here.

> **NOTE** For a comprehensive list of Photoshop plug-ins, visit *www.lesa.in/psplugins* or open the new Adobe Exchange panel by choosing Window→Extensions→Adobe Exchange. The latter lets you find, buy, and install all manner of plug-ins, brushes, and actions from within Photoshop.

■ Noise Reducers

If you've taken a photo in low light or if you set your camera to a high ISO (a setting that increases its sensitivity to light), chances are the image has a ton of *noise*—grainy-looking speckles—in it. While you'll find a couple of noise-reducing tricks in Chapter 11, if the image is *really* important, you can spring for one of these noise-reducing plug-ins instead.

TROUBLESHOOTING MOMENT

Disabling Plug-Ins

If Photoshop starts acting weird after you install a plug-in, you can temporarily disable that plug-in to see if it's the culprit by locating it on your hard drive and adding a tilde (~) to the beginning of its file name. Some manufacturers nest their plug-ins inside yet another folder; for example, you'll find a folder called Mask Pro *inside* your Plug-Ins folder. In that case, you can put the tilde to the beginning of the *folder's* name to disable everything inside it. Either way, adding the tilde means the plug-in won't load the next time you launch Photoshop. When you want the plug-in to load again, just delete the tilde and relaunch Photoshop.

You can also get Photoshop to temporarily disable *all* plug-ins (great for narrowing down why the program might be acting strange). Simply press and hold the Shift key when you launch Photoshop and you'll see a dialog box asking if you'd like to "Skip loading optional and third-party plug-ins" (that is, anything installed in the *Adobe Photoshop CC→Plug-Ins* folder). Your choices are Yes and No (you don't get to pick and choose *which* plug-ins Photoshop skips; it's an all or nothing kind of deal).

Noiseware

This plug-in has quickly become the noise reducer of choice for professional photographers. Instead of blurring the whole image to make the noise less visible, Noiseware analyzes the image and reduces noise only in the areas that really need it. You also get a handy before-and-after view so you can see what it did. It's available from *www.imagenomic.com* and costs around $50.

TIP You can often get plug-ins much cheaper if you buy 'em bundled together, or if you're upgrading from a previous edition. Be sure to look for special deals on the developer's website!

Dfine

This plug-in reduces noise in a very simple and nondestructive way. When you launch Dfine and click its Measure button, it scours your image for noise in areas without much detail (where noise is easiest to see). Start by trying the factory setting and then increase or decrease the noise-reduction level with the easy-to-use sliders (see *Figure 19-2*). When you find a setting you like, click OK to make Dfine create a copy of the currently active layer and apply the noise reduction to the duplicate instead of the original.

FIGURE 19-2

Dfine's handy split-screen view lets you see how much noise the plug-in will remove from the image before you commit to the change. Here, the original is on the left side of the vertical red line and the result on the right.

Thanks to Nik Software's amazing *control points* technology, Dfine lets you reduce noise in certain areas of an image without adding a mask. It also figures out which kind of camera you used to take the photo and then applies the right amount of noise reduction for your particular model (which makes sense because your camera is what introduced noise in the first place). Before Google purchased Nik Software in late 2012, you could buy Dfine as a separate product, but these days it only comes bundled with the rest of their plug-ins, including Sharpener Pro, Color Efex Pro, and Viveza (all discussed later in this chapter) for $150. One nice thing about Nik Software's plug-ins is that they all have the same appearance and controls, so once you learn how to use one, you can easily use 'em all (*www.niksoftware.com*).

> **NOTE** As of this writing, the Nik Software plug-in bundle is *free* to anyone who owns the current version of *any* Nik Software plug-in. While that's one heck of a deal on fabulous software, this kind of thing smells *suspiciously* like the end of a product's lifecycle, which is a real shame.

Photo Ninja (previously Noise Ninja)

Long considered the king of noise-reduction software, Noise Ninja has been used by photographers and newspaper production artists for years (though Noiseware has become extremely popular, too). It helps reduce noise (speckled imperfections) and grain (textured imperfections) while preserving details. It can tackle 16-bit images, handle batch processing, and work as a Smart Filter. These days the noise-reducing part has been rolled into a *new* product named Photo Ninja, which you can use in place of Adobe's Camera Raw plug-in to edit and convert raw images into other formats. The new software will set you back about $130, though Noise Ninja owners can upgrade for $80 (*www.picturecode.com*).

◼ Making Selections and Masking

As you've learned in previous chapters, selecting stuff like hair and fur is *really* hard. Sure, there are some tricks that make it simpler, but a plug-in specifically designed for that task can make your life a heck of a lot easier and save you tons of time (especially if you do this kind of thing a lot). That said, you'll need a bit of patience when you start working with masking plug-ins, because they're not for the faint of heart. But with practice, you can use them to create selections you just can't make any other way.

> **NOTE** Adobe put a lot of work into improving the Refine Edge command back in Photoshop CS5. So before you plunk down cold hard cash on a masking plug-in, make sure you're up to speed on the enhancements discussed starting on page 165.

Fluid Mask

This is a *powerful* plug-in that helps you mask around complex areas like hair and fur. As soon as you open Fluid Mask, it analyzes your image and marks what it thinks are edges with blue lines (see *Figure 19-3*) so you can decide which edges keep and which ones to zap. Then it creates a cutout of the image you can send back to Photoshop to use as a mask. You can also save your project and return to it later—a nice touch. Fluid Mask costs about $150 (*www.vertustech.com*).

FIGURE 19-3

These blue lines mark the edges that Fluid Mask found in this image. You can use the plug-in's tools (on the left) to mark edges you want to keep and ones you want to throw away.

UP TO SPEED

Finding Built-In Plug-Ins

Plug-ins come in two flavors: those that are installed with Photoshop and those that aren't. Back in CS6, Adobe changed where the program installs built-in plug-ins. This change keeps built-in plug-ins separate from plug-ins you install yourself—whether they're from another company or an optional plug-in from Adobe—which makes troubleshooting plug-in related problems a little easier for the poor souls at Adobe Technical Support. So where on earth does Photoshop put the built-in ones?

The standard plug-ins—filters, extensions, the "Save for Web" dialog box, and the like—are squirreled away in a folder named *Required*. To see this folder on a Mac, Control- or right-click the Photoshop CC application icon (which lives in *Applications/ Adobe Photoshop CC*), choose Show Package Contents, and then navigate to *Contents/Required/Plug-ins*. On a PC, the path is *C:\Program Files\Adobe\Adobe Photoshop CC (64Bit)\ Required\Plug-Ins* for the 64-bit version of the program, and *C:\Program Files (x86)\Adobe\Adobe Photoshop CC\Required\ Plug-Ins* for the 32-bit version.

You really don't need to root around in the Required folder, but at least now you know why the regular Plug-Ins folder is practically empty!

Perfect Mask

Perfect Mask helps you pick the precise colors you want to keep or remove as you build image masks. It gives you two eyedroppers to work with: Use one to select colors you want to keep and the other to select colors you want to throw away. Then you can use its Magic Brush to paint away the image's background while the plug-in helps you along by referring to the Keep and Drop color palettes you made. It can also extract *partial* color from a pixel, leaving you with a partially transparent pixel—important when you're selecting hair or fur (the edges are so soft that they have to be partially see-through to blend in with a new background). You can also view the image in mask mode, which helps you see what the selection looks like because it's displayed in shades of gray (just like a layer or channel mask). Perfect Mask can handle 16-bit images and works as a Smart Filter, though you have to turn the layer into a Smart Object first; otherwise, the plug-in deletes the selected pixels as soon as you apply it.

This plug-in costs around $100, though it's cheaper if you buy the Perfect Photo Suite bundle, which includes Perfect B&W, Perfect Portrait, Perfect Effects, Perfect Resize, and FocalPoint (some of which are covered in this chapter). The whole enchilada costs $300 and gives you access to the plug-ins through Photoshop, Photoshop Elements, Photoshop Lightroom, and Apple's Aperture; however, you can pick up a stand-alone version of the whole suite that runs *independently* of Photoshop for a mere $80 (*www.ononesoftware.com*).

> **TIP** When you install plug-ins from onOne Software, be sure to peek in both the Window→Extensions menu as well as the File→Automate window to find your new goodies.

■ Color Correction and Enhancement

The plug-ins in this category can spruce up or fix the color in your images and produce a startling array of special effects while they're at it. Read on for the scoop!

Viveza

As you've learned in previous chapters, before you can adjust the color of a specific part of an image, you need to *select* that area first. Not so with Viveza. Since this plug-in made its debut in 2008, it has revolutionized selective color and light adjustments. By marking the areas you want to change with *control points* (the small gray circles shown in *Figure 19-4*), you can adjust the saturation, brightness, and contrast of those areas at warp speed. And Viveza performs its magic on a duplicate layer, so you don't have to worry about destroying your original image. It's available from *www.niksoftware.com*, bundled with the rest of their plug-ins (including Sharpener Pro, Color Efex Pro, and Viveza) for $150. (See the Note on page 780 regarding the current state of Nik plug-ins.)

FIGURE 19-4

By dropping a control point on an image (the circular gray dot near the cowgirl's neck), you can adjust each area's saturation, brightness, and contrast individually.

Notice that in the right side of the image, the contrast and saturation of the woman's vest has been increased while the sky remains untouched.

Color Efex Pro

If you could buy just one plug-in, this would be a darn good choice. Using the same control points as other Nik Software plug-ins, Color Efex Pro lets you selectively apply up to 55 enhancement filters to your images—all nondestructively. You can use them to enhance images in creative ways, as well as to fix color casts, smooth skin, and so on (see *Figure 19-5*). Drop as many control points as you want and use them to set the effect's opacity in certain areas of the image, or click the Brush button to paint the effect where you want it. This plug-in is included in the $150 Nik Software bundle available at *www.niksoftware.com*. (The Note on page 780 has info about the current state of Nik plug-ins.)

Perfect Portrait

With the click of a single button, this plug-in scans your image for faces and facial features so it can whiten eyes and teeth, define lips, soften wrinkles, and reduce shines and blemishes. Perfect Portrait can also zap color casts based on the ethnicity of each face in the image; it now includes the power of SkinTune, which was part of the now-discontinued PhotoTune plug-in. And age- and gender-specific presets give you a head start for a slew of common problems. A handy set of sliders let you adjust each and every improvement, and tools let you paint away stray hairs, blemishes, and wrinkles. When you find a combination of settings that works, you can save it as a preset for use on other photos. You get to choose whether to apply these amazing fixes as a Smart Object or as an additional Image layer. Perfect Portrait is available for $100 from *www.ononesoftware.com*, though it's also included in their $300 software suite.

FIGURE 19-5

Top: This split-screen preview shows you before and after versions of an image. This particular filter, called Bleach Bypass, creates a high-contrast grunge look.

Bottom: The Glamour Glow filter gives the original image (left) a seriously dreamy look (right). But because Color Efex Pro applies the effect on another layer, you can always lower the filter layer's opacity to blend it with the original and produce a more realistic result.

Miscellaneous Plug-Ins

Most of the plug-ins in this section relate to specific tasks like creating black-and-white images, making enlargements, merging HDR images, building websites, creating actions, and so on.

Silver Efex Pro

This plug-in isn't a black-and-white converter; it's a virtual black-and-white *darkroom* that helps you create stunning black-and-white images (*Figure 19-6*) from color ones (though you can also use it to improve images that are already black and white). It has more than 30 black-and-white presets and also lets you create your own. You can make global adjustments using the plug-in's sliders or drop control points to tweak the brightness, sharpness, contrast, and structure (level of detail) in specific areas of an image, such as eyes, patterned clothing, and so on. You can also add a color filter just as if you'd put a filter on your camera lens. Silver Efex Pro lets you choose from over 20 different film types to simulate the look and grain of real film, add tints, or burn the edges of your images. It works as a Smart Filter and is included in the $150 Nik Software bundle (*www.niksoftware.com*). (See the Note on page 780 regarding the current state of Nik plug-ins.)

FIGURE 19-6

Silver Efex Pro, currently the most powerful black-and-white plug-in on the market, includes a gazillion gorgeous presets that you can fine-tune.

It even helps you create the look of black-and-white images captured on real film. If you want to add a little grain to an image, you can pick from several different options that look like real film grain.

Perfect Resize

This plug-in (which used to be called Genuine Fractals) will save your bacon if you need to *enlarge* an image. It lets you create printable versions of even low-resolution images (like those made for the Web or captured with a low-quality setting on your digital camera). It can blow images up to over 1,000 percent to make honkin' big panoramas, enlarge still frames from old videos to create higher-quality versions, and so on. It can scale any Photoshop document—even if it's brimming with Smart Objects, paths, or Type layers—without losing resolution or harming the image's quality. Just pick the pixels, dimensions (if you know them), enter a percentage for the enlargement, or enter the print size and resolution you want. If the image's proportions don't match those of the paper size you pick, Perfect Resize offers you a cropping grid. It also batch-processes images. The premium version costs $150, the stand-alone version runs $50, though it's also available as part of OnOne's $300 bundle (*www.ononesoftware.com*).

HDR Efex Pro

High Dynamic Range photography is all the rage these days, and while Photoshop lets you merge multiple exposures of the same image (page 395), this plug-in makes the process super simple. HDR Efex Pro offers an easy-to-use workspace, mathematical formulas to take your images from great to galactic in a flash, the ability to fine-tune the resulting image with precise adjustments, and a slew of incredible presets. This plug-in is included in the $150 Nik Software bundle available at *www.niksoftware. com*. (Read the Note on page 780 for info on the current state of Nik plug-ins.)

Eye Candy

This ever-popular set of special effects plug-ins now comes in one big honkin' set. It includes 30 filters that replicate the texture of everything from metal; glass; gel; and natural phenomena like fire, ice, and smoke; to textures like lizard, fur, and stone. The Eye Candy plug-in set runs $200 and is available from *www.alienskin.com*.

SiteGrinder

If you've designed a website in Photoshop and shudder at the thought of slicing it up and turning it into actual code, this plug-in will do that for you in just two steps. SiteGrinder builds a web page based on *CSS* (Cascading Style Sheets) and HTML5 straight from Photoshop, so you never have to *see* (much less tweak) any code. You can also make photo galleries, Flash slideshows, CSS-based menus, and other amazing stuff without losing the design you've painstakingly crafted in Photoshop. The magic lies in naming your layers and layer groups things like "button," "roll-over," and "pop-up" so the plug-in can figure out how each part of the web page should work. The basic program is $347, though add-ons for e-commerce, remote content management, and the ability to generate WordPress themes start at $197 each (*www.medialab.com*).

Dashboard Pro

Need help with Photoshop actions? Look no further. Longtime pro photographer Kevin Kubota created Dashboard Pro (it's free!), a collection of 50 actions that are organized so you can easily find them (categories include black-and-white, color, creative enhancements, romantic, edgy, and so on). You can also assign keywords to your own actions and then search by keyword, name, or category. You can mark favorites for quick recall, and write a searchable description for any action. Kubota also sells dozens of action packs—including a collection of borders, textures, and artistic styles based on popular photographers—and you can try *any* of 'em inside Dashboard Pro before you buy 'em, which is a nice treat (*www.lesa.in/kkdashboardpro*).

Photoshop and Video

Everybody's shooting video these days, whether it's with a smart phone, video camera, point-and-shoot camera, or fancy digital SLR. You might not realize it, but Photoshop has been able to edit videos since CS3, though only in the more expensive Extended version (which, as you know from page xxiii, doesn't exist anymore). Back in CS6, Adobe moved the video-editing features into the more affordable standard version of Photoshop. This is great news; since you already know how to use Photoshop, you don't have to learn another program just to edit videos.

Now, while you *can* create an extensive video project in Photoshop complete with animation and dancing flamingos, other tools are much better suited for that, such as Adobe Premiere Pro and After Effects, Apple's Final Cut Pro, Sony's Vegas Pro, and Avid's Media Composer. Instead, you'll want to use Photoshop for creating small- to medium-sized video projects that contain only a handful of clips, or for cleaning up clips for use in those other programs. That being said, Photoshop is ideal for creating promotional pieces for nearly any business type, portfolio-based slideshows, as well as sellable add-ons to your photography business (just imagine a combo of stills and video clips from a romantic wedding or family portrait sitting!).

Here's a more detailed list of what you can do with video in Photoshop:

- Trim and split clips, as well as add a nice array of transitions between 'em.

- Clean up unwanted objects or blemishes, frame by frame.

- Correct the color and lighting in a clip, as well as sharpen clips.

- Use Adjustment layers and filters to give clips creative color, as well as shallow depth of field effects.

- Add still images, text, and other graphics (like logos) as well as animate 'em in a variety of ways.

- Add and control multiple audio tracks, so you can include background music *and* sound effects, for example.

- Export your project as a ready-to-use video file, or in a format suitable for further editing in an advanced video-editing program.

What makes Photoshop so great for editing video is that everything you know about working with images applies to working with video, too—you just have to learn a few details about video formats and how to use Photoshop's Timeline panel to work with clips. Once you know that, you'll be ready to hop into the director's chair!

Creating Your First Video Project

The *first* step in creating your video masterpiece is to gather and *organize* the files you want to use. Start by creating a folder for your project and then create two *more* folders inside the first: name one *Audio* (for background audio and sound effects) and the other *Content* (for video clips, still images, logos, and so on). Inside the Content folder, take some time to figure out the order in which you want the content to play *before* you open it in Photoshop. For example, by including a letter or number at the beginning of each filename, the content will sort itself alphabetically or numerically when you import it into your Photoshop document. Because the Timeline panel is so small, organizing your content beforehand makes your life a *lot* easier.

Another reason to organize content up front is that Photoshop doesn't embed video files into your document. Instead, it links to the *original* file, keeping your Photoshop document's file size manageable and leaving the original video file untouched. The downside to this setup is that if you move the video file on your hard drive, you'll break the link. But the upside is that this linking lets you perform nondestructive editing—Photoshop applies your edits to a *copy* of the original clip when you export your project (page 818).

TIP Before starting any video project in Photoshop, change your workspace to one that Adobe designed specifically for video editing; simply choose Window→Workspace→Motion. When you do, Photoshop pops open all the panels that are most useful for video editing, including the Timeline panel, which appears at the bottom of the program's window. Once the Timeline panel opens, you can open its panel menu and choose Panel Options, and then click the largest thumbnail size in order to make the previews in the panel a little easier to see.

Using Video Document Presets

Although you could begin your video project by opening existing clips (as explained in the next section), it's nice to start a video project with a fresh, empty Photoshop document. Not only do you get a slick set of guides (explained in a sec), but you also get a wonderfully handy set of commonly used video presets. To do that, choose File→New and, in the resulting New dialog box, choose Film & Video from the Preset menu. Photoshop then displays a slew of video-related settings in the dialog box, so you have to know a lot about your *final* video format in order to pick the right ones. Your myriad options include:

- **Size**. This menu lets you tell Photoshop what size document to create, and includes presets for NTSC (North American) and PAL (anything outside North America) televisions, high-definition video, and professional film industry standards. The choice you make here affects the Width and Height fields below this menu (which, not surprisingly, control the width and height of your project), as well as the Pixel Aspect Ratio setting at the very bottom of the New dialog box.

- **Resolution**. This field determines the size of your pixels. Straight from the factory, it's set to 72 ppi (perfect for onscreen use), so you probably won't need to change it because you're dealing with onscreen video (which doesn't get printed).

- **Color Mode**. Just as with any new Photoshop document, you can choose the color mode you want to use. Leave this menu set to RGB Color and the drop-down menu to its right set to 8 bit.

- **Background Contents**. This menu lets you pick a background color for your project, which is visible whenever there's a transparent area in a *frame* (one of the many still images that make up your video). The most flexible option is Transparent, which results in a gray-and-white checkerboard pattern. However, if you're planning to start your video with a solid black or white screen that gently fades into your first image, go ahead and pick black or white here.

- **Color Profile**. A *color profile* is a set of instructions that determine how computer monitors and printers display or print your document's colors, and they're discussed in depth back in Chapter 16. When it comes to video, a good choice is Adobe RGB (1998).

- **Pixel Aspect Ratio**. This menu changes automatically to suit the choice you make in the Size menu near the top of the dialog box. This setting determines the *shape* of the pixels by changing their aspect ratio (the ratio of width to height of a single pixel in a video frame). Your best bet is to leave this set to whatever Photoshop picks.

NOTE If you choose a video format that uses a pixel aspect ratio that's different from your monitor (say, rectangular or anything not perfectly square), Photoshop automatically changes your view to the aspect ratio of your document so your clips don't look vertically stretched. This bit of preview magic is handled by the View→Pixel Aspect Ratio Correction command, which is turned on from the factory.

When you click OK, Photoshop opens a new, empty document that includes handy guides that indicate where it's safe to place *titles* (text) and important parts of your video, as shown in *Figure 20-1*. In the Timeline panel, you'll see a Create Video Timeline button. (If you don't, click the down-pointing triangle in the middle of the panel and choose Create Video Timeline to display this button.) Give it a swift click and Photoshop adds a video and audio track to the panel. To add clips, click the tiny filmstrip icon next to the track's name in the Timeline panel, and then choose Add Media. In the resulting dialog box, navigate to where the clip(s) live (Shift- or ⌘-click [Ctrl-click on a PC] to choose more than one file), and then click Open.

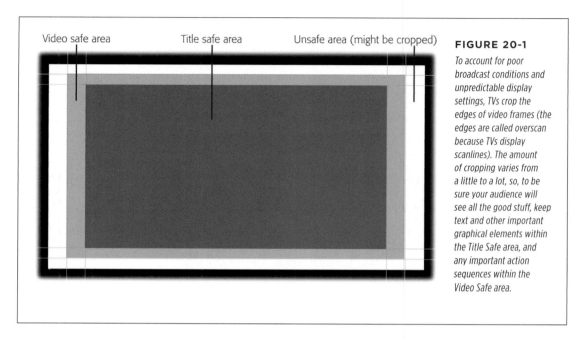

Video safe area   Title safe area   Unsafe area (might be cropped)

FIGURE 20-1

To account for poor broadcast conditions and unpredictable display settings, TVs crop the edges of video frames (the edges are called overscan because TVs display scanlines). The amount of cropping varies from a little to a lot, so, to be sure your audience will see all the good stuff, keep text and other important graphical elements within the Title Safe area, and any important action sequences within the Video Safe area.

NOTE   If you're preparing a video for the Web (say, for posting on YouTube or your own website), you can ignore the safe areas shown in *Figure 20-1* because, online, the entire video image is always displayed.

■ Opening and Importing Video Clips

Another way to create a new video project is by opening an existing clip. You won't get the handy guides that you do when you create a blank video project as described in the previous section, but you can always add 'em yourself (page 60).

NOTE   Photoshop understands MPEG-1, MPEG-2, MPEG-4, MOV, AVI, and FLV files (if Adobe Flash is installed on your computer), as well as the Image Sequence formats (where each frame of the video is saved as an individual file) BMP, DICOM, JPEG, OpenEXR, PNG, PSD, TARGA, TIFF, Cineon, and JPEG 2000. Whew!

To open a video clip as a new document, choose File→Open, navigate to where the clip lives on your hard drive, and then click Open. Photoshop creates a new document whose size matches the size of the frames in the video, opens the Timeline panel, if

it's not already open (*Figure 20-2*, top), and plops the clip into a video track. Photoshop also creates a group in the Layers panel (named Video Group 1) and places
the clip in that group on its own Video layer (*Figure 20-2*, bottom).

Clips in a single video track play one after another. To add more clips to your track,
click the tiny filmstrip icon next to the track's name in the Timeline panel, and then
choose Add Media; alternatively, click the + sign to the right of the video track (on
the right side of the panel). In the resulting dialog box, navigate to where the clip(s)
live (Shift- or ⌘-click [Ctrl-click] to choose more than one file), and then click Open.
The new clip(s) appear to the right of the first clip and in the Layers panel as a new
layer (or layers) at the top of the currently active video group.

FIGURE 20-2

*Top: Once you import a video
clip, it appears in its own video
track in the Timeline panel.
New in Photoshop CC is the
Playback Options menu (the
gear icon circled here), which
lets you control the video's resolution while you're previewing
it, as well as whether or not the
track loops (starts over). Being
able to control the resolution is
handy because you can lower
it to make Photoshop play the
video a bit more smoothly.
Your choices are 25, 50, or 100
percent (straight from the
factory, this menu is set to 50
percent).*

*Bottom: Over in the Layers
panel, you see a new video
group that contains the clips
you imported. (Four clips have
been imported here.) Clicking a
Video layer in the Layers panel
activates it in the Timeline
panel and vice versa.*

Alternatively, you can add a single clip to your document by choosing Layer→Video
Layers→"New Video Layer from File"; in the resulting Add Video Layer dialog box,

locate a clip, and then click OK (you can't add multiple clips with this method). Photoshop imports the clip as a Video layer and places it on a video track named Layer 1. (You can also click the Create Video Timeline button in the Timeline panel to do the same thing, though you only see that button if you haven't created any Video layers yet.) To add more clips, use the methods described in the previous paragraph and Photoshop adds 'em to the track and plops them into a new group in your Layers panel. You can also use Bridge or Mini Bridge to open or add clips to your project (see Chapter 22).

Keeping your video clips in one track (and thus, in a single video group in your Layers panel) is handy for organizing your project. For example, you could use the video track for clips that you want to play in succession, and then add another track for text (Chapter 14) or other graphical elements (say, your logo). If you want one clip to play at the same time as another (say, for a special effect), add another video track by clicking the filmstrip icon next to the track's name in the Timeline panel and choosing New Video Group.

> **TIP** If you want import a clip into a *new* video track instead of the current one, make sure you don't have any clips active by clicking an empty spot in the Layers panel, and *then* import the clip.

If you're working with multiple Video layers (whether they're in a video group or not), be sure to give each one a meaningful name. This helps you keep 'em straight in your head and prepares the document for additional tweaking in a professional video-editing program, which may get confused by duplicate layer names (say, if you import the same video clip *twice* instead of just duplicating the Video layer in Photoshop).

WORKAROUND WORKSHOP

Videos as Smart Objects

Once you've added some video clips to your document, you might want to turn 'em into Smart Objects. When you do, the clips are primed and ready for applying filters nondestructively. In fact, using Smart Objects is the *only* way to apply a filter to a whole video clip (otherwise Photoshop only applies the filter to a *single frame*; you'll learn more about that on page 816). Using Smart Objects is also handy if you want the clip to be smaller onscreen than other clips (for a picture-in-picture effect), because using Smart Objects means you can resize it without losing quality.

While it seems logical that you could *import* a video clip as a Smart Object by choosing File→Place...you can't. Sure, doing so adds the clip to your document as a Smart Object, but Photoshop treats the clip as a *still image* instead of a video. The only way to turn a Video layer into a Smart Object is to add the clip using the techniques described on page 790 and then Control-click (right-click) near the layer's name in the Layers panel and choose "Convert to Smart Object." You can also activate one or more layers and then choose Filter→"Convert for Smart Filters."

Meet the Timeline Panel

The Timeline panel is mission control for your video projects (*Figure 20-2*, top). It appears at the bottom of your workspace when you create a new video document or open an existing clip. It lets you play, rewind, or fast-forward through your project, trim or split clips, skip to a specific spot within a clip, apply motion to stills and text, and more. Before diving into all that, it's good to know the basics of using the Timeline panel.

The first thing you'll want to do is to play the clip to determine whether it needs trimming or splitting. When you first import a clip, Photoshop positions the *playhead* (labeled in *Figure 20-2*, top) at the beginning of the clip; it looks like a tiny blue triangle with three dots on it, and a thin red line extending down through all your tracks. The playhead moves across the track during playback to indicate which part of the track you're viewing. You can move the playhead manually by dragging the blue triangle, or control its position by using the first four buttons at the top left of the Timeline panel (labeled in *Figure 20-2*, top):

- Click the **First** button to move the playhead to the first frame of your project (in other words, the very beginning).

- Click the **Previous** button to position the playhead one frame to the *left* of the playhead's current position.

- Click the **Play** button to, well, play your project; when you do, the playhead moves rightward through your tracks. As soon as you click this button, the icon on it changes to a Pause symbol (two vertical lines); click it to halt playback. (You can do the same thing by tapping your space bar once to play and again to pause.) As your project plays, the *timecode* at the bottom of the panel lets you know exactly where you are in the video. Photoshop also displays the *frame rate* (the speed at which it plays the individual frames) to the right of the timecode.

> **NOTE** Even new machines can struggle with video playback, especially if the clips are high definition. If the Timeline panel's frame rate turns *red* during playback, you aren't seeing all the frames (Photoshop shows how many you *are* seeing, instead of the intended frame rate). You'll also spot a row of tiny cyan-colored dots beneath the time ruler.

- Click the **Next** button to position the playhead one frame to the *right* of the playhead's current position.

Here's what the Timeline panel's other settings do:

- The **Mute** button lets you silence any audio that you've included in the document's tracks (page 803).

- Clicking the new **Playback Options** button (it looks like a gear and is circled in *Figure 20-2*, top) displays two settings. The Resolution menu lets you tell Photoshop what resolution to use during playback (it's automatically set to 50 percent). And you can use the Loop Playback checkbox to make your video start over once it finishes.

- Use the **Split** button to slice a clip in two at the playhead's current position (page 798).

- The **Transition** icon summons a menu of interesting effects that you can use to *transition* (hence the name) from one clip to another.

- The **time ruler** tells you where you are in your project. From the factory, it's set to display time intervals, but you can have it show frame numbers instead by heading to the Timeline panel's menu and choosing Panel Options→Frame Number.

- Use the **playhead** to tell Photoshop where to start playing back your project (just position it and then press your space bar or click the Play button in the Timeline panel) or where to split clips (position it and then click the Split button). You can also use the playhead to precisely position elements in your project. For example, if you put the playhead where you want a sound effect to occur, you can click and drag the sound effect in the audio track and it'll automatically snap to the playhead's position.

To rearrange your clips to change the order in which they play, just click a clip in the Timeline panel and drag it left or right; when you drag, your cursor turns into a closed fist and you see a ghosted image of the clip. When you get it in the right spot, release your mouse button. That said, it's *much* easier to drag clips up or down in the Layers panel instead, as explained in the following Tip.

TIP In the Layers panel, layers that are *lower* in the stack within a video group appear *earlier* in that video track, and layers that are *higher* in the stack appear *later*. (In other words, the bottom-to-top order of Video layers in the Layers panel is the same as the left-to-right order of video clips in a video track.) So dragging a Video layer down or up in the Layers panel also moves the clip left or right in the video track, respectively.

◼ Editing Video

Very few, if any, video clips begin and end at the perfect moments. That's why it's important to know how to trim or split clips in Photoshop, both of which are incredibly easy to do (and nondestructive to boot!). In this section, you'll learn how to do just that as well as add transitions, text, other images, and as audio. Read on!

Changing Clip Length

Fortunately, Photoshop makes it easy to trim a clip—just drag its endpoints left or rightward in the Timeline panel. As you shorten one clip in a video track, the others slide over to keep the track seamless, as shown in *Figure 20-3*.

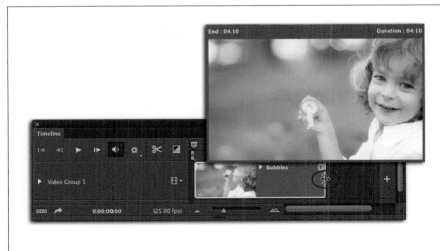

FIGURE 20-3

Point your cursor at the start or end point of a clip and it turns into a bracket with a double-sided arrow (circled). The direction of the bracket indicates which clip will be affected (here, the bracket faces left). Click and drag the bracket left or right and Photoshop opens the preview window shown here, which shows exactly which frame you're trimming the video down to. Handy, eh?

You can also adjust the length of a clip by clicking the triangle in the clip's upper-right corner clip in the Timeline panel. When you do, Photoshop opens a panel containing Video and Audio buttons (circled in *Figure 20-4*, top). Either way, trimming clips is a nondestructive process; if you decide to *undo* your trimming, just drag the clip's endpoint to the left or right (happily, Photoshop won't let you extend a clip beyond its original length).

FIGURE 20-4

Top: Click the little triangle at the top right of a video clip to open this panel, which lets you enter a precise duration for the clip. You can also adjust each setting by dragging its slider, as shown here.

Bottom: The Audio portion of this panel lets you set the volume and fade-in/ fade-out times of any sound in the clip. You can also silence the audio by turning on the Mute Audio checkbox. (If only that worked in real life!)

If you've converted a Video layer into a Smart Object (page 792), clicking the triangle in the clip's top right opens the *Motion* panel instead (it includes presets such as Pan, Zoom, Rotate, etc.). You can use it to add Ken Burns-style motion to still images in order to produce a pro-level slideshow, as described on page 802.

To regain access to the Audio panel (say, in order to mute any audio contained in a video clip), double-click the Smart Object in the Layers panel to open it in a separate (temporary) document. In the new, temporary document, click the clip's triangle in the Timeline panel—use the zoom controls at the bottom of the Timeline panel to enlarge the clip if you don't see the triangle—and then adjust the audio controls as necessary. Finally, choose File→Save or press ⌘-S (Ctrl+S) to save the file, and then close it to return to your main project document, where Photoshop reflects your changes.

The Video portion of the panel includes the following controls:

- **Duration** sets the length of the clip by trimming frames from the end.
- **Speed** sets the playback speed of the clip, from 25% to 400%.

NOTE If you *increase* the speed, Photoshop will shorten the clip's duration. Likewise, if you *decrease* the speed, Photoshop will lengthen the clip's duration, though not beyond its original length (it just slows the clip down...to...a...crawl).

When you click the panel's Audio button, you get these options instead:

- **Volume** sets the clip's sound level from 0% to 200% of its original volume.
- **Fade In/Fade Out** controls the time at which the clip's sound fades in or out.
- **Mute Audio** does just that; turn on this checkbox to hear nothing but the sound of silence.

When you're finished tweaking the panel's settings, press Return (Enter on a PC) to accept your changes, and then click anywhere in the Timeline panel or within your document to close the Video/Audio panel. If you change your mind about editing the clip, press the Esc key instead to dismiss the panel and cancel your changes.

Adding Transitions

If your video project contains more than one clip (and it will), you can add a *transition* that connects the two clips by fading them together in a variety of ways. You can also add transitions at the beginning and/or end of your project, which is a classy way to fade the video in from a solid color (say, black) when it starts, and then fade it out to a solid color when it ends. Photoshop offers the following transition styles for your video-viewing pleasure:

- **Fade**. Fades the clip in or out depending on which end of the clip you apply it to (the beginning or the end). Use this transition on *layered* video elements, such as text or a graphic (say, a logo) that appears atop *other* clips that you've placed in a separate video track that lives *beneath* this one. If you've only got one video track, try using one of the last three fades in this bulleted list to fade to a solid color instead of transparent (empty) pixels.

- **Cross Fade**. This transition is used *between* clips to fade the first clip out as the second clip fades in, so you see a blending of the two video clips (or stills).

- **Fade With Black**. Fades the clip to solid black, which is handy for using at the beginning or end of your project (as are the next two options).

- **Fade With White**. Fades the clip to solid white.

- **Fade With Color**. Fades the clip to the solid color of your choice. You can choose the color *before* you add the transition by clicking the color chip that appears in the Transition panel when you pick this style, or *after* you add the transition by Control-clicking [right-clicking] its icon in the Timeline panel.

To add a transition to a clip, click the Timeline panel's aptly named Transition button that's circled in *Figure 20-5*. In the resulting panel (*Figure 20-5*, top), drag a transition style and drop it onto the beginning or end of a clip, or *between* two clips, as shown in *Figure 20-5* (bottom). When you drop the transition, an icon appears on the clip where you placed it (it looks like one or two light-colored triangles inside a rectangle, depending on which transition you pick). If you drop the transition between two clips, the icon appears at the end of the first clip and the beginning of the second.

FIGURE 20-5

Choose a transition style and duration from the Transitions panel shown here, and then drag it onto the beginning or end of a clip. If you add a transition to the beginning of a clip (so it fades in), you can adjust its length by dragging its right edge leftward to shorten the clip or rightward to lengthen it. If you add a transition to the end of a clip (so it fades out), drag its left edge instead. As you drag, a handy info overlay appears showing the transition's duration.

> **TIP** If you add a Cross Fade transition, you can drag either end of it to adjust its length asymmetrically (to create a longer fade out and shorter fade in, or vice versa). To adjust a Cross Fade transition's length symmetrically, Option-drag (Alt-drag on a PC) one end of it. This lengthens or shortens the transition equally on both ends.

You can control a transition's duration either by adjusting the Duration slider in the Transition panel *before* dragging the transition onto the Timeline panel, or by dragging the edge of the transition's icon *after* you've dropped it on the Timeline panel. You can also Control-click (right-click) the transition's icon in the Timeline panel to make Photoshop display the Transition panel, which lets you change the transition's style and duration (see *Figure 20-6*).

FIGURE 20-6

Control-click (right-click) a transition's icon to display this handy panel. To delete the transition, click the trash can icon at the bottom of this panel. You can also delete a transition by clicking its icon in the Timeline panel and then pressing the Delete key (Backspace on a PC).

Splitting and Trimming Video Clips

Another kind of edit you'll likely need to make is to *split* a long clip into multiple pieces, or to chop a section out of the middle of a clip. The first maneuver is super easy; the second takes a little more effort.

To split a video clip into two pieces, click the clip in the Layers or Timeline panel to activate it, and then position the playhead where you want the split to occur. When it's in the right spot, click the "Split at Playhead" icon (the scissors) at the top of the Timeline panel, as shown in *Figure 20-7*.

FIGURE 20-7

When you split a video clip, Photoshop cuts it wherever the playhead is and a new Video layer appears in the Layers panel (not shown) within the video group at the top of the layer stack. Photoshop cleverly names adds the word "copy" to the end of the original layer's name.

Removing a section from the *middle* of a clip is only slightly more complicated and there are a couple of ways you can do it. If all you want to do is to delete a section of a clip, simply split the clip twice to isolate that section, click the section to activate it, and then press Delete (Backspace on a PC). Photoshop scoots the clip segment on the right side over to the left so the clips play one right after the other.

Another way to remove part of a clip is to define a *work area*, which lets you tell Photoshop which section of the clip you want to work with. To do so, first drag the Video layer *out* of its video group in the Layers panel, even if there's just one clip in the group—simply drag it above or below the video group to liberate the layer. (As *Figure 20-8* explains, you don't *have* to perform this step, but you'll have more options if you do.) Then, click and drag the work area sliders labeled in *Figure 20-8* (top) so they're on either end of the portion of the clip you want to work with. Alternatively, you can position the playhead where you want the work area to start and then, from the Timeline panel's menu, choose Work Area→"Set Start at Playhead." Then set the end of the work area by repositioning the playhead and, from the same menu, choosing Work Area→"Set End at Playhead." Either way, the next change you make applies only to the work area, whether you delete that section from the clip or export that portion to see what the final version will look like.

Once you've defined the work area, you can delete that section of the clip by using the Timeline panel's menu. The menu gives you two different ways to accomplish this deletion, depending on the result you want. If you want the original clip to play uninterrupted where the axed section used to be, choose Work Area→Extract Work Area. This *divides* the original clip into two and places the pieces on separate video tracks; the second piece plays immediately after the first one, as if the missing section never existed (*Figure 20-8*, middle). If you instead want to leave a hole the duration of the deleted section, choose Work Area→Lift Work Area. This also divides the original clip into two and places the pieces on separate video tracks, though it leaves a *gap* between 'em the duration of the section you zapped (*Figure 20-8*, bottom).

Adding Text, Logos, and Still Images

One of the more common video-editing tasks is to add text, still images, logos, and other graphics to a video project (*Figure 20-9*). These are all great ways to add brand identity to a project, navigation elements to a video disc or kiosk, or visually interesting bits and pieces that you can animate.

Work area sliders

FIGURE 20-8

If you don't drag a clip out of its video group before defining a work area in it, the Timeline panel menu's Work Area→Extract Work Area and Work Area→Lift Work Area commands are grayed out (though that doesn't keep you from defining a work area and then using it just to preview or export that portion of your clip). After you liberate the Video layer from its video group, these commands become active.

Top: Use these sliders to define your work area.

Middle: Extracting *the section you defined by creating a work area leaves the two remaining parts on separate video tracks with no gap between 'em (circled).*

Bottom: Lifting *a section of a clip instead leaves a gap between the two remaining parts of the original clip (circled). This kind of thing is handy when you want to add other graphics between the clips (say, a caption on a solid colored background).*

Adding such items to a video in Photoshop is super simple. You can drag and drop 'em directly from Bridge or your computer's desktop; use the File→Place command so they arrive as Smart Objects; copy and paste 'em from another Photoshop document; drag and drop a layer from another Photoshop document; or create 'em from scratch in your current document. Whichever method you use, the new goodies appear on their very own layer, either above the currently active layer or, if no layers are active, at the top of the layer stack. If a video track or video group is active when you add the text or image, then the associated clip appears at the far *right* of that track in the Timeline panel; if not, then the text clip appears on its *own* track.

In the Timeline panel, these added items look and behave just like video clips; the length of their segments determines how long they stay onscreen.

FIGURE 20-9

Left: Adding text gives you a chance to personalize the video and add branding, as shown here. Also, mixing still images with video clips adds visual interest to the piece (the rose background is a still image). The top image is the first thing the happy couple will see when they play the video, and the bottom image is what they see when the video ends (a great way to remind clients how to contact you for more photo shoots!).

Right: This Layers panel shows how the video project was set up. As you learned on page 794, the layer stacking order determines the order in which the contents of those layers play in the video (layers on the bottom play first). By adding a separate video track for the text, you can position the Type layer clips in the Timeline so they play simultaneously with the video and stills in the first video track (shown in Figure 20-10, top), so you can see the text atop the still image of roses and the solid black Fill layer.

Adding text to video works just like any other text: simply press T to activate the Type tool, click within the document where you want the text to appear, and then start pecking away (be sure to commit the text by clicking the checkmark near the right end of the Options bar or by clicking any other layer in the Layers panel). Photoshop creates a new Type layer that you can format and reposition however you'd like. (For more than you ever wanted to know about formatting text, flip back to Chapter 14.)

To add a still image—be it a photo, vector, or whatever—choose File→Place, navigate to where the file lives on your hard drive, and then click Place. Photoshop surrounds the item with a bounding box that you can use to resize or rotate it; to move the item, click and drag within the bounding box. When you're finished, press Return (Enter on a PC) to accept the transformation and Photoshop adds the item as a Smart Object.

TIP When you're preparing still images for viewing on a TV (from a DVD, say), make sure the images are 720×534 square pixels or 720×480 non-square pixels. Also, the color gamut on a TV isn't the same as it is on your monitor. For the best reproduction, try adding a Levels Adjustment layer and then, in the Properties panel, entering *16* into the Output field at the panel's bottom left and *235* into the Output field on the right (see page 377 for more on these fields). Doing so should pull any colors that are too bright back into the TV color gamut.

Once you've added a few still images to your project, you may as well make 'em move around a little! As you learned earlier, clicking the little triangle on the right side of a clip in the Timeline panel opens the Motion panel. However, as *Figure 20-10* shows, the panel gives you a *different* set of options for still images (even if they're vector based) and text than you do for video clips (though once you convert a video clip into a Smart Object, you get these same options).

TIP If you're a photographer, make sure you capture some video along with stills (easy since most new DSLRs do both). For example, if you're a portrait photographer, capture some video between poses (especially if you're working with kids). Once you put it all together in Photoshop, you've got a fabulous video that you can sell to your clients.

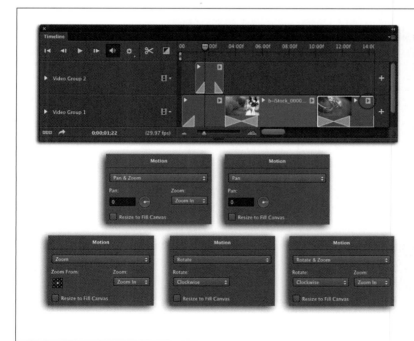

FIGURE 20-10

Top: The Motion panel's presets make it easy to animate still images and text. To open it, click the triangle circled here or Control-click (right-click) the clip itself.

Bottom: Here's each Ken Burns-style preset and its various settings. These options also let you make a pro-level slideshow of your own photography. Simply create a new video document and video timeline as described back on page 788. Next, click the little filmstrip icon on the video track and choose Add Media, and then steer the resulting Add Clips dialog box to your best photos. Once they appear in a video track in the Timeline panel, use the Motion panel to add slightly different movement to each one for a custom effect.

TIP When using the Motion presets to create a slideshow of still images, it's helpful to tweak their file names to number them in the order you want 'em to appear in the slideshow *before* you import 'em.

The five Ken Burns-style presets in the Motion panel are a great way to quickly get still images (or text) moving, whether you're using 'em on stills mingled with video or making a custom slideshow of your artwork. Each preset offers different controls that you can tweak (they all include a "Resize to Fill Canvas" checkbox, which fills your frame with the image or text, regardless of its original size). Here's what each preset does:

- **Pan & Zoom**. *Panning* is the act of moving the image or text across the frame; the Pan dial controls the *direction* of this movement. The Zoom drop-down menu lets you choose whether the image or text grows (Zoom In) or shrinks (Zoom Out) during the panning.

- **Pan**. Use the Pan dial to adjust the direction of the movement.

- **Zoom**. The Zoom From setting controls where the zoom starts—click the upper-left square in the microscopic box at the left of this panel to make the image or text grow or shrink from the screen's upper-left corner, click the center square to make it grow or shrink from the screen's center, and so on. The Zoom menu determines whether Photoshop zooms in or out.

- **Rotate**. Use the Rotate menu to control whether the image or text rotates clockwise or counterclockwise.

- **Rotate & Zoom**. This preset lets you choose which direction the image or text rotates and whether Photoshop zooms in our out.

If you're an artist, designer, or photographer, animating stills in this way is just the ticket for creating a digital portfolio of your work. Just don't forget to add branding—text or your logo on an image or Fill layer—at the beginning and end of the project. To keep the text readable atop an image, add a drop shadow to it or create a subtle block of color *beneath* the text. Once you've added the text, grab the Rectangular Marquee tool and draw a selection that's a little bigger than the text, and then add a Solid Color Fill layer. If your image is mostly dark, add a white Fill layer; if it's fairly light, use black instead. Last but not least, lower the Fill layer's opacity to about 15 percent (you'll need to experiment with that setting to see what works best for you) to give the text a nice soft landing spot.

Adding and Controlling Audio

Photoshop automatically gives you one audio track that appears at the bottom of the Timeline panel, primed and ready for you to add a little background music to your project (you can add *more* audio tracks, as explained later in this section). The advantage of using audio tracks is that doing so lets you control the volume of each audio clip, as well as how they fade in and out. (If you add an audio clip to a *video track*, Photoshop treats it like a video and you have far less control over it.)

To add an audio file to the audio track, mouse over to the Timeline panel and click the musical-note icon to the right of the words "Audio Track" (circled in *Figure 20-11*). From the drop-down menu that appears, choose Add Audio, and then navigate to where the audio file lives on your hard drive. When you click Open, Photoshop plops the file into the audio track.

NOTE Happily, Photoshop understands most common audio file formats, including AIF, WAV, MP3, and AAC (but not FLAC). Basically, if iTunes can play it, Photoshop can import it. And if Photoshop *refuses* to import it, then it may be protected by a digital rights management (DRM) system (for example, an M4P file).

Just like a video, text, or image clip, you can adjust the start and end points of an audio clip to trim off its beginning or end. You can also drag the entire clip left or right to control when it plays. If you click the triangle at the right end of the audio clip in the Timeline panel (circled in *Figure 20-11*), you summon a panel that lets you set the time in which it takes the clips to fade in and out, as well as adjust its volume, as shown in *Figure 20-11*.

Timeline Tricks

To master the Timeline panel, you'll need a few tricks up your sleeve. Here are some of the most useful ones to memorize:

- **Switch units**. From the factory, the Timeline panel's unit of measurement is *time*, and it displays this info both in the time ruler at the top of the panel and in the timecode at the bottom (both are labeled back in *Figure 20-2*, top). To see frame numbers instead, Option-click (Alt-click on a PC) the timecode. To change the units back to time, simply Option-click (Alt-click) it again.

- **Show or hide track properties**. To expand a track to see any layer properties that you can animate such as the position of an image or Type layer, its opacity, and so on, click the flippy triangle to the left of the track's name. When you do, Photoshop expands the panel to show each property of that track.

- **Show or hide clips**. To show only some of the clips in a document, first designate the ones you want to display by Shift- or ⌘-clicking (Ctrl-clicking on a PC) in the Timeline panel to activate 'em, and then choose Show→Set Favorite Clips from the Timeline panel's menu. Then, to specify which clips are displayed, choose Show→All Clips or Show→Favorite Clips Only (also from the Timeline panel's menu).

- **Create a new video group from multiple clips**. If you have multiple clips in your Timeline panel that are related and you *didn't* import them into a video group (say, you added your logo or Type layers to the document), you can click and drag a clip from one video track onto another and Photoshop combines them into a new video group (just double-click the group's name in the Layers panel to change it), making your Layers panel a bit more organized.

When it comes to moving the playhead, you can move it manually by dragging it or using the playback control buttons, or do any of the following:

- Click anywhere on the time ruler to reposition the playhead at that point.

- Point your cursor at the timecode and, when the cursor turns into a double-sided arrow, click and drag left to move the playhead left, or right to move it, well, right.

- Double-click the timecode and, in the resulting Set Current Time dialog box, enter a time or frame number, and then click OK.

- From the Timeline panel's menu, choose Go To→Time, and then enter a specific time in the resulting dialog box. (The other options in the Go To submenu are Next Frame, Previous Frame, First Frame, Last Frame, "Start of Work Area," and "End of Work Area.")

FIGURE 20-11

To add, duplicate, delete, or replace audio files in the automatic Audio Track, click the icon that looks like musical notes (circled), and then choose a menu item from the resulting menu.

To turn off the audio track (and all the audio clips it contains), click the Mute Audio checkbox shown here.

Mute Audio Track

NOTE Unlike all other tracks in the Timeline panel, audio tracks *don't* appear in the Layers panel, and you can't change their names.

To create a more complex and *layered* audio effect in which audio clips overlap each other, you can add *additional* audio tracks and place audio clips in them. (This is how you add sound effects to your project.) To do so, click the musical-note icon circled in *Figure 20-11* (top) and then, from the resulting menu, choose New Audio Track. Position your playhead where you want the sound effect to occur—say, when your superhero descends from the sky and lands on the ground—and then drag the audio clip to the playhead and it snaps into place. If you're searching for such a sound effect online, try the keywords "cinematic hit." Unfortunately, there's no way to duplicate sound effects you've added to an audio track, so to add multiple cinematic hit sounds to the same audio track, for example, you have to bring 'em in one at a time.

WARNING *Don't* drag an audio file from Bridge, Mini Bridge, or your computer's desktop into your Photoshop document. If you do, it appears as a new *video* track in the Timeline panel (and as a new layer in the Layers panel). This method gives you absolutely no control over the audio: You can't adjust its fade-in and fade-out times or its volume. Also, *don't* steal audio for use in your projects. Audio is subject to the same copyright laws as imagery, so either create the audio yourself or purchase it from a royalty-free service such as *www.Pond5.com*, *www.PremiumBeat.com*, or *www.StockMusicStore.com*.

■ Animating Objects and Effects

In Photoshop, the term *animation* refers to anything that changes over time. For example, an object can change position in your document and it can also change in size. For example, if the starting position of some text is outside the document's margins, then it can appear to move across the screen. If an object starts out micro-scopically small, it can appear to magically zoom itself into view. Along those same lines, an *adjustment* you apply to a layer can change its opacity over time or even the area to which it's applied. Layer styles can also change over time. This section shows you how to include all those exciting changes, and more, in your video projects.

Adding and Deleting Keyframes

The key concept (ha!) to grasp about animations is that everything happens around a *keyframe*: the moment in an animation when something changes. This could be the direction of an object's movement, the object's size, the properties of a filter or image adjustment, or whatever. To create an animation in Photoshop, you create multiple keyframes, and then Photoshop creates the appropriate frames between them (these in-between frames are called *tween* frames). For example, to create a bouncing ball animation, you'd place the ball on the ground in one keyframe, then you'd move it to the sky in another keyframe, and then you'd place it on the ground again in yet another keyframe; Photoshop then adds all the frames in between to make it look like it's really bouncing.

UP TO SPEED

A Word on Text in Videos

When it comes to adding text to videos, less is more. And aside from formatting it correctly (by using kerning, leading, and so on—see Chapter 14), there are a couple more things to consider:

Color. The most common color for text in video is white (though an extremely light gray is a better choice because it's slightly lower in contrast). The second most common color is black. Both colors are quite legible, even atop a moving background. Feel free to choose other colors to complement the ones in your project, though be sure to pick a very light or very dark shade. If you're working with a corporate client, they may have an official corporate color that you can specify using the Pantone Matching System (page 492) to make your project appear similar to their other projects.

Readability. Your computer monitor has a much finer resolution than most TVs (the pixels on TVs are bigger), and you're physically closer to the screen than your audience will be. For those reasons, what you're seeing in Photoshop *isn't* what your audience will see. To ensure that your text is readable, put Photoshop into full-screen mode (press the F key repeatedly to cycle through the different views). Next, zoom in so the project fills your whole screen (press ⌘-+ or Ctrl-+), and then step back at least 10 feet and see if you can easily read the text.

Last but not least, be sure to *preview* your text on the intended output device (if possible) after you export the video (page 818), as the encoding process—the way Photoshop converts the project into a specific file format—can cause unexpected results.

To create your first keyframe, drag the playhead to the spot in the video where you want the keyframe to be (in other words, set the playhead at the starting point of whatever it is that you're going to make happen). Then set your object's location, size, layer opacity, and so on exactly the way you want it; once you've got it just right, click the flippy triangle to the left of the track's name in the Timeline panel and Photoshop displays several layer properties beneath the track's name (see *Figure 20-12*). Next, click the stopwatch icon to the left of the property you want to use. When you do, Photoshop creates a keyframe and a yellow diamond appears to the left of the stopwatch, between the Previous and Next triangles, as well as in the Timeline panel where the playhead is, also shown in *Figure 20-12*.

FIGURE 20-12

Click the stopwatch icon to activate a layer property and Photoshop adds a yellow diamond to the property's left, as well as beneath the playhead (circled). This diamond is called a keyframe indicator.

When you move the playhead to another position and then make a change to the contents of that particular clip (this change can be as subtle as changing layer opacity from 100% to 50%), Photoshop automatically adds another keyframe.

You can use the triangles labeled here to move the playhead from keyframe to keyframe in order to see the results of your hard work. In this example, the Type layer "Throttle" was positioned beyond the document's right margin in the first keyframe (top) and then left-aligned with the rest of the text in the second keyframe (bottom), to make it appear as if it slides onto the screen during playback. Pretty cool, eh?

Now it's time to tell Photoshop when in the video you want the animation to *end*. To do that, move the playhead to a spot in the time ruler where you want the change or motion to stop. Then change your object's location, size, layer opacity, and so on, and when you're finished—say, when you accept a size change using Free Transform or finish moving an object with the Move tool—the program *automatically* adds another keyframe for you (that is, so long as you adjust the *same* layer property as you did in the first place). And that, dear Grasshopper, is all there is to creating animations in Photoshop. (Okay, there's a *little* more to it, but that's the basic process.)

> **TIP** If you press and hold the Shift key as you drag the playhead, it snaps to the next keyframe. However, if you're working with a long project, an easy way to move the playhead to the previous or next keyframe is to click the Previous or Next Keyframe triangles labeled in *Figure 20-12*.

Because Photoshop *automatically* adds a keyframe any time you move the playhead and then change the contents of that clip (or rather, layer) in any way, it's easy to add too many. To delete a keyframe, click it to activate it and then press Delete (Backspace on a PC) or choose Keyframes→Delete from the Timeline panel's menu. Alternatively, you can position the playhead atop the keyframe you want to delete and then click the yellow diamond between the Previous and Next triangles, or Control-click (right-click) the keyframe and then choose Delete from the resulting menu. To remove *all* keyframes for a property on that layer, click the stopwatch icon next to its name.

Editing and Copying Keyframes

Once you've created keyframes, you can easily move 'em around by dragging them left or right, or by copying them from one place to another. The quickest way to edit or copy a keyframe is to Control-click (right-click) its yellow diamond in the Timeline panel. When you do, Photoshop displays a shortcut menu that lets you delete, copy, or paste that keyframe (of course, you can't *paste* a keyframe until you've *copied* one first). You can also use these commands on *multiple* keyframes by choosing Select All from the same shortcut menu, or by clicking and dragging *around* them in the Timeline panel; you won't see a selection marquee but if the keyframes turn yellow, then you've activated 'em. (Once you're finished making changes, reopen the shortcut menu and choose Deselect All.) You'll also find these options in the Timeline panel's menu whenever one or more keyframes are active (meaning they're yellow).

Pasting a copied keyframe (or several) to another location is a three-step process. First, copy the keyframe(s) as described above, and then move the playhead to the new spot where you want the keyframe(s) to appear. Next, click the diamond between the Previous and Next Keyframe navigation triangles and Photoshop adds a keyframe to that position. Finally, Control-click (right-click) the new keyframe (the yellow diamond that appeared beneath the playhead), and then choose Paste from the shortcut menu that appears. Whew!

NOTE Don't try to use keyboard shortcuts such as ⌘-C (Ctrl+C) to copy, paste, or cut (delete) keyframes. If you do, Photoshop applies the commands to the *entire* Video layer instead of individual keyframes!

Choosing an Interpolation Method

The most common use for keyframes is to indicate points in time where something changes, and then let Photoshop *interpolate* (make up) the frames in between. This process is called Linear Interpolation. When you have one or more keyframes activated, both the Timeline panel's menu and the shortcut menu you get by Control-clicking (right-clicking) a keyframe offer another choice: Hold Interpolation. This option tells Photoshop *not* to change the frames *between* the keyframes—instead, the program leaves the property the way it's set at the first keyframe and simply makes an abrupt change at the *new* keyframe.

Most often, you'll leave Photoshop set to Linear Interpolation, but there are creative uses for Hold Interpolation, such as when you really *want* to introduce an abrupt and shocking change in your video.

NOTE If you have a lot of keyframes and tracks, your project can begin to slow down and stutter when you preview it. One way to avoid this is to choose Allow Frame Skipping from the Timeline panel's menu. This tells Photoshop that it's okay to *skip* frames when you click the Play button in the Timeline panel, making the preview run more smoothly. (Photoshop still *creates* all the frames correctly when you export the final video file.) One way to tell whether Photoshop is skipping frames is to look for a tiny, light blue line just beneath the time ruler: If it's a solid line, you're seeing all the frames; if it's broken, you're not. In Photoshop CC, you can also try to speed up video playback by temporarily reducing the video's resolution using the Playback Options icon (the tiny gear circled back in *Figure 20-2*, top).

Warping Text

If you've arrived at this point in the chapter by reading the whole thing, you've already learned how to animate text in a couple of different ways: by using the Motion panel (page 802) or the Transform layer property (page 810). However, with text, you get an *additional* layer property called Text Warp (see page 596 for the scoop on warping text.) When you create a Type layer, any Text Warp you apply appears in the Text Warp property in the Timeline panel, as shown in *Figure 20-13*.

Animating Masks

When you add a layer mask to a layer, it becomes a property that you can animate in the Timeline panel. (See page 109 for the scoop on creating layer masks.) This lets a background image or video poke *through* the mask. You can animate the mask's position and control whether it's turned on or off, but that's it.

Rotoscoping and Onion Skins

Rotoscoping is the process of creating new animations from scratch: You create a new video frame, put something on it, duplicate the frame, change its content a tiny bit, and repeat the process until you have a video (you need about 30 frames per second). If you have the patience, you can theoretically create a masterpiece this way.

Starting text position keyframe   Ending text position keyframe

Starting text warp keyframe   Ending text warp keyframe

FIGURE 20-13

Top: In this example, a Type layer was placed and then distorted using the Wave Text warp, and two keyframes were added using the controls in the Timeline panel. Next, the playhead was moved to the position in the time ruler where the animation should end, the text was repositioned at top right and a Flag warp was applied to it. Photoshop added the second keyframe automatically.

Bottom: The yellow diamond marks the keyframe that controls the ending text warp. The gray diamond to its left (at the beginning of the clip) marks the keyframe where the first text warp was applied. The diamonds on the Transform property timeline indicate the beginning and ending positions of the text on the screen (starting at bottom left and ending at top right).

While Photoshop gives you a tool for rotoscoping called *onion skins*, you're much better off using a program like Adobe After Effects instead because the process in Photoshop is just too tedious to bear. Nevertheless, onion skins let you see a ghosted image of a certain number of frames before and after the one you're working on (you tell Photoshop how many frames to display), which helps guide your edits.

To use onion skins, turn 'em on by choosing Enable Onion Skins from the Timeline panel's menu, and then set the frame options by choosing Onion Skin Settings from the same menu. When you do, Photoshop displays the dialog box shown in *Figure 20-14*.

The Onion Skin Options dialog box contains these options:

- **Frames Before/After**. Sets the number of frames that will show through the current frame. You can display up to eight frames before and eight frames after.

FIGURE 20-14

This dialog box lets you control how many ghosted frames you see before and after the current frame, as well as the spacing, opacity, and blend mode of those frames.

You can change these settings anytime (to see more frames or fewer, say).

- **Frame Spacing**. Often, consecutive frames don't change much, so it's helpful to skip some. This setting lets you show only every other frame, every third frame, or whatever. Setting this field to 1 means Photoshop shows *all* the frames, setting it to 2 means Photoshop only shows every other frame, and so on.

- **Max/Min Opacity %**. When viewing more than one frame before and after the current frame, you may want to see the closer frames at a higher opacity than those that are farther away. Max Opacity sets the opacity of the closest frame, while Min Opacity sets the opacity of the farthest frame. The frames in the middle range are between the two opacities.

- **Blending Mode**. Just like with layers, you can assign a blend mode to onion skins. Why? Because some videos are easier to see as onion skins when you use a different blend mode. Your four blending options are Normal, Multiply, Screen, and Difference.

Global Lighting

When you add a layer style that includes embossing, a shadow, or other depth-related effect to a Video layer, you can set its lighting angle. And if you apply layer styles to *multiple* layers in a video project, you probably want *all* the light to look like it's coming from the same angle. To ensure consistent lighting, you can add a global lighting track by heading to the Timeline panel's menu and choosing Show→Global Light Track. The global lighting track overrides any *other* lighting angles that may have been set in individual layers. (To change the angle of the light over time, you can add *multiple* global lighting keyframes that have different lighting angles.)

To set a global lighting angle and apply it to your video project:

1. **From the Timeline panel's menu, choose Show→Global Light Track.**

   Photoshop adds the Global Lighting track to the top of the track stack in the Timeline panel.

2. **Create a new layer by clicking the New Layer icon at the bottom of the Layers panel.**

3. **Add a layer style by clicking the *fx* icon at the bottom of the Layers panel.**

   Pick Bevel & Emboss, Inner Shadow, or Drop Shadow, as those are the layer styles that offer a Use Global Light option. When you make a choice from this menu, Photoshop opens the Layer Style dialog box.

4. **In the Layer Style dialog box, set the lighting angle and turn on the Use Global Light checkbox.**

   Use the Angle dial to set the angle you want for the first portion of your project (you can also type a number into the field to its right), click the Use Global Light checkbox, and then click OK to close the dialog box.

5. **In the Timeline panel, move the playhead to the *beginning* of your project and then add a keyframe.**

   To position the playhead at the beginning, just click the First Frame button (labeled back in *Figure 20-2*, top) or drag the playhead all the way left. To add the keyframe, click the diamond in the global lighting track. When you do, the keyframe automatically adopts the lighting angle you set in the Layer Style dialog box.

   If you want the lighting angle to be the same throughout your project, you're done. If you want to change the angle anywhere in the project, continue to the next step.

6. **Move the playhead to where you want the light to change, and then adjust the lighting angle of the layer style you added in step 2.**

   Back in the Layers panel, double-click the name of the effect you applied to the layer you created in step 1. In the resulting Layer Style dialog box, change the Angle setting, and then click OK.

7. **Set a new keyframe where your playhead is.**

   Click the diamond in the global lighting track to add a new keyframe. The keyframe adopts the new lighting angle you set in the layer style and *keeps* this setting through the end of your project, or until you create a new global lighting keyframe.

■ Adding Comments

Just like Photoshop's Note tool lets you add a hidden comment to a Photoshop document (see online Appendix C), you can use the Comments track to add a hidden *comment* at a specific time in your *video* (handy if there are multiple people working on the project and you need to explain an edit or mark a certain spot for additional editing).

To get started, turn on the comments track by going to the Timeline panel's menu and choosing Show→Comments Track. To add your first comment where the playhead is, click the stopwatch to the left of the word "Comments," and Photoshop displays the Edit Timeline Comment dialog box so you can enter some text (*Figure 20-15*, top). Once you click OK, a yellow square appears at that point on the comments track (*Figure 20-15*, bottom). To add more comments, position the playhead, and then click the yellow diamond near the left end of the comments track. To edit an existing comment, double-click its icon in the Timeline panel and Photoshop displays a dialog box containing your note. You can also copy, paste, edit, or delete a comment by Control-clicking (right-clicking) its icon (the yellow square) in the Timeline panel to reveal a shortcut menu.

FIGURE 20-15

Once you add a comment, it appears as a tiny yellow square in the Comments track beneath the time ruler. If you double-click it, Photoshop opens a dialog box that contains your note (and lets you edit the comment). When you're finished editing or reading it, click OK to close the dialog box.

To export all the comments in a video project, click the Timeline panel's menu and choose Comments→Export As HTML or Comments→Export As Text. Either way, Photoshop creates a document containing your comments along with their frame numbers and timecodes. This is a great way to see *all* the comments in a single project.

■ Adding Fill and Adjustment Layers

Just like still images, video clips often look better after you adjust their color and contrast or apply a creative color effect to 'em (think black-and-white or sepia), all of which is easily done with an Adjustment layer. There will also be times when you want your video to begin or end with a fade in or out to a solid color (say, black), which is the perfect use for a Fill layer.

Happily, you can add Fill or Adjustment layers to a video project exactly the same way you add 'em to any other Photoshop document. In the Layers panel, activate the layer that you want the Adjustment or Fill layer to appear above, and then click the half-black/half-white circle at the bottom of the panel. From the resulting menu, choose the kind of Fill or Adjustment layer you want to add, and then tweak the settings that appear in the Properties panel. For example, to start your video with solid black, you can add a black Fill layer to the bottom of your video group in the Layers panel (or drag it to the beginning of the video track in the Timeline panel). To add solid black at the *end* of your video, duplicate the Fill layer and drag it to the top of the video group (in the Layers panel) or end of the track (in the Timeline panel).

When you add an Adjustment layer, Photoshop automatically *clips* it to the active Video layer, so you don't have to worry about it affecting other Video layers. (Fill layers, on the other hand, *don't* get clipped to the active Video layer and are visible across the whole video screen.) If you *want* the Adjustment layer to affect all the Video layers underneath it, click the "Clip to layer" button at the bottom of the Properties panel (see page 309). However, unlike still images, the lighting in a video clip often changes over time. Fortunately, the Timeline panel also lets you control the *duration* of Adjustment layers you apply to video clips (you'll learn how in a moment).

Adding a Color Tint

You can change the mood of a video by adding a color tint like, say, a sepia tone, which is easy to do with a Black & White Adjustment layer. Just click the half-black/half-white circle at the bottom of the Layers panel and choose Black & White. Then, in the Properties panel, turn on the Tint checkbox (*Figure 20-16*), and Photoshop adds a nice brown tone to your video. (You can change that color by clicking the color swatch next to the word "Tint" in the Properties panel, and then choosing another color from the resulting Color Picker.)

Changing Fill and Adjustment Layers' Duration

What if you want one Fill or Adjustment layer to affect part of a clip, and then you want *another* Fill or Adjustment layer to affect the rest? No problem—just make sure the Video layer isn't part of a video group (if it is, simply drag it out of the group in the Layers panel). Next, add the Fill or Adjustment layer (it appears in the Timeline panel on its own track above the video track). Then change the layer's *duration* in the Timeline panel by dragging its start and end points, just like you would with any clip or transition, as shown in *Figure 20-17.* Then use the same process to add the second Fill or Adjustment layer.

FIGURE 20-16

The Properties panel's Tint checkbox makes it a snap to add a nice sepia tone to your project, giving it a vintage feel.

FIGURE 20-17

After liberating this Levels Adjustment layer from a video group, it appears on its own video track. This lets you adjust its end points to match the duration of the video clip below it. (Unfortunately you can't add transitions to Adjustment layers in order to make 'em fade in or out with a clip. Bummer!)

NOTE You can also restrict the effects of a Fill or Adjustment layer to one Video layer by converting the Video layer to a Smart Object before adding the Fill or Adjustment layer. Just activate the Video layer in the Layers panel, and then choose Filter→"Convert for Smart Filters." Then double-click the Smart Object's layer thumbnail to display it in a new (temporary) document window. Add your Fill or Adjustment layers to it, and then choose File→Save (*not* File→Save As). Photoshop automatically updates the Video layer in your main document.

Adding Layer Styles

You can apply any of Photoshop's layer styles to a Video layer by clicking the *fx* button at the bottom of the Layers panel or by choosing Layer→Layer Style. For example, if you've placed a small video clip on top of larger one (for a picture-in-picture effect), you can make the small clip appear to *float* on top of the larger one by adding a drop shadow to the smaller clip's layer. Another useful layer style is Inner Shadow, which can create the darkened-edge vignette effect shown in *Figure 20-18*.

FIGURE 20-18

To add a darkened-edge vignette effect to a video clip, apply an Inner Shadow layer style. (Any layer styles you add apply to the whole the video clip—you can't adjust their duration.)

As you can see here, a well-placed layer style can make quite a difference!

Using Smart Filters with Video

The good news is that you can run Photoshop's filters on video clips. The bad news is that if you run a filter on a *regular* Video layer, it only affects *the current frame* of that video. To make the filter affect *all* the frames in the clip, convert the clip to a

Smart Object before applying the filter. To do so, activate the Video layer(s) in the Layers panel, and then choose Filter→"Convert for Smart Filters"; *then* run the filter. (As you learned in the box on page 792, you can't use File→Place to import video as a Smart Object because Photoshop turns it into a still instead.) Alas, you can't adjust the duration of the Smart Filter—it affects the *entire* Video layer.

In Photoshop CC, the Field Blur, Iris Blur, and Tilt-Shift filters work with Smart Filters, too, meaning they're primed and ready for use with video clips. In fact, the Tilt-Shift filter produces a nifty effect when applied to time-lapse video (video that's captured at a very slow frame rate so that when played back, it appears to be moving really fast, making the movement much more pronounced that it is in real-time), as *Figure 20-19* shows.

FIGURE 20-19

By rotating the Tilt-Shift filter's band of focus, this speeding shopping cart stays in focus while everything to its left and right is blurred.

There's simply no end to the creative effects you can add to video using Photoshop's amazing filters. Chapter 15 teaches you all about 'em!

Cloning and Healing

You can use Photoshop's cloning and healing tools on video clips, but it's *incredibly* tedious—you have to edit each frame individually (yawn!). Unfortunately, there's no magic technique that lets you follow an object through a whole scene to fix it in one go. So pour yourself a nice beverage, settle into your chair, tweak one frame, and then use the navigation buttons in the Timeline panel to go to the next frame and repeat the process. And repeat. And repeat again.

> **NOTE** When using the Clone Stamp tool to fix multiple frames of a video, consider turning on the Lock Frame option in the Clone Source panel (page 298). This makes Photoshop keep your source in the same frame you sampled, rather than moving it to the next frame as you clone onto a new frame. If your video clip is fairly stable, this will give you a clean source to clone from. However, if the video is unstable, it may work better to set the Clone Source panel's Frame Offset field to 1 or 2 so that the source is more similar to your target frame.

■ Exporting Videos

Once you're satisfied with your project, you can export it to a new video file via a process called *rendering*. Choose File→Export→Render Video or click the Render Video button at the bottom left of the Timeline panel (the curved arrow). In the resulting Render Video dialog box, adjust the following settings (shown in *Figure 20-20*):

- **Name**. Use this field to name the video file you're about to export.

- **Select Folder**. Click this button to tell Photoshop where to save the exported file.

- **Create New Subfolder**. If you turn this checkbox on, Photoshop creates a new subfolder *inside* the folder you specified in the Select Folder option and puts your video file in it. Enter a name for the subfolder in the text field next to this checkbox.

- **Export Encoder**. This unlabeled menu includes two options: Adobe Media Encoder and Photoshop Image Sequence. What you choose here determines the *other* settings you see in this section of the dialog box.

  Choosing **Adobe Media Encoder** tells Photoshop to render your project as a video file, and you see these settings:

  — **Format**. DPX (Digital Picture Exchange) is commonly used in the TV and movie industries. H.264 is used for consumer gadgets such as TVs, handheld devices, and iOS devices, as well as websites like YouTube.com and Vimeo.com. QuickTime format is used by desktop video programs.

  — **Preset**. This menu includes a number of useful options. When you choose one, the controls below this menu reflect the settings appropriate for that preset, though you can change any of those settings manually.

  — **Size**. Choose a video frame size appropriate for your intended viewing device. This menu includes sizes for common uses such as North American (NTSC) and PAL TVs, high-definition video systems, and professional film-editing systems. You can also enter a custom size.

  — **Frame Rate**. Determines how many frames Photoshop includes in each second of video. Choose from common rates or enter a custom one.

Export Encoder menu

FIGURE 20-20

Behold, the Render Video dialog box! This is where you can give the exported video a new name, save it to a specific location on your hard drive, and tell Photoshop exactly which format to use. You can also choose to render the whole video or only certain frames.

Once you click the Render button, Photoshop applies all of your edits to your clips, creates new video frames for any animations you've added, and then exports a video file or a sequence of image files, depending on the settings you picked.

— **Field Order**. While computers display video in a progressive series of complete frames, TVs slice each frame into two interlaced fields, each containing half the image. This option lets you choose whether the exported video should have complete frames (Progressive) or interlaced frames that start with the Upper or Lower Frame first. Choose Progressive if you're creating a video folks will watch on their computers, or one of the other options if they'll watch it on a TV.

— **Aspect**. This determines the video's aspect ratio—the frame's ratio of width to height.

— **Color Manage**. Turning on this checkbox tells Photoshop to pay attention to any color-management information that's included in your project. You'll probably want to leave this setting turned on to take advantage of color profiles included in any images you've added to your project.

Choosing **Photoshop Image Sequence** tells Photoshop to render your project as a sequence of images instead of a single video file, and you get these options:

— **Format**. Choose a format for your rendered frames. Some formats let you set various options by clicking the Settings button, including compression, transparency, metadata, and so forth. (If the Settings button is grayed out, the format you chose doesn't include any additional options.)

— **Starting #** and **Digits**. Since Photoshop will render each frame as a separate file, each file needs a unique name. Photoshop names each file beginning with what you entered into the Name field at the top of the dialog box, and tacks on a sequence of numbers to the end of it. The Starting # field lets you specify the number it starts with, while the Digits field lets you tell Photoshop how many numerals to add to the end of the filename. The "Ex:" item to the right of these fields shows you a preview of how your filenames will look.

— **Size** and **Frame Rate**. These settings are the same as the ones described earlier in this list.

- **Range**. Lets you to specify whether Photoshop renders all the frames in your project, a range of frames you specify, or only the currently active work area.

- **Alpha Channel**. This setting lets you specify how Photoshop should combine alpha channels with the video so that transparency can be preserved when you place your video on top of *other* videos or images. Your options are:

— **None**. Photoshop doesn't include alpha channels in the rendered video.

— **Straight - Unmatted**. Photoshop uses the alpha channel to generate transparency when it's rendering.

— **Premultiplied with Black/White/Color**. These three options make Photoshop place the transparency in the alpha channel over a black background (common in video that will be displayed on TVs), a white background, or a background color (which you choose by clicking the color swatch to the right of this setting), respectively.

- **3D Quality**. If your project includes 3D objects, this setting controls how Photoshop renders their surfaces. Interactive is suitable for video games and other on-screen uses; Ray Traced Draft results in a low-quality version but renders quickly; and Ray Traced Final is very high quality but takes a long time to render.

When you've adjusted all the settings in the Render Video dialog box to your liking, click the Render button and Photoshop goes to work creating your video file.

Using Your Project in Other Video Editors

To go beyond Photoshop's editing capabilities, you can import your video project into *another* video-editing program. To do that, simply save your Photoshop document and then open it in the other program. If you're handing the project off to another member of your team, be sure to include all the fonts, audio files, and video files that you used in your project. (Your Photoshop document merely *references* those files—it doesn't actually include the source files—so the other video editors will need 'em, too.)

■ Additional Video Resources

This chapter is by no means a comprehensive guide to video editing. When you're ready to learn more, here are a few resources worth checking out:

- *www.lesa.in/clvideos*. Your author is continually pushing the limits of video editing in Photoshop and frequently records online video workshops for your viewing pleasure. If you like learning by watching videos, be sure to check out the 90-minute course *Practical Video Editing*. (New classes will be added to this same URL.)

- *www.RodHarlan.com*. Author and video-editing expert Rod Harlan has a website chock full of links to tutorials, tips, and tricks.

- *www.RichardHarringtonBlog.com*. Another author and video-editing pro, Richard Harrington has an informative blog that's worth visiting.

Photoshop and 3D

One of the big new features in Photoshop CC is the inclusion of all the 3D tools that used to live only in the now-deceased Photoshop Extended. But if you don't know anything about 3D, do all these features mean anything to you? They could. If you've ever dreamt of dabbling in 3D modeling, Photoshop is a great place to start. Just as you can buy stock images, video clips, and audio clips, you can also buy 3D objects. Do a quick Google search and you'll find oceans of 3D models for sale. If those objects are already painted and lit (some aren't), you can bring all that info into Photoshop. You've also got a fair amount of control over the object's textures and lighting in Photoshop. If the object comes with a separate texture file, you can edit that file in Photoshop and then see your updated model when you save it. You can also add and adjust lighting to make the model blend into your scene better.

If you're feeling particularly brave, you can paint directly on the surface of a 3D model in real time (meaning you see your brushstrokes as you make them). It's really nice to be able to do this kind of painting in Photoshop, especially if you don't have a dedicated 3D painting program. You can even *render* (apply lighting and reflections using a technology called *ray tracing*) a portion of an object and even pause the process, which is a great timesaver when you want to focus on an important area of detail.

Learning to do a little 3D work can be both fun and beneficial. For example, you can build your own props. Let's say you forgot to include a stick of butter in the croissant shop shoot last week in France. Do you fly back and redo the lighting, hire talent, and so on? Heck, no! You can churn a stick of butter right in Photoshop and then toss it into your shot. Adobe has made it fairly easy, too, since Photoshop treats 3D objects like souped-up layers—you can run filters on them, add Layer styles, and so on (they're similar to Smart Objects).

Here's what you can realistically expect to do with 3D in Photoshop CC:

- Create 3D text, shapes, and logos.

- Create *flying* postcards and billboards.

- Wrap artwork around basic 3D shapes.

- Animate 3D objects in a video file.

- Import 3D models created in other 3D programs.

- Export the result as a ready-to-use image file, or in a format suitable for further editing in advanced 3D software.

Photoshop CC includes a 3D panel that works a lot like the Layers panel: It lets you delete, reorder, group, and duplicate 3D objects. Also new in this version of the program: just like in Adobe Illustrator and Flash, you can make *instances* (copies) of a 3D object so that they all update whenever you make a change to any one of 'em (kind of like linked Smart Objects; see page 120). And when you're painting on a 3D object, the new Live 3D Painting mode lets you *see* your changes on the 3D object as you paint on the texture file that's wrapped around it, in real time.

All this power comes at a cost: Your computer needs to have at *least* 512 MB of video RAM (a.k.a. VRAM) on its graphics processor if you want to work in Photoshop's 3D environment. Previously, Photoshop would *attempt* (poorly) to let you work with less VRAM, but Photoshop CC won't even try. (With less VRAM, you can still work with 3D-ish features on a 2D image—such as the Blur Gallery, Lighting Effects, Oil Paint, Liquify, and so on—but the 3D environment isn't available to you.)

Photoshop CC can't do everything a traditional 3D-modeling program can (such as Autodesk's 3ds Max), so while it's *not* a smart choice for 3D professionals, it's still useful for photographers, graphic designers, web designers, and motion graphic designers. For example, photographers can add objects or forgotten props to existing shots and graphic designers can add 3D text or 3D objects to photos (say, their clients' products or packaging). Web designers can easily make buttons and banners with transparent shadows and materials, and motion graphic designers can create special graphics that appear in the lower third of a video (with 3D text), or an unfinished wireframe mockup for use in other 3D applications. This chapter explains the basics of working with Photoshop CC's 3D features.

◼ 3D Basics

If you're new to 3D, all the parts and pieces can be baffling. Here's the gist: A *3D object* starts with a *mesh*, which has one or more *surfaces*, each of which can have a *texture* applied to it. You can envision the mesh as chicken wire molded into a 3D shape, like one of those animal-shaped wire structures that you sometimes see in gardens (normally, they're covered by ivy to create topiary critters). A *texture* can be made from one of your own images, or you can choose a *material* preset that resembles a real-world material such as fabric, stone, wood, glass, or plastic, or something fanciful like a checkerboard pattern. To customize the material, you can apply a color to it, or apply separate *textures* to its reflective areas.

This 3D object lives in a *scene* that has one or more *lights* illuminating it, and one or more *cameras* providing different *views*. The scene may have more than one 3D object in it, and the entire scene lives in an *environment* that has its own global lighting for all the objects in the scene, as well as a *ground plane* on which shadows may fall, and an optional *background* image or panorama.

And of course, everything is customizable!

Photoshop's 3D Environment

When working with a 3D object, you'll use the 3D menu, the Move tool, and the 3D Mode tools that appear in the Options bar when you have the Move tool and a 3D object active, along with a few panels: the 3D panel as well as the familiar Properties and Layers panels. You'll also encounter a 3D *object cage* (Photoshop's representation of the 3D area that *encloses* the object—it looks like a rectangular wireframe), a special tool that lets you control the *view axis* (the angle in which you're viewing the object), and a set of other clever HUD (heads-up display) features, explained later in this chapter.

> **TIP** To prepare for your first foray into the realm of 3D, head to the right end of the Options bar and choose 3D from the unlabeled workspace menu. When you do, Photoshop opens the Properties and 3D panels on the right side of the workspace, and plops the Timeline panel at the bottom of the document window (but it's collapsed, so all you see is its tab).

To create a 3D object, you start by activating an Image, Type, or Shape layer, or even a selection or a path you've drawn with a shape tool or the Pen tool. Then you use the 3D panel shown in *Figure 21-1* to *extrude* the item into a 3D object. One of the easiest ways to create a 3D scene is to activate one or more layers in the Layers panel, and then make a choice from the 3D panel. (You can also create a 3D object from a selection, a work path, or a separate file—the process is the same as the one described in the next section.)

Creating a 3D Postcard

The simplest way to dip your toes into Photoshop's 3D realm is to convert an existing image into a flying postcard that you can slide, roll, and rotate in 3D space.

Pop open an image and then, in the Layers panel, activate the layer you want to convert into a 3D object. (Don't worry if the layer is locked—Photoshop will unlock it for you.) If your image consists of multiple layers—say, an image and some text—activate those layers and create a stamped copy of them by pressing ⌘-Option-E (Ctrl+Alt+E), and then hide the original layers by turning off their visibility eyes. Next, locate the 3D panel on the right side of your screen (if you don't see it, choose Window→3D). Turn on the 3D Postcard radio button as shown in *Figure 21-1*, and then click Create.

TIP To follow along, visit this book's Missing CD page at *www.missingmanuals.com/cds* and download the practice file *Rome.zip*.

FIGURE 21-1

The 3D panel lets you easily create a 3D postcard from single layer or multiple layers; the other options shown here are covered later in this chapter.

Enjoy the simplicity of these controls while you can because they change drastically the second you click the Create button!

Once you've created an object, the 3D panel changes to display the many editable attributes of your new 3D object (see *Figure 21-2*). The panel lists all your 3D objects (also known as *meshes*) and all their parts, as well as the environment (the world in which your 3D object lives), the current scene, and its lights and camera.

FIGURE 21-2

As soon as you create a new 3D object, Photoshop places it into a scene complete with cameras and a lighted environment. You can filter (limit) the kinds of items listed in the panel by clicking one of the icons near the top of the panel. The icons at the bottom let you add a new light, render your scene (page 837), or delete an item.

When you activate a 3D object by clicking its name in the 3D panel, you can then adjust its properties in the Properties panel. You can use the Layers panel to activate layers and convert them to a 3D object, or to control the visibility of an object or its various properties such as textures and illumination. (You can also control visibility in the 3D panel.)

Press V to grab the Move tool, and in the document window Photoshop displays the *ground plane* and controls for manipulating your *scene* (*Figure 21-3*). (The ground plane helps you visualize where your object is in relationship to an imaginary grid that represents the ground, while the scene contains your object(s), cameras, lights, and so forth.)

Select View/Camera   Swap Views   Main view

Ground plane   View axis (HUD)

Render

FIGURE 21-3

Photoshop's document window has features that help you navigate your 3D world, such as the Secondary View window (described in the box on page 828) and the View Axis for manipulating your camera angle. When you drag your mouse near the View Axis, the way the view angle changes depends on which 3D mode is active in the Options bar. The Properties panel displays 3D camera options, including several helpful presets in the View menu.

The following sections explain some of the things you can do with your new 3D postcard, as well as how to create other kinds of 3D objects. Grab a frosty beverage and buckle up, because there's heady stuff ahead!

Moving Objects in 3D Space

When you're working with 3D objects, the tool you'll use the most is the Move tool. After you activate it, you then tell Photoshop what kind of movement you want to perform by either choosing one of the 3D modes from the Options bar (*Figure 21-4*) and then clicking in the 3D space, or by using the 3D Axis HUD covered in the next section.

Now you can use the Move tool to adjust the camera's view of the scene. In the Options bar, click the first 3D mode icon (Rotate). Then click and drag anywhere in the document window to see your postcard from various angles.

PHOTOSHOP'S
3D
ENVIRONMENT

Rotate Drag Scale

Roll Slide

FIGURE 21-4

The five 3D mode options labeled here control what kind of movement the Move tool will apply to your 3D object. To see these modes, first activate a 3D layer, and then grab the Move tool.

To work with the 3D object itself, click its name in the 3D panel to activate it. (It's named the same as the layer it was made from, plus the word *Mesh*.) Photoshop displays a colorful 3D HUD in the middle of your postcard, but you can ignore it for now. Still using the Move tool in Rotate mode, click and drag anywhere *outside* your object to rotate it in 3D space. Drag the object down to make it advance toward you, or up to make it retreat away from you.

Give the other 3D modes a try by clicking their icons in the Options bar. If you change the 3D mode to Roll, then you can click and drag around the outside of the object to rotate it around its center. With the 3D mode set to Drag, you can—you guessed it—drag the object around the window. With the 3D mode set to Slide, you can slide the object along the ground plane. And with the 3D mode set to Scale, you can enlarge or shrink the object in relation to its background. Try shrinking it to about a quarter of its original size by clicking and dragging your mouse downward on the area outside the postcard.

UP TO SPEED

Room with a (Secondary) View

It can be difficult to work with 3D objects in 3D space when all you can see is one 2D view of it! To make things easier, Adobe includes a Secondary View window in the upper-left corner of Photoshop's document window that helps you place objects and lights (see *Figure 21-3*). When at its standard size, the Secondary View window is small enough to stay out the way, but big enough to give you an idea of how your 3D object looks from a different perspective. If you want to resize the Secondary View window, just drag on its lower-right corner.

You get to decide which view is displayed in the Secondary window: Just click the Select View/Camera icon in its upper-

left corner (labeled in *Figure 21-3*) to display a drop-down menu. Your options include Left, Right, Top, Bottom, Back, Front, Vanishing Point Grid (if you've set one up by choosing Filter→Vanishing Point), and any additional camera views you've saved (page 831). (In the flying postcard example used in this chapter, the only meaningful views are Front and Back.) If your scene has multiple 3D objects, the current camera angle for each one appears at the bottom of this list.

You can even *swap* the main view and secondary view. Just click the Swap Views icon in the upper-right corner of the Secondary View window (labeled in *Figure 21-3*).

NOTE The 3D modes are sticky, meaning that Photoshop remembers which one you were using the last time you worked with 3D objects and uses that same mode the *next* time you work in 3D (until you activate a different one).

At first, Photoshop's various 3D modes may seem mysterious, but once you get the hang of them, you'll know which one to use to get just the view you want.

■ USING THE HUD TO POSITION AN OBJECT

When you use the Move tool and the 3D modes in the Options bar, you'll be doing a lot of clicking to change the 3D mode to the one you want at any given time. A more fluid way to work with 3D objects is to use the HUD features (see *Figure 21-5*). These context-sensitive controls appear on or near the active object, and let you manipulate it. They provide circles, arrows, and handles you can grab and move to make adjustments.

Y axis

X axis

Z axis

FIGURE 21-5

The 3D Axis shows the current X-, Y-, and Z-axis orientation of models, cameras, lights, and meshes in 3D space. It appears when you activate the Move tool, and rotates in space along with your 3D object.

Adobe helpfully used the colors red, green, and blue for the X, Y and, Z axis controls (respectively). So, if you can remember RGB, you can remember XYZ. Neat, huh?

Other handy HUDs include the Deform HUD that controls Taper, Twist, Extrude, Bevel, Bend, and Shear. It appears when a 3D object is active and you click the Deform icon in the Properties panel. The Cap HUD controls Bevel and Inflation. It appears when a 3D object is active and—you guessed it—you click the Cap icon in the Properties panel.

The best way to get comfortable working with the 3D Axis on the object itself is to give it a try. The 3D Axis behaves the same regardless of which 3D mode is active in the Options bar. In fact, it can replace *all* those modes once you get the hang of using it!

> **NOTE** You can snap your object to the ground plane by choosing 3D→"Move Object to Ground Plane."

As you point your cursor at the various parts of the 3D Axis, that particular part turns yellow and a tooltip appears letting you know what it does. For example, dragging the big white box in the center of the HUD scales the object uniformly, while the smaller boxes farther out on the control handles scale the object in only one dimension (X, Y, or Z). (You can think of X as left to right, Y as top to bottom, and Z as front to back.) Dragging the curved pieces on the control handles rotates the object along the X , Y, or Z axis, while dragging the arrowheads at the end of the control handles moves the object along the X , Y, or Z axis. This seems about as logical as one could hope for! (It makes more sense once you try it yourself.)

Next, let's make sure that the layer containing the map of Italy is turned on (this layer is included in *Rome.zip*, which you can download from this book's Missing CD page): In the Layers panel, click the visibility eye next to the Background layer. Make sure your postcard layer is active, and then use the 3D Axis or the Move tool to drag and rotate the postcard to a location that looks good to you (see *Figure 21-6*).

FIGURE 21-6

Your flying 3D postcard hovers over a map of Italy, complete with a subtle stroke (outline) and drop shadow that was added to offset it from the map, as shown in the Layers panel.

To finish your project, you need to tell Photoshop to use all its graphics muscle to generate a high-quality rendition of your art, taking into account all the lighting options, reflections, and other 3D goodness. To do that, click the Render button at the bottom of the 3D panel or Properties panel (it looks like a tiny 3D cube inside a square). Or, choose 3D→Render. (Rendering is discussed in detail on page 837.)

When Photoshop is done rendering your file, you can save it as in PSD format to retain all your 3D editing capabilities. You can also save or export the file in any of Photoshop's regular 2D formats for use in print, on the web, or in other projects.

Working with the Camera

Everything you've done so far places a 3D object in its 3D space. This section explores how to control your view of that 3D object. In Photoshop's 3D world, a "camera" is a combination of viewing angle, location, and camera-specific settings such as Perspective, Field Of View, and Depth Of Field.

Cameras are listed in the 3D panel. When a 3D object is active in the Layers panel, the item in the 3D panel named Current View represents the virtual camera that's at the location and direction from which you're viewing that 3D object.

The View Axis in the lower-left corner of the document window (labeled in *Figure 21-3* back on page 827) indicates the orientation of your Current View camera and lets you adjust it. You can change its orientation by activating it (just click Current View in the 3D panel), and then grabbing the Move tool and dragging anywhere in the document window other than on top of the 3D object. As you drag, the camera moves based on which 3D mode is active in the Options bar. (Photoshop reminds you that you're manipulating your view—and not the 3D object itself—by putting a gold border around your canvas.)

TIP As you mouse over the View Axis, a shaded square appears around it. Drag within this shaded square to make big changes to the Current View camera; drag outside the shaded square to make more subtle changes.

The Properties panel lets you make dozens of changes to the camera's characteristics, and it also has several useful camera presets in its View drop-down menu, such as Front, Back, Top, Bottom, Left, and Right. The View menu also includes presets that match the Current View of other 3D objects in your project—their names match the names of your other objects.

If you're into 3D stereoscopic imaging or lenticular printing, you can even turn on the panel's Stereo checkbox (*Figure 21-7*) and then customize to your heart's content!

Let's say you've found a camera position and a set of properties that you'd like to be able to use again later. You can save the location of the Current View camera and its properties by either Control-clicking (right-clicking) the View Axis and choosing Save, or by choosing Save from the Properties panel's View menu when Current View is active in the 3D panel. Give your new camera a name, and you can then call it up later from the View menu in the Properties panel.

FIGURE 21-7

The Properties panel includes camera options that a cinematographer would love!

(Unfortunately, a detailed explanation of these settings is beyond the scope of this book.)

FREQUENTLY ASKED QUESTION

Working in a Cage

Dude, what's with the wireframe box around my object?

When you point your cursor at a 3D object or activate the object in the Layers or 3D panel, a wireframe box appears around it. This is called the *cage*, and in addition to indicating your current object, it also gives you another way to move and rotate your object. (Other ways include using the HUD features or the Move tool with a 3D mode activated in the Options bar.)

If you click the edge of the cage and drag, your object moves around in 3D space. To move the object closer to you, drag downward (like you're pulling the object toward you); to move it farther away from you, drag upward (pushing it farther away).

If you click just outside the cage and drag, you can move or rotate your object, based on the 3D mode that's active in the Options bar. You can also click and drag on one of the cage's faces to move or rotate the object, again based on the current 3D mode.

It's helpful to remember that using the cage is just one way to manipulate a 3D object—depending on the object, you may find it easier to use a HUD feature or the Move tool combined with a 3D mode in the Options bar. Using the cage takes some practice, but once you get used to it, it can begin to feel intuitive.

■ Creating Other 3D Objects

The flying postcard described earlier in this chapter is the simplest 3D object to work with, because it has no depth. The second-simplest 3D object to create and work with is 3D text or a 3D shape, which you'll learn how to create in this section.

Making 3D Text

Creating a 3D object from some text is as simple as clicking the 3D button in the Options bar. To get started, activate the Type tool and add some text to your document and format the text to your liking (see Chapter 14 for details on working with text).

> **NOTE** A 3D Type layer is *very* different from a normal 2D Type layer—it's more like a 3D object rather than a string of text. You can still edit the characters and formatting as described below, but you can't convert it back to a 2D layer. If you want to keep a copy of your Type layer handy for future use as a regular 2D Type layer, first duplicate the layer by dragging it onto the New Layer icon at the bottom of the Layers panel. You may also want to turn off its visibility so it doesn't get in the way—just click its visibility eye in the Layers panel.

Once you're happy with the text's formatting, click the 3D icon at the far right of the Options bar. Photoshop converts the Type layer to a *3D* Type layer, and displays all the 3D controls. The new 3D Type layer appears in the 3D panel, and in the Layers panel, the Type layer now has a 3D cube on its thumbnail. (If you don't see the 3D icon in the Options bar, click your original Type layer in the Layers panel to make it active, and then grab the Type tool; the 3D icon should then appear. Alternatively, you can open the 3D panel, turn on the 3D Extrusion radio button, and then click the Create button.)

Using the tools and panels described earlier in this chapter, you can manipulate the text to your heart's content. In addition to those tools, you'll also see the Extrusion Depth slider in the Properties panel; it lets you control the depth of your 3D text. The center point of the slider is 0, which means no extrusion. Drag this slider to the right to increase the extrusion behind the front face of the object. Drag the slider to the left to decrease that extrusion. If you drag the slider far enough to the left, you'll start seeing negative numbers in the slider's value field and the front of your object will begin moving forward while leaving an extrusion behind it.

The Shape Presets in the Properties panel are also fun to play with—they let you make your text puffy, or beveled, or just plain. *Figure 21-8* shows how 3D type looks when set in Josip Kelava's free Metropolis 1920 typeface (this free font is available online from several sources; just Google its name).

Even after you convert your Type layer into a 3D Type layer, you can still edit the text it contains, so feel free to make changes in the Character and Paragraph panels; simply click the Type layer in the Layers panel to activate it, and then tweak away. To change the characters themselves (say, to correct a typo), click the Edit Source button in the Properties panel. Photoshop opens a new document window containing only your Type layer, so you can edit the text using any of the techniques described in Chapter 14. When you're done editing the text, just choose File→Save to update the text in your 3D Type layer. Then simply close the Type document that Photoshop opened for you—you can always get back to it by clicking the Properties panel's Edit Source button again.

FIGURE 21-8

This 3D text is sitting on the ground plane. Its cage and 3D Axis are displayed because the Move tool is active and the 3D Type layer is active in the Layers panel.

Making 3D Shapes

Using Photoshop's vector shapes is another easy way to experiment with 3D features. For example, create a new Photoshop document and then use the Custom Shape tool in Shape mode to draw a heart (it's one of the built-in shapes you can choose from the Custom Shape picker; see page 555). For fun, use the Options bar's Fill setting to make it red.

TIP You can also apply layer effects to the custom shape—just be sure you convert it to a Smart Object before you turn it into a 3D object.

Then, with the Shape layer active, use one of the following methods to create a 3D object out of the heart:

- Control-click (right-click) the object and choose "New 3D Extrusion from Selected Path"

- From the 3D menu at the of the Photoshop window, choose "New 3D Extrusion from Selected Path"

- In the 3D panel, click the 3D Extrusion radio button, and then click the Create button

You should end up with something like the heart in *Figure 21-9*. Then use the tools and panels described above to customize your new 3D shape!

TIP   A quick way to create a 3D object from an image layer is to draw a shape or selection on the image layer (you can use any tool to do so), and then, from the 3D panel's Source menu, choose either Work Path or Selection. The panel's 3D Extrusion radio button will automatically be selected, so just click the Create button. Photoshop will then extrude your path or selection into 3D with the image on its front surface.

FIGURE 21-9

Photoshop's built-in heart shape, extruded to 3D, with its cage and 3D Axis showing.

You can add your own custom shapes to the 3D panel's shape menu. Photoshop CC accepts Collada (.dae) 3D model files, so to add a shape, simply place its Collada model file in the Meshes folder inside the Photoshop program folder (Adobe\Adobe Photoshop CC\Presets\Meshes).

Wrapping Art around Basic Shapes

If you have an image that you'd like to wrap around a standard shape such as a soda can or wine bottle, Photoshop makes it really easy. Just head to the Layers panel and activate the layer(s) containing your artwork, and then, in the 3D panel, click the radio button labeled Mesh From Preset. Next, choose one of the shape options from the unlabeled drop-down menu below the Mesh From Preset label, then click the Create button, and Photoshop wraps your artwork around the shape.

Photoshop's preset shapes are Cone, Cube Wrap, Cube, Cylinder, Donut (torus), Hat, Pyramid, Ring, Soda (can), Sphere, Spherical Panorama, and Wine Bottle.

Once your art is wrapped around the 3D shape, you can move it by using the hidden Texture Properties dialog box. To get there, pop over to the Layers panel and click your object to activate it. Then switch to the 3D panel and click the Label Material item nestled under your object's name. In the Properties panel, the Materials properties should now be displayed. The top item is labeled Diffuse. To its right is a color swatch and a document icon that represents your art, which Photoshop now considers a texture. Click that icon, and then choose Edit UV Properties from the pop-up menu that appears. This opens the Texture Properties dialog box, where you can change the scale of the art, along with its position (called Offset). A real-time preview helps while you're positioning your artwork.

Making a Plane, Cylinder, or Sphere from Scratch

Here's a powerful feature that average Photoshop users will never use, but 3D professionals formerly used all the time to build 3D shapes such as planets, mountains, or monsters. It works like this: You provide a grayscale image, and Photoshop builds a 3D model from it, making the white areas the highest points on the model and the black areas the lowest points. The results can be quite surprising if your brain doesn't think in terms of mapping grayscale to 3D!

To use this feature, start with a grayscale image on its own layer. Be sure the image includes both white and black areas. Activate the layer (or multiple layers, if you like), and then in the 3D panel, click the radio button labeled Mesh From Depth Map. Next, use the drop-down menu below that label to choose one of the four options: Plane, Two-Sided Plane, Cylinder, or Sphere. Plane uses your art to raise and lower the surface of a one-sided flat plane; Two-Sided Plane raises and lowers both sides of a plane; Cylinder maps it outward from the center of a cylinder; and Sphere maps it radially outward from one center point. It can be hard to predict what kind of results you'll get from this feature, so the best way to find out is to simply click the 3D panel's Create button. If you don't like the results, go back to the original grayscale image and change it, remembering that black is the "floor" and white is the "ceiling." Easy, right?

Making a 3D Object from a Medical Scan

If you've ever had a medical imaging scan, the results were likely converted to a DICOM file (Digital Imaging and Communications in Medicine). So if you've ever been interested in playing around with your scan results, here's your chance! Photoshop CC lets you open and work with DICOM files using the .dc3, .dcm, .dic, or no extension.

DICOM files sometimes contain multiple frames, each of which represents a different layer (slice) of a scan. Photoshop can convert those frames to layers, or open them as a 3D object (also called a *volume*) you can rotate in 3D space. To create a 3D object from a DICOM file, choose File→Open, navigate to the folder containing your DICOM files, and activate some or all the files in the folder (the Select All button is handy for that). In the resulting Import Options dialog box, turn on the "Import as volume" radio button under Frame Import Options, and then click the Open button. Photoshop creates a 3D object of the DICOM frames and places it on a 3D shape layer in the Layers panel. You can then use Photoshop's 3D tools to view the 3D object from any angle, render a scene, and save or export to any format Photoshop understands.

Importing a 3D Model

In addition to building your own models from scratch in Photoshop, you can also import models and materials created in other programs, such as 3ds Max, Maya, modo, Cinema 4D, Poser, DAZ Studio, and SketchUp, as well as from online services such as Google 3D Warehouse, TurboSquid, and 3DVIA.

> **TIP** One way to get additional 3D content is to choose 3D→Get More Content. This takes you to an Adobe web page with links to free and paid content.

To import a 3D model, choose 3D→"New 3D Layer from File," and then in the resulting Open dialog box, navigate to where the file lives on your hard drive and click Open. Photoshop then generates a 3D layer containing the object, which you can manipulate just like a 3D object you created yourself!

You can import the following types of 3D files into Photoshop CC: 3D Studio, DAE (Collada), KMZ (Google Earth 4), STL, U3D, and Wavefront|OBJ.

Rendering

While you're working on a 3D object, Photoshop is actually only showing you a low-resolution preview. When you're finished with your work, or when you just want a glimpse of the fabulosity of your talent, you need to tell Photoshop to render the scene. This generates a high quality version of your scene that you can use online, in print, or in an animation. Rendering uses ray tracing and a higher resolution than what you see on Photoshop's preview to generate more realistic lighting and shadow effects. (*Ray tracing* follows rays of light as they emerge from their sources, pass through semi-transparent objects, and reflect off surfaces to generate realistic reflections and shadows.)

When Photoshop renders a scene, it uses the render settings in the Properties panel. (These settings only appear when you have a scene active in the 3D panel.) The Properties panel has 21 rendering presets; some are useful only to 3D pros, while others are fun for everyone (wireframe presets, for example).

You can make hundreds of choices in the Properties panel's Cross Section, Surface, Lines, and Points sections. And there are a handful of simplification options that do things like remove shadows, hide back faces, and lines. Unless you're a 3D pro, stick with the presets.

You can also choose to render only a *portion* of a scene, which saves time when you just need to see a higher-quality version of part of your object, such as a shadow. To do that, first activate the object in the Layers panel, and then use any tool to select the area of the object that you want to see in higher detail. That way, Photoshop will render only the selected area.

There are several ways to tell Photoshop to start rendering your 3D scene: Choose 3D→Render, Control-click (right-click) the 3D layer in the Layers panel and choose Render, or click the Render button at the bottom of the 3D panel. Whichever method you use, Photoshop goes to work.

Rendering takes time—Photoshop keeps you informed of its progress by displaying a Time Remaining progress bar in the lower-left corner of your document window, and you can also entertain yourself by watching dashed lines move around your window as it processes each area multiple times. You can press the Esc key at any time to cancel the rendering—Photoshop will pick up where it left off the next time you tell it to render.

> **TIP** If the rendering process is taking longer than you'd like, you can speed it up by changing Photoshop's 3D Preferences (File→Preferences [Edit→Preferences on a PC]). If you change the High Quality Threshold in the Ray Tracer section from 5 to 4, the rendering quality will be just slightly lower, but the speed will be dramatically faster.

■ Saving and Exporting 3D Objects

When you want to share your 3D masterpiece with the world, you can either render your 3D scene and then save it in any of Photoshop's 2D image formats just like a regular file (page 38), or you can export your 3D model for additional manipulation in another 3D program. To do the latter, choose 3D→Export 3D Layer, and then choose one of these file formats: Collada DAE, Flash 3D, Google Earth 4 KMZ, STL, or OBJ.

The easiest way to save your file in a way that preserves all your 3D editing magic is to simply save it in native Photoshop (PSD) format. However, you can also save it in PDF or TIFF format. Here's how: Choose File→Save or File→Save As, choose Photoshop (PSD), Photoshop PDF, or TIFF from the format drop-down menu, and then click the Save button.

> **NOTE** Want to affordably generate your own 3D objects in the *real* world (not in Photoshop)? No problem! 3D printers are now a reality. Industry experts are predicting that enterprise-class 3D printers will be available for less than $2,000 by 2016. Meanwhile, there are 3D-printing services such as Shapeways (*www.shapeways.com*) and Sculpteo (*www.sculpteo.com*) that will create a 3D object from your exported 3D file.

Budget 3D Scans

You may have heard about this up and coming technology: 3D scanners! A professional model, such as Artec's Eva 3D scanner, costs $12,899 (if you just want to capture an object's shape), or $17,999 (if you want to capture its texture as well). Artec also makes a larger scanner that can scan big objects such as cars and people. However, you also need to buy their Artec Studio software for $649, so 3D scanning can get *real* expensive real quick.

However, there is a way to scan objects to create 3D models without taking out a loan. Buy Arctec's software (which costs about $650) and use it with a gaming sensor, such as Microsoft Kinect for XBox/Windows, the Asus Xtion/Xtion Pro Live, or another sensor based on PrimeSense technology (*www.primesense.com*). The software can export the result into several 3D formats, including OBJ, which you can open into Photoshop.

■ Editing 3D Objects

Once you've created an object, you can do all kinds of things with it, such as apply materials to its surfaces, shine various kinds of lights on it, paint on it, run filters on it, adjust its opacity and blend mode, or even animate it over time. This section explains all these creative options.

Working with Materials

In Photoshop, a *material* is just what it sounds like: a flat image that gets applied to one side or all sides of a 3D object. To get started working with materials, activate a 3D object in the Layers panel, and then look for a material nested under that object in the 3D panel—every 3D object has them. When you activate a material in the 3D panel, Photoshop displays the Materials settings in the Properties panel (*Figure 21-10*). (You can activate multiple materials to adjust their properties all at once.)

FIGURE 21-10

This heart is much more interesting with one of the Fun Textured materials applied to it. To see the name of each material, click the material thumbnail (the ball) to show a list of materials, and then put your cursor over one of them (without clicking). To see all the names at once, click the gear icon in the upper-right corner of the list of materials, and then change the view to either Text Only, Small List, or Large List.

Materials can appear in lots of places on an object, so the Layers and 3D panels' filter feature can really help when you want to adjust them. Here's an effective approach:

1. **In the Layers panel, activate the object you want to work with.**

2. **In the 3D panel, click the Materials icon (labeled in *Figure 21-2*).**

   This limits the panel to showing only the materials in the active object(s).

3. **Still in the 3D panel, activate the materials you want to edit.**

   To activate all of 'em, click the top one and then Shift-click the bottom one; to activate only some of them, click one and then ⌘-click (Ctrl-click) on each of the others.

4. **In the Properties panel, make your changes to the materials using the controls shown in** *Figure 21-10*.

You choose or switch a material by clicking the Material thumbnail at the upper right of the Properties panel. Photoshop CC comes with 36 built-in materials—including fabrics, gemstones, metals, woods, glass, plastics, and even moss and bricks. If you need something different, you can download more than 100 additional materials by choosing 3D→Get More Content. Then, to load them, click the Material thumbnail in the upper right corner of the Properties panel, and then click the gear icon at the top right of the list of materials. Finally, choose Load Materials and navigate to the set of materials you just downloaded.

The top part of the Properties panel also lets you apply colors and textures to the reflective areas of the current material (using the Diffuse, Specular, Illumination, and Ambient settings). To change the color, click on the color swatch, and then choose a new color in the Color Picker that pops up. To add a texture, click the folder icon to the right of the Diffuse, Specular, or Illumination setting to create or load a texture. Once you've assigned a texture, the folder icon changes to a file icon that you can click to edit, replace, or remove the texture. Point your cursor at the file icon to see a thumbnail of the texture and info about it.

TIP   You can also edit the UV properties of a patterned texture (such as a checkerboard or wood grain) to adjust how Photoshop scales or offsets the texture when you apply it to the surface. The UV Properties option appears in the Properties panel when you've applied a texture to an object and you click that texture's icon in the Properties panel. (In case you're curious: In the same way that X, Y, and Z refer to the three directions in a 3D space, U and V refer to the coordinates on a surface.)

In the Properties panel, the final two Materials settings—Normal and Environment—let you apply a texture to the object's entire surface or to the environment around the object, respectively. (The environment texture is visible in any reflective areas of the object.) These settings are mainly used by advanced 3D professionals.

You can also copy and paste materials from one object surface to another by using the 3D tools in Photoshop's Tools panel:

- The **3D Material Eyedropper** is located in the Eyedropper toolset. It works similarly to how the Eyedropper tool works on 2D images: Click a 3D surface to sample its material, and then Option-click (Alt-click on a PC) another 3D surface to apply that material to it.

- The **3D Material Drop tool** is located in the Gradient toolset. It works exactly the *opposite* of the 3D Material Eyedropper: Option-click (Alt-click) to sample a material, and then click to apply it to another surface.

Painting on a 3D Object

If you have a creative soul, you've probably been eagerly awaiting the part of this chapter that explains how to paint directly on a 3D object. Well, you made it! You can use any of Photoshop's brush tools on either the object itself or on the texture file attached to it, and watch as your strokes are applied to both.

To paint an object in Photoshop's spiffy Live 3D Painting mode, first activate a 3D object in the 3D or Layers panel. Then, open the texture document that you want to paint by double-clicking its name in the Layers panel. Alternatively, you can click the texture in the Properties panel, and then choose Edit Texture from the drop-down menu that appears. Either way, the texture opens into its own window so you can edit it.

> **TIP** Another way to paint on a texture is to grab the Brush tool from the Tools panel, and then click the surface of the 3D object. In the resulting dialog box, click "Change Texture Target," and Photoshop opens the texture document in a new window.

Choose Window→Arrange, and then pick one of the Tile options to view your 3D model and the texture document side by side. Using the Brush tool, paint either the 3D model or the texture document, and your brushstrokes automatically appear in the other view, too. (How cool is that?) When you're done painting, close and save the texture document, and the texture will permanently update on the 3D object.

> **TIP** Photoshop CC also lets you make 3D objects look like a sketch or illustration. To do so, activate your object in the Layers panel, and then, in the Properties panel, click the Presets menu. Scroll through the sketch, illustration, and wireframe options to see them applied to your object!

Lighting Your 3D Scene

Just like in your home or on a movie set, the final appearance of your 3D scene depends not only on the materials, textures, and camera angles you've chosen, but also on the number and types of light sources in the scene. Photoshop has three kinds of basic lights and one advanced light. To add a new basic light to a scene, just click the New Light button at the bottom of the 3D panel, and then choose from the drop-down menu that appears:

- A **Point light** has a location and *falloff* (meaning it tapers off, so objects far away from it won't be affected by it), but no direction—like a bare incandescent light bulb.

- A **Spot light** has a location, direction, and *cone of illumination* (like the cone of light created by a real-world flashlight or ceiling spotlight). And, like a Point light, it also has a falloff.

- An **Infinite light** sends light into the scene from a specific direction but its light doesn't taper off—it's infinite (the sun is a good example of this kind of light).

Adjusting the details of any basic light is easy: Just activate the light in the 3D panel, and then tweak the settings in the Properties panel (see *Figure 21-11*). The Properties panel's Preset menu has 14 really useful options: Red, White, Blue, CAD Optimized, Cold, Dawn, Day Lights, Hard Lights, Fire, Lush, Mardi Gras, Night Lights, Primary Colors, and Purple Faze. If you get confused, you can just choose Default Lights to get back to where you started.

FIGURE 21-11

The Properties panel lets you adjust your scene's lighting in all sorts of ways. Here you see the options for an Infinite light, but the panel offers similar settings for Point lights and Spot lights. (The 3D panel shown here has the Light filter turned on, so only light-related items are listed.)

The strange-looking object in the middle of this extruded heart is the Infinite Light HUD; its control handle points to the source of its light.

> **TIP** If you get lost while moving a light around, click the Properties panel's "Move to view" icon to reposition the light near your object. Or, in the Coordinates area of the Properties panel, click the Reset Coordinates button to move the light to the center of your 3D object.

After you've chosen a lighting Preset, you can adjust its Color and Intensity settings, whether it casts shadows or not (if so, you can tweak the softness of its shadow), and for directional lights, the light's falloff, cone, *hotspot* (width of its bright center), and other properties. You can also change the light's location by clicking the Coordinates icon at the top of the Properties panel—but dragging the light around in the main view window is more intuitive. Just click and drag one of the handles on the light's HUD to move it.

Besides those three basic lights, Photoshop also lets you use a much more advanced light known as an *Image Based Light* (IBL), which is generated from an image file that was specifically created to shine light in various ways all the way around your scene. (Photoshop also has its own IBL that it applies to every scene for you.) It acts like a sphere around your scene and lights it from all directions based on the color and intensity of the IBL's image. The IBL also shows up in the reflections of your materials if the Reflection value in the Properties panel is greater than 0%.

The IBL applies to your scene's whole environment, so to add one you need to activate the Environment item in the 3D panel. Then, in the Properties panel, turn on the IBL checkbox. Photoshop then applies its built-in IBL to the environment, and you can adjust its many settings in the Properties panel. If you click the IBL's thumbnail in the Properties panel, you can edit the image file that's used for the IBL or replace it with a new image file.

> **TIP** Once you've created a set of lights that you like, you can save them as a preset by choosing Save Lights Preset from the 3D panel's menu. There, you can also delete or replace the current lights preset, or add a new preset from a file.

■ POSITIONING LIGHTS

How you reposition a light depends on what kind of light it is. But no matter what kind it is, you first have to activate the light in the 3D panel. To make it easier to find your lights in the 3D panel, click the Lights icon at the top of the panel (labeled in *Figure 21-2*), so you only see lights in the panel's list.

> **NOTE** You can't reposition IBLs, since they wrap around your whole scene.

To reposition a Point light, grab the Move tool and drag the handles of the HUD that appears. If you lose control of your light, you can reset its position by clicking the helpful "Move to view" button in the Properties panel. This puts the light to the lower left corner of your object.

You reposition a Spot light the same way: Grab the Move tool and drag the handles of the HUD that appears. Another option is to click and drag anywhere in the window. The light moves based on the 3D mode that's active in the Options bar (see page 827). A couple of buttons in the Properties panel can be helpful when you're moving a Spot light: The "Point at origin" button resets the light's angle to point directly at your object, and the "Move to view" button moves the light to the lower-left corner of your object.

To reposition an Infinite light, grab the Move tool and, in the Options bar, set the 3D mode to Rotate (the first icon). If you've activated an Infinite light in the 3D panel, you'll see a HUD in the center of your window that looks like a giant satellite dish (see *Figure 21-11*). Click and drag anywhere in the window to change the light's angle.

Instances

3D objects are complex, so keeping track of multiple copies of an object can be challenging. Also, each object contains lots of data, so Photoshop gives you a way to keep your files slim *and* save you the headache of keeping track of multiple copies of the same object. The trick is to make one or more *instances* from one object, so that when you make a change to the properties of the original object or any instance, they all reflect the change. (If you use Adobe Illustrator, Fireworks, or Flash, you're familiar with this concept, which is similar to using a linked Smart Object in Photoshop.)

To create an instance from a 3D object, activate the object in the 3D panel. Then, from either the panel menu or the contextual menu that appears when you Control-click (right-click) the object in the 3D panel, choose Instance Object. This adds a copy of the object to the 3D panel, named the same as the original object but with a number at the end of its name. (Its icon is dark to remind you that it's an instance.) If you activate the original object or any instance and then make changes in the Properties panel, those changes will also apply to the original and any other instances.

If you want to *break* the link between an instance and the original (so that you can continue to make changes to the instance without affecting the original or the other instances), just activate the instance in the 3D panel and choose Bake Object from either the 3D panel's menu or the contextual menu that appears when you Control-click (right-click) the item in the 3D panel.

Combining Objects

At some point, you may want to combine two or more 3D objects to act as one, so that it's easier to position and light them. Here's how: In the Layers panel, activate the 3D layers you want to combine. Then hold down the Shift key while you choose 3D→Merge 3D Layers. Photoshop combines the separate 3D layers into one 3D layer in the Layers panel.

Running Filters on a 3D Layer

Just like regular 2D layers, you can apply Photoshop's filters to 3D layers. It's always a good idea to first convert the 3D layer for use with a Smart Filter (choose Filter→"Convert for Smart Filters"). For the full scoop on Smart Filters, flip back to page 632.

Changing a 3D Layer's Blend Mode and Opacity

Just like regular 2D layers, you can change the blend mode and opacity of a 3D Layer. Simply activate the 3D layer in the Layers panel, and use the panel's Opacity and Fill settings, as well as the unlabeled blend mode menu near the top of the panel (it's set to Normal unless you change it). To change any of these settings on multiple layers at once, simply activate all the layers first.

Rasterizing a 3D Layer

At some point, you may want to simplify a 3D project by boiling down a complex, multi-part 3D layer into a simple 2D Image layer—essentially flattening it into a static picture. That's where rasterizing comes in. (Remember: Rasterizing [described on page 43] is different than *rendering* [page 837].)

Rasterizing a 3D layer is similar to rasterizing a Type layer in that it removes all of the layer's 3D-editing goodness. So either make a duplicate of your layer for future 3D editing before you rasterize it, or be *real sure* that you're completely finished adjusting it! When you're ready to rasterize, either choose Layer→Rasterize→3D, or Control-click (right-click) the name of the 3D layer in the Layers panel, and then choose Rasterize 3D from the resulting shortcut menu. Either way, Photoshop squishes your 3D layer down into a flat version of its former self, as if you'd taken a photograph of it.

◼ Creating 3D Animations

Using the Photoshop Animation timeline, you can create animations that move a 3D object through space and change the way it appears over time. The trick is to click the Create Video Timeline button in the Timeline Panel (Window→Timeline). (If you don't see this button, click the triangle in the middle of the panel, choose Create Video Timeline panel, then click the button.) When you do so, Photoshop adds all the layers in the Layers panel to the Timeline as video layers.

To access a 3D object's properties in the Timeline panel, click the flippy triangle next to its name. To create a keyframe animation for properties such as Scene (object) Position, Camera Position, Render Settings, Cross Section, Lights, Materials, and Meshes, just click the stopwatch icon next to the property's name. You can then treat each object and property exactly the same as you would any other object you're animating in the timeline. (See page 806 for details on creating animations.)

◼ Additional 3D Resources

This chapter is by no means a complete guide to 3D modeling—it's more of an heroic attempt to simplify a complex art form! To learn more, check out these resources:

- **CGSociety** (*www.lesa.in/3dcgtalk*) is a huge community of professionals who are helpful and insightful. Be sure to check out the 3D sections if you want to have your mind blown by what others are doing with professional-level 3D applications.

- **3Dtotal** (*www.3dtotal.com*) has endless resources for all things 3D (and 2D).

- **PSD tuts+** (*www.lesa.in/3dpstuts*) has a fine selection of free 3D tutorials for Photoshop CC users. However, some are for older versions of Photoshop that had a very different set of 3D tools, so you may have to figure out how to accomplish them with the current toolset.

- **"60 Excellent Free 3D Model Websites"** (*www.lesa.in/3d60free*) is an article by Kay Tan that highlights 60 valuable 3D resources.

- **Archive3D** (*www.archive3d.net*) has 35,000+ 3D models and props, and they're all free!

- **CG Textures** (*www.cgtextures.com*) has zillions of free textures.

- **Blender** (*www.blender.org*) is a free, open-source, cross-platform suite of tools for 3D creation.

Using Adobe Bridge

As digital images pile up on your hard drive, the ability to sift through 'em quickly and efficiently becomes more and more important. Enter Adobe Bridge, an image-browsing and -organizing program that's been shipping with Photoshop for years. Its special purpose in life is to let you browse, compare, sort, manage, import, and even *manipulate* (to an extent) the files on your hard drive. The important thing to remember about Bridge is that you can use it to see preview thumbnails of most any file on your machine, whether you used Bridge to import 'em or not.

And just like nice clothing stores display goodies from multiple designers, Bridge can display thumbnail previews of *multiple* file formats—more than either the Mac or Windows operating systems currently can. For example, you can see multiple pages of PDFs and at least *two* pages of Adobe InDesign files (you can see *more* than two by tweaking InDesign's preferences, but that's fodder for another book). Bridge also lets you watch movie files and listen to audio files, all without opening the files themselves. However, Bridge *can't* peek into your iPhoto library because Macs squirrel that away for safekeeping, nor will you see thumbnail previews of QuarkX-Press files (a popular page-layout program) even though the document preview is embedded in the XPress file (Adobe programs just don't take advantage of it).

Because *everything* you do to files in Bridge happens to those files on your *hard drive* (in the Mac Finder or Windows Explorer), Bridge is typically the easiest place to perform mundane file-management tasks such as renaming, moving, copying, and deleting files. It also gives you easy access to several automated tasks that work on multiple files; for example, you can use it to copy and paste edits made in Camera Raw to other images without actually *opening* Camera Raw.

If you used Bridge years ago, you'll likely remember that browsing images was painfully slow and the program wasn't very intuitive. That's all changed in recent versions. Bridge CC is fast (it's a 64-bit program just like Photoshop; see page xxviii), user-friendly, and sports an eye-relieving dark gray coat of paint. Bridge also includes a super useful Review mode that photographers adore (see page 854).

Now for the bad news.

In CC, unlike in previous versions, you have to install Bridge (and the Mini Bridge panel—page 866) *separately* from Photoshop (though after reading this section you might not think that's bad news *after* all). In order to optimize Bridge CC for Retina displays (super-high-resolution displays made by Apple, called HiDPI on PCs), Adobe *removed* some relatively new and, unfortunately, useful features from the program. The most glaring omission is the entire Adobe Output Module, which was responsible for creating web galleries and PDFs. And if you go rootin' around for the Export panel—useful in converting images from one format to another and quickly posting images on Flickr, Facebook, and Photoshop.com—you won't find it, either. Also missing is the New Synchronized Window command, which let you have *two* instances of Bridge open at the same time.

Will any of these features return in future versions? Only time will tell. However, if your current workflow *depends* on that stuff, there is a workaround: Keep using Bridge CS6. That said, if you're new to the program or if you never used those features, you won't miss 'em and you'll be pleasantly pleased by the zippier performance of Bridge CC. But a lot of folks depend on these features, so keep your eyes peeled for a way to restore the AOM to Bridge CC via a separate installation. For the latest info, download online Appendix A from this book's Missing CD page at *www.missingmanuals.com/cds*.

In the following pages, you'll learn the basics of browsing, importing, and rating your images in Bridge. By the time you're finished reading, you'll likely be one of Bridge's *biggest* new fans.

■ Installing Bridge

In order to keep the file sizes of Adobe's downloadable Creative Cloud programs as slim and trim as possible, Bridge and its Mini Bridge panel are no longer automatically installed when you load Photoshop onto your machine. The installation process is simple—but as of this writing, it was still in flux. For the most up-to date info on installing Bridge CC, download online Appendix A from this book's Missing CD page at *www.missingmanuals.com/cds*.

Happily, Bridge CS6 and Bridge CC seem to *coexist* peacefully on a single machine, so if you need the missing features mentioned back on page 848, feel free to keep the CS6 version hanging around.

NOTE Once you install Bridge CC, you can access it *inside* Photoshop using the Mini Bridge panel. Choose File→"Browse in Mini Bridge" or Window→Extensions→Mini Bridge. Either way, it appears at the bottom of your screen; flip to page 866 for a sneak peek. (The Mini Bridge panel is installed along with Bridge CC.)

Unfortunately, Bridge doesn't have an equivalent of Photoshop's Migrate Presets feature (page 29), so if you've customized an earlier version of Bridge with favorites (page 850), collections (page 857), and so on, you need to copy those files over to the new version *manually*. To do that on a Mac, find the *Macintosh HD/Library/Application Support/Adobe/Bridge CS6 Extensions* folder, and then open it to reveal your presets folder. Drag those files into the into the same folders inside the Bridge CC Extensions folder, and then restart Bridge.

Browsing through Photos

If you're working in Photoshop CC, you can open Bridge by choosing File→"Browse in Bridge." If Photoshop *isn't* running, you can double-click the Bridge icon in the Adobe Bridge application folder (on a PC, go to Start→All Programs→Adobe Bridge CC). Either way, you see the window shown in *Figure 22-1*.

NOTE If you open Bridge and it looks different from *Figure 22-1*, try clicking the word Essentials near the top of the Bridge window. That will switch you over to the built-in workspace shown here.

The Bridge window displays a variety of info about your images in collapsible panels—just double-click a tab to collapse or expand a panel or group of panels. You can use the Folders panel on the left to navigate to a specific spot on your hard drive to view the images stored there. When you click a folder in this panel, Bridge displays its contents as thumbnails in the Content panel in the middle of the window (use the slider at the bottom right of the Bridge window to control how big these thumbnails are). Click an image in the Content panel to see a larger version of it in the Preview panel on the right.

TIP To see a *larger* preview of an image whose thumbnail is displayed in Bridge, click the file to activate it and then tap the space bar; Bridge displays the image in all its full-screen glory. Press the space bar again to go back to the Bridge window.

At the top of the Bridge window are controls that help you find the files you want (shown in *Figure 22-1*):

- **Forward and back arrows**. Click these buttons to move through the folders you've recently viewed. For example, if you went to your Pictures folder and then opened the Blackmail folder inside it, click the back arrow to return to the Pictures folder. (These buttons don't activate files, just folders.)

Back/Forward
Go to parent folder/Favorites
Recent files/folders
Go to Photoshop — Rotate photo   Path bar   Search

Drag to resize panels   Thumbnail size   Thumbnails | List
                                                    Details

FIGURE 22-1

You can use Bridge to browse all the images on your hard drive, not just ones you've downloaded from your camera using Bridge (as explained on the next page).

The program's various panels harbor different kinds of info, and they're all movable and resizable: To move one, drag its tab; to resize one, drag the bar that divides it from other panels; and to combine two panels, drag one panel's tab into another panel.

TIP   For quick access to certain folders, add them to Bridge's Favorites panel: Activate a folder in the Folders or Content panel, Control-click (right-click) it, and then choose "Add to Favorites" from the resulting menu. (You can also choose File→"Add to Favorites" or simply drag a folder from the Content panel into the Favorites panel.) From then on, you'll have one-click, timesaving access to that folder in the Favorites panel.

- **Go to parent folder→Favorites**. Like the back-arrow button, this button lets you move up a folder level. For example, if you're perusing the Midnight Madness folder that lives inside your Photoshop World folder, you can click this button to reveal a menu that lets you quickly pop back to the Photoshop World folder (which is called the *parent* folder because it's one level above the Midnight Madness folder in your computer's file-organization family tree). You can also use this button to access folders that you've added to the Favorites panel.

- **Go to recent files/folders**. Click this button to see a menu that lists all the files and folders you've recently viewed in Adobe programs, which includes a list of files and folders categorized by the program that made 'em. When you choose an item from this menu, Bridge displays a preview of the item along with its location on your hard drive.

- **Path bar**. This outrageously useful bar is a clickable, virtual trail of breadcrumbs that helps you keep track of where you are on your hard drive. It shows which folder you're in, so if you want to jump to a different spot in the trail, simply click the name of another folder in this bar. Since the path bar shows you how you arrived at the folder you're in, you always know exactly where you are (and the clickable links offer a fast track backward). If you don't see this bar—or if it's mysteriously disappeared, as it sometimes does—choose Window→Path Bar.

TIP If the folder you're currently perusing contains *subfolders* (folders within folders), you can see a list of all those subfolders by clicking the > symbol at the far right of the path bar. To view the contents of *one* of those subfolders, simply choose it from the list. To make Bridge show you the individual files *inside all subfolders*, choose "Show Items from Subfolders." (You'll still see the subfolders, but you can hide them from view by choosing View→Show Folders; the same command lets you turn 'em back on.) This maneuver is called *folder cruising*, and it's a great way to force Bridge to create thumbnail previews of everything inside a folder (handy when the folder contains a slew of images and if Bridge hasn't cached them yet [page 23], meaning you can't find 'em using Bridge's search field). To turn folder cruising off, click the > and choose Stop Folder Cruising.

- **Search field**. If you know the name of the file you're looking for but don't remember where it lives, type its name (or the first few letters of it) into this field and then press Return (Enter on a PC). Bridge scours the current folder and its subfolders and shows you a list of files that best match what you typed. You can also use this field to find images with specific keywords (page 852). Click the magnifying glass for a list of recent searches or to switch to a Spotlight search (a Windows Desktop search on a PC) to find specific filenames anywhere on your hard drive (the latter doesn't work on keywords or metadata, however).

TIP For a more *powerful* Bridge search feature, choose Edit→Find. In the resulting dialog box, you can tell Bridge exactly *where* on your hard drive you want it to search, and set myriad search criteria such as date created, date modified, file size, document type, and so on. You also get access to your image's metadata (page 852), which lets you search for stuff like Focal Length, ISO, and so on. Who knew?

▇ Importing and Managing Photos

Bridge makes importing images a snap, and it can perform all kinds of wonderful housekeeping chores for you. For example, it can automatically rename photos and add keywords, descriptions, and copyright info to each file. You can also have it back up your files (either to an external hard drive you've plugged in or to another spot on your internal hard drive) as part of the process of importing photos from your digital camera or memory card.

Customizing the Bridge Window

You can customize the Bridge workspace just like you can in Photoshop, or use one of its built-in layouts. Near the top of the Bridge window is a row of workspace buttons that arrange the program's panels in a variety of ways (see *Figure 22-1*). Here's what each one does:

- **Essentials** is the arrangement you see when you first open Bridge: The Favorites and Folders panels are on the left, the Content panel is in the middle, and the Preview panel is on the right. It's a handy workspace for sifting through files.

- **Filmstrip** is great for looking at photos you've imported. The Favorites and Folders panels are still on the left, but the Content panel is down at the bottom of the window as a wide, thin strip, and the Preview panel takes center stage. Photographers like this workspace because it gives 'em a nice big preview area.

- **Metadata** shows you all kinds of info about your images. There's no big Preview panel in this workspace; the Content panel takes precedence, displaying a list that includes each file's creation date, size, type, and so on. The Favorites panel is on the left along with the Metadata panel, which includes stats about the active file like its dimensions, resolution, and so on.

- **Keywords** is similar to Metadata except that, in the Preview panel, you see the folder icons displayed with

info such as the date the image was captured or created, date modified, and color profile. This workspace also sticks the Keywords panel at the Bridge window's bottom left for easy access.

If these workspaces don't float your boat, you can make your own. Simply move and resize the panels just the way you like, and then click the tiny down-pointing triangle to the right of the Keyword button and choose New Workspace. Give it a meaningful name in the resulting dialog box, and then click Save. Your custom workspace appears as a button at the top of the Bridge window, just like the built-in workspaces. If you want to get rid of it, click the triangle again, choose Delete Workspace, pick the offending workspace in the resulting dialog box, and then click Delete.

You can also customize the color theme in Bridge, just like you can in Photoshop. Simply choose Bridge→Preferences (Edit→Preferences on a PC) and then click the General category in the left-hand list. You'll see various color squares that you can click to change the color scheme, as shown here. You can also use the sliders underneath 'em to tweak the program's overall brightness, change its image backdrop (the background color Bridge displays your images on), and its accent color (the highlight color Bridge puts around an image's thumbnail when you click to activate it).

To import images, make sure your card reader is attached to your computer (see the box on page 855), and then choose File→"Get Photos from Camera" or click the tiny camera icon at the top left of the Bridge window. Either way, Bridge opens the Adobe Photo Downloader in *standard mode*, which isn't very impressive; its most redeeming feature is the Advanced Dialog button at the bottom left. Click it to switch to *Advanced mode*, shown in *Figure 22-2*. (If this is the first time you've downloaded photos with Bridge, you'll see the dialog box mentioned in the Tip on page 854.)

FIGURE 22-2

Importing photos from a camera or memory card with Bridge is a huge timesaver. Plus, if you've got an external hard drive plugged into your computer, you can turn on the "Save Copies to" checkbox (circled) and sleep better knowing you have extra copies of your photos stored somewhere other than your main computer.

For more tips on importing photos from your camera, flip to the box on page 855.

At the top of this extremely useful dialog box, tell Bridge where to save your precious pictures by clicking the Choose button (the Browse button on a PC). The Downloader also lets you pick which images to import (turn on the appropriate checkboxes like the one circled in *Figure 22-2*, left), give the images meaningful names, *and* instruct Bridge to back 'em up (by turning on the "Save Copies to" checkbox circled in *Figure 22-2*, right). Once you've got these options just right, click Get Media, and then sit back and relax.

TIP The first time you choose File→"Get Photos from Camera" or click the camera icon on a Mac, Bridge asks if you want it to *automatically* open each time you attach a card reader to your computer (or plug in your camera's USB cable). If you want to always use Bridge to import photos, click Yes. This saves you a couple of clicks each time you import images, because Bridge automatically launches and opens the Photo Downloader dialog box. If you've already hightailed it past this dialog box, you can access it in Bridge's preferences. Choose Bridge→Preferences→General and turn on the "When a Camera is Connected, Launch Adobe Photo Downloader" setting.

In Windows, you need to choose your memory card from the "Get Photos from" menu at the top of the Photo Downloader dialog box each time you import photos. Alternatively, you can go to Start→Control Panel→AutoPlay and, from the Pictures drop-down menu, choose Download Images Using Adobe Bridge CC, and then click Save. That way, each time your computer detects a memory card, the Photo Downloader dialog box automatically opens and picks your memory card as its source.

Review Mode

After you import images, you can use Bridge's most excellent Review mode to view them in a giant, floating carousel (see *Figure 22-3*). It's a quick and easy way to check out your images, mark the ones you don't like, and apply star ratings to the ones you do.

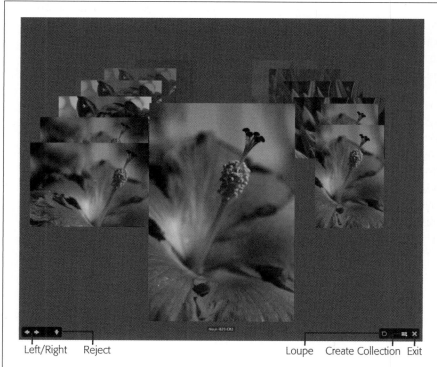

Left/Right   Reject   Loupe   Create Collection Exit

FIGURE 22-3

In Review mode, press ⌘-1, 2, 3, 4, or 5 (Ctrl+1, 2, 3, 4, or 5 on a PC) to give an image a rating of 1 to 5 stars, or click the down arrow button in the window's lower left to remove an image from view (this doesn't mark the image as rejected; it simply removes it from view and deactivates it).

To take a closer look at part of an image, either click the Loupe button in the window's bottom right or just click the image.

NOTE To mark an image as *rejected* (meaning you're tagging the photo as one you don't want to keep), simply activate the image's thumbnail in the main Bridge window (not in Review mode), and then press Option-Delete (Alt+Backspace on a PC). Once you do that, you can delete all your rejected images in one fell swoop, as explained in the next section.

Tips for Importing Photos

Here are a few pointers for importing photos from a digital camera quickly and safely that will also help you find the little boogers on your hard drive later:

- **Always use a card reader**. The slowest way to import photos is by using the USB cable that came with the camera. It's sweet that the camera manufacturer included it, but those cables are super cheap. The cable's low quality also makes using it dangerous—the cheaper the cable, the greater the chance that something will go wrong. Fortunately, you can avoid this risk by getting a *card reader*, which imports photos much faster and more reliably. You simply take the memory card out of your camera, stick it in the card reader, and then connect the reader to your computer. Card readers are inexpensive (for example, you can get a SanDisk ImageMate 12-in-1 for around $20) and most models can read several different kinds of memory cards (that's what the "12-in-1" part means), which is a nice bonus if you have more than one brand of camera. Also, if you're on a Mac, take care that you don't yank a memory card out of the card reader until you've properly ejected or unmounted it from your computer by choosing File→Eject in the Finder.

- **Erase memory cards only in your camera**. Most photo importing/organizing software offers to erase photos from your memory card after it imports them onto your computer. Resist the urge to say yes, and instead stick the memory card back into your camera, and then use the *camera's* menus to reformat the card to erase the images. This protects you from losing files if there's some

kind of crash or stall while they're being imported, which can corrupt the photos (and, if the software has already erased them from the memory card, you can't reimport them). Also, many folks believe that reformatting memory cards rather than erasing them helps reduce the risk of cards getting corrupted and losing your photos. To learn how to reformat your memory card, dig out the manual that came with your camera.

- **Give photos meaningful names**. Instead of sticking with the completely useless names your camera assigns to photos, give them meaningful names when you import them. Programs like Bridge can automatically number the files for you and tack on a name like *Photoshop World*. You've got to admit that the name *Photoshop World 2013_1.jpg* is a lot more descriptive than *DCS_00102.jpg*.

- **Use several small memory cards instead of one big one**. No matter how well you care for them, memory cards—like any storage device—can fail and lose all the precious images stored on 'em. For that reason, consider carrying four 8 GB cards instead of a single 32 GB card; that way, you'll lose fewer photos if one of the cards goes south. When buying memory cards, do a little research to find a good brand. The cheapest cards can be unreliable and are usually slow. The faster the card, the faster your camera can take photos (and the faster your computer can import 'em). Checking reviews on Amazon.com is always a good idea, though as of this writing the SanDisk Extreme cards are blazing fast and are especially useful when shooting video.

To use Review mode, activate a folder in the Folders panel or choose multiple images (more than four) in the Content panel by ⌘-clicking (Ctrl-clicking) or Shift-clicking them. Then either press ⌘-B (Ctrl+B) or click the Refine button at the top of the Bridge window (it looks like a stack of paper) and choose Review Mode. Either way, Bridge takes over your screen and displays the images on a dark gray background. The left and right arrow buttons at the bottom left the window let you quickly flip through images (you can also use the arrow keys on your keyboard). You can also click any image in the background to bring it to the front, or drag an image off the bottom of your screen—or click the down arrow button at the bottom of the window—to remove it from Review mode (it doesn't get deleted or tagged as rejected, just removed from view). To exit Review mode and return to the Bridge window, click the X in the bottom-right corner of the window or press Esc.

> **TIP** To rotate an image in Review mode, click the image to activate it, and then press the left or right bracket key to turn the image clockwise or counterclockwise, respectively. (To rotate images in one of Bridge's workspaces, add the ⌘ [Ctrl] key.) To see a list of all the keyboard shortcuts you can use while you're in Review mode, press H while in that mode.

Sorting and Filtering Images

Bridge gives you a lot of flexibility when it comes to viewing images. For example, you can use the Sort menu at the top of the Bridge window to arrange 'em by name, date modified, size, and so on (see *Figure 22-4*, bottom). You can also sort 'em manually: In the Content panel, drag them into any order you want.

Filtering is a quick way to toss the images you've rejected (see the Tip on page 855). To do that, head to the "Filter items by rating" menu (it looks like a star), choose Show Rejected Items Only, and then choose File→"Move to Trash."

The Filter panel lets you weed out images by displaying only those that match certain criteria, like a specific star rating (see *Figure 22-4*, top). (In most workspaces, this panel lurks near the bottom left of the Bridge window; if you don't see it, choose Window→Filter Panel.) If you didn't use Review mode to rate your images after importing them, you might want to rate them now so you can quickly view the best ones. Rating and sorting is handy if you're a stock photographer: You can give future submissions a 5-star rating and then find 'em quickly using the 5-star filter.

If you applied keywords when importing the files, you can use those keywords to filter your images. To see a list of keywords applied to the files in the folder you're viewing, head over to the Filter panel and click the word "Keywords." (If you don't see the Filter panel, just open the Keywords panel instead by choosing Window→Keywords Panel). Click a keyword (it turns bold and a checkmark appears to its left) to make the Content panel display only images with that keyword applied. Nice!

FIGURE 22-4

Top: The Filter panel (Window→Filter Panel) lets you limit the images Bridge displays. For example, if you've rated your images, you can filter your collection by clicking the panel's stars. In this example, Bridge is displaying only 4-star images; just click the star rating you want to see and a little checkmark appears (circled). To view all your images again, click to the left of the words "No Rating."

To filter images using other criteria like the date they were created or their orientation, click a category in the Filter panel to expand that section, and then click to the left of an item to turn on that particular filter. For example, click Orientation, and then click again to place a checkmark next to Landscape or Portrait.

If you've filtered your images but now want to see 'em all, press Opt-⌘-A (Alt+Ctrl+A) to clear all filters.

Bottom: The star menu at the top of the Bridge window also lets you filter images. The Sort menu to its right controls the order in which Bridge displays the thumbnails. If Bridge is taking a long time to display images as you scroll or after you filter them or perform a search, you can use the square icons labeled here to lower the thumbnails' quality, which makes Bridge display them a little faster.

Grouping Images into Collections

Another way to organize images is to put them into folders called *collections*. Bridge lets you create two types of collections:

- **User-defined collections** are ones you make by dragging and dropping images into a special folder. To create this kind of collection, click the Collections panel in the bottom-left part of the Bridge window or choose Window→Collections

Panel (if the panel is already open, this command closes it, so you may have to choose it *twice* to spot the panel!). Activate the images you want to include, click the New Collection button (labeled in *Figure 22-5*, top), and Bridge asks if you want to include the active files in the new collection. Click Yes and Bridge adds your new collection to the Collection panel and highlights its name so you can enter something meaningful than "New Collection." To add more images, use the Folders or Favorites panel to find the ones you want to include, and then drag 'em onto the collection's brown envelope icon. To remove an image from the collection, make sure you're actually viewing the collection (it'll be highlighted in the Collections panel), and then in the Content panel Control-click (right-click) the image and choose Remove From Collection from the resulting shortcut menu.

TIP You can also create a user-defined collection while you're in Review mode by clicking the Create Collection button shown back in *Figure 22-3*.

- Bridge creates **smart collections** based on criteria you set in the dialog box shown in *Figure 22-5* (bottom right). Just click the New Smart Collection button at the bottom of the Collections panel and then enter your criteria. Click save when you're finished, and Bridge finds all the images that match your requirements. (If you've told Bridge to look through your *whole* hard drive, this may take a while!) Later, if you then import a new image that meets your criteria, Bridge automatically adds it to the collection. Smart collections have blue envelope icons.

Grouping Images into Stacks

If you typically use your camera in burst mode (meaning it captures three or more images in rapid succession each time you press the shutter button), you can group those images into *stacks*. This is a great way to organize similar images and simplify what you see in Bridge's Content panel. For example, instead of scrolling past *several* versions of the same image, you see a single stack of 'em instead, as shown in *Figure 22-6*.

To create a stack, activate the images by Shift- or ⌘-clicking (Ctrl-clicking) them, and then choose Stacks→"Group as Stack" or press ⌘-G (Ctrl+G). You can then expand the stack by choosing Stacks→Open Stack, and Bridge displays the images as individual thumbnails (to close the stack, choose Stacks→Close Stack). If you ever want to *free* images from a stack, click the stack to activate it and then choose Stack→"Ungroup from Stack" or press Shift-⌘-G (Shift+Ctrl+G). To change the image at the top of a stack (think of it as *representative* of what the stack contains), just expand the stack, click the image you want to appear at the top, and then choose Stacks→"Promote to Top of Stack."

FIGURE 22-5

Top: Once you create a user-defined collection, you can drag several photos into it at once, as shown here. (You can tell this is a user-defined collection because its envelope icon is brown.)

Bottom: To create a smart collection, use this dialog box to tell Bridge which photos to fetch. Use the "Look in" menu to tell the program where to look, and then set criteria using the menus below it. To add more criteria, click the + button.

Once you've made the smart collection, you can go back and tweak your criteria by clicking the Edit Smart Collection button (labeled in the top image here).

Edit Smart Collection   New Collection   Smart Collection   Delete Collection

Opening Images in Camera Raw

One of the many benefits of organizing and browsing images in Bridge is that it gives you easy access to the Camera Raw plug-in. In fact, Bridge offers *several* ways to open images in Camera Raw:

- Double-click a raw file in the Content panel.

- Activate an image in the Content panel and then press ⌘-R (Ctrl+R). This method lets you open raw files, JPEGs, and TIFFs in Camera Raw.

- Activate an image in the Content panel and then choose File→"Open in Camera Raw."

FIGURE 22-6

Top: Photoshop automatically creates image stacks when you stitch photos together into a panorama or a High Dynamic Range image, though you can create 'em manually, too. Bridge even lets you know how many images are in a stack by displaying a number at the top-left corner of each one, as shown here.

Bottom: To see all the images in a stack, put your cursor over the stack and a little Play button appears (you may need to increase the thumbnail size to see it; it looks like a right-pointing triangle, though it turns into a Pause button—as shown here—when you click it.) Give the button a click and Bridge slowly displays the images in the world's tiniest slideshow. To speed up the playback rate, choose Stacks→Frame Rate, and then choose a larger value in the list.

- Control-click (right-click) the image in the Content panel and then choose "Open in Camera Raw" from the shortcut menu that appears.

- Activate an image in the Content panel and then click the camera-iris icon at the top of the window (next to the Refine icon).

Once you've edited an image in Camera Raw, a microscopic icon appears next to the image's preview in Bridge's Content panel that represents the edit you made (see *Figure 22-7*). If you've got several images that need the same edits, you can copy the changes you made and apply them to others right in Bridge. Just Control-click (right-click) the image in the Content panel and then choose Develop Settings→Copy Settings. Then activate the images you want to apply the edits to, Control-click (right-click) one of them, choose Develop Settings→Paste Settings, and Bridge applies those same edits to the active images. Now that's working smarter instead of harder!

Renaming Multiple Files

If you forgot to rename your photos when you imported them or if you'd like to rename other files on your hard drive, you don't have to change their names one at a time—that'd take *weeks*. Happily, Bridge can rename entire folders of images for you using a simple process called *batch renaming*. To get started, press Shift-⌘-R (Shift+Ctrl+R) or head to the Refine menu at the top of the Bridge window (it looks like a stack of paper) and choose Batch Rename (you need to have a least one image active in Bridge's Content panel, or else the command is grayed out).

In the Destination Folder section of the resulting dialog box, tell Bridge whether you want to rename the images without moving them, or move or copy them to a different folder. The New Filenames section includes several options for customizing the files' names. Click one of the fields on the left side of this section to see the following options in a drop-down menu:

- **Text**. Choose this option to replace the file name with something more meaningful. For example, if you shot a series of photos at Photoshop World, you could use "PSW" for your file name—short and sweet!

- **New Extension** adds whatever you enter in this field to the *end* of the images' names, replacing the original extension. Beware, though: Changing a file's extension or adding a new extension to a file's name doesn't change the file's format, so your computer may not know what kind of file it is in order to open it if, for example, you add a .tif extension to the end of a .jpg file's name.

- **Current Filename** tells Bridge to keeps the file name that's already assigned to each image and add your other custom name changes to it (such as changing it to upper- or lowercase).

- **Preserved Filename** tells Bridge to keep the original metadata file name—the cryptic one assigned by your camera that tags along with your image—as part of the new file name.

- **Sequence Number** adds a unique number to each image's name. You pick the starting number, and Bridge counts up by one for each file it renames.

- **Sequence Letter** works just like Sequence Number, but it adds a unique *letter* to each file name instead.

- **Date Time** adds a date and time stamp to each file's name.

- **Metadata** lets you include metadata in each file's name. You can choose from several pieces of info that your camera embedded in your image files.

- **Folder Name** includes the name of the folder the images are in as part of the new file name.

- **String Substitution** lets you tell Bridge to find an element in the old file name (a piece of text, for example) and replace it with something else.

You can add and remove items from the New Filenames section by clicking the + or − button to the right of each one. Be sure to remove items you don't plan on using so Bridge doesn't include info you don't want.

In the Options section, turn on the "Preserve current filename in XMP Metadata" checkbox to leave the current file name that's stored in the file's metadata alone (in case you ever need to go back to it). And if there's a chance your renamed images will end up on different computer platforms, be sure to turn the Compatibility checkboxes for the appropriate operating systems. For example, if you use a Mac but your client uses PCs and Unix computers, turn on the Windows and Unix checkboxes.

At the bottom of the dialog box, Bridge displays an example of what your files *are* named and what they *will* be named. (If you think you'll use these settings again in the future, save 'em as a Preset by clicking the Save button in the Presets section at the top of the Batch Rename dialog box.) If everything looks good, take a deep breath, click Rename, and Bridge makes your changes in the blink of an eye.

FIGURE 22-7

When you edit an image in Camera Raw and then click Done in the Camera Raw window, tiny icons representing the edits you made appear next to the image in Bridge. The icons circled here indicate that this image was cropped and its exposure was changed.

Control-clicking (right-clicking) an image in Bridge's Content panel brings up this shortcut menu that includes all kinds of timesaving choices.

Showing Off Your Work

Bridge CC includes a nifty slideshow generator that lets you quickly display your work onscreen. *Previous* versions of Bridge had even *more* features for showing off your work, including the now deceased Output panel for creating PDFs and Web galleries and the equally dead Export panel for automating the process of uploading photos to popular websites (such as Facebook, Flickr, and Photoshop.com), as well as creating JPEG versions of raw files (though the latter can be done using the Image Processor Script, as described on page 247).

This section teaches you how to create spectacular slideshows and if you (wisely) kept Bridge CS6 on your machine, you'll also learn how to use the now-missing features mentioned above. Read on!

NOTE Keep your eyes peeled for a way to restore the AOM in Bridge CC (via a separate installation) so you can create PDFs and web galleries. For up-to-date info, download online Appendix A from this book's Missing CD page at *www.missingmanuals.com/cds*.

Making a Slideshow

If you need to show your work to a client or family member, you can quickly filter for your top-rated images (flip back to *Figure 22-4*) and then have Bridge play them as a full-screen slideshow. Here's how:

- **To start an instant slideshow**, activate a folder or several images by Shift- or ⌘-clicking (Ctrl-clicking) them, and then choose View→Slideshow or press ⌘-L (Ctrl+L). That's it! Your photos immediately appear onscreen, one after the other (each one stays onscreen for 5 seconds). To exit the slideshow, press Esc.

- **To customize the slideshow's settings first**, choose View→Slideshow Options or press Shift-⌘-L (Shift+Ctrl+L). In the resulting dialog box, you can make the slideshow repeat, control how many seconds each image stays onscreen, resize the slideshow window to fit your monitor, and add transitions between slides (see *Figure 22-8*). The only thing you *can't* do here is add music—though you can always open iTunes and play music in the background. When the settings are the way you want, click Play to start the show.

Bridge CS6's Export Panel

If you're using Bridge *CS6* and you like displaying your images on social-networking and photo-sharing websites such as Facebook, Flickr, and Photoshop.com, the Export panel can help you out (sadly, this panel was removed from Bridge CC and, as of this writing, it's not expected to return). It's also handy for converting a slew of images to JPEGs. The export process takes a few steps, but once you get things set up properly, it goes quite quickly.

Open the Export panel by clicking its tab at the bottom left of the Bridge CS6 window (if you don't see it and you're sure you're using Bridge *CS6*, choose Window→Export Panel). This panel includes icons for uploading photos to Facebook, Flickr, and Photoshop.com. If that's what you want to do, double-click the appropriate icon (for example, Flickr). The first time you do this, you'll then need to double-click the Flickr icon and enter your account info in the resulting dialog box. This same dialog box also lets you choose which album to put the images into, as well as *if* and *how* you want 'em resized. Click the Save button, and Bridge CS6 displays a status bar showing you the upload's progress.

FIGURE 22-8

By adding a transition and making sure the Zoom Back And Forth checkbox is turned on (which makes Bridge zoom in and then back out of each image), you can create a pretty slick slideshow in no time flat. This is a great way to assess your images.

To make a slideshow you can export, use the PDF option explained in the next section or the PDF Presentation option covered on page 713.

If you want to create JPEGs from raw files, click the Export panel's "Save to Hard Drive" icon and then click the + at the bottom of the panel to add a new preset (set of instructions). In the resulting dialog box's Destination tab (*Figure 22-9*, top), pick the folder where you want the exported images to land. Then click the Image Options tab and let Bridge CS6 know whether you'd like it to make the images smaller and/or reduce their quality (both great for images you want to post on the Web; not so much if you plan to send the JPEGs to a stock-image site). At the bottom of the dialog box, enter a meaningful name for the preset, click Save, and Bridge CS6 adds a new hard drive icon with that name to the Export panel, as shown in *Figure 22-9* (bottom).

Exporting Images from Bridge CS6 as PDFs

PDFs are really handy because you can open them on any kind of computer without having to buy any software. Bridge CS6 has a few templates you can use to create PDFs, and a slew of settings for customizing exactly how they look. You can even add watermarks to individual images in your PDFs, instead of one watermark per PDF page.

FIGURE 22-9

Top: If you're a stock photographer, you can use the Export panel to create high-quality JPEGs from raw files so you can submit them to your favorite stock image service, such as Fotolia.com or iStockphoto.com.

Bottom: Once you've created a preset, you can drag images onto its icon on the Export panel (left) and Bridge CS6 adds 'em to its "to export" list (right). You can delete items from the list by pointing your cursor at the image's name and then clicking the tiny X to its right. When you get the list just right, click the upward-pointing arrow (labeled here) to the right of the preset to send the images on their merry way.

TIP You can't create PDFs in Bridge CC, but you *can* create a PDF in Photoshop CC by choosing File→Automate →PDF Presentation or Contact Sheet II. See page 713 for step-by-step details.

To get started, activate the image(s) you want to export and then choose "Output to Web or PDF" from the Output menu at the top of the Bridge CS6 window (it looks like a piece of paper with a down-pointing arrow and is labeled in *Figure 22-10*). The Output panel opens on the right side of the Bridge window.

At the top of the Output panel, make sure the PDF button is active (if not, click it), and then choose an option from the Template menu. To see a preview of the template you picked, click the Refresh Preview button. The Output Preview panel appears in the center of the Bridge CS6 window (circled in *Figure 22-10*). Bridge CS6 offers some nice templates to choose from, though you can always customize them using the Output panel's various settings (use the scroll bar on the panel's right side to see all the settings—there are a ton of 'em). To make your PDF to run as a slideshow, be sure the Playback options near the bottom of the panel are turned on. When everything looks good, click the Save button at the very bottom of the panel and Bridge exports your file as a PDF.

Output menu   Click to save settings as template

FIGURE 22-10

The Template menu includes precious few options, though you can add your own. To see what your PDF will look like, click the Refresh Preview button (circled); the preview appears in the Output Preview panel. And as you make changes to the Output panel's gazillion settings, you have to keep clicking the Refresh Preview button to make Bridge CS6 update the Output Preview panel.

Happily, you can save your custom settings by clicking the icon labeled here, which is a welcome option after you've worked hard to create a PDF template or web gallery style that meets your needs.

Making a Web Gallery

You can also use Bridge CS6 to make a quick online gallery of your images. Heck, it'll even upload the images for you! Flip back to page 750 for the scoop. (This feature was removed in Bridge CC.)

■ Using Mini Bridge

Once you install Bridge CC, you can open a *smaller* version of it—cleverly named Mini Bridge (*Figure 22-11*)—as a panel *within* Photoshop by choosing Window→Extensions→Mini Bridge in Photoshop. It looks and works like big Bridge, but you get the added bonus of not having to switch program windows to find and open images.

FIGURE 22-11

The Mini Bridge panel gives you easy access to images right inside Photoshop. Just like any other panel, you can grab its tab and drag it anywhere else on your screen to make it free-floating (like the version shown here) or dock it elsewhere, though the size slider only appears in the floating version. Use the drop-down menu and list of folders on the panel's left to navigate to images, and then drag and drop 'em from the Mini Bridge panel right into your Photoshop window (or document), as shown here. As soon as you release your mouse button, Photoshop opens each image in its very own tabbed document (or, if you already have an image open, it'll place the images as new layers within the document).

> **NOTE** If you undock the Mini Bridge panel and then accidentally close it, don't panic. You can always reopen it by choosing Window→Extensions→Mini Bridge, or by choosing File→"Browse in Mini Bridge." Whew!

When you first open Mini Bridge, it checks to see if big Bridge is running. Why? Because the Mini Bridge panel works only when Photoshop *and* big Bridge are open on your machine. If big Bridge isn't running, you'll see a message in the Mini Bridge panel that says, "Bridge must be running to browse files" and a Launch Bridge button is underneath it (if Bridge was open and suddenly isn't, the message reads, "Bridge has disconnected" and the button is labeled Reconnect instead). Just click the button and Photoshop sends a message to big Bridge to get its tail in gear. Once Bridge launches, you'll see a drop-down menu and a list of folders on the left side of the Mini Bridge panel that you can use to navigate to your images (labeled in *Figure 22-11*). Double-click a folder in the list, and any images inside it appear as thumbnails on the right.

To change the size of the thumbnails within the panel, you have to *undock* it first and then use the slider labeled in *Figure 22-11*. To resize the panel itself, just grab its left or bottom side and then drag leftward or downward to make it bigger (or any side if it's floating).

> **TIP**   Mini Bridge displays only *image thumbnails* in its content area, not folders. To navigate to another folder, you have to use the navigation list on the panel's left, its path bar, or its Search field.

Here's what the various buttons labeled in *Figure 22-11* let you do:

- Click the **Reveal in Bridge** button to open the active image(s) in big Bridge, where you can do things like create collections (page 857) and use commands that run on multiple files such as Batch Rename (page 861), "Load Files into Photoshop Layers" (page 45), "Merge to HDR Pro" (page 396), and Photomerge (page 294). You can also summon these options by Control-clicking (right-clicking) an image thumbnail (see *Figure 22-12*).

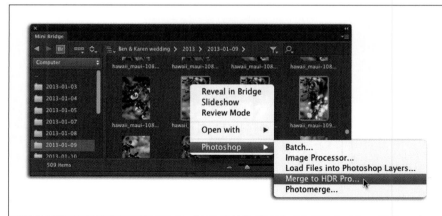

FIGURE 22-12

The shortcut menu you get by Control-clicking (right-clicking) an image in the Mini Bridge panel differs slightly depending on how many images are active when you open it (here, three images are activate). The Photoshop submenu includes several automation goodies, as you can see here.

- The **View menu** lets you refresh (update) the Mini Bridge panel's contents, as well as show and hide rejected files (page 855). You can also choose Select All, Deselect All, or Invert Selection (so the images that *were* active aren't, and what *wasn't* active is). This menu also lets you start a slideshow containing active images, enter Review mode (page 854), and control what info is displayed beneath each thumbnail, such as file name, ratings, file size, and so on.

> **TIP**   Tap the space bar to see a full-size preview of any image you activate in the Mini Bridge panel. Tap it again to go back to Photoshop.

- The **Sort menu** lets you determine in what order the thumbnails are shown: by file name, type, date created, and so on.

- Use the **Filter menu** to make Mini Bridge display files that have a certain star rating, label, and so on.

You can also Control-click (right-click) a thumbnail—or several—to summon a menu that gives you quick access to handy commands such as "Reveal in Bridge," Slideshow, Review Mode, "Open with," and the ever-useful Photoshop menu (see *Figure 22-12*).

Index